THE YEAR'S WORK 1997

*This volume is dedicated to the memory
of Rex Stainton-Rogers.*

The Year's Work in Critical and Cultural Theory

7

Edited by
KATE McGOWAN

Advisory Editors

STEVEN CONNOR (Birkbeck College, London)
TERRY EAGLETON (St Catherine's College, Oxford)
LAWRENCE GROSSBERG (University of North Carolina,
Chapel Hill)
STUART HALL (The Open University)
LINDA HUTCHEON (University of Toronto)
FREDRIC JAMESON (Duke University)
CHRISTOPHER NORRIS (University of Wales, Cardiff)
ELAINE SHOWALTER (Princeton University)
ALAN SINFIELD (University of Sussex)
STAN SMITH (University of Dundee)
GAYATRI CHAKRAVORTY SPIVAK (Columbia University)
PATRICIA WAUGH (University of Durham)

Published for
THE ENGLISH ASSOCIATION

by

First published 2000

2 4 6 8 10 9 7 5 3 1

Blackwell Publishers Ltd
108 Cowley Road
Oxford OX4 1JF
UK

Blackwell Publishers Inc.
350 Main Street
Malden, Massachusetts 02148
USA

British Library Cataloguing in Publication Data
A CIP catalogue record for this book is available from the British Library.

ISBN 0 631 21930 7 (hbk)

Typeset in 9 on 10pt Times
by SetSystems Ltd, Saffron Walden, Essex
Printed in Great Britain by MPG Books, Bodmin, Cornwall

This book is printed on acid-free paper.

Preface

The Year's Work in Critical and Cultural Theory is a companion volume to *The Year's Work in English Studies*, also published for The English Association by Blackwell Publishers. It provides a narrative bibliography of work in the field of critical and cultural theory, recording significant debates and issues of interest in a broad field of research in the humanities and social sciences. This volume covers books and journal articles published in 1997, and will be of interest to scholars working in many areas of literary and cultural studies as well as in media and visual arts, and law and policy.

This year the volume consists of nineteen chapters, including two new chapters on 'Marxism(s) and Post-Marxism(s)' and 'Multiculturalism'. These additions reflect our continuing commitment to developing the work in critical and cultural theory with which we deal. We also value, wherever possible, the opportunity of encouraging contributions from scholars working in critical and cultural theory outside of the British Isles. While every effort is made to consider the expansion of the volume in the direction of new and developing areas of critical and cultural theory, suggestions and proposals will always be welcomed by the editor.

We are unable this year to include the usual chapter on 'Discourse Analysis' by Beryl C. Curt. As you may know, 'Beryl C. Curt' is the pseudonym for a collective of writers working in a variety of areas of discourse theory. Sadly, this year a key member of that collective died and this volume is dedicated to his memory. Beryl C. Curt may reform herself for future ventures in future years.

Readers will note that the volume is again divided into two sections: Part I Critical Theory, and Part II Culture and Communications. Though arbitrary, this division is intended once again to emphasize a commitment to developing work in areas of cultural concern which may not necessarily be encompassed in the traditional canon of poststructuralist critical theory. This is a feature which will remain in place in future volumes.

No bibliography of this kind can claim to be complete in its review of new publications. Authors, publishers and editors are therefore invited to submit review copies of journals, books and articles for inclusion in future volumes. Items for review should be addressed to The Secretary, The English Association, The University of Leicester, University Road, Leicester LE1 7RH.

Kate McGowan
The Manchester Metropolitan University

The English Association

This bibliography is an English Association publication. It is available through membership of the Association; non-members can purchase it through any good bookshop.

The object of the English Association is to promote the knowledge and appreciation of the English language and its literatures.

The Association pursues these aims by creating opportunities of co-operation among all those interested in English; by furthering the recognition of English as essential in education; by discussing methods of English teaching; by holding lectures, conferences, and other meetings; by publishing a journal, books and leaflets; and by forming local branches overseas and at home.

Publications

The Year's Work in English Studies. An annual evaluative bibliography. Published by Blackwell Publishers, Oxford and Malden, MA.

The Year's Work in Critical and Cultural Theory. The first issue of this new critical theory volume appeared in 1994. Published by Blackwell Publishers, Oxford and Malden, MA.

Essays and Studies. An annual volume of essays by various scholars assembled by the collector covering usually a wide range of subjects and authors from the medieval to the modern. Published by Boydell and Brewer, Woodbridge, Suffolk.

English. The journal of the Association, *English*, is published three times a year by the English Association.

Use of English. This journal is published three times a year by the English Association.

English 4–11. This journal is published three times a year.

Benefits of Membership

Institutional Membership
Full members receive copies of *The Year's Work in English Studies, Essays and Studies, English* (three issues) and three *News-Letters*.

Ordinary Membership covers *English* (three issues) and three *News-Letters*.

Schools Membership covers one copy of each issue of *English*, one copy of the *Use of English*, one copy of *Essays and Studies*, three *News-Letters*, and preferential booking for Sixth-Form Conference places.

Individual Membership
Individuals take out basic membership, which entitles them to buy all regular publications of the English Association at a discounted price and three *News-Letters*.

For further details write to The Secretary, The English Association, The University of Leicester, University Road, Leicester LE1 7RH.

Contents

Part I

Critical Theory

Critical Theory: General

DAVID WALKER

This chapter is divided into five sections: 1. Poststructuralisms; 2. Marxism; 3. Introductions; 4. Literature and Theory; and 5. Reference Works.

1. Poststructuralisms

In the wake of Derrida's *Spectres of Marx* comes his *Politics of Friendship*, translated from the French edition of 1994 by George Collins. This is a text, which, like the aforementioned *Spectres*, will please those who are invigorated by Derrida's later works and more directly by 'political' content. Derrida, as has often been noted, is the most 'literary' of philosophers writing today. The opening chapter, 'Oligarchies: Naming, Enumerating, Counting', takes as its starting point the statement, 'O my friends, there is no friend', which is often attributed to Aristotle. From this beginning, Derrida opens a dialogue in the ensuing chapters with thinkers from the past as diverse as Aristotle, Plato, Cicero, Montaigne, Kant, Nietzsche, Schmitt, Blanchot, and Foucault, as well as bouncing off a host of lesser philosophical luminaries. In the first chapter, for instance, Derrida brings a deconstructive analysis to the relationship between Cicero's *Laelius de Amicitia* (*On Friendship*), Montaigne's essay 'On Friendship', and both writers' echo of Aristotle's supposed dictum quoted above. According to Derrida, 'In reading Montaigne, Montaigne reading Cicero', we are brought back to Aristotle as it is Aristotle 'who stands guard over the very form of our questions'.

The search for friendship, as it is read through Cicero, is the search for oneself, with the friend being defined as the '*exemplar*', 'which means portrait', but also the '*exemplum*', 'the duplicate, the reproduction, the copy as well as the original'. The scene is therefore set for the deconstruction of an array of binary oppositions with which Derrida is familiarly associated: 'the absent becomes present, the dead living, the poor rich, the weak strong'. For Derrida, friendship supposes a level of political commitment. In his analysis of Aristotle and primary friendship Derrida extends the discussion in to justice and politics, a community of good friends which represents an ideal state, measured against bad friends who 'invert or pervert this hierarchy'. On the one hand it would appear that 'fraternal friendship' is antithetical to the maintenance of the *res publica*. On the other hand, however, according to Derrida's reading of the great philosophical tradition in the West – 'from Plato to Montaigne, Aristotle to Kant, Cicero to Hegel' – philosophical discourses on friendship as elaborated by these writers, 'have explicitly tied the friend-brother to virtue and justice, to moral reason and political reason'. Friendship and justice are apparent in all forms of non-tyrannical government and constitutions.

As one would expect, this is a complex book written in a complex and dense style. The closest of readings is applied to the texts with which Derrida engages. Nevertheless, on the whole *The Politics of Friendship* is more accessible than many of Derrida's previous works and demonstrates a level of overt political engagement which critics of the pre-*Spectres of Marx* writings have excoriated for its absence.

Gerard Genette is primarily known for his contribution to the theory of narratology. In *Palimpsests: Literature in the Second Degree*, Genette, as the title of the volume would suggest, is concerned with the relationship which texts have with previous texts. The aims and objectives of the book are admirably laid out at the very beginning. As Genette states, he is not concerned with the analysis of texts *per se*; that is the job of the literary critic. Rather, he is interested in poetics, which he defines as *'transtextuality'*, which is in turn defined as 'all that sets the text in a relationship, whether obvious or concealed, with other texts'. That all texts are essentially a rewriting of other texts, to varying degrees, forms the basis of Genette's analysis of a wide range of writings from the classical and French tradition. Genette, however, is truly cosmopolitan in his outlook and includes in his analysis writers as diverse in their cultural and political assumptions as Ariosto, Joyce, Calvino, Eugene O'Neill and Thomas Mann, among others. As a consequence Ariosto's *Orlando Furioso* is focused upon by Genette as a continuation and rewriting of Boiardo's *Orlando Innamorato*; Joyce's *Ulysses* and Homer's *Odyssey*; O'Neill's trilogy *Morning Becomes Electra* and its Greek ancestors by Euripides, Aeschylus, Sophocles, and Homer. According to Genette O'Neill lays waste a plot Greek tragedy had bequeathed him, and rewrites the motivations of Orestes, Agamemnon, Clytemnestra, and Electra in fascinating ways. 'Only Aegisthus/Brant pre-served solid family reasons for wishing the demise of Agamemnon/Ezra'. Thus O'Neill's rewriting of Greek tragedy is based on 'a pseudo-Freudian theory'. The above does not do justice to the complexity of Genette's argument which draws on such a wide range of material in the literary tradition of many countries. Imitation and rewriting takes a great deal of forms: parody, pastiche, homage, travesty, transposition, and forgery, all of which are woven into a complex and fascinating web by Genette.

Manfred Frank's work takes issue with the so-called 'death of the author' which is so closely associated with French poststructuralism. A collection of his work has been edited by Andrew Bowie. In *Manfred Frank: Essays on Literary Theory and Philosophy*, we are presented with four essays which address the poststructural project in its interpretation of literary texts. The most interesting of these is 'What is a literary text and what does it mean to understand it?'. As Bowie's erudite introduction to the volume explains, Frank's current work is an extension of, and further dialogue with, the early

German Romanticists, Novalis, Schlegel, and particularly, Schleiermacher. This is apparent in the opening pages to the essay referred to above. For Frank, post-Romantic hermeneutics are modern only when they adopt Schleiermacher's methodical doubt. From this premise Frank starts to answer the question what is a literary text, and how does one interpret it? He begins from the following observation: 'nothing is self-explanatory, everything calls for the act of interpretation. One never knows from the outset what a passage of text is supposed to mean'. Frank argues that the interpretation of a text should not be ungoverned by rules and that critics should first of all discover what 'grammar' – here interpreted as 'the totality of social and cultural codes of an age' – is altered by the author's construction of the text. This approach obviously offers an alternative approach to the one favoured by poststructuralists such as Derrida, Foucault, and Barthes. Indeed, Frank is much closer in his interpretative model to the work of Ricoeur and Hans Georg Gadamer. Throughout 'What is a literary text?' Frank engages vigorously with poststructural theory. Always, however, he brings us back to the German Romantics with their emphasis on selfhood.

The conflict of interpretations which is central to the difference between hermeneutics and poststructuralism as figured in the work of Paul Ricoeur, is approached by Frank through the hermeneutics of Schleiermacher, which is used as a basis for counter-acting deconstruction's preoccupation with the death of the subject, which in part forms the topic, through an analysis of Derrida's debate with Searle, of the last chapter in the volume. Georges Bataille is being increasingly recognized as a significant figure in the cultural history of twentieth-century Europe. A follower of the surrealist movement in art in the 1920s, of Marx in the early 1930s, and a student of Nietzsche's thought from 1936 onwards, Bataille exercised an important influence on structuralist and poststructural figures, such as Barthes and Foucault in the post-war years. It is therefore fitting that Fred Botting and Scott Wilson have edited *The Bataille Reader*, a volume which presents texts written by Bataille in the 1930s and 1940s. The volume is usefully divided into five sections subdivided as follows: Inner Experience; Heterology; General Economy; Eroticism; and Sovereignty. *The Bataille Reader* is a useful introductory volume to the work of an influential thinker and is accompanied by an introduction which is thoughtful and intelligent in mapping Bataille's development as a thinker.

Christopher Norris's *New Idols of the Cave: On the Limits of Anti-realism*, is a polemical dispute with what he sees as 'the errors and confusion' of a 'widespread relativist trend' in philosophy of science. This is fuelled and maintained by the preoccupation of paradox mongerers 'on the woollier fringes of literary academe', concerned as they are with 'chaos theory . . . and the like'; such are the purveyors of the 'new obscurantism'. Norris's attack on postmodern theories of science – based '(one suspects) on minimum acquaintance with the relevant scientific and philosophical literature' – quickly and predictably exempts Derrida from such shoddy intellectual paradox mongering. Indeed, it is Derrida and Empson who come to dominate this book. Chapters two, three, and four are specifically concerned with Empson and truth, deconstruction and philosophy and science, and deconstructing anti-realism, as read through Derrida's essay 'White Mythology'.

Throughout *New Idols of the Cave*, Norris is keen to uphold the importance of truth claims. Hence in a chapter on realism and semantics, Norris has recourse to Empson's *The Structure of Complex Words*, a book little read by philosophers, but which is none the less a rigorous analytical text which supports 'a more confidently realist outlook with regard to belief-content and propositional attitudes'.

Later in the book Norris deploys a deconstructive reading to critique postmodern views of science held by Lyotard, the proponent of 'paralogism, narrative pragmatics, and "performativity" as the measure of scientific truth'. All such theories, says Norris – and he includes Foucault's 'relentlessly sceptical genealogies of power/knowledge', as well as 'Heidegger, Gadamer, and expositors of a depth-hermeneutical approach' – have as their common ground 'a turn toward language . . . as a counter to realist claims of whatever variety'. Norris meets Lyotard et al. on their own ground by reading Empson and Derrida on metaphor in science, where once again he has recourse to *The Structure of Complex Words* to argue for the 'impossibility of doing without metaphor'. Typically Norris gives short shrift to what he sees as sloppy and ill-informed readings of scientific and philosophical texts. *New Idols of the Cave* is extremely well written and accessible for the non-specialist, but also has much food for thought for those more fully informed about the current state of the debate.

2. Marxism

Caryl Emerson's *The First Hundred Years of Mikhail Bakhtin* is a fascinating history of Bakhtin's reception in Russia from his first publication in 1929 until his death in 1975, and beyond to assess his posthumous rediscovery. Emerson's book is at once a literary history of Russia in the twentieth century, an intellectual biography, and a treatise on Russian literary criticism and the history of Russian ideas. The emphasis is on studying Bakhtin in his 'contexts', 'in this dizzying shift from centripetal Marxism–Leninism to the centrifugal currents of neo-humanism, neo-nationalism, and postmodernism'. Emerson's introductory chapter is discursive and puts Bakhtin's thought within a Russian intellectual context which is deeply pessimistic about recent movements in Western philosophical trends, particularly postmodernism, quoting Mikhail Epstein to the effect that in Russia ' "The concept of postmodernism is beginning to sound absurd" '. Once past her introductory remarks Emerson begins to analyse Bakhtin's contribution to European cultural history in its various and often very different contexts. There is an interesting and suggestive analogy made between Bakhtin's politics and Greek stoicism, a credo Bakhtin was familiar with through his undergraduate classics courses at Petrograd University. Emerson states that there are parallels between Bakhtin and those Greeks who were living in a *polis* which was in 'disarray', implying that Bakhtin's survivalist instinct was bolstered by the Epicurean notion that heroic martyrdom was a pointless activity in a state which was characterized by 'a corrupt body politic'. For Emerson, Bakhtin's 'resonance with [stoicism] is one index of his distance from mainstream Russian revolutionary activism'.

The First Hundred Years of Mikhail Bakhtin is organized along simple and helpful lines: part one is concerned with Bakhtin's reception history – recent and more distant – while part two is mainly expository and considers Bakhtin's writings, covering the main areas for which Bakhtin is most well known in the West: his poetics as they relate to his work on Dostoevsky, and his analysis of carnival. Overall this is a highly commendable book on a most important theorist.

Walter Benjamin's Other History: Of Stones, Animals, Human Beings, and Angels, by Beatrice Hanssen, is a thought-provoking study which aims to bring Benjamin closer to poststructuralist philosophy. Benjamin's writings on history and nature, as argued by Hanssen's deconstructionist analysis, 'needs to be placed in the context of a distinct ethico-theological tradition, one to be found in the work of Levinas and Derrida, no less than in Adorno's critical philosophy'. In *Walter Benjamin's Other History*, Hanssen 'calls for another kind of history', one which is not grounded in the history of the human subject, 'namely the category of natural history'. Benjamin's turn to natural history is predominantly argued through Benjamin's work on German baroque drama, the *Traurspiel*, particularly the chapters on 'The Ruin', and on allegory (1–3). The book itself is organized into two parts. In 'Part One: Towards a New Theory of Natural History', Hanssen places Benjamin's thought within the context of his times, comparing his work with that of Adorno and the Frankfurt School. Hanssen states that Benjamin shared with Adorno a desire to 'explode the hermeneutic circle', derived from Heidegger.

3. Introductions

In *Walter Benjamin* by Norbert Bolz and Willem Van Reijen, *Reading Knowledge* by Michael Payne, and in Niall Lucy's *Postmodern Literary Theory*, we are presented with three textbooks aimed at an undergraduate audience. Bolz and Van Reijen are concerned with the manner in which Benjamin continues to exercise a significant amount of influence on current cultural theory. They offer chapters in what is a very short though highly instructive introduction, on Benjamin and language, Benjamin and theology, and history, and aesthetics. Of these, language looms largest. For Bolz and Van Reijen 'Benjamin's reflections on language stand at the center of his philosophy'. Through his philosophy of language Benjamin forces the early twentieth century to face up to its 'failed reception of technology'. Language is the medium in which the world reveals itself to us' and the means by which Benjamin expressed his ideas on the centrality of the critic and criticism as fundamental to the 'completion of the work of art'. While there is nothing in this book with which the specialist will not be familiar, Bolz and Van Reijen make understandable the work of a philosopher and critic who is notoriously difficult to classify.

Similarly Michael Payne attempts to introduce the work of Barthes, Foucault, and Althusser to those not familiar with their ideas. For the purposes of his exposition Payne chooses to focus on how each author, through a brief analysis of their major writings, demonstrates their 'common interests in the forms and conditions of knowledge'. The heart of the book concerns readings of Barthes's *S/Z*, Foucault's *The Order of Things*, and

Althusser's *Reading Capital*. Like Bolz's book on Benjamin referred to above, the specialist will find nothing he or she does not already know. What makes this book valuable is the manner in which Payne relates complex ideas without appearing simplistic, a considerable skill in itself as any teacher of literary theory to the uninitiated will testify.

Niall Lucy's introduction is of a more complex order. More advanced than the previous volumes referred to in this section, Lucy's is a polemical book which deliberately states a strong case for the usefulness of reading literary texts from an informed theoretical basis. This is made apparent from the very beginning of the book when he distinguishes between reading from a liberal-humanist perspective, one which begins from the assumption that authors produce literature, as opposed by the idea that authors, like literature, are themselves produced 'by forces beyond their control'. The latter, he maintains, 'could be seen as leading to the development of postmodern literary theory'. As the book develops one becomes aware that Lucy is not an enthusiastic adherent of postmodern theory. This makes the book all the more reader friendly in that Lucy is clearly not trying to 'sell' postmodern theory to the unwary undergraduate. In a provocative chapter entitled 'The Death of Theory' Lucy draws the surprising conclusion that 'Despite the many apparent differences between them ... it is possible to see Harold Bloom and Jean-François Lyotard as being on the same side of "art against theory"'. This is even more surprising, says Lucy, when one considers how very differently both see Kant's *The Critique of Judgement*, in very negative and very positive terms, respectively. On this point, as on many others, Lucy is witty, provocative, and often erudite. His reference to Habermas's desire not to debate with postmodernism, but to silence it, and to Habermas's unjust accusations against Derrida, align Lucy with Norris whose systematic defence of Derrida is a consistent feature of his writing throughout the last decade. Though he clearly does not sympathize with postmodernism as such, Lucy's critique is never less than fair-minded.

4. Literature and Theory

This section reviews three books which demonstrate something of the theoretical differences illustrated in the previous sections and the writing of literary criticism. David Wallace has written what is arguably the most significant addition to Chaucer studies produced this decade. In *Chaucerian Polity: Absolutist Lineages and Associational Forms in England and Italy*, we are presented with an extremely sophisticated comparative analysis of English and Italian literature in the fourteenth century written from a Marxist perspective. From the beginning Wallace is keen to collapse the distinctions between the Medieval and Renaissance periods which he believes have been falsely constructed within the discipline of literary history. His analysis of Chaucer is placed within a European context and is deeply informed by a Marxist literary-historiographical methodology. Hence Chaucer's trips to Italy in the 1370s were not the experiences of a naive country bumpkin travelling from the darkness of the northern European dark ages to the bright lights of the Italian Renaissance, but an easy transition within a world which was dominated by 'capital, warfare and wool'. Constantly in *Chaucerian Polity* Wallace keeps in the foreground the integrated relationship between politics and economics, always viewed in this study from a Marxist perspective. The cities of northern Italy, particularly Florence and Milan, represent two points of political conflict which is specifically ideological, the former being the period's best representation of republican *libertas*, and the latter, the embodiment of despotism as personified by the Visconti dukes. *The Canterbury Tales* revisits these political territories in a variety of ways: in the arbitrary Thesian polity of *The Knight's Tale*, and in the Lombardy of *The Clerk's Tale*, and *The Merchant's Tale*, a place which 'comes to represent for Chaucer a spatial metaphor for the tyrannical cast of mind'. Wallace takes the latest work in Marxist and feminist theory to create an inordinately powerful rendering of the medieval political and economic state.

Jonathan Goldberg's *Desiring Women's Writing: English Renaissance Examples* also pursues linkages, but in contrast to Wallace Goldberg is more concerned with feminine virtue in the period and the status of women's writing within the canon. *Desiring Women's Writing* is deeply informed by poststructuralist thought, and the manner in which Derrida's texts have been filtered through feminist theory. Goldberg sees through a reading of Elaine Hobby's work that 'gender is a relational category that exceeds the binary men/women'. With this in mind Goldberg does not read early modern women's writing from a biographical perspective; rather, he chooses to focus on a wide range of women writers from the late sixteenth to the late-seventeenth centuries and to approach them through a gendered reading which pays close attention to their relationship to the centres of power. As this is the early modern period, this centre of power is for the most part the court. This, and the fact that what unites Aemilia Lanier and Aphra Behn in the first section of the book is 'structures of desire', signpost Goldberg's analysis as one which is indelibly marked by the governing tropes of New Historicism. In his final chapter Goldberg argues in his analysis of Elizabeth Cary's *Tragedy of Mariam* that a deconstructive reading is an altogether plausible one. The character Graphina, *Graph-ina*, 'genders writing as female'. From this point Goldberg states that – glancing at Derrida's *Of Grammatology* – 'writing occupies the same idealized and prescriptive space that women do' in early modern England. And so on. Goldberg is a deft reader of Renaissance literature, as any one who has read his *James I and the Politics of Literature* can testify. The book is on the whole uneven. The chapters on early seventeenth-century women writers work much better than his comments on Aphra Behn, a writer working in an entirely different context from the Elizabethan and Jacobean figures he treats so well.

Timothy Clark's *The Theory of Inspiration: Composition as a Crisis of Subjectivity in Romantic and Post-Romantic Writing* offers an extremely sophisticated analysis of writers as diverse as Plato, Wordsworth, Shelley, Nietzsche, Breton, H. D. Blanchot, and finally, Derrida. Clark's subject is inspiration, an unfashionable term in literary criticism nowadays, as he quickly informs us in his introductory remarks. Yet the legacy of Romantic inspiration is a powerful one and writers continued to idealize the act of writing well into the twentieth century. Rather than approach the topic of inspiration from a liberal humanist perspective, Clark argues that 'the term inspiration comes increasingly to name a crisis of subjectivity at odds with any humanist mythology of psychic power'. The figures which Clark focuses on to elaborate his thesis are Nietzsche, Shelley, and Hölderlin especially, although there are chapter-length studies on Blanchot and Derrida which draw heavily on poststructural theories of subjectivity. Overall this is an extremely thorough study of a much-neglected subject. Clark's grasp of aesthetics is never less than invigorating and his exposition of complex texts is always stimulating and to the point.

5. Reference Works

The following three books are additions to a growing market of dictionaries and encyclopaedias designed to help the undergraduate student through the complexities of literary theory. In Michael Payne, ed., *A Dictionary of Cultural and Critical Theory* we have an A–Z which is arguably the most affordable and complete single volume edition available to date. Some of the entries such as 'Marxism and Marxist Criticism', 'Postmodernism', and 'Philosophy of Law' amount to extremely informative small essays. Payne's dictionary is wide-ranging and discursive and will suit the needs of undergraduates in the social sciences as well as the humanities. *The Bedford Glossary of Critical and Literary Terms* (Murfin and Supryia, eds), however, as the title would suggest, is more clearly aimed at the student of literature. Accordingly the entries are more specifically geared to the terminology involved in analysing poetry, prose, and drama. That said, where cultural and philosophical movements have had the most impact on literature (postmodernism, poststructuralism, Marxism, feminism), there are lengthy and detailed expositions. Finally, in Mark Baurlein's *Literary Criticism: An Autopsy*, we have a glossary which attempts to do more than give an uncontroversial explanation of technical terms. Instead, Baurlein takes issue with the currency of critical and theoretical jargon, offering opinions as well as potted explanations. A good case in point is his explanation of the term 'deconstruction', which some critics and philosophers, such as Lucy and Norris, have attached political value to. According to Baurlein 'political deconstruction has three benefits: the escape from metaphysics, the elevation of political discussion, the incisiveness of interpretation', making for 'extra-textual involvements with politics'. Baurlein's *Autopsy* is much narrower in scope than the other reference works reviewed. However, in its aims to clarify terms current in cultural and critical enquiry and ask questions about the politics behind glib assertions of postmodern and poststructural theories, Baurlein's text makes readers think about the terms they are using rather than simply regurgitate bite-sized explanations.

Books Reviewed

Baurlein, Mark. *Literary Criticism: An Autopsy*. University of Pennsylvania Press. pp. 156. £15.50. ISBN 0 8122 1625 3.

Bolz, Norbert and Willem Van Reijen, *Walter Benjamin*. Trans. Laimdotta Mazzarins. Humanities Press. pp. 106. pb £11.50. ISBN 0 391 03942 3.

Botting, Fred and Scott Wilson, eds. *The Bataille Reader.* Blackwell. pp. 353. pb £14.99. ISBN 0 631 19959 4.

Clark, Timothy. *The Theory of Inspiration: Composition as a Crisis of Subjectivity in Romantic and Post-Romantic Writing.* Manchester University Press. pp. 312. hb £40.00. ISBN 0 7190 5064 2.

Derrida, Jacques. *Politics of Friendship.* trans. George Collins. Verso. pp. 308. pb £15.00. ISBN 1 85984 033 7.

Emerson, Caryl. *The First Hundred Years of Mikhail Bakhtin.* Princeton University Press. pp. 293. hb £25.00 ISBN 0 691 06976 X.

Frank, Manfred. *The Subject and the Text: Essays on Literary Theory and Philosophy,* edited with an introduction by Andrew Bowie. Cambridge University Press. pp. 199. hb £40.00. ISBN 0 521 56121 3.

Genette, Gerard. *Palimpsests: Literature in the Second Degree.* Trans. Channa Newman and Claude Doubinsky. University of Nebraska Press. pp. 490. pb £28.50. ISBN 0 8032 7029 1.

Goldberg, Jonathan. *Desiring Women's Writing: English Renaissance Examples.* Stanford University Press. pp. 255. pb £11.95. ISBN 0 8047 2983 2.

Hanssen, Beatrice. *Walter Benjamin's Other History: Of Stones, Animals, Human Beings, and Angels.* University of California Press. pp. 207. £30.00. ISBN 0 520 20841 2.

Lucy, Niall. *Postmodern Literary Theory: An Introduction.* Blackwell. pp. 283. hb £45.00. ISBN 0 631 20000 2.

Murfin, Ross and Supryia M. Ray. *The Bedford Glossary of Critical and Literary Terms.* Bedford Books. pp. 457. pb £11.99. ISBN 0 333 69096 6.

Norris, Christopher. *New Idols of the Cave: on the Limits of Anti-realism.* Manchester University Press. pp. 253. hb £40.00. ISBN 0 7190 5092 8.

Payne, Michael. *Reading Knowledge: An Introduction to Barthes, Foucault and Althusser.* Blackwell. pp. 121. pb £14.99. ISBN 0 631 19567 X.

Payne, Michael. *A Dictionary of Cultural and Critical Theory.* Blackwell. pp. 644. pb £16.99. ISBN 0 631 20753 8.

Wallace, David. *Chaucerian Polity: Absolutist Lineages and Associational Forms in England and Italy.* Stanford University Press. pp. 555. hb £40.00. ISBN 0 8047 2724 4.

2

Semiotics

ADRIAN PAGE

Jonathan Bignell's *Media Semiotics, an Introduction* offers students a guide to the semiotic study of advertisements, newspapers, magazines, television and film. This is an ambitious attempt to present the vast literature on semiotics in both an informative and critical manner for students who are new to the subject. The various approaches to the study of signs in the media are illustrated by applying them to media texts and a careful evaluation of each approach ensures that further issues are left open to be explored. Bignell rightly suggests that the approaches to semiotics range from the rather rigid theory of structuralism to the much looser style of ethnography. The author himself chooses to situate his own approach somewhere between these two extremes and argues that texts 'position' their readers but that audiences can also negotiate meaning.

This is a very subtle balance to maintain, and it is interesting to observe how a range of alternatives can be made available to students in each case study. To be entirely consistent in this strategy requires constant self-criticism. Bignell warns students that it is dangerous to assume that all texts compel us to accept one meaning and that audiences can decode texts in eccentric or deviant ways. The analysis of a *Wonderbra* advertisement seeks to exemplify this state of affairs by both specifying the position that the advertisement advances for us, and speculating on the ideological diversity it represents. Can a *Wonderbra* ad really be read as both a cynical attempt to persuade women to emulate others by buying consumer goods and also as a feminist statement? It might have been helpful in this instance to relate the analysis more closely to the overall issues in semiotics. It is, of course, debatable whether certain images and signs are irredeemably harmful and cannot always be recuperated by imaginative decoding.

The *Wonderbra* study includes a picture of a model wearing a green *Wonderbra* with the caption 'Terrible thing Envy'. There is also a *Wonderbra* label and a statement, 'Now available in extravert green'. The view that this image can be read as a feminist statement is based on the slender evidence that the word 'extravert' *anchors* the meaning that women can choose whether to project their sexuality or not. This suggests that the meaning is fixed, yet it is also stated that the ad invites us to enjoy the 'unanchoredness' of its signs.

Barthes' term 'anchorage' is in fact used of two signs which can be seen as substitutable for each other. Hence the picture's meaning is anchored by the word '*Wonderbra*' which specifies exactly what the picture is meant to signify. Both the word and image signify the same in this context. The use of two signifiers with the same signified specifies clearly what is meant. Bignell refers to the *relay* between the bra denoted iconically in the ad and the linguistic sign '*Wonderbra*', whereas it should surely be anchorage.

Barthes' term 'relay' seems more appropriate in the case of the relationship between the word 'extravert' and the image. Relay establishes a complementary relationship between the two elements so that they can play a part in a larger syntagm, according to Barthes. The caption and the image here are clearly an example of relay since juxtaposing them invites the observer to contemplate multiple ways of completing the syntagm of the advertisement. Although the analysis Bignell provides is subtle and aware of multiple possibilities, it would be immensely valuable to students if such useful terms were defined and used to define a methodology which can accommodate ambiguities.

In an introductory textbook, students may need to know how to arrive at such analyses rather than be exposed to highly complex interpretations made by authors. This book, however, illustrates the problems in contemporary semiotics, since the methodological choices are not presented. Consequently, it is difficult to see the borderline between our positioning by signs and our freely produced readings. Is all positioning inevitable, or can we always resist? Although students will undoubtedly find this a stimulating introduction to the subject, the examples seem to suggest at times that film can successfully and pleasurably resolve ideological issues in our culture. On these occasions, the fundamental theoretical position as outlined seems to be obscured.

Appropriating Images: the Semiotics of Visual Representation (1996) by Keyan G. Tomaselli takes an unashamedly anthropological approach to the study of cultures in film. Tomaselli argues that semiology 'excludes the category of experience' and that an approach which is based on Saussurean dichotomies such as subject and object can only deal with what can be known. The anthropological approach must incorporate an appreciation of the diversity and strangeness of cultures. Semiotics, for Tomaselli, therefore, is the study of signs in their cultural context with a full recognition of their uniqueness. Tomaselli exposes the difficulty in an approach such as Bignell's which attempts to synthesize semiology and semiotics. Semiology insists on a kind of cultural supremacy whereby all signifying systems can be assimilated into existing symbolic structures.

As an academic working in South Africa, Tomaselli is able to produce some very pertinent examples of resistance and domination in the field of visual sign production. The taxonomic style of semiology does little to illustrate the dynamic struggle for power in representation, which Tomaselli is concerned with. In one case study, the author describes the reaction to a film, *Indaba Ye Grievance*, which was made to represent the legal battles for workers' rights that Zulu workers engaged in by an ethnographic style. The workers were recorded expressing themselves as they normally would, including gesture and dance. The film counterbalanced the more conventional style of the white South African attempt to capture the same topic in the documentary, *A World of Difference*. As Tomaselli observes, the reason for discrepancies in interpretations of the same situation lies in the cultural contexts of the two groups of viewers. It is not the case that all discrepant interpretation can be classified as 'aberrant decoding'. Tomaselli explicitly rejects much of the positioning which is inherent in many South African films and leads the viewer to accept apartheid. Tomaselli therefore rejects the view that texts inevitably position their audiences, and raises the question of whether freedom of interpretation and attempts at 'positioning' audiences can ever co-exist. This is a stimulating development of the anthropological study of signs and for once also investigates the far-reaching political consequences of the discipline. This work also does a great deal to justify the claim that the ethnographic film cannot be understood by linguistic means and that the precise ideology and values of the film crew also make a considerable difference to the presentation of the material.

Roy Harris sets out to elaborate a linguistic theory in *Signs, Language and Communication* (1996), which adds further weight to Tomaselli's arguments. Harris distinguishes between the *segregationist* theories of communication which see the study as a subdivision of human activity with its own rules and procedures, and the *integrationist* theories which stress that communication has to be studied as an integral aspect of human behaviour. Harris subscribes to the integrationist theory and argues for an understanding of 'the participants' activities, both physical and mental'. Harris emphasizes the role of signs as creative in fashioning our perception of the world rather than simply echoing the rules of an immutable system. He is therefore at one with Tomaselli in stressing that not all non-verbal behaviour is describable in linguistic terms and that context is all-important. This book, however, takes the whole debate further by reminding us that the simple dichotomy may be theoretically attractive but merely 'postpones' the problem of interpretation. When an integrationist discovers some consistency in human uses of signs, for example, can this not simply be seized upon by the segregationist as a system? Whereas Tomaselli wishes to address substantial issues of politics through visual texts, Harris is primarily concerned with theory and having stated his belief, then proceeds to defend it against a range of other theories in linguistics. Umberto Eco's distinction between intentional signs and natural signs (e.g. smoke as a sign of fire) is dismissed by the integrationist as a *semiological* distinction. This lays the axe to the root of much of Eco's thinking. For the integrationist, the sign is defined by the human activities it integrates. Thus the marriage ceremony is analysed as a ritual which, although closely defined, none the less establishes a complementary relationship with preceding social practices by the participants. The artificier fallacy, by which the maker of a work of art can endow that work with a meaning, is also attacked.

The most fundamental distinction which Harris draws between the two theories is that they are, in fact, rival epistemologies. He cites Lacan as an example of the segregationist fallacy through his theory of the mirror stage. For Harris, the theory presupposes that knowledge of oneself depends on interpersonal communication, and he vigorously denies this. Just how self-communication can be achieved without some form of pre-existent signs is still unclear, however. Harris is highly consistent in his theory and maintains that all communication occurs as if for the first time, but this is perhaps still the most difficult assumption to accept. When Robinson Crusoe communicates with himself it is through keeping a diary, which, of course, ironically depends on the available signs of language. This is an important work which challenges much contemporary thinking in a disciplined manner.

Peter Bondanella's survey of Umberto Eco's entire work is concise, lucid and also at times polemical. In *Umberto Eco and the Open Text* he manages to summarize a vast oeuvre in an engaging manner. Bondanella describes Eco's early encounter with medieval scholasticism as an early introduction to a type of structuralism and a counter to the aesthetic intuitionism of Croce. He uses the title of one of Eco's early books, *The Open Work* (1962), as a condensed appraisal of Eco's lifetime ambitions. Having detected that the artist's vision was not enshrined forever in an immutable form, Eco's intellectual progress can be seen as an attempt to promote the written work of art as the property of the reader as opposed to the writer. The valuable feature of this account of Eco's intellectual development is that it does enable us to see the progression of ideas. The opening up of the text ironically also makes it less penetrable in that its depth and complexity continually frustrate the postmodern reader in search of stable meaning. Bondanella explores how this theoretical perception underlies the fiction Eco has produced. In novels such as *Foucault's Pendulum* Eco attempts to thwart any clever readings which will seek to expose a fundamental meaning and continues to deny even himself the privilege of the status as a writer of unique insight. What Bondanella does not quite perceive perhaps, is that Eco both dismisses the uniqueness of modern culture and demonstrates how even postmodern theories had their origins in antiquity, but does so in a unique and instantly distinguishable manner. Even if he can be classified as a segregationist, Eco has created an artistic practice that seems to transcend the semiotic principles upon which it is based.

As Brian Stock reminds us in *Listening for the Text*, a work which incorporates a number of essays on history and language, Ricoeur wrote that the problem of writing must be separated from the text. Stock's focus on history reminds us that semiotics may concentrate on discourse, but that history is concerned with *events*, the particularity of events will not be arrived at by studying the rules of discourse. For Stock it is not the text which historians need to study in detail but the uses and interpretations that are made of it. Daniel Punday, in an article entitled 'Meaning in Postmodern Worlds: the Case of *The French Lieutenant's Woman*' (*Semiotica* 115, 3/4 (1997) 313–343), argues that in a postmodern novel such as this, there is no sign which simply signifies the past, but that any sign has to be seen as enmeshed in multiple relationships.

Many works on contemporary semiotics appear to have subscribed to one or other of two camps. Whereas some specify the rules and principles which can be abstracted from textual studies to establish a systematic approach to interpretation, others adopt a more descriptive approach and attempt to elaborate on the breaking of rules and the establishment of new artistic practices. In work on linguistic theory and signs, however, these two positions are not always seen as mutually exclusive. Paul J. Thibault, in *Re-Reading Saussure: the Dynamics of Signs in Social Life* argues that Saussure is not guilty of repressing the role of the individual in meaning making and attempts to defend his reputation which is sometimes easily dismissed these days. Thibault reads Saussure carefully to extract the view that *langue* and *parole* are, in fact, interdependent and not rigidly separable. *Langue*, for example, is interpreted as a phenomenon which cannot exist without *parole*, and Saussure's stress on semiotics as a branch of social psychology, means that he saw *langue* as existing in some kind of inter-individual understanding.

Thibault suggests that Saussure conceives of the individual as a social type and that there is not, therefore a clear dichotomy between the individual and society as is generally believed. This also accounts for the interdependency of *langue* and *parole*. *Langue*, in other words, is realized in individual acts of *parole*. Thibault also describes how *parole* is the seed of change in the language system and dispels a common belief that Saussurean linguistics cannot accommodate linguistic change. The arbitrariness of the signifier is also scrupulously explored and critics such as Jonathan Culler are argued to have missed the point. The signifier is motivated within any one language system, although its arbitrariness is evident in an absolute sense. In defending Saussure against the criticisms of rigidity voiced by Terence Hawkes and Ruqaiya Hasan, Thibault makes an interesting comparison between Saussure and Volosinov and presents an argument to show that they are remarkably similar. The sole exception is that Volosinov lacks a theory of *langue*. In conclusion, the relations between language and other semiotic systems in social semiosis are referred to and some interesting examples drawn from visual communication. This is a spirited defence of the richness of Saussure's work, and although it may sometimes appear to be an ingenious elaboration based on Saussure rather than an interpretation, it none the less indicates the direction in which semiotic thought is progressing.

This defence of Saussure's semiotic theory may help to reverse the trend towards Peircean thought that has been evident in recent publications. C. S. Peirce's vast collection of theoretical writings has often seemed to be more amenable to writers such as Umberto Eco and Julia Kristeva. *The Portable Kristeva*, edited by Oliver Kelly, was published in 1997 and contains some of the classic essays on semiotics. In particular in 'The Semiotic and the Symbolic', Kristeva distinguishes between the psychoanalytic concept of the semiotic *chora* which exists in an inchoate flux along with the drives, and the symbolic which can be represented. This chapter from the much earlier *Desire in Language* (1974) makes a differentiation between that towards which signs can only gesture and the knowable universe. It is a powerful challenge to more rigid materialist theories and helps Kristeva to theorize on women's experience in terms which are not predominantly patriarchal.

In Floyd Merrell's *Peirce, Signs and Meaning*, the primacy of the individual is again challenged as simply another 'sign amongst signs'. Merrell begins with a witty fictional dialogue to summarize Peircean theory in which the familiar triadic diagrams proliferate until every sign is also an interpretant and enmeshed within an inescapable network. This is a further attempt to break down the self/society dichotomy. The result is a schematic representation of language which shows considerable similarity to Derrida's deconstructionism.

Merrell also attacks 'linguicentrism' which seeks to concentrate almost exclusively on symbolic sign systems to the exclusion of iconic and indexical signs. The issue at stake behind this very detailed study of Peirce's theories is the illusion of individuality. To risk a vast simplification, the sign is either at the disposal of the individual or composes the individual and dictates his or her activity. Meaning in Peircean philosophy seems to revert to a socially determined *fait accompli*, which no amount of individual creativity can subvert. Pragmatism, which attempts to put an end to the disputes of philosophers concerning the meanings of words, may ultimately seem to be a counsel of despair. Can we really allow the meanings of all words to be dictated by the network of relations implicit in the sign system, and forgo our opportunity to put forward values and beliefs?

Peter Bogh Andersen could be described as making full use of the pragmatists' arguments in his book, *A Theory of Computer Semiotics*. He compares the designer of a computer system to a playwright who first sketches a plot and only later fills in reactions to each element. The theory of computer design outlined by Andersen is based on the view that semiotics is now so refined that it can be adapted in programming. Andersen cites Peirce as one of the theorists used in the earliest attempts to systematize programming. The interface was argued to be an example of the representamen. The structuralist attempts at classification have paved the way for programming which is based on signs and their meanings. Of the three types of reasoning identified by Peirce: deduction, induction and abduction, only abduction cannot as yet be successfully modelled. Abduction involves inventing rules to cover an unanticipated occurrence, sometimes without logical justification. Andersen quotes Eco's use of this term to illustrate how language cannot be entirely modelled on a logical basis. To return to the issue of whether signs compel us to accept certain meanings or not, Ibrahim Taha, in an article entitled 'The Literary Communication Pact: a Semiotic Approach' (*Semiotica* 114, 1/2 (1997) 131–150), develops a theoretical model which stresses that both the author and the reader enter into a voluntary agreement to read signs in a particular manner.

Books Reviewed

Andersen, Peter Bogh. *A Theory of Computer Semiotics*. Cambridge University Press. pp. 405. pb $29.95. ISBN 0 521 44868 9.
Bignell, Jonathan. *Media Semiotics, an Introduction*. Manchester University Press. pp. 223. pb £11.99. ISBN 0 7190 4501 0.
Bondanella, Peter. *Umberto Eco and the Open Text: Semiotics, fiction, popular culture*. Cambridge University Press. pp. 218. hb £30.00. ISBN 0 521 44200 1.
Harris, Roy. *Signs, Language and Communication*. Routledge. pp. 279. hb £30.00. ISBN 0 415 10089 5.
Merrell, Floyd. *Peirce, Signs and Meaning*. University of Toronto Press. pp. 384. pb $24.95. ISBN 0 8020 4135 3.
Oliver, Kelly, ed. *The Portable Kristeva*. Columbia University Press. pp. 410. pb £12.99. ISBN 0 231 10505 3.
Stock, Brian. *Listening for the Text: on the Uses of the Past*. University of Pennsylvania Press. pp. 197. pb £10.95. ISBN 0 812 1612 1.
Thibault, Paul J. *Re-reading Saussure: the Dynamics of Signs in Social Life*. Routledge. pp. 360. pb £17.99. ISBN 0 415 10411 4.
Tomaselli, Keyan G. *Appropriating Images: the Semiotics of Visual Representation*. Intervention Press. pp. 332. pb $31.00. ISBN 87 89825 05 5.

3

Psychoanalysis

ANNE-MARIE SMITH

It may not be inappropriate to play with a double meaning of 'The Year's Work in Psychoanalysis', the implied title of this chapter. It may refer not only to books produced in the field of psychoanalysis, often by academics for academics, but also in a more literal sense, to the joint venture of analyst and patient, session after session, season after season, which becomes theory when the analyst takes up his or her pen to become a writer of psychoanalysis. What concerns me in this ambiguity is an academic separation between the two which leads us to consider only one side of the question, commonly called psychoanalytic theory. This is a serious rift since it forgets origins. Psychoanalysis needs patients, patients with stories.

The books I have chosen to review all bridge this rift in various ways. John Forrester takes us behind the scenes of psychoanalysis' controversial and ongoing history. Ilse Grubich-Simitis captures the material aspects of its production in the raw. She documents in detail the painstaking construction of a science, discipline and corpus of texts by Freud, whom she represents writing, living through the history of his time, listening to patients, note-taking, sifting, talking with colleagues, letter-writing, hoarding dream material, collating, publishing, crossing frontiers, fleeing persecution, and being translated. Kristeva, reading Proust, reminds us that psychoanalysis and literature are the reliable guardians of subjective experience and singularity, which enable us to breach the gap between the realm of the 'sensible', of sensory experience, akin to Irigaray's definition of the 'natural', on the one hand and language, culture and the socio-political corpus on the other. Poetic activity has the same function for Cixous. Irigaray draws our attention to how this gap is instituted by the breach between nature and culture onto which femininity and masculinity are mapped, preventing a full realization of sex and gender within the individual, for both sexes.

University humanities departments, especially in America and the UK, are often characterized by the rapid consumption of theory, often French theory in translation, forgetting its origins, spinning off into the production of more theory. Psychoanalysis has been left somewhere far behind. In this situation, precisely because it is cut off from, even from thinking about, practice – poetic and clinical practice, and psychoanalysis is concerned with both, theory, to quote Hélène Cixous, 'take[s] the spare wheel for the bird':

There is a continuity in the living; whereas theory entails a discontinuity, a cut, which is altogether the opposite of life. I am not anathematizing all theory. It is indispensable, at times, to make progress, but alone, it is false . . . So I am worried when I see certain tendencies in reading: they take the spare wheel for the bird.

I have included Cixous' book in this collection because although she consistently avoids all psychoanalytic terminology, her reflections on the practice of writing come very close to the meaning of psychoanalysis' legacy to reading: the unconscious in language, language's return to the poetic, which as readers of literature is perhaps what concerns us most: 'this urgency, this need to decipher what cannot be said, what is expressed otherwise than in verbal speech which nonetheless arouses the desire for words'.

Cixous is primarily a poet and a writer on poetics even if her more polemical texts are those best known outside France. The text, *Rootprints*, presented in the form of a dialogue with Mireille Calle-Gruber, reader and interlocutor who spans two worlds: France and Canada, and with a contribution from Jacques Derrida in the appendix, sets the record straight. Cixous and Derrida write, hearing language as quickly as it speaks, with the ear of a foreigner: 'like a second language: as one reads languages by the roots'. They share 'a foreign relationship to the French language'. Lacan called this 'l'autre du langage', the other side of language heard in words resonating strangely from the analyst's couch. Psychoanalysis is about language's otherness and only language can reveal it.

Derrida says the same of sexual difference:

There cannot be sexual difference without trace, . . . sexual difference is to be interpreted, to be deciphered, to be decoded, to be read and not to be seen. Readable, thus invisible . . . it passes by, it is in passage, it passes from the one to the other, by the one and the other.

The translator of this volume, Eric Prenowitz, is to be congratulated for his attention to the intense poetization which is a proverbial feature of both Cixous' and Derrida's prose and which Mireille Calle-Gruber cites as fundamental to Cixous' enterprise, often cast as theoretical rather than poetic outside France: 'through poetry . . . in the course of the work of fiction, you pursue an effort of lucidity: in the place of writing's blindness – of which you are conscious'.

Cixous is arguing for taking language by the roots, for a return to roots – the volume is illustrated with photos of her past: *Photos de Racine*, the French title of the book – against the secateur grip of theory. Kristeva, in Columbia University Press' translation of her overwhelming study of Proustian language: *Time and Sense*, is arguing for a return to sentient time – the inscription of sensation in language through the metaphor of the Proustian sentence. Ross Guberman's rendering of the French title (*Le temps sensible* 1994), like Stephen Bann's before him: *Proust and the Sense of Time* (1993), a UK edition (Faber) which in fact appeared before the French original, does not translate this notion of sentient time. Sentient Time would be a more sensitive translation. Kristeva's title looks three ways: backwards – nostalgically, fowards – with inspiration, and pauses at Proust's texts as that to which we must return. The lyricism is lost in translation. Lyricism is the living source of the theory: for Kristeva, time in Proust is an association of two sensations. Past sensation inhabits us. Involuntary memory returns to it when a present perception associated with the past, as Freud argues, by the desire which traverses time, links up with the past. Proust's metaphors are lined with sensation. They are analogies – maintaining two different terms in reciprocity or contradiction. We cannot talk about the word or the sign as the minimal element of Proust's writing. We have to talk about a style amalgamating the sensation and the idea, the image incarnate. Sensations associated in this way across time and space lose their specificity and become impression which the reader shares as a sensory experience. The reader reading participates in a communion, an identification with something both at once inside and outside himself. This real and symbolic presence in sensation recalls the complexity of sacrament in theological discourse and Merleau-Ponty's account of 'le sensible' in phenomenology. So sentient time, *le temps sensible*, integrating the movement of history and personal history is what enables images and text to emerge, lyrically, from the silences of the dark-room. According to Kristeva, psychoanalysis and literature are guardians of subjective experience and the Proustian text both provides us with and demands of us a time and space accorded to the exploration of subjectivity and of sexual desire, to a form of revolt which is fundamentally poetic. And she does not forget patients, drawing a poignant analogy between reading Proust and treating the autistic child, between literary and analytic receptivity, which, the book shows, go hand in hand.

Two of the books I have chosen to review belong to the New Library of Psychoanalysis, edited by Elizabeth Bott Spillius and published by Routledge in association with the Institute of Psychoanalysis. 'Its purpose is to facilitate a greater understanding of what psychoanalysis is about and to provide a forum for increasing mutual understanding between psychoanalysts and those in other disciplines. The series also aims to make some of the work of Continental and other non-English-speaking analysts more readily available to English-speaking readers, and to increase the interchange of ideas between British and American analysts'. One of the assets of this collection is its demonstration of how theory both emerges from and shapes practice. Its translation policy is moreover a visible espousal of the transculturality which is inseparable from the history and dissemination of psychoanalytic thought. Anna Potamianou is an analyst and university teacher whose practice spans two worlds: Paris and Greece. *Hope: A Shield in the Economy of Borderline States* is a translation from French by Philip Slotkin. To follow Potamianou's theorizing the reader will need to be familiar with the psychoanalytic terminology of cathexis, decathexis and countercathexis, terms derived from the science of energy in a perhaps deliberate reiteration of the physical as indissociable from the psychical, to refer to the preservation, spending and channelling of energy, to libidinal economy. Potamianou is concerned with symptoms of breakdown in libidinal economy and more radically with how serious borderline states may be screened by clinging to an immutable form of hope which amounts to delusion.

Her exposition draws its dynamism equally from related case histories and the literature of Greek myth. There is then a timeless, theatrical resonance in her scenarios which not only breathes new life into the ancient figures, gods and men, of Greek drama, but also provides the tenor of her psychoanalytic listening: to witness, wonder and reflect like a spectator in the ampitheatre, 'The ego addresses itself to its ideal as a child to the omnipotent parents. ' "Give me all . . ., Papa", says Artemis to Zeus. And Zeus replies: "Take, child, everything you want, and Father will give you other things even better" '.

Potamianou defines as a 'central problem of analytic practice' Freud's hesitation and after Freud, the analyst's hesitation between 'on the one hand, what is rediscovered (memories, traumas, the truth of the past), i.e. the plot of a substantially prerecorded text which must be remembered – and on the other, fantasy, everything that is created in the bipersonal relationship of the treatment, the transformations achieved in the transference, which is not a copy but a new production'. This is an important question since it addresses the controversial issue of the place of fantasy in any reconstruction and indeed of truth – or psychic reality in fantasy. It is the question of objectivity which can only be illuminated by a proper understanding of, that is the ability to read, formations of fantasy at all levels.

Different analysts profess different degrees of objectivity as we again see in *Back to Freud's Texts* by the German psychoanalyst, writer and Freud editor, Ilse Grubrich-Simitis. This book is also translated by Philip Slotkin who deserves mention for his vast contribution to the English translation of European psychoanalysis. Grubich-Simitis is making a stance, against over-interpretation, for patient, attentive listening to texts, Freud's texts:

> *Back to Freud's texts* is meant not in the sense of Jacques Lacan's *Retour à Freud*, that collective appeal for a fundamental reinterpretation and « retrointerpretation » of psychoanalysis, or even in the sense of Jean Laplanche's rigorous translation imperative *Le texte, tout le texte, rien que le texte*, but in an even more concrete and simpler, literally literal sense: back to Freud's texts in their original manuscript form.

The subtitle of the book is *Making Silent Documents Speak* 'an advocacy of the texts as intense as it is sober . . . making the documents speak for themselves, so as to reveal Freud's thought in new and fresh light in the materiality and myriad details of his manuscripts.' This is a critical position which requires considerable modesty and humility as well as the sobriety to which she refers and which leads her to cite in the epigraph Starobinski's essay 'Le texte et l'interprète' in her argument for relative objectivity over *furor biographicus*. She returns to Starobinski's argument as paradigmatic of her approach in the introduction: 'to guarantee a maximum of presence and independence for the object of our study' so that 'it [is] able to assert its difference and maintain its distance', or to intensify its 'material aspects' causing it 'to stand out in bolder relief with a sharper outline' and aiding and abetting it precisely 'in its ability to resist us'. She goes as far as to evoke, again via Starobinski, the phenomena of abuse in the form of the ill-treatment of the text by interpreters who appropriate it for themselves in terms of their own desire. This definition of approach, in which we are alerted to the words of a practitioner who has listened to patients suffering the intrusion of the other's desire, sketches an ethics of reading which sets up scientific rigour against the incursions of desire into any act of interpretation. It might be more appropriate, as readers, to analyse the ways in which desire itself resists this kind of policing and Grubich-Simitis displaces her own onto a reverant concern for the material aspects of Freudian production, a loving concern for sources and hand-written traces, which the French call Genetic Criticism. Such rigorous and loving attention to the detail and conditions of history makes this book an invaluable reminder against theory's forgetting of origins. Our glimpses of Freud at work, none the less stage-managed by Grubich-Simitis' pen, and not only focuses our attention upon the pleasure and pain of Freud writing and attempting to establish a psychoanalytic press, but also recalls his own revolutionary attention to the power of words: Freud listening to patients speaking, convinced they have something to say about the nature of suffering, which in the process of writing becomes the discovery and theory of the unconscious, in language. Analytic listening, writing as a form of interpretation, and the dissemination of these processes as shaped by editorial and translation history, as well as the material evolution of theory – itself an aspect of reading, are all nicely bound together in this story of origins.

Adam Phillips is a writer of paradoxes, neat paradoxes which he continues to inhabit when one wishes he would somehow find a way out, but that is perhaps the very point of his style. *Terrors and Experts* inhabits that space between personal terrors and the reassurance of experts, a fictional space in which we hover between symptoms and authorities, 'fascination with fictions' and recourse to the 'experts on the canon', each embodied in the figure of the psychoanalyst. Phillips elaborates the psychoanalytic paradox: the double status of the analyst, the quest for certainty to which the answer is always more uncertainty. At least of that we can be sure:

> We may be unacceptable to ourselves, Freud the confident
> Enlightenment scientist suggests, but we are not unintelligible
> to ourselves ... Pain, the psychoanalyst must believe, can be
> translated, like a language ... But the post-Freudian analyst –
> the man who was always ahead of himself, and who we are
> beginning to catch up with – was the ironist of exactly this
> Enlightenment project. He was an expert on the impossibility of
> self-knowledge, on the limits of expertise ...

Phillips lightens and demystifies. He defines psychoanalysis as 'a conversation in which people cannot help but experiment with themselves'. He draws attention to the fundamental importance of bisexuality, examining the Freud/Ferenczi relationship as, like the transferential relationship, one in which 'people speak each other's disowned voices'. He affirms the place of the Oedipus complex, but then he has very little to say about the transference and refutes Oedipal sexuality as 'a limiting binary system'. So Phillips is playing games, Enlightenment games and post-Freudian games and he is engaged in a conversation outside the parameters of both a theory of the transference and the Oedipus complex. This is the argument:

> Starting with two sexes – described as opposites or alternatives or complements – locks us into a logic, a limiting binary system, that often seems remote from lived, spoken experience, and is complicit with other binary pairs – inside/outside, primary process/secondary process, sadism/masochism, patient:analyst, and so on – that are such a misleading part of psychoanalytic language.

Phillip's alternative is a thoroughly postmodern narrative in which the rule seems to be free-play, the landscape extremely flat, the climate generally mild and the tone one of ordinary conversation. One wonders whatever happened to the dramas and antinomies of childhood, of myth, of Greek or Shakespearian tragedy, even to dream language or poetic language which is forever constructing itself around these disowned antinomies?

The argument is daring and provocative but it is not convincing, yet that is precisely the point. The text is laced with aphorisms, maxims, the paper-darts of a seventeenth-century French moralist, terse little bits of conviction undoing other people's conviction: 'The self as expulsive is the self as exclusive', 'difference makes competition possible; and competition is a cure for shame', 'Defences are always defences against the provisional' and so on. In fact the style of the whole speaks of such a convinced undoing of conviction that one takes the full brunt of the paradox of trying to do away with conviction.

The most inspiring chapter is the final one, previously published as an essay on Winnicott 'The Mind Object' and here called 'Minds'. It refers to Winnicott's theory of the birth of the mind, of thought, as a result of the trauma of impingement. So thought is an obsessional defence against intrusion but it may just run away with itself. Phillips, after Winnicott, stresses the importance of regression, for the restoration of psychic health. Regression in this sense means getting lost again, leaving the trauma of thought behind and recovering the body – as one does in play. Phillips does not forget to play and in this he is a true exponent, expertise aside, of Winnicott.

Regression in the sense defined above, with regard to Winnicott, links to both Kristeva's theory of 'le sensible' and to Cixous' taking language by the roots. It is tantamount to a poetic return to origins, in the sense that the poetic always enacts a return to the senses, and in this respect Winnicott's theories of the mind, of language and of transitional phenomena hold great potential for the reading of psychoanalysis in culture, a potential that has yet to be realized in academic psychoanalysis.

Hanna Segal's *Psychoanalysis, Literature and War* is a collection of papers written between 1972 and 1995 and published by The New Library of Psychoanalysis. Hanna Segal has been for many years the leading exponent of Melanie Klein's ideas in Britain, Europe, South America and the United States. The book is divided into two sections: Clinical Psychoanalysis and

Literature and Politics. In clinical, literary and political analyses she uses Melanie Klein's elaboration of the theory of the life and death instincts; as well as showing how shifts from archaic fantasy organisation to an integration of reality – Klein's depressive position – mark not only a successful analysis but a stable political situation. Integration amounts to a healthy incorporation of the death instinct.

Segal also draws an interesting parallel between Chomsky's theory of grammar as a deep structure and the structure of object relations:

> The development of language springs from the grammar of object relations . . . Having an inborn grammatical structure and yet being able to acquire the different grammars of different languages, is like our view that the Oedipus complex is an inborn structure but that its actual realization will vary in different cultures and in different individuals within a culture.

Her analyses of literature do not, however, carry the full import of Melanie Klein's theories for critical theory. Jacqueline Rose's work, reviewed in the 'Psychoanalysis' chapter, is perhaps a better example of this. Segal remains a clinician in her literary analyses yet a clinician who remains fascinated by creativity and the creative process: the way in which every work carries within it the story of its own genesis. She reads Joseph Conrad's text *Heart of Darkness* in relation to midlife crisis (as theorized by Elliot Jaques in 1965) and draws attention to the way the text at once stages the crisis and demonstrates the implications of the crisis for creativity. Segal nevertheless fails to read any transcendence of despair in this text: 'It is the story of almost unremitting destructiveness and despair'. Yet if we consider her argument that psychic integration is a sign of the increased capacity for symbolization and verbalization, surely Conrad's writing in *Heart of Darkness* amounts to sublimation at its most eloquent?

One cannot but admire the breadth and energy of Hanna Segal's psychoanalytic and political commitment. Her personal elaboration of the theories of Melanie Klein leads her to plunge into the murky waters of the death instinct in the attempt to release creativity in the individual and undo the mechanics of war-mongering where true integration has failed, for 'the defences against the death-instinct create vicious circles leading to severe pathology'. This is a statement whose complexity – since it refers not to the death instinct *per se*, which must be integrated, but to the defences brought to bear upon this instinct as the true source of suffering – is readable not only in the psychopathology of individuals or of texts, but also in any war situation.

One of the central philosophies of *Dispatches from the Freud Wars* written by John Forrester, historian of psychoanalysis and of its controversies, is that it is in the very nature of psychoanalysis to be 'attested or viewed with suspicion'. Forrester inhabits both sides of the argument for if critique is the 'constant companion of psychoanalysis', he is a faithful, artful and playful critic. In the chapter reiterating the book's title he addresses Freud's critics, especially Frederick Crews, face on as it were, considering the demand for scientific truth and objectivity which they claim psychoanalysis cannot meet. One cannot help wondering whether the sort of tabloid smear campaigning against psychoanalysis that we associate with Frederick Crews merits this amount of consideration, but nor can one help wondering whether Forrester is really taking him seriously.

Forrester devotes a chapter called 'Casualties of Truth' to the scandal of transference love:

> It is the foundation of psychoanalysis, and its inevitable and irremediable scandal, that patients develop passionate relations to their analysts. The scandal becomes a double scandal ... when the passions of life have added to them the pursuit of scientific truth and professional achievement.

Whose argument is this, whose scandal? Forrester claims to be concerned with 'how the analysts and colleagues, Freud and Ferenczi, negotiated their ways through the minefield of love and truth, psychoanalysis and science' and furthermore to be demonstrating psychoanalysis' resolute lack of concern for ethical principles. Again he is hovering somewhere between the sceptics and the believers. One wonders whether this is a subtle way of pouring scorn on the truth debate, by a theatrical staging of events and characters whom he skilfully removes to a more textual level of consideration, in a manner akin to Phillip's playing with paradox?

The chapter devoted to Freud's passion for collecting antiquities 'Collector, Naturalist, Surrealist' explores the various metaphorical significances of this activity. It is an analogy of Freud's theory of the mind which hoards psychic events from different epochs so preserving its past. It is a surrealist celebration of the transvaluation of all values, and also perhaps, since Forrester emphasizes that the intrinsic objects in Freud's collection were worth very little and that he bore little attachment to individual items preferring the activity of collecting and exchanging *per se*, it is a concession to a symbolic form of play which none the less represents the activity of analysis:

> Every problem that Freud confronted, then, took on the same character: a riddle of the Egyptian Sphinx that this new Oedipus must answer, whose solution would allow him to take possession of the mysterious space over which, like the gods in his collection arrayed silently on his desk, the statues stood guard.

The most compelling chapter in the book is perhaps 'Dream Readers' which draws complex parallels between Freud's self-analysis through dreams, his autobiographical writing – the account of his discoveries with Fliess as reader, and this activity as 'exemplary and originary of psychoanalysis itself'. Forrester quotes Derrida, 'How can an autobiographical writing, in the abyss of an unterminated self-analysis, give birth to a world-wide institution?' He explores all sides of the question, reiterating Lacan's observation that just as in analysis the dream is already addressed to the analyst, so Freud in the dreams dreamt for self-analysis is already addressing himself to the readers of psychoanalysis and so their search for the truth of the dream becomes through transference the search for Freud's hidden secret, that is the truth of their own inner-dream life. The links drawn here between the poetic activity of dreaming and interpretation within the transference as paradigmatic of reading are invaluable. Forrester also highlights the play of seduction: exchange of roles between desirer and censor, the dance of disclosure and withdrawal, which emerges from Freud's writing, the textual history of early psychoanalysis, in which 'dreamer, patient and reader are articulated closely together'. Reading itself can be assimilated to dreaming activity as well as to interpretation. The differences between the two are relative. The different positions shade into one another. Forrester suceeds masterfully in showing how the Freudian text constructs any one and all of three readers: the dreamer, the resisting critic and the common reader. These positions are, of course, representative of all acts of reading. Their definition depends upon the shape of the transferential activity taking place. This chapter on the constitution of the reader as integral to the evolution of psychoanalysis at all levels and which discloses illuminating parallels between reading and analytic activity is the most convincingly complex.

'A Whole Climate of Opinion' furthers the argument, showing how for the historian of psychoanalysis' intellectual history, biographical history and personal history are all irrevocably intertwined and furthermore how the history of psychoanalysis is itself shaped by cultural context. Forrester draws particular attention to France's contribution to the history of psychoanalysis. Evoking *Vocabulaire de la psychanalyse* (1967), produced by Laplanche and Pontalis working within the French epistemological tradition of textually accurate internal history, Foucault working within the French philosophical tradition of hermeneutics, aesthetics, archaeology of concepts, genealogy of practices and Elisabeth Roudinesco's history of French psychoanalysis: *La Bataille de Cent Ans* (1983), Forrester observes how only a psychoanalytic environment open to alliances with the human sciences as it is in France, rather than with medicine as in the Anglo-American tradition, can produce histories of such interest for the humanities.

In *I love to you* translated by Alison Martin, Luce Irigaray continues her enquiry into the ethics of sexual difference, using Hegel's philosophical exclusion of woman from love as a labour of the universal, to argue that woman must renounce claims to equality, or inclusion in this abstract universal and occupy a transitional position between nature and culture. This will be a culture particular to her sex and gender 'which it is important for the woman to realize without renouncing her natural identity'. Irigaray thus refuses to occupy either side of the essentialist/militant tendency divide, a common characterization of French feminism, and enters into the issue of the ethics or uses of parity. She also addresses masculinity as consistently as she does femininity and shifts the universal away from the sphere of men onto sexual difference itself, as universal, suggesting that the heterosexual couple, formed by man and woman, should be cultivated, not for means of reproduction, nor the creation of a family and the acquisition of property, nor for the exchange of women, but of itself, for itself as 'the manifestation of and the condition for the production and reproduction of life'. Thus the lovers' culture of sexuality will be transmitted through speech to the child who will then in turn be formed in this 'new economy of existence or being which is neither that of mastery nor that of slavery but rather of exchange'.

There is a translation problem here, not just at a linguistic level but in the transmission of a whole philosophical and cultural tradition which provides the vocabulary of the argument, decidedly continental, and which leaves one wondering whether it can carry, be translated in the most general sense. One imagines the hackles of separatist feminism rising all over the UK and the United States. The same problem affects readings of Kristeva and Cixous in translation. Each has refuted labels of essentialism coming from Anglo-American reading and one is forced to consider very deeply what is actually happening when the baggage emerges into a different culture, language, and philosophical tradition and how much mislabelling inhabits the misreading.

Irigaray's prescription for a culture which does not abolish the natural, is here introduced as the foundation for her familiar argument in favour of cultural representations of the mother-daughter relationship, 'The mother-daughter relationship reminds woman, women, of their lack of subjective identity, and arouses affects for which there is no corresponding cultural organization'. This argument uses psychoanalysis – the importance of intro-jection, of primary metaphorization, of the emergence from melancholia – against classical psychoanalysis in which a language does not exist which adequately mediates and represents the mother-daughter relationship, and in which, as Irigaray has argued elsewhere, many of the characteristics of melancholia are in Freud mapped onto his description of the little girl's psychic development. In *I love to you*, Irigaray circumvents the Oedipal itinerary and argues the case for gender as a fulfilment of sex, 'All we need do is become our gender in order to get away from an undifferentiated relation with the mother ... *I am* born a woman ... I must *still become* this woman that I am by nature'.

In the formula *I love to you*, the 'to' points to a fundamentally intersubjec-tive passage between separate identities, a passage interrupting a relation-ship which appropriates the other as the direct object of desire and accords space, difference, autonomy, speech and silent listening. We are not far from a paradigm of psychoanalytic listening in which, to use Irigaray's term, civility may be introduced into passion in the name of love, in which it is impossible to divorce a culture of sexuality, either from the body, or from generic identity and in which belonging to a gender involves a dialectic of alterity and intersubjectivity. Irigaray leaves us with an essential definition of the work of psychoanalysis.

Because it draws together questions of fantasy, desire, alterity, seduction, transference and cultural activity with such finesse, complexity and poign-ancy I conclude with Jean Laplanche's essay 'The Theory of Seduction and the Problem of the Other'. In this text Laplanche proposes a new vocabulary for thinking these questions which he elaborates in terms of self-centred (Ptolemian) and other-centred (Copernican) systems. Since it regards the originary gravitation of man as taking place around the other, internal or external, the Copernican model is both inspirational and revolutionary. It is also a paradigm of the psychoanalytic revolution. Indeed both models exist in Freudian thought since the domain of psychoanalysis is inseparable from its approach. First the Freudian revolution discovers the unconscious as off-centre and then the seduction theory maintains the unconscious in its alien-ness. We recognize the stamp of Laplanche: the unconscious is made up of scenes and these scenes are essentially sexual. So otherness is everywhere because of sexuality, 'because the primacy of sexuality opens directly onto the question of the other, and in the case of the child, on to the adult other in his alien-ness'. Following Freud's text 'A Difficulty in the Path of Psychoanalysis', Laplanche argues that the alien-ness of seduction is tantamount to the ego being subject to a foreign invasion, as if by alien thoughts. Laplanche suggests that a return to centring is only achieved when the unconscious is brought back to an 'intimor intimo meo' ('something more inward than my own inwardness'), even if the unconscious is only guaranteed by the other person. He goes on to argue that representation – the sign-making relation – as a solution to the trauma of seduction and an exit from the magic circle of subjectivity is what the child both lacks and is crying out for:

> The way Freud and all his followers theorize the first experience of the child, is cruelly marked by the absence of precisely this 'sign-making' relation . . . What is important in the scenes of seduction is that the adult transmits a message in it, that he 'makes a sign' from his own unconscious.

In this sense both the subject traumatized by seduction, and Freud in complicity with his object, are susceptible to a form of Ptolemaism, 'a closing-in-on-itself of the Freudian psychical system' which Laplanche qualifies as a going-astray. Yet the Ptolemian scenario also corresponds to 'a conviction *acquired* by the psyche itself: its narcissistic re-centring follows – as if after a presupposition – a "Copernican" stage, in which the infant nursling is caught in the orbit of the other and has a passive relation to its messages'.

The analytic situation reproduces the upheaval of the individual's encounter with the enigma of the other and Laplanche sketches how two possible forms of the transference – '"a filled-out transference", with unconscious imagos and fantasies coming to fill the hollowed-out space presented by the analyst' with the analysand remaining none the less 'so to speak, closed in on himself', and a '"hollowed out transference" . . . re-elaboration in the space which opens up of the inevitably unresolved enigmas left behind by the other', mimic the Ptolemian and Copernican models. He proposes these perspectives as an alternative to 'the old notion of projection' and relates cultural activity to the 'hollowed-out transference' – 'an opening-out on to the other . . . caused by the other', which can in turn be transferred out-side analysis' in the form of creative activity. This 'transference of transference . . . captures what is innovative in analytic sublimation', as this essay captures what is innovative in Laplanche's analytic writing – his illuminating definition of the scenarios which may emerge from the confusion of seduction each time fantasy returns to the primal scene.

Books Reviewed

Cixous, Hélène. *Rootprints: Memory and Life Writing*. Hélène Cixous and Mireille Calle-Gruber, translated by Eric Prenowitz. Routledge. pp. 254. hb £40.00. ISBN 0 415 15541 X.
Forrester, John. *Dispatches From the Freud Wars: Psychoanalysis and its Passions*. Harvard University Press. pp. 309. pb £18.50. ISBN 0 674 53961 3.

Grubich-Simitis, Ilse. *Back to Freud's Texts: Making Silent Documents Speak.* Translated by Philip Slotkin. Yale University Press. pp. 322. hb £25.00. ISBN 0 300 06631 7.

Irigaray, Luce. *I Love to You: Sketch of a Possible Felicity in History.* Translated by Alison Martin. Routledge. pp. 150. hb £35.00. ISBN 0 415 90732 2.

Kristeva, Julia. *Time and Sense: Proust and the Experience of Literature.* Translated by Ross Guberman. Columbia University Press. pp. 432. pb £26.00. ISBN 0 231 10250 X.

Laplanche, Jean. 'The Theory of Seduction and the Problem of the Other', *The International Journal of Psychoanalysis*, August 1997, 78(IV), 653–66. ISSN 0020 7578.

Phillips, Adam. *Terrors and Experts.* Faber and Faber. pp. 110. pb £12.99. ISBN 0 571 17583 X.

Potamianou, Anna. *Hope: A Shield in the Economy of Borderline States.* Routledge, The New Library of Psychoanalysis. pp. 120. hb £45.00. ISBN 0 415 12176 0.

Segal, Hanna. *Psychoanalysis, Literature and War: Papers 1972–1995.* Routledge, The New Library of Psychoanalysis. pp. 178. hb £45.00. ISBN 0 415 15328 X.

4

Feminisms

JILL LEBIHAN

Like a number of books published in this year, Naomi Wolf's *Promiscuities* deals with the sexualization of adolescent girls. Wolf incorporates entries from her own memoirs, as well as quotations from interviews with girlhood friends, along with her more usual journalistic commentary on women's issues, to produce a story of becoming a woman in San Francisco in the 1970s. She gives accounts of encounters with flashers, date rapists, woman-beaters and dangerous strangers, as examples of many young women's early encounters with heterosexuality and patriarchy. This is a readable explanation of the conflicts, embarrassments and risks that characterize female adolescent experience in Western culture, and the partly confessional style encourages the reader to empathize strongly. Some of the integration of discursive material is rather laboured: there is one long section that consists mostly of a gloss on Laqueur's history of the clitoris, and there are other unhappily integrated mini-lectures on the sexual and initiation procedures undergone by girls in other ages or other cultures.

Her main point of argument is hard to contest: that girls and women have little access to ways and means of expressing their sexual desire. Being lustful or even sexy women makes us bad girls, and sluts have never traditionally occupied positions of social power and regard. Her revised model of becoming a woman is a predictably, and rather depressingly, individualistic one: 'I think we became women, in our culture, when we made the decision that, even if we didn't know for sure, all the markers imposed on us were flawed, and that we were somehow going to find a way, through whatever struggle I might take, to determine the meaning of "becoming a woman" for ourselves' (240). It is hard to argue with this in experiential terms, but it is equally difficult to turn a model of personal development like this into a useful political strategy. Women manage, despite everything. They're copers. So why is there any need for political change?

Despite some of her more sensible criticisms on sex education and the doctrines of femininity, when it comes to raising teenagers, Wolf perhaps has more to learn. She blames the historical and cultural period for the inappropriate lack of boundaries provided to her and her teenage friends in terms of sexual experimentation. Nevertheless, despite her criticisms of parental complacency, arguing that many mothers were too busy finding themselves to pay proper attention to their children's growth and provide sexual guidance and restriction, the moment she finds herself in a restrictive environment, as part of an Israeli kibbutz complete with chaperones *in loco parentis*, she rebels and runs off with an Irish field-worker whom she has been explicitly banned from seeing. Whatever one might wish for one's daughters, and it certainly wouldn't be a repetition of some of Wolf's and her friends' sad experiences, one cannot give them the experience they need to deal with their sexuality. One can only help to arm them with enough information and self-defence skills to take care of themselves, for their dangerous encounters with male violence will necessarily occur when their mums are not there to save them.

In *Ruling Passions*, Sue Lees also discusses the difficulties inherent in expressions of female desire. This book is a collection of a number of different essays covering issues such as girls' sexual reputation, sex education, male rape, marital rape, and the inequalities inherent in the criminal justice system when dealing with sexual violence. In her research on sex education, Lees interviewed a number of school-aged girls and boys about their experience of talking about sexuality in a school context, and she also examines broader cultural attitudes to the matter in 90s' Britain. She concludes, not surprisingly, that young people find communicating about sexual issues embarrassing and difficult. She adds, again uncontroversially, that girls and boys talk about sexual matters in different ways, and that girls operate under a double standard, expected to be both sexually responsive and responsible, but also constantly aware of their 'reputation'. Like Wolf, she insists that 'schools reinforce the suppression of female desire through the lack of discourse about female desire in sex education discussion' (51). None of the conclusions reached in these essays raises eyebrows: girls police their own behaviour to avoid the 'slag' label; women are shattered by the rape trial process; women's sexual reputations are always brought into sexual assault cases; marital rape prosecutions are rarely successful; women cannot claim provocation for retaliation for male violence – they can only claim temporary insanity. However, there are many useful details, such as rape-trial statistics, and particularly interesting are the studies of individual cases involving sexual violence of different kinds.

Whereas Wolf's American, journalistic style spins out small incidents for many pages, Lees' essays are concise and to the point, but this is at the cost of important analytical detail. There are many places where an interesting point is raised and immediately dropped without any explanation or elaboration. The essays contain material that is barely or carelessly connected. For instance, one incident where Lees confronts a rape trial barrister is repeated verbatim in two different places (63–4 and 85). Elsewhere, in a discussion on contraception among young women, the issue of love is raised out of nowhere and immediately dropped without further exploration:

> Intriguingly, the phrase 'letting yourself go' has connections with both sexual excitement and becoming sluttish. Love seems to play an important ideological role in permitting the former while offering some protection from the latter' (50).

These sentences seem to lead the previous discussion into a more abstract realm, and have potential for interesting analysis, but Lees consistently steers away from this kind of development of her ideas. The overall result is rather stilted writing and unsatisfying reading. It also means that some of the more paradoxical problems raised by the treatment of rape victims go unexplored. For instance, we're told that in rape trials, 'absence of injuries is taken of evidence of consent' rather than fear of death, but Lees fails to connect this comment with other evidence in the book that demonstrates that even women with the most horrific injuries and harrowing tales cannot secure convictions against their assailants. What this depressing text shows the reader, although Lees nowhere says this, is that women's injuries or lack of them, their 'good' or 'sluttish' reputations, their age, their marital status and any other personalizing details are largely irrelevant in a criminal justice system that is reluctant to confront the extent of male sexual violence, and is completely unwilling to change its methods to make successful prosecutions against such perpetrators more likely.

Bernard Lefkowitz's *Our Guys* provides an extremely detailed study of a community in which this refusal to confront the extent and significance of violent male behaviour results in devastating personal tragedy. What has become known as the Glen Ridge rape involved a number of wealthy young men, known in the New Jersey community and in their high school for their athletic abilities rather than their intellectual ones. They assaulted a young woman with learning difficulties who wanted nothing more than to belong to the in-crowd. The Jocks, as they are referred to in Lefkowitz's lengthy essay, invited the young woman into the basement of one family home, and forced her to perform fellatio; they also assaulted her with a broomstick, a baseball bat and another stick that was found in the park. The assaults were committed by three main perpetrators, but witnessed by many more. Lefkowitz documents how this terrifying group assault on a woman who had a very poor understanding of adult social relations was simply an extension of the kind of behaviour that was tolerated among the young men themselves and particularly within the school environment. One of the young men, for instance, repeatedly exposed himself to fellow students and masturbated *in the classroom*, but although his behaviour was noted in his school file, he was never reprimanded for this activity. The teenagers repeatedly invited young women into their homes, where their sexual activity was watched by other members of their sports teams (not always with the knowledge or consent of the women involved). One of the ringleaders was also accused of serious sexual assault by another woman in another town, although her complaints were not taken into account in the sentencing. Despite the guilty verdict reached by jury, and the sentence of a maximum of fifteen years in prison passed by the judge, all the perpetrators were given indeterminate minimum terms in young offenders' institutions. They were also allowed free on bail during the course of the appeals procedure and so had actually served no time in jail at all at the time of the account's publication. Like Lees and Wolf, Lefkowitz comments on the impact that this 'Jock' behaviour has on young women in the community. One girl came to the conclusion that 'All guys are perverts' (423) and Lefkowitz concludes:

Because adults did not intervene to stop the abuse, many girls questioned their own worth, not only to boys but also to adults whose judgement really counted. This theme of submissiveness to the abusive demands of the boys, coupled with a sense of adult abandonment, was sounded early and often . . . For those girls who lacked self-esteem to start with, it was potentially devastating. It could undermine their future relations with men and impair their chances of succeeding in school and in the workplace (423).

While being critical of the legal system that showed such leniency towards young men who had exhibited extreme violence, Lefkowitz places the blame more clearly on the local treatment of the behaviour of young men: encouraging athletic success over academic achievement, school failure to treat early signals as indicators of anti-social attitudes, parental 'benign' neglect.

Joan Smith's *Different for Girls*, advertised as a late 1990s' version of *Misogynies*, shares the concerns of Wolf and Lees with the construction and policing of femininity and female behaviour. A collection of accessible essays on a variety of cultural images, Smith's book is more obviously popular than the other texts considered in this section, but she nevertheless makes some of the most direct assaults on patriarchy and male assumptions about women. In a very personal chapter on women's rights to choose not to have children, she concludes bluntly: 'Birth statistics and population tables may not appear exciting at first glance, but their message, in this instance, is both consistent and revolutionary. All women are not the same. This is good news. It makes life more interesting. Get used to it' (91–2). Smith's point – illustrated by a wide variety of essays on such subjects as female killers, *film noir*, Jackie Kennedy, dress designers and supermodels, fertility treatment, marriage, and motherhood à la Paula Yates – is that women are persistently deemed different (to men), but all the same as one another. This leads to assumptions, such as mothers should be self-sacrificing whereas 'fathers are let off the hook in this culture' (117); and women who do not have children are selfish (despite the ever-increasing global population expansion). Women who do not conform to or comply with patriarchal models of helplessness, powerlessness and sexual modesty are criticized heavily: how can the articulate Hillary Clinton be any match for the silent, widowed Jackie Kennedy? Why is it that the test 'of a real woman, at the end of the twentieth century . . . is the lengths to which she will go . . . in the hope, however vain, of conceiving a child'? (62). In a discussion of the relation between the bodies of supermodels and male-designed catwalk fashion, Smith looks at an advertisement that replaces the bodies of real models with those of Barbie dolls. She concludes that the effect is 'not so much that women and dolls were interchangeable but that Barbie, with her moulded plastic breasts, tiny waist and pert bottom, represented the ideal female figure at the end of the twentieth century'. While Wolf analyses how we have managed to get to this point, Smith gives numerous clever examples that illustrate precisely the complexities of *fin de siècle* femininity. Nothing could do so more than Smith's strangely clairvoyant essay on Diana, Princess of Wales, published in 1997 but before Diana's death. Titled 'To Di For: the

Queen of Broken Hearts', the essay shows how Diana was treated not so much as 'a semi-detached member of the British royal family' but more like 'the survivor of some terrible ordeal' like 'a train crash or massacre' (4). Smith draws parallels between Diana and other tragic heroines from literature, such as Miss Haversham from *Great Expectations* and Anna Karenina, but also suggests that Diana would like to be seen more like a tragic queen on the scale of Medea, Clytemnestra and Phaedra: a '*donna abbandonata*', the 'young, glamorous, wronged woman' (16). Shockingly though, in the light of later events, Smith points out that 'Greek tragedy . . . is the original genre of which it might accurately be said that "no one gets out of here alive" ' (10). Diana created the tragic role for herself, argues Smith, but then asks: 'is it a role she is prepared to die for?'(17). The answer would appear to be 'yes'. What is more, many women remain enthralled by this model of victim femininity, while still failing to acknowledge its fatal consequences.

Another text that discusses personal and political issues in the context of a deep understanding of feminism is Nancy K. Miller's *Bequest and Betrayal*, published at the very end of 1996 and received to review too late for last year. Miller inserts italicized paragraphs of her own memoir about her childhood and about the illness and death of her father within this collection of essays on Philip Roth, Simone de Beauvoir, Carolyn Steedman, Art Spiegelman and Susan Cheever. Miller works through a number of important psychoanalytic issues, as one might expect in a text of mourning for dead parents, but she does this with a great deal of subtlety and manages to avoid the most obvious psychoanalytic discourse. Instead she uses texts like Steedman's, which specifically foregrounds class issues over those of gender in the discussion of not good enough mothering; and like Spiegelman's *Maus* cartoon series as a means of analysing the nature of father-son relationships after the Holocaust. Within these careful commentaries on the work of others who have looked at parental relations, Miller explores how these texts resonate with her own experience. So her analysis of Steedman allows her to be both critical and appreciative of her own mother, and her analysis of Spiegelman allows her to analyse her own sense of her Jewishness. Although Wolf in *Promiscuities*, for instance, is attempting to emulate this kind of feminist writing, Miller's sensitivity towards the texts that she is examining, and her own analytical sense of herself, produce a much richer, more rewarding piece of work. *Bequest and Betrayal* manages to both incisive critical commentary on a range of known, but not over-exposed, twentieth-century texts, as well as offering a moving portrayal of Miller's own personal struggles to find meaning for herself as a middle-aged, Jewish, American, feminist, childless, woman intellectual. This is one of those rare pieces of academic writing that can be read with the same kind of pleasure as a novel.

Lynne Tillman also writes about the death of her Jewish father in one essay included in her collection, *The Broad Picture*. She covers some similar ground here to Miller, including a mild curiosity about his penis, a concern for his depression, and a fear of his violent mood changes, 'from a charming Dr Jekyll into a snarling Mr Hyde' (6). Tillman recounts how her father used to pretend to be the Bogeyman, to scare her, but on adult reflection she observes that 'the people who are most afraid make and become the best monsters' (7). Her account of her father, and her consideration of how she might feel about him, is clearly influenced by, and sometimes explicitly acknowledged as, psychoanalytic, but unlike Miller, Tillman is less critical about her theoretical framework. The short essays in this collection cover a wide range of topics, including Derek Jarman, Andy Warhol, Spike Lee, *The Bodyguard*, *The Godfather*, multiple personality disorder, and a deranged cat named Boots. Readable and sometimes insightful, the essays provide good commuter reading, but are ultimately less politically motivated, and less sustaining, than Miller's detailed and carefully formulated work. They are also rather out of date for a 1997 text, most of them dating from the 1980s, and the rest from the early 1990s.

From autobiographical essays, we move to a series of critical essays on significant twentieth-century autobiographies by women. Linda Anderson's *Women and Autobiography in the Twentieth Century* is a restrained, focused work on four important figures in British autobiographical writing this century: Alice James, Virginia Woolf, Vera Brittain and Sylvia Plath. Anderson is fully informed by recent studies on autobiography, aware and critically astute about appropriations of contemporary critical theory, and entirely committed to a feminist project in literary analysis. Above all, Anderson is careful not to simplify any of the issues regarding conditions of production and reception of autobiography. In her essay on Alice James, for instance, Anderson articulates two crucial questions for feminist critics of autobiography: 'to whom is she speaking?' and 'who is speaking?' (40). She rejects a poststructuralist formation of this last question ('does it matter who is speaking?'), but suggests that it may be impossible to make a critical decision about the primacy, for feminist theorists, of 'contesting the limits of female subjectivity and its inscription within those limits' (41). Anderson returns to this issue in the concluding chapter, in her consideration of Adrienne Rich's use of the first person pronoun. Anderson contests Rich's triumph in the union of the woman in the poem with the woman writing the poem. She argues that Rich's conflation 'effects a powerful reversal of the negative identification of woman in Western discourse ... but it could also be said to lead to an impasse, for women are still locked into the same system of meaning, reabsorbed within a wholeness which recognises no "other" identities, no otherness within the concept of identity' (131). Throughout her essays, Anderson treads a careful line between being swayed by the force of the experiential voice, and understanding the dangers, as well as the value, of identity politics.

Another text that makes us consider subjectivity and personal identity, although in an entirely different context, is Alan Hyde's *Bodies of Law*. This is not strictly a feminist text, but could prove immensely useful to those wrestling with the body ethics that are involved in issues such as rape and abortion. Although primarily an American legal specialist, Hyde demonstrates a thorough understanding of the implications of poststructuralist and postmodern thought for the construction of the human body within contemporary discourse. The recent challenges posed by cultural theory to our conception of the body as bounded, individual and personal property also have legal examples, Hyde demonstrates. His discussion includes consideration of the 'legal vagina', which is constituted in the discourse in such a way as to make 'it fairly easy for law's eye to get inside a woman's shorts' (171). His examples are of internal searches for drugs and he looks closely at legal reports, focusing particularly on a text in which a request is made of 'search warrants for appellant's apartment and vagina'. Conducting searches of body cavities is justified partly in the interest of public good, but also partly in the interest of the individual: a woman is taking a grave physical risk in transporting drugs in this way, and legal practitioners like to construct these intimate searches as beneficial to the woman. As Hyde points out, this constructs the vagina as 'dangerous to women except as tamed by male authority' (172). Hyde looks at a number of other examples where our belief in bodily integrity and ownership comes into conflict with the law and with public good, such as public nudity and pornography, donations of body material for medical use, compulsory testing for certain diseases, offensive bodily odours and use of urine in compulsory random drug-testing. His conclusion calls for the creation of a 'body fantasia'. He argues for a law that is self-conscious 'about its discursive construction of the body', and under which, bodies are 'visualizations, not legal entities'. Importantly, the sexual, pleasurable body is not, under Hyde's utopian law, a legal body; it is a body that can be imagined as a different legal person, and it is that person that may have different legal interests or rights (263–4).

Hyde is primarily concerned with the adult body, since this is what is inscribed within most legislation, but the body and mind of the child remains a thoroughly contested site, and a particular concern of feminist theory this year. As shown earlier, much contemporary feminist work acknowledges the role that education in girlhood has when those girls grow up to become women. In *Waking Sleeping Beauty*, Roberta Seelinger Trites contributes analyses of a large number of American novels aimed at younger people. And here lies the first criticism, in that Trites' text consistently talks about books for children, when most of the texts she talks about are for adolescents. This is a significant difference, since the possibilities for androgynous power are much greater in works for a younger audience than those for teenagers. The texts that Trites looks at deal with runaways, drug abuse, pregnancy, lesbian and heterosexual relationships, as well as a number of less controversial themes that would nevertheless be inappropriate in books for smaller children. Much about this text is laudable in intention. Studies of fiction for children and young adults remain hopelessly untouched by the corrupting hand of contemporary literary theory, and so a work that has feminist theory underpinning its main aims, with influences from poststructuralism and psychoanalysis, is most welcome. However, the type of feminist literary analysis engaged in is never fully explained, since Trites argues that feminist children's novels are those 'in which the main character is empowered regardless of gender' (4). In fact, in the tradition of 'images of women' criticism, Trites deals with texts with young women as protagonists, and which are mostly authored by women.

As desirable as it is to have theoretical analyses of literature written for children and adolescents, in this text, the attempt to integrate a different theoretical issue in each chapter produces an unconvincing and formulaic effect. Each chapter begins with a couple of paragraphs of synopsis, followed by a literary illustration of one main theoretical point. So for instance, the chapter on deconstruction offers us a definition of aporia, followed by an aporia-hunt through a selection of novels. The chapter on 'subjectivity as a gender issue' introduces Jacques Lacan as a literary critic (26). We are given a quotation: 'The unconscious is that which, by speaking, determines the subject as being', and the gloss that 'according to Lacan, language is the sole determinant of being' (26). Clearly, there is a big difference in Lacan's view that the speech of the unconscious determines the *subject*, and the gloss that says language is the sole determinant of *being*. For Lacan, subjectivity and existence are not the same thing. Trites then says she will go on to explore the production of subjectivity through language in two novels with female protagonists, but in fact she investigates object relations through window metaphors, and, supposedly, the production of the subject through intertextual reference. She argues that texts that were once used to govern behaviour can be reclaimed through contemporary interpretation, and that this demonstrates the dialogic nature of subjectivity. However convincing this latter claim might seem, and as a reader of this book I required far more in the way of explanation to be persuaded, it has nothing whatever to do with the discussion of Lacanian subjectivity that opened the chapter. Indeed, in this chapter and in others, the theoretical discussions are introduced but never put into practice in the textual analysis.

In contrast, Cristina Bacchilega's *Postmodern Fairy Tales* offers a series of persuasive and sophisticated readings of well-known folktales as they have been retold in contemporary media. The text claims to explore 'the production of gender, in relation to narrativity and subjectivity in late twentieth-century literature and media for adults' (4). Unlike Trites' superficial glance at revisionary intertextuality, Bacchilega provides a coherent argument for the use of postmodern theory in understanding the place of fairy tales in the contemporary imagination. The text includes chapters on 'Snow White' as it is reformulated in Carter's 'The Snow Child', Coover's 'The Dead Queen' and Barthelme's *Snow White*; 'Little Red Riding Hood' in three stories from *The Bloody Chamber*; 'Beauty and the Beast' as it is refigured by Carter again, and by the 1980s CBS television series; and finally, Bluebeard as he appears in Atwood's 'Bluebeard's Egg', Campion's *The Piano* and, of course, 'The Bloody Chamber'. Throughout, Bacchilega pays scrupulous attention to the numerous versions of the fairy tales, and the differences between them, before going on to understand their significance in contemporary fiction. For instance, she examines 'Bluebeard', 'Fichter's Bird', 'How Toodie Fixed Old Grunt', 'Mr Fox' and 'The Robber Bridegroom'. She argues that despite the morals of the earlier versions of the tale, which operate as violent warnings against women's curiosity and agency, modern retellings offer an alternative view in their albeit ambiguous celebration of women's boldness. She concludes her chapter with the point that:

> Put to different feminist uses, then, a gruesome fairy tale often deployed against women becomes recuperated as the story of successful, socially meaningful female initiation. 'Bluebeard's' plot-sustaining dynamics of simultaneous doubling and duality are reformed to articulate and further our knowledge of gendered relationships in varying scenes (138).

Despite this largely positive conclusion to this gruesome chapter, Bacchilega is sensitive to the entirely different emphases put on their interpretations of the tale, from Atwood's ironic ambiguity, to Carter's 'seductive and confessional self-portrait of the "victim"' and Campion's more affirmative discussion of self-discovery and empowerment (138). She insists throughout the text on the many possibilities offered not just by the numerous retellings of familiar tales, but the way in which the reader's projected desires depend on social, political, historical and gendered context.

While Bacchilega and Trites produce their feminist analysis through consideration of literary texts, Elaine Millard, in *Differently Literate*, takes adolescent readers as her subjects for research on the effects of gender on patterns of reading and literacy. In this text, Millard lays out the results of painstaking research with Y7 pupils (11–12 years, in their first year at secondary school). Part of the interest of this work is the revelation of what children on the edge of their teens find pleasurable to read. *The Diary of Adrian Mole*, the story of a teenaged boy told by an adult woman, came out most popular with both girls and boys, but this was practically the only area of overlap between the sexes. While Roald Dahl remains popular with both sexes, the actual texts chosen by girls and boys are sharply divided. Dahl's novels featuring male protagonists, such as *Danny*, the *Charlie* stories, and *Boy*, appealed to the boys, while the girls chose *Matilda* and *The BFG*. Surprisingly also, the girls chose the reactionary *Anne of Green Gables*, whose most important lesson in life is to finally hold her tongue, way above the stories of Jacqueline Wilson, whose contemporary, feisty heroines contend with familial disasters with courage and wit. Less surprisingly, lads on the edge of puberty chose texts such as the *Alien Trilogy*, *Conan the Barbarian* and assorted football novels as indicators of their masculinity.

Millard has done considerable research on how patterns of reading within families affect children's perceptions of this activity, and to read fiction is clearly seen as an activity for women and girls. In one fabulous extract from an interview, a boy is asked what his dad reads. The boy explains that his dad reads 'newspapers 'bout horses and er, what time they're running and everything' and he also 'reads football results on the telly' (84). The reading of 'factual' material is clearly associated with the men in the family, while mothers, sisters and grandmothers read novels, novels which they will then often recommend to the younger girls in the family. She concludes that teaching of English based on reading and analysing fiction alone is rather outmoded, and is leading to a significant disadvantage for less able boys in the classroom. Millard's solution is an eminently reasonable one, which still retains a place for feminist teaching methods:

> Positive action to compensate for the neglected narrative interests of boys and the likely influence of this on their weaker performance in English would mean that teachers would need to make some changes to the fiction chosen for classroom study. This would involve supplementing the choice of predominantly authentic realist texts to include narratives that emphasised action and plot rather than 'knowledge of the human heart'. I am of course arguing for an injection of fantasy and adventure into the texts chosen for class study so that a wider range of genres become identified as appropriate to English lessons. Some space might be afforded to works of popular fiction such

as 'blood and thunder' stories, with their powerful images of masculinity that were so roundly condemned as 'rubbish' by previous generations of teachers and which have been described recently as stories 'of and for the boys' (161).

Millard explains that the use of such texts, which are likely to offer some problematic images of women, might easily be incorporated via the work of feminists such as Atwood, Carter, Warner, and I would add Bacchilega, who have all used mythical representations of women to produce refigurations of femininity.

Turning, finally, from the education of girls to the education of students in further and higher education, feminist lecturers can do far worse than recommend Mary Evans' *Introducing Contemporary Feminist Thought* to their students. Evans' text is a clear, historically located and remarkably concise account of the influence of women's studies within British academic thought. One of the most remarkable things about this book is its ability to conjoin the sociological dimensions of feminist thought with the theories that emanate primarily from cultural studies. Given the often rigid divisions between these disciplines, the seamless shift of the discussion from one issue to another is quite admirable and valuable. The other extremely valuable aspect to Evans' work is its absolute clarity and readability. This is less like a textbook and more like a story of academic feminist theory, without any of the intimidating jargon. In this sense, I'm not sure how well it will prepare students for what awaits them in the women's studies section of the library, since few texts have the lucidity of this, nor its narrative claims on the attention. In addition, it would be difficult to see how this book would work in a seminar setting, in the way that some other texts might, since it presents matters in such a clear and apparently uncontentious way. However, it could be recommended as preliminary reading material for a range of feminist courses, and students would arrive already having a strong overview of the field. Evans covers the work of a wide but unpredictable range of theorists, including Coward, Moi, Jagger, Grosz, De Beauvoir, Stanley, Lorde and Sayers. She uses numerous examples from literature (Tolstoy, Hardy, Austen, Brontë, Jong) to illustrate her arguments, as well as insisting on a view of social and world politics as essential to feminism. Although there are many introductions to feminist thinking, Evans' text comes across as fresh and accessible, and its coherence makes it useful even to a reader who is familiar with the ground covered.

Another useful text for lecturers, especially those with students looking for dissertation topics, is Kathleen Wheeler's *A Guide to Twentieth-Century Women Novelists*. This guide contains a series of short essays on 135 different writers, ordered in historical and contextual bands, covering biographical and stylistic details, and there is a separate bibliography of critical sources for each of the main entries. Students who go to the library with a vague idea of the historical period in which they wish to work for an extended essay, and perhaps a single writer on whom to focus, will be delighted to find it possible to put that author in an understandable context with no more effort than required to read one of the eleven historical overviews. It is then possible to find all the secondary material required on a particular writer in well-ordered lists at the back. There is also a helpful essay offering hints on more general research on women in this period. The Guide includes a survey titled 'More Women Writers World-wide', which helpfully lists authors by national affiliation, followed by subgroups which are both chronological and ordered in informal subgenera, such as detective writing, lesbian fiction, Native North American writing and so on.

There are some problems with this volume, however. The groupings of writers in historical periods (for instance 1895–1925) seems sensible enough, but each group is accompanied by a contextual essay (for example, 'The Influence of Psychological Writings on Literature'), which does tend to force each description of a writer's oeuvre into some kind of comparison with the chosen thematic framework, and this gives an illusory sense of coherence to some of the groups of writers. One of the supplementary essays, on 'Feminist Theory and Feminist Writing', is really quite inadequate, and fairly irrelevant in a volume like this. It gives a very cursory account of theoretical developments in feminist literary criticism, something which is done much better by texts dedicated to this subject. The theoretical influences are not really evident in the individual essays on each author anyway. It would be better to replace this essay either with a more comprehensive and up-to-date list of references to the area, or to have the theoretical perspectives more carefully integrated into the main body of the work. One final complaint is that the alphabetical list of writers, included at the beginning as part of a series of different kinds of contents pages, infuriatingly doesn't include any page references. However, there are compensations in the excellent index. This is a potentially useful text to keep in a library's reference section, but there are a lot of typographical errors in a text costing £65.

Books Reviewed

Anderson, Linda. *Women and Autobiography in the Twentieth Century: Remembered Futures*. Harvester/Wheatsheaf. pp. 174. pb £18.95. ISBN 0 13 355034 6.

Bacchilega, Cristina. *Postmodern Fairy Tales: Gender and Narrative Strategies*. University of Pennsylvania Press. pp. 208. hb £30.95. ISBN 0 8122 3392 1.

Evans, Mary. *Introducing Contemporary Feminist Thought*. Polity Press. pp. 170. hb £39.50. ISBN 0 7456 1475 2. pb £11.95. ISBN 0 7456 1476 0.

Hyde, Alan. *Bodies of Law*. Princeton University Press. pp. xii + 278. £11.50. ISBN 0 691 01228 8.

Lees, Sue. *Ruling Passions: Sexual Violence, Reputation and the Law*. Open University Press. pp. 211. pb £12.99. ISBN 0 335 19613 6. hb £40.00. ISBN 0 335 19614 4.

Lefkowitz, Bernard. *Our Guys: The Glen Ridge Rape and the Secret Life of the Perfect Suburb*. University of California Press. pp. 443. hb £22.95. ISBN 0 520 20596 0.

Millard, Elaine. *Differently Literate: Boys, Girls and the Schooling of Literacy*. Falmer Press. pp. 211. pb £13.95. ISBN 0 7507 0661 9.

Miller, Nancy K. (1996) *Bequest and Betrayal: Memoirs of a Parent's Death*. Oxford University Press. pp. 194. hb £19.50. ISBN 0 19 509130 2.

Smith, Joan. *Different For Girls: How Culture Creates Women.* Chatto and Windus. pp. 176. pb £10.99. ISBN 0 701 16512 X.

Tillman, Lynne. *The Broad Picture: Essays.* Serpent's Tail. pp. 175. pb £11.00. ISBN 1 85242 440 0.

Trites, Roberta Seelinger. *Waking Sleeping Beauty: Feminist Voices in Children's Novels.* University of Iowa Press. pp. 170. hb £23.50. ISBN 0 87745 590 2. pb £11.95. ISBN 0 87745 591 0.

Wheeler, Kathleen. *A Guide to Twentieth Century Women Novelists.* Blackwell. pp. 442. hb £65.00. ISBN 0 631 16493 6.

Wolf, Naomi. *Promiscuities: A Secret History of Female Desire.* Chatto and Windus. pp. 288. pb £12.99. ISBN 0 7011 6572 3.

5

Colonial Discourse/
Postcolonial Theory

PATRICK WILLIAMS AND NAHEM YOUSAF

'No discussion of the "postcolonial" should proceed without participants making known their understanding of the term.' So begins Benita Parry's opening salvo 'The Postcolonial: Conceptual Category or Chimera?' in *The Yearbook of English Studies*, 27. (This special issue on 'The Politics of Postcolonial Criticism' is the most wide-ranging collection to appear in 1997, and as such requires more space than it might otherwise get.) No doubt many would agree with Parry, though for some such as Edward Said it is precisely the fact that postcolonial critics endlessly explain their understanding of the term which makes postcolonial criticism seem so debilitatingly inward-looking. Parry goes on to provide a typically forthright summary of the emergence of postcolonial theory, its forms, strategies, and weaknesses. While it is not clear how far she really answers the question in her title (nor how far she is fair to that kind of postcolonial work which happens not to be obsessed with poststructuralism or 'the linguistic turn') this, like her earlier 'Problems in Current Theories of Colonial Discourse', is a useful polemical survey.

An even more polemical piece is Nicholas Visser's 'Postcoloniality of a Special Type: Theory and its Appropriations in South Africa'. Visser is scathing of the nature and functioning of postcolonial theory in the South African context. The problems he sees as partly attributable to its (implicit or explicit) inclusion of theories positing South Africa as 'Colonialism of a Special Type' (CST), where the issue is 'national' rather than class-based, and partly to its belief that South African identities and politics are fundamentally racial (rather than, for instance, class-based). In addition, Visser sees postcolonialism as involving the assumption and celebration of having 'arrived', with the understanding that no further social transformation is necessary (though quite where he gets the latter from, I'm not sure). Finally, the desire of South African critics such as Paul de Kock and David Atwell to promote a postcolonial theory shorn of certain theoreticist excesses is ridiculed on various counts: what is left isn't worth bothering with; 'moderate' postcolonial theory merely reinstalls safe liberal-pluralism; etc. (There is an irony here, that Visser, who is arguing from a minimally articulated Marxist position, should find those postmodernist, poststructuralist or postcolonial theorists who concern themselves least with material conditions to be the most interesting and provocative.) Ultimately, Visser's political stance may be persuasive, but I'm not sure his reading of postcolonial theory matches it.

Against those (like Visser) who criticize postcolonial theory's apparent neglect of the material, Helen Tiffin quotes Bourdieu: 'symbolic struggles are always much more effective (and therefore realistic) than objectivist economists think'. In 'Colonialist Pretexts and Rites of Reply', Tiffin examines the politics of postcolonial reinscription of colonial texts, in this case, Randolph Stow's rewriting of Conrad, Malinowski and Australian popular fiction in *Visitants* and (in a move which would no doubt amaze Aijaz Ahmad) worries about the (US) tendency to apply terms such as postcolonial to any form of domination. Whether or not her article constitutes the sort of inappropriate application that worries Helen Tiffin, in 'Black American Literature and the Postcolonial Debate', Christine MacLeod thinks the (for some) unthinkable, and suggests that not only does black American experience have a legitimate place within postcolonial debate, but also that aspects of the debate would be improved by theoretical engagement with African-American culture. MacLeod argues that 'black America's precise geo-political contours are ultimately less important than the perspectives that emerge when its culture is *conceptualized* as postcolonial', and goes on to read a number of novels (*Invisible Man, Native Son, Dessa Rose, Beloved*) for the ways in which they articulate postcolonial issues.

Among the pieces which focus on Africa, Ato Quayson's 'Protocols of Representation and the Problems Constituting an African "Gnosis": Achebe and Okri' consists of pretty much what its title says, though its subtle reading of Achebe (and to a lesser extent Okri) is more successful than its analysis of the problems of an African gnosis. Patrick Williams' '"Like Wounded Birds?": Ngugi and the Intellectuals' analyses Ngugi's engagement with intellectuals (both colonized and postcolonial): his fictional representations of them, his discussions of them in his non-fiction, and his own instantiation of the theory-and-praxis combination.

Ngugi is also the focus of two of the contributions to *The Politics of (M)Othering: Womanhood, Identity and Resistance in African Literature*, edited by Obioma Nnaemeka. In 'Bound to Matter: The Father's Pen and Mother Tongues' Cynthia Ward uses Ngugi in a Bakhtin-influenced discussion of the politics of language (oral/written, vernacular/literary, African/European) in Africa, while Celeste Delgado Fraser in 'MotherTongues and Childless Women: The Construction of "Kenyan" "Womanhood"' focuses on Ngugi's play *maitu Njugira (Mother Sing For Me)* and Rebecca Njau's novel *Ripples in the Pool*. Both pieces are concerned with the problematic relation of woman and nation, and Delgado draws on Homi Bhabha's well-known 'DissemiNation' essay, though there is no consideration of the relevance of Bhabha's undifferentiated category of 'the modern nation' to the specificities of postcolonial Africa. For her part, Ward concludes that 'a project of decolonizing of the mind by embracing "the mother" in the creation of national literatures is a trap that will at best ensnare women.'

Charles Sugnet's '*Nervous Conditions*: Dangarembga's Feminist Reinvention of Fanon' offers a different and more optimistic perspective on the relation of women to questions of national identity. Sugnet sees the coming to consciousness of Tambu, the novel's female narrator, as a parallel for the war of liberation in Rhodesia/Zimbabwe which forms the unspoken contemporary backdrop to the narrative, though it is not clear in what way, apart from foregrounding women, Dangarembga is 'reinventing' Fanon here. The status of Mariamma Bâ's *So Long A Letter* as 'one of the most widely read African novels in the American academy' is reflected in its centrality in two of the contributions, Uzo Esonwanne's 'Enlightenment Epistemology and "Aesthetic Cognition": Mariamma Bâ's *So Long A Letter*' and Obioma Nnaemeka's 'Urban Spaces, Women's Places: Polygamy as Sign in Miriamma Bâ's Novels', (and arguably inappropriate appearance in a third, Renée Larrier's 'Reconstructing Motherhood: Francophone African Women Autobiographers'). There is not a lot on urban spaces in Nnaemeka's piece, though there is on polygamy, which she feels has had a bad press, and therefore wants to distinguish between the (potentially) beneficial institution and the routinely oppressive contemporary practice. The unfair stigmatizing of African customs looks to Nnaemeka like the self-perpetuation of Western superiority: 'If polygamy did not exist, imperialism would invent it.' Or, 'If circumcision did not exist, Western feminism would have invented it.' Which seems a mite paranoid in respect of feminism (though not of imperialism). Esonwanne prefers to talk about polygyny rather than polygamy, and like Nnaemeka he feels it has not been well analysed or understood. Following Johannes Fabian's argument about the way in which the Enlightenment produced its Other through a process of space/time distanciation, Esonwanne sees polygyny as 'produced' by African nationalist and anti-colonialist discourse (which is obviously a long way from its invention by imperialism).

Huma Ibrahim's 'Ontological Victimhood: "Other" Bodies in Madness and Exile – Toward a Third World Feminist Epistemology' wobbles between seeing victimhood as a Western discursive construct, 'a definitional understanding imposed on the postcolonial world by our friends in the "same movement" who have enjoyed our collaboration and are loath to lose it' and as (ontological) fact of life. This lack of clarity is perhaps no surprise in the context of remarks of the editor's, such as: 'The feminization of "victim" is inscribed in the French language, for example. It is very interesting to note that in a dual-gendered language such as French the word "victim" (la victime) is feminine even when the victim is male. The implications are many among which are: that victims are supposed to be female; or that to reduce the male to the level of victim is to feminize him.' This elementary confusion of linguistic gender with the operations of the social construction of gender is deeply worrying in a professor of French.

Like E. Anne Kaplan (see below) Peter Hitchcock takes up the difference between the gaze and the look in his interesting discussion of 'The Eye and the Other: The Gaze and the Look in Egyptian Feminist Fiction'. Hitchcock follows different positions on veiling and unveiling, looking and gazing in texts by Nawal el Saadawi and Alifa Riffaat, and is at pains to emphasize that 'even when the subaltern subject cannot speak or is not speaking she is always looking'. The desire to foreground subaltern (ocular) agency leads him to oppose Malek Alloula's influential study *The Colonial Harem* on the grounds that it accords too much power to the gazing 'eye of the beholder' and not enough to the resistant look of the colonized/subaltern. (It may be worth mentioning in passing that Hitchcock's efforts to differentiate between the gaze and the look in this way are complicated by Homi Bhabha – who, one assumes, ought to get this kind of thing right – and who talks of the relation Hitchcock analyses as 'this process by which the look of surveillance returns as the displacing gaze of the disciplined' (*Location of Culture* p. 89) – i.e. precisely the opposite. Or perhaps it doesn't matter.) Overall, *The Politics of (M)Othering* is a useful collection where the range of issues covered outweighs problems with individual contributions – not that the volume as a whole is without its problematic side: editorial assertions such as 'The colonialist/imperialist enterprise is first and foremost an epistemic violence' really don't help.

Although it opens with surprisingly dogmatic and problematic claims such as 'the "male" gaze and the "imperial" gaze cannot be separated within Western patriarchal cultures', E. Anne Kaplan's *Looking for the Other: Feminism, Film and the Imperial Gaze* goes on to debate in rather more encouraging fashion a range of important issues relating to race, gender, postcolonialism and imperialism in connection with the gaze. Kaplan usefully distinguishes between the often elided concepts of the 'look' (as process and relation) and the 'gaze' (as one-way, non-relational, objectifying and marked by anxiety), though having established the gaze as in some senses the mark of the dysfunctional (or, at the very least, a problematic activity) she then goes on to talk about 'the gaze of the Other', apparently without these negative connotations, which seems somewhat contradictory. (The fact that the 'imperial gaze' turns out to be 'the gaze structures specific to representing ethnic others in Hollywood' doesn't *necessarily* undermine Kaplan's project, but such a sense of imperialism certainly complicates – if not confuses – things.)

Another worrying opening assertion (worrying not least for those postcolonial writers and critics who spend their time trying to distance their work from postmodernism) is that postcolonial theory is part of postmodern theorizing – though fortunately this line is not particularly stressed in the book. Once past these initial hiccups, Kaplan develops a series of interesting and accessible discussions both of dominant Hollywood practices, forms of representation, gaze structures and the like, and of the different returns, reversals or refusals of the gaze by black, Third World, postcolonial, and, above all, women film-makers. There is also a laudable determination to make connections – between theories, issues and disciplines, but also between chapters of the book (though this can lead to some repetitious summarizing and signposting). The films covered range from the silent era (Griffiths' *Birth of a Nation*) via the 1930s (*King Kong*), 1940s film noire (*Cat People*), through to the 1990s (*Bhaji on the Beach, Daughters of the Dust, Warrior Marks*), and from the mainstream (old and new Hollywood) to the experimental or marginal (most of the rest, in different ways).

The only person to get a whole chapter to herself is Trinh Minh Ha, perhaps the most theoretically informed and critically self-reflexive of contemporary film-makers, though it is arguably time that her complex, challenging and sometimes controversial work was more widely known and better discussed. As a way out of the endless dilemmas of representation – speaking for/ speaking about the Other – Trinh, in her first film *Reasemblage*, advocates 'speaking nearby'; and looking for ways out of theoretical binds, or certain well-trodden polemical paths, is very much part of Kaplan's approach. Sometimes it all seems so simple, and a sentence like 'There is a big difference between *failing* to approach the subjectivity (including the body) of the Other, and its being *impossible* to approach such an Other subjectivity (body)' cuts through so much attitudinizing. Kaplan also suggests that the unsatisfactory alternative positions (attempting to know the Other is inherently dominative; attempting to know the Other is a waste of effort since the Other is unknowable) are very much 'Western *male* modes of knowing which ignore psychic energies, psychoanalytic operations and concern with subjectivity or interiority. Equally, Kaplan is good at offering level-headed assessments of debates – for instance, the famous Fredric Jameson/Aijaz Ahmad dispute, or whether *Warrior Marks*, Alice Walker and Pratibha Parmar's film about female genital mutilation, repeats imperialist assumptions in its opposition to indigenous practices – and there is a refreshing refusal to (over)praise black or women's oppositional efforts simply for existing: 'Reversing the predominant gaze, as Moffat does, or as Dhenjan does in a different way, is important, but . . . this strategy does not necessarily move things forward'. A book like *Looking for the Other*, on the other hand, might just help to do that.

A different perspective on feminism is offered by *Black British Feminism: A Reader* edited by Heidi Safia Mirza. This is a welcome exploration of a long-neglected area, and while sceptical in various ways, avoids the demonizing of feminism which is rather too prevalent in *The Politics of (M)Othering*. Locating itself within 'the postcolonial diaspora', the book brings together extracts from a number of earlier debates, including such minor classics as Hazel Carby's 'White Woman, Listen' or Valerie Amos and Pratibha Parmar's 'Challenging Imperialist Feminism'. Unusually for a reader, however, it contains more new pieces than reprinted ones. A substantial number of the new pieces are grounded in the lived experience of black women (authors and others), though the contributors are at pains to emphasize that this is done very differently from the naive way in which earlier feminism prioritized experience. Nevertheless, there is the feeling that, within the constraints of a short book chapter, recounting experience can occur at the expense of analysis.

A number of the pieces address the question of diaspora. Magdalene Ang Lygate's 'Charting the Spaces of (Un) location: On Theorizing Diaspora' highlights the problematic relation of Chinese and Filipino women to the category of 'black', here perceived as homogenizing, silencing particular groups, and insufficiently attentive to difference. This downfall of what was intended to be positive, liberatory, etc., is paralleled by anti-racist discourse, which has supposedly 'adopted what was originally an imperiality enterprise, when colonial powers imposed identities on colonized peoples and refused them power to name themselves'. Problems of 'black' are also explored in Naz Rasool's 'Fractured or Flexible Identities? Life Histories of "Black" Diaspori women in Britain'. The focus on the experiences of Afro-Caribbean, Iraqi-Kurdish, Kenyan-Indian and South African-Asian women indicates the complex nature of identity and identification in the postcolonial context. Cultural hybridization emerges not just as a social fact of diaspora but also as a survival strategy for women in this kind of situation. Jayne Ifekwunigwe's 'Diaspora's Daughters, Africa's Orphans? On Lineage, Authenticity and "Mixed Race" Identity' also focuses on the experiences of a diverse group of women in contemporary Britain, though unlike other contributions it wants to authenticate itself as ethnography. Ifekwunigwe argues for the value of *métis/métisse* in describing people with parents from different ethnic groups, though her usage broadens (unhelpfully) to include, among other things, 'oscillation, contradiction, paradox, hybridity, creolization, mestizaje, "blending and mixing", polyglot, heteroglossia, transnationalities, multiculturalism, so-called multi raciality', leaving the reader wondering what analytical work it does which these other terms do not, and how it can be so many things at once.

Mapping Men and Empire by Richard Phillips offers, according to its subtitle, 'A geography of adventure'. It covers adventure narratives from (broadly) Defoe to Tournier and Coetzee; from eighteenth-century attempts to justify colonialism to twentieth-century postcolonial resistance to it; and includes stories set in areas less studied in this context such as Australia and Canada. The book represents a substantial opportunity: to revise earlier untheorized studies of adventure such as Martin Green's *Dreams of Adventure, Deeds of Empire*, to relate this to the rapidly growing body of work on masculinity, and at the same time, bringing to bear a geographer's perspective, to temper the metaphorical excesses of work in the postcolonial field which has been characterized by over-enthusiasm for cartographic images. The extent to which any of these is achieved is, however, debatable, and problems can occur both with the way issues are framed in the introduction and the way they are followed up in the various chapters. For example, 'While adventure is sometimes labelled a "masculinist" narrative . . . adventures do not reinscribe archetypal singular masculinity: they map historical masculinities.' While this misunderstands the difference between masculinity as a gender formation and masculinist as an ideology which particular masculinities may or may not promote, it does at least recognize the existence of 'historical masculinities'; unfortunately, the chapters dealing with eighteenth-, nineteenth- and twentieth-century texts do not examine what these differences might consist of. Further, important recent studies such as Graham Dawson's *Soldier Heroes* are mentioned but not engaged with, which undoubtedly weakens what Phillips has to say. The understanding of empire is similarly problematic: '*Robinson Crusoe* marked a shift towards a *petit bourgeois* colonialism, founded more on emigration, settlement and practical work'. Apart from the fact that emigration and settlement are not class-specific (and certainly not petit bourgeois), they are generally a long way from the early eighteenth-century world of *Robinson Crusoe*, and if colonialism is a function of the global spread of capitalism, then it cannot be a petit bourgeois phenomenon. Also, 'Colonies, like masculinities, are mapped in the geography of adventure. They are conceived in spaces of adventure and reflect the characteristics of those spaces.' However, the idea that colonialism is produced by, and reflects, 'the spaces of adventure' is, to put it mildly, highly tendentious. Phillips argues for more complex readings of adventure narrative, which is fine, but it is hard not to feel that his own stated preference for 'paying particular attention to plot' is perhaps not the best way to achieve this. Part of the complexity is to want to see texts as critical or resistant, when arguably they are doing no more than displaying new ideological contradictions which in no way disturb their overall political stance. Recuperatory reading of, for example, Rider Haggard's racism as critical and resistant seems like something other than 'complex'.

Resistance and geographers turn up again in *Geographies of Resistance*, edited by Steve Pile and Michael Keith. This is a very interesting collection which reflects some of the ways in which postcolonial theory intersects with work done in other disciplines, and is more satisfactory than Phillips' both at the level of theory (postcolonial and other) and of 'real' geography. In 'Resisting Reconciliation: The Secret Geographies of (Post)colonial Australia', Jane Jacobs revisits some of the territory covered in her excellent *Edge of Empire* (see *YWCCT* 6). Jacobs examines the project of 'reconciliation' as an attempt to deal with the violences of the colonial period towards Aboriginal people and as 'an official strategy of correcting the national sense of self'. She also discusses the relation of Aboriginal resistance to such a strategy, particularly in regard to land ownership/access. Ironically, 'reconciliation' has resulted in a postcolonial racism which claims that Aborigines have too much – 'too much of the nation's history, too much land, too many special rights and services'. As if.

Two of the other contributions focus on postcolonial Africa: Michael Watts' 'Black Gold, White Heat: State Violence, Local Resistance and the National Question in Nigeria', and Donald Moore's 'Remapping Resistance: "Ground for Struggle" and the Politics of Place', which concentrates on Zimbabwe. Moore provides a relevant survey of positions on resistance before moving on to examine the struggles over resettlement and other issues in Zimbabwe and returning to resituate his discussion in relation to a range of theoretical stances. Watts' piece is much more 'straight' geography, but its study of the politics of petrol in Nigeria's Ogoni delta includes the judicial murder of postcolonial writer and activist Ken Saro-Wiwa.

This year also sees the publication of two books with similar agendas (introductory/survey), but rather different organizational rationales – Peter Childs and Patrick Williams' *An Introduction to Post-Colonial Theory* and Bart Moore-Gilbert's *Postcolonial Theory: Contexts, Practices, Politics*. The former follows Patrick Williams and Laura Chrisman's successful *Colonial Discourse and Post-Colonial Theory*, and the two make for an interesting partnership, with the *Introduction to Post-Colonial Theory* doing a neat job of filling the gaps where the reader did not provide detailed summaries on the essays or commentaries on the various positions.

An Introduction to Post-Colonial Theory is organized in a user-friendly manner with each chapter split into sections and a number of theorists, concepts and differential positions are examined in detail. Nevertheless, there is a certain lack of consistency across chapters. Where the 'Introduction: Points of departure' raises a number of salient questions ('when is the post-colonial'; 'where is the post-colonial?; 'who is the post-colonial?'; and 'what is the post-colonial?'), complicating each response to emphasize the danger of easy answers or comfortable solutions, deferring judgement at this stage, 'Lines of resistance' does not even attempt a summation. However, by the time the reader reaches 'Metropolitan theorising' and the remaining chapters, an evaluative commentary is offered together with further reading. There is little doubt, however, that this book is an invaluable intervention in the field. It is much more elucidatory and more carefully and cogently theorized and argued than, for example, Ashcroft et al.'s *The Empire Writes Back*.

The first three chapters of *An Introduction to Post-Colonial Theory* are especially welcome since the authors draw on the work of a range of critics, a number of whom may be described as the dissenting voices in postcolonial studies and postcolonial theory, in particular. Their perspectives are interrogated and their anxieties explored. 'Lines of resistance' is important in establishing the work done in India to re-evaluate European colonizing processes and, consequently, addresses Gandhi and Nehru, albeit rather too briefly. In contextualizing the Black Atlantic, Senghor and Cesaire are examined in relation to Negritude and the impact of thinkers and commentators C. L. R. James, Edouard Glissant and Wilson Harris is exemplified, as is the writing of Fanon and Ngugi on resistance.

Refreshingly, the 'Holy Trinity' (to borrow Robert Young's phrase) of Said, Bhabha and Spivak, although discussed in individual chapters, are not set up as the sole agents of postcolonial theory. Childs and Williams do nevertheless succeed in explicating the key theories and concepts associated with each critic. Chapter and section titles direct the reader in the case of Bhabha, for example, to 'hybridity', 'ambivalence and colonial discourse' and 'stereotype as fetish'. Each section is followed by the criticism levelled against him and by further reading. But, Childs and Williams do not allow these notable critics to dominate. Their final chapter, 'Post-colonial intersections', examines the ways in which post-colonial theory intersects with other theoretical positions, via issue-based discussion of 'language, gender, and nationalism', for example. The major strength of this book lies in its authors' ability and willingness to explore issues in a multidisciplinary way, drawing on historical analysis, race and gender theories and those critical theories now firmly embedded in 'literary studies'.

Bart Moore-Gilbert in *Postcolonial Theory: Contexts, Practices, Politics* is similarly concerned with 'recent controversies about postcolonial theory, which have led to what seems to some observers to be a growing divide between postcolonial theory . . . and the rest of postcolonial criticism . . .' The strengths of his book lie with the sustained and detailed analysis of Said, Bhabha and Spivak along with the specific ways in which postcolonial theory has made an intervention in the academy. This is a stimulating study. However, given the breadth of the field of postcolonial studies, Moore-Gilbert perhaps unsurprisingly misses the opportunity to intervene in some of those areas where Childs and Williams make an impact. The two books have their strengths and weaknesses but, taken together, they provide a very valuable introduction to postcolonial theory and the debates currently taking place in the field. Undergraduate and postgraduate students of the discipline will benefit greatly from exploring the ideas discussed in both books.

In a (surprisingly?) lucid and readable editorial to *Cultural Inquiry* (23 Spring 1997, 431–459) entitled 'Maneuvers and Unsettled Negotiations,' Homi Bhabha explores precisely what occurs when one writes 'from the middles of difference', which he describes as 'a *movement between third and first persons*'. This is a movement wherein 'a narrative of historical becoming is constituted not as a dialectic between first and third persons but as an effect of the ambivalent condition of their borderline proximity – the first-in-the-third/the one-in-the-other.' To explain this idea Bhabha focuses on ambivalence, proximity and anxiety via a reading of Adrienne Rich's poem 'Movement'. Ideas of movement or location are also the focus of Rajeswari Sunder Rajan's 'The Third World Academic in Other Places; or, the

Postcolonial Intellectual Revisited' (*Cultural Inquiry* 23 Spring 1997, 596–616). Rajan reads three different modes of writing: Arif Dirlik's 'The Postcolonial Aura', Salman Rushdie's *The Satanic Verses* and Gayatri Spivak's critical reading of *The Satanic Verses*, in order to 'establish a recurrent preoccupation in contemporary postcolonial discourse with the politics of its practitioners based on their residence in one of two postcolonial spaces, the First or Third World'. Focusing on self-location, she argues for a critical consideration of the local as well as the global. Strangely, she conflates postcolonial theory with postmodernism: 'In common with other postmodernisms, postcolonial theory itself refuses the epistemological transparency of the theorizing subject' but fails to develop this, preferring to point the reader in the direction of Kwame Anthony Appiah's essay 'Is the Post- in Postmodernism the Post- in Postcolonial?'

In 'Creole Skin, Black Mask: Fanon and Disavowel' (*Cultural Inquiry* 23 Spring 1997 578–595), Francoise Verges analyses the black body in Fanon's work. She argues that Fanon's philosophy of the alienated subject 'that presupposed a *before* of truth and integrity and an *after* of regained authenticity could not be applied to the Creole subject'. This is primarily because there is no precolonial space to which one may return and therefore little to valorize in the context. Verges asserts that: 'Fanon disavowed a society [Antillean society] to which the Master is always present, on the scene of history and in the primal scene'. In her view, Fanon disavowed the Creole filiation: 'the enslaved father and the raped mother could not be his parents. Nor did he symbolize *metissage*, this encounter, violent or loving, between people of different races of which he was a product.' For Fanon, the Antilleans were 'emasculated men. Algeria gave Fanon his dreamed filiation.' The trope of the body also figures prominently in Helen Gilbert and Jacqueline Lo's 'Performing Hybridity in Postcolonial Monodrama' (*Journal of Commonwealth Literature* xxxii: 1, 1997, 5–19). Gilbert and Lo examine four monodramas (plays for one actor) in order to establish how 'performative articulations of hybridity' arise in the plays' particular uses of dialogic devices'. They go on to argue that performance 'positions the postcolonial body as a particularly charged site of cultural contestation in the process of constructing a hybrid subjectivity'. They draw on Bhabha's formulation of hybridity and his notion of 'Third Space' in order to demonstrate 'that the multiple signifying systems of theatre' provide a Third Space which 'enables writers and performers to dramatize cultural hybridity and the resignification of cultural difference'.

In 'Allan Seely's *The Trotter-Nama*: A Postcolonial Synchronicle' (*Journal of Commonwealth Literature* xxii: 1, 1997, 67–78), Geetha Ganapathy-Dore states that 'Anglo-Indians are modern India's first metamorphic children . . . insiders and outsiders to the society in which they were born'. This opening and, indeed, her title suggest that the reading might draw on the work of some theorists, but instead, Ganapathy-Dore makes brief and uncritical use of Salman Rushdie's *Imaginary Homelands*. What this article actually demonstrates is the way in which the term 'postcolonial' can be unhelpfully employed as an untheorized periodizing marker. This is a charge that cannot be levelled at Kyung-Won Lee. In 'Is the Glass Half-empty or Half-Full? Rethinking the problems of postcolonial Revisionism' (*Cultural Critique* 1–2 Spring 1997, 89–117), Lee proposes to examine the very problems that arise from 'critiques of the reductive tendencies in postcolonialism', and considers whether 'the critiques against postcolonial binarism can be made valid when applied to the specific sociocultural conditions of English history'. By focusing on Bhabha's notion of 'ambivalence', Lee demonstrates how an 'insistence on the ambivalence of colonial discourse is itself grounded on an ambivalent epistemological framework ... [Bhabha] obscures, deliberately or otherwise, the boundaries between colonizer and colonized. The result is a dehistoricisation of colonialism'. Lee subsequently develops Abdul Jan-Mohamed's idea (itself derived from Gramsci) of the dominant and hege-monic phases of European colonial history, in order to show that this model is also too broad and potentially all encompassing. Lee states that 'popular concepts in recent discourse analysis – Bakhtin's dialogism, Foucault's interdiscursivity, Gramsci's hegemony, all of which stress a mode of dialogi-cal interplay between dominant and dominated – constitute an alluring paradigm for postcolonial reconstruction; but it is a paradigm incompatible with the historical facts of colonialism. Given the silence of the natives and the relative absence of discursive interactions between metropole and periphery, colonist discourse was not a dialogue in the Bakhtinian sense'. In conclusion, Lee suggests that the search for a postcolonial theory that is free of the 'logic of Manichean duality' ignores the 'always-already-there reality of colonial history'.

Books Reviewed

Childs, Peter and Patrick Williams. *An Introduction to Post-Colonial Theory.* Prentice Hall/Harvester Wheatsheaf. pp. 240. pb £11.95. ISBN 0 132 32919 0.

Kaplan, E. Anne. *Looking for the Other: Feminism, Film and the Imperial Gaze.* Routledge. pp. 333. pb £12.99. ISBN 0 415 91017 X.

Mirza, Heidi Safia, ed. *Black British Feminism: A Reader.* Routledge. pp. 306. pb £14.99. ISBN 0 415 15289 5.

Moore-Gilbert, Bart. *Postcolonial Theory: Contexts, Practices, Politics.* Verso. pp. 242. pb £14.00. ISBN 1 859 84034 5.

Nnaemeka, Obioma, ed. *The Politics of (M)Othering: Womanhood, Identity and Resistance in African Literature.* Routledge. pp. 233. pb £13.99. ISBN 0 415 13790 X.

Phillips, Richard. *Mapping Men and Empire.* Routledge. pp. 208. pb £14.99. ISBN 0 415 13772 1.

Pile, Steve and Michael Keith, eds. *Geographies of Resistance.* Routledge. pp. 315. pb £14.99. ISBN 0 415 15497 9.

6

Historicism

SCOTT WILSON

A number of books published this year and last, plus a new journal, *Rethinking History*, published by Routledge and edited by Alun Munslow and Robert A. Rosenstone, suggest that there is currently a lot of activity in anglophone history departments concerned with the future of the discipline. These books include Keith Jenkins' *The Postmodern History Reader*, Alun Munslow's *Deconstructing History*, C. Behan McCullagh's *The Truth of History* (all Routledge), along with Michael S. Roth, *The Ironist's Cage: Memory, Trauma and the Construction of History* (New York: Columbia, 1995), F. R. Ankersmit and Hans Kellner's *A New Philosophy of History* (Chicago University Press, 1995) (reviewed *YWCCT 95*), Joyce Appleby, Elizabeth Covington, David Hoyt, Michael Laytham and Allison Sneider's *Knowledge and Postmodernism in Historical Perspective* (Routledge, 1996) and Beverley Southgate's *History: What and Why?* (Routledge, 1996) (both reviewed *YWCCT 96*). History, as a discipline, seems to be finally grappling, in a serious way, with critical and cultural theory and postmodernism. As Keith Jenkins writes in the Introduction to *The Postmodern History Reader*, there have been many Readers over the past fifteen years or so concerned with postmodernism itself, or on aspects of postmodernism and something else like feminism, literature, architecture and so on, but there has yet to be a Postmodern History Reader. Jenkins has stepped into the breach marshalled by the massed ranks of commonsense empiricists, anti-theoretical realists, dyed-in-the-wool Marxists, 'traditionalists' and so on and produced an excellent Reader that is ideal for history students and courses on the Theory and Practice of History. It should become the cornerstone of the core courses that are necessary to provide some semblance of intellectual coherence and critical self-reflection in those areas where the study of history has become complacent, unreflecting and fragmented. Though the selection is slightly biased towards postmodern approaches to history, these are vigorously contested in other anthologized pieces. Selections from Jean-François Lyotard's *Postmodern Condition*, Baudrillard's *Illusion of the End* head the collection and the section on 'History in the Upper Case', supported by complementary and contestatory selections from Elizabeth Ermath, Diane Elam, Robert Young, Iain Chambers, Elizabeth Fox-Genovese, Christopher Norris and Bryan Palmer. Selections on 'History in the

Lower Case' begin with Roland Barthes' 'The discourse of history' and Michel Foucault's 'Nietzsche, Genealogy, History' and are followed by essays by Hans Kellner, Robert Berkhofer, Gertrude Himmelfarb, Geoffrey Elton and Gabrielle Spiegel. The group of so-called 'undecided or nuanced others' are represented by Joyce Appleby, Lynn Hunt, Margaret Jacob, Tony Bennett and Susan Stanford Friedman. There is also a lively section that reproduces debates that have continued in key history journals such as *Past and Present* and *Social History* featuring Lawrence Stone, Patrick Joyce, Catriona Kelly, Gabrielle Spiegel, F. R. Ankersmit, P. Zagorin, Neville Kirk, Geoffrey Eley and Keith Nieldand. The concluding section uses a 'The Holocaust Debate' as a means of testing various approaches and selections from *History and Theory* and Saul Friedlander's *Probing the Limits of Representation* with contributions by Hayden White, Hans Kellner, Wulf Kansteiner, Robert Braun and Berel Lang.

A useful companion to Jenkins' *Reader* would be Alun Munslow's *Deconstructing History* which also believes that the discipline of history has been put into crisis by the advent of postmodernism. It should be stressed, however, that the 'deconstruction' of the title has nothing to do with Jacques Derrida, Paul de Man, Geoffrey Bennington or writers normally associated with the term. Munslow disassociates himself from Derrida – his book has chapters on Michel Foucault and Hayden White as exemplifying deconstructive history – and defines his term 'deconstruction' in relation to 'reconstructive history' and 'constructive history'. 'Reconstructive history' is the method of 'conservative empiricists and practical realists' who 'envisage the role of language and narrative as cognitive elements in the reconstruction of the past' (188), and 'constructive history', exemplified by the Marxist and *Annales* schools, deploy social theoretical constructions as models for social change and exchange (8). 'Deconstructive history', however, is determined by a critical process that views all history as 'the creation and eventual imposition by historians of a particular narrative form on the past', an understanding that Munslow calls 'the deconstructive consciousness' (2). The problem with 'deconstructive history', it seems to me, is that it enables, on the one hand, the deconstructionist subject of history to engage both in neat pedagogical analyses of other historians' textual strategies, all the while affirming him or herself (and his or her consciousness) as the 'creative' metaphor for whatever historical category – race, class and gender – that the historian believes he or she creates and represents for no particular purpose other than sustaining a career in history: 'the past is not discovered or found', writes Munslow, 'it is created and represented by the historian as text, which is in turn consumed by the reader' (178). While there is nothing wrong with trying to sustain a career in history, the very nature of that career is changing, as Munslow's use of the metaphor of 'consumption' indicates. As Munslow also writes in his Editorial to the first issue of *Rethinking History*, history departments are being made ever more 'accountable' to external forces and funding sources from the 'museum, collective memory, and public history business' (not to mention theme park and heritage sites) and financial managers working in the name of 'the public' who are allegedly 'demanding firm and fixed insights into the roots, identity, and heritage of our culture' (2). The 'deconstructive' marketization of history into easily consumable ready meals threatens to dissolve History into nothing other than a shopping mall of local, ethnic identities to be consumed and enjoyed by tourists. It seems to me that Munslow's 'deconstructive history' is precisely the method that justifies the Lakeland Disney Department of Virgin University (North West) impelling its new appointment, say, to dress up as Dorothy Wordsworth in order to creatively represent Romanticism for the paying punters.

For Alun Munslow, the 'deconstructionist view of history . . . results from the wider end-of-century postmodern intellectual context' outlined in Lyotard's *Postmodern Condition* (14). It is also evident from the organization of Jenkins' *Reader*, that Lyotard's seminal Report on Knowledge is the defining text around which many of these debates in history are organized. Jenkins' division of 'History into the upper case', broadly corresponding to Lyotard's notion of master or metanarratives, and 'history in the lower case', 'particularist' or 'academic' forms that have a less obvious correlation with Lyotard's '*petit recits*' and appear to have more to do with disciplinary specialisms that, in their Anglo-American empiricist way, eschew 'metanarrative claims that [they are] discovering in the past meaningful trajectories, purposes and teleologies' (6). This misreading of Lyotard, on behalf of commonsense empiricists who never believed in grand narratives anyway, is compounded by their complacent blindness to the metanarrative implied by empiricism and the set of generalizations, classifications, modes of description, rules of interpretation and so on that govern their practice and generate the truth-form that has gained institutional acceptance. C. Behan McCullogh's *The Truth of History* has the virtue of acknowledging this. Noting that 'many historians today prefer to tell "little stories", which focus upon the activities of individuals, rather than upon generalizations and abstract social structures', not least because 'it sells better' (300), he nevertheless insists that 'we should not avoid seeking and testing limited generalizations about causal processes in particular societies, which will illuminate our history' (302). Confident in the essentially nineteenth-century 'mirror and lamp' idea of representation in which the 'illumination' is predicated on a prior reflection, this is also, perhaps, mistakenly complacent with regard to the universality of its second person singular. It is not certain that the subject 'we' (presumably academic historians) are given much credence by nonhistorians (or nonprofessional historians) with regard to 'their' history. As Keith Jenkins cogently argues in the first issue of *Rethinking History*, current academic models of historical representation determine that these histories simply reflect the interests, professional or otherwise, of historians: historical problems and solutions are always *historians'* problems and solutions.

> Given that history is constituted by the work of historians (historiography) the idea that we can 'learn lessons from the past/history', actually translates out as simply, 'we can learn lessons from historians'. At which point the fairly obvious question arises as to how many of us would trust historians as 'moral guides', as 'lesson givers', and as providers of and legitimators of our identities, any further than we could, how can I put it, throw them? (Jenkins, 'Why Bother with the Past?' *Rethinking History* 1.1, pp. 56–66, 64.)

This quotation amply illustrates Lyotard's point about an 'incredulity towards metanarratives' and the devastating implications that this incredulity has not just for historians but for the whole notion of a 'University' that has any pretention towards 'universality' or a governing cultural idea, implications that have barely been addressed. The severity of these implications have very little to do with the deconstruction of history, and attempts to reconnect historical narrative to some external authority or authorizing reality will have no effect because its credit has been withdrawn (and with the credit, the credence that it bought). Universities have to move towards becoming self-funding now, no funding authority is going to credit them just because they claim access to the truth. For nearly the last twenty years, one of the ironies of the ubiquity Lyotard's *Postmodern Condition* has enjoyed is how little notice scholars have paid to the paragraphs that directly follow the discussion of metanarratives and *petit recits*, as if the latter provided the answer to the dissolution of the former. Lyotard notes the passing of the University and the beginning of patchy Institutes, 'local determinisms' that arise on the basis of different language games. However, this 'heterogeneity of elements' is deployed in a significantly uniform and homogenizing way:

> The decision makers, however, attempt to manage these clouds of sociality according to input/output matrices, following a logic which implies that their elements are commensurable and that the whole is determinable. They allocate our lives for the growth of power. In matters of social justice and of scientific truth alike, the legitimation of that power is based on its optimizing the system's performance – efficiency. The application of this criterion to all of our games necessarily entails a certain level of terror, whether soft or hard: be operational (that is, commensurable) or disappear. (Lyotard, *The Postmodern Condition*, in Jenkins, p. 37)

History departments, and the academics within them, will operate efficiently according the economic logic of input/output matrices, or they will disappear. The 'terror' that this criterion implies will not be combatted through recourse to academic apparati of legitimation, or through recourse to rational or moral judgements concerning the right, the true, the just, or even the good. 'The operativity criterion is technological; it has no relevance for judging what is true or just', and it is utterly indifferent to human ideas of the good, apart from the maximization of technological goods and the training of those experts, technicians, managers and IT engineers that operate, and are operated by, them. The computer, its absolute ubiquity in techno-bureaucratic institutions, is the simile for the system even as the PC becomes the metaphor for the operativity of the working subject operating and operated by it, a subject rendered obsolescent when it can no longer be upgraded to the optimum level. The operativity criterion is indifferent to the 'human' content that is deployed within or on the surface of it, indifferent to which historical identities, roots or heritage function as the most efficient indicators of maximal performance: it may be the history and heritage of queer masculinities in Welsh mining villages one day, a paedophiliac Ruskin or Catholic Shakespeare the next. Such creative innovations are necessary, however, to provoke demand for more consumable history. As Lyotard writes, 'the novelty of an unexpected "move", with its correlative displacement of a partner or group of partners, can supply the system with that increased performativity it forever demands and consumes' (Lyotard, *The Postmodern Condition: A Report on Knowledge*. Manchester University Press, 1984, p. 15).

'Imagine', writes C. Behan McCullagh, 'the terror of living in a world without any idea of the causal processes at work in it' (302). But that is precisely the condition that 'we' find ourselves in: there are no rational, moral or aesthetic grounds for determining the 'causal processes' that determine social life. No one knows much in advance what the next technological transformation of 'our' life-world will be, or how it will come about. Perhaps we will never know until a different kind of intelligence, one attuned to the machinic logic of technological development writes a history of its own causal processes from the point of view of the machine. While it is unlikely that some future machinic intelligence will be interested in its own heritage, a sufficiently anthromorphic and therefore readable robot historian may one day be programmed to write its own history. In that history, as Manuel De Landa writes in his *War in the Age of Intelligent Machines* (New York: Zone, 1991, pp. 2–10), the robot historian would of course emphasize the way machines affected human evolution by providing it with models for the human subject and society – the clock, the motor, the computer etc. – but ultimately 'the role of humans would be seen as little more than industrious insects pollinating an independent species of machine-flowers that simply did not possess its own reproductive organs during a segment of its evolution' (De Landa, p. 3). De Landa is one of a new generation of historians who use models from 'hard' science – physics, biology, meteorology and geology – to account for historical transformations, rather than those subject-centred models drawn from the human sciences.

Though subject-centred history may be inadequate to account for the historical 'causal processes' that determine social life, the subject is still the uncertain and ambiguous space where such transformations are 'experienced' even though that experience may not be comprehended as such, or only belatedly or retroactively as a misperception and a miscomprehension. A number of books this year are looking again at the invention of the modern subject or self from the early modern period to the present day. The most disappointing is *Rewriting the Self: Histories from the Renaissance to the Present* edited by Roy Porter, despite the starry names it has gathered together. From Porter's rather tired introduction which runs, in a perfunctory way, through the usual suspects: Burckardtian Renaissance individualism, the Reformation, Protestantism, Montaigne's scepticism, Hamlet, English empiricism, the rise of capitalism, French rationalism, Rousseau's confessions, Robinson Crusoe, Romantic egotism, and finally Freud. The collection follows this well-worn narrative and is divided into four parts: the Renaissance and the early modern with essays by Peter Burke, Jonathan Sawday, Roger Smith; the Enlightenment with essays by Jane Shaw, E. J. Hundert, Sylvana Tomaselli, Carolyn D. Williams, John Mullins; Romanticism with essays by Roger Cardinal, Kate Flint, Lynda Nead, Daniel Pick on stories of the eye; and the modern and postmodern period with essays by Steven Connor, Nikolas Rose, Jonathan Dollimore and Terry Eagleton.

A more focused study is Michael Mascuch's *Origins of the Individualist Self: Autobiography and Self-Identity in England 1591–1791*. This book takes as its focus James Lackington's *Memoirs of the First Forty-Five Years of the Life of James Lackington* (1791) which it claims as the first truly modern autobiography. Lackington, Mascuch argues, is the first characteristic English individualist. His text looks at the emergence of this characteristic English individual and the forms that contributed to the appearance of the autobiographical genre and the subject that it helps to shape. From religious papers and manuscript devotional diaries, confessions, secular diaries and personal papers through to criminal biographies and the quasi-autobiographical apologetic narratives produced by scandalized gentlewomen (actresses, poets and courtesans), the form that Lackington would ultimately embody takes shape. Looking at Charlotte Charke, Laetitia Pilkington and Constantia Phillips, in particular, who 'by deliberate manipulation of autobiographical discourse' created and maintained an original and autonomous place for herself in the public domain as a kind of woman warrior, or female outlaw, liberated from the prison of the family, the domestic economy, patronage, religion, and ultimate subordination to traditional corporate authority, public and private. 'In their work', writes Mascuch, 'we find individualist self-identity displayed in its most pronounced form before the appearance of Lackington's memoirs' (189).

David Hillman and Carla Mazzio's *The Body in Parts: Fantasies of Corporeality in Early Modern Europe* is a richly illustrated, attractively edited volume of essays by noted writers associated with New Historicism. Rather uneasily anticipating the criticism of incoherence by citing Montaigne's description of his own collection of essays as 'grotesques and monstrous bodies, pieced together of diverse members, without definite shape, having no order, sequence or proportion other than accidental' (xviii), the Frankensteinian editors have assembled together Marjorie Garber on joints, Stephen Greenblatt on bodily marking and mutilation, David Hillman on the entrails, Sergei Lobanov-Rostovsky on the eye, Jeffrey Masten on the anus, Carla Mazzio on the tongue, Katharine Park on the clitoris, Gail Kern Paster on the nervous system, Katherine Rowe on the hands, Michael Schoenfeldt on the belly, Kathryn Schwarz on the breast, Peter Stallybrass on the foot, Scott Manning Stevens on the heart and the brain, Nancy J. Vickers on corporeal fragments. Hillman and Mazzio's hideous progeny has no penis, it seems, or rather no noted New Historian to work upon it, and so, as they say, it surfaces throughout the volume in 'the most unexpected of places' (xx). Needless to say, with the scholarly talent on show here, the essays are always enjoyable, informative and fascinating. Again, the most common theme is how the various exhibited and examined body parts contribute to the fashioning of subjectivity. Hillman argues that the entrails were 'a crucial locus of subjectivity' in Renaissance culture; Paster looks at the interior passageways of the body as 'the early modern subject's imagined physiology of self'; Masten probes the anus as the 'fundamental' site of alterity upon which the early modern subject's knowledge of itself and its health was predicated; Schwarz considers the missing breast of the legendary and mythically significant Amazon warrior as an embodiment (or disembodiment) of loss: 'loss of the mother, of gender stability, of referential certainty'; Park looks at the rediscovery of the clitoris as symptomatic of anxieties about gender and sexual difference; Lobanov-Rostovsky considers the gendering of the eye and the gaze; Greenblatt discusses the shift from predominantly religious to anthropological understandings of mutilations such as circumcision, scarification and so on; Schoenfeldt discusses how the stomach is imagined at the site of human, specifically devotional, inwardness; Stevens notes how the centre of mental and emotional activity moves from the heart to the brain as the former's function as a mechanical pump became more evident; Rowe looks at the hand of God working in the anatomist's touch; and Stallybrass looks at how the Renaissance cobbler could become a 'member of bad Soules' in both senses. Given this almost total overdetermination of the body by theological, literary and ideological discourses concerned with subjectivity, inner life, mental health, gender identity and so on, it is tempting to suggest that despite what is popularly believed about the corporeality of the early modern period, there was no body in the Renaissance.

If the body is a human fiction, it is no less so than death, as Michael Neil convincingly shows in his well-illustrated, elegant and critically accomplished *Issues of Death: Mortality and Identity in English Renaissance Tragedy.* Neil's book discusses how human self-consciousness is defined in relation to a consciousness of death, and how the understanding of this self-consciousness takes a secular shift during the Renaissance. From the cultural construction of death in Genesis, where 'death comes into existence . . . only when a living being can imagine dying' (2), where death is imagined incorporeally, to Milton's corporeal rewriting of Genesis, where death takes on 'its startling physical presence' (3). Neil argues that the tragic drama of Elizabethan and Jacobean England plays a crucial role in this secularizing process; tragedy was 'among the principal instruments by which the culture of early modern England reinvented death (3). Given this statement, it is odd that Neil's book actually argues that the primary secularizing and corporealizing forces were the plague and the study of anatomy, connecting the latter up with the tragic theatre because of 'its habitually moralized iconography and through its highly theatricalized practice' (43). Neil looks at how the 'new science of anatomy contributed to an emerging discourse of interiority by representing the human body as a multi-layered container of "secrets"' (44), and looks at a number of 'psychological' tragic dramas that seem to do the same on the Jacobean stage. Shakespeare's *Othello* and Middleton and Rowley's *The Changeling* are selected for particularly close and insightful re-readings. If I have a criticism it is that Neil neglects an obvious and highly literary dimension to the secularlization of death in the Renaissance – the eroticization of death. Of course this eroticization is linked to the transgression of religious conceptions of death, hence, in Genesis the self-consciousness of death is figured as the self-consciousness of nakedness and sexual shame. However, as Neil cites in a footnote, the taboo on nakedness was virtually absent from medieval culture and re-emerges in the Renaissance for a number of complex reasons to do not least 'with the changing attitudes towards death as with a stricter policing of sexuality' (11). These changing attitudes and stricter policing cohere on the Jacobean stage where sex is frequently censored *and* represented by death, most famously in *Othello* where Desdemona is murdered in a jealous passion on her marital bed by her husband, and in *The Changeling* where, hidden in a closet, Beatrice-Joanna and De Flores 'rehearse again their scene of lust' with the latter violently stabbing the former, Beatrice-Joanna's exclamatory 'oh!s' being indistinguishable, to an audience, from cries of ecstasy. While Neil of course acknowledges the sexual dimension of these scenes, it merely serves as an example of theatrical 'disclosure' analogous to scientific or anatomical disclosure. Thus, the violent turning point of European eroticism, and the repressive-transgressive history of sex that followed in its wake, is overlooked. John Twyning's *London Dispossessed: Literature and Social Space in the Early Modern City* is a book about Thomas Dekker, 'the quintessential urban writer of his period', and the low-lives that populated London from the 1590s: the prostitutes, pimps, huxters, cheaters, gamesters, gulls, gallants, rogues and so on that feature in his writings. Twyning reads Dekker's 'underworld literature', his *Honest Whore* plays, his plague pamphlets and other nondramatic works to look at the City of London, its notorious institutions such as Bedlam and Bridewell and its 'mad' population, where the term 'mad' is used variously to 'symbolize the stress of metropolitan life' (11). As a 'theatrical trope', madness 'encodes infra-class and inter-class antagonism, urban stress, social dislocation and courtly emblems, as well as the genuinely, and somewhat anarchically, insane' (11). The book also devotes chapters to prostitution, London's languages of fashion and Puritanism's conception of Hell and purification. It is fascinating throughout.

Paul Innes' *Shakespeare and the English Renaissance Sonnet* looks at the courtly fashion for sonnet making in the 1590s and provides a subtle, sophisticated yet entirely readable account of Shakespeare's sonnets. Deploying a lighter touch than the heavyweight combination of Lacan and Paul de Man in Joel Fineman's rhetorical analysis *Shakespeare's Perjured Eye* (1986), Innes' account nevertheless draws on the theoretically informed Shakespeare criticism of the 1980s and 1990s to provide a nuanced, materialist account of the text. Innes' reading is particularly indebted to Lorna Hutson's *The Usurer's Daughter: Male Friendship and Fictions of Women in Sixteenth-Century England* which is published in paperback for the first time this year. Hutson's excellent work addresses the socio-economic and gender implications of a shift in the meaning of male friendship in which the term moves from being a marker of economic dependency and patronage to an affective bond defined, romantically, in opposition to such dependency. The code of faithful friendship that was tied up with an aristocratic system of gift-friendship, in which bonds of loyalty are maintained in relations of credit, is gradually replaced by 'a humanist reading programme' that transformed the education of Englishmen and led to the invention of 'an altruistic, non-instrumental' form of friendship (3). Hutson argues that this new form of friendship emerged out of a certain practice of persuasive rhetoric and writing that had women as its subject, initially as objects of exchange between men, and latterly as objects of a homo-sociality. Hutson looks at 'the importance of women as signs of credit between men [both] in the traditional anthropological sense of alliance formation, and in a sense peculiar to the literary culture of humanism, in which the claim to be able to "fashion" women by addressing them through persuasive fictions of themselves lent a special social credibility to the masculine activity of authorship' (7). It is in this context that Paul Innes places the writing of Shakespeare's sonnets. Thus the special 'friendship' that liberal humanist Shakespeare scholars have often romanticized, idealized, and even homoeroticized is here firmly located in a relationship of patronage, the sonnets being inscribed, for Innes, 'within a dynamic relation with "friends" who are most precisely not necessarily friends in the modern sense' (7). Innes seeks to refute the reading of the sonnets that 'assumes mutuality, even . . . homosexuality' between the persona and the friend. However, while it seems to me perfectly correct to note the fundamental differences, the lack of mutuality between the male protagonists, relations of patronage, debt and credit do not foreclose the possibility of sexual relations, quite the contrary. Greek homo-eroticism, for example, was predicated on relations of patronage and 'friendship' in this precise sense.

James Loxley in *Royalism and Poetry in the English Civil Wars* aims to correct the 'golden moments' view of Cavalier poetry, 'the image of Izaak Walton and the younger Charles Cotton fishing in the Dove on a fine day' (1). Instead of reading Cavalier verse as a celebration of love, friendship and the good life of rural retirement, Loxley locates the poetry at the heart of the struggle over the political future of England as a fiercely partisan, royalist contender in the Civil War. Loxley examines the political instrumental uses of the poetry, questions what it means to construct a verse practice in accordance with partisan needs, and finds an intensely self-reflexive verse that continually questions how it represents itself to itself and its own role in the political and military struggles of the 1640s. For the puritans and the supporters of Parliament, Cavalier verse betrayed 'a terrifying rapacity', a threatening evil that earned them the epithet 'malignant'.

Longman's *Literature and Culture in Modern Britain* series is a three-volume sequence that attempts to give 'the reader the intertextual cultural history of modern Britain'. While literature is foregrounded, and the series is designed for use by literature departments, the series attempts to show how literary, cultural and historical processes are intimately connected. The second volume, covering the years 1930–55 is published this year, edited by Gary Day. Day's Introduction considers the economy, social policy and cultural issues during this time, in which the rise of consumerism was beginning to shape Britain, and it was facing a growing, popular cultural Americanization after the war, following in the wake of the very real American presence during it. Other essays in the book focus on a variety of cultural forms. Jessica Maynard discusses British poetry 1930–55, particularly Tomlinson, Eliot, Auden, MacNeice, and Betjeman, and looks at themes of landscape, ruin and renewal, nostalgia, social waste and the social hope that, variously, hoped to revitalize Britain from the perception that it was 'a backward and dilapidated province' (47). Maggie Clune, Gary Day and Chris Maguire consider the novels of this period and discuss the supposed 'decline and fall' of the form that, with some notable exceptions, largely returned to the conventions of realism after the modernist experimental heights of the 20s. Michael Hayes looks at the popular fiction of the age, particularly the economic success of best-selling genre fiction – romance, (*Rebecca*), adventure (Bull-Dog Drummond etc.), westerns (*Shane* etc.), thrillers (James Bond etc.), detective stories (Agatha Christie etc.) all of whom met with the vigorous disapproval of the Leavises and their circle.

Michael Woolf discusses the theatre of 1930–55, particularly those 'major theatrical experiences' *An Inspector Calls* and *The Winslow Boy*, and the brief flourishing of the poetic drama with *Murder in the Cathedral* and *Under Milk Wood*. Nicholas Rance discusses the newspapers of the period, Robert Giddings the radio and Lez Cooke the cinema; David Masters looks at the British response to modernism in art during the period, Rober Bleil, Peter Driver and Benedict Sarnaker discuss the cultural importance of popular music, the relationship between Broadway and the West End, dance bands, swing, the new radio and record markets and, ultimately, the emergence of 'youth culture'; John Morris discusses the increasing importance and speed of technological development, 1930–55 in many ways (because of World War II) being the crucial period of the century for determining what the next century will be like. The book also includes a useful chronology in which literary events are juxtaposed with other cultural and political events, hence we are reminded that Noel Coward's *Private Lives* (1930) is contemporaneous with the first issue of *The Daily Worker*, the publication of Freud's *Civilization and its Discontents*, the beginning of Mahatma Gandhi's civil disobedience campaign in India and the invention of the photo flashbulb and perspex.

Lynda E. Boose and Richard Burt's (eds) *Shakespeare the Movie*. Boose and Burt's own essay discusses the 1990s' vogue for Shakespeare in Hollywood not just adaptations of particular plays such as *Hamlet*, *Romeo and Juliet* with A-list stars like Mel Gibson, Glenn Close and Leonardo di Caprio, but also the regular references to Shakespeare and his plays in mainstream Hollywood movies like *Clueless*, *L.A. Story*, *Last Action Hero*, *The Lion King*, *Renaissance Man* and so on, though are themselves clueless about the significance of the current vogue and find nothing of interest to say about individual movies. Barbara Hodgdon discusses the interest in *Othello* that developed in commentaries surrounding the O. J. Simpson case, arguing that Shakespeare's play provided a 'literary logic not only for containing blackness within the white imaginary but also, by dreaming the death of "woman", for re-enclosing women's voices and bodies within a male imaginary which sanctions its own destructive desires' (41). Donal K. Hedrick looks at the political ambiguities of 'Dirty Harry V' and Kenneth Branagh's martial mud-wrestling in his versions of Shakespeare's plays; James N. Loehlin locates Richard Loncraine's *Richard III*, starring Ian McKellen, in the cinematic conventions of both the British heritage film and the American gangster movie, a strange combination; Robert Hapgood admires the popularizing 'artistry of Franco Zeffirelli', Valerie Wayne looks at Merchant Ivory's *Shakespeare Wallah* in the context of 'colonial specularity', Laurie E. Osborne contributes an interesting essay on *Shakespeare: The Animated Tales*, the innovative series of short animated films that originated in Wales, England and the Soviet Union; Tony Howard looks at the controversial 1953 CBS *King Lear* that had Orson Welles in the title role, directed by Peter Brook, a version watched by 15 million people that became the focus of 'scholarly panic' over the violation of sacred texts for mass consumption; Kenneth S. Rothwell also looks at the Brooks/Welles production of *Lear* along with a range of others throughout the twentieth century; Diane E. Henderson discusses *Kiss Me Kate* and a variety of *Shrews*; Peter S. Donald looks at 'sexual and electronic magic' in Peter

Greenaway's *Prospero's Books*; Lynda Boose appears again to commend Jonathan Miller's production of *Othello* despite his decision to cast Anthony Hopkins rather than a black actor in the title role; Katherine Eggert, in an essay called 'Age Cannot Wither Him', ingeniously reads Warren Beatty's *Bugsy* as a 'Hollywood Cleopatra'. Not only does the gangster movie reproduce the plot of Shakespeare's play, as mediated through Joseph Mankiewicz's 1963 epic *Cleopatra*, but Warren Beatty's performance as Bugsy betrays an ambivalent masculinity that 'is amplified by his taking on both gender roles, not only Antony's but Cleopatra's' (208). Ann Thompson contributes a short meditation on Asta Nielson and the mystery of *Hamlet*, Susan Wiseman looks at *My Own Private Idaho* and Richard Burt provides a guide to the 'New Shakesqueer Cinema' that shows how recent cinematic productions of Shakespeare have provided a vehicle for gay and queer appropriations, identifications and fantasies. Notable examples include Richard Dreyfus's gay version of Richard III in *The Goodbye Girl*, Caliban as 'Prospero's taste-of-latex love slave' in *Prospero's Books*, Don John's gay sadomasochistic relationship with Conrade (Keanu Reeves in black leather pants being massaged by his manservant) in Branagh's *Much Ado About Nothing*, and tips on how to get off 'on Iago getting off on Cassio getting off on Desdemona' in Zeffirelli's *Otello* (241, 248–250).

A number of cultural and critical theory journals have published interesting and important historical essays, and even special issues, this year. *Textual Practice* (11.1) has a fine essay by Paul Hamilton on the New Romanticism (109–132), but much of this issue is given over to a pointless 'heated debate' over Shakespeare's 'materiality' between Edward Pechter (51–68) and Margreta de Grazia and Peter Stallybrass (69–80) and Graham Holderness, Bryan Loughrey and Andrew Murphy (80–88). Pechter seems to have taken over from Richard Levin as the self-appointed defender of Shakespeare's liberal humanism whose sole mission and *raison d'être* is to goad New Historicist and cultural materialist critics. I do not know why it needed six critics to reply to him, or why he felt the need to repeat himself in the next issue (11.2). The autumn issue (11.3) is a special issue on 'Luxurious Sexualities: effeminacy, consumption and the body politic in eighteenth-century representation' edited by May Peace and Vincent Quinn. It contains some excellent and fascinating essays covering themes familiar to *Textual Practice* but from a century that has perhaps been under represented: Cath Sharrock writes on sodomy, masturbation and the body (politic) in eighteenth-century England (417–428), Philip Carter raises the dilemma of an 'effeminate' 'or efficient' nation (429–444), Miles Ogborn looks at luxury, sexuality and vision in Vauxhall gardens (445–462) and Robert W. Jones pens some 'Notes on *Camp*: Women, effeminacy and the military' (463–491). There are also two superb essays by Sue Wiseman on the luxurious to the virtuous breast and Marcia Pointon on jewellery, royal bodies and luxurious consumption (493–517). *English Literary History* (64.4) has a special issue on Jacobitism and eighteenth-century literature, with Lawrence Lipking, Toni Bowers, Manuel Schonhorn, J. A. Downie, Howard Erskine-Hill, Nicholas Hudson, Howard D. Weinbrot, Allan Reddick, Dustin Griffith and J. C. D. Clark, that comprises mostly traditionalist critics, but is no less interesting for that. *Literature and History* (61.2) this year has a special issue on 'Placing Travel' with essays by May Baine Campbell on seventeenth-century space travel and the impulse of ethnology (1–17), Peter Hulme 'In the Wake of Columbus: Frederick Ober's Ambulant Gloss' (18–36), John Lucas discovers England by rail (37–55), Peter Bishop glimpses Tibet (56–72) and Tim Youngs discusses the travel writing of Paul Theroux and Bruce Chatwin (73–88). *New Literary History* has given its whole volume over to themed issues, from a special on Medieval Studies (28.2) to Cultural Studies in China (28.1). The latter opens with a familiar denunciation of 'culturalists' by Terry Eagleton (1–6) and essays on the Chinese reception of, and confrontation with, postmodernism, postcolonialism and globalization by Shaobo Xie, Ersu Ding, Henry Y. H. Zhao, Wang Fengzhen, Wang Ning, Liu Kang, Jerry Aline Flieger, Sheldon Hsiao-Penglu, Jonathan Arac and Rey Chow. Issue 28.3 of *New Literary History* is devoted to 'Critical Exchanges' in which Suzanne Gearhart condemns Stephen Greenblatt for 'taming Michel Foucault' and Greenblatt worries, in reply, about sadomasochistic practices (457–486), there is an exchange between Richard Levin and Valerie Traub, (525–542), and Amrohini Sahay and Gregory Ulmer debate 'cybermaterialism and the invention of the cyber-cultural everyday' (543–600), Jeff Humphries and Masao Miyoshi discuss 'theory in Japan' (601–648). In the final theme issue of the year, 'Philosophical Thoughts', Terry Eagleton again opens the collection of essays with a valedictory 'Ballad of Marxist Criticism' in which he apparently bids farewell to theorized Marxist approaches to literature and culture. To the tune of 'Say Something Stupid Like I love You', Eagleton recalls 'the day I found Dick Hoggart was a populist reformist sentimentalist / Nostalgic petty-bourgeois social democrat subjectivist empiricist / I saw the light of day, I turned to Ray, my structure of feeling it was born anew / Until I went and spoilt it all by writing something stupid in *New Left Review*'. Several verses follow in which Eagleton recalls a gradual disillusionment with, successively, Lukacs, Brecht, Benjamin, Adorno, Jameson and Macherey until he concludes that:

> Though Althusser is smart his views on art and
> ideology don't ring quite true,
> So hello Helen Gardner, Donald Davie, Denis Donoghue
> I love you (v).

Books Reviewed

Boose, Lynda E. and Richard Burt (eds). *Shakespeare the Movie*. Routledge. pp. 277. hb £45.00. ISBN 0 415 16584 9. pb £14.99. ISBN 0 415 16585 7.

Day, Gary (ed.). *Literature and Culture in Modern Britain* II (1930–55). Longman. pp. 260. hb £40.00, ISBN 0 582 07551 3. pb £14.99. ISBN 0 582 07550 5.

Hillman, David and Carla Mazzio (eds). *The Body in Parts: Fantasies of Corporeality in Early Modern Europe*. Routledge. pp. 344. pb £14.99, ISBN 0 415 91694 1. hb £45.00. ISBN 0 415 91693 3.

Hutson, Lorna. *The Usurer's Daughter: Male Friendship and Fictions of Women in Sixteenth-Century England*. Routledge. pp. 295. pb £15.99. ISBN 0 415 16261 0.

Innes, Paul. *Shakespeare and the English Renaissance Sonnet.* Macmillan. pp. 238. hb £42.50. ISBN 0 333 68371 4.

Loxley, James. *Royalism and Poetry in the English Civil Wars.* Macmillan. pp. 251. hb £45.00. ISBN 0 333 66075 7.

Mascuch, Michael. *Origins of the Individualist Self: Autobiography and Self-Identity in England 1591–1791.* Polity. pp. 277. hb £39.50. ISBN 0 745 60874 4.

McCullagh, C. Behan. *The Truth of History.* Routledge. pp. 327. pb £14.99. ISBN 0 415 17111 3.

Jenkins, Keith (ed.). *The Postmodern History Reader.* Routledge. pp. 443. pb £14.99. ISBN 0 415 13904 X.

Munslow, Alun. *Deconstructing History.* Routledge. pp. 226. pb £11.99. ISBN 0 415 13193 6.

Munslow, Alun and Robert A. Rosenstone (eds). *Rethinking History: The Journal of Theory and Practice* 1.1. Routledge. pp. 109. Subscription rates: EU: £96.00 (institutional), £35.00 (individual). ISSN 1364 2529.

Neil, Michael. *Issues of Death: Mortality and Identity in English Renaissance Tragedy.* Clarendon Press. pp. 404. hb £45.00. ISBN 0 19 818386 0.

Porter, Roy (ed.). *Rewriting the Self: Histories from the Renaissance to the Present.* Routledge. pp. 283. pb £14.99. ISBN 0 415 14280 6.

Twyning, John. *London Dispossessed: Literature and Social Space in the Early Modern City.* Macmillan. pp. 258. hb £45.00. ISBN 0 312 17652 X.

7

Queer Theories/Cultures

BRETT BEEMYN

This chapter has three sections: 1. Introduction; 2. Readers/Anthologies; 3. Books by One Author.

1. Introduction

The early 1990s witnessed such a phenomenal rise in the number of texts examining the cultures of lesbians, gay men, bisexuals, transgenders, and other sexual and gender communities that a recognized academic and publishing field took shape under the rubric 'queer theory', or more generally, 'queer studies'. While not all writers whose work focuses on the constructions of sexuality and gender accept this appellation – including, no doubt, some of the writers discussed here – it nevertheless represents the most inclusive and comprehensive designation for texts in this area of critical and cultural theory. Indeed, among the ways in which the field can often be distinguished from its 'lesbian and gay studies' precursor is its recognition of a variety of sexual and gender expressions and perspectives that are not readily reducible to narrow, essentialized identity categories. For example, one of the most dynamic and influential areas of queer theory during 1997 was work in transgender studies. Building on the groundbreaking writing of Leslie Feinberg, Kate Bornstein, and others, texts such as Riki Anne Wilchins' *Read My Lips: Sexual Subversion and the End of Gender* and Holly Devor's *FTM: Female-To-Male Transsexuals in Society* offered important critiques of the ways in which gender and sexuality are constructed, challenging binary frameworks that utterly fail to capture the complexities of individual lives and the diversity of the broader society.

Another distinguishing characteristic of queer theory/studies is how work in the field often questions and violates established disciplinary and subject boundaries. Consequently, as a previous reviewer for 'Queer Theories/ Cultures' argued, the texts in this chapter cannot adequately be grouped according to traditional academic categories, much less be reduced simply to sexual and gender identities. Therefore, like previous volumes, I am dividing the works according to the means through which they were published: readers and anthologies, and books by one author.

2. Readers/Anthologies

Two of the most impressive works published in 1997 were anthologies produced by the Center for Lesbian and Gay Studies (CLAGS) and edited by Martin Duberman, its founding director. Both *A Queer World* and *Queer Representations* are based on a number of the papers presented at colloquia and conferences organized by the Center during its first decade (1986–96) of existence as part of the City University of New York Graduate School. The larger volume, *A Queer World*, is divided into five sections, each of which addresses an important theme in the field: the meanings of sexual and gender identities; the recovery of lesbian, gay, bisexual, and transgender histories; the struggles for economic and legal rights; the implications of scientific and psychological research on sexuality; and the sexual politics of adolescence, aging, and AIDS. Like most volumes that draw exclusively from a body of material that was originally presented in a different context, *A Queer World* provides a somewhat uneven treatment of its general themes and at times leaves some gaping holes (for example, the subsection on AIDS doesn't address the devastating impact that the pandemic continues to have on Black gay and bisexual men, and bisexuality is completely ignored throughout the anthology). Still, it is much more comprehensive than many similar compilations, and the tremendous quality of the essays and the inclusion of many of the leading writers in queer studies should make it an indispensable teaching and research tool for many years to come. Among the contributors are M. V. Lee Badgett, Nan Alamilla Boyd, Jewelle Gomez, Gilbert Herdt, Jonathan Ned Katz, Elizabeth Lapovsky Kennedy, Joan Nestle, Cindy Patton, Ruthann Robson, Judith Roof, Will Roscoe, and Carmen Vazquez.

Like *A Queer World*, *Queer Representations* insightfully explores a number of critical themes in queer theory, focusing on the creation and interpretation of literary and cultural images. It is also equally as wide-ranging, covering such subjects as the depiction of homosexuality in Bronze Age Cretian art, the epistemology of the Latin American literary closet, the historical portrayals of Langston Hughes and Radclyffe Hall, and the autobiographical narratives of writers such as Essex Hemphill and Sarah Schulman. One particular highlight of the text are symposia addressing the development and contemporary status of lesbian and gay literatures in the US, with participants including Dorothy Allison, Samuel R. Delany, Allen Ginsberg, Melanie Kaye/Kantrowitz, Assoto Saint, and Barbara Smith.

In addition to Duberman's two readers, 1997 also saw the publication of *The Gender/Sexuality Reader* edited by Roger Lancaster and Micaela di Leonardo. As its title suggests, Lancaster and di Leonardo's work has a larger scope than its CLAGS counterparts, enabling queer theory to be part of and to inform discussions of feminist theory, the history of sexuality, and body politics. As a result, John D'Emilio's classic essay, 'Capitalism and Gay Identity', for example, can be read alongside Susan Bordo's 'Material Girl', a thoughtful discussion of the construction of beauty and women's bodies in postmodern consumer culture, and Arlene Stein's insightful article on 'The Decentering of Lesbian Feminism' in the late 1980s and 1990s can be read alongside Carole S. Vance's critical analysis of the work of the US Attorney

General's Commission on Pornography in the mid-1980s. Other especially valuable essays include Siobhan Somerville's 'Scientific Racism and the Invention of the Homosexual Body', Darlene Clark Hine's 'Rape and the Inner Lives of Black Women in the Middle West', and Anne Fausto-Sterling's 'How to Build a Man'. The book's thirty-seven works are divided into nine sections: 'Moving Borders: Genders, Sexualities, Histories'; 'Modes of Reproduction: Kinship, Parenthood, States'; 'The Social Construction of Identities: Comparative Sexualities'; 'Bodies of Knowledge and the Politics of Representation'; 'Marks and Signs: The Social Skin'; 'Polyvalent Pleasures: Resistances, Reinscriptions, and Dispersals'; 'Sex Wars, Culture Wars'; 'Traveling Theory: Transnational and Postcolonial Interlocutions'; and 'Re-Imagining Bodies'.

A further exploration of the intersections and commonalities of sexuality and gender is provided by *Feminism Meets Queer Theory*, a reprint of a special 1994 issue of *Differences* edited by Elizabeth Weed and Naomi Schor. In addition to essays by Judith Butler, Evelynn M. Hammonds, Biddy Martin, Kim Michasiw, Carole-Anne Tyler, and Elizabeth Weed, the collection includes interviews by Butler with Rosi Braidotti and Gayle Rubin, a dialogue between Braidotti and Trevor Hope over Hope's reading of Braidotti's work, and a similar exchange between Elizabeth Grosz and Teresa de Lauretis over Grosz's review of de Lauretis' *The Practice of Love*.

A number of other pioneering collections published during the year had a more specific focus. Given the substantial contributions that queer theory has made to literary analysis in recent years, it is surprising that Eve Kosofsky Sedgwick's *Novel Gazing: Queer Readings in Fiction* was the first anthology of queer criticism on the novel. Building upon a 1996 special issue of the journal *Studies in the Novel* edited by Sedgwick, *Novel Gazing* brings together both new and established literary theorists to examine a variety of works, including traditional canonical texts, best sellers, Jewish and African-American literatures, and science fiction. However, only five of the eighteen contributors are women (and almost all of the novels discussed are by men) and, without explanation, the book is limited to an analysis of British, French, and US works. These weaknesses aside, *Novel Gazing* breaks much new ground, beginning with Sedgwick's introduction, in which she challenges the 'hermeneutic of suspicion' that dominates contemporary literary criticism (4). Rather than automatically jumping to a paranoid or cynical approach, she outlines the possibility for what she calls 'a reparative impulse', and the essays in the collection largely take up her call, engaging in new critical practices that are additive and richly textured (28–9). For example, Maurice Wallace's exploration of 'Dance, Desire, and the Black Masculine in Melvin Dixon's *Vanishing Rooms*' suggests that a recognition of the transformative roles of dance and movement in the novel adds to an appreciation of the much undervalued work of Dixon and provides greater insights into the lives of Black gay men. Kathryn Bond Stockton's '*Beloved* in the Cybernetic Age of AIDS' also points to the need for new, accretive approaches, as she reads the novel as a text born with its 1987 publication – in another time of 'untimely deaths and dangerous transmissions' (42).

The Best of **The Harvard Gay and Lesbian Review** features some of the most notable works published in the first three years of *The Review*, edited by the journal's editor, Richard Schneider Jr. Because of its unique position as an independent, nonpartisan quarterly, *The Review* has been the setting for some of the major literary, political, and cultural debates among lesbians and gay men in the 1990s – several of which are captured in the collection. Barney Frank and Rich Tafel confront each other over electoral political strategy, and David Bergman and Bruce Bawer argue over assimilation and gay male identity. While not involving direct, individual exchanges, two other sections of the book also address important areas of difference between lesbian and gay scholars, activists, and writers: one discusses the basis of sexuality and another the significance of postmodernism. Additional sections offer perspectives on history and literature, with particularly interesting essays on a newly rediscovered 'gay Civil War novel', the persecution of gay men during the Holocaust, the lesbian dance scene in early 1970s' New York, and re-readings of the works of writers including Emily Dickinson, Gertrude Stein, and Sapphire.

Noting at the outset that 'We have seen much more theoretical attention paid to the social constructions of homosexual identities than to theories explaining heterosexist discrimination' (5), James T. Sears and Walter L. Williams' *Overcoming Heterosexism and Homophobia: Strategies that Work* goes a long way towards opening up this undertheorized research area. The thirty-two original essays in the collection present concrete, hands-on approaches to reducing heterosexism within a wide range of local institutions, from elementary schools, senior highs, and universities, to churches, the media, grassroots multicultural communities, law enforcement agencies, and the corporate world. Collectively, the contributors make a powerful case for looking not just to the political and legal realms for bringing about societal change, but also engaging in direct, more personal efforts to root out prejudicial attitudes and institutionalized discrimination (and, in fact, the editors decided not to include essays discussing political and legal strategies because these areas have been overemphasized, while other methods for challenging heterosexism and homophobia remain relatively unexamined). Grounded in social scientific research and theory, many of the essays offer case studies and practical strategies, including suggestions for beginning a conversation about the experiences of lesbian, gay, bisexual and transgender (LGBT) people, successful methods for coming out to family members and coworkers, and information on conducting different types of sensitivity trainings and workshops.

Mark Blasius and Shane Phelan's *We Are Everywhere: A Historical Sourcebook of Gay and Lesbian Politics* brings together some of the most important historical, legal, psychological, and theoretical documents discussing the development of the category 'homosexual'; the rise of political and cultural movements based on lesbian and gay identities in France, England, Germany, and the US; the impact of AIDS and AIDS activism; the experiences of different LGBT communities; and the debates over outing, same-sex marriage, and forms of political resistance. Among the classic writings included in this impressive 844-page collection are the Wolfenden Report, the US Senate's McCarthy-era report justifying the exclusion of gays from federal employment, the statements of purpose of the Mattachine Society and the Daughters of Bilitis, the Radicalesbians' 'The Woman-Identified Woman', Huey Newton's letter to 'the Revolutionary Brothers and Sisters About the Women's Liberation and Gay Liberation Movements', Harvey

Milk's 'The Hope Speech', Audre Lorde's 'I Am Your Sister', and the 1992 open letter to the organizers of the Michigan Womyn's Music Festival condemning the exclusion of transsexual women. Another weighty collection, both literally and figuratively, is Gary David Comstock and Susan E. Henking's *Que(e)rying Religion: A Critical Anthology*. Consisting of forty-one contributors from a range of academic disciplines, the volume demonstrates that same-sex sexuality has been an integral part of the spiritual lives and practices of believers from a variety of religious traditions, including Judaism, Islam, Buddhism, Native American spiritualities, and different Christian denominations, throughout history. Although all of the essays in *Que(e)rying Religion* have been published previously, some were in small, relatively difficult-to-find journals, and many of the more well-known works have not been anthologized before. Among the most noteworthy contributions are John Boswell's examination of homosexual traditions within the early Christian church, Christine Downing's exploration of lesbian mythology in ancient Greece, Nicholas Bradford's research on transgenderism in South Indian goddess worship, Michael Warner's reflections on his Pentecostal childhood, and Makeda Silvera's description of how Afro-Caribbean lesbians have been rendered invisible by the colonial and postcolonial imposition of Christian values.

My work, *Creating a Place for Ourselves: Lesbian, Gay, and Bisexual Community Histories*, sets out to document the vibrant US gay communities that existed for decades prior to Stonewall in places far from the traditional gay coastal meccas of New York and San Francisco. The histories of these communities, particularly those in the South and Midwest, have often been ignored, in part because the popular framework for understanding communities is based on the experiences of lesbians and gay men in large cities with predominantly gay neighborhoods. But in recent years, more and more historians have begun to examine the richness of gay life in areas not well known today for their lesbian, gay, and bisexual communities, inspired in part by such pioneering works in the field as Elizabeth Lapovsky Kennedy and Madeline D. Davis' work on Buffalo, George Chauncey's work on New York, and Esther Newton's work on Cherry Grove. In addition to chapters based on these studies, *Creating a Place for Ourselves* also includes new research on relatively small cities (Flint, Michigan and Birmingham, Alabama), large cities not often recognized for their long-standing gay communities (Chicago, Philadelphia, Detroit, and Washington), and a 'gay mecca' (San Francisco). Along with Chauncey, Davis, Kennedy, and Newton, the contributors are myself, Nan Alamilla Boyd, Allen Drexel, John Howard, David K. Johnson, Joan Nestle, Tim Retzloff, Marc Stein, and Roey Thorpe.

Further shifting the focus of US gay history away from the East and West coasts and away from urban areas, John Howard's *Carryin' On in the Lesbian and Gay South* provides fresh, innovative perspectives on the role of place in lesbian, gay, and bisexual identity and community development, paying particular attention to the significance of race, religion, and rurality in much of the region. The fourteen essays included here cover a broad range of southern history, from the antebellum and postbellum periods, to the Jim Crow and Cold War eras, to lesbian feminist activism in the 1960s and 1970s, to 'AIDS and beyond'. Certain to become a classic text, *Carryin'*

On includes Martin Duberman's recovery of the correspondence between two prominent male 'bedfellows' in antebellum South Carolina; Katy Coyle and Nadiene Van Dyke's description of lesbian life among prostitutes and college students in turn-of-the century New Orleans; Daneel Buring's discussion of the parameters of Memphis' lesbian community from the 1940s through the 1960s; James Schnur's and John Howard's analyses of state crackdowns against gays in Florida and Atlanta, respectively; and Donna Jo Smith's call for new theories that can better incorporate southern queer experiences.

Another critical but undertheorized area of queer theory/queer cultures in which important works were published in 1997 was cross-cultural studies of sexuality and gender. Two texts focused on Latin American cultures: Daniel Balderston and Donna J. Guy's collection *Sex and Sexuality in Latin America* and David William Foster's *Sexual Textualities: Essays on Queer/ing Latin American Writing* (reviewed in the section on books by one author). Balderston and Guy's volume is the more comprehensive, with essays that range from a study of bisexuality in a popular Mexican film, to examinations of transgenderism in a 1960's Spanish novel and contemporary Nicaraguan society, to the 'multiple masculinities' evident in Puerto Rican literature, the nineteenth-century Brazilian military, and the two leading Argentine cultural exports: football (soccer) and tango music. Among the central themes covered in the text are the policing and repression of sexuality in Latin America, sexual and gender transgression as forms of cultural expression and resistance, and the need to re-evaluate how sexual and gender identities are viewed in different historical and cultural moments. It concludes with an extensive bibliography by Balderston and Guy of works in Latin American gender and sexuality studies.

Two other works published in 1997 addressed same-sex sexuality in Islamic and Arabic cultures. *Islamic Homosexualities*, edited by Stephen O. Murray and Will Roscoe, offers historical, anthropological, and literary studies that document the ways in which homosexuality is viewed and practised in various Muslim societies from medieval times to the present. In the process, it 'challenge[s] the dominant, Eurocentric model of gay/lesbian history' and the implication 'that nothing at all preceded modern homosexuality or that whatever homosexual behavior occurred earlier was too disorganized, spontaneous, and insignificant to compare with modern homosexualities' (5). The contributors to the collection demonstrate that not only can same-sex desire and behaviour in the Islamic world be documented for centuries, but that 'before the twentieth century, the region of the world with the most visible and diverse homosexualities was not northwestern Europe but northern Africa and southwestern Asia' (6). However, sexual relations between women has generally remained more hidden in Islamic cultures, and the limited research done to date has contributed to this invisibility by focusing almost exclusively on men. *Islamic Homosexualities* does not entirely break with this practice, but it does contain two important essays describing female gender-crossing roles and Murray's short review of 'Woman-Woman Love in Islamic Societies'. Other notable works include essays that discuss 'the symbolism of male love in Islamic mystical literature', reports of homosexuality in Asia and North Africa in the nineteenth century, and the experiences of contemporary Pakistanis who pursue same-sex relationships. Although male homoerotic allusions and imagery are pervasive in medieval Arabic writing, these motifs have heretofore been either ignored or misunderstood. Thus J. W. Wright Jr. and Everett K. Rowson's *Homoeroticism in Classical Arabic Literature* represents an important breakthrough in the field of Arabic literary studies, and hopefully it will prompt a great deal of additional research. The eight essays in this collection employ a variety of critical perspectives to examine homoeroticism in traditional lyric poetry, courtly narratives, shadow plays, dreambooks, and other genres of Arabic literature dating from the eighth to fourteenth centuries. Besides Wright and Rowson, the contributors are James T. Monroe, Steven M. Oberhelman, Franz Rosenthal, Richard Serrano, Paul Sprachman, and Suzanne Pinckney Stetkevych.

Má-ka: Diasporic Juks, Contemporary Writing by Queers of African Descent takes its main title from the name that many Africans in the diaspora give to a thorny plant that is so prevalent in tropical regions that it is frequently taken for granted until it 'juks' or pricks you. Like the má-ka, this collection describes an important part of the landscape and should not be ignored. Edited by four Caribbean-born people of African descent now living in Canada (Debbie Douglas, Courtnay McFarlane, Makeda Silvera, and Douglas Stewart), *Má-ka* consists of poetry, fiction, memoirs, and essays from more than forty contributors from Africa and throughout the diaspora. Among the notable works are Cheryl Clarke's 1996 Outwrite speech on 'Audre Lorde's Legacy to Lesbian and Gay Writers' and Wesley Crichlow's articulation of a 'Black same-sex consciousness'.

Two-Spirit People: Native American Gender Identity, Sexuality, and Spirituality, edited by Sue-Ellen Jacobs, Wesley Thomas, and Sabine Lang, signals a much-needed shift from the white domination of academic discourses about gender and sexuality in Native American and First Nations communities to the communities themselves. The term two-spirit represents just such a change. It was coined at the 1990 Native American/First Nations Gay and Lesbian Conference in Winnipeg to refer to contemporary Native American and First Nations people who are lesbian, gay, bisexual, or transgendered, as well as to people who had been historically described by anthropologists and other social scientists as 'berdache' – a term now often considered inaccurate and insulting. As the title of the essay by Clyde M. Hall (Lemhi Shoshoni) suggests, 'You Anthropologists Make Sure You Get Your Words Right' (272).

The collection is divided into five sections. The first two re-examine anthropological research, challenging not only the inappropriate terminology of scholars, but also their entire concepts of how gender and sexuality are constructed among different Native American peoples. Along with essays by each of the editors, this part of the book brings together articles by Jason Cromwell, Carolyn Epple, Jean-Guy A. Goulet, Beatrice Medicine (Standing Rock Lakota), Arnold R. Pilling, and Terry Tafoya (Taos/Warm Springs). The third section consists of personal narratives in which two-spirit people urge the reader finally 'to listen to who I am' (228). The fourth section offers, in the words of Evelyn Blackwood, new readings 'beyond anthropological models and misrepresentations' (284). In addition to Blackwood's and Hall's works, it includes groundbreaking essays by Gilbert Herdt, Sue-Ellen Jacobs, Alice B. Kehoe, and Lee M. Kochems. *Two-Spirit People* concludes with the text of a 'talking circle' that was held among many of the contributors and others discussing how they deal with heterosexism and homophobia in their everyday lives.

Although coming out stories are so ubiquitous in queer literature that they are hardly worth mentioning, Lisa C. Moore's *Does Your Mama Know?: An Anthology of Black Lesbian Coming Out Stories* is notable and long overdue. Not only is it one of the first collections to focus on the lives of Black lesbians, but it also brings together an impressive array of lesbian writers from the US and Canada, including Donna Allegra, Becky Birtha, Cheryl Clarke, Alexis De Veaux, Jewelle Gomez, Terri Jewell, Makeda Silvera, and Shay Youngblood. The forty-nine works in *Does Your Mama Know?*, which range from short stories and poems to interviews and essays, reinforce the need for new, more complicated theories of sexuality, ones that place the experiences of Black lesbians at the centre.

Another much-needed work is Laura Harris and Elizabeth Crocker's *Femme: Feminists, Lesbians, and Bad Girls*. As the editors note, 'few histories have been written from perspectives that recognize and respect femmes' (1), and as a result, even today they remain largely marginalized in queer theories, with their identities considered only in relation to butch identities. Through enabling femmes to articulate their own experiences, this volume constructs a 'sustained gender identity' model that historicizes the lives of femmes and allows for a recognition of femme importance to US lesbian and butch-femme history, feminism, and queer thought. The book's three sections facilitate this process by considering femmes in relation to lesbian 'Histories', feminist 'Generations', and queer 'Futures'. Among the important works in *Femme* are selections from Elizabeth Lapovsky Kennedy and Madeline D. Davis' research on femmes in Buffalo, New York during the 1940s and 1950s; Harris and Crocker's reinterpretation of perhaps the earliest study of an African-American butch-femme community (from St Louis, Missouri in the 1960s) and their theorization of 'bad girl' role models in femme personal narratives and fictional representations; Lilith Albrecht-Samarasinha's reflections on being a bisexual femme; Alex Robertson Textor's analysis of femme as a model for queer male identities; a conversation between Joan Nestle and Barbara Cruikshank; and interviews with Davis, Jewelle Gomez, Amber Hollibaugh, Mabel Maney, and Minnie Bruce Pratt.

Dana Heller's *Cross-Purposes: Lesbians, Feminists, and the Limits of Alliance* likewise considers the intersections and incongruences between lesbian studies, women's studies, and queer theory. The collection's fourteen essays extend a critical dialogue about the history, current status, and possible future of the relationships between lesbians and straight feminists in the US. As Heller states in her insightful introduction, 'Throughout the twentieth century, lesbianism has been viewed as both everywhere and nowhere within feminism, a cause as well as an effect. Lesbians have been idealized as both the "vanguard of the women's movement" and the movement's greatest liability, a contradiction that renders the very idea of lesbian feminism at once a redundancy and a contradiction in terms' (4).

Heller divides *Cross-Purposes* into three parts, each examining different aspects of lesbian-feminist alliances. The first section, 'Crossings', focuses on the multiple involvements and linkages between feminist and lesbian studies, and includes Carolyn Dever on 'dykes in the mainstream of feminist theory', Teresa de Lauretis on the discourses around female sexuality and 'the lesbian postmodern', Ruth Salvaggio on the language connected to lesbian bodies, and Tania Modleski on the intersections of race, gender, and sexuality in the work of Sandra Bernhard. The second section, 'Collisions', describes historical and cultural moments of intersection and inconsistency between lesbian and feminist realities, and includes Colleen Lamos on the unchallenged dichotomy of sexuality and gender, Michèle Aina Barale on the interworkings of sexual and gender dynamics in film analysis, Katie Hogan on the need for both lesbian and feminist studies to recognize the urgency of the AIDS crisis, Annamarie Jagose on how feminism often tends to negate lesbian existence, and Karman Kregloe and Jane Caputi on the ways that Camille Paglia and Susie Bright represent 'supermodels of lesbian chic' but poor models of lesbian feminism. The final section, 'Coalitions', considers possible sites 'where lesbian studies and feminist studies might redefine their alliance and work toward common goals in the context of their acknowledged differences' (11), and includes Bonnie Zimmerman on being a lesbian feminist critic, Kathleen Chapman and Michael Du Plessis on the misguided attacks against transpeople in feminist, lesbian, and queer academic discourses, Karin Quimby on the development of women's music, and Sue-Ellen Case on the lack of feminist affinity among 'queer dykes'.

As *The Bisexual Imaginary: Representation, Identity and Desire* demonstrates, one of the important contributions that queer theory in general and bisexual theory in particular have made to academia is debunking the notion that identities are stable, immutable, and dichotomous. Edited by five members (Phoebe Davidson, Jo Eadie, Clare Hemmings, Ann Kaloski, and Merl Storr) of Bi Academic Intervention, a network of UK teachers, researchers, and writers whose work addresses bisexuality, this collection gives a more nuanced reading of sexual identity than many previous bisexual texts. Rather than simply considering what bisexuality is or what it means, *The Bisexual Imaginary* also examines how it functions – how it is represented, deployed, and elided. Among the many provocative, groundbreaking essays included here are Clare Hemming's demarcation of a bisexual theoretical perspective that can account for the multiple and sometimes contradictory meanings of bisexuality, Phoebe Davidson's rereading of two psychoanalytic case studies from the 1920s that were influential in how bisexuality was constructed in medical and popular cultural discourses, Merl Storr's examination of the racial marking of bisexuality in the studies of sexologists Havelock Ellis and Richard von Krafft-Ebing, Nick Selby's contextualizing of the works of Walt Whitman and Allen Ginsberg within a bisexual poetics, and Jo Eadie's discussion of the bisexual character in film as an indicator and embodiment of cultural transgression.

Some of these same issues are addressed in Carol Queen and Lawrence Schimel's *PoMoSexuals: Challenging Assumptions About Gender and Sexuality*. 'Pomosexuals', according to the editors, are '*queer* queers', people who cross, live on the borders of, or simply do not fit into, existing identity categories, and the fifteen contributors here represent a broad spectrum of lived experience. Yet, while the essays are intriguing and at times quite provocative, most only relate personal stories; few of the writers consider the theoretical implications of their experiences or place them within larger social, historical, or political contexts. Some notable exceptions are Pat Califia's discussion of using different personas to write pornography for a variety of audiences, David Harrison's description of using personal ads as a transsexual man, and Schimel's examination of parallels between queer and Jewish identities.

In contrast to *PoMoSexuals*, *Lesbians in Academia: Degrees of Freedom*, edited by Beth Mintz and Esther Rothblum, seeks to use personal narratives to elucidate theory. Beginning with the stories of more than thirty women, Mintz and Rothblum capture the diversity of lesbian academic experience in the US and demonstrate that lesbians' degree of outness and level of acceptance are not predicated on region or type of college or university, but are more closely related to their 'academic generation', with the latest generation more likely to come out very early in their careers and to advocate for LGBT rights. Subsequent sections of the work provide further analyses of the narratives by comparing the general academic experiences of lesbians to nonlesbian women of colour, older women, and working-class women and by describing common interests and areas of difference that affect the coalition-building abilities of women faculty members. The anthology concludes with two opposing lesbian-feminist perspectives on the ramifications of queer theory for lesbian academics.

Gabriele Griffin and Sonya Andermahr's *Straight Studies Modified: Lesbian Interventions in the Academy* takes a very different approach. While *Lesbians in Academia* focuses on how race, age, class, and other aspects of identity affect individual academic lesbian experience, *Straight Studies Modified* examines the state of lesbian scholarship and visibility in different academic disciplines in the UK, US, Australia, and Canada. The collection breaks new ground by not only considering fields where there has been significant research on lesbians and a number of well-known out lesbians – such as literary criticism, film studies, theatre, history, and psychology – but also much less explored areas such as philosophy, legal theory, health studies, geography, biology, linguistics, and computer science.

The Gay '90s: Disciplinary and Interdisciplinary Formations in Queer Studies, a volume of *Genders* edited by Thomas Foster, Carol Siegel, and Ellen E. Berry, addresses the institutionalization of queer theory and how this process has impacted on both academe and the field itself. The first section, 'Disciplinary Reflections', looks at the potential opportunities and pitfalls of queer studies, whether in 'queerying the academy', producing different forms of 'queer knowledge', or interrogating heteronormativity. The second section, 'Interdisciplinary Readings', brings other fields to bear on queer studies and vice versa. Essays include the search for a Black gay legacy in James Baldwin's *Giovanni's Room*, an examination of dyke comic strips as both a medium and a cultural phenomenon, and the production of commercial homoerotic imagery in 1950s' America.

A special volume of *Social Text* (52–53) edited by Phillip Brian Harper, Anne McClintock, José Esteban Muñoz, and Trish Rosen also explores the relationship between queer theory and various political and cultural formations. Based around the theme of 'Queer Transexions of Race, Nation, and

Gender', the collection provides transnational readings of sexuality, race, and gender, combining queer analytical perspectives with feminist, postcolonial, and critical race theories to interrogate conceptions of social and sexual identity. Among the many valuable essays included in the volume are David L. Eng's 'Queerness and Diaspora in Asian American Studies', Judith Halberstam's 'Gender, Race, and Masculinity in the Drag King Scene', Don Kulick's 'The Boyfriends of Brazilian *Travesti* Prostitutes', Rachel Holmes' 'Queer Comrades: Winnie Mandela and the Moffies', David Valentine and Riki Anne Wilchins' 'Gender, Genitals, and Hermaphrodites with Attitude', and C. Jacob Hale's 'Leatherdyke Boys and Their Daddies'.

Chris Holmlund and Cynthia Fuchs' *Between the Sheets, In the Streets: Queer, Lesbian, Gay Documentary* seeks to interrogate both documentary representations and queer, lesbian, and gay identities, while also questioning the meanings and boundaries of these terms. Each of the anthology's four sections 'blur distinctions among documentary, avant-garde, and fiction as genres, and lesbian, gay, and queer sexualities as identities' (7). The first section, 'Markers', highlights the importance of location to the process of perception, with essays on southern lesbian and gay documentary, media representations during Oregon's 1992 anti-gay ballot initiative, and the positioning of queer youth in several television series. The second section, 'Memories', centres on remembering and representations of the past, and includes works that discuss documentaries by and about older lesbians and aspects of performance in lesbian and gay documentaries from the 1970s and early 1980s. 'Marriage and Mourning', the subject of the third section, examines how meanings of the family and AIDS are inscribed in contemporary queer autobiographical documentaries. Rounding out the collection, 'Mirrors' reflects upon the relationship between the performative and cultural identities through essays that address the reception of works by lesbians of colour among white lesbian viewers, the creation of alternate gender narratives in transgender documentaries, and the ways in which the 'queering' of documentary challenges the construction of fixed, visible, 'real' identities.

While the lives of lesbians, gay men, bisexuals, and transgendered people have been the subject of scholarship in many areas of the humanities, including literature, history, political science, anthropology, women's studies, African-American studies, and film, same-sex sexuality has been almost completely ignored in the field of economics, enabling misinformation and propaganda to take the place of empirical research. Without evidence to the contrary, the US Far Right has been free to portray the gay community as a wealthy, privileged elite who could only gain 'special rights' from anti-discrimination laws. This makes Amy Gluckman and Betsy Reed's *Homo Economics: Capitalism, Community, and Lesbian and Gay Life* especially timely and valuable. For not only does the collection document how such prosperity is limited to just a narrow segment of the gay community, but also several studies included here show that the majority of lesbians and gay men actually earn comparatively less than straight women and men. Moreover, as many contributors argue, the LGBT movement must be about ending class oppression, and for some that means advocating for a radical restructuring of economic and political systems. Beyond being the first work of its kind, *Homo Economics* is also noteworthy for the breadth and quality of its contributors. The twenty-one writers are among the leading voices in academia, union and queer activism, publishing, the arts, journalism, and economic policy, and include M. V. Lee Badgett, Jeffrey Escoffier, Pat Hussain, Tony Kushner, Barbara Smith, and Kath Weston.

Like the unproven but nevertheless highly touted belief in gay economic prosperity, substantial popular attention in the 1990s has been devoted to research on a biological basis for homosexuality, despite insubstantial and often dubious scientific findings. For example, the intense media coverage given to finding a supposed 'gay gene' is hardly warranted, since even the researchers themselves do not contend that genes entirely determine sexual orientation. Yet, as Vernon A. Rosario's *Science and Homosexualities* reminds us, biological explanations for same-sex sexuality are nothing new, but have been widely circulated for most of the past century and a half. The thirteen essays in this volume, along with Rosario's well-crafted introduction, examine these various genetic, neurobiological, hereditarian, and hormonal theories and place them in broader social and cultural contexts, including documenting the assumptions and biases of medical researchers and the role that clinical subjects have played in the scientific process. Among the contributors, Hubert Kennedy considers how Karl Heinrich Ulrichs relied on existing research in embryology to develop his scientific theories; Alice Dreger describes the challenge that intersexed people posed to French and British classification systems of gender and sexuality; Harry Oosterhuis discusses how letters received from homosexuals shaped the beliefs of Richard von Krafft-Ebing; Margaret Gibson traces how late nineteenth-century medical literature on the clitoris was used to pathologize independent, 'masculine' women; Julian Carter shows how Havelock Ellis and his white, bourgeois colleagues mapped their norms of racial and class progress onto the sexological models they developed; and Jennifer Terry explores why biological determinist theories of homosexuality are currently in vogue.

Going back even further than Rosario, Ian McCormick's *Secret Sexualities: A Sourcebook of 17th and 18th Century Writing* traces British attitudes toward same-sex sexuality before the emergence of modern categories and practices. Consisting of excerpts from nearly seventy-five primary documents, many of which have not been published since the period, McCormick's work demonstrates that contrary to popular belief today, opinions about people who transgressed the established sexual and gender boundaries of the times were complex and often contradictory, and while secrecy was a critical concern (hence the book's title), there was also a surprising level of openness as well. Thus while sodomy was considered scandalous and harshly punished, such forms of criminality also held a certain public fascination, and reprints of the trial proceedings were extremely popular. The text is divided into four sections: 'Anatomies', which examines how eunuchs and 'hermaphrodites' were constructed in early British society; 'Crimes and Punishments', which describes some of the famous sodomy cases; 'Representations', which addresses the depictions of 'fops', 'sodomites', and 'mollies' (effeminate sodomites); and 'Sapphic Texts', which considers female crossdressers, 'mannish women', and 'female husbands'. Along with an extremely insightful general introduction and brief introductions to each section, McCormick provides endnotes that explain more obscure references, a glossary of terms, and an extensive bibliography.

3. Books by One Author

As I mentioned in my introduction, some of the most significant works published in queer theory/cultures during the year were in transgender studies. Until recently, transgendered people were generally either ignored or misunderstood and maligned in feminist, lesbian, and queer theories. Outside of an occasional passing reference to their involvement in Stonewall, drag queens and kings were reduced to their gender performativity, while transgendered women and men were misrepresented as patriarchal infiltrators into the lesbian community and anti-feminist traitors, respectively. But now, with transgendered individuals increasingly speaking for themselves and having their voices heard, there has been a greater appreciation of their experiences and more complicated understandings of gender, sexuality, and the body. As a result, the number of informed, well-crafted works by and/or about transgendered people has grown dramatically in the last few years, and 1997 saw the publication of three such texts.

The most insightful and revealing is Riki Anne Wilchins' *Read My Lips: Sexual Subversion and the End of Gender*. Combining theoretical analysis, political treatise, and personal narrative – each with healthy doses of wit, anger, and sadness – *Read My Lips* reclaims transpeople from the margins of academic abstraction and discursive otherness, providing compelling descriptions of their day-to-day struggles for personal and political survival. Like the powerful photos in the middle of the text showing Wilchins and other trans activists lobbying Congress, serving as witnesses to the murder of transpeople, and protesting intersex genital mutilation, the book places transgendered lives unapologetically at the centre of the lens. Documented here are the responses of transpeople to their exclusion from the New York City Gay Games and the Michigan Womyn's Music Festival, a Transexual Menace confrontation with outspoken transphobe Janice Raymond, and a chronology of some of the activities of Transexual Menace and GenderPAC (a national coalition of trans-supportive groups, of which Wilchins is the Executive Director) from 1993–97.

Alongside these important historical accounts, Wilchins explores the actual problems facing 'hirself' and other 'transexuals', which do not involve being 'trapped in the wrong bodies', but rather being 'trapped in a society which alternates between hating and ignoring, or tolerating and exploiting us and our experience' (47). To these discussions, Wilchins brings not only the clarity and acumen gained from first-hand knowledge, but also a pointed sense of humour and irony that is evident in essays like '17 Things You DON'T Say to a Transexual' and section titles such as 'Honest Officer, They Were Sexed Here When I Arrived' and 'Oh Yeah? Well, My Mom Says Your Body Is Just a Discursively Produced Event Based on Highly Variable Cultural Norms'. As this last title suggests, Wilchins situates hir analysis within a postmodern framework, providing forthright, accessible readings of often unnecessarily complex theoretical material, including 'a good English-language translation' of the works of Judith Butler and Michel Foucault.

In *Sex Changes: The Politics of Transgenderism*, Pat Califia similarly offers a well-formulated critique of medical, psychological, feminist, and lesbian readings of transpeople's lives, and like Wilchins, she begins by positioning herself in relation to her subject matter. Many long-time readers of Califia's work will be surprised to learn that she had investigated the process of sex-reassignment surgery, but 'deciding that [she] could not separate [her] personal ambivalence about being female from the misogyny and homophobia of the surrounding culture', chose instead to become 'a sort of psychic hermaphrodite', with 'strong personas as both male and female' (5–6). Such stories demonstrate the interconnections between trans and lesbian oppression, and Califia admits that she wrote the book in part to bolster alliances between activists in gay and transgender communities.

Sex Changes covers a great deal of ground. Califia begins by examining the pioneering transsexual autobiographies of Christine Jorgensen, Jan Morris, and Mario Martino and the work of doctors and sex researchers like Harry Benjamin, John Money, and Richard Green – dubbed 'the father figures of gender science' by Califia – who formulated US medical policies and practices on transsexuality and sex reassignment. Much of Califia's analysis is quite critical, and nowhere is this criticism more effective and to the point than in her chapters on Janice Raymond's 'fundamentalist feminism' and the misappropriation of Native American 'berdaches' (a term which she unfortunately does not challenge), Indian hijras, and 'passing women' by gay male academics such as Jonathan Ned Katz, Walter L. Williams, Will Roscoe, and Ramón A. Gutiérrez. The other chapters examine the second wave of transgender narratives (considering the work of Renée Richards, Mark Rees, Lou Sullivan, Leslie Feinberg, and Kate Bornstein), trans activism in the 1990s, and the experiences of the significant others of transpeople, including Virginia Prince and Minnie Bruce Pratt. This latter essay is especially important, for as Califia notes, trans partners are the 'invisible gender outlaws'.

To say that Holly Devor's FTM: Female-to-Male Transsexuals in Society is thorough is seemingly stating the obvious; at nearly 700 pages, the text represents the most meticulous, in-depth study published to date on the experiences of transgendered people. Based on a series of detailed interviews with transgendered men, a group much less frequently discussed in research than transgendered women, FTM traces their everyday experiences, from childhood and adolescence to 'changing over' and life after transition. Devor extensively uses her narrators' own words, so they speak for themselves about their relationships with family members, peers, and lovers and their developing identities, sexualities, and self-images. The amount of personal description here is impressive, but Devor is relying on the experiences of just forty-five female-to-male transsexuals – far too few participants for such a massive undertaking, especially given that only one narrator was African American and one was Latino. Still, with so little direct, accurate information on the lives of transgendered men, FTM is a tremendous step forward and an indispensable resource for both scholars and professionals.

Somewhat less useful is Richard Ekins' Male Femaling: A Grounded Theory Approach to Cross-Dressing and Sex-Changing. Ekins, a social psychologist and the director of the Trans-Gender Archives at the University of Ulster, develops a theory that 'conceptualise[s] male cross-dressers and sex-changers as males who "female" in various ways, in various contexts, at various times, with various stagings and with various consequences' (2). He delineates five major phases of 'male femaling': 'beginning femaling', 'fantasy femaling', 'doing femaling', 'constituting femaling', and 'consolidating femaling', each of which is discussed in a separate chapter, using examples from the lives of his British informants. While Ekins captures some of the complexity of transgender experience, recognizing, for example, that there is much more to cross-dressing than just donning a different set of clothes, the model he presents is nevertheless structurally and culturally limited. Considering the ways in which Wilchins, Feinberg, Bornstein, and other US trans writers and activists have completely undermined traditional conceptions of gender and sexuality, his privileging of 'biological sex', exclusive focus on transsexuals and cross-dressers who identify as heterosexual or bisexual, and insistence that transgendered women 'seek to display as females while hiding aspects of their male identities' (51) seem too narrowly conceived, essentialistic, and politically regressive. Also troubling is Ekins' disregard for race; he provides absolutely no information on the racial composition of his sample, much less considers how race often plays a critical role in the construction of trans identities and communities.

In addition to the important studies on the lives of transgendered people, two impressive, groundbreaking texts published this year consider the development of lesbian and bisexual women's identities and communities. In *Sex and Sensibility: Stories of a Lesbian Generation*, Arlene Stein eloquently traces the origins and legacy of lesbian feminism through the experiences of the postwar generation of women who shaped and, in turn, were shaped by it, and the 1990s' generation of women who established lesbian identities that challenged many of the assumptions of their predecessors. Beginning with an examination of the historical and cultural contexts in which baby-boom lesbians came of age and then came out, she analyses the 'identity work' involved for different women to 'become lesbian', which for many meant resisting dominant gender and sexual norms and creating a shared sense of community (67). However, not everyone fit easily into this community; Stein devotes carefully drawn chapters to lesbian-identified women who consider themselves to have a bisexual orientation and to lesbians who have 'gone straight'. Another chapter considers the shifts in the meaning of lesbian identity among the baby-boom cohort in the 1980s, as they grew older and many became more focused on careers and children. For lesbians who came of age in the 1990s, the notion of a single community was even more contested, and apparent inconsistencies between desire, sexual practice, and identity were even more pronounced and tolerated. But despite all of these changes, Stein finds that 'the *salience* of lesbian identification among younger women did not seem significantly different from that of baby boomers at the same age' (187).

Stein's study is based on interviews with self-identified lesbians in the San Francisco Bay Area, which given the often greater visibility and politicization of lesbians there, might seem to skew her results. But as she notes in discussing her work, 'the San Francisco Bay Area is a trendsetter for lesbian/gay life in this country, and therefore my findings are generalizable to other parts of the country – at least to other urban areas. . . . To a large extent, as San Francisco goes, so goes the Lesbian Nation – if not immediately, then several years later' (207). Kristin G. Esterberg's *Lesbian and Bisexual Identities: Constructing Communities, Constructing Selves* appears to confirm Stein's premise. Esterberg conducted interviews and surveys with approximately 120 lesbians and bisexual women from 1988 to 1991 in the small Northeast college town in which she then lived to determine how they came to see themselves as lesbian or bisexual, what their identities mean to them, and how they characterize their community. Three years later she returned to re-interview some of the women to see how they and the community had changed. She found that the lesbian community had changed relatively little over that time, but the identities of some of the women had changed fairly dramatically; for example, one woman began dating a man, another legally married, and a third began thinking of herself as celibate. Yet, as Esterberg points out, these differences did not make the women's previous identities any less valid. Drawing from social science theories of identity and community, she describes how identities are multiple and contingent – how, for the women involved, both narratives can represent who they are.

Perhaps the greatest strength of *Lesbian and Bisexual Identities* is Esterberg's ability to weave together the women's stories in their own words to create a study that is both very readable and highly informative. In addition to discussing the women's identity formation and the changes they experienced over time, Esterberg dedicates chapters to the women's sometimes contradictory interpretations of community, the role of race and class in their lives, the spoken and unspoken standards set for behaviour in the community, and the experiences of bisexual women. She concludes with a call for lesbians and bisexual women to move beyond a notion of community that is based on some mythical shared identity – which inevitably excludes many women and requires the policing of boundaries – to one based on concrete projects and actions, allowing commonalities to develop out of a shared sense of struggle.

Like *Sex and Sensibility* and *Lesbian and Bisexual Identities*, James T. Sears' *Lonely Hunters: An Oral History of Lesbian and Gay Southern Life, 1948–1968* uses personal narrative to create a vivid, richly textured portrait of US gay experience during specific historical and political moments. Southerners of this generation were profoundly affected by the Cold War and the civil rights movement, but as Sears illustrates, the lives of LGBT Southerners were also dramatically shaped by anti-gay violence, state-sponsored witch hunts, sensationalist press coverage, and a growing sense of self-worth and empowerment. In chapters that flow together into a seamless narrative, Sears describes in compelling detail the eight-year reign of terror carried out against people suspected of being gay by a special investigative panel of the Florida legislature; the simultaneous development of the civil rights movement and an awakening gay consciousness in North Carolina; the race, class, and gender ruptures revealed within Charleston society by Dawn Langley Hall, a wealthy, white transsexual who married a working-class black man; and the rise of more militant gay activism in Florida and Washington, D.C. At the end of the book, Sears provides a bibliography of the extensive primary and secondary sources he consulted, broken down by subject.

Undoubtedly the most hyped queer studies text of the year was long-time New York journalist Charles Kaiser's *The Gay Metropolis: 1940–1996*. Although it contains some interesting anecdotes (much press attention has focused on the story of a threesome involving John F. Kennedy), *The Gay*

Metropolis largely doesn't live up to its billing. 'This book tells the story of an amazing victory over adversity', Kaiser states in his introduction. '[H]ow America's most despised minority overcame religious prejudice, medical malpractice, political persecution and one of the worst scourges of the twentieth century to stake its rightful claim to the American dream – all in barely more than half a century' (vii). Leaving aside for a moment the fact that LGBT people still encounter a tremendous amount of bigotry and oppression and don't necessarily feel embraced by, much less buy into, the mythos of the 'American dream', *The Gay Metropolis* offers few sophisticated arguments and little in the way of historical analysis. The contrast here to George Chauncey's incredibly well-researched and comprehensive study, *Gay New York: Gender, Urban Culture, and the Making of the Gay Male World, 1890–1940*, is striking. But, at times, Kaiser's work does shine, especially in his description of the social and sexual connections that developed among an elite group of mostly white gay male writers, artists, and celebrities (he pays little attention to people of colour, white women, and those who weren't young and 'beautiful' – groups who frequently cannot use privilege to escape oppression or lay 'claim to the American dream'). Kaiser excels at name dropping, and *The Gay Metropolis* includes stories involving the likes of Gore Vidal, Jack Kerouac, Truman Capote, and Leonard Bernstein; however, like the superficial and sensational conversations of his cocktail party habitués, Kaiser's reliance on celebrity gossip grows tiresome after a while. One looks forward to Chauncey's follow-up volume on the same years.

An important contribution to non-US cultural history, Alkarim Jivani's *It's Not Unusual: A History of Lesbian and Gay Britain in the Twentieth Century* is based on the narratives of thirty-six women and men. The informants range from a friend of Radclyffe Hall and Vita Sackville-West in the 1920s to a lesbian who came out in the 1990s, at the age of thirteen. In between are fascinating accounts of the ways that British lesbians and gay men recognized each other from the 1930s through the 1950s, how London became what Quentin Crisp characterized as a 'vast double bed' during wartime blackouts, the rise of gay coffee bars in the 1950s despite police crackdowns, the creation of the Homosexual Law Reform Society and the country's Gay Liberation Front in the 1960s, the advent of AIDS and AIDS activism, and the outrage generated by Clause 28 (a 1987 law which prevents local authorities from 'promoting homosexuality').

Patricia Juliana Smith's *Lesbian Panic: Homoeroticism in Modern British Women's Fiction* considers Britain in the twentieth century through an examination of some of the country's most important contemporary literature. Although texts such as Virginia Woolf's *The Voyage Out* and *Mrs. Dalloway*, Doris Lessing's *The Golden Notebook*, and Elizabeth Bowen's *The Little Girls* have received a substantial amount of critical attention, they have not been acknowledged as what Smith calls narratives of 'lesbian panic': novels in which 'a female character, fearing discovery of her covert or unarticulated lesbian desires . . ., lashes out directly or indirectly at another woman, resulting in emotional or physical harm to herself or others' (2). In this approach, her work is similar to Eve Sedgwick's articulation of a 'homosexual panic' in male narratives. But whereas the motivating factor in

Sedgwick's model involves a threatened loss of male privilege, in Smith's it is a woman's 'fear of the loss of identity and value as object of exchange, often combined with the fear of responsibility for one's own sexuality' (6). Smith devotes her first chapter to an examination of Woolf's work, recognizing that not only was she an important modernist figure, but that this aesthetic sensibility was directly tied to her desire to explore and articulate nontraditional expressions of gender and sexuality. Her second chapter, entitled ' "Are You a Lesbian, Mumbo?": Freudian Discourse, Shame, and Panic in Postwar Prefeminist Fictions', considers how novels by writers such as Bowen, Lessing, Anita Brookner, and Muriel Spark may have centred on a female character's search for heterosexual domesticity, but that this narrative was driven by repressed homoerotic desire, and thus these works serve as 'isolated examples of lesbian representation' in mid twentieth-century Britain (83). Smith's final chapter presents some of the strategies that novelists from the 1970s to the present, including Fay Weldon, Jeanette Winterson, and Emma Tennant, have used to move beyond the narrative limitations of lesbian panic.

The lesbian panic narrative outlined by Smith can be considered part of a wider representational strategy that Sherrie A. Inness refers to as 'the lesbian menace' in her book of the same name. Focusing on twentieth-century US popular cultural texts, Inness delineates not only the ways in which the dominant society perpetuates stereotypes about lesbians – including the notion that they are evil temptresses seeking to seduce innocent, unsuspecting heterosexuals – but also how lesbians create more supportive images for themselves through alternate readings of these and other works intended for a heterosexual audience. In her first chapter, she examines Radclyffe Hall's *The Well of Loneliness* and Edouard Bourdet's *The Captive* in the context of popular conceptions of lesbians in the 1920s, persuasively arguing that Hall's masculine heroine could be more easily contained because she conformed to conventional wisdom about the mannish lesbian, while Bourdet's feminine protagonist was potentially more subversive because she disrupted common assumptions. Inness' second chapter also addresses how lesbians were depicted in the early twentieth century through an analysis of popular fiction that represented women's colleges as, in the words of one novel, 'the soil where Sapphism flourishes' (33). While the representation of lesbians today is seemingly more positive, Inness demonstrates in her third chapter that the ways in which contemporary women's magazines portray lesbians as identical or nearly identical to heterosexual women can often be as damaging as the lesbian menace imagery of the past.

Switching perspective, the fourth and fifth chapters of *The Lesbian Menace* consider the ways that lesbians subvert texts aimed at a heterosexual audience or develop their own narratives by examining how lesbian readers bring a distinctly 'queer' perspective to Nancy Drew mysteries and how the portrayal of lesbians has changed in children's books during the past two decades. Inness' last three chapters look at the specificity of lesbian lives, discussing 'the ways that lesbians, themselves a marginalized group, have created a society that, in turn, relegates some of its members to the outskirts' (7). She perceptively describes how 'queer geography' shapes and influences lesbian identity, how all lesbians are part of a process of passing, and how individual butch identities and butch-butch relationships are often ignored by lesbian scholars.

'This book was as much born from excitement as indignation', writes renée hoogland at the outset of *Lesbian Configurations*. '[E]xcitement about the growing visibility of lesbian sexuality in Western cultural production, and indignation about the particular settings, or configurations, in which mainstream "lesbian" images consistently (re)appear and, more often than not, subsequently disappear' (vii). hoogland demonstrates the liberatory potential of the growing body of lesbian cultural criticism through chapters that provide a detailed analysis of specific literary and cinematic texts which invoke lesbian desire only to obscure and then frequently suppress it (some of these representations also involve bisexuality, but hoogland does not address this fact). Included are fresh, valuable readings of Alice Walker's *The Color Purple*, Sylvia Plath's *The Bell Jar*, and Elizabeth Bowen's *Friends and Relations*, and the films *Basic Instinct* and *Bitter Moon*. She concludes by considering the historically ambivalent relationship between lesbian cultural studies and mainstream feminist scholarship, calling attention to the ways that feminism has also sought the discursive containment of female same-sex desire.

Building upon his landmark book *Gay and Lesbian Themes in Latin American Writing* (1991), David William Foster's *Sexual Textualities: Essays on Queer/ing Latin American Writing* offers queer readings of a range of Latin American literary and cultural texts. Foster begins by outlining the parameters of a gay male literary heritage in different Latin American cultures, focusing on works from Argentina, Mexico, Puerto Rico, Cuba, and Brazil. In subsequent chapters, he considers Eva Perón as a cultural and sexual icon, the development of a Latin American 'feminine pornography', the subversion of Mexican patriarchy in Jaime Humberto Hermosillo's classic 1985 film *Doña Herlinda y su hijo*, the depiction of homoerotic desire in the writing of Chicano/Chicana authors such as Cherríe Moraga and Francisco X. Alarcón, the coming together of Cuban-American politics and issues of gay identity in Matías Montes Huidobro's 1988 play *Exilio*, the representation of the body in Alejandra Pizarnik's poetry, and the crisis of masculinity in Argentine fiction from 1940 to 1960.

A mid-century crisis in masculinity is also the subject of Richard J. Corber's *Homosexuality in Cold War America*. While Foster demonstrates how changing societal roles were represented in Argentine literature, Corber considers how gay and bisexual writers in the US resisted a political climate that saw homosexuality as simultaneously everywhere and nowhere. Examining the work of Tennessee Williams, Gore Vidal, and James Baldwin, Corber argues that all three authors treated gay male identity less as a sexual preference than as a means of opposition to the developing Cold War consensus around a domesticated and consumer-focused model of masculinity. Rather than reducing homosexuality to a discrete subculture, they stressed its broader political possibilities, including the opportunity for alliances between disenfranchised groups and the structural links between racism, sexism, and heterosexism.

To better situate his literary analysis in relation to 'the operations of power in postwar American society and the modes of resistance those operations both enabled and precluded' (3), Corber begins by examining 1940s' film noirs, specifically *Laura* and *Crossfire*. He suggests that the frequent inclusion of characters marked explicitly as homosexual in film noir rendered gay men visible, but the genre's ability to undermine the Cold War re-organization of masculinity was limited by its perpetuation of gay stereotypes. He therefore concludes that Williams, Vidal, and Baldwin engaged in more productive forms of resistance than film noir and, although he offers no direct evidence, claims that they laid the groundwork for the emergence of the gay liberation movement a decade later.

Scott Tucker's *The Queer Question: Essays on Desire and Democracy* is an important addition to discussions of US gay politics, culture, and activism. At a time when it is often hard to differentiate Democrats from Republicans, when gay male conservatives have become the poster boys of much of the gay and straight press, and when the traditional Left continues to distance itself from LGBT people, Tucker's call for queer liberation – for 'our right to the world' – is refreshing and inspiring. Consisting of essays published in left and gay magazines over the past fifteen years, *The Queer Question* presents a democratic socialist vision for the future while reclaiming the radical roots of democracy and addressing a range of contemporary social and political issues, including same-sex marriage, acceptance in the military, sexual censorship, and the search for 'the gay gene'.

In *The Sodomite in Fiction and Satire, 1660–1750*, Cameron McFarlane demonstrates that the concepts of 'sodomy' and 'buggery' had much broader, more 'confused' meanings during the Restoration and the first half of the eighteenth century than they commonly do today, referring to 'a category of undifferentiated debauchery that included acts that we would call "homosexual" *and* "heterosexual" as well as behavior that could be deemed sacrilegious or a challenge to political authority and cultural purity' (3). Yet during this period these terms were increasingly being used just to describe sexual contact between two men as the image of male same-sex desire began to achieve cultural prominence. To his credit, McFarlane does not assume that this greater visibility necessarily signalled the emergence of a proto-modern 'homosexual identity', but instead sees it as an indication that sodomy was becoming a definable social act – what he refers to as 'sodomitical practices' – with specific cultural meanings. He begins by effectively tracing the discursive emergence of the sodomite as a destructive social type in a number of texts from the late seventeenth and early eighteenth centuries, including *The Tragedy of Nero*, *Faustina*, and *Plain Reasons for the Growth of Sodomy*. Through a detailed reading of the Biblical destruction of Sodom, *Love Letters Between a Certain Late Nobleman and the Famous Mr. Wilson*, and *Sodom; or the Quintessence of Debauchery*, McFarlane then considers the ways in which times of social upheaval were characterized as sodomitical, with the sodomite not only serving as a convenient figure for the displacement of cultural anxieties, but also being constituted through this displacement. Finally, by examining the works of Tobias Smollett and John Cleland, he analyses 'the instabilities and discursive ruptures in sodomitical inscription in an attempt to locate the place of desire within the language that would negate it' (107).

Books Reviewed

Balderston, Daniel and Donna J. Guy, eds. *Sex and Sexuality in Latin America.* New York University Press. pp. 288. hb £44.00 ($55.00), pb £16.00 ($20.00). ISBN 0 8147 1289 4, 0 8147 1290 8.

Beemyn, Brett, ed. *Creating a Place for Ourselves: Lesbian, Gay, and Bisexual Community Histories.* Routledge. pp. 300. hb £45.00 ($70.00), pb £12.99 ($16.99). ISBN 0 4159 1389 6, 0 4159 1390 X.

Bi Academic Intervention, eds. *The Bisexual Imaginary: Representation, Identity and Desire.* Cassell. pp. 216. hb £45.00, pb £14.99 ($18.95). ISBN 0 3043 3744 7, 0 3043 3745 5.

Blasius, Mark and Shane Phelan, eds. *We Are Everywhere: A Historical Sourcebook of Gay and Lesbian Politics.* Routledge. pp. 844. hb £50.00 ($75.00), pb £16.99 ($24.99). ISBN 0 4159 0858 2, 0 4159 0859 0.

Califia, Pat. *Sex Changes: The Politics of Transgenderism.* Cleis Press. pp. 309. pb £13.99 ($16.95). ISBN 1 5734 4072 8.

Comstock, Gary David and Susan E. Henking, eds. *Que(e)rying Religion: A Critical Anthology.* Continuum. pp. 552. pb £21.99 ($34.50). ISBN 0 8264 0924 5.

Corber, Richard J. *Homosexuality in Cold War America: Resistance and the Crisis of Masculinity.* Duke University Press. pp. 240. hb £47.50 ($49.95), pb £16.50 ($16.95). ISBN 0 8223 1956 X, 0 8223 1964 0.

Devor, Holly. *FTM: Female-To-Male Transsexuals in Society.* Indiana University Press. pp. 696. hb £40.50 ($49.95), pb £11.99 ($14.95). ISBN 0 2533 3631 7, 0 2532 0533 6.

Douglas, Debbie, Courtnay McFarlane, Makeda Silvera and Douglas Stewart, eds. *Má-Ka: Diasporic Juks, Contemporary Writing by Queers of African Descent.* Sister Vision Press. pp. 212. pb $17.95. ISBN 1 8967 0514 6.

Duberman, Martin, ed. *Queer Representations: Reading Lives, Reading Cultures.* New York University Press. pp. 410. hb £48.00 ($60.00), pb £19 ($23.50). ISBN 0 8147 1884 1, 0 8147 1883 3.

Duberman, Martin, ed. *A Queer World: The Center for Lesbian and Gay Studies Reader.* New York University Press. pp. 705. hb £52.00 ($65.00), pb £20.00 ($25.00). ISBN 0 8147 1874 4, 0 8147 1875 2.

Ekins, Richard. *Male Femaling: A Grounded Theory Approach to Cross-Dressing and Sex-Changing.* Routledge. pp. 185. hb £47.50 ($75.00), pb £14.99 ($20.99). ISBN 0 415 10624 9, 0 415 10625 7.

Esterberg, Kristin G. *Lesbian and Bisexual Identities: Constructing Communities, Constructing Selves.* Temple University Press. pp. 201. hb £39.95 ($49.95), pb £15.50 ($18.95). ISBN 1 5663 9509 7, 1 5663 9510 0.

Foster, David William. *Sexual Textualities: Essays on Queer/ing Latin American Writing.* University of Texas Press. pp. 180. hb £16.64 ($28.00), pb £10.07 ($16.95). ISBN 0 2927 2501 9, 0 2927 2502 7.

Foster, Thomas, Carol Siegel and Ellen E. Berry, eds. *The Gay '90s: Disciplinary and Interdisciplinary Formations in Queer Studies.* New York University Press. pp. 254. hb £44.00 ($55.00), pb £14.50 ($19.50). ISBN 0 8147 2672 0, 0 8147 2673 9.

Gluckman, Amy and Betsy Reed, eds. *Homo Economics: Capitalism, Com-*

munity, and Lesbian and Gay Life. Routledge. pp. 283. hb £45.00 ($74.95), pb £14.99 ($19.99). ISBN 0 415 91378 0, 0 415 91379 9.

Griffin, Gabriele and Sonya Andermahr, eds. *Straight Studies Modified: Lesbian Interventions in the Academy.* Cassell. pp. 244. hb £45.00 ($89.50), pb £16.99 ($29.95). ISBN 0 3043 3633 5, 0 3043 3630 0.

Harper, Phillip Brian, Anne McClintock, José Esteban Moñoz and Trish Rosen, eds. 'Queer Transexions of Race, Nation, and Gender', Social Text, 52–53 (Fall/Winter). Duke University Press. pp. 289, pb $19.00. ISBN 0 8223 6452 2.

Harris, Laura and Elizabeth Crocker, eds. *Femme: Feminists, Lesbians, and Bad Girls.* Routledge. pp. 222. hb £45.00 ($70.00), pb £14.99 ($17.99). ISBN 0 415 91873 1, 0 415 91874 X.

Heller, Dana, ed. *Cross-Purposes: Lesbians, Feminists, and the Limits of Alliance.* Indiana University Press. pp. 238. hb £29.50 ($35.00), pb £12.50 ($14.95). ISBN 0 2533 3246 X, 0 2532 1084 4.

Holmlund, Chris and Cynthia Fuchs, eds. *Between the Sheets, In the Streets: Queer, Lesbian, Gay Documentary.* University of Minnesota Press. pp. 304. hb £45.00 ($54.95), pb £17.95 ($21.95). ISBN 0 8166 2774 6, 0 8166 2775 4.

hoogland, renée c. *Lesbian Configurations.* Columbia University Press. pp. 168. hb £27.03 ($45.00), pb £9.91 ($16.50). ISBN 0 2311 0906 7, 0 2311 0907 5.

Howard, John, ed. *Carryin' On in the Lesbian and Gay South.* New York University Press. pp. 402. hb £44.00 ($55.00), pb £15.25 ($18.95). ISBN 0 8147 3513 4, 0 8147 3560 6.

Inness, Sherrie A. *The Lesbian Menace: Ideology, Identity, and the Representation of Lesbian Life.* University of Massachusetts Press. pp. 256. hb £31.95 ($40.00), pb £11.95 ($16.95). ISBN 1 5584 9090 6, 1 5584 9091 4.

Jacobs, Sue-Ellen, Wesley Thomas and Sabine Lang, eds. *Two-Spirit People: Native American Gender Identity, Sexuality, and Spirituality.* University of Illinois Press. pp. 331. hb £27.00 ($44.95), pb £11.98 ($19.95). ISBN 0 2520 2344 7, 0 2520 6645 6.

Jivani, Alkarim. *It's Not Unusual: A History of Lesbian and Gay Britain in the Twentieth Century.* Indiana University Press. pp. 224. hb £14.99 ($35), pb £9.99 ($15.95). ISBN 1 854 79205 9, 1 854 79279 2.

Kaiser, Charles. *The Gay Metropolis: 1940–1996.* Houghton Mifflin. pp. 404. hb £20.00 ($27.00), pb £8.99 ($14.00). ISBN 0 297 84217 X, 0 753 80662 2.

Lancaster, Roger N. and Micaela di Leonardo, eds. *The Gender/Sexuality Reader: Culture, History, Political Economy.* Routledge. pp. 574. hb £47.50 ($75.00), pb £15.99 ($27.99). ISBN 0 415 91004 8, 0 415 91005 6.

McCormick, Ian, ed. *Secret Sexualities: A Sourcebook of 17th and 18th Century Writing.* Routledge. pp. 262. hb £55 ($65), pb £15.99 ($18.99). ISBN 0 415 13953 8, 0 415 13954 6.

McFarlane, Cameron. *The Sodomite in Fiction and Satire, 1660–1750.* Columbia University Press. pp. 216. hb £36 ($45), pb £13 ($16.50). ISBN 0 231 10894 X, 0 231 10895 8.

Mintz, Beth and Esther D. Rothblum, eds. *Lesbians in Academia: Degrees of Freedom.* Routledge. pp. 298. hb £45 ($70), pb £13.99 ($20.99). ISBN 0 415 91701 8, 0 415 91702 6.

Moore, Lisa C., ed. *Does Your Mama Know?: An Anthology of Black*

Lesbian Coming Out Stories. RedBone Press. pp. 313. pb £8.99 ($19.95). ISBN 0 9656 6590 9.

Murray, Stephen O. and Will Roscoe, eds. *Islamic Homosexualities: Culture, History, and Literature.* New York University Press. pp. 331. hb £40 ($55), pb £17 ($21). ISBN 0 8147 7467 9, 0 8147 7468 7.

Queen, Carol and Lawrence Schimel, eds. *PoMoSexuals: Challenging Assumptions About Gender and Sexuality.* Cleis Press. pp. 192. pb £11.99 ($14.95). ISBN 1 5734 4074 4.

Rosario, Vernon A., ed. *Science and Homosexualities.* Routledge. pp. 308. hb £40 ($70), pb £12.99 ($19.99). ISBN 0 4159 1501 5, 0 4159 1502 3.

Schneider, Richard Jr, ed., *The Best of* The Harvard Gay and Lesbian Review. Temple University Press. pp. 363. £16.79 ($27.95). ISBN 1 5663 9596 8.

Sears, James T. *Lonely Hunters: An Oral History of Lesbian and Gay Southern Life, 1948–1968.* Westview. pp. 317. hb £21.50 ($28), pb £11 ($15.95). ISBN 0 8133 2474 2, 0 8133 2475 0.

Sears, James T. and Walter L. Williams, eds. *Overcoming Heterosexism and Homophobia: Strategies that Work.* Columbia University Press. pp. 456. hb £40 ($49.50), pb £12.95 ($18.50). ISBN 0 2311 0422 7, 0 2311 0423 5.

Sedgwick, Eve Kosofsky, ed. *Novel Gazing: Queer Readings in Fiction.* Duke University Press. pp. 518. hb £57.00 ($59.95), pb £20.95 ($21.95). ISBN 0 8223 2028 2, 0 8223 2040 1.

Smith, Patricia Juliana. *Lesbian Panic: Homoeroticism in Modern British Women's Fiction.* Columbia University Press. pp. 236. hb £40.00 ($49.50), pb £12.95 ($16.50). ISBN 0 2311 0620 3, 0 2311 0621 1.

Stein, Arlene. *Sex and Sensibility: Stories of a Lesbian Generation.* University of California Press. pp. 256. hb £35.00 ($45.00), pb £13.95 ($16.95). ISBN 0 5202 0257 0, 0 5202 0674 6.

Tucker, Scott. *The Queer Question: Essays on Desire and Democracy.* South End Press. pp. 257. hb £24.03 ($40.00), pb £13.99 ($18.00). ISBN 0 8960 8578 3, 0 8960 8577 5.

Weed, Elizabeth and Naomi Schor, eds, *Feminism Meets Queer Theory.* Indiana University Press. pp. 341. hb £33.50 ($39.95), pb £14.99 ($17.95). ISBN 0 2533 3278 8, 0 2532 1118 2.

Wilchins, Riki Anne. *Read My Lips: Sexual Subversion and the End of Gender.* Firebrand. pp. 231. hb £17.39 ($28.95), pb £13.99 ($16.95). ISBN 1 5634 1091 5, 1 5634 1090 7.

Wright, J. W. Jr and Everett K. Rowson. *Homoeroticism in Classical Arabic Literature.* Columbia University Press. pp. 239. hb £40.00 ($49.50), pb £15.95 ($20.00). ISBN 0 2311 0506 1, 0 2311 0507 X.

8

Marxism(s) and Post-Marxism(s)

GLYN DALY

In the 150th anniversary of the publication of *The Communist Manifesto* contemporary reflection on Marxism appears generally less assured and more speculative. Undermining the univocal tradition and the search for the one true message of Marx, a number of recent texts take for granted the idea of a basic heterogeneity in Marx; a multiplicity of voices, spirits, philosophies and so on. Moreover, the traumatic dislocations between the promises of nineteenth-century Marxism and their twentieth-century actualizations have tended to open up spaces for more creative forms of intellectual engagement.

This process of creativity can be discerned, to greater and lesser extents, in the texts reviewed here. On the other hand, however, there exist opposing kinds of intervention, which have insisted on a more traditional defence of Marxist orthodoxy. Probably the best example is the book edited by Ellen Meiskins Wood and John Bellamy Foster, *In Defense of History: Marxism and the Postmodern Agenda*. The book is divided into two basic sections – Postmodernism and Intellectuals; and Postmodernism and Movements – and includes, among a number of others, contributions from Terry Eagleton and Fredric Jameson. As the title suggests, the book comprises something of a traditionalist polemic, which engages in a series of refutations of what is characterized, in a rather sketchy manner, as 'postmodernism'. For Wood, the so-called 'agenda' of postmodernism is unmistakable: it is 'rooted in the "Golden Age of Capitalism"' (16) and is 'traceable to an obsession with consumer capitalism and to the conviction . . . that the old political agencies (the labor movement in particular) have been permanently "hegemonized" by capitalist consumerism' (9). In a similar vein, Eagleton states in his contribution – 'Where do Postmodernists Come From?' – that postmodernism reflects 'the ideology of a particularly jaded, defeatist wing of the liberal-capitalist intelligentsia' (25). While J. B. Foster asserts that the 'irony of postmodernism is that while purporting to have transcended modernity, it abandons from the start all hope of transcending capitalism . . .' (193).

Now it is easy to see how these types of argument work. By simply turning the idea of postmodernism into some kind of ideological-cultural epiphenomenon of late capitalism, it can be authoritatively denounced with the entire weight of Marxist critique. But is this actually the case? Is postmodernism such an undifferentiated monolith or are the authors simply assuming what they need to demonstrate?

Let us focus for a moment on the question of modernism and its historical development. As Hans Blumenberg (1985) makes clear in his outstanding study, *The Legitimacy of the Modern Age* (London: MIT Press), modernity develops through a paradoxical faith in Reason in which the dominant philosophico-intellectual tradition – that of teleological mastery – curiously reflects the very theological culture it sought to overturn (the belief in the earthly possibilities for salvation, reconciliation, grace, and so on). The point is that the Enlightenment-based enthusiasm for Reason and secular endeavour begins to be mobilized in a number of different directions – liberal, socialist, nationalist, totalitarian, fascist . . . – without being essentially linked to any one of them. On the contrary, what emerges is a complex and diverse history in which modernity can be seen as a *terrain* of struggle for competing ideologies with different, and characteristic, claims on universal truth.

Now in the context of postmodern thought this type of heterogeneity and open-endedness is made even more explicit. In this regard, the idea of a pre-given politics or agenda *of* postmodernism is simply nonsensical. If postmodern thought affirms the *lack* of an ultimate foundation – if it affirms the lack of an algorithm for determining decisions – then the political consequences of this are wholly indeterminate; in Derrida's terms, they are radically undecidable. Everything depends, therefore, on the ability of concrete social forces to politically constitute their definition(s) of reality in a historical context of possibilities. In a social formation, any 'foundation' or 'ground' is always the result of hegemonic struggle, which, because it is partial and incomplete, is always vulnerable alternative hegemonic interventions. And if the processes of grounding are undecidable – if they are a historical matter of political encounter – then this clearly does not rule out the possibility of developing a radical postmodern tradition.

This is precisely what Laclau and Mouffe set out do with their project of re-conceiving Marxism within an anti-foundationalist context; what they term post-Marxism. Moreover this type of project enables us to approach the whole issue of the metanarrative in a rather different way. Thus it is not a question of simply abandoning the metanarrative, as indicated by Lyotard, but rather of critiquing its ontological/essentialist status. To replace the metanarrative with an unqualified conception of atomized narratives would finally amount to an inversion on the terrain of necessity: either we have a necessary unity or a necessary dissolutionism; in other words, a new kind of 'endism' with no scope for universalistic forms of activity. In this sense both Universalism and Particularism are equally essentialist. By contrast, what Laclau and Mouffe demonstrate is that it is possible to cut through this exclusivist alternative and to construct a metanarrativity, or universalist-type politics, which is perfectly compatible with a postmodern perspective provided it is based upon political argumentation rather than epistemic foundation. Indeed, their conception of radical democracy, as based upon the continual amplification of the Enlightenment values of freedom and equality *without final completion*, precisely constitutes a metanarrativity that is postmodern in character.

However, Wood and Foster et al. are not willing to analyse postmodern thought as a differentiated terrain of political struggle and offer no discussion of alternative projects of postmodern radicalism. On the contrary, they focus exclusively on the way in which their version of postmodernism functions as a support to the globalizing logics of a consumer-liberal-capitalism. Moreover, Marxism itself tends to be presented in rather general and unitary terms without any significant conceptual history of its own. This is regrettable because it lifts Marxism out of any philosophico-intellectual context and portrays it as something of a back-to-basics common sense, which naturally coincides with rather impressionistic ideas about 'realism' and so-called historical materialism. In this way, the authors systematically evade all the problems in Marxism of theoretical inconsistency and dualistic tensions between economic determinism and ethical practice, between objectivism and the primacy of the political, between science and ideology, and so on.

As with Hilferding's famous contention that History was that best of all Marxists, the impression which is given in the book is that Marxism, and in particular 'historical materialism', is simply short-hand for the language of truth and objectivity. Indeed the authors quite explicitly fall back on some of the most basic positions of positivism in order to support their claims. E. M. Wood, for example, simply asserts that there are universal and immutable laws of nature and that scientific knowledge is invariable (5–6). While M. Nanda – in her chapter 'Against Social De(con)struction of Science – argues that we share the same natural world and that there is a 'common book of nature' (93) to be deciphered. Now we can immediately ask, which common book of nature is this and which particular laws of nature are being referred to? The ones identified by Ricardo, Smith, Hobbes, Locke . . . for example? Moreover, if scientific knowledge is so invariable would we have ever moved from the Newtonian paradigm to Einsteinian and post-Bohrian physics? Will not twenty-first-century science re-describe twentieth-century science in the same way that the self-evident truths of the nineteenth century have been re-described and radically transformed? Furthermore what does the common book of nature tell us about such thorny issues as HIV/AIDS, abortion, cloning, space technology, and so on? Decisions about such issues, let alone questions of historical interpretation and political organization, will involve a whole range of ethical, social and cultural considerations that cannot be read off from any basic algorithm.

Perhaps the ultimate irony with this book is that in seeking a defence of history, and a materialist conception of it at that, it ends up doing precisely the opposite. That is to say, in the classic manner of all idealism – i.e. the attempt to reduce the real to the concept – the authors set out to re-affirm rational mastery and the idea of a universal set of *a priori* truths which are above and beyond history, which do not depend on any context and which are not prone to the historico-political processes of subversion and transformation.

Edward Reiss's *Marx: A Clear Guide* is very much designed as an introductory textbook. It possesses bite-size, and easy-to-digest, chapters complete with 'suggested questions' at the end of each one. It is written in a lively and accessible way, covering a considerable amount of ground and incorporating some refreshing anecdotal detail (e.g. that Marx was sometimes referred to as 'Doctor Crankey' by his family members). This is a useful text for students who are new to the topic. Moreover, it also manages to develop a sophisticated critical perspective. For example, it highlights the contradictory views of history in Marx (as class struggle and as a forces/relations of production dialectic) and also explores some important ambiguities surrounding the issues of class, ideology, gender and so on. At certain points, however, the book suffers from over-condensation. On one page, for example, Reiss dizzies the reader by moving the discussion from M. Bakhtin to K. Mannheim to A. Gramsci to L. Althusser and, finally, to S. Hall. Nevertheless, in contrast to our defenders of historical materialism, this is a book that keeps the debates around Marxism alive by setting them within contemporary contexts.

Ethical Marxism and its Radical Critics, by Lawrence Wilde, develops an alternative but equally essentialist approach to Marxism. For Wilde the most enduring legacy of Marxism is not so much a theory of history but rather, returning to Marx, the discovery of a common humanity which is in need of liberation through the overcoming of capitalism and its structures of alienation. Attempts to re-conceive Marxism in ethical terms (in contrast to the thinkers of the Second International) were initially undertaken by such Austro-Marxists as Max Adler and Otto Bauer. As Wilde acknowledges, these authors sought to develop a creative and non-dogmatic approach. Breaking with the 'scientific socialism' of Engels, Bauer, for example, took up a radically anti-foundationalist position by declaring that Austro-Marxism was 'nothing but the ideology of unity of the workers' movement' (cited in Bottomore, T. and P. Goode, 1978, *Austro-Marxism*, Oxford). Adler, on the other hand, completely re-formulated the Marxist project through the moral philosophy of Kant. This had the effect of widening the scope of socialist politics by investing it with a universal kind of moral force that transcended notions of class pre-destination. At the same time, Adler tended to present a far more open-ended approach to questions of history, society and the economy in terms of (politically) competing forms of consciousness rather than the determinist movement of the forces of production. The central point is that this ethical re-articulation of Marxist ideas involved crucial departures from the logics of inevitability and necessity and stimulated a new kind of theoretical inquiry.

Wilde, however, does not wish to develop this inquiry – simply rejecting it as being in contradiction to Marx's stated position (1) – and returns instead to a far more traditionalist position. For Wilde, 'ethical; Marxism' is one which takes the idea of a human essence to be central (5) and sets out to solve 'the question of how alienation can be overcome so that the human essence of creative social activity can be enjoyed by all citizens' (6). Unfortunately, this appears to amount to something of a re-statement of a rather familiar story about Marxism as 'committed to the full realization of human potential', and that 'capitalism creates a working-class opposition capable of emancipating both itself and all humankind' (142). This kind of romanticism – e.g. the approval of Bloch's 'warm stream' of Marxism as conjuring the 'unexhausted fullness of expectation' – ultimately raises far more questions than it solves. What is this human essence? Who is this humankind that Wilde refers to? Given the advances of psychoanalysis and the demonstration of the historico-contingent nature of 'the self' and its fragmentary and antagonistic constitution, it seems quite eccentric to insist on a classical notion of a positive and non-contradictory human essence which only needs to be fully realized (by Marxists, of course). Moreover, when Wilde speaks of the 'species' *telos* (146) and the 'commitment to solidarity and revolution as the means through which the "new man" will emerge' (147), we must surely ask what *telos* and which new man? The ones represented accurately by socialists but not by fascists? The attempt to disengage ethics from politics, to present it as a reflection of historical necessity and/or as the culmination of an immanent necessity, is surely the ideological fantasy *par excellence*.

'Wrong' declares *Marxism Today* under an iconic, and rather glaze-eyed, representation of Tony Blair. After folding in 1991, *Marxism Today* has re-animated itself for a spot check of New Labour's first term of office. All the usual contributors are rounded up here and the overwhelming (if unsurprising) consensus is that New Labour has not been radical enough and has tended to lose its way. The one dissenting voice is that of G. Mulgan who accuses leftist intellectuals like S. Hall and E. Hobsbawm of scholastic isolation and of preferring a kind of self-satisfied and hysterical opposition to the realities of government.

I have some sympathy with Mulgan's position (which, apart from some notable exceptions, livens up some rather hackneyed journalism), and the view that *Marxism Today* itself cannot stand apart from its own responsibilities in contributing to the very foundations of Blairite politics. However, organic anti-intellectuals like Mulgan and Co. cannot be allowed to get away with trotting out the same old alibi for authoritarian pragmatism. Stifling radical critique in the name of effective government is the miserable excuse of all guillotinists.

The Communist Manifesto: New Interpretations, edited by M. Cowling and put together by members of the Political Studies Association (UK) Marxism Specialist Group, celebrates the 150th anniversary of the eponymous text. The book boasts a new translation of *The Communist Manifesto* by T. Carver and includes a collection of concise essays that cover a wide range of themes in the *Manifesto*. This is a refreshing book that dispenses with familiar clichés of eulogy and engages with the thought of Marx and Engels in a warts-and-all fashion. In this way, the authors are concerned to analyse the historical contribution of the much-vaunted *Manifesto* and, at the same time, to de-divinize its near Gospel status in order to show the limitations of this mid-nineteenth-century document. It is divided into four sections. The first deals with the text itself and the way in which the surrounding contexts influenced both its construction and subsequent interpretations. The second examines the category of revolution and its vicissitudes. The third explores the various ambiguities associated with the constitution of the working class, while the final section addresses the continuing relevance of the *Manifesto*.

It is one of the merits of the book that the authors interrogate the *Manifesto* with a healthy irreverence and that they seek to analyse the thought of Marx within a certain sense of historical context. M. Gane, for example, offers an interesting commentary on Marx and Engels' view of the transgendering of the classes, and in particular the proletariat, under capitalism and the ambiguous effects this might hold for the historical transformation of the family structure (132–141). Similarly, W. Suchting points out that there are major questions concerning the uses of the term 'class' in the *Manifesto* and the way it appears to refer to rather vague and impressionistic ideas about oppression and exploitation (161–162). S. Wilks-Heeg, on the other hand, takes the irreverence even further and commits what many might regard as cardinal blasphemy against Marxist orthodoxy:

> The historical evidence falls squarely on Bernstein's side of the argument. Class fragmentation has meant that labour leaders have been unable to assume that workers are a homogenous block united by a common desire to overthrow capitalism (128).

This contrasts markedly with the routine incantations about the working class rising up, like the Second Coming of Christ, to deliver us from the ravages of global capitalism. The category of class has occupied such a central, and even sacred, position in the Marxist canon that to criticize it is to be guilty of heresy and of turning one's back on the most vulnerable in society. This no doubt is, in part, due to a process of metonymical sliding and an overwhelming tendency to conflate the notion of class with generalized descriptions of poverty, disaffection, oppression and so on. In Marx and Engels the concept of class, in its analytical status, clearly referred to productive position and the argument concerning the political centrality of the working class (as the agent of social transformation) was linked to the observation that the industrialized nineteenth-century economy was producing a relatively unified industrial working class (similar work patterns, habitat, life styles and so on). In the post-industrial age this class is very much in decline. In response to this situation, Marxist thinkers began to develop a broader notion of worker in terms of wage slave and/or seller of labour power. But this notion would apply literally to the vast majority of the population (from miners to corporate managers) with no pre-given basis for political solidarity. Now this analytic *a priori* view of class has evidently broken up and will not perform the role that was meant for it. Moreover, the desperate conditions of poverty which persist today, as an integral logic of capitalist development, are more often than not marked by fragmentation and isolation and do not fit into any traditional framework of class.

However, I would add two further points to Wilks-Heeg. The first pertains to his discussion of Kautsky. Kautsky was to observe that towards the end of the nineteenth century the working class was not only becoming less homogenous, it was also revealing a far greater predisposition towards social democracy and trade unionism which were quite compatible with (even supportive of) the continuing existence of capitalism. For these reasons, and despite all his leanings towards economic determinism and classism, Kautsky began to affirm a crucial mediating role for socialist intellectuals in order to stimulate a revolutionary consciousness. These tentative movements towards a political pragmatism – inexorably undermining the logic of inevitability – are considerably widened with Lenin and, of course, Gramsci.

The second point concerns Bernstein. Bernstein's radicalism consists in his break with determinism and class essence and of showing how proletarians could be transformed into national citizens through a logic of politico-ideological articulation. However, this does not necessarily lead to societies that are more integrated and conformist, for by this very logic the political character of identities (including class identities) cannot be predicted in advance. Indeed, what we are witnessing today is not the steady absorption of social conflict by a new universalism (an end of history), but quite the opposite: an increasing diversification of particularistic identities and political demands constituted around new sites of antagonism including gender, sexuality, ethnicity, cultural autonomy . . . as well as economic position. Thus the critique of classism is not one which leads to an inevitable embracing of some kind of liberal utopia. On the contrary, by developing Marx's very point that capitalism is constituted on the grounds of its own impossibility, it becomes possible so to speak to democratize the approach to the various antagonisms in a given social formation; antagonisms which do not naturally or spontaneously converge but which undermine all forms of absolutism and ontologically guarantee the conditions for alternative forms of political subversion and hegemonic practice.

Now, in this sense, while Marxism cannot simply master the multiplicity of antagonisms (the construction of a socialist-feminist-ecologism, for example, is not a unity foretold but is something which has to be made through negotiation and mutual modification), it can nevertheless make a fundamental contribution to an ongoing emancipatory project. However, such a contribution can only be *dimensional* and not totalizing. Here I would thoroughly endorse J. Townshend's conclusion that a reconstituted and 'de-teleologized' Marxism has a fundamental and vibrant role to play in the articulation of a new radical democratic 'universalism' which takes as its starting point 'the presumption that "history" has no fixed end-point' (187).

Terrel Carver's *The Postmodern Marx* is premised on the idea that there are multiple Marxes and that 'each one is a product of a reading strategy' (234). Carver rightly points out that Marx is not 'one' and that we should abandon the search for 'the "real" or the "relevant" Marx' (235). Drawing inspiration from hermeneutics, deconstruction and contextualism, Carver's strategy is based on what he calls a textualization of Marx and is situated in the progressive philosophical tradition of what Rorty, among others, have called the 'linguistic turn'. I have considerable sympathy with Carver's approach of 'de-divinizing' Marx and support his attempts to introduce some complex ideas and formulations in such an accessible and student-friendly manner. However, I would make three main criticisms for the purpose of further debate.

The first concerns the characterization of capitalism. According to Carver 'it is only when money is established that capitalism becomes possible in practice' (40). At first glance this appears self-evident. However, what actually drives the logic of commodification – in which money is increasingly revealed as an empty signifier, and at the same time the ultimate fetishized object, in the system of exchange – is not the invention of money itself (which pre-dates capitalism) but the way it functions within the capitalist mode of *production*.

The second relates to Carver's rather curious rejection of Derrida's *Specters of Marx*. Indeed Carver's own position would seem to endorse Derrida's central point concerning the heterogeneity of the spirit(s) of Marx (the more than one/no more one). For Carver, Derrida's reading of Marx is altogether too whimsical and even 'perverse':

> Overall, Derrida's reading of Marx leaps from trope to trope, text to text, in a way that is bereft of political contextualisation

in any very extensive sense, much as one would expect in plenary lectures, I suppose. Nonetheless for me his discussions of what may or may not be important distinctions in Marx's choice of, and use of, various related metaphors (*Geist, Gespenst, Spuk*, etc.) are largely empty in terms of argumentative context (13).

Now I find this rather disappointing, as it seems to undermine the very kind of heterogeneity that Carver initially endorses. Derrida's *Spectres* is certainly a work of intellectual imagination and intertextual richness. However, what appears to be at stake is not merely aesthetic or academic preference but a broader question of what can be done with a text. While Carver clearly does not adhere to any notion of the rationality of the text that is independent of its possible uses, is there not a danger of reproducing this very form of singularity at the level of the context? Something of this kind appears to occur in the work of Q. Skinner in which the author's intentions, what s/he was actually trying to say, can be discerned through a pinning down of the context of the relevant speech-acts. The problem, therefore, is precisely that of one-ness; of always placing the text within a *single* context. The radicalism of Derrida, by contrast, consists in doing something which is virtually the opposite: conjuring with contextual deformation itself and showing not only the limits of any context but its ultimate failure to constitute itself as 'one' (i.e. an ontology) and, therefore, how concepts and categories can always slip their moorings and go on to form new contexts. In short, the process of deconstruction.

In this way, Derrida is able to cast new light on the *Manifesto* precisely through contextual shifts and excursions through Shakespeare, Stirner, Fukuyama and so on. At the same time, what is absolutely central to Derrida's perspective is the demonstration of precisely that which stands outside any context: in paradoxical terms, the ontological presence of 'hauntology'. Derrida develops the idea of hauntology (or the logic of the specter) in respect to a basic undecidability, or contamination, between flesh and spirit; between the one and the universal. This impossible but necessary relationship gives rise to a permanent haunting in which time is always out-of-joint; in which society can never reach its final 'destination'. In other words, ontology can never overcome hauntology and that this constitutes a basic starting point for keeping alive the promise of an emancipation and democracy which is always to come. For Derrida, this means that while the ontological aspirations of Marxism can never be realized, it is something which nevertheless must/will remain integral to a haunting which is the condition of possibility for the future development of social justice.

This connects with the third point, which is that in focusing on the 'postmodern Marx' Carver tends to elude any encounter with the 'modern Marx'. Thus there exists little or no engagement with all the problems of teleology, class reductionism, economic determinism and so forth, which are clearly present in Marx himself (they are not simply distortions by Engels et al. as is sometimes claimed). What is revealed in Marx is precisely the tension *between* modernity and postmodernity, between the ontological and the hauntological, which cannot be resolved and which have been played out, in various directions, in the subsequent intellectual development of Marxist thought.

Sean Homer's *Fredric Jameson: Marxism, hermeneutics, postmodernism* is a timely reminder of the influence and importance of Jameson's work. As Homer points out, Jameson does not fit in with any obvious intellectual genre but has, instead, sought to combine the insights of poststructuralist, psychoanalytic and postmodern theory within a general Hegelo-Marxist framework.

In *The Political Unconscious*, for example, Jameson develops a conception of history in terms of the Freudian–Lacanian unconscious. In this way, Jameson characterizes history as a subtext in which 'our' narrated reality – about who 'we' are, 'our' destiny and so on – is always a retroactive construction of an infinitude (the real) which can never be fully mastered: i.e. history as the impossible process of constructing the one from the many. This view is a compelling one in that it presents the movement of history in terms of symbolic overdetermination. History is that which is accessible to us only through discourses that never manage to fully constitute themselves as ontologies. This is why the unconscious remains irreducible – in Derrida's terms it will always be produced as the shadowy 'double', the hauntology of any ontology.

Homer, however, resists this kind of reading of Jameson as it would inevitably 'lead down the poststructuralist and postmodernist path of relativism and the reductive notion that there is nothing outside the text' (65). Indeed, Homer would prefer a stronger defence of an 'independent reality' along the lines of Bhaskar (65). This does not convince me, as I think the very tensions in Jameson's thought point beyond any naturalistic return to the idea of an independent reality. In the first place, the assertion of the discursive character of reality-history is not one that necessarily admits to relativism where everything is in a constant state of flux. On the contrary, we only have to secure Lacan's argument about persistence of the *points de capitons* (nodal points), to appreciate how the socio-symbolic order achieves a *relative* consistency and stability through the repression of alternatives. For Laclau and Mouffe, this is the very 'game' of hegemony that can never be finally resolved through some imaginary conformity with an independent reality. Indeed, Jameson's position appears to be more subtle than this. For example, when Jameson speaks of history as that which 'hurts' as a kind of existential limit, and as that which 'can be apprehended only through its effects, and never directly as some reified force' (cited in Homer, 65–66), he would appear to be designating an ontological impossibility which constitutes the very 'ground' upon which historical possibilities and their subversions take place.

Jameson is probably more well known for his thesis that postmodernism is merely a cultural expression of late capitalism. This brings together all the main tensions in Jameson's thoughts. Jameson is not only adroit at identifying postmodern themes and developments in the socio-cultural arena, but also goes beyond writers like Baudrillard and Lyotard in historicizing their historicism: that is, contextualizing postmodernism in terms of late capitalist development. Now while the dangers of economism are clearly apparent, I think that Jameson's position is perhaps more compelling than that of Laclau whose central assertion regarding capitalism is that: 'There is no . . .

"capitalism", but rather different forms of capitalist relations which form part of highly diverse structural complexes' (Laclau, 1990, *New Reflections on the Revolution of Our Time*, London: Verso, p. 26). While I would tend to agree with this, an immediate observation is that it is nevertheless *capitalist* relations which are being globally constructed (albeit in diverse ways). What Laclau plays down – and what Jameson is fully cognisant of – is the extent to which capitalism *tendentially* affects the contemporary forms of political subjectivity. Thus capitalism, as a relentless process of commodification, actively requires and conjures with logics of socio-cultural difference through cycles of valorization and, thereby, reproduces a certain promise of emancipation through modes of consumption (technology, cuisine, habitat, style . . .). In this respect, there exists a certain affinity between Jameson and Deleuze and Guattari who point out that while capitalism is a liberating force in deterritorializing desire, at the same time it reterritorializes that desire within a far more extensive and insidious regime of capitalist exchange.

In this context, there can be no doubt that capitalism is intrinsically bound up with the construction of modern forms of subjectivity: or as Žižek puts it, modern capitalism tends to produce subjects which 'are prone to inconsistent forms of enjoyment' (in *Tarrying with the Negative*, Durham USA: Duke University Press, p. 216). However, as Homer points out, this raises the question of how totalizing Jameson's postmodern culture actually is: does it simply reproduce itself uniformly across the different developed/undeveloped regions of the globe. In addition, it also raises the question of resistance. Is postmodern culture (with all the ambiguities that are present in this term) simply an epiphenomenal expression of late capitalism, or is there the possibility of developing a postmodern radicalism that is opposed to capitalist logics? I think the answer can only be in the affirmative. Evidence of postmodern forms of radicalism (in the sense that such radicalism tends not to be teleologically grounded) can surely be found in the new types of ecologism, the various opt-out/alternative life-style movements, the diverse struggles against capitalist expansion and property development, widespread oppositions to nuclear power, the arms race, new technology and the waste of natural resources, to name but a few. Jameson, however, does not countenance the subversive potential of postmodern culture. And this is perhaps where the Marxist orthodoxy kicks in. Instead of exploring the contemporary forms of complex political subjectivity, as contingently structured around new sites of antagonism (which are neither pre-given nor predetermining), Jameson wants to maintain a totalizing conception of the 'single great adventure of class struggle' (Homer, 79). Nevertheless Jameson's interventions continue to endure and remain a powerful antidote to elated forms of postmodern hype.

Psycho-Marxism: Marxism and Psychoanalysis Late in the Twentieth Century, edited by R. Miklitsch, brings together a number of essays which are loosely organized around the current renaissance in psychoanalytic and post-Althusserian thought. As part of a multi-faceted project which Miklitsch tendentiously refers to as 'political psychoanalysis', the essays intervene in a range of areas from political economy to postcolonial and literary theory to 'queerness' and the unconscious, and the cultural phenomenon of 'conspiracy'.

As the introduction acknowledges, S. Žižek is a central figure in this type of endeavour. Indeed, the book opens with a chapter by Žižek entitled 'Psychoanalysis in Post-Marxism', and Žižek's perspective is discussed extensively by Miklitsch. Without engaging in the extremely rich and nuanced thought of Žižek, I will rather comment here on three important elements that I think are crucial for the development of a political psychoanalysis.

The first is the psychoanalytic identification of a ubiquitous surplus enjoyment – that which is 'in me more than me' as a kind of human excess (a monstrous inhuman) – which drives the subject towards an ultimate resolution/satisfaction (an end of drive). In the case of nationalism, for example, what tends to be overlooked in the deconstructivist emphasis on artificial construction (the iterable play of signification, and so on) is precisely the power of nationalism to organize the deep forces of enjoyment – and, thereby, to establish a strong sense of reconciliation for the subject. As Lacan points out, while humanism has tended to deny the 'inhuman' drives of enjoyment through lofty idealizations, the capitalist economy thrives on precisely this element of the inhuman and obscenely parallels it with its own relentless logic of commodification.

The second is that against the fashionable debunking of the Lacanian subject as a negative *a priori* (i.e. no structure without a subject), Žižek insists on the validity of this term. For Žižek, the subject is *both* the ontological gap (the Kantian 'night of the world' of radical self-withdrawal) and the gesture of subjectivation that attempts to close up that gap. Moreover, the very endeavour to fill in this gap, or void, is what generates and sustains it.

The third is that the great calamities and holocausts of our history have not resulted from morbidly embracing 'the void', or something dark in the human soul, but on the contrary from 'our endeavouring to avoid confronting it (the void) and to impose the direct rule of Truth and/or Goodness' (258). However, this does not automatically lead to a politics of deferral, as in the various notions of 'to come'. For Žižek the true revolutionary is not the one who wishes to remain in permanent opposition, but the one who is not afraid to 'pass to the act' and to assume the responsibilities of the Hegelian Master in wielding actual power. In this way, Žižek conceives the possibility of a new type of revolution which does not rely on any ideological promise or elimination of the gap/void, but which seeks to inscribe the latter as a positive feature of a new order of being.

New Theories of Discourse: Laclau, Mouffe and Žižek, by J. Torfing, and *Laclau and Mouffe: The Radical Democratic Imaginary*, by A. M. Smith, explicitly engage with the type of post-Marxist perspective which has been principally developed by Laclau and Mouffe. While both books cover similar ground and are very competent in elaborating the main themes and concepts of post-Marxism, there are clear differences in tone and character. If Torfing's analysis tends to be more theoretical in orientation, Smith is more concerned with politics and the potential for developing a 'radical multiculturalism'.

Smith develops a well-argued critique of essentialism (especially in reference to Marxist orthodoxy) and mobilizes a number of clear and informative examples from contemporary political and cultural life. Smith, however, is critical of certain aspects of Laclau's more recent work and argues that there is a risk that Laclau and Mouffe's 'radical democracy' (with the emphasis here on democracy) might be used to curtail and/or threaten a radical multiculturalism. And in this regard, Smith is perhaps more concerned with defending pluralism and heterogeneity against the universalizing tendencies of democracy. I have some sympathy for Smith's point of view as it highlights the basic tension in modern politics between liberty and equality, and which is also present in Laclau and Mouffe. It is because of the irresolvability of this tension, moreover, that the universalist dimension of radical democracy can (and to some extent *must*) do violence to particularism. Indeed, the consistency of any political order depends on excluding some forms of particularism.

However, I am less sympathetic to Smith's playing down of the opposite risk, i.e. that particularism can become so extreme and withdrawn that it does excessive violence to universalism and thereby destroys the conditions for democracy and social tolerance. Where Smith objects to Laclau's use of the term 'apartheid' as a *logic* which is present in certain extreme forms of particularism, I would tend to support this usage as an accurate characterization. One only has to think of the situation in Kosovo to see how sociocultural particularism can produce an absolute polarization which destroys any basis for universalist discourses of social equality and tolerance. Nevertheless, Smith has produced a compelling work that puts to rest some of the more conservative objections to post-Marxist theory and, at the same time, raises new and important issues.

Torfing's text comprises a comprehensive, if rather literal, explication of the main elements of Laclau and Mouffe's discourse theory. Moving from Gramsci and Althusser to the more recent perspectives of Levinas and Derrida, Torfing explores the practical applications of discourse theory for political study and ends by affirming the utility of a postmodern ethics.

While the scope is impressive, Torfing's contribution is not as irreverent as that of Smith. Indeed, at times the discussion appears to run almost too smoothly in its attempts to hegemonize disparate, and even opposed, theoretical and philosophical currents. Žižek, for example, remains an extremely problematic figure for discourse theory and cannot be unambiguously linked with the perspective of Laclau and Mouffe. As in Ridley Scott's *Alien*, Žižek's status is rather that of the 'supplementary' passenger who resists any automatic integration with the order of discourse theory. In the last decade or so, Žižek has developed a consistent critique of poststructuralism and deconstruction and has repeatedly emphasized the persistence of fantasy and enjoyment that remain, in a certain sense, both before and beyond discourse. Moreover, from the psychoanalytic perspective, the various deconstructive notions of emancipations and democracies 'to come' can be seen as so many hysterical evasions of the event. For Žižek, acting politically means addressing precisely this issue.

I am also unconvinced by Torfing's assertion that 'deconstruction involves an ethical openness towards the alterity of the Other' (280). In the manner of Levinas, Torfing seems to be implying that being open to the heterogeneity of the other is an ethical injunction that can be found in the theory of deconstruction itself. But as Laclau has already pointed out (E. Laclau, *Emancipation(s)*, London: Verso, pp. 77–78), this argument can be refuted on at least two counts. First, if deconstruction affirms an ultimate undecidability then it cannot be made the source of any decision or ethico-political imperative. It is perfectly possible to be a deconstructivist and a fascist. In the sense of Wittgenstein, everything depends on the way in which deconstruction is *used* (the fascist rationale might very well be that because of the deconstructive problems of openness and instability, then closure has to be imposed as strongly as possible). Second, it cannot be a question of an ethical obligation to be open to the other simply on the grounds that s/he is *different* (like an ethnic cleanser, for example). A democratic culture, if it is to remain democratic, will always have to impose a certain closure against anti-democratic otherness. Just as there is the potential of Derrida's democracy 'to come', there is always the threat of opposing forms of 'to come'. In certain circumstances, therefore, the ethical gesture may have to be radically rejectionist. The point is that there is no *theoretical* solution to the vicissitudes of ethico-political discourse.

On these grounds too, I would also tend to disagree with Torfing's contention that 'postmodernity is modernity without illusions' (275). This surely risks producing the same kind of unqualified conception of postmodernity which, although opposite to that of Wood et al., is equally totalizing. While for Wood et al. postmodernity is necessarily full of illusions, for Torfing it would appear to be necessarily anti-illusional. I don't think the question of illusion, and especially ideological illusion, is one that can be solved by adopting either a modern or postmodern orientation. One only has to think of the contemporary phenomenon of postmodern racism, Rorty's 'postmodern bourgeois liberalism' or, indeed, Lyotard's (essentialist) rejection of the metanarrative, to appreciate how the dimension of illusion is constantly resurfacing within the postmodern tradition.

Books Reviewed

Carver, T. (1998). *The Postmodern Marx*. Manchester University Press. pb £12.99. ISBN 0 719 04919 9.

Cowling, M. (ed.) (1998). *The Communist Manifesto: New Interpretations*. Edinburgh University Press. pb £14.95. ISBN 0 748 61035 9.

Homer, S. (1998). *Fredric Jameson: Marxism, Hermeneutics, Postmodernism*. Polity. pb £13.99. ISBN 0 745 61686 0.

Marxism Today. Special Issue, November/December, 1998.

Miklitsch, R. (ed.) (1998). *Psycho-Marxism: Marxism and Psychoanalysis Late in the Twentieth Century*. Special Issue of *The South Atlantic Quarterly*, Spring 1998, Vol. 97, No.2.

Reiss, E. *Marx: A Clear Guide*. Pluto Press. pb £11.99. ISBN 0 745 3101 5.

Smith, A. M. (1998). *Laclau and Mouffe: The Radical Democratic Imaginary*. Routledge. pb £14.99. ISBN 0 415 10060 7.

Torfing, J. (1999). *New Theories of Discourse: Laclau, Mouffe and Žižek*. Blackwell. pb £14.99. ISBN 0 631 19558 0.

Wilde, L. (1998). *Ethical Marxism and its Radical Critics*. Macmillan. £45.00. ISBN 0 333 62054 2.

Wood, E. M. and J. B. Foster (eds.) *In Defense of History: Marxism and the Postmodern Agenda*. Monthly Review Press.

Part II

Culture and Communications

9

Cultural Studies: General

ANGELA WERNDLY

One of the most useful books for lecturers and students is John Storey's second edition of *An Introduction to Cultural Theory and Popular Culture*. As in the first book, this highly accessible introduction to cultural studies focuses upon key moments in the history of the study of popular culture but with an emphasis on its ideological function in the present. Storey explains a wide range of theoretical approaches and key debates through the analysis of specific examples drawn from popular culture including music, film and television. The updated edition incorporates revisions that reflect recent developments in cultural studies. The revised book is enhanced with the addition of new sections on Popular Culture and the Carnivalesque, and Postmodernism and the Puralism of Value. Storey has also expanded five sections: Neo-Gramscian Cultural Studies; Popular Film; Cine-psychoanalysis and Cultural Studies; Feminism as Reading; Postmodernism in the 1960s; and The Cultural Field. The new edition retains the clear and lively style which made the first book a widely used foundational text. It remains the ideal introduction to cultural studies.

Cultural Methodologies edited by Jim McGuigan should be recommended to students who are either doing research or aiming to do research in cultural studies. A book written specifically to help students embarking on postgraduate dissertation or thesis research is a great idea and will be appreciated by those who need clarification on what cultural studies is methodologically. In his introduction McGuigan explains that the book 'does not give a great deal of advice in terms of methodical procedure; instead it addresses methodological issues as they relate to theory and practical research in real conditions'. Speaking from my own experience, this kind of information is exactly what new researchers are looking for when setting out on substantive cultural studies projects. The book is divided into three sections: Methodologies; Researches; and Reflections, and there are contributions from a number of well-known figures including Tony Bennett, Ann Gray, Carolyn Steedman and Michael Green.

The first chapter of the book, written by Douglas Kellner, is at pains to emphasize what he sees as the need to include the Frankfurt School's political economy approach in any major cultural studies project. For a more positive discussion of consumption, Ann Gray's final chapter in this section,

'Learning from Experience: Cultural Studies and Feminism', is an excellent review of a relationship that has been both prolific and tense. Gray discusses feminist contributions to cultural studies that have produced research on women's experiences of culture as well as proposing practical methods, such as the interview, for the researcher who does not want to rely wholly on abstract theory. Finally, Michael Green's excellent concluding chapter 'Working Practices' is a 'how to go about things' piece aimed at 'researchers writing PhDs or engaged in funded research projects'. However, I agree with his belief that much of this 'nuts and bolts' contribution will also be useful to students involved in writing dissertations on BA and MA programmes.

Cultural Studies in Question, edited by Marjorie Ferguson and Peter Golding, is a collection of thirteen chapters by some of the most prominent scholars in the field including Nicholas Garnham, David Morley, Jim Mc-Guigan and Angela McRobbie. Their aim is to critically evaluate cultural studies, focusing on its contribution to the understanding of media, communication and popular culture.

As a body of work, one of the main issues the volume addresses is the conflict between cultural studies and the political economy of culture. Jim McGuigan, for example, claims that the study of the popular in cultural studies has become fixated on consumption at the expense of political economy. Arguing that consumptionist cultural populism 'now provides little space for transformative struggle of any kind', McGuigan critiques Fiske's analysis of Madonna to illustrate his view. Asserting that Fiske produces a simple inversion of the mass culture critique in his 'discovery' that Madonna subverts 'patriarchal systems of representation', McGuigan suggests Kellner's (1995) multidimensional approach which combines interpretive and political economy perspectives, offers a more satisfactory explanation of Madonna as an icon.

The editors Marjorie Ferguson and Peter Golding support McGuigan's pessimistic view insisting that cultural studies often 'loses all purchase on the institutional and structural context of cultural practice'. Indeed, cultural studies' supposed obsession with textual analysis and its failure to engage with economics and matters of cultural policy is another theme of the book. The authors are all careful to point out that they are not advocating a return to elitist and disparaging conceptions of culture but a pessimistic tone pervades most of the chapters. One of the most convincing pieces is Angela McRobbie's interesting contribution 'The Es and the Anti-Es: New Questions for Feminism and Cultural Studies' in which she also argues for new directions in cultural studies that involve looking back. Calling for a more applied feminist cultural studies, she urges a return to the 'three Es': the empirical, the experiential and the ethnographic 'alongside and in relation to what has been happening in the theoretical world of anti-essentialism, psychoanalysis and poststructuralism'. The book will be of interest to lecturers and students who are looking for reviews and clarification on current issues and debates about contemporary cultural studies and its direction.

These issues are also discussed in Lawrence Grossberg's introduction ' "Birmingham" in America' in *Bringing It All Back Home*. Responding to the criticism that cultural studies ignores economics and is little more than a populist celebration of culture, Grossberg points out that often such criticisms are selective to say the least and that cultural studies in general does not assume that all pleasure is good or politically progressive. However, Grossberg does agree that cultural studies 'must confront the globalization of culture' and he also challenges its direction, particularly its reconstitution around questions of identity and difference.

The book contains fifteen essays that have been written over a twenty-year period. They reflect Grossberg's own intellectual development as well as his 'fraught and ambivalent' relationship to cultural studies. The book is divided into three sections: 'Cultural Theory, Cultural Studies'; 'Locating Cultural Studies'; and 'Subjects, Audience and Identities'. It is an impressive collection of essays by one of cultural studies' leading scholars.

The year 1997 also saw the publication of a collection of work by Phil Cohen. *Rethinking the Youth Question: Education, Labour and Cultural Studies* brings together material produced over a twenty-year period from 1969 to 1989. Cohen employs the useful and engaging strategy of providing an introduction to each chapter 'which tells a story about its genesis . . . so as to anchor each chapter to its other scene – that once familiar time and place whence it came, but which has now become a foreign country, and to the author as much as the reader'. As a collection of work, this book, like Grossberg's, is a book that should be of interest to anyone involved in cultural studies. It includes published works (many of which are difficult to trace) and three substantive unpublished pieces as well as a highly readable introduction in which Cohen integrates autobiographical and political contexts in his discussion of the collection.

The book *Music and Cultural Theory* written by John Shepherd and Peter Wicke is recommended by Grossberg who, on the dust cover, says:

> This book actually moves popular music studies forward and offers a significant challenge to cultural theory. It is one of the most important and exciting contributions in recent years to the study of popular music and popular culture.

In this book the central issue that the authors' focus upon is that 'sound in music functions in a manner distinct from sound in language' but as a signifying practice, music has been theorized as though it were language. Further, cultural studies usually examines the 'linguistic discourses that are constructed around musical practices' rather than music itself. The authors develop this argument through their examination and evaluation of a range of approaches to music including linguistics, poststructuralism and psychoanalysis. In the final section Shepherd and Wicke integrate musicology with cultural studies developing their own challenging theory of music as a material form of human expression.

John Street's *Politics & Popular Culture* is an examination of the collapse of the distinction between political power and popular culture. The book is divided into three sections: 'The Political and the Popular'; 'Governing the Global'; and 'Political Theory/Cultural Theory'. The first section, in which Street explains the ways in which popular culture is always political, is arguably the most impressive of the book. Written in a clear and engaging style and with some excellent examples of politics as popular culture, this section is well-suited for students in cultural studies:

In 1996, Tony Blair, leader of the Labour Party, gave a speech of fulsome tribute. It was not to celebrate some great event or tradition in the labour movement's history, nor was it to announce plans for export-led growth or indeed for any other worthy political initiative. He was speaking at a music industry awards ceremony, and he was there to praise David Bowie ... He was working on his image; he was soliciting votes; he was using popular culture as part of his political armoury.

Street's final section, in which he discusses political theories of culture, is less coherent. He argues that John Storey's rejection of Jim McGuigan's call to reinsert qualitative judgement and instead ask more 'interesting questions' seems to either offer an uncritical populism or push him back into the arms of the very thesis he begins by criticizing. But to say this is to misread Storey's proposition that we should not have unquestioned authority to say what is or is not worthy and that particular texts are not in *themselves* radical, rather, radical meanings may or may not be produced in their consumption.

Balmurli Natrajan and Radhika Parameswaran's 'Contesting the Politics of Ethnography: Towards an Alternative Knowledge Production' (*Journal of Communication Inquiry* 21:1 27–53) is a discussion on the need for research that does not depend solely on knowledge produced within academia. Their view that 'distorted and disempowering representations of Orientalist knowledge' can be challenged through 'ethnographies of everyday life' is illustrated effectively through the use of examples of ethnographic research on the lives of Third World women that have produced 'alternative knowledge'.

Michael Pickering's *History, Experience and Cultural Studies* is a discussion of the 'stand off' between social history and cultural studies. Pickering's project is to 'foster a more interactive relationship between history and cultural studies'. *The Emergence of Cultural Studies 1945–65* by Tom Steele traces the history of British cultural studies in the work of adult educators in the immediate pre-war and post-war period. The book begins with Steele's argument that rather than coming from a university school of English, British cultural studies emerged through the work of 'adult educationalists who were shifting politics into the realm of symbolic values in the immediate post-war period'. The rise of English studies and pedagogic 'wars' are two of the main topics of the book and over three chapters the book also analyses the individual contributions of Richard Hoggart, E. P. Thompson and Raymond Williams 'to the emergence of cultural studies as an adult educational project'. Despite its examination of well-known topics and founding figures in cultural studies, Steele's book covers new ground and is both informative and interesting. Indeed, Steele draws upon unique archive material throughout his work to produce new areas for teachers and students of the historical aspect of cultural studies.

Books Reviewed

Cohen, Phil. *Rethinking the Youth Question: Education, Labour and Cultural Studies.* Macmillan Press Ltd. pp. 414 pb £18.99. ISBN 0 333 63148 X.

Grossberg, Lawrence. *Bringing It All Back Home.* Duke University Press. pp. 431 pb £18.99. ISBN 0 8223 1916 0.

Ferguson, Marjorie, and Peter Golding eds. *Cultural Studies in Question.* SAGE Publications Ltd. pp. 247. pb £13.99. ISBN 0 8039 7924 X.

McGuigan, Jim, ed. *Cultural Methodologies.* SAGE Publications Ltd. pp. 215 pb £13.99. ISBN 0 8039 7485 X.

Pickering, Michael. *History, Experience and Cultural Studies.* Macmillan Press Ltd. pp. 274 hb £45.00, pb £13.95. ISBN 0 333 62110 7.

Shepherd, John, and Peter Wicke. *Music and Cultural Theory.* Polity Press. pp. 230. hb £45.00, pb £13.95. ISBN 0 7456 0864 7.

Steele, Tom. *The Emergence of Cultural Studies 1945–65 Cultural Politics, Adult Education and the English Question.* Lawrence and Wishart Limited. pp. 217. pb £14.99. ISBN 0 85315 826 6.

Storey, John. *An Introduction to Cultural Theory and Popular Culture.* Prentice Hall/Harvester Wheatsheaf. pp. 269. pb £13.99. ISBN 0 13 269218 X.

Street, John. *Politics & Popular Culture.* Polity Press. pp. 212. hb £39.50, pb £12.95. ISBN 0 7456 1214 8.

10

Media Studies

JEFFREY WALSH

This chapter has four sections: 1. Research Methods; 2. Media and Cultural Identities; 3. Audience Studies; 4. Interdisciplinary Approaches.

1. Research Methods

Media studies, together with its related disciplinary fields such as mass communication research, is increasingly re-examining its methodological principles. The parameters of such debates are not exclusively intellectual, and are at least partly driven by an academic climate that emphasizes measurable research output and encourages the recruitment of increased numbers of undergraduates. The organization of this chapter is intended to exemplify some of these concerns about the coherence and identity of media studies. Several of the books reviewed question whether systematic approaches can offer a specific disciplinary core, while others employ wider interdisciplinary perspectives which demonstrate the cogency of comparative and cross-disciplinary study.

Barry Gunter's *Measuring Bias on Television* develops the author's longstanding research into television news and current affairs. It also analyses a wide range of evidence from the most prominent news scholars in Britain and the United States. Gunter's premise is that no one approach to measuring bias is 'necessarily more legitimate or valid than any other', and he proposes that the most significant theories and research methodologies should be studied comparatively. *Measuring Bias on Television* succinctly evaluates the relative strengths and weaknesses of the most influential of these approaches, and provides a comprehensive overview of two decades of scholarship into one of the most relevant topics in contemporary media studies.

In seeking to examine 'the issue of television's impartiality or bias with special reference to news and current affairs' the volume establishes in its opening chapter operational definitions which link the concept of bias with other associated terms such as objectivity. These definitions, although problematical, set ground rules for exploring such cognitive criteria as accuracy, completeness or factualness, and for differentiating them from more evaluative modes of discrimination which seek to measure balance, neutrality, ideology, propaganda etc. Gunter's own model for analysing the issue of impartiality concentrates upon two broad bands of criteria: output criteria including the appraisal of narrative content and styles of presentation; and audience criteria which surveys research into the opinions, competencies and expectations of viewers.

The middle chapters of the book focus upon the output of news, and upon how news broadcasts are received and understood by audiences. Both of these topics are analysed from cognitive and evaluative perspectives. In assessing cognitive aspects of news output, for example, the volume adduces ways of appraising performance quality: these range from methods of testing the breadth of information in a news presentation, to examining programme formats, journalistic practices and values. Research carried out by a range of scholars suggests how the news agenda may 'exhibit certain biases in relation to the selection of certain news categories and the way they are presented, thus determining what audiences will think about or learn of current news events and issues'. The detailed evidence that supports it endorses the validity of this hypothesis.

The most compelling parts of *Measuring Bias on Television* are those which consider audience-based assessment. The way cohorts of viewers respond to broadcast news is immensely complex and contradictory, and measuring such responses is necessarily fraught with difficulties. Gunter's discussion understandably encounters problems in analysing the television audience's subjective impressions about the accuracy, completeness and relevance of factual content: clearly the widely divergent backgrounds of viewers and their idiosyncrasies render the measurement of more 'subjective' evidence liable to inexactness.

In contrast research into the more cognitive aspects of bias from an 'objective' audience perspective seems to hold more promise. Studies are designed which test memory and comprehension in apparently significant ways: among the factors that demonstrably influence viewer understanding are: the packaging of news, the structure of texts, sequencing, writing style, visual narration, and whether stories are presented thematically or episodically, anecdotally or contextually. Measuring the way viewers perceive the news to be balanced, neutral, credible, impartial or hegemonic is thus at least partly dependent upon how it is presented. The qualitative aspects of news communication for audiences are still to a large extent determined by professional journalistic practice according to Gunter's thesis.

Like other approaches to studying the media, semiotics is an imperfect analytical method, yet it provides a powerful resource for theorists through its capacity to explore both verbal and visual sign systems. Jonathan Bignell's critical overview, *Media Semiotics: An Introduction*, is one of the few books to critique the methodology of semiotics by evaluating it against other contingent academic approaches such as psychoanalytic criticism, ethnographic research, theories of ideology, film theory and postmodern studies. This comparative mode of study is applied to a variety of media, including advertising, magazines, newspapers, television, and cinema, thereby allowing distinctions to be made between semiotics' methods in exploring one medium, say newspapers, vis-à-vis its procedures for analysing the more elaborate codes of television. The volume considers representative texts in order to evaluate the claims made for semiotics by early theorists such as Barthes and later ones such as Metz and Eco.

During the course of *Media Semiotics* a variety of semiotic methods is demonstrated through a sophisticated range of examples ranging from a VW Golf advertisement to analyses of television news programmes and Hollywood films including *Four Weddings and a Funeral* and *Unforgiven*. The author proposes that semiotics benefits considerably from being studied alongside other methodologies which support its approach such as psychoanalysis and film theory, and suggests that it gains also from being contrasted with those approaches which seem to undermine it theoretically, for example, audience research and postmodernism. In an account of the collision between postmodernism and semiotics, the latter assuming a set of meanings signified by discernible signs, Bignell offers a fruitful discussion of television's ways of encoding the subject position of viewers 'by locking their signs together in particular ways'. The polysemic nature of television is thus illuminated by the concept of multi-accentuality and its generation of multiple subject positions. Here semiotics is demonstrably enhanced by a different yet related approach to television and its audience, which suggests that both signs and texts have a fluid and dynamic identity: 'meanings are perpetually being made but are at the same time perpetually being fractured from within, scattered by their interaction with other meanings.'

For a scholar of media theory a coherent and systematic understanding of semiotics is a valuable analytical tool. Bignell's lucid book assists such an understanding by demonstrating how major forms such as film construct diverse meanings through specific codes and sign systems.

In a broad evaluation of the nature and validity of the data produced by mass communication research James D. Halloran asks fundamental questions about whether 'the scientific approach' is appropriate or indeed possible as a method for studying the field. Halloran's sceptical overview is one of a book of essays by his colleagues from the Leicester Centre for Mass Communication Research, and his is a salutary admonition, arguing as it does for critical eclecticism and a holistic approach which takes cognizance of 'several disciplinary positions'. This recognition of other scholarship from the areas of literary criticism, social philosophy, the arts, education and even 'within social science (for example, psychology, sociology, economics, anthropology and political science)' will provide, he says, other necessary 'empirical, theoretical, critical and humanistic perspectives'.

Halloran's salient questions about the boundaries and linkages of social scientific approaches frame the attempts by his colleagues to seek out more objective, rigorous and systematic research methods. *Mass Communication Research Methods* is a co-authored book by Anders Hansen, Simon Cottle, Ralph Negrine and Chris Newbold, which 'aims to provide an introduction to key research methods and approaches in the study of media and mass communication processes'. The perspective taken by the joint authors is to exemplify a number of 'coherent' and 'productive' methods in action, after firstly locating them theoretically and historically in their contexts. Acknowledging that their fundamental approach is sociological, they hypothesize that within this disciplinary dimension each topic is best served by 'those methods, or combinations of methods, which can light up the most angles and dimensions of what are invariably multidimensional and complex processes and phenomena'. For the researcher pragmatic advice is also offered on the systematic steps which help to guide one through a research project.

The various research procedures explored in the volume range from well-known approaches such as content analysis and audience research to less well-known methods such as 'epistemological analysis' which examines how visuals contribute to the underpinning and validation of knowledge constructed by media conventions and genres. Much of the work demonstrated builds upon established practices such as those adapted from structuralism and semiotics, which are then deployed to evaluate the narratives and generic patterns commonly encountered in still and moving images. The pseudo-scientific structuralist methodology applied to folk tales and westerns gives way in the later chapters of the book to examples of statistical techniques, which measure data from audience research and explain computer-assisted handling and analysis. There is also a useful appendix, which lists sources of information for researchers in mass communication.

It is stereotypical to critique a book co-authored by four men and advocating a highly systematic perspective upon mass communication research as masculinist, yet the gendered image of such a methodology as positivist, absolutist and patriarchal is sometimes loosely bandied about in feminist discourse. Certainly the emphasis upon methodological rigour and 'objective' models of evaluation gives Hanson, Cottle, Negrine and Newbold's study a very different ground tone from a collection of essays by women edited by Charlotte Brunsdon, Julie D'Acci and Lynn Spigel.

Feminist Television Criticism: A Reader sets out to 'trace some of the contradictions and reciprocities of the relationships between feminism and television that have emerged over the last twenty years, with a concentration upon the anglophone US/UK axis'. The volume is organized to suggest the evolution of feminist scholarship over the last three decades, moving from textual analysis which studies representations of women to 'audience and reception contexts', and finally to more problematical issues surrounding 'the public/private divide' at the heart of much contemporary feminist research. Brunsdon and her co-editors have made a thoughtful selection of material which brings together work from a diversity of sources. The book's identity is best illustrated by the way it combines case studies of programmes, icons and specific genres with more theoretically speculative essays such as Charlotte Brunsdon's 'Identity in Feminist Television Criticism' or Annette Kuhn's 'Women's Genres; Melodrama, Soap Opera and Theory'. These wider-ranging pieces contextualize the papers on feminist icons such as Kathleen Rowe's celebration of Roseanne, 'Unruly Woman as Domestic Goddess' or audience studies such as Lyn Thomas's 'In Love With Inspector Morse' which explores how 'feminist subcultures' consume 'quality television'.

As in any good compilation of feminist research those essays which are politically controversial tend to stand out. *Feminist Television Criticism* offers four or five of such polemical articles, notably Jacqueline Bobo and Ellen Seiter's study of *The Women of Brewster Place* which rebukes white feminists for neglecting to study the relationships between women of colour and television, and Prabha Krishnan and Anita Dighee's 'Affirmation and Denial: Construction of Femininity on Indian Television' which provides an Asian perspective. Perhaps the outstanding essay in the book is Purnima

Mankekar's study of Indian television's treatment of *The Mahabharata* which analyses one particular episode involving the public disrobing of one of the epic's most significant female characters, Draupadi, wife of the five Pandava brothers. Mankekar, in considering the multiple interpretations of this episode, explores its cultural repercussions for Indian women and discusses how it enabled them to understand their own oppression in an increasingly nationalist state where Hindu chauvinism is rife.

2. Media and Cultural Identities

The part played by media in shaping cultural identity may perhaps be conceptualized in the struggle between programme makers seeking to maintain indigenous traditions and those wider global forces motivated by international capitalism that seek to appropriate them. The national and local appear to be everywhere under threat from internationally standardized formats.

Compared to some research-orientated texts, Andrew Crisell's *An Introductory History of British Broadcasting* appears untheoretical and essentialist. The author who is known principally for his book, *Understanding Radio*, chooses to address what he calls 'the broadcasting process and the way in which audiences experience it' and to construct 'a crowded chronology of events, facts, personalities and trends around a simple account of technological evolution'. Crisell's central thesis is that it is the 'actual character' of radio and television that primarily determines content rather than the operations of institutions. *An Introductory History of British Broadcasting* focuses, therefore, upon the emergent nature of radio and television from the early 1920s with emphasis upon how these two media became distinctive from other forms such as print journalism and cinema, how the activity of audiences shaped their different identities, and how the convergence of media is accelerating in contemporary culture.

Crisell's historical survey which is structured in the loosely impressionistic manner of a continuous narrative lacks sophistication for a reader alert to the nuances of advanced media theory. It does, however, have compensations. Punctuating the factual and informational summaries there are passages of opinion and interpretation which offer valuable insights into the growth of broadcasting institutions and the connections which radio and television have to wider socio-political contexts. For example, there is a thoughtful discussion running throughout the volume about the resistance of radio to attempts whether by early Reithians, high-minded intellectuals in the post-war years, or regulators in the last two decades to impose blueprints that ignored listeners' preferences. Crisell's examination of the evolution of local radio is extremely illuminating, demonstrating that no matter how much such ideas as mixed programming are advocated as a desirable concept, listeners ultimately exert more pressure than members of committees, no matter how worthy the latter's intentions or their intellectual disdain for commercial imperatives. Such tendentious ideas, Crisell suggests, reveal a truth, that the history of broadcasting relates, albeit fortuitously, to the principle of democratic choice.

The issue of whether or not television and radio are implicitly or explicitly democratic is examined intermittently. In a key chapter entitled 'Television and its Social Effects' a balanced debate critiques the 'equivocations' of television, its banality and tendency to elide fictionality and 'the diffuseness and indeterminacy of real life'. The author, however, takes a sanguine view of its potential: it is, in some ways, 'a strongly democratizing medium' which creates a 'global pressure towards open government, democracy and fair play'.

Audiences during the last two decades are credited with shaping this more favourable climate. In analysing the impact of the Peacock Committee, the advent of cable and satellite, and the outcome of the 1990 Broadcasting Act, the author chronicles the ambiguous relationships between established broadcasters such as the BBC and ITV, media moguls such as Murdoch and Turner, and 'millions upon millions of viewers of every social background' who consume their products individually and privately. Crisell apparently has faith that misdeeds and tyrannies will be exposed and hierarchies demystified by broadcast media. It is a comforting hypothesis, although not necessarily a convincing one.

The ecology of broadcasting is rapidly changing, nowhere more so than in the problems facing the makers of documentaries for television. On British television during the last two or three years there has been a perceptible shift from formats which necessitate a long gestation period of research towards softer-focus programmes that foreground human interest and popular entertainment values. The drive for rating is, of course, responsible for this and also the further erosion of public service broadcasting. Some of these issues are treated by Richard Kilborn and John Izod in *An Introduction to Television Documentary: Confronting Reality*, one of Manchester University Press's valuable series of books on documentary and ethnographic film.

The volume is primarily concerned with 'giving an account of the ways in which documentary has had to adjust to the requirements of the television medium', and it explores contemporary practices in documentary programming. Written in an accessible manner, Kilborn and Izod's study synthesizes existing research rather than offering new conceptual or theoretical insights. It has the virtues of a soundly written introductory work, which provides synopses of the debates currently surrounding documentary as a medium struggling to remain viable. Ranging over an orthodox agenda, including the integrity of the form, its relationships with 'real-world' issues, the strategies employed by practitioners, the power exerted by institutions upon producers and artistic directors, and the responses and changing tastes of audiences, *An Introduction to Television Documentary* fulfils its objective of differing slightly from other projects by 'showing the full impact of television on documentary's development', and placing attention on 'the broadcaster-audience interface'. The book's emphasis upon interpenetrations of form in evolving docu-drama formats is also interesting, as is its attention to both the threats and the opportunities open to documentary producers, for example, through niche programming such as the Discovery and History Channels. The co-authors are cautiously optimistic that new technology will contribute to the genre's survival.

Global Television and Film by Colin Hoskins, Stuart McFadyen and Adam Finn deploys the research methodologies of economics and business research to explore the international trade in audio-visual products. The volume addresses some pivotal factors in the global market for television programmes and feature films; for example, why does the United States dominate the business? Why do certain genres, for example, action drama, prevail over others? How are pricing mechanisms decided for the export of audio-visual goods? Are there ways to maintain and ensure competitiveness when initial production costs are so high? Does dumping take place? What are the economics affecting cultural transference, when one country's television series, for example, is exported to another country? As well as this kind of hard-nosed business approach the authors also venture opinions about issues of regulation, public policy, cultural imperialism, and the economic evolution of media in a future where convergence and digitization prevail.

The microeconomic mode of analysis adopted offers insights into the pricing of television and film. The enormous costs of making original series may be offset, for instance, by having a vast indigenous market such as that in the United States and China. When a programme made in America is exported these start-up costs may be recouped, although there is what Hoskins, McFadyen and Finn call a 'cultural discount' when one nation's audio-visual products are reproduced within a different country: this reduces the profit of the exporting country but ensures economic viability to importers. The sharing of production costs through joint national production is another essential strategy for television companies, extending to three or more markets, those of the two partner countries plus export potential. In these cases linguistic and cultural factors are significant, and countries such as the United States, Britain and Canada have an inherent advantage over producers in Japan whose indigenous television culture is too esoteric for wider global distribution.

Difficulties associated with the globalization of television, film, video and other audio-visual products are, according to the authors, frequently of a qualitative nature: should a government intervene, for example, to support the growth of a native industry in television or film if cultural 'benefits' to society as a whole are perceived to accrue from it? Are theories of public interest television susceptible to economic criteria? Are regulators necessary: if they are, should they be industry-controlled or external? The book, in general, argues that each case should be carefully assessed on its merits, although it supports the idea that television programmes and films contribute centrally to the 'preservation and promotion of distinctive values', thus nurturing 'the well-being of a nation state'.

Hoskins, McFadyen and Finn espouse the values of 'mainstream economics' in considering matters of international trade agreements, protectionism, and regulation of programme content. They advance orthodox free market principles, that over-regulation inhibits a smaller country's media industry, as does protectionism. What matters is the fostering of creative talent and the harnessing of business and imaginative skills. From an economic perspective the possession of libraries of material, recognizable brand names such as Disney or the BBC, and copyright of classics, are vital in the globally competitive market. A stream of new talent is crucial in an international environment where pirating and unauthorized duplication is increasingly threatening the concept of 'intellectual property'.

When *Global Television and Film* looks to the future its speculations envisage a fluidity of economic circumstances. Although the United States is predicted to be market leader, its hegemony may be soon challenged by China. Other challenges to established hierarchies will be located in digitization, the exponential spread of the Internet, and the accelerating process of media evolution: all will weaken the power of regulators. Further deregulation, decentralization and cost-cutting will erode monopolies and shift power to individual consumers. A lowering of transaction costs and the costs of information services will radically alter the global landscape in media trade, destroying further the 'distance' between users and distributors, enhancing audience sovereignty and speeding up the search for the ultimate 'killer basket' which will instrumentalize media convergence for untold profit. *Global Television and Film* is a scholarly book, ranging from global economic considerations to microeconomic details such as the reasons why themed television channels are extremely viable while dubbed TV programmes are less so.

Internationalizing the news is a concept also fundamental to Ted Turner's high sense of mission which is celebrated rather uncritically in Don M. Flournoy and Robert K. Stewart's study of the master, *CNN: Making News in the Global Market*. Providing an insider's perspective, Flournoy and Stewart's volume chronicles the history of CNN from a company based in Atlanta to a 'global entity, not just an American company with linkages abroad'. Inevitably the authors address the 'vision' of Ted Turner, his idealism, strong opinions and determination to transcend American imperialism by foregrounding the interests and values of indigenous cultures and 'humanizing' them through effective journalism.

Flournoy and Stewart argue a coherent, although not an impartial case for CNN's internationalism. The company is described as being like a 'family' imbued with the ethics of its founder whose principal belief is that 'social responsibility and making money can go hand in hand'. CNN's nurturing of its brand, its negotiations with different governments such as the Chinese, and its investment in state-of-the-art technology, for example in satellites, computer technology and the Internet, is adduced to explain what is called 'The Turner Paradox'. This is conceptualized as having enough entrepreneurial acumen to compete with hungry competitors like Rupert Murdoch, and conversely an enlightened advocacy of environmentalism, good international relationships between east and west, and numerous charitable and humanitarian projects. *CNN: Making the News in the Global Market* reads like a paean to global free marketing in news media, and is a guide to CNN's innovations, for example, its ethnically diverse programme, *World Report* which airs stories by local reporters in over eighty countries all over the world.

3. Audience Studies

This section discusses two works from the United States which differ significantly in their scope and methodology. *The National Television Violence Study* (*Volume One*) is the first of three annual studies which intend to monitor changes over a precise period of time in order to show how 'problematic' depictions of violence on television influence audiences. The project which began in 1994 combines the input of leading media scholars from four US universities, the University of California at Santa Barbara, the University of Texas at Austin, the universities of Wisconsin, Madison, and North Carolina, Chapel Hill. The common assumption underlying the research is that television violence is a 'partially preventable social ill', and has affinities with parallel public health issues, especially those concerned with mental well being. Broadly the study has two aims: to identify the contextual elements that surround violent television depictions which notably increase the risk of a harmful effect upon the audience; and to analyse empirically 'the television environment' so as to demonstrate the character and extent of portrayals of violence, especially the 'relative presence' of the most disturbing representations.

Building upon social science research methods, the *National Television Violence Study* is primarily driven by content analysis conducted on an impressively wide scale. Rather pompously the project claims that its launch-pad was 'a review of the entire body of existing scientific knowledge, regarding the impact of televised violence'. Its conclusions and recommendations inevitably do not justify such claims, although they are proactive in tone, and aim to promote 'anti-violence', mainly through social learning and relevant public service announcements. Because the project is arguably the most comprehensive ever conducted to study the connection between television violence and the audience response of young people its findings are of special interest.

These conclusions contain only one positive outcome: that television violence is usually not explicit or graphic. On the adverse side, violent programmes do not warn against violence's ill effects: perpetrators frequently go unpunished, and anti-violent themes are rare. Research demonstrates that the context in which violence is presented poses risks for young viewers.

Practical suggestions from experts for mitigating the effects of violence on television upon young people testifies to the belief by American academics in the medium's power to exert malign influence. E. Graham McKinley, a researcher and teacher of journalism, has explored other effects of TV on young adults in *Beverly Hills, 90210: Television, Gender and Identity*. Her premise is that this prime-time soap, which narrates the lives of affluent girl students who attend two upmarket fictitious schools in southern California, has a major impact upon the lifestyle, values, opinion and behaviour of its young female viewers. By drawing on an eclectic mix of theoretical approaches, including discourse analysis, cultural studies, social constructionism, and poststructuralist feminism McKinley analyses the interview responses to the show of thirty-six girls and young women whose ages ranged from eleven to twenty two. The sample consisted of a range of 'socio-economic classes' and was primarily white, with three Asian respondents.

When the author outlines her sampling techniques which seem to be highly informal when compared, say, with the more rigorous methodologies of social scientists towards mass communication research (*pace* Halloran and the Leicester Centre) she slips into what the book's publicity calls its 'intimate style' which 'has the urgency of a heart to heart conversation' with plenty of 'rich anecdotal moments and revelations of self'. The unease arising from these claims is not entirely allayed by the volume's mode of study which has no qualms about approving of readers who skip difficult theoretical chapters and concentrate upon less challenging topics. Perhaps the desire to reach a popular readership is responsible for this unwise advice which undermines the author's theoretical procedures.

The inconsistency pointed up here does at times detract from the integrity of the study. It draws upon complex theoretical work, and yet its address to the reader is contradictory as the authorial voice intermittently moves from academic discourse to a chatty and impressionistic mode which tends to encourage essentialism rather than critical engagement. Despite this, *Beverly Hills, 90210* reaches some firm conclusions, in general by reinforcing what McKinley calls 'hegemony theory'. In a summary chapter, 'Swimming with the Tide', she suggests that her data confirms the work of other cultural theorists that the active engagement of young women viewers 'contributed to perpetuating an impossible and disadvantaging standard for female identity'. Patriarchal and capitalist culture, therefore, through processes of enculturation win consent to hegemonic definitions of femininity.

4. Interdisciplinary Approaches

The wide remit of media studies, its amorphous nature and continuing incursions into adjoining terrain, is enacted in an increasing number of books which subvert disciplinary boundaries. Many include the term 'media' in their subtitles, others fight out intellectual battles within their own area of mass communication research such as advertising or journalism. This section considers five such studies which typify cross-disciplinary or interdisciplinary approaches to media studies.

Timothy Murray in *Drama and Trauma: Specters of Race and Sexuality in Performance Videos and Art* examines 'the artistic struggle over traumatic fantasies of race, gender, sexuality and power'. His analysis ranges from psychoanalytic and epistemological studies of Shakespeare to gendered and postcolonialist readings of contemporary drama, and exploration of visual culture including television, installation art and video. The erudite cross-disciplinary methodology of the volume which draws upon psychoanalysis, contemporary philosophy and literary theory, fuels the media-orientated discussions in its final part which is entitled 'Televisual Fear'.

Murray here refers to 'television's drive to control the world picture', and explores its ideological impact upon perception and consciousness as evidenced through artistic practice. Mary Kelly's installation *Gloria Patri*, for example, 'provides a polished reflection on the media blitz that subjected all telespectators, willing or not, to the censored images and soundbites of the Gulf War'. Televisual 'incorporations', including video and digital photography, teleconstructions and computer graphics, are shown to construct new versions of reality. Throughout Murray's book the image of Shakespeare's canonical work revisioned experimentally by television and video acts as a summative metaphor for his primary thesis.

In a way that parallels Murray's interest in 'interdisciplinary perspectives not delineated or curtailed in terms of content or research methodology'

Susan J. Drucker and Gary Gumpert's edited collection, *Voices in the Street: Explorations in Gender, Media and Public Space*, recognizes media technology as a vital agency in changing consciousness because 'contemporary media offer convenient, cost-effective, safe and fascinating options to the social life once available almost exclusively in public space'. In examining the construction of gender and its interactions with public space *Voices in the Street* emphasizes how television, telephone, video and electronic media collapse the boundaries between public and private domains.

In her essay 'The Telephone and Women's Place' Lana Rakow, for example, considers how the lives of women in a midwestern town in the USA have been shaped by their use of the telephone. Her conclusions are broadly that they are not radically empowered in an economic sense by their use of the telephone, although their 'creative' use of it allows them to transcend 'both the barriers of space that once dissolved family ties and the distinction between family and work'. The telephone itself is gendered differently in the public and private worlds.

A similarly ambiguous conclusion is reached by Jonathan David Tankel and Jane Banks in studying whether Lifetime Television, a niche US television service primarily aimed at women viewers, constitutes a gendered electronic space allowing female viewers to connect with other actual women. The authors conclude that Lifetime Television is only 'an initial step in that direction, waiting only for true interactive capability to fulfill its potential'.

Other research, pursuing a similar line of enquiry such as an essay on the attempts of women to communicate with each other both locally and globally, holds out equally tantalizing prospects about the construction of an international feminism through the use of radio which will promote women's issues that 'transcend national, race, class, and ethnic dividing lines'. One station called FIRE, established in Costa Rica, offers a putative model for such a development, although the limitations of radio as a medium may hamper such aspirations, especially in US and European cultures. In these more affluent parts of the world it is likely that cyberspace may become the genuinely open medium that utopians aspire to. The final essay in *Voices in the Street* addresses this issue, while warning that information superhighways are at present perpetuating existing gender biases.

Another book which recognizes the significance of media in fashioning our perceptions of ourselves is Arthur Asa Berger's *Narratives in Popular Culture, Media and Everyday Life* which, as its title might imply, draws upon well-known theories of narrativity ranging from Aristotle through to Propp, Bal, Barthes, Scholes, Bakhtin and Chatman. Using these and some related Freudian techniques of analysis loosely applied, Berger considers a number of media products including comic books, television commercials, a radio script and film narratives. While some of these analyses are illuminating such as the discussion of the Macintosh '1984' television commercial which promotes Macintosh computers, others are constrained by structuralist approaches as in the author's exegesis of Zinnermann's film *High Noon*.

Berger's book is useful as a textbook which popularizes narrative theory, and has the quality of succinctness: its treatment of narrative in comics is both informative and a model of brevity. By providing a glossary of terms relating to the study of narrative, and an appendix which recommends 'simulations, activities, games and exercises' the author reinforces the volume's pedagogical value as an introductory study.

Advertising, which supplies one brief case study in Berger's book, is a major concern of *Buy This Book: Studies in Advertising and Consumption*, edited by Mica Nava, Andrew Blake, Ian MacRury, and Barry Richards. This volume, in a manner similar to those already discussed in this section, foregrounds its interdisciplinarity. Through a central concern with consumption the study 'both interrogates assumptions within specific disciplines and demands a reassessment of the relationships between disciplines'. Such disciplines include media studies alongside art and design history, psychoanalysis, cultural studies, social history, philosophy, sociology, politics and business studies.

Buy This Book is structured around six themes which all address the practices or ethics of consumption: these are: theories and histories; the advertising industry; case studies; textual strategies; readers as producers of meaning; and consumption and identity. Because the study of consumption has no disciplinary core it acts as a 'meeting place' for these other disciplines, a 'multidisciplinary site for critical analysis which makes possible theoretical links across subjects'. This lack of a unified theoretical project is posited in Nava's study as presenting significant opportunities for analysing the workings of commodity capitalism, and the 'disciplinary transformations' manifested in the collection further this aim. Celia Lury and Alan Wardle, for example, in their essay, 'Investments in the Imaginary Consumer: Conjectures Regarding Power, Knowledge and Adversity' refer to a spectrum of methodologies, alluding to the relationship between 'social scientific and marketing knowledges'. This interface between academic and commercial discourse is pursued in dialectical fashion throughout the essay and, indeed, throughout other pieces in the volume, thereby giving theory a cutting edge when discussing an increasingly consumerized society.

The role of newspaper and television journalists in articulating British cultural identity is one of the issues addressed in *A Journalism Reader*, edited by Michael Bromley and Tom O'Malley, which contains 'a series of inter-connected readings on specific topics within, and of specific views on journalism', and aims to cultivate understanding of journalism's role in 'the development over time of cultures commonly given the epithets "democratic", "popular", "mass" and "consumer"'. In their preface to the volume the editors write of their objectives to 'foster cross and interdisciplinary contacts and approaches.' Although not as overtly apparent as the interdisciplinarity of *Buy This Book*, such eclecticism of method is operationally effective.

The broad selection of varied pieces, including material from previously unpublished sources, constitutes a critical conspectus of the practice and ideologies of journalism. From different perspectives and traditions the writers represented include philosophers, historians, cultural theorists, novelists, academic specialists on journalism, and journalists themselves. To a general reader two aspects of the collection are perhaps of most interest: writing by canonical figures such as George Orwell, James Cameron, Nicholas Tomalin and C. P. Scott, and more symptomatic articles which testify to the problematic sense of identity and status of the practising journalist. The anxieties of practitioners, and their reflections upon how their craft is subject to commercial and political influences, is a common theme. As Bromley and O'Malley comment: '... there is a sense of uncertainty – about the proper role of government in relation to the media; about the role of commerce; about standards; about regulations and training; about the effects of technological changes'. Journalism, it seems, like media studies has always been in crisis.

Books Reviewed

Berger, Arthur Asa. *Narratives in Popular Culture, Media and Everyday Life.* Sage. pp. 199. pb £13.99. ISBN 0 7619 0345 3.

Bignell, Jonathan. *Media Semiotics: An Introduction.* Manchester University Press. pp. 223. pb £11.99. ISBN 0 7190 4501 0.

Bromley, Michael, and Tom O'Malley, eds. *A Journalism Reader.* Routledge. pp. 394. pb £15.99. ISBN 0 415 14136 2.

Brunsdon, Charlotte, Julie D'Acci and Lynn Spigel, eds. *Feminist Television Criticism: A Reader.* Clarendon Press. pp. 387. pb £14.99. ISBN 0 19 871153 0.

Crisell, Andrew. *An Introductory History of British Broadcasting.* Routledge. pp. 280. hb £40.00. ISBN 0 415 12802 1.

Drucker, Susan J. and Gary Gumpert, eds. *Voices in the Street: Explorations in Gender, Media and Public Space.* Hampton Press. pp. 312. pb £21.50. ISBN 1 57273 017 X.

Flournoy, Don M. and Robert K. Stewart. *CNN: Making News in the Global Market.* University of Luton Press. pp. 227. pb £15.00. ISBN 1 86202 542 9.

Gunter, Barry. *Measuring Bias on Television.* University of Luton Press. pp. 186. pb £14.95. ISBN 1 86020 526 7.

Hansen, Anders, Simon Cottle, Ralph Negrine and Chris Newbold. *Mass Communication Research Methods.* Macmillan. pp. 350. pb £14.99. ISBN 0 333 61710 X.

Hoskins, Colin, Stuart McFadyen and Adam Finn. *Global Television and Film: An Introduction to the Economics of the Business.* Oxford University Press. pp. 176. pb £14.99. ISBN 0 19 871147 6.

Kilborn, Richard and John Izod. *An Introduction to Television Documentary: Confronting Reality.* Manchester University Press. pp. 258. pb £12.99. ISBN 0 7190 4893 1.

McKinley, E. Graham. *Beverly Hills, 90210: Television, Gender and Identity.* University of Pennsylvania Press. pp. 274. pb £13.75. ISBN 0 8122 1623 7.

Murray, Timothy. *Drama and Trauma: Specters of Race and Sexuality in Performance, Video and Art.* Routledge. pp. 304. pb £15.99. ISBN 0 415 15789 7.

National Television Violence Study (Volume 1). Sage. pp. 568. hb £45.00. ISBN 0 7619 0801 1.

Nava, Mica, Andrew Blake, Iain MacRury and Barry Richards. *Buy This Book: Studies in Advertising and Consumption.* Routledge. pp. 355. hb £45. ISBN 0 415 14131 1.

11

Popular Culture

HILLEGONDA RIETVELD

For a simplified reading experience, this chapter has been divided into the following sections: 1. Approaches to Popular Culture, which shows a variety of research methodologies and entering points into the study of popular culture; 2. Politics of Identities, which addresses power relations and identity formations in a wide range of popular cultural contexts; 3. Dance Culture, which is a particular category for this year, since a large amount of (British) texts have addressed the legacy of a decade of dance parties that have affected popular cultural production and consumption; and 4. Popular Fantasies, which addresses not only the fantastic in narrative fiction, but also the creation of a fantastic public image for USSR leader Stalin.

1. Approaches to Popular Culture

From Subcultures to Club Cultures: An Introduction to Popular Cultural Studies is a collection of Steve Redhead's writing covering the years that the UK 'New Right' experienced a long stretch in government. The bulk of the texts stem from the mid-1980s, with one contribution from the late 1970s that provides an early example of his work on the treatment by the UK government of football (soccer) subcultures, which culminated in his establishment of the Unit for Law and Popular Culture at the Manchester Metropolitan University. The notion of 'clubculture' has been borrowed from Thornton (1995) and shows his increasing academic interest in popular music and (especially Manchester's) club and party scenes. In Redhead's own words:

> What I proclaimed as 'Popular Cultural Studies' in *Unpopular Cultures* . . . builds on the rich legacy of Contemporary Cultural Studies – and especially the 'Birmingham School' – but also repairs some of the theoretical, political and methodological problems generated by that previous body of work (ix–x).

In particular, Redhead argues that the notion of 'subculture' cannot be sustained from the hedonist mid-1980s onwards; instead, the concept 'clubculture' would provide appropriate complementary ways of making sense of contemporary British culture. In addition, he advocates the research approaches developed by the Centre for Contemporary Cultural Studies at Birmingham, such as a mixture of ethnography and 'exciting and innovative social theory and political commentary' (x). Although Redhead does not go into much detail with regards his specific methodologies and critical influences; the collection provides ample illustrations. The collection is complemented by another collection, *The Clubcultures Reader*, an exciting streetwise academic collection of research and theory papers in the field of popular cultural studies edited by Redhead with Wynne and O'Connor, which will be discussed below.

In *Post-fandom and the Millennial Blues: The Transformation of Soccer Culture* Redhead provides a practical application of some of the ideas introduced in *Subculture to Clubcultures*. Hereby we get a closer peek at his methodology, which in this case is applied to his initial research subject, football (soccer) fandom in the UK. Influences from cultural studies are again evident in his approach; Redhead shows a tendency to follow his own fandom interests (both in football and pop music) and to interpret this within a theoretical framework which is quite loosely defined. For example, Redhead points to the work of French 'marginalized' cultural theorists such as Baudrillard and Virilio as sources of inspiration. He introduces the idea of '"pulp theory" . . . to go along with "pulp culture"' (8); in other words, a type of 'low modernism', whereby the theory is on a similar wavelength to the cultural activities studied. It is argued that 'youth' as a concept is disappearing; it existed as a mediated invention, for example in marketing. 'Fandom' is also addressed as being a mediated conceptual tool within cultural and social theory and it is argued that within subcultural theory a blindness has existed to youth who do not show the spectacular commitment of fans. Redhead uses liberal doses of the notion 'post-' (post-youth, post-culture, post-fandom) in order to present updated versions of these concepts. However, rather than undertaking a traditional social study of football fandom, attempting to create a representational map of its existence, Redhead follows Baudrillard in his pessimism that this would be an impossible ideal, especially in a thoroughly mediated society. Data is derived from an eclectic mixture of mediated forms of fandom, a particular source being football fanzines; a large list of fanzine titles is supplied at the end of the book.

An example of Redhead's particular approach to popular culture can also be found in *Imprinting the Sticks: The Alternative Press beyond London*. Thoroughly researched and lovingly written by Robert Dickinson, this book is based on a postgraduate study, supervised by Steve Redhead. This insider's view shows how small press and fanzines in the area of Manchester (covering pop music, entertainment, comics and critical politics) are part of a tradition of underground press which established itself in the mid to late 1960s.

While on the subject of fanzines, the San Francisco based publisher V/Search, formally known as Re/Search, is well known for its chronicling of US counter cultural interests. The second volume of *Zines!*, edited by V. Vale, is witness to this. It provides a series of in-depth interviews with makers of some of the better-known American underground zines and small press; hereby it is an example of a useful research resource (as opposed to an academic text).

The small press provide a particular form of articulation of the creativity of everyday life. The latter is the subject of Celia Lury's sociological contribution to academic studies of popular culture, entitled *Consumer Culture*. Here, Lury specifically analyses patterns of consumption within the context of Western material culture:

> *Material culture* is the name given to the study of ... person-thing relationships; it is the study of things- or objects-in-use. . . . The thesis that will be put forward here is that consumer culture is a particular form of material culture that has emerged in Euro-American societies during the second half of the twentieth century (1, italics by the author).

Lury proposes that the acquisition of material goods is 'a moment of consumption *and* production' (1, italics by the author); once possessed, objects are converted and customized to aid the lifestyles and needs of the user. Lury discusses forms of material culture in specific ideological contexts, such as the construction of youth, race and women. Clarity of presentation makes this an excellent textbook for courses in cultural studies, sociology and media studies.

Consumption and production are also closely related in Paul Theberge's *Any Sound You Can Imagine: Making Music/Consuming Technology*. Recent digital musical instruments (such as drum machines, sequencers, synthesizers and samplers) are discussed in terms of their relatively new relationship with popular electronic musicians:

> Popular musicians who use new technologies are not simply the producers of prerecorded patterns of sounds (music) consumed by particular audiences; they, too, are consumers – consumers of technology, consumers of prerecorded sounds and patterns of sounds that they rework, transform, and arrange into new patterns (3).

Like consumers elsewhere within Western capitalism, electronic musicians are in a consumption race to keep up with the latest technologies and the latest sound textures. Theberge's thorough study, based on his PhD, addresses the musical instrument industry; the mediation of knowledge of new music technologies; and the musical practice in the context of new music technologies.

Of interest within the theme of the study of sound technologies in popular culture is the winter issue of *Convergence: The Journal of Research into New Media* Technologies (edited by Knight et al.). This issue is subtitled 'More Than Meets The Eye: Special Issue on Music and Sound Performance, Perception and Interactivity'. It addresses subjects as varied as use of sound in multimedia environments; employment of Web sites and CD-ROMs; the history of the Theremin; an overview of sound in cinema; and creative use of acoustics.

The issue of research methodologies in cultural studies is explored in detail in *Cultural Methodologies*, edited by Jim McGuigan. In his introduction, McGuigan points out that, due to the success of cultural studies in both research and educational terms, it is now a legitimate academically institutionalized subject. Cultural studies therefore merits an overview of research methodologies which could help both undergraduate and postgraduate researchers. Soon it became clear that not all approaches could be included in one book, since cultural studies is 'eclectic in the methods it uses, drawing liberally from across the humanities and social sciences' (1). The contributors are mostly employed in departments that cater for cultural studies, although sociology features highly as well, in addition to philosophy and social history. Issues in methodologies are illustrated in the first part by Douglas Kellner, Tony Bennett, Nick Stevenson and Ann Gray. Case studies are provided by Carolyn Steedman, Martyn Lee, Helen Thomas and Sabina Sharkey. Graham Murdock and Michael Green close the book each with a reflective chapter.

Back to Reality? Social Experience and Cultural Studies, edited by Angela McRobbie, is an attempt within cultural studies to redress the politics of 'difference and diversity' within the field of cultural studies, with a 'commitment to understanding the social experience of culture, the way in which culture is lived and the use of culture as a structure for the articulation of experience' (1). Most of the papers in this collection are written by well-known theorists in the field, each characterized by carefully considered and researched arguments. The dense writing style in most contributions prohibits this collection to an undergraduate readership, except, perhaps, third-year research projects. The first part of this book puts cultural studies in a theoretical framework that reaches beyond Britain and is provided by Lawrence Grossberg, Meaghan Morris, Graham Murdock and bell hooks. The second part features specific case studies of popular cultural production, with contributions by Paul Gilroy, Dave Laing, Vrin Ware, Maria Pini, Sean Nixon and Angela McRobbie (the latter an updated version of an elsewhere published chapter), from artefacts such as popular music and raves to magazines; and from black politics to sexual identities.

2. Politics of Identities

A sense of identity in terms of social background and relationships (class, gender, ethnicity) seems to have been high on the agenda this year. Although being produced within the subject area of literary, rather than sociological, studies, *British Cultural Identities* is one such publication. Edited by Mike Storry and Peter Childs, this textbook features anonymous contributions by Jo Croft, Edmund Cusick, Ross Dawson, Roberta Garrett, Frank McDonough and Gerry Smith, as well as by the editors. It addresses clearly defined subjects, such as sense of place and nation; notions of lived time, like education, work and leisure; gender and sexual relations; understanding the idea of youth; class and democracy; ethnicity and language; religion and cultural heritage. Like a unit guide, the sections are accompanied by exercises and recommended reading, which is useful for introductory undergraduate higher education.

Within this context, the summer issue of *Soundings: A Journal of Politics and Culture* (edited by Stuart et al.) is relevant. In addition to reviews, poems and European matters, this issue addresses 'Young Britain', from the use of the dance drug Ecstasy to black politics, DiY politics, trade unions and popular music.

Virtual Politics: Identity and Community in Cyberspace, edited by David Holmes, deals with issues of identity in the contexts of technoscience, virtual reality and cyberspace. Holmes distinguishes postmodern technoscience from 'earlier forms of Enlightenment science in that it transforms its object – be it natural or cultural – into the likeness of *scientific representation*' (2, italics by Holmes) and that '"human needs" . . . are as much the product of the way the world is changed as are the commodities produced to satisfy them' (2). The collection displays a thin line between technological determinism and social construction of cultural uses of technologies such as the Internet. The two parts show critical literary and sociological approaches in their broadest sense, addressing the effects of new technologies on society and subjectivity as well as the popular fantasies in which sense is being made of such technologies. Its contributors are active in academic fields such as literary studies, media studies, cultural studies, law, architecture and sociology. The first part deals with notions of self, identity and the body with contributions by David Holmes, Nicola Green, Chris Chesher and Simon Cooper, as well as Paul James and Freya Carkreek. The second part homes in on social aspects of virtual realities, in terms of politics and community, with contributions by Michael J. Ostwald, Michelle Wilson, Mark Nunes, Patricia Wise, Christopher Ziguras and veteran theorist Mark Poster. Patricia Wise's chapter is an example of a feminist critique of cyberspace and virtual reality that often display articulations of male fantasies, of a sense of omnipotence, which at the same token disintegrates on encounter with (feminized) cyber technologies.

A major feminist contributor to the debates of identity and new technologies is Donna J. Harraway, who this year published *Modest_Witness @Second_Millennium. FemaleMan_Meets_OncoMouse: Feminism and Technoscience*, in which, as in the above title, both life sciences and information sciences are discussed. Some of the chapters have appeared elsewhere, but are now combined in a larger conceptual framework. Harraway displays a critical feminist approach in a witty and flamboyant manner, which integrates a specific style of presentation with her argument. She is as much interested in technoscience as in the popular representations that it inspires:

> I learned early that the imaginary and the real figure each other
> in concrete fact, so I take the actual and the figural seriously as
> constitutive of lived material-semiotic worlds (2).

For example, as in the above introductory writing by Holmes, in the chapter 'Gene' she states: 'Technoscience's work is cultural production' (154); it produces certain historical forms of biological entities. Therefore, popular and populist discourses about technology and the body are part of technoscience, which should be addressed with the critical tools at our disposal in a joining of 'anti-racist feminist studies, cultural studies and science studies' (270).

1997 also saw the publication of Sadie Plant's long-awaited cyber feminist book, *Zeros and Ones: Digital Women and The New Technoculture.* The title signals that one needs to approach this work with caution; the 'the' relating to 'technoculture' seems naively all-encompassing – echoing McLuhan's notion of the global village. 'Technocultures', in plural, would have shown a more carefully presented argument that includes a diversity of social and cultural contexts. Therefore, one could presume that the book would be technologically determinist and essentialist in its outlook. Yet, it is also an intervention in the spectacle of the history of digital technology. Plant returns to its history, starting with the nineteenth-century invention of the Difference Machine by Ada Lovelace, or Ada Byron, which is usually ascribed to Charles Babbage (who also worked on its development). The critical basis of her argument leans towards an adaptation of psychoanalytical theory, using sources such as Freud, Lacan, Deleuze and Irigaray. The latter has been criticized for producing an essentialist version of gender identities, which again could be justified as an intervention – the right action at the time of publication, a creative play with concepts in a European philosophical tradition, which ultimately may lead to some interesting 'alternative' insights into (popular and populist) cultural discourses.

A more 'traditional' area in which gendered identity construction is studied is film studies. However, the analysis of the male as erotic spectacle, both for heterosexual women and gay men, is a relatively recent event. With *Uneasy Pleasures: The Male as Erotic Object*, Kenneth MacKinnon makes such an attempt. He notes that his undergraduate students feel great unease in making public their desire for a male object – for some reason, it always seems to be someone else, elsewhere, who may have such a desire – therefore, this desire is disavowed. MacKinnon starts with a return to Laura Mulvey's mid-1970s' feminist intervention, which asserted that within patriarchal Hollywood narrative cinema, a male cannot be sexually objectified. He then shows in various case studies from popular culture that men can indeed be portrayed as erotic objects, especially in the 1990s, from film and pop stars to visuals in art, dance, advertising and comics as well as pornography for 'women' and for 'men'. MacKinnon notes that disavowal of the erotic male is produced by finding acceptable contexts for male nudity – most strongly found in the depiction of sportsmen. He also argues that the eroticization of the male in popular imagery is possible when imagined as only available to a desiring heterosexual female gaze. Thereby, the objectified (hetero-sexualized) male is not 'castrated' and feminized and therefore patriarchal values are kept in place. However, although the female gaze is still problematic to some extent for MacKinnon, he also points out that 'the amorality and directionlessness of consumerism opens up a space within patriarchy' (192), which may offer some potential for change.

The issue of sexualities and gendered identity construction in the area of musical production and consumption is explored further in *Sexing the Groove: Popular Music and Gender*, edited by Sheila Whitely and partially based on contributions to a conference that took place several years earlier. This 353-page update of discussions around issues of gender in rock and pop are mostly written by academic veterans in the field of popular music studies. The first part shows several approaches to the subject, with contributions by Will Straw (on connoisseurship, or the male 'train spotter'); Sara

Cohen (on male dominance in pop music scenes); Mavis Bayton (on the female rock musicians); and Norma Coates. The second part analyses several notions of masculinity in popular music, with case studies by Sheila Whitely (on Mick Jagger's sexualized image); Gareth Palmer (on Bruce Springsteen); and Stan Hawkins (discussing the pop image of The Pet Shop Boys). Part three deals with femininities in mostly rock guitar music, with musings by David Sanjek, Charlotte Greig, Keith Negus, Stella Bruzzi, Mary Celeste Kearney and Marion Leonard. The last part takes a closer look at identity and visual language of performance, with Sheila Whitely (links between music and image in pop videos); Paul McDonald (Take That as a spectacle of desirable boys); Sean Cubitt (providing another revisit to Mulvey and related film theory – arguing a similar point to MacKinnon). The chapters are characterized by an uncluttered style, which makes the book a welcome help in the teaching of popular music studies and of popular culture and gender in undergraduate courses from level two onwards. The grouping of recommended reading into recognizable categories at the end of the book is a further help, as is an extensive index and a useful discography.

Popular music can also be a vehicle to discuss ever-changing cultural identities. *Perfect Beat: the Pacific Journal of Research into Contemporary Music and Popular Culture* (edited by Hayward et al.) bears witness to this. The July issue shows a wide range of genres, which are associated with various cultural user groups, such as Goa Trance (Euro-American-Australian-Japanese-Israeli), electronic dance music associated with a holiday destination in Indian province, Goa; Rap and authenticity; Aboriginal Rock; 1920s Australian Orientalism; and guitar music on the Solomon Islands (Choiseul/Lauru in particular). This shows that cultural formats and certain identity formations travel around the globe in dialogue and monologue, affecting cultures and hybridizing in the process. Especially the informal mode of communication of popular music can be a first manifestation of such cultural crossroads.

Within the context of the mobility of popular music, it is appropriate to finish this section with a mention of a book on yet another popular cultural activity, tourism. *Touring Cultures: Transformations of Travel and Theory*, edited by Chris Rojec and John Urry, provides an overview of insights into cultural tourism. The (less) fashionable concept of 'post-' appears here as well, in the form of 'post-tourism', in a chapter by George Ritzer and Allan Liska. This piece is part of a group of contributions which address theoretical approaches to the notion of tourism; additional contributors are Eeva Jokinen and Soile Veijola, Chris Rojek and Celia Lury. Part two deals with various contexts and case studies by Jennifer Craik, Philip Crang and Sharon Macdonald, as well as a useful piece on tourism in the English Lake District and the photographic gaze by Carol Crawshaw and John Urry.

3. Dance Culture

Several authors, such as Steve Redhead in *Subculture to Clubcultures*, Maria Pini in *Back to Reality?*, Jonathan Keane in *Soundings* as well as Fred Cole and Michael Hannan in *Perfect Beat*, have addressed specific features of what during the last ten years has become known in Britain as 'dance culture'. This term includes rave culture and club culture, whereby raves are large nightly gatherings of people that dance to amplified repetitive electronically produced dance music – to stay in the rhythm of some of the above authors, perhaps a (post-)useful term for this music could be 'post-disco'(?). Additional titles that address this area of study in popular culture will be discussed in this section.

Maria Pini contributed yet another imaginative chapter this year; 'Cyborgs, Nomads and the Raving Feminine' includes references to cyber feminism and poststructuralist subjectivity theory and addresses a young (working class) female experience of UK raves. It can be found in Helen Thomas' edited collection *Dance In The City*. Also Georgiana Gore contributes with a chapter on rave, approaching it from a (hippie-like) trance and tribalism perspective. The rest of the book addresses other cultural aspects of dance, in art settings as well as in social dance, from black identity in dance hall and hip hop to issues of ballroom dance, from ballet classes to the club stripper; contributors are Helen Thomas, Andrew Ward, Paul Gilroy, Valery A. Briginshaw, Sanjoy Roy, Nicola Miller, Lesley-Anne Sayers, Barbara O'Connor, Les Back, Stacey Prickett, Sheril Dodds and Stephany Jordan.

Steve Redhead's *From Subcultures to Club Cultures* (see above) is complemented by The *Clubcultures Reader: Readings in Popular Cultural Studies*, edited by Steve Redhead with Derek Wynne and Justin O'Connor. The title promises more about club culture than it offers; its main themes are cultural resistance, subcultures and dance culture-associated activities. It is the definitive collection of work produced by academic researchers who, in one way or another, have associated with the Unit for Law and Popular Culture (ULPC) and/or the Manchester Institute for Popular Culture (MIPC), both based at the Manchester Metropolitan University. The ULPC is a postgraduate study centre supervised by Redhead within the School of Law, which for a few years was part of the MIPC. Wynne and O'Connor are still active within the MIPC, which is a research centre that also provides supervision to postgraduate students. The list of contributors is impressive and includes: well-published academics Simon Frith, Will Straw, Steve Jones and Lawrence Grossberg; writers Jon Savage, Marek Kohn and Ted Polhemus; and academic researchers Cressida Miles, David Muggleton and Beverly Best. Within the context of the study of dance culture, the following authors are relevant: Simon Reynolds (a polemic critique of rave culture), Sarah Champion (her adventure at an American open air rave), Hillegonda Rietveld (research chapter on House Music in Chicago), Dave Haslam (his role as DJ in Manchester) and Katie Milestone (research chapter on Northern Soul), as well as Adam Brown (research chapter on democratization of popular music and football industries).

Dance culture does not only feature dance and DJ produced music; it has also been plunged into sensationalized tabloid notoriety and wrangles with the administrators of law and order due to its association with hedonist use of illegal chemical substances (in this case dance drugs). This has led to a popular belief that dance parties, which trace their ontology to the Acid House parties of 1987–88, are synonymous with drugs, not only 'acid' (LSD) and 'speed' (amphetamines) but especially the relatively new dance drug Ecstasy (mostly MDMA). It is appropriate here to draw attention to *Disco*

Biscuits: New Fiction for the Chemical Generation, a well-selling pulp fiction collection of short stories edited by Sarah Champion (see also above). Although it is fiction, the stories give examples of insights into what the period and the events felt like, in a subjective sense. Some of the contributors, but definitely not all, are able authors, such as Irvine Welsh, Jeff Noon, Martin Millar, Douglas Rushkoff or Alan Warner. Especially Nicholas Blincoe (a hilarious story set at a small club in Ardwick, Manchester) and Gavin Hills (a fast-paced profile and a dodgy yet fashionable warehouse party in London) have succeeded in conveying a real ethnographic sense of dance culture in well-written prose.

In *Altered State: The Story of Ecstasy Culture and Acid House*, Matthew Collin, now editor for street magazine *The Big Issue*, set out to write a comprehensive history of events that led to the explosion of drugged-up dance gatherings, featuring 'amplified repetitive beats' which grabbed the nation's imagination for up to a decade. With contributions by John Godfrey, editor of cutting-edge magazine *i-D* during the dance party explosion, Collin traces the disparate events which came together to provide an intensely energized focus point for the production and consumption of contemporary popular culture in the UK. He then takes the story further, to show how a short-lived coming together of people from very different social backgrounds crumbled, each group or locality taking some of the influences and mixing them with their own cultural references. The book covers the buzz of the initial parties around South London; the explosion of dance parties around the M25 orbital road; the way that the East End of London put its own stamp on events; the explosion of dance clubs around Manchester and the hybridization of its attitudes with local independent bands; the free-of-charge travellers' techno sound systems in open fields; the development of jungle and drum and bass; and the various struggles with government, new laws and police actions. The details are crammed within 308 pages and are accompanied by a useful index.

The concern with the (ab)use of dance drugs such as Ecstasy by 'the chemical generation' or 'culturE' (as Henderson names it) in the context of sexual behaviour, especially of young women, led to a research project by drugs advisor and social researcher Sheila Henderson. *Ecstasy: Case Unsolved*, is a feminist approach to the study of teenage women and drug use within specific cultural contexts, such as going to raves in Manchester. Most of the data was gained through a mixture of diaries and interviews. Of concern to drugs outreach workers is to find out how to deal with ecstasy users. However, Henderson was also interested in the way that her subjects reported that a certain type of unpatriarchal behaviour was found among their male friends who used the drug, which was partly due to its empathy enhancing effect. The girls too had shifted in their role – in previous subcultural studies, the girl is presented as a normalizing force, while the boy has leanings towards deviance. Now young women took equal part in these nocturnal dance events. However, Henderson remarks that:

> ... to begin with, the boys loved it too. It was liberation to roam this girly world of physicality, sensuality and emotion, especially for the white, straight boys.... But the boy punters didn't stay all girly and united, didn't stay punters for long (116).

Like Collin, Henderson notes how boys from various backgrounds 'went their separate ways' (116). She also points out that several of the boys left the crowd in order to take control, for example, as a DJ (I like to add that some girls aspired to become DJs as well, but it seems they were in a minority). Henderson does not offer a solution to how one should socially deal with Ecstasy and finishes her book with a discussion of a generational divide between parents and youth.

Antonio Melechi was one of Redhead's first research assistants who, after several research trips to dance clubs in the UK and the continent, immersed himself into an experience of 'the chemical generation' and returned to the publishing world as the editor of *Psychedelica Britanica: Hallucinogenic Drugs in Britain*. A foreword is provided by Swiss pharmacist Albert Hofmann, who in 1943, at the age of thirty-seven, discovered the psychedelic properties of LSD-25 (Stevens, 1987). Melechi introduces the collection and contributes two historical chapters, one addressing changes in social use of LSD, from clinical setting to recreational drug, and one tells the remarkable tale of the slightly shady Michael Hollinghead's World Psychedelic Centre in mid-1960s' London. Michael Carmichael muses about the psychedelic influences of Lewis Carroll's story writing; Dr Ronald Sandison provides a retrospect of his clinical work with LSD; the literary underground of the 1960s is represented by Alexander Trocchi; Sheila Whitely (see above) addresses psychedelic influences in popular music; Simon Reynolds (see also above) looks at the regressive and pastoral aspects of psychedelic music; Stuart Metcalfe gets on with the subject of Acid House and Rave parties and associated uses of Ecstasy; Fraser Clarke finishes the book with a prophetic piece which brings a 1960s' 'shamanic' interpretation to the Rave parties of late 1980s and early 1990s.

4. Popular Fictions

The Commissar Vanishes: the Falsification of Photographs and Art in Stalin's Russia, by David King, is a fascinating document of unique archive photographs which show how the mediation of political relations was purposely manipulated, producing a popular fiction. One sees how those who fell out of Stalin's favour were not only arrested, but were also removed from public memory by deleting their image in photographic prints. Those photographs that depicted proximity to Stalin were especially affected, but also family photo albums did not escape the violence of selective erasure of the photographic record of the USSR's political history. Photographs were also cut and altered to give Stalin an aura of increased importance, adding to the Stalin cult that was carefully crafted to justify his despotic regime. This book shows how values of authenticity in leadership as well as in documentary photography are transgressed and how a fantasy image can be successfully presented as authentic due to a strong popular (and naive) belief that 'the camera never lies'.

The fantastic as a genre provides a focus for *West Virginia University Philological Papers Volumes 42–43: Special Issues Devoted to The Fantastic and Related Genres and Revising the Canon: Culture and Pop Culture*. This American conference-based refereed journal addresses narrative in literature, popular fiction, television and cinema. It makes a good resource for seminar discussions and specific research. Themes vary from the representation of America in French popular fiction to vampires, gothic imagery and magic realism. Subject matter moves from authors such as Toni Morrison, Rachel Ingall or Guy de Maupassant to film director Francis Ford Coppola or the popular influences on the work of Brecht.

The theme of the vampire in contemporary fiction and film is also explored in the American collection *Blood Read: The Vampire as Metaphor in Contemporary Society*, edited by Joan Gordon and Veronica Hollinger. The main thesis is that within postmodern culture, the vampire works as a kind of mirror image with which the reader or viewer can partially identify. Part One provides historical insights into the fictional development of a notion of the vampire, with contributions by Nina Auerbach, Jules Zanger, Margaret L. Carter and Joan Gordon; Part Two concentrates on the production of vampire texts, with Suzy McKee Charnas, Brian Stableford, Jewelle Gomez; and Part Three analyses contexts of consumption of vampire tales, with Sandra Tome, Nicola Nixon and Rob Latham. Part Four takes issue with the production of the Other in vampire stories, such as the monstrous by Miriam Jones; Gay Males and Queer Goths by Trevor Holmes; Japanese Techno-Gothic imagination by Mari Kotani and a deeper focus on the postmodern vampire as metaphor by Veronica Hollinger.

Happily Ever After: Fairy Tales, Children and the Culture Industry is the last title in this review. It is a varied range of essays by academic fairy tale specialist Jack Zipes, which are based on various talks and guest lectures. His concern is with modes of story telling and the relationship between oral, literary and filmed fairy tales. The film industry of Hollywood, for example, releases both animated Disney productions and live-action films; the latter not only depict classic fairy tales but also follow similar narrative structures with an inevitable happy ending. Zipes is interested in the socialization of children through fairy tales and shows a concern for the effects of the culture industry. Unlike optimists about contemporary popular culture, Zipes argues that 'commodified culture' (7) is not really very liberating and that people are not autonomous in their cultural choices. To Zipes, popular culture is not 'by the people, for the people', but rather a commodified version of culture and he stresses that especially children can be susceptible to the patriarchal and consumer values represented by the culture industry. Without wanting to run into a romanticized notion of folklore (as intellectuals during various stages of the development of an industrial society have done), Zipes suggests that the practice of oral story telling is a useful manner for various peoples to (re-)gain a sense of history. The act of story telling produces pleasure in itself, which adds to the happy ending of the fairy tale.

Books Reviewed

Champion, Sarah. *Disco Biscuits: New Fiction for the Chemical Generation.* Sceptre/Hodder and Stoughton. pp. 300. pb £6.99. ISBN 0 340 68265 5.
Collin, Matthew, with contributions by John Godfrey. *Altered State: The Story of Ecstasy Culture and Acid House.* Serpent's Tail. pp. 314. pb £10.99. ISBN 1 85242 377 3.

Dickinson, Robert. *Imprinting the Sticks: The Alternative Press beyond London*. Popular Cultural Studies: 12. Arena/Ashgate. pp. 251. pb £19.95. ISBN 1 85742 235 X.

Gordon, Joan, and Veronica Hollinger, eds. *Blood Read: The Vampire as Metaphor in Contemporary Society*. University of Pennsylvania Press. pp. 264. pb £15.50. ISBN 0 8122 1628 8.

Hall, Stuart, Doreen Massey and Michael Rustin, et al. eds. *Soundings: A Journal of Politics and Culture* Issue 6 Summer. Lawrence and Wishart. pp. 208. individuals £35.00, institutions £70.00 for three 1997 issues. ISSN 1362 6620.

Harraway, Donna J., with paintings by Lynn M. Randolph. *Modest_Witness@Second_Millennium. FemaleMan_Meets_OncoMouse: Feminism and Technoscience*. Routledge. pp. 361. pb £14.99. ISBN 0 415 91245 8.

Hayward, Philip, and Mark Evans et al., eds. *Perfect Beat: The Pacific Journal of Research into Contemporary Music and Popular Culture*, Volume 3, Number 3, July. John Libbey and Company. pp. 105. A$15.40 incl. surface post or A$18 by Airmail. Copies are not stocked in UK. ISSN 1038 2909.

Henderson, Sheila. *Ecstasy: Case Unsolved*. Pandora/Harper Collins Publishers. pp. 132. pb £5.99. ISBN 0 04 440917 6.

Holmes, David, ed. *Virtual Politics: Identity and Community in Cyberspace*. Politics and Culture – A Theory, Culture and Society Series, Sage Publications. pp. 248. pb £14.99. hb £45.00. pb ISBN 0 7619 5610 7.

King, David. *The Commissar Vanishes: The Falsification of Photographs and Art in Stalin's Russia*. Canongate Books. pp. 192. hb £25.00. ISBN 0 86241 724 4.

Knight, Julia, and Alexis Weedon et al. eds. *Convergence: The Journal of Research into New Media Technologies*, Volume 3, Number 4, Winter. John Libbey Media, University of Luton Press. pp. 144. varied subscription rate, from £30.00 p.a. to £80.00 p.a. ISBN 1 86020 024 9.

Lury, Celia. *Consumer Culture*. Polity Press. pp. 273. pb £13.95. ISBN 0 7456 1441 8.

MacKinnon, Kenneth. *Uneasy Pleasures: The Male as Erotic Object*. Cygnus Arts/Golden Cockerel Press. pp. 262. hb £17.50. ISBN 1 900541 30 0.

McGuigan, Jim, ed. *Cultural Methodologies*. Sage Publications. pp. 215. pb £14.99. hb £45.00. pb ISBN 0 8039 7485 X.

McRobbie, Angela, ed. *Back to Reality? Social Experience and Cultural Studies*. Manchester University Press. pp. 216. hb £40.00. ISBN 0 7190 4454 5. pb ISBN 0 7190 4455 3.

Melechi, Antonio, ed. *Psychedelica Britanica: Hallucinogenic Drugs in Britain*. Turnaround. pp. 212. pb £9.99. ISBN 1 873262 05 1.

Plant, Sadie. *Zeros and Ones: Digital Women and The New Technoculture*. Fourth Estate. pp. 305. hb. £14.99. ISBN 1 85702 386 2.

Redhead, Steve. *From Subcultures to Club Cultures: An Introduction to Popular Cultural Studies*. Blackwell Publishers. pp. 120. pb £12.99. ISBN 0 631 19789 3.

Redhead, Steve. *Post-fandom and the Millennial Blues: The Transformation of Soccer Culture*. Routledge. pp. 160. pb £13.99. ISBN 0 415 11528 0.

Redhead, Steve, with Derek Wynne and Justin O'Connor, eds. *The Clubcul-*

tures Reader: Readings in Popular Cultural Studies. Blackwell Publishers. pp. 230. pb £14.99. hb £50.00. pb ISBN 0 6312 1216 7.

Rojec, Chris, and John Urry, eds. *Touring Cultures: Transformations of Travel and Theory.* Routledge. pp. 214. pb £13.99. hb £45.00. pb ISBN 0 415 11125 0.

Singer, Armand E. et al., eds. *West Virginia University Philological Papers Volumes 42–43: Special Issues Devoted to The Fantastic and Related Genres and Revising the Canon: Culture and Pop Culture.* The West Virginia University Foundation. pp. 156. $12.00.

Stevens, Jay. 1987. *Storming Heaven: LSD and the American Dream.* Paladin. pp. 539. £5.99. ISBN 0 586 08796 6.

Storry, Mike, and Peter Childs, eds. *British Cultural Identities.* Routledge. pp. 350. pb £13.99. ISBN 0 415 13699 77.

Theberge, Paul. *Any Sound You Can Imagine: Making Music/Consuming Technology.* Wesleyan University Press. pp. 291. pb £19.99. ISBN 0 8195 6309 9.

Thomas, Helen, ed. *Dance In The City.* Macmillan Press. pp. 254. pb £15.99. ISBN 0 333 64961 3.

Thornton, Sarah. *Club Cultures: Music, Media and Subcultural Capital.* Polity Press. pp. 191. pb £11.95. ISBN 0 7456 1443 4.

Vale, V., ed. *Zines!* Vol. 2. V/Search. pp. 147. pb £15.99. ISBN 0 9650469 2 3.

Whitely, Sheila, ed. *Sexing the Groove: Popular Music and Gender.* Routledge. pp. 353. pb £13.99. hb £45.00. pb ISBN 0 415 14671 2.

Zipes, Jack. *Happily Ever After: Fairy Tales, Children and the Culture Industry.* Routledge. pp. 171. pb £13.99. hb £45.00. pb ISBN 0 415 91851 0.

12

Australian Popular Culture and Media Studies

TARA BRABAZON

Australian history has been punctuated by figures of excessive masculinity. From Ned Kelly to Gough Whitlam, and Barry MacKenzie to Crocodile Dundee, popular culture has revelled in the complexities of the Aussie bloke. However, 1997 is a year of difference, paranoia, confusion and pain. These affective disturbances emerged from debates triggered by two powerful and provocative women. Pauline Hanson and Helen Demedenko/Darville have been major characters in the theoretical palate of 1997 popular culture and media studies. The major sites of investigation in this review spiral from these alternative traces of Australian history, displaying the ambiguities emerging from a proto-republican, (post)colonial, multicultural nation.

This chapter is divided into eight sections: 1. Media Scares and Journalist Responsibility; 2. Public and Private Broadcasting; 3. A Question of Reception; 4. Hip Hop, Dancing and a Didjeridu; 5. Gender and Performance Anxiety; 6. Technology as a Commodity; 7. Pedagogy and Popular Culture; 8. Writing the Republic.

1. Media Scares and Journalistic Responsibility

Complex and convoluted contexts raise questions of speaking and writing positions, and the responsibilities involved in being part of public debates. These concerns are not only legal and institutional, but are a constitutive part of citizenship. Debates about journalistic restriction and freedom are a significant part of media policy.

Clem Lloyd and Cratis Hippocrates, in 'Public Journalism, Public Participation and Australian Citizenship' (*Culture and Policy*, 8, 9–22), consider how journalism builds a community. They desire an increased interactivity between newspapers and the society they serve. Particularly significant is the discussion of public journalism in the United States and how these principles and practices may be applied to the race debate in Australia.

There has also been an increasing discussion of the structural limitations imposed on Australian journalists. Martin Hirst evaluates the 'MEAA Code of Ethics for Journalists: An Historical and Theoretical Overview' (*Media International Australia*, 83, 63–77). He discusses reasons why the post-war eight-code system had been lifted to twenty points by 1995. In terms of ethics and responsibility, two ideas in particular have caused problems to journalists. First, the movements between news and entertainment have resulted in contradictory understandings of value. Secondly, accountability has become an increasingly vague phrase, particularly considering the spectrum of journalistic sites in both community newspapers and ethnic-based information sources. Hirst has provided a solid, empirically useful and theoretically subtle exploration of how freedom of speech has transformed into a free market in ideas.

While journalists are among the first to make rhetorical claims about the freedom of information and speech, there are serious legal repercussions for the activation of this ideology. Mark Pearson has written a timely text, titled *The Journalist's Guide to Media Law*. The book is written in a simple style, providing an overview of the legal system, including the freedom of information acts, privacy measures and the legislative initiatives that change the way in which newspapers print and frame stories. Pearson states that 'every day of their working lives journalists make decisions which could have some legal implications'. The manner in which an interview is handled, the changing of a photograph or the editing of footage leave journalists vulnerable to legal charges.

Most significantly, Pearson investigates *sub judice* contempt in light of the Port Arthur massacre. He ponders how crime is to be reported while still respecting the rights of all parties in a court of law. Radio journalist Derryn Hinch presented *sub judice* broadcasts about a former Catholic priest on molestation charges, naming the accused during the programme. Pearson presents the reasons why Hinch went to jail for this legal breach.

Aimed at both journalists and journalism students, this book grants these groups an understanding of media law. This attention to the journalistic context ensures that readers evaluate how legal constraints function in a series of divergent workplaces. He includes provisional considerations of how new media technologies will change the law. The presentation of case studies reinforces how a particular piece of legislation operates. With a question and answer section at the end of each chapter, it is an ideal textbook. Yet Pearson's research remains easy to read, consult and consider long after a course has concluded.

An obvious case study for a further edition of Pearson's book is the way in which print and televisual journalists reported stories arising from one woman: Pauline Hanson. The Member for Oxley has kept cultural critics and political journalists busy during 1997. Pauline Hanson was elected to the Federal parliament in 1996 after being disendorsed by the Liberal Party for racist comments. She, like John Howard's Liberal Party, went on to win the election. Yet the Pauline Hanson narrative actually starts in October 1996, when she made her maiden speech in the Australian Parliament. After this event, she came to dominate talkback radio, newspapers, television and magazines in a way rarely seen in Australia. Her attacks on indigenous Australians, migrants, 'fat cat' bureaucrats, the family court and academics took a scattergun approach to the public sphere. Most of the pellets missed their target, but some did permanent damage. Media theorists repeatedly dipped their pen in the ink well of the Hanson phenomenon.

Although John Howard guided the liberal/national coalition government back into office after thirteen years, 1996 was not his year. Nicholas Economic asks the question most Australians pondered after Hanson's success: 'How Did She Do It?' (*Arena Magazine*, 27, 35–36). As Economic reminds readers, five independent candidates won the election. While conscious of this trend, he is amazed at the speed in which she 'has become one of the media's favourite topics, and her Australian community now knows much, much more about her views on everything from race matters to growing outdoor plants'. The scale of interest has rendered her a major irritant to the coalition government, deflecting attention from their political agenda.

Television is Hanson's sphere of most success. Bill Bainbridge has investigated how a media phenomenon such as this is started and, most importantly, continued ('A Hanson Affair', *Arena Magazine*, 27, 34). After a few uncomfortable appearances on the Australian Broadcasting Corporation, the public television channel, she focused her efforts on commercial stations. Bainbridge argues that by 'advocating the banning of the ABC she is presumably endorsing commercial television as the cultural space for all of her "ordinary," average Aussies on the street'. Welfare mothers, youth unemployment, Aboriginal bureaucrats, foreign investment and Asian gangs became the ill-defined, but repetitive, target of her televisual performances. Bainbridge invokes a textual analysis of particular segments, such as her *60 Minutes* interview, and asks why the producers utilized the celebrity, rather than the political, genre. Most importantly, he recognizes that Hanson 'is offering the inarticulate and reactionary response to globalization'. This is a significant realization, as most theorists of the Hanson phenomenon forget that her greatest success occurs in the working class areas which have been neglected by both major parties. Although she promotes discussions of race, she is actually using the regional and linguistic spaces of class difference.

Hanson's electoral success is not an isolated circumstance. Australia has a damaging and sustained history of race-based prejudice. Philip Bell, in '(Yet Another) Race Row Looms' (*Metro*, 109, 79–81), activates a longer-term analysis of the entanglements of race and immigration. Bell also interrogates the role of the media, both the quality press and populist television programmes, in transforming a debate into a 'race row'. He states that 'the media did not initiate this cycle of events, nor are they the "cause" of racism'. However, he highlights the significance of the media in defining the public agenda and reproducing a certain way of understanding social relationships and political conflicts linked to 'race'. His argument gains credibility through demonstrating how the media can ignore particular elements of Hanson's message, like withdrawal from the United Nations or the re-introduction of national service, while promoting the link between race and immigration. Hanson operates at the borders of consensus, mobilizing phrases like the ordinary Australian, mainstream and the silent majority. Ironically, the more mistakes she makes, the increasing stumbles reported by the media, the more she is represented as the ordinary 'battler'. Bell documents how Hanson, as a topic, moved from the sphere of political reporting to a human-interest story. This transition was eased by emphasizing nation over race. Those who disagreed with her, or critiqued her arguments or evidence, were labelled as politically correct, the supposed intellectual plague of the 1990s. Bell does not blame the media for racism, but strongly implicates journalists in repeating and naturalizing the category of race as a sign of difference and inferiority.

Andrew Jakubowicz is even more damning of the media's treatment of the Hanson issue. In 'She's Not There: Pauline Hanson and the Australian Media' (*Metro*, 109, 82–85), he states that 'the populist media see in Hanson a source of continuing entertainment: racism can be fun and her fundamental morality may be skewed but it speaks, as we do, for/to the great unwashed'. Jakubowicz is very concerned with the media's social responsibility, arguing that they contravened most standards of argument, evidence and debate. Like Bainbridge, he also realizes that multiculturalism and immigration are class-based issues. Multicultural policies are attractive to the young, the urban and the cosmopolitan. Resistance to these forces forms the basis of Hanson's success and comes from the poor, the aged and working class communities. These are the groups most threatened by the deregulated economy. Memorably, Jakubowicz describes Hanson as 'the corporeal realization of the convulsive local response to globalization'. Ironically, this response ties Australia to the past, to the British Isles and a colonial history.

While the class-based analysis of the Hanson success is significant, Michael Meadows is concerned with the complex interchanges of power in the media ('Perfect Match: The Media and Pauline Hanson', *Metro*, 109, 86–90). He shows that few voices of indigenous people or migrant populations are granted currency. Instead, 'Hanson began her attacks on the disadvantaged – from her position of privilege'. Political correctness or 'PC' is being used as a phrase to inhibit discussion and debate. The simple terms in which both the media and Hanson present stereotypes and naive representations as a truth means that they serve each other's purposes. Meadows argues that too much stress has been placed on one woman. He suggests that 'our attention should focus on the media, rather than on the individual'. His point is important, as most Australians gain their only knowledge of indigenous affairs from television and newspapers.

Considering Meadows' maxim that media structures, rather than the individual politician, need to be granted analytical attention, Glen Lewis instigated a research project into the Australian media from October–December 1996. In 'The Media and the Pauline Hanson Debate: Cheap Talk or Free Speech?' (*Australian Journal of Communication*, 24, 9–22), Lewis shows how commercial television, talkback radio and the tabloid press are the channels for the Hanson ideology. Talkback is particularly important as it is responsive, impulsive and aggressive, not the most balanced emotional triggers for a discussion of immigration in Australia. Lewis's work is most convincing in the discussion of how claims for freedom of speech are used to block vigorous, informed public debate. The minimal role of intellectuals in the discussion, which would have slowed down the plethora of issues emerging from Hanson's mouth, means that a myriad of moral panics about race, law and order, immigration and education were granted a credibility that rarely occurs when many voices contribute to a discussion. Instead, Hanson and Howard were allowed to inter-cut nightly news stories, to form what Lewis described as 'a collage of cheap talk and free speech'.

Similarly, Peter Putnis utilizes the Hanson case study to reveal the rules of media reporting. In 'The Nature of the News Discourse' (*Metro*, 109, 91–93), he shows how Hanson is such a revealing example of news because there is a central symbolic figure and triggering word, like racism and multiculturalism. Putnis shows that 'news needs controversy'. Through her presence on gardening programmes like *Burke's Backyard* at the height of her media reign, every action became newsworthy.

A stance against the stream of articles tying Hanson to the popular media is Stuart Cunningham's 'Influences on the Idea of Media "Influences"' (*Metro*, 111, 31–34). He generates a non-legal framework to discuss the concept of media power, attempting to evaluate and rank significance and importance. Governments and media theorists work from the thesis that the media is efficacious. This maxim serves as the rationale for national broadcasters. Cunningham reviews the psychological and cognitive models of text and audience engagements. Even after the Hanson debate, he affirms that 'there is no evidence to suggest that the traditional agenda setting function of the elite print media has been eroded in Australia'. While other writers have demonstrated how talkback, tabloids and commercial television follow Hanson through the mire of race-based prejudice and anti-immigration, Cunningham is suggesting that the older media continue to set the political and social agenda.

While Cunningham's argument is convincing, it is difficult to block the power and passion of Australian talkback radio. While this mode of broadcasting has been present throughout the medium's history, in the last few years Australia's talkback hosts have been at the centre of controversy. Not surprisingly, 1997 saw the rise of a book and several articles that questioned the power held by these men. Phillip Adams and Lee Burton produced *Talkback: Emperors of the Air*. The text is a fascinating amalgam of commentary, transcription, history and systematic analysis. Lee Burton, a teacher of media studies at the Royal Melbourne Institute of Technology, and Phillip Adams, of the public broadcaster's Radio National, ask how the 'Emperors of the Air' influence public policy. There are also more tentative inquiries into the reasons why callers contact talkback programmes. Ironically, the period in which they monitored the stations coincided with the rise of Pauline Hanson, which provided powerful textual fodder for the consideration of broadcasting responsibility and the construction of a media public. Phillip Adams states that 'our shock jocks are, by any measure, very low in the media food chain'. Even though their credibility is minimal, the right wing ascendancy in Australian radio has formulated a political climate of slogans and pontification, rather than argument and evidence. The talkback hosts have successfully sutured conservatism, populism and racism in a way not seen before in the Australian media. The idea that this ideological mix has transpired on radio is not surprising. It is an intimate medium, and mostly heard alone. This is an ideal venue to describe the injustices to 'little Aussie battlers', and to enfranchise the seemingly disenfranchised.

A strength of the book is an emphasis on the localism of the shock jocks. Each city has distinct frameworks and perspectives. Ron Casey's Sydney is distinct from Howard Sattler's Perth. While Casey is obsessed with Asia and Asians, Sattler is focused on law and order, crime and punishment. Both Lee Burton and Phillip Adams argue that the use of talkback is a site where nationalism is tested, reviewed and provoked.

As Burton and Adams have suggested, an analysis of talkback requires a clear grasp of local issues. Steve Mickler has instigated a careful and important discussion of Howard Sattler, Perth's king of talkback. Mickler describes the radio host as 'The "Robespierre" of the Air' (*Continuum*, 11, 23–36). He is focused on the way that class and Aboriginality function within the programme. He views Sattler as the 'impassioned champion of the people, patriot and scourge of the vested interests and their political sympathizers'. The formation of a 'battler constituency' ruthlessly excludes Aboriginal people and stresses the Anglo and the masculine, those groups diminished through multiculturalism. At times, the race hatred is so vitriolic that Steve Mickler remarks, 'I don't think we have been terribly well equipped as media critics to respond to discourses hostile to indigenous concerns such as heard on talkback radio'. The antagonistic formations of race and class mean that theorists must mobilize a very precise series of analytical tools. The key is to concentrate on case studies. Mickler continues this work in the article 'Talkback Radio and Indigenous Citizens: Towards a Practical Ethics of Representation' (*The UTS Review*, 3, 46–66). He reviews the case of an indigenous family who had been pursued by the police. The result of this campaign was the death of an eighteen-year-old man when his stolen car collided with another vehicle. His parents blamed police harassment. Mickler details how Peter Newman and Howard Sattler, the resident talkback hosts, handled this story. His argument demonstrates that Aboriginality and citizenship are oppositional categories within the talkback discourse.

These case studies are politically significant and textually incisive. However, Keith Galash believes that the talkback climate is generating a negative and angry social environment. In 'The Culture Target' (*Culture and Policy*, 8, 187–197), he argues that John Laws and other radio ranters are generating 'the current meanness ... to reverse much affirmative action of some 30 years'. He sees talkback as one part of an attack on the arts and funding strategies. Anything that promotes critical engagements with the past is being labelled as 'politically correct' or the 'black armband view of history'.

The past, nostalgia, myth, legend and lies are entangled in the second major media crisis of the year, encircling Helen Demidenko/Darville. Her text, *The Hand that Signed the Paper*, was awarded and lauded in literary circles. Unfortunately critics and award committees became tangled and perhaps bewitched by ideologies of authenticity. Helen Demidenko claimed Ukrainian ancestry, which seemed to almost justify, or at least explain, anti-Semitic tendencies. The third edition of her book revealed the ruse. Demidenko transformed into Darville and Ukrainian parentage disappeared from the literary justifications of her greatness. The best analysis of these remarkable events is Kateryna Olijnyk Longley's 'Fabricating Otherness: Demidenko and Exoticism' (*Westerly*, 42, 29–70). As a Ukrainian-Australian academic, her interest in the case is personal and political. Her theoretical frame is strong. She uses the exotic to understand the Demidenko case. The way in which ethnic authenticity constructs insiders and outsiders grants an ambivalent edge to cultural knowledge. By exoticizing ethnicity, it is removed from the mainstream, meaning that racism and xenophobia are not disclosed or discussed. For Longley, the Demidenko-Darville couplet 'exposed, by means of this double twist, Australian mainstream culture's complicity in her act by way of its fascination with the exotic'. This was the site of betrayal: a potent but hidden ideology of Australian literary culture was revealed.

Longley met Demidenko: she found the writer used the Ukrainian language with accuracy and fluency and could not understand 'why ... anyone [would] go to such lengths to create a false identity for literary purposes'. Probably her critical and popular success were part of the attraction. Longley's narrative demonstrates that literary awards offer a safe site to acknowledge difference, without questioning the structures and institutions of Australian culture.

McKenzie Wark continues this fascination with the most complex of media and literary confluences in 'The Demidenko-Effect and the Virtual Republic' (*Continuum*, 11, 61–71). He argues that this media event resulted in a critical loss of faith in the authorial voice. It is remarkable that even after Barthes, Foucault and Kristeva, there is a desire for origin and truth which serves to return critics to the hand that wrote the words. As Wark suggested, Demidenko-Darville 'is a story about the limits of liberalism and the lengths old cold warriors will go to fend off their own obsolescence'. Theories of writing require a fluidity and critical reflexivity that was not shown throughout this media event.

Far more effective is Megan Watkins' investigation of the mechanism through which the media framed and questioned Helen Demidenko-Darville. 'The Damnation of Demidenko – Interview or Inquisition?' (*Social Semiotics*, 7, 53–74) generates a close study of genre through the television current affairs interview. Framed by Deleuze and Guattari's map, the fluidity of genre is seen to be far more appropriate when compared to the metaphors of the frame or template. The interview of Demidenko is taken from the Australian Broadcasting Corporation and occurred before the revelations of her identity. The interview is not a dyadic structure, as there were two interviewees, but the writer was baited by two journalists: one a guest and the other an interlocutor. The interview follows the structure of a trial, but 'she is denied the support of a judge or mediator'. The interview becomes a complex multigeneric formation, demonstrating how televisual mapping can position a victim.

Media imaginings are rarely benign, but they can be revealing. Elspeth Probyn, a theorist who chose to move from Quebec to Australia during 1996/7, is disturbed but fascinated by the differences around her. As she states in 'Bloody Metaphors and Other Allegories of the Ordinary Nation' (*Continuum*, 11, 113–125), 'my emigration from Quebec to Australia has been an immersion course in the ways in which the ordinary can sometimes loom up ... when the taken-for-granted isn't'. The ordinary and the everyday nature of popular culture, in divergent national regimes, is revealed through the media crises emerging from Hanson and Demidenko-Darville. Through such events, new and compelling modes of media analysis do emerge.

2. Public and Private Broadcasting

Conflicts in the political arena are frequently matched by disquiet in intellectual circles. These concerns overlap through theorists' attention to financial cuts to the Australian Broadcasting Commission. It seems odd that at the very moment when the Australian public sphere requires a plurality of voices and some evidence to accompany shrill slogans, public broadcasting is under threat.

Attacks on public broadcasting are not new. As Ken Inglis demonstrates in 'ABC Shock Crisis Threat' (*Media International Australia*, 83, 5–10), government confidence in the broadcaster has wavered through its history. Major questions remain unasked of the ABC, such as the values promoted by a public broadcaster in an environment of postcolonialism and multiculturalism. Through dependency on governmental funding, issues like broadcast freedom, standards and convictions become decentred. Because of the continual environment of financial crisis, other ideological concerns are not addressed, which result in long-term dissonances between the government of the day and an 'independent' ABC.

Gay Hawkins is more ascerbic in her discussion of the 'ABC and the Mystic Writing Pad' (*Media International Australia*, 83, 11–17). She asks 'exactly what needs to be saved in the ABC and how should this rescue operation be mounted?'. A politics of despair about public broadcasting is not assisting the discussion of the present and future of the ABC. Hawkins criticizes the broadcaster for its minimal contribution to multicultural, postcolonial national imaginings. The station promotions, which feature black and white vignettes of diverse populations drawing the logo, have been concurrent with a decline in funding for programmes that perform that diversity beyond a fifteen-second commercial. With quality still being defined as what Gay Hawkins describes as 'authoritarian paternalism', attacks on the bias of the ABC are actually missing their critical mark.

Paul Jones takes a wider reading of public broadcasting's role in debate. In 'The Public Media in Review' (*Arena Magazine*, 28, 40–41), he argues that the ABC is important because it offers an alternative to the commercial media, thereby activating an informed citizenship. As the media is a source of public information, journalists in the public and private sectors must be accountable. Jones demands a greater attention to communications policy, believing that public culture will suffer greatly without attention from critics, scholars and legislators.

Part of the ABC's charter is that it offers audiences a model of effective citizenship. While television gains most attention from media theorists, radio is becoming increasingly important in the confusing representations of public opinion. Anne Dunn investigates 'The Role of ABC Radio in the Creation of Citizenship Models (*Culture and Policy*, 8, 91–103). As recently as 1994, Australians were reported as listening to radio more hours in the week than watching television. This makes national, publicly funded broadcasters a significant instrument in the building of an informed citizenry. Yet Dunn, like other writers, is uncertain as to the extent and place of pluralism in the textual suite of a national broadcaster.

Andrew Funston also ponders the relationship between 'The ABC and Citizenship' (*Overland*, 147, 59–62). He argues that the savagery of the recent cuts is particularly serious as they undermine the agenda setting and educative roles of the public broadcaster. Funston states that 'perhaps our parliamentarians and major parties are not too concerned with the quality of public communication. Informed communities give parliamentarians a hard time, and they also poke their noses into the excesses of the market place'. Besides the issue of accountability, he also asks how to present diversity within a national model, and affirms that radio handles this task far more effectively than television. Most significantly, he is concerned by the threats to Radio Australia (RA), the ABC short wave service that broadcasts through the Asian and Pacific region. He demonstrates that short wave is not a dying transmissional mode, with the BBC World Service and the Voice of America expressing an interest in taking the frequency space if Radio Australia closes.

It is the threats to Radio Australia that are most concerning critics. It certainly seems an odd victim of cuts. RA broadcasts twenty-four hours a day in English, and also in Indonesian, Mandarin, Cantonese, Thai, Vietnamese, Khmer, Tok Pisin (Papua New Guinea Pidgin) and French. Yet in a governmental review of the ABC, Radio Australia was the first target. Errol Hodge takes issue with this decision in 'International Broadcasting: The Reluctant ABC' (*Media International Australia*, 84, 87–90). He argues that the image projected of Australia through RA is pivotal to trade, investment, tourism and education, while also incorporating a foreign aid dimension. Hodge states that 'if the nation abandons RA ... it will convince millions of listeners and viewers in Asia and the Pacific that Pauline Hanson is typical of Australians, and that the government has lost interest in the region'. The timing of this debate is unfortunate and undermines political and social imperatives that bind Australia into an Asian and Pacific future. Hodge continues his defence of Radio Australia in 'Decision on Darwin Redolent of Colonial Era' (*Metro*, 111, 35–36). Responding to the closure of Darwin transmitters for Radio Australia announced by the Australian Communications Minister Richard Alston, the article is saturated by an amazed frustration in the government's narrow view of public broadcasting. Simultaneously, RA axed programmes in Thai, French and Cantonese, two months before the People's Republic of China took over Hong Kong. The Cantonese service would have been internationally important in this new context. Hodge affirms that 'like a ghost from the colonial past, Radio Australia's enfeebled voice will be limited mainly to English, the language of the colonial masters of yesterday, and pidgin, the language those colonial masters used to communicate with the native'. The ill-defined and hostile 'Asia' of Pauline Hanson's imagining is reinforced by millions of listeners who no longer hear their language or an alternative view of Australia's political climate.

The language of rancour and concern dominates discussions of the ABC, yet as Monroe Price has suggested there is a transnational tendency that is actually being revealed in Australia. In 'The Global Weakening of Public Service Broadcasting' (*Media International Australia*, 83, 18–23), he situates the debates about the ABC into a more universal trend. Most significantly, public broadcasters are placed into a broad range of cultural authorities, like the church, schools, universities and families. He believes we are witnessing the transformation of the medium through globalization, providing a hint of how transnational networks will appear.

While these globalizing tendencies are percolating through public broadcasters, pressure groups are debating over definitions of Australian content. Jock Given, in 'Are New Zealand Programs Australian?' (*Media Inter-*

national Australia, 83, 38–40), assesses the debate over the place of non-Australian programmes under content regulations. Under Closer Economic Relations (CER), New Zealand broadcasters and producers had assumed that their programmes would be granted a freedom of movement into the Australian market, just like wool, clothing and foodstuffs. Indeed, Australian programmes have a major presence on New Zealand screens. The New Zealand lobby group, Project Blue Sky, was set up in 1993 to encourage the growth of a New Zealand production industry, particularly in the Australian market. Given demonstrates how the Australian government sent ambiguous legislative messages about the content quotas to New Zealand broadcasters.

A more oppositional position is assumed by Anne Britton in 'True Blue takes on Blue Sky' (*Media International Australia*, 83, 40–45). She confirms the need for content protection, arguing that 'local broadcasters are unlikely to be able to resist the temptation to replace some Australian programs with heavily discounted NZ substitutes'. Unfortunately, Britton does not engage with the sentiments and legal parameters of CER, and continues to include New Zealand producers in the category of 'foreign sellers'. Trans-Tasman agreements are meant to counter such definitive determinations of home and foreign markets.

Quite rightly, Geoff Lealand counters the arguments of Anne Britton. In 'A Fair Suck of the Sav: Project Blue Sky and the New Zealand Case' (*Media International Australia* 83.46–50), he reminds Australian readers that New Zealand is even more disadvantaged than her trans-Tasman neighbour in the arena of international television distribution. CER, and the demise of the ANZUS treaty, has resulted in an increasing economic, social, political and military dependence of New Zealand on Australia. A cursory glance at New Zealand television reveals that the trans-Tasman audiovisual space has advantaged Australian producers. Lealand is completely justified in remarking that this 'argument is not really about opportunism or about freeloading. It is essentially about fairness in trade relations – and most particularly – the more willing compliance of one partner to the provisions of the CER treaty'. From both Australian media theorists and practitioners, there seems an ignorance and discrimination against New Zealand product. While some differences are welcomed politically and socially, others are seen as economically damaging.

Determining the level of acceptable differences is an increasingly complex task in Australian broadcasting. Rod Webb investigates these limits and boundaries in 'Enter the Dragon: SBS-TV and the Remaking of Australian Culture' (*Culture and Policy*, 8, 105–113). The Special Broadcasting Service (SBS) is a public broadcaster that aims to both promote awareness into the diversity of Australia's population and assist the settlement of migrants. During the Hanson debate, SBS became increasingly important in providing alternative information to an unsettled citizenry. Rod Webb is highly critical of other broadcasters who did not critique racism. He states that 'racism is rarely an issue of national importance unless it has the active approval of either a government or, at the very least, a major component of the ruling structure'. As Head of Scheduling at SBS Television, Webb is extremely sensitive to his role in promoting tolerance and diversity. He programmed SBS to feature a film at 9:30 every night of the week, drawing from a pool of fifty-five languages. Yet the reviewers investigating this remarkable array of cultural product were inconsistent and sloppy, with the *Sydney Morning Herald* film reviewer terming Turkish, Iranian and Egyptian films to be Arabic. Webb argues that media organizations can preach intolerance both through a lack of thought and intentional prejudice.

There are other broadcasting options apart from the public and commercial sectors. Community broadcasting is finally gaining some attention from media theorists. Stuart Cunningham, in 'Community Broadcasting and Civil Society' (*Metro*, 110, 21–25), displays how this medium can provide examples of effective civic virtues. Community broadcasting in Australia was delayed by the confusions over pay television, with the Labor Party relying on a corporatist model of government and society. The Howard government has increased the budget for community broadcasting, moving to a civic responsibility model. Cunningham instigates an intricate discussion of this movement, recognizing that 'the purpose of community media is not in itself to advocate a multiplication of group differentiated rights, but the implementation of communal responses to group differentiation'. This is a significant realization, as it moves theorists from vague claims for difference and diversity to more solid mobilizations of audience needs and activities.

David Barlow also looks to the community media sector as a democratic option to the public/private division. His 'Whither Non-profit Community Media in the Information Society' (*Culture and Policy*, 8, 119–138) presents an important discussion of how media convergence will impact on the sector. Convergence is a word with a free-floating meaning – and an even looser application – in contemporary theorizing. Barlow discusses how rhetorical mobilization of words like locality, convergence and identity are producing new community networks. These networks offer both opportunities and threats to the delicate non-profit community media in Australia. By 'reconstructing the local', a new site of argument, and a new voice of critique, will emerge.

With the ABC under threat, few theorists and commentators have time to consider broader questions about the current public/private model of broadcasting. In the present political climate, such a discussion may be misconstrued as discrediting another critical, public voice. However, Christina Slade offers a fresh analysis of 'The Public/Private Divide' (*Media International Australia*, 84, 102–111). She grants attention to the way in which new technologies make media regulation, such as suggested by anti-New Zealand ideologies in Australian broadcasting, difficult to sustain. Technological change has always altered the boundaries between the public and the private. That demarcation is necessary for regulation of the media sector. Slade discusses how Taiwan handles its viewer-pays television, suggesting advice to Australian writers and legislators. She explores how vague mentions of the public domain in communication debates are actually quite destructive to any effective regulation of the media.

At times of public underconfidence and swift media change, metaphors of citizenship offer an anchor for media theorists. There is a need during such a time for precise definitions and a subtle mobilization of evidence. The present limits of Australia's media imaginings are drawn at the Tasman Sea. However, technological changes, and the awareness of them, are rendering such discussions either redundant, or at least marginal in their importance.

It is necessary to study how media audiences are altering their perceptions and ideologies in response to transnational, multicultural and postcolonial ideologies.

3. A Question of Reception

As any media teacher knows, an effective, succinct first-year text that does not reify abstract theoretical frameworks is rare to find. Stuart Cunningham and Graeme Turner have edited one of these texts. *The Media in Australia* enters its second edition in 1997, after a highly successful first run in 1993. This completely revised publication continues the strength of the first, by working well with both history and contemporary politics. The new material is focused on the expanding areas of magazines, new technologies, electronic publishing and the Internet. Such books are very significant, as they shape a generation of media students. Six sections structure the chapters: 'The Media in Australia Today'; 'Media Industries'; 'Media Institutions'; 'Media Texts and Messages'; 'Media Audiences'; and 'Media Futures'. This text is effective because it grants attention to a spectrum of cultural industries. The press, radio, film, television, magazines, advertising, popular music, multimedia, video and pay television are all featured. In 'The Media in Australia Today' (1–20), Graeme Turner and Stuart Cunningham frame the second edition around convergence, showing how fibre optics allow the connection of the Internet, cable television, banks, shopping and mail. They also discuss how 'at the same time as the media technologies converge and the ownership structure of the industry which sells them becomes more concentrated – nationally and internationally – the audience for their products has begun to fragment'. Turner and Cunningham display a strong understanding of how industrial deregulation operates in Australia. They also reveal the tools available for media studies, affirming the importance of both ethnography and textual analysis.

Frances Bonner in 'Magazines' (112–123) displays a spectrum of techniques for investigating media audiences. She observes that while the circulations for individual titles are failing, the overall readership of magazines is increasing. Media diversification is significant in this context, as Australians are the highest per capita consumers of magazines in the world. Bonner presents a carefully constructed theoretical framework between television and magazines and advertising client and editorial content. Through this attention to text, she generates a convincing reading of the gendered world of magazines. She argues that 'women's interests are seen to be more homogeneous across the field of gender specific magazines than men's are'. This interesting thesis will be tested as the sphere of men's magazines continues to increase in both number and circulation.

Gillian Appleton also grants attention to 'Converging and Emerging Industries; Video, Pay TV and Multimedia' (163–188). The terrain of media technologies is notoriously littered with jargon, rendering the prose difficult for the non-specialist. However, Appleton has provided an accessible account of what happens to audiences and cultural industries as different delivery technologies overlap. Australians are known for their quick uptake of new technologies. Multimedia is no exception. Gillian Appleton suggests that theorists wishing to observe the workings of convergence, should monitor sport broadcasting, a continual site of innovation and audience interest.

As to 'Media Futures' (397–449), Stuart Cunningham and Terry Flew provide tentative suggestions of how the information economy is changing. Affirming the unpredictability of technological uptake, the writers remind us that innovation is 'wasteful by nature'. Their advice for theorists of the new media is to explore the impact of networking through the Internet by granting attention to 'genuinely enhanced participatory possibilities rather than achieved virtual communities'. These technological changes demand an even stronger grounding in empirical, textual or ethnographic research into media audiences.

An example of the deployment of this manner of research is John Frow's 'Class, Education, Culture' (*Culture and Policy*, 8, 73–88). This article emerges from the Australian Cultural Consumption Project, a large survey-based analysis of cultural taste. Initiated in 1992, consumption includes not only concerts, television and radio, but also sport, gambling, furniture, clothing and cars. Of the 5,000 copies of the questionnaire randomly distributed – 2,756 responses were received. The data demonstrates that aesthetic decisions are not autonomous, but grafted from, and situated by, social relations. Particular variables that were granted attention include education level, class and age. The project leaders, Tony Bennett and John Frow, attempted to reproduce – with theoretical changes – a framework similar to Pierre Bourdieu's *Distinction*. There were many surprises in the data, but one result most fascinated Frow. He found 'the relatively strong proportion of manual workers . . . reporting that they watch SBS; the figure is higher than of the other working-class groups and for both groups of employers'. This evidence adds a complexity to an evaluation of how cultural distinction can become a model of social domination.

Tony Bennett also assesses this data in 'Consuming Culture, Measuring Access and Audience Development' (*Culture and Policy*, 8, 89–113). For him, the primary problematic is how to measure an audience. One of the difficulties emerging from cultural policy is how to theorize the readership of cultural production, particularly as the arts sector is becoming less reliant on government funding. By considering how statistics of consumption have a role in the development of modes for audience access, attention is needed in the area of educational levels. Bennett found that the more highly educated the respondent to the survey, the more likely they were to use new media. As a reading of the relationship between education and publicly funded culture, the survey offers enormous potential to researchers. Bennett also realizes that 'those who are . . . culturally dispossessed are the least likely to be aware of this dispossession'. Clearly, the rhetoric of cultural access is only partly useful. Education generates a consciousness of distinction.

The work of Bennett and Frow needs to be taken seriously throughout Australian popular culture and media studies. It means that theorists must spend more time evaluating educational frameworks and institutions before audience judgements can be made. Such an understanding clarifies many of the general points made by Tina Kaufman in 'Finding an Audience: The Challenge for Australian Cinema' (*Metro*, 112, 9–12). She asks serious questions about the aberrant audience appreciation for Australian films. Why was *Shine* successful and *Children of the Revolution* not as auspiciously received? Similarly, *The Castle* was a surprise Australian hit, while *The Well* could not find an audience. Kaufman recognizes that 'just what works for a film to succeed at the box office is still a mystery. The most carefully planned, assiduously promoted, professionally advertised release of a "surefire" hit can be for nothing if all that work doesn't attract the audience into the cinema'. Clearly, in the case of *The Castle* and *The Well*, educational levels of the audience are a particular factor to explain the success. *The Castle* is a vibrant, contemporary film that activates a plurality of literacies, enacting a crossover between televisual and filmic genres. *The Well* grafts literary, poetic and filmic discourses, making the film slow and opaque for televisually literate audiences.

One of the more provocative political connections made in *The Castle* is between the working class and indigenous Australians. Aboriginal land rights are summoned in the film, but in a decontextualized way. Little attention is paid to the very specific needs and aims of indigenous people. This film continues the invisibility of race as a marker in Australia's visual field. Alan McKee recognizes this absence in 'Films vs. Real Life: Communicating Aboriginality in Cinema and Television' (*The UTS Review*, 3, 160–182). He grants attention to the way in which texts only become activated through audience interrogation. By focusing on how texts of Aboriginality are produced, he realizes that dark skin is the primary marker of indigeneity in Australian film and television. By focusing on skin, Aboriginality is rendered voiceless. Importantly, McKee suggests that cinema is 'a colonial medium', but television has far less requirement for dark skin. Other modes of recognition and presentation are deployed. McKee continues this study in 'Marking the Liminal for True Blue Aussies: The Generic Placement of Aboriginality in Australian Soap Opera' (*Australian Journal of Communication*, 24, 42–57). This article presents a history of Aboriginal characters in soap opera, granting attention to *GP*, *Neighbours*, *Home and Away* and *Flying Doctors*. Being 'issue-bearing characters', indigenous men and women rarely feature in romantic plots. The long-term repercussion of these roles is that fixed generic expectations are emerging for the representation of Aboriginality.

The survey instigated by Frow and Bennett demonstrates that education levels are a crucial theoretical marker for understanding consumption practices. Such recognition means that childhood must be granted much more attention in media studies. Jan Kociumbas's *Australian Childhood: A History* is a carefully researched narrative. The book's argument bounces off the romantic ideals of childhood, with particular attention to Aboriginal childhood – both before and after invasion, class differences and the role of medicine and the media. She suggests that 'childhood history must always be as much about adults as children'. Recreation, toys and sport are all significant popular cultural contributions to her study. Similarly, American television, cars and clothing offer case study for the movement of popular cultural symbolism through both time and space.

Many theorists claim cultural populism as the house style of Australian cultural studies. Conversely, in the contemporary era, few sites of cultural resistance are being hailed as significant or of value. Instead, theorists are far more tentative in speaking of, and for, an audience. The impact of Frow and Bennett's research is a pivotal movement to new types of research into reception. The binary of textual analysis versus ethnographic investigation is no longer as clear as it was in the late 1980s. The spectrum of techniques offers much subtlety in understanding a plurality of contexts and a myriad of texts.

4. Hip Hop, Dancing and a Didjeridu

An area of expanding interest in Australian popular culture and media studies is popular music. In the last two years, a minority interest has transformed into a solid site for the investigation of localism, indigenous politics and gender. One of the most fascinating and original publications of the year is Karl Neuenfeldt's edited collection of *The Didjeridu: From Arnhem Land to Internet*. This text displays several renderings of the instrument: those who play it, use it for pedagogical purposes, read it as a signifying system or preserve it as a portal of indigenous history. Two specialist threads recur in the text: the issue of gender and notions of authenticity.

The book opens, appropriately and productively, with Mandawuy Yunupingu's 'Yidaki' (vii–viii). Australian of the Year in 1993 and lead singer of Yothu Yindi, he explains the role of the Yidaki – the Yolngu description of the instrument known commonly as the didjeridu – in the presentation of dance, music, art and history. He outlines the role of the instrument in the maintenance of rhythm, rather than pitch, in song and dance. He reminds readers that while Yolngu accept non-Yolngu use of the instrument, 'its origins are sacred and secret to Yolngu men'. From the opening chapter, gender, place, rhythm and history are emphasized as being especially significant. These interests are carried through the book.

Philip Hayward and Karl Neuenfeldt ('One Instrument, Many Voices', 1–10) ask that readers respect the didjeridu's history and usage. Increasingly, the instrument is becoming a generic symbol for the nation. This was displayed at the eightieth anniversary of the Gallipoli landing in Anzac Cove. With no bugle to play the last post, Michael Lucas, a white backpacker, pulled out his didjeridu. Similarly a netsite – *didjeridu@eartha.mills.edu* – is a space for fans and players to dialogue about the instrument. From an aural signifier of Aboriginality to a retail object, the didjeridu is an increasingly global commodity. Hayward and Neuenfeldt focus on the social relationships and theoretical frameworks that dance around the instrument, arguing that it provides an ideal and evocative sign of both localism and globalism.

Much popular music theory is critical about the lack of musicological knowledge of writers. An even more telling absence is with regard to performance theory. Kev Carmody and Karl Neuenfeldt address this concern in 'Ancient Voice – Contemporary Expression' (11–19). Carmody, as both an Aboriginal musician and social activist, is highly conscious of how the didjeridu is a living instrument that is politically charged at the moment of the performance. He outlines the three components of performance:

pitch, rhythm and voice interval. By utilizing the three techniques, a representational field is constructed.

A characteristic of this book is the attention paid to the didjeridu's role in schools. Mick Davison and Karl Neuenfeldt focus on this sphere in the chapter 'Education, Empowerment and Entertainment: An Aboriginal Perspective on the Didjeridu' (21–29). For Davison, the Aboriginal and Torres Strait Islander Students' Cultural Support Officer at the University of Newcastle in New South Wales, the instrument offers a point of connection between past and future, and non-Aboriginal and indigenous people. Peter Dunbar-Hall also discusses this temporal movement ('Continuation, Dissemination and Innovation: The Didjeridu and Contemporary Aboriginal Popular Music Groups', 69–88). This chapter investigates commercialized popular music. Besides the customary Yothu Yindi, he investigates Coloured Stone, Tiddas and the Warumpi Band. He shows how the didjeridu functions as a member of the rhythm section in bands, but can also have solo roles. Changes are also taking place, particularly with regard to pitch and alignments with the rock discourse.

Contemporary inflections of the didjeridu are having a major impact on its meaning. Linda Barwick ('Gender "Taboos" and Didjeridus', 89–98) and Karl Neuenfeldt ('The Issue of Gender: A Discussion of the Use of the Didjeridu by Women', 99–105) work through the rights of women, both indigenous and non-indigenous, in playing the instrument. Both writers agree that because of the varied indigenous rule systems, international exploitation and appropriation is possible, and perhaps inevitable. Fiona Magowan extends this discussion beyond gender to explore how the didjeridu is played in Britain and Ireland ('Out of Time, Out of Place: A Comparison of Applications of the Didjeridu in Aboriginal Australia, Great Britain and Ireland' 161–183). She utilizes ethnomusicological approaches to access the constitution of tradition, hybridity and synthesis. From Rolf Harris's 'Tie me Kangaroo down, sport', contemporary playing is situated in neo-primitivist or neo-shamanistic frameworks. This de-contextualized, appropriated instrument may sound like a didjeridu, but its meaning has changed beyond recognition. The problem for contemporary theorists is to assess how and why authenticity matters to the instrument, while evaluating the nature of sonoric seizure.

The issue of appropriation becomes more convoluted when considering how other musical instruments and genres are being imported into the Australian context. Ian Maxwell has, over the years, developed a strong series of articles about Sydney hip hop. It is a thriving community with its own magazine, rappers and discourse. Hip hop arrived in Australian during the early 1980s, through the records and tours of Run DMC and Ice T. Complex resonances of culture, nationalism and community ground a hip hop social imagining, based on rapping, breakdancing and graffiti. Maxwell argues that Sydney hip hop culture is present at its own making, being written (and rapped and tagged) into existence through continual discourse. He has witnessed what he describes as 'the process by which a local experience becomes marked as being "authentic"'.

Kurt Iveson extends Maxwell's ground breaking and theoretically inspired work, through exploring 'Partying, Politics and Getting Paid: Hip Hop and

National Identity in Australia' (*Overland*, 147, 39–44). Iveson recognizes the expansion of alternative music, but suggests that rap is offering a radical edge to contemporary music, a site where social commentary is emerging. Rap is lyric-focused, de-emphasizing melody and chord structure. While hip hop has its roots in New York, Iveson argues that very specific cultural productions are being generated in Sydney. As he argues, 'most successful Australian bands have one thing in common that makes them pretty irrelevant to increasing numbers of young people in Australia – they're all very white'. Rap actively discusses racism. In Australia, a diversity of languages is being used. The Brethren's song 'Pasa la Cuchara' uses Spanish to convey an immigration narrative. Other rappers use Australian slang and accents to generate a provocative new interchange between local sounds and global genres. A 'progressive multicultural lyrical project' is being formed in hip hop.

While the hip hop discourse is activating new and interesting sonoric spaces, colonial agendas are still framing many musical genres. World music is becoming a marketing phrase to present non-Western sounds to a Western audience. Graeme Smith assessed this formation in 'WOMADELAIDE '97' (*Arena Journal*, 8, 17–22). WOMAD festivals started in 1992, organized in Britain by Peter Gabriel. The idea was imported into Australia, with half the programme featuring Aboriginal and Torres Strait Islander performers. Smith mounts a strong argument that the world music movement only presents a level of difference that is acceptable to Western middle class listeners. He suggests that 'the overall shape of the world music alliance of genres is set by the view from Europe'. While, in a positive way, world music seems to form affective alliances between fourth world people and European clubbers, a more cynical critic recognizes that exhausted rockers need an infusion of new sounds and rhythms.

The easy rhetoric of localism and globalism seems to permeate popular music theory more than other popular cultural spheres. This tendency is overcome by a careful attention to place and space. Peter Dunbar-Hall initiates such a study in 'Site as Song – Song as Site: Constructions of Meaning in an Aboriginal Rock Song' (*Perfect Beat*, 3, 58–76). A fascinating article, the writer works through music's space-producing qualities, with particular attention to the Warumpi Band's 'Warumpinya'. A short history of Aboriginal rock music is presented, with special attention paid to how place recurs in the repertoire. While it is an overstatement to argue that 'the topic of place … appears enough to seem characteristically Aboriginal', he offers a succinct analysis of how the naming of a place through music can access knowledges that change the conditions of consumption and reception.

While authenticity and indigeneity entwine comfortably in Australian musical theory, femininity and feminism remain an underdiscussed category. Maree Macmillan attempts to fill in some of this absence through 'Women Find a Voice in Music' (*Overland*, 147, 19–24). She investigates the role of women in Australian music from the colonial era, summoning the phantoms of Englishness in Antipodean drawing rooms. The reconstructed history of female composers is starting to overcome the absences of feminism in musicology. More usefully framed through feminism are theories of the mobile, dancing body. Tara Brabazon's 'Disco(urse) Dancing: Reading the Body Politic (*Australian Journal of Communication*, 24, 104–114) offers a textualization of the dancing body from disco to techno. In contextualizing modern dance, identity and gender become negotiated territory. Dance music defamiliarizes the semiotic encounter with the mobile body, offering a new approach to theorizing consciousness and meaning. Both these articles offer distinct interventions in theories of music, one through musicology and the other through dance.

Australian popular music has a rich and provocative history. Although working within Anglo-American genres, Aboriginal instrumentation and histories are offering alternative modes of thinking about sound, sensibility and landscape. Women and migrant groups are also considering a very different history of meaning that operates in distinct languages and semiotic systems. Popular music theory is obviously becoming increasingly important to new theories of race, age and identity.

5. Gender and Performance Anxiety

Australia has a critical, quirky feminist history. It has left a politicized and passionate impact on cultural and media studies. Yet the oddity of the last few years of the 1990s is that men and masculinity have claimed much theoretical attention. However, three strong feminist research projects have been undertaken.

Helen Meekosha and Leanne Dowse have produced a surprising, innovative and provocative analysis. In 'Distorting Images, Invisible Images: Gender, Disability and the Media' (*Media International Australia*, 84, 91–101), the writers investigate the gendered nature of disability images. Two narratives of spinal injury commence the piece. The first records a payout of $31.8 million to Jon Blake, an Australian actor who received compensation for an accident. This is compared with $100,000 compensation for a woman who also suffered a car accident. Her compensation was 'justified' for the loss of financial benefits through the support of a husband. It was argued that the accident reduced the plaintiff's prospect of marrying.

By investigating the relationship between gender and disability, Meekosha and Dowse argue that the media promotes very narrow public perceptions of disability. While 1981 was the year of disabled people, theoretical frameworks have moved faster than journalists and editors. Metaphors have remained unchanged, with 'crippled' used to describe an economy and blind and deaf carrying negative meanings. They make the realization that 'photographs usually accompany stories of disabled men, but stories of disabled women are both fewer in number and less likely to be illustrated'. Their interpretation of this phenomenon is that disabled women are rarely considered to be desirable. A woman who is not desirable is not newsworthy. Therefore eroticism, in the case of a feminist disability theory, is not a negative formation, but works against the dominant ideologies of the disability experience. While a victim ideology frames women with disabilities, men are more likely to be discussed as struggling to overcome the odds. This article is important, as it offers the start of a new 'gendered disability studies of the media'. They open the way for new types of research, with attention to different lived experiences of disability.

Similarly innovative is Gillian Swanson and Patricia Wise's *Going for*

Broke: Women's Participation in the Arts and Cultural Industries. Arts Queensland and the Australia Council commissioned this study. The aim was to investigate the status of women as artsworkers in Queensland, and how to identify and overcome disadvantages. Their research is based on surveys and demonstrates the diverse packaging of women's employment as freelance, commercial and sponsored arts. The writers present a regionally nuanced picture, with a network of agencies, corporate sponsorship, government agencies and private patronage. They also make comments about women's use of cultural venues and libraries, demonstrating that they are 'a key client group for the cultural industries'. The study demonstrates that women working in the cultural industries manage work and family patterns and broken career paths through being flexible and maintaining the mix of divergent funding sources and work practices.

Women who also manage long working hours and diverse employment conditions has been the focus of Diane Kirkby's *Barmaids: A History of Women's Work in Pubs.* This is an example of original scholarly research, exploring the role of the pub in Australian life. This history is distinct from the American saloon, with the temperance movement having a distinct effect on the ideology of public drinking in both countries. The book is a contribution to popular cultural studies, labour history and cultural history, serving as a reminder that the pub is a place of work for the barmaids. The operation of gender relationships is particularly pivotal, as not only did female bar staff attend a predominantly male clientele, but women also dominated ninteenth-century temperance movements. Female drinkers were relegated to the Ladies Lounge that was also more derogatively termed the Virgin's Parlour. While the pub is a central icon in Australian popular culture, Kirkby reveals that it circulates in a highly gendered semiotic system. Although the barmaid had to confront prejudice and condescension, the work was better paid than most of the opportunities available to women, and the hours were more regulated than the domestic service.

While gender relations are highlighted, it is significant to realize that the text is the first history of Australia's drinking culture. It is fortunate that such an important text, both historically and theoretically, is well written, effectively referenced and structured into two clear parts: the nineteenth and twentieth century. Excellent primary research, from government documents and photographs, grants the text a depth and breadth that is rare in popular cultural studies. The reason for the barmaids' special stature in popular culture is believed by Kirkby to be caused because 'they have been the mainstay of the hotel trade, and the subject of paintings, plays and films in a way that no other group of workers has'. The infamous six o'clock swill, where men would pack out a bar to order large quantities of beer before closing time, made barmaids' work arduous and threatening. With the masculine drinking and pub culture enshrined in law throughout much of the colonial and national history of Australia, women occupied a highly ambivalent place. Kirkby's argument is that although the barmaid is central to the popular mythology of the pub, women were never considered as drinking companions.

These feminist research projects are important and change the way in which truth and reality are represented. Yet men, masculinity and media have dominated gender studies. David Buchbinder's *Performance Anxieties:*

Re-producing Masculinity, is the key text in this area. He manages a wide spectrum of cultural texts with the aim of exposing the way in which 'culture often works to *prevent* us from seeing them as *representations*, so that we take them instead for reality, for truth'. Masculinity must be performed without error and flaw, so that discussions of power relations and inequality are avoided. Yet Buchbinder argues that ideological excess is being carried in masculine representations. From advertisements for men's underwear to Shakespeare and Bram Stoker's novel *Dracula*, competitive masculinity sorts out the patriarchal order. Confirmation of masculinity is derived through other men, rendering the anomalous dangerous. The book presents a careful analysis of *Strictly Ballroom*, showing how masculinity operates through popular culture and particularly in dance.

Tom Morton has written a more populist rendering of the masculine realm. *Altered Mates: The Man Question* is based on a radio series broadcast by the ABC. The book provides theoretical, political and social commentary about men during the era of Family Court battles, divorce, wife battering and child abuse. Morton considers the concrete struggles that occur in popular culture and everyday life within the group that are labelled as 'mainstream Australia' by politicians and advertising executives. He discusses the highly segregated nature of the Australian work force, emotional investments in family life and sexuality. Popular culture is a constant source of evidence and enlightenment, from the Hunters and Collectors' song 'The Slab' to television commercials presenting family life. Morton recognizes that men have benefited enormously from their power over women, but makes the realization that if men are being oppressed, then it is other men enacting that oppression. This book has a strong structure, and presents a highly convincing argument verified by interviews and popular cultural texts.

Morton's book is impressive because he never argues that feminism is responsible for men's current 'problems'. Bob Lingard and Martin Mills, in 'Masculine Politics: An Introduction' (*Social Alternatives*, 16, 4–6), ask why media stories in the last few years have claimed that feminism is the winner and men are the new victims who require the considerations of public policy. Not discussed is the class question: while middle class women have gained some success, there has been a simultaneous feminization of poverty. Importantly, the writers recognize the context in which they are working. They state that 'much of the reactionary "men's movement" as with Pauline Hanson in respect of race politics, plays on the fears of those who have not been part of the progressive social movements, such as feminism, gay and lesbian liberation, identity politics'. Lingard and Mills try to construct a new type of masculine space, that is not part of a feminist backlash.

R. W. Connell is one of Australia's most distinguished scholars. He has been important to both progressivist teaching movements and the theorizing of masculinity. His article 'Men, Masculinities and Feminism' (*Social Alternatives*, 16, 7–10) provides an investigation of how feminist principles can operate in public life. The importance of childcare and flexible working hours are the most important ways for men to claim alternative roles and identities. He dismisses the New Lads and Promise Keepers, but also realizes how modern primitivism, and the media's discussion of it, is having a detrimental impact on new theories of a masculine self.

Two institutions are ideologically imperative to the formation of masculinity: the military and sport. The latter category has been the focus of a number of articles during the year. David Brown and Russell Hogg, in 'Violence, Masculinity and Sport: Governance and the Swinging Arm' (*The UTS Review*, 3, 129–141) evaluate the emblematic coverage of television sporting events. They investigate why particular violent moments are plucked from the sporting narrative and repeated. There is a socially damaging linkage between violence, masculinity and sport and while the writers acknowledge the dangers in an essential approach to each element in that link, they recognize the need to theorize the place of the video replay in sport. They affirm that 'the crude, essentialist equation – violence=masculinity=sport – actually closes off a whole series of questions opened up by a more detailed analysis of the particular practices involved in the formation of male bodies, masculine identities and specifically violent practices'. The writers do not argue for generalized or reified claims about the effects of violence in sport. Instead, they demand precise semiotic analysis, and provide an example of how it works in rugby league coverage.

Rugby league is also of concern in Martin Mills' exploration of 'Football, Desire and the Social Organization of Masculinity' (*Social Alternatives*, 16, 10–13). He investigates how strong feelings for football have a consequence for other social relationships. As sport, and in particular football codes, represents a valorized masculinity, it is integral to 'the Australian hegemonic masculine project'. By valorizing violence and pain as a way to sort out 'the real men', Mills suggests that sport needs to be analysed with other modes of masculine force, like domestic violence and rape. Most significantly, he discusses how concepts like civilization, race and class function in the football discourse. Australian Rules Football, for example, features many high profile and successful Aboriginal players. Mills suggests that 'these marginalized men are seen as being well suited to football, but not to activities which require intellectual ability'. Sport is therefore highly hegemonic, serving to order and categorize divergent modes of successful masculinity.

Australian Rules Football is a site of changing gender relationships. 1997 saw the arrival of the Nine Network programme *The Footy Show*. Without the right to show video footage, the commentators had to consider other means to fill the hour of television. It became a comedy programme. Women flocked to the show, and it became the most popular show in Melbourne. On first textual reading, it appears misogynist, anti-disabled, anti-working class and anti-gay. To understand the reasons for its success, Robert Pascoe discussed 'Television Humour and Australian Rules Football' (*Metro Education*, 11, 22–24). He focuses attention on Sam Newman, the show's star. An ex-footballer, he presents what Pascoe has described as 'exaggerated masculinity'. Indeed the show is far more about men than football. To explain the high level of female audience, Pascoe believes that the show (and Australian Football more generally) 'follows the same rule of narrative as the soap opera, so it is hardly surprising that . . . [they] share so much of the same audience'. With 'Real Men' valorized and 'Wimps' condemned, Pascoe's argument has much credence.

Outside of Melbourne, a rugby league-based *Footy Show* plays in Sydney and Brisbane. The codes of football in Australia are still incredibly regional, with Victoria, Tasmania, the Northern Territory, Western Australia and

South Australia being centres of Australian Rules, while New South Wales, the Australian Capital Territory and Queensland are saturated by League. Heather Brook investigated the intense gendering of the other *Footy Show* in 'Big Boofy Blokes in Frocks: Feminism, Football and Sexuality' (*Social Alternatives*, 16, 5–9). She explains why women viewers of sport are increasing, by focusing on the increasing presence of footballers in women's magazines, where they are 'presented as erotic spectacles'. The eroticization of class and race-based differences is performed through drag and humour. Yet Brook reminds readers that while rugby league, and *The Footy Show*, presents working class men and women with some erotic possibilities, the dire attention to women's sport should remain a primary concern of feminist researchers.

A courageous feminist researcher attended a cricket match at the Sydney Cricket Ground to observe crowd behaviour. In ' "Spewin', Mate!" – A Day at the Cricket' (*Social Alternatives*, 16, 26–30), she had a close encounter with 'the mythical Aussie Larrikin'. Drinking became pivotal to the determination of hegemonic masculinity, with amateur trumpeters, pitch invasions and blow-up dolls being significant accoutrements to the hard work of being one of the boys. Nikki Wedgwood suggests that 'anyone who was not actively doing hegemonic masculinity was considered "fair game" by those who were'. This humorous, but disturbing piece, displays how the goals of white, working class masculinity are negotiated and ranked through popular sporting events.

Through much of the theoretical work of the year, masculinity is not defined through an opposition to femininity, but via its hierarchical relationship with other modes of masculine performance. This is most clearly revealed in Yong Zhong's discussion of 'Sex Acts: Coverage of a Sex Debate by Australian Chinese Community Media' (*Media International Australia*, 84, 59–66). Shi Guo-ying triggered a media storm, both inside and outside the Chinese community media, by writing a controversial article. She explained why Chinese women prefer a cross-ethnic sexual preference. Her words generated an uproar, with (male) Chinese leaders construing her as a sick, promiscuous woman because of her preference for 'Western' men. In response to this controversy, Yong Zhong shows how this furore revealed the highly volatile performance of Chinese masculinity in Australia.

Both Chinese and Western working class masculinity are absent voices from one of the more disturbing texts of the year, Jill Julius Matthews' edited collection *Sex in Public: Australian Sexual Culture*. Although the title suggests that Australian culture is the sphere of interest, the overwhelming majority of writers are from Sydney, with a few from Canberra and Melbourne. The rest of Australia, outside of the southeast corner of the continent, appears to be doing, thinking and theorizing little of interest. Although Jill Julius Matthews in her 'Introduction' (xi–xxix) mentions this absence, she states that 'there is considerable reference to the abstract internationalism of cyberspace'. The key for Matthews is to find groups that use and define sex as central practices of identification. Most importantly she argues that sex is not necessarily a community building practice, because it centres on individual desires and actions. Catherine Lumby's chapter, 'Nothing Personal: Sex, Gender and Identity in the Media Age' (1–15), is the most successful of the collection. She uses Baudrillard's work on the seduction and the feminine to survey a range of Australian magazines, from the tabloid weeklies to the new men's magazines like *Men's Health*, and large circulation women's magazines. She argues that 'the Bad, Literal Feminist reading' and the 'Knowing, Cultural Hip reading' both lack a subtle mechanism through which to explore the flow of desire between media and audience. By wishing to view audiences and readers as textual objects, Lumby restates much of John Hartley's argument about the collapse of the public sphere, and its rebirth through the media. However, discussion is lacking as to why magazine circulation, for both men and women, is expanding. What type of public sphere is being created? What are the new rules of textual engagement and who holds power?

Barbara Creed discusses the way in which new technologies are changing the power relations of sexuality in 'Screen Sex: From Television to Teledildonics' (16–30). She investigates the world of computer pornography and Internet relay chat. She theorizes the nature of sexual harassment on the net and the meanings of disembodied sex. Quite importantly, she explores how the division between the public and private sphere is splintering through the intervention of technology. Fiona Patten continues this discussion through 'The Economy of Pleasure and the Always of Desire' (31–49). She emphasizes the regulation and judgements upon sexual pleasure, notably through prostitution, erotic dancing and X-rated videos. Once more, technology is changing and challenging legislative frameworks. Patten questions how *Penthouse* on CD-ROM will alter censorship provisions.

Other chapters investigate bisexuality (McKenzie Wark, 'Bisexual Meditations: Beyond the Third Term', 63–77) and the gay community (Gary Dowsett, 'Sexual Conduct, Sexual Culture, Sexual Community', 78–89), but overall the book has major weaknesses. First, the text is too presentist and hyper-individualistic. Outside of the technology-based chapters, further research is needed into the history of Australian sex in public. Such an absence is remarkable considering Jill Julius Matthews' reputation as one of Australia's finest historians. Also, there is no reason to prioritize Sydney culture in this way. Sydney is not Australia, and must not masquerade as such. The other major concern is that heterosexuality, particularly for women, is rarely mentioned as a public discourse outside of the magazines that they read and the (gay) men they meet. To tackle such a wide-ranging topic as sex, and to subtitle the book *Australian Sexual Culture*, necessitates a far more diverse study in terms of regions covered, theoretical frameworks utilized, deployed writing styles and political agendas.

Far more effective in addressing this range of issues is John Tulloch and Deborah Lupton's *Television, AIDS and Risk*. The text is so competent because it not only moves through a series of historical tensions, but also is methodologically innovative. The writers use cultural studies approaches in a way that also encompasses social science methodologies. Quantitative analysis and ethnographic data are assembled, and matched with theories of reading. Health communication is an underinvestigated part of popular cultural studies, as television and advertising is used in a highly pedagogic function. This book represents Australian cultural studies at its most sophisticated, constructing knowledges but also being reflexive about the differences in knowing systems.

Language, power and AIDS is the key relationship of the text. It is monitored through a diversity of texts, from graffiti to television advertisements, from soap opera to documentaries. The Grim Reaper advertisement is probably Australia's most famous contribution to the AIDS awareness campaign. Launched in April 1987, it features a dark, skeletal figure standing at the end of a bowling alley and, upon rolling the ball, knocks over women, children, men and the aged. Tulloch and Lupton grant much attention to this most famous of advertisements, assessing how risk is embedded in the culture of the young, the feminine, the masculine and the black. As they state 'risk is used to distinguish between self and other, to project anxieties and cast moral judgements and blame upon marginalized social groups'. They reinforce this argument by a careful discussion of televisual documentaries and the place of the AIDS body in soap opera.

Besides risk, the writers also discuss how knowledge is owned and presented in public. Health professionals rarely use media theory to construct or decode health messages, just as cultural studies theorists rarely evaluate health campaigns. Tulloch and Lupton suggest throughout their book that research must always 'seek to explore the broader context in which audiences respond' to textual material. This excellent text is a reminder of the importance, both politically and theoretically, of effective cultural studies research.

6. Technology as a Commodity

During 1997, Australian publishers and journal editors discovered the Internet. While there were occasional articles and a few metaphoric references before that time, this year signals the commencement of a sustained questioning of how technology changes social conventions or reinforces conventional ideological frameworks. The balance and rigour of this debate is a welcome corrective to many of the excessive affirmations or attacks on computer-based operations.

P. David Marshall presents an array of services and industries that spiral from the Internet in 'The Commodity and the Internet: Interactivity and the Generation of the Audience Commodity' (*Media International Australia*, 83, 51–62). He uses the word 'reorientation' to describe how the Internet is altering the uses of other media. By discussing the new definitional spaces arising through technology, he monitors the continual integration of media forms. For example, the radio will be an important site of innovation for the Internet, as users wish to listen to music while working. Clearly, the Internet is a commodity, which contravenes many of the historical freedoms associated with cyberspace. Marshall focuses on the way that Internet advertising actually materializes the users and stabilizes the way that theorists understand media audiences.

The rhetoric of freedom, in both information and ideas, is also being criticized through empirical study. Mark Balnaves and Peter Caputi critique how class and the level of educational attainment shape patterns of technological adoption ('Technological Wealth and the Evaluation of Information Poverty', *Media International Australia*, 83, 92–102). They focus on the case study of Gungahlin, a suburb of Canberra. This technology-rich population provides 'an excellent vignette' of how the ownership of other media also triggers an entry into computer-based ownership. Balnaves and Caputi recognize that 'there is currently no comprehensive methodology to assess the impact of new networked series on quality of life'. The affiliation between information change and societal transformation requires more attention.

Concerns with the social role of technology are also stressed by Peter Spearritt in 'Content, Access and Equity in the New Communications Environment' (*Culture and Policy*, 8, 115–132). This article, written by a historian with an interest in cultural policy, acknowledges 'both ambivalence and confusion' with the new communications environment. He suggests that all new technologies raise old questions about the theoretical and political repercussions for the distribution and analysis of material. He remains conscious of how both online services and CD-ROM are increasing the distinction between classes. This makes the provision of computer-based learning a highly charged decision for universities. The research potential is enormous, but the World Wide Web provides information without knowledge, and millions of texts without a context. Spearritt's article outlines these concerns as they apply to universities, scholars, librarians and students.

Journalists are also asking how new modes of knowing interact with their modes of working. Mark Pearson, in 'Look Who's Talking' (*Media International Australia*, 84, 112–121), asks how new technologies are applied within Australasian journalism. Of particular interest is the way in which electronic discussion lists can be used in journalistic work. Importantly, Pearson reminds readers that the United States' domination of discussion lists and the Internet generally means that virtual and general knowledge is revealed, but without concrete and tangible evidence.

Electronic publishing is new, fast and threatening. It offers enormous opportunities, but has high establishment costs in both equipment and training. A guide through this new field is John Colette and Meredith Quinn's edited collection, *The Business of Electronic Publishing*. The readership for this text varies from cultural studies theorists who desire an understanding of the digital environment to those wishing to enter the discourse of electronic imaging. The wide format of the book makes it easy to read and use. John Colette's 'The Big Picture' (1–35) investigates how markets and technologies are changing, with opportunities for early adopters being matched by miscued movements into multimedia. He reminds readers that it still is very difficult to make judgements about the success of net-based advertising, with 'market share' being difficult to measure or assess. Yet he argues that the net is different, as it gathers audiences or consumers at a phenomenal rate, being the first communication technology with a global media footprint. Other chapters discuss the role of 'The CD-ROM Producer' (Jonathon Delacour, 45–58) and 'Publishing on CD-ROM' (Erica Dale, 79–85). Yet the most useful technical chapter is John Colette's 'Toolchest: Electronic Imaging' (87–99). He discusses the importance of Adobe PhotoShop, presenting examples of its work. For media technology theorists or technicians moving into the area, this is a solid work that can take a beginner to more advanced levels.

Trying to understand the Internet is difficult. It is growing and moving faster than most can imagine. It is a cultural formation that seems to work in dog years. The best publications in the area combine applied knowledge with theoretical reflexivity about publishing in the new environment. Technological change is altering the way in which journalists collate news, students study and teachers teach. However, too much time is being spent in questions of copyright and graphic quality, without considering the pedagogical repercussions of the modifications. The next review section assesses these concerns.

7. Pedagogy and Popular Culture

New literacies are formed and changed through the proliferation of computers. Ilana Snyder's *Page to Screen: Taking Literacy into the Electronic Age* is a relevant and diverse edited collection. The book has four sections: the spaces of electronic literacies, emerging literacies, the problems and possibilities of hypertext, and changing the cultures of teaching and learning. The research bounces off Stuart Hall's proclamation of 'New Times'. This drift to differentiation and fragmentation, and away from homogeneity and standardization, offers a rethink into how information is produced and accessed. The transformation from page to screen is not only a movement of media, but also a shift in politics, identity and philosophy.

In 'Page to Screen' (xx–xxxvi) Ilana Snyder investigates how literacy practices have changed through the use of electronic mail, hypertext and word processing. Through modification of language use, a different interlacing of technology and literacy takes place. Yet Snyder argues that the promise of technology as an educational tool was discussed when television arrived fifty years ago, but few curriculum changes resulted from these debates.

Gunther Kress always offers fresh insight into the relationship between ocular and linguistic codes. The chapter 'Visual and Verbal Modes of Representation in Electronically Mediated Communication: The Potentials of New Forms of Text' (53–79), investigates the social application of knowledge. Careful consideration is attended to the way in which e-mails reshape a social situation and the language used. Kress's thesis is 'information that displays what the world is like is carried by the image; information that orients the reader to that information is carried by language'. This chapter inserts writing into a visual mode of communication.

This discussion is continued in the context of e-mail by Charles Moran and Gail E. Hawisher's 'The Rhetorics and Languages of Electronic Mail' (80–101). The chapter discusses computer-mediated communication as a new writing space, revealing new concerns with access. The writers analyse the 'warmth' of e-mail communications, and the reasons for the sense of immediacy and intimacy. They also discuss the ease with which these short messages can be composed, copied and stored.

The World Wide Web and hypertext offer theorists a new and changing site to consider the nature of literacy. Nicholas Burbules, in 'Rhetorics of the Web: Hyperreading and Critical Literacy' (102–122), evaluates how hypertext alters the way in which readers engage with information. It is the links that make the World Wide Web distinctive. Yet Burbules reveals his concern for the over-synthesizing tendencies of the web. As most of the Web is organized around statistics, visuals, dates, lists and charts, a greater responsibility rests on users transforming information into knowledge. Ilana Snyder continues this discussion in 'Beyond the Hyper: Reassessing Hypertext' (125–143). She draws this use of hypertext into the educational sphere. Snyder argues that 'if teachers are prepared to transfer to students much of the responsibility for accessing, sequencing and deriving meaning from information, hypertext can provide an environment in which exploratory or discovery learning may flourish'. By removing the hyperbole and placing technology into longer histories of change, clearer applications emerge. Overall, *Page to Screen* is a well-balanced text. The chapters are diverse in their methods and topics, but reveal deep scholarly research and a careful grafting of new technologies onto classroom models of literacy.

While *Page to Screen* is a text aimed at helping teachers confront and understand the changes in their classrooms, Erica McWilliam is interested in how the 'embodied' practices of education are altering through technological change ('No Body to Teach With? The Technological Makeover of the University Teacher', *Australian Journal of Communication*, 24, 1–8). She discusses a sometimes controversial and frequently underplayed component of teaching – 'the (corpo)realities of university pedagogy'. She asks how teachers' bodies operate within the pedagogical process and how this will change through online delivery of materials. By keeping students' bodies 'off campus', teaching and learning become cheaper and faster. However, McWilliams is arguing that many of the problematic teaching methods are not being addressed. She realizes that 'the current excitement over learning packages, e-mail, on-line delivery and related cyber-pedagogical activities can be explained in part by the great relief of many lecturers who need no longer be betrayed by their embodied performance in large group lectures or tutorials'. She ponders how technologies will alter the subjectivities of both teachers and students.

A misleading title betrays a remarkable example of popular cultural pedagogy in Robyn Quin and Barrie McMahon's article, 'The Case of *Babe* on the Internet: New Paradigms of Curriculum Development' (*Metro Education*, 9, 9–21). While a side argument does discuss the sites dedicated to the most famous pig in Australian cinema, far wider analytical judgements are made of media education and the new opportunities available. After a brief history of the area, the writers determine that a dynamic cultural context is best suited to a vibrant media pedagogy. They argue that the world outside of the text must be emphasized at all times, stating that media teachers do not grant enough attention to reading public texts, like policy statements or economic literature. Also, Quin and McMahon are far more interventionist with regard to shaping students' relationship with the Internet. They state that 'students should not be allowed to begin their search until they have a clear idea of what information they are looking for and some directions on how they might find it'. Quin and McMahon are interested in fostering a dynamic relationship between text and context: non-interventionist 'net surfing' by students does not interest them. This article offers a new way of thinking about (and through) media education, crystal-lizing how teachers can move beyond semiotic and audience paradigms, which can over-emphasize specific texts.

Alison Lee and Bill Green consider 'Pedagogy and Disciplinarity in the "New University"' (*The UTS Review*, 3, 1–25). They begin their investigation with a set of simple questions about the relationship between higher education and the University, education and training, teaching and learning, information and knowledge. They argue that the work currently being conducted by the academy is being placed under much stress and is remoulding into a new form. Clearly, 'it is certainly not the case . . . that it is Business as Usual in terms of efficacy and effects of what people do in the name of teaching'. With a new and continually changing definition of knowledge, 'everyone has become an expert on education'. While department, faculties and schools of education are under much stress, other specialist areas of knowledge are claiming a credibility in pedagogy that may be unwanted. The relationship between a critical pedagogy and cultural studies is of much interest to the writers, who believe a theoretical and political edge will be added to analysts utilizing this frame. They affirm that a qualified researcher is not necessarily a good teacher, and with few academics trained as teachers, a sloppy approach to curriculum and methodology is being produced. This article is strongly argued and highly provocative. For cultural studies theorists wanting to explore how pedagogy can be theorized in the Australian context, this piece is crucial.

Terry Flew also investigates the changes in media studies 'From Demountables to Foundations' (*Media Education*, 10, 22–27). He assesses the credibility issues that have dogged the development of media studies, yet recognizes that the area is now continuing to grow, while the other areas of the arts and humanities are in structural decline. Flew affirms that media studies must be resituated, particularly in its relationship with literary theory, and there is a need to consider policy issues. The explosion in Australian communication services, with national growth trebling in 1994–45, results in challenges for Australian teachers to grasp new theories of audience, markets and industries. The two trajectories of media studies, in tertiary and secondary education, means that there must be a far greater attention paid to teaching practices. Flew argues for a cultural politics which has a justifiable significance outside the educational sector, rather than replaying the 'ethical registers of the traditional humanities'. The only criticism of Flew's work is that he does not acknowledge that most teachers of media and cultural studies come from 'the traditional humanities'. Anne Waldron Neumann's writing offers a counter to Flew's theoretical vectors. She asks, 'Should you Read Shakespeare?' (*Meanjin*, 56, 17–25). She addresses her words to secondary school students, asking what they may gain from knowledge of the literary canon. She offers a way to think about Shakespeare as a politicized formulation, offering much historical insight. Her words effectively counter contemporary scholars who claim that Shakespeare is either of 'benefit' or 'harm'. Ian Hunter justifies the importance of this type of analysis in 'The Critical Disposition: Some Historical Configurations of the Humanities' (*The UTS Review*, 3, 26–55). He argues that the humanities is a site for historical pedagogy, tracing definitions of terms like critical, criticism and critique. This theoretical training has one aim: 'the teaching of students to mistrust or suspend experiential judgement'. Hunter's work is significant, as he reminds teachers that their aim is discuss modes of negotiation that are appropriate for a precise context.

The crisis of the humanities is a maxim saturating scholarly journals. It is ironic that this fear and concern emerges during the era that critical thinking is most required. In this context, R. W. Connell offers 'Notes on the World Intelligentsia' (*The UTS Review*, 3, 74–86). He discusses the role of debate in European and North American intellectual life. While no longer using the Arnoldian language of philistines and barbarians, Connell charts the way intellectuals operate within a class system. His major concern is how the rhetoric of access to higher education is balanced against the abstraction of intellectual work. In offering 'an industrial sociology of knowledge', Connell tempers talk of crisis with a reflexive debate about the nature and place of intellectual work in universities and beyond.

Australian theorists of popular culture and media studies are thinking, actively and critically, about education inside and outside the university. With the humanities suffering economic threats and structural changes, the study of a popular pedagogy and critical thinking is becoming more significant. Matched with this interest in classroom politics is a desire to arch beyond university confines and intervene in Australia's political and social system – to write a republic.

8. Writing the Republic

Some Australian critics have described their struggle against the baby-boomer generation as a culture war. These scholars are mostly based in Sydney, white, affluent and older than they seem. The most controversial book to emerge during 1997 is Mark Davis's *Gangland: Cultural Elites and the New Generationalism*. Although he repeatedly denies that his book is an example of boomer bashing, he draws his combatants precisely. An 'older generation of cultural apparatchiks' are blind to 'young people['s] ... suffering'. He critiques the clubbishness of intellectual groups, but argues that 'never has a "generation" looked over its shoulder so constantly and with such fear'. His strongest work is placed in evaluating the cultural wars over political correctness, victim feminism, censorship and literary theory. His least convincing arguments are ahistorical ramblings that state that 'old guard' journalists are representing young people as dole bludgers, irresponsible students or apolitical feminists. He ignores the sizeable historiography of youth culture, particularly Australian-based research on the moral panics encircling the bodgies and widgies in the 1950s.

His overarching argument is that Australia has a powerful cultural establishment that will not relinquish editorial control or influence. While these culture wars may appear real and suffocating in Sydney, the book refuses to look beyond a very narrow group of editors, writers, critiques and publishers in the southeast corner of Australia. Why does he share with his readers that 'none of my own friends voluntarily reads Elizabeth Jolley or Helen Garner or Barry Hill or Robert Drewe or Rodney Hall or David Malouf'? This poorly aimed dismissal of Australian writers is not necessary, and actually undermines the credibility of his argument. Instead, he blithely defends young writers from the savagery of baby boomers. Attacks on Helen Demidenko-Darville are oddly sandwiched with censorship of death metal and gangsta rap. While he rightly suggests that 'I've taken the attitude throughout this book that the media aren't any one thing ... all sorts of media from talkback radio to 'zines ... are context-sensitive at the point of reception', he has not applied his own thesis. The text is too generalized, moving between disparate sites with a confidence that belies an awareness of bodies of theoretical writing in radio, fanzines and popular music. While he places much emphasis on new knowledges and new practitioners, he underestimates how many other Australian critics are developing new and insightful research projects into cultural policy, communication technology and pedagogy. He asks, 'What is it about the past? The present certainly doesn't seem to be the place where anybody wants to be lately'. This review into Australian popular culture and media studies during 1997 demonstrates that there are many researchers who are interested in contemporary questions. Actually, if there is a major overarching criticism of contemporary Australian cultural studies it is a lack of historical awareness.

This presentist ideology is displayed in Catherine Lumby's *Bad Girls*. Like Davis, she establishes 'a vast cultural gap' between generations. Instead of a distinction through age, Lumby confirms a cultural difference formed by the experience of television. She argues that a new generation of women have encountered a diverse experience of politics and corporate life through the medium. Her attack on feminism includes a denunciation of the way in which television's role in representational politics has been underestimated and undermined. The major flaw in the text is a shadow boxing of feminists who 'are clinging to a literal-minded and narrow view of the relationship between the media and their consumers'. The book ends with a demand that feminists learn from 'the mass media'. Yet women who are already constructing this productive work are unacknowledged.

There is a network of writers, including Mark Davis, Catherine Lumby and McKenzie Wark, who are being defined and limited as much by geography as age. While these writers produce much work of importance and merit, their more high-profile material demonstrates a lack of careful consideration of its impact, particularly out of Sydney. Also, their 'establishment' enemies are increasingly being misrepresented. Paul Dawson, for example, analyses 'Grunge Lit: Marketing Generation X' (*Meanjin*, 56, 119–125). Unlike Davis, Dawson is careful to separate Generation X as a marketing device and as an age-based category. He describes Grunge as being used 'to fuel the myth, beloved of the Australian media and book publishing industries, of a conflict between generational cultures'. By providing a brief literary genealogy of grunge, he recognizes that the autobiographical element of the texts dooms the genre to being a collection of first books by new authors. He unwinds the affiliation between baby boomer/establishment and Generation X/other. Instead, Dawson summons critics to 'bemoan the ways in which mediating institutions like the press can equate a genre of writing with the voice of a generation'. Davis did not attempt such a careful argument.

After Meaghan Morris and John Frow, the most acknowledged writer in Australian cultural studies is McKenzie Wark. His first book, *Virtual Geography*, has entered the cliched paradigm of undergraduate students, while his regular contributions to *The Australian* newspaper's *Higher Education Supplement* ensure that his ideas have a wide currency and diverse readership. Therefore, his second text, *The Virtual Republic: Australia's Culture Wars of the 1990s*, was greeted with much anticipation in cultural studies circles. Certainly, the book represents a depth of argument and consideration beyond Davis's *Gangland*, but is uneven in its quality. As it progresses, it becomes more assured and wide ranging. However, the first ninety pages are a series of vignettes looking for an argument. Too much is being discussed: the republic, scholarly writing, institutional change, Sydney, Sydney postmodernism, Sydney culture and Sydney intellectual culture. Like Davis, Wark confirms that Sydney-based scholars have yet to realize that there is life beyond Oxford Street, Manly and Glebe. As with all Wark's work there is much to ponder and consider. He suggests that 'a republic . . . can only converse, in these "postmodern" times, in a virtual space composed of media, rather than in the public square of the old renaissance republics'. This important idea needs much greater attention. Wark throws off a series of important concepts, texts and cheeky slogans that are remarkable in their scope. Yet he rarely doubles back to elaborate on his, at times quite controversial, maxims. For example, he offers the charming mantra that 'the tyranny of distance gives way to the tyranny of difference'. These brilliant stylistic sorties are rarely verified against historical or textual evidence. Although he claims that *Virtual Republic* is a book of essays, invoking a writing process rather than a fixed research path, there are few excuses, literary or pedagogic, for presenting too many ideas and too little explication. A recurrent problem throughout the book is his shifting (and quite shaky) usage of 'culture'. It is used to describe (at the very least) sociological groupings, disempowered collectives, texts, contexts and intellectual work.

Virtual Republic is at its best through its discussion of Australian cultural studies. There is an international tendency, most witnessed in the journal *Cultural Studies*, to ignore, decentre or forget the Australian contribution to the field. Wark offers a significant corrective, providing an important history of the movement. The forces of feminism, multiculturalism, Aboriginal cultural activism and environmentalism generate a broad theory of difference. The political contribution of the book is the unravelling of the 'fair go' legend against the challenges of Pauline Hanson. Who is a mate, and who is outside this imagining?

Ironically, the disparity of issues means that *Virtual Republic* does not unpick the topic of its title. Clare O'Farrell, in 'Media Republics: Intellectuals Strike Back' (*Continuum*, 11, 54–60), assesses how the anti-intellectualism of Australian popular culture will be changed through the Republican Movement. She argues that 'intellectuals . . . are on home territory when it comes to debate over symbols'. Governmentality and nationalism provide rich fodder for scholarly debate. However, O'Farrell remains critical of many university-based academics for their inability to present ideas in a diversity of media fora. This discussion of modes of knowing and modes of presenting knowledge is also addressed in Tara Brabazon's 'Making it Big: Julie Burchill and Writing in Public' (*The UTS Review*, 3, 96–106). She evaluates how the 'dangerous' politics and prose of Burchill can provide options and triggers for Australian cultural studies. There is also a discussion of how Burchill's map, and those of other writer/academics like Camille Paglia, rarely include Australia, New Zealand or the Asian and Pacific region. It is argued that a blending of cultural studies and cultural journalism will generate an apparatus for intellectuals to present ideas beyond the offices and corridors of a university.

A superb and far-reaching transnational approach to critical thinking is

Andrew Milner's 'Cultural Studies and Cultural Hegemony' (*Arena Journal*, 9, 133–155). He critiques current theorists for 'an endemic lack of historical memory'. Because of the sociological and semiological domination of contemporary cultural studies, theoretical frameworks become over-archingly synchronic. Milner situates British cultural studies into a desire for a practical political agenda that would extend beyond class-based relationships. Yet he argues that Australian cultural studies has a distinct radical tradition, located in history rather than literature. These early historical writers, like Ian Turner, Stephen Murray-Smith and the journal *Overland*, have been sidelined in an attempt to 'keep up' with international cultural studies. Quite provocatively, Milner argues that Australian cultural studies focuses on the nation, not out of patriotic loyalty or an intense interest in the popular sphere, 'but rather as a means to secure a place of its own, a niche market in fact, in the increasingly globalized business of Anglo-American higher learning'. With Commonwealth literature an untrendy enterprise, Australian postcolonial theory is far more marketable.

Milner's article will hopefully challenge Australian scholars to invoke indigenous historical paths, while also pondering transnational and regional affiliations. This earlier task can be assisted through Michael Pickering's *History, Experience and Cultural Studies*. Working off Carolyn Steedman and E. P. Thompson, this text presents an overlay of social history and cultural studies. The aim is to not only take popular culture seriously, but also to use popular culture to unsettle more determinist forms of Marxism. He produces a thorough and convincing reading of how history and cultural studies separated into divergent traditions. Pickering reminds cultural studies theorists that 'historical practice is about keeping faith with those ordinary men and women'. While presentist or poststructuralist approaches have value, there is a significant intellectual resource not currently being deployed in Australian cultural studies.

While the nation is the primary node of contemporary cultural studies analysis, an under-theorized framework of proto-Republicanism is the landscape. George Seddon is a remarkable academic who has a diverse career, taking a first degree in English, followed by a PhD in geology. These knowledges have joined in *Landprints: Reflections on Place and Landscape*. A popular cultural Australia is constructed, with attention to the environmental aspects of history and regionalism. The motif of landprints is deployed to convey how the land is used, abused and read within Australian popular culture. Discussion focuses on both the project of Australianness and the role of universities in that formation. His writing is stylish, evocative and engaging, ideally suited to assessing Australia as 'Europe's "geographic unconscious"'. The way in which language structures both our maps and reality is applied to photographic sources, gardens, the backyard and literacy criticism. The book is an ocular pleasure: innovative graphics, in both colour and black and white makes this book a textured guide through both the Australian landscape and critical writing.

Chris Healy, like George Seddon, is drawn to the undulations of the land. *From the Ruins of Colonialism: History and Social Memory* offers an application of postcolonial theory and popular memory to contemporary Australian life. His aim is for contemporary citizens to 'learn ... to inhabit landscapes of memory which are, in part, landscapes littered with ruins'.

Healy works through the iconic status of James Cook, and how such colonial memories have entered history. For Aboriginal Australians, history has been a destructive force, a constitutive element in dispossession and inequality. Yet Healy believes in the realm of 'social memory', a more fluent and just rendering of British 'ruins' can be revealed in the Australian present.

A smaller, but more obvious presence of Britishness in Australian popular culture is found in footwear. Tara Brabazon's 'Boot Politics: Pondering the Antipodean Doctor Marten Boot' (*Continuum*, 11, 59–73) follows movements of meaning within a 'transnational podiatrist paradigm'. After providing a brief history of Docs, she argues that the shoes and boots claim a trope of marginality throughout the world, but this marginality resonates differently in distinct places. The case study of Doc Marten advertising in both Australia and New Zealand is worked through multiculturalism and biculturalism to investigate the functions of English ideologies within the Antipodean present. Such a presence was also summoned after the death of Diana, Princess of Wales. Kevin McDonald, in 'Global Emotion' (*Meanjin*, 56, 596–613) investigates how Diana's death became a world event. He reviews Australian newspapers' response to the death and offers a critique of easy globalization. He demonstrates how a search for ritual, when combined with a global attention to private lives, results in an intense visibility on not only a death and funeral, but the British people's public mourning.

On a much smaller scale, but over a much longer time, Australia's Anzac myth has operated as a site of both nation building and collective mourning. Anna Rutherford and James Wieland have edited a diverse and exciting book, *War: Australia's Creative Response*. A wide range of material is investigated from postcards and photographs, to cartoons, diaries, film and history. Rutherford and Wieland in their 'Foreword' (xi–xii) do not aim to celebrate war, but to convey both the celebratory and traumatic ideologies that have greeted its arrival. The myth of Anzac is a constant presence, however, they remind readers that 'hardly a decade has passed when Australian troops have not been fighting on foreign shores in someone else's war'. The strongest chapters offer an amalgamation of cultural history, cultural studies and film theory. Livio and Pat Dobrez open out 'Old Myths and New Delusions: Peter Weir's Australia' (215–227). The writers provide a careful review of *Gallipoli*, to show how the film structures sentimentality into the final scenes of death and destruction. The political concerns, such as the place of indigenous Australians, and the relationship between the Irish and English in the new nation, are underplayed. As the writers realize, 'Absurdities abound here. A blond (read British) Australian lays down his life for a reluctant Irish Australian ... Obviously Weir has not heard of Easter 1916'. Maintaining a similar argument, Graeme Turner researches the television series 'Anzacs' (229–238). This mini series screened in Australia during November 1985, and received much criticism at the time for its 'Pommy-bashing'. Turner situates this programme into a 'more widespread revision of Australian entanglement with colonial ties'. The objectivity of the text is not relevant to Turner: instead it is a subjective deployment of confidence in a future without British leadership. Most importantly, he argues that the mini series occupies a positive role in recognizing that television, and popular cultural generally, is important for reimagining and reconstituting Australian history.

The search for a (re)public, an audience, a nation and a readership has dominated the attention of writers during 1997. While computer-mediated communication has raised new questions about the role of the university and academics in society, it is clear that it is a reflexive interpretation of history that demands most attention. The balancing of multiculturalism, postcoloniality, economic rationalism and a morphing nation state is generating a difficult, dynamic and productive context in which to conduct scholarly work. While Pauline Hanson may fade from power, and the culture wars subside, it is obvious that Australian popular culture and media studies is a vigorous and volatile terrain.

Books Reviewed

Adams, P. and L. Burton. *Talkback: Emperors of the Air*. Allen and Unwin. pp. 246. pb A$16.95. ISBN 1 86448 325 3.

Buchbinder, D. *Performance Anxieties: Re-producing Masculinity*. Allen and Unwin. pp. 210. pb A$24.95. ISBN 1 86448 425 X.

Colette, J. and M. Quinn. *The Business of Electronic Publishing*. Allen and Unwin. pp. 229. pb A$35. ISBN 0 642 27093 7.

Cunningham, S and G. Turner. *The Media in Australia: second edition*. Allen and Unwin. pp. 492. pb A$35.00. ISBN 1 86448 272 7.

Davis, M. *Gangland: Cultural Elites and the New Generationalism*. Allen and Unwin. pp. 308. pb A$17.95. ISBN 1 86448 340 7.

Healy, C. *From the Ruins of Colonialism: History as Social Memory*. Cambridge University Press. pp. 249. pb £14.95. ISBN 0 521 56576 6.

Kirkby, D. *Barmaids: A History of Women's Work in Pubs*. Cambridge University Press. pp. 244. pb A$29.95. ISBN 0 521 56868 4.

Kociumbas, J. *Australian Childhood: A History*. Allen and Unwin. pp. 276. pb A$24.95. ISBN 1 86448 059 9.

Lumby, C. *Bad Girls*. Allen and Unwin. pp. 228. pb A$17.95. ISBN 1 86448 076 9.

Matthews, J. *Sex in Public: Australian Sexual Culture*. Allen and Unwin. pp. 197. pb A$24.95. ISBN 1 86448 049 1.

Morton, T. *Altered Mates: The Man Question*. Allen and Unwin. pp. 322. pb A$16.95. ISBN 1 86448 333 4.

Neuenfeldt, K. ed. *The Didjeridu: From Arnhem Land to Internet*. John Libbey and Company. pp. 184. pb A$29.95. ISBN 1 86462 004 8.

Pearson, M. *The Journalist's Guide to Media Law*. Allen and Unwin. pp. 272. pb A$24.95. ISBN 1 86448 434 9.

Pickering, M. *History, Experience and Cultural Studies*. Macmillan Press. pp. 274. pb £14.50. ISBN 0 333 62110 7.

Rutherford, A. and J. Wieland. *War: Australia's Creative Response*. Allen and Unwin. pp. 356. pb A$29.95. ISBN 1 87104 918 9.

Seddon, G. *Landprints: Reflections on Place and Landscape*. Cambridge University Press. pp. 254. hb A$39.95. ISBN 0 521 58501 8.

Snyder, I. *Page to Screen: Taking Literacy into the Electronic Age*. Allen and Unwin. pp. 260. pb A$29.95. ISBN 1 86448 435 7.

Swanson, G. and P. Wise. *Going for Broke: Women's Participation in the Arts and Cultural Industries.* Australian Key Centre for Cultural and Media Policy. pp. 229. pb A$22.00. ISBN 0 86857 915 7.

Tulloch, J. and D. Lupton. *Television, AIDS and Risk.* Allen and Unwin. pp. 236. pb A$29.99. ISBN 1 86448 224 9.

Wark, M. *The Virtual Republic: Australia's Culture Wars in the 1990s.* Allen and Unwin. pp. 314. pb A$19.95. ISBN 1 86448 520 5.

13

Popular Music

DAVID BUCKLEY

This chapter has five sections: 1. Biography, Autobiography and Critical Surveys of Artists; 2. Anthologies, Collections and Encyclopaedias; 3. History and Analysis; 4. Short Notices; 5. Articles.

1. Biography, Autobiography and Critical Surveys of Artists

The editor of one of the leading rock monthly publications in the UK recently said that only two sorts of books ever made it big in the popular music publishing world. Either you had to write a tacky biography to cash in instantaneously on the latest teeny-pop sensation, and fill your book with cut 'n' paste derivative prose and as many photos as possible. Or you had to write a biography so well researched, so compelling, so weighty, that it could stand comparison to any other biography from any other academic discipline. Pop star biographies had to be as well put together as, say, one on Field Marshal Montgomery or some other 'serious' figure deemed worthy of weighty biographical probing. Sadly, most pop academics do not write pop biographies. Rather, within popular music studies the individual tends to be endlessly theorized, displaced, removed, seen as a 'star text', a signifier or an embodiment of a mood, a zeitgeist, an environment, an embodiment of media myths. Taking a lead from film studies critic Richard Dyer and his groundbreaking work, *Stars* (British Film Institute, 1979), popular music scholars have evaded the discussion of individuals by stripping them of their individuality. While almost every other academic discipline treats biography as valid, popular music studies is usually apologetic. Wary of hagiography, or the blind partisanship of the fan, scholars are traditionally loath to nail their colours to the mast. The result is that popular music studies is a world curiously under-populated by famous individuals within the pop process. Biography is still overwhelmingly the province of the journalist-fan critic. At its worst, the product of this tradition is mere froth: ill-advised and poorly written press releases emanating from within the industry, or pamphleteering masquerading as literature. At its best, however, there are biographies that pass the 'Field Marshal Montgomery test' with flying colours.

Take Barry Miles' *Paul McCartney Many Years From Now*, for example.

Almost a decade in the writing, this expansive and erudite biography is a major work of learning. It does have its flaws: as an official biography it is perforce mildly compromised and partisan. Although McCartney has understandably sought to answer all those critics who have dubbed him the 'soft' side to Lennon's caustic genius, the result is a refreshingly balanced and honest take on the 1960s. Miles is the perfect biographer for McCartney. Active on the scene as editor of *International Times*, he knew his subject well. Compared with George Harrison's mid-1970s autobiography, *I Me Mine*, which woefully underplayed the role of the other individuals' contribution to the Beatles, *Many Years From Now* is charitable and level-headed. Miles expertly discusses McCartney's Liverpool working-class roots, and shows how it was primarily McCartney, and not Lennon, who had a love for bringing in literary and cultural references and ideas into the Beatles' work. Finally, the exhaustive analyses of the nuts and bolts of record composition and production, together with detail on managerial, promotional and music business wheels and deals, makes the book essential reading.

Part of the rationale behind *Many Years From Now* was to show that, despite McCartney's (justified) reputation as a purveyor of the less-than-radical, maudlin dirge, he was, in fact, more attuned to the subterranean rumblings of the 1960s' underground than Lennon. *We All Shine On: The Stories Behind Every John Lennon Song 1970–1980* not only restates the case for Lennon's superior radical clout, but also draws our attention to his post-Beatles work (where Miles skirts over McCartney's platinum-selling post-1970s' work in a mere thirty pages), while also claiming that, solo, Lennon was just a potent as force as when he was a Beatle. Du Noyer, himself a scouser, as well as a veteran UK journalist and founder of *Mojo* magazine, is laconic, dry and economic in his prose. His analysis of Lennon's solo work is always insightful and his handle on Lennon's brand of feckless, excessively emotional sloganeering is succinct. Du Noyer's claim that New York provided the perfect emotional and creative climate for the renegade Liverpudlian because of its similarities with Lennon's hometown is also important: 'a couple of tough old seaports, self-obsessed and self-mythologizing, where Irish-featured stevedores barked in accents that practically overlapped ("Youse guys over dere, shift dis") (54). Lennon spent most of the 1970s in exile in the USA, and in 1976 was finally awarded his green card after years of struggle over his citizenship. It was a battle won, but, with a terrible irony, as it was the US government's decision to grant Lennon the right to live in what he called 'a big Liverpool', which led to him being where he was on 8 December, 1980.

Although seldom shown nowadays on network television, the Beatles' five films, *A Hard Day's Night*, *Help!*, *Magical Mystery Tour*, *Yellow Submarine* and *Let It Be*, did much to solidify the band's success, particularly in the post-split 1970s, when the films were frequently rerun on British television, thus reactivating their back catalogue for those born too late to remember the band in action. Film studies critic Bob Neaverson is one such fan. His book, *The Beatles Movies*, is perhaps the first serious study of the band's film oeuvre, and is thus unique. Neaverson points out that 'the generic status of the pop musical, to which the films for the most part belong, has, for reasons largely unknown to me, never garnered much interest within British film history and theory. In addition, much film history still favours an exclusively auterist approach, and, since the five Beatles movies were made by four different directors (or sets of directors), they do not form part of the auterist canon' (2). What follows is a cogent and succinct analysis of the Beatles films from the trajectory of film studies which wears its theory lightly and ultimately reads more like a journalistic history than an academic work. The music, for the most part, is under-theorized, but no matter. Neaverson's book reactivates an interest in a neglected body of work, and popular music students will be rewarded with an evaluation of the texts and 'historical insight into the production, marketing and reception of the Beatles films' (4).

The most obvious link between the Beatles and 1990s' popular music can be found in the rise and rise of Oasis in the mid-1990s. Located in the Manchester suburb of Burnage, these aspirant Britpoppers shared the Beatles' Celtic roots, being as they were second-generation Irish immigrants. They also shared their mentors' penchant for melodic pop, if not their industry (in the space of half-a-dozen years Oasis released just three studio albums). Paolo Hewitt's *Getting High: The Adventures of Oasis*, was written with the co-operation of the band. Rather than explore how Oasis reassembled a simulacra of the 1960s' experience in the 1990s, or delve further into how Oasis' immigrant roots translated themselves through sound (Hewitt has a lot to say about Irish identity, though his handling of the theme is often cliché), Hewitt turns in an almost novelesque account of the rise to fame of the Gallagher brothers, with a superabundance of triviality (month-by-month detailing of records and tickets sold, gigs played, interviews conducted, set-list changes, fluffed opening bars of live renditions, television shows suffered, sound-checks endured). The result is that Hewitt, despite being granted access to the band, loses the big picture in a litany of minutiae.

The diffident, difficult, hard-drinking machismo of the Gallaghers, a paradigm of behaviour attributable, according to Hewitt, to their Irish ethnicity, is the stuff of 1990s' rock myth. Beneath the tabloid sensationalism devoted to the arrogant misdemeanours of rock stars is the more revealing structure of pop mythology. Pop superstardom (and pop fandom) is often predicated on an insatiable quest for temporal oblivion through excess. Lesley-Ann Jones' *Freddie Mercury: The Definitive Biography* attempts a sympathetic account of Queen's bravura lead-singer, but ends up as a classic portrayal of rock-star abuse. The reader is presented with a picture of man for whom it is hard to find much sympathy: recklessly self-destructive and almost incapable of interaction with others on a common-sense, everyday basis, Mercury led his life as an intriguingly, cocooned adventure play-park of carefully stage-managed hedonism. The most interesting part of the opening chapters relates to the evidence unearthed by Jones in Mercury's (Bulsara) native Zanzibar (now Tanzania), which shows how singer and country disowned one another.

With little to say on Queen's actual music or the reasons for their huge, enduring popularity, beyond blithe assertions of their self-evident greatness, Jones' account is no more than a well-told story of Mercury's nauseating self-importance, and a sympathetic detailing of his protracted illness and death from AIDS-related causes in November 1991.

As a piece of hands-on investigative journalism, Robert Greenfield's *A Journey through America with the Rolling Stones*, is worth further inquiry.

A reprint of a long out-of-print 1974 book, it stands, along with recently reactivated books such as Ian Hunter's *Diary of a Rock'n'Roll Star* (Independent Music Press, 1996) and Michael Braun's *Love Me Do* (Penguin, 1995), as a piece of warts 'n' all reportage and will be of interest to anyone concerned with the organization of the rock business in the first half of the 1970s. His close monitoring of the interpersonal tensions and aspirations of the Stones also provides ample evidence of the conventions and constraints of a band who were one of the first to capitalize on the global restructuring in the 1970s of pop's counter-cultural 1960s' roots.

The book is not without its fair share of the rock-star stroppiness that is so central to the pop experience. For example, a woman serving Jagger a subpoena relating to the group's disastrous Altamont gig of December 1969, when fan Meredith Hunter was beaten and stabbed to death by the band's security for the evening, the Hell's Angels, was greeted with a punch.

'Crikey!' was allegedly the dumbstruck response of Conservative MP Sir Norman Fowler when a civil servant advising him on the spread of AIDS explained to him what oral sex was. Readers of a similar disposition would doubtless find the reprint of Jenny Fabian and Johnny Byrne's 1969 novel, *Groupie*, an education. Middle-class and educated, Fabian was one of the most high-profile and successful British groupies. Sleazy and self-serving the novel may be, but as a cultural artefact it is significant, providing as it does a snapshot of rock life during the counter-culture – the pubs, clubs, venues, promoters, managers and stars, albeit in thinly veiled pseudonymous disguise. According to Jonathon Green's preface to this edition of the book, 'Groupie' is cited 22 times in the *Oxford English Dictionary* for neologisms such as 'downers', 'trippy', 'spliff' and 'uptight'. Sir Norman would doubtless be interested to learn of another word for fellatio, 'to plate' (from cockney rhyming slang, 'plate of meat': eat).

Electronica pioneer Gary Numan initially traded on the machismo of rock iconography. Shy but obsessional, famous at twenty, and largely abandoned by the mainstream by the age of twenty-five, Numan has spent the last fifteen years worrying away at the pop politic with his own distinctive, and influential, brand of electronic experimentalism. His autobiography, *Praying to the Aliens* (co-written with *Q*'s Steve Malins), is a trusting, personal and paradoxical read. Refreshingly honest about his own personal foibles the book details the meteoric rise of an angst-ridden, Bowie-obsessed suburbanite who, for the year of 1979, was the biggest male pop star in the UK. Numan's rightist politics, his love of aviation, his sci-fi interests, and his devotion to gadgetry and machinery are faithfully attested, and the result is an eminently readable excavation of a career more influential than many would credit. Numan's imagined future of mechanized humanity predicted many of the recent developments in ritual body art and performance art, his fascination with simulacra (his 1979 album *Replicas* being a prime example), predated much 1980s' postmodernist writing, and his music was a direct influence on 1990s' industrial acts such as Nine Inch Nails and Marilyn Manson.

While Numan has been somewhat neglected, then Elvis Presley suffers from gross over-exposure. The subject of countless biographies (Professor Albert Goldman's controversial *Elvis* (Allen Lane, 1981), is one of the biggest-selling rock biographies of all time), Presley has always fascinated serious-minded cultural critics and academics alike as the work of Simon Frith, Dave Marsh, Greil Marcus and Peter Guralnick amply shows.

In Search of Elvis: Music, Race, Art, Religion, edited by Vernon Chadwick, gathers together the papers delivered at the first annual International Conference of Elvis Presley, which was held in August 1995 at the University of Mississippi in Oxford, USA. Chadwick argues for the existence of the 'Elvis text', 'a gateway into issues of race, class, religion, and everyday existence' (xi). He goes on: 'Just as Elvis Presley rebelled against the taboos of segregated society in the 1950s, so too does the new Elvis scholarship marshalled in this book – which embodies the spirit of Elvis – dissent significantly from the academic status quo in the 1990s. The reader will encounter no disembodied, professorial talking heads in these essays but rather real people, with personal histories and human voices, conversing, conferring among their peers'. These are bold claims. At stake seems to be not only a new Elvis but also a whole new scion of engaged academia. Articles include Bill Malone's 'Country Elvis', Will Campbell's 'Elvis Presley as Redneck' and Mark Gottdeiner's 'Dead Elvis as Other Jesus'. This engaged, and often personal, collection of papers attempts to portray a progressive Elvis, and a taboo-smashing progressive rocker who embodied all that was best in Southern society. The problem, however, even disregarding the more voracious and vicious claims contained in Goldman's book, is that the true Elvis was a combination of, or a compromise between, these two extremes. Chadwick claims that 'the "Elvis" of this book is the thinker's Elvis who changes everything we thought we knew' (xi). But the small-minded, childish, drug-addled, gun-toting, sheriff-badge-wearing, massively hypocritical, Nixon-loving, hardcore porn-addicted, drugged-up Elvis was as much a 'reality' as the libertarian progressive portrayed in these pages, and it would be foolish, indeed unhistorical, to claim otherwise. The seamier side of Elvis is, however, absent from these pages. A more compelling 'academi-cization' of Presley would take the bad along with the good, and engage with the huge paradoxes of the first pop star of the rock 'n' roll era, rather than render the paradoxes invisible. Furthermore, despite the claims for the articles' engaged character, the prose is often arcane and elitist, or embarrassingly confessional.

Another seminal American rock star to stammer and stutter artistically after an initial burst of creativity was Brian Wilson of the Beach Boys. This creator of some of the most perfect pop of the 1960s spent the following two decades emotionally and creatively bankrupt, before experiencing a middle-aged mini-renaissance and a return to calmer personal waters in the 1990s. *Back to the Beach: A Brian Wilson and The Beach Boys Reader*, edited by Kingsley Abbott, collects chronologically some of the most important articles on Wilson and his band, concentrating on such totems of rock mythology as the never-completed *Smiley Smile* album and Wilson's relationship with his psychiatrist and mentor, Dr Eugene Landy. The pick of the anthology is a haunting article by the British iconoclast, Nick Kent, whose 'High and Bri' is an anatomy of a rock star's psychic collapse and makes for harrowingly compelling reading. For all those interested in the band and its enduring musical legacy, and in the collapse and reformation of a pop personality broken by the business and its pressures, *The Beach Boys Reader* is worth seeking out.

Finally, Johnny Rogan's *The Byrds: Timeless Flight Revisited*, an update of his 1977 biography, *Timeless Flight: The Definitive Biography of the Byrds*, is a painstakingly researched and hugely impressive rock biography. Sympathetic, illuminating, though never flinching from the massive personality defects of the band members, the book concludes with a 250-page addenda and documents section, including moving, and graphic, obituaries of two past members, Gene Clark and Michael Clarke, and a detailed discography covering all the manifestations of the Byrds and its scions. Rogan's highly personal preface, 'The Ghost of Electricity', which recalls his own pre-teenage fascination with pop in a London dwelling still lit by glass lamps at the time of 'Swinging London', is an essential piece of fandom-cum-scholarship, while the book itself not only tells the story of the band in exhaustive (and exhausting) detail, but also intertwines a sage critique of the twists and turns of folk, rock, and psychedelia along the way. Seldom has a rock biography been so detailed and so well researched.

2. Anthologies, Collections and Encyclopaedias

Anthologies are very popular within popular music studies, as either documentations of conferences, or collections of themed pieces of original research, although it is the academic anthology that has the biggest intellectual kudos within the discipline. It is also the most uneven of publications in terms of overall quality: excellent, eloquently written articles rub shoulders with arcane mystification and neophyte careering.

In view of the pressure on institutions to be seen to be proactive in terms of producing new bodies of knowledge for research assessment purposes, the academic anthology is often the most contrived, and the least successful, of projects, very often bloated with substandard work. The most successful anthology of the year originates not from popular music studies *per se*, but from the wider intellectual domain of cultural studies, although it will certainly be of use to the historian of popular music. *Visions of Suburbia*, edited by Roger Silverstone, is an excellent collection of articles dealing with that locale of liminal 'pleasures' which define, for some, mundanity, for others the quintessence of the English creative experience. Popular culture, and indeed popular music, particularly in the UK, has been fired by arty bedsit dreamers who, concertinaed by suburban conformity, yearn to be numbered among the urban cool. In an excellent introduction, Silverstone names the southeast suburb of Bromley as perhaps the quintessential suburban town and an unlikely crucible of talent (Bowie and many of the punks grew up there, as did writers H. G. Wells and Hanif Kureishi). 'Bromley is both unique and entirely typical', writes Silverstone. 'In this it is exemplary. Suburbia, the product of the complex and untidy histories and geographies of urbanization and modernization, is just such. Instantly recognizable though never entirely familiar. Ubiquitous but invisible. Secure but fragile. Desired but reviled. Suburbia is neither singular nor unchanging' (4). Since so much pop has originated out of the suburban experience (from the Beatles in the 1960s to Suede in the 1990s), it is perhaps surprising that its relationship to popular music has yet to be discussed in any great detail. *Visions of Suburbia* partially addresses this need with a typically thought-provoking article by Simon Frith, 'The Suburban Sensibility in British Rock and Pop', which concentrates on Suede. 'Anderson's lyrics suggest a continuingly ambiguous attitude to the city', writes Frith, 'which is described less as a real place than as something made up in suburbia itself and imagined, inevitably, in media imagery, through Hollywood scenarios and sci-fi cartoons. The city, London, is not a place in which to live but a backcloth against which to imagine living' (274). Full of good things (as his articles always are), I would heartily recommend Frith's analysis of suburbanity to anyone wishing to make sense of what makes English pop tick. However, Frith's self-parodying style and trademark (annoying) soundbites ('But then British suburbia is as much a product of pop as British pop is a product of suburbia,' [275] leave the reader's palate jaded. 'When I was young, suburbia was what stood between me and pleasure', writes Andy Medhurst in 'Negotiating the Gnome Zone: Visions of Suburbia in British Popular Culture', another very worthwhile article in *Visions of Suburbia*. Although not directly concerned with pop music, Medhurst's depiction of suburbia as a 'topography of conformity', his personal analysis of the southeast commuter-belt, and his witty analysis of British cinema, sitcom and soaps, provides excellent contextual reading for historians of pop.

The Subcultures Reader, edited by Ken Gelder and Sarah Thornton, collects together fifty-five previously published articles and extracts which give a taste of the variety of theoretical protocols developed in subcultural theory. Some of the selections are useful, familiar, and predictable, such as an extract from Dick Hebdige's canonical *Subculture: The Meaning of Style*, Gary Clarke's famous rebuttal, 'Defending Ski-Jumpers: A Critique of Theories of Youth Subcultures' and Robert Walser's 'Eruptions: Heavy Metal Appropriations of Classical Virtuosity'. Some of the older extracts, such as Paul G. Cressey's 'The Life-Cycle of a Taxi-Dancer', originally published in 1932, impress more by virtue of their relative unfamiliarity (at least to this reader). Two articles, however, are worthy of special attention: Laud Humphrey's 'The Sociologist as Voyeur', originally published in 1970, is a remarkable account of a participant observation experiment into the activities of male homosexuals in public toilets, Wendy Fonarow's 1995 essay, 'The Spatial Organization of the Indie Music Gig', anatomizes the space occupied by the audience at a gig, dividing this area into three zones. Zone one contains the most vibrant activity (moshing, dancing, crowd surfing). In zone two, 'participants are visibly and physically oriented towards the band and stand facing the stage. There is a modest amount of physical response in some participants – rocking back and forth, gentle moving the head, and tapping one's feet in rhythm to the music' (365). Zone three, 'the mediation zone between inside and out' (366), the furthest away from the stage, confers the most prestige, an area where journalists file their reports, managers and pop businessmen confer, and merchandising is bought. Fonarow makes a convincing case for an explicit ageism at work at the gig, organizing the audience and segregating awareness and partici-pation: 'As individuals age, they move back through space until they are aged out of the venue all together. When older people stop going to gigs, they do not stop attending musical performances. They attend concerts – concerts that are performed in venues with seats, a move that compels even more reserved bodily composure. The gig is an event that communicates the expected behaviors associated with ageing: youth as the time of physical and emotional expressiveness, and adulthood as a time of reserved, composed demeanor and sedentary lifestyle' (369).

Sexing the Groove, edited by Sheila Whitely, is dedicated to the International Association for the Study of Popular Music (IASPM), and is unfortunately marred by several contributions which revel in trendy cultural studies doublespeak and careerist jargon. The rationale for the book is sound: to present 'a diverse range of perspectives, discussions and debates with one common mission in mind: to explore the ever-changing modes of expression within popular music and, in particular, its relationship to genders and sexualities' (xiii). Whitely goes on to say: 'The contributors thus hail from diverse theoretical backgrounds while retaining their identity as first- and second-generation academics in this new field of study. They are all actively involved in their own music scenes as performers, critics or fans. They have all delivered papers at major international conferences devoted to the study of popular music and culture' (Idem). The result is that a goodly proportion of the articles speak to and for an intellectual coterie. Endless referencing, cross-referencing, acknowledgements and summaries of each other's work, as well as attacks and counter-attacks, cloud many of these articles, obfuscating the usually interesting material under discussion. Consequently, the best contributions are the least overtly academic, and those that talk imaginatively and interestingly about important themes, rather than situating and summarizing existing bodies of knowledge. Mavis Bayton's assertion that 'lead guitarists are made, not born. The reasons for women's absence are entirely social' is compellingly elucidated with ethnographic research in her article, 'Women and the Electric Guitar'. Charlotte Grieg writes eloquently about the female persona within pop in 'Female Identity and the Woman Songwriter'. Such articles do not cloak learning in heavy theoretical clothing, and reveal many truths.

Another handicap is *Sexing the Groove's* out-of-touch-ness. The articles on Riot grrl, Springsteen, Sinead O'Connor, the Pet Shop Boys, Seal, Take That and k.d. lang are interesting and worthwhile, but, as examples, are curiously out of date. Why not Marilyn Manson, Nine Inch Nails, the Smashing Pumpkins, ritual body art – the late-1990s' cultural mix of polysexuality? Yet again, popular music studies has its finger on the pulse, but the pulse of 1992, not 1997. Whitely says that popular music is a 'new' discipline. This is palpably not true. Almost twenty years on from the first IASPM conference, and around thirty years since the earliest published work by Dave Laing and Simon Frith, popular music studies has confidently, if not completely, embedded itself within the Academy, if not always accepted with open arms. However, on the evidence of this collection, it is still nervous, twitchy and troubled, and far too self-referential and knowingly academic.

Doing Cultural Studies: The Story of the Sony Walkman, written by Paul Du Gay, Stuart Hall, Linda Janes, Hugh MacKay and Keith Negus, focuses on one ubiquitous cultural artefact and uses it as a test case for students of cultural theory. The tone and design of the book (numerous sub-*Face* photos of young people actively 'consuming' their Walkman), together with the title of the collection, are self-consciously trendy. However, the book is useful in that it guides the reader through all points of contact between the Walkman and culture (dealing with issues of production, design, consumption and regulation), while also including eight related extracts from the cultural studies canon (including Benjamin, Williams, Chow, Chambers). A useful, though perhaps not entirely essential, study guide.

Popular Music Studies: A Select International Bibliography, edited and compiled by John Shepherd, David Horn, Dave Laing, Paul Oliver, Philip Tagg, Peter Wicke and Jennifer Wilson, is a genuinely indispensable research tool for all students and scholars of popular music. This is the first fruit of the *Encyclopaedia of the Popular Music of the World* (*EPMOW*) project, which began almost a decade ago. With bibliographical information on popular music genres, the music industry, social and cultural contexts (such as bibliographical entries on 'advertising', 'journalism', 'racism' and 'urbanization'), musical practices, locations, and theory and method, *EPMOW* breaks new ground. For the first time, popular music studies has a bibliographical tool which accurately reflects the interdisciplinary and international character of the discipline. No popular music institution can afford to be without this reference work.

Finally in this section, two worthwhile popular music encyclopedias: although the *Virgin Encyclopedia of Popular Music*, Concise Edition, claims, at over 1300 pages, definitive status, it is in fact not so much a popular music encyclopaedia as a biographical listing, with critical analyses of varying quality, of the major names in twentieth-century popular music. In essence, therefore, it is a *Who's Who* of rock stars, rather than an encyclopaedia, avoiding as it does any discussion of cultural context, the music industry, musical genres and styles, and suchlike. Edited by Colin Larkin, the book is nevertheless a useful reference guide, with short biographical sketches backed with discographical data, a sometimes controversial rating system which betrays the over-forty-something bias of the editorial policy, and a guide to further reading. Better still is *The Great Psychedelic Discography* by Martin C. Strong. This never pretends to dress subjective fandom in learned objectivity, offering as it does biographical entries and style analysis of individual acts with an idiosyncratic touch. Strong also includes a mass of other useful factual information (including transatlantic chart positions, catalogue numbers) and while there's an air of anality, the fun presentation (including cartoon caricatures by Harry Horse) makes it an essential factual guide.

3. History and Analysis

One distinctive and heartening aspect of popular music publications this year has been the emergence of a number of books dealing with specific styles of popular music. Progressive rock, for example, has been characterized in the public imagination by arcane virtuosity, pseudo-intellectualism and overblown on-stage vacuity. Although massively outselling punk rock, a musical moment which was deemed by the critical consensus to have killed off the progressive rock movement, progressive rock acts such as Genesis,

Pink Floyd, Jethro Tull, King Crimson and the Moody Blues are conspicuous by their absence in the discursive formation of pop's history, with the odd honourable exception, such as Alan F. Moore's accessible musicological analysis, *Rock: The Primary Text* (Open University Press, 1993). Punk was seen as dealing with dangerous signs, as being musically and culturally subversive, its style warfare a totem of the new spirit of post-capitalistic nihilism. Yet its impact has been overstated at the expense of other styles with prog-rock, along with disco, the prime injured parties. A poll conducted among working-class youth in Liverpool in the early 1980s revealed that the most popular groups were none other than Pink Floyd and Genesis. This album-based music, long thought of as the preserve of the middle-class male nerd, had taken over popular culture. The reality of this surprising hegemonic control by music dubbed by the cognoscenti as desperately unhip has always been hidden away. Until now, that is. Edward Macan's *Rocking the Classics: English Progressive Rock and the Counter-culture* is a musicological analysis originating out of the mainstream of popular music studies, while a second study, Paul Stump's *The Music's All That Matters: A History of Progressive Rock*, is a narrative cultural history. Unfortunately, neither of these two new studies of the progressive rock moment really gets to grips with the consumption of progressive rock. An ethnographic slant to the research, a la Robert Walser in his seminal study of heavy metal, *Running With The Devil* (Weslyan University Press, 1993), would have been welcome. Nevertheless, these first book-length analyses of the style to date, are very worthwhile.

For readers primarily interested in the music, Macan gives the fullest account, analysing what he considers to be the four seminal prog-rock texts by ELP, Yes, Genesis and Pink Floyd. However, Stump is more engaged, providing much the better overall history of the genre, and is knowledgeable about the work of popular music scholars too. He is also good at situating progressive rock in its ideological, economic and cultural context, and his book successfully balances a fan's-eye view of the style with telling contextual passages. Championed by hip media figures such as disc jockey John Peel, progressive rock emerged from the same background as the art rock of Roxy Music and Bowie, but took a different turn in the late 1960s, reaching its zenith in the early-to-mid-1970s, before imploding in the late 1970s. Stump's theory that progressive rock's demise in the 1970s was due to a combination of the rise of grass-roots populist heavy metal (not punk), together with an alarming drop in the actual quality of the music itself (the uneven quality and critical mauling of Pink Floyd's *The Wall* in late 1979 is seen as a key moment), and fat-catism (as certain progressive rockers became corporate whores), deserves a fair hearing. Like Greil Marcus on punk, Stump sees progressive rock as a Geist, with elements of its style cropping up in the music of artists not traditionally spoken of as progressive, such as Kate Bush, Propaganda and Grace Jones. As a result of his work, scholars can no longer disregard progressive rock and its scions.

In contrast, the music press and style magazines, at least in the UK, have been full of comment about dance music. Whereas progressive rock was perfect for the adolescent bedroom, with many a teenager, headphones on, being entranced by the alarm-clock cacophony of Pink Floyd's *Dark Side Of The Moon*, or the 13/8 time-signature of Genesis' 'Watcher Of the Skies',

1990s' dance music is overwhelmingly a public and shared experience, hedonistic, centred on the body and dance. Jungle music, an accelerated, polyrhythmic mulatto music, drew on, and ironized, late 1980s' and early 1990s' dance music (techno, ambient house, Balearic beat), turning into music literally too quick to actually dance. DJ and journalist Martin James' slight *State of Bass: Jungle: The Story So Far* seeks to introduce a genre considerably more talked about than bought (as was the case with punk). Indeed, the dopey tunes, anonymous soundscapes and personality-less practitioners meant that, despite the critical plaudits and Mercury Music Awards, the scene never crossed over to the mainstream, and its effects seem limited at best. *State of Bass* does not, however, concede any of this. Written by an insider keen to aggrandize and to restate the 'purity' of drum 'n' bass over those within the movement and in the media who might 'corrupt' its vision, the narrative skirts across the musical terrain rather too quickly, the music adumbrated rather than dissected. 'Tracing the roots of Jungle back to a definitive starting point is nigh on impossible', writes James as early as page 6. Such an admission of defeat before the analysis has been given a chance to develop unsettles the reader, whose sympathies are subsequently never regained. A sketchy discographical and biographical section weaken this personalized account further.

Rather better is *Altered State: The Story of Ecstasy Culture and Acid House* by Matthew Collin, with contributions by John Godfrey. This meticulously researched study of dance culture from the origins of house music in Chicago in the immediate post-Stonewall 1970s, the rise of 'DJ culture' and the 'Second Summer Of Love' in 1988, when the ecstasy drug went mainstream amid a wash of Balearic beat and techno, to 1997's chemical generation, is an invaluable piece of popular cultural writing, which deals with issues of regulation, policing and state policy as well as the formations of the various music scenes themselves. Collins and Godfrey write:

> Ecstasy culture seemed to ghost the Thatcher narrative – echoing its ethos of choice and market freedom, yet expressing desires for a collective experience that Thatcher rejected and consumerism could not provide. Thatcherite Conservatism offered a blueprint for achievement with a Victorian morality built in; Ecstasy culture ran with the blueprint but inverted the morality, firing a vibrant black economy not only in illegal drugs but cash-in-hands deals for all manner of ancillary services, from DJ careers to home-produced records, creating an unprecedented number of cultural artefacts (7).

It is a shame, however, that, in places, *Altered State* becomes so delirious and so absorbed with its object of study that critical distance dissolves into hyperbole. Such aggressive self-recommendations as 'this is the story of how we reached the peak of human experience – and what happened afterwards' (9) may easily dissuade potential readers from exploring further what is in fact a worthwhile book.

In terms of critical debate, writers and critics return time and again to punk. With so much of the terrain covered, it is remarkable that Gina Arnold has been able to find a new slant. Committed, partisan and eloquent,

Kiss This: Punk in the Present Tense is a personalized account of how the punk legacy, particularly that bequeathed by the Sex Pistols, has been emasculated by big business and the new American punk groups such as Green Day and the Offspring (and by the reformed Sex Pistols themselves). In a sense, this is an old-hat style analysis. The original punks were artistes but their vision became co-opted by big business and now, so claims Arnold, the Pistols are close bedfellows to the likes of Kiss, playing better music, but less successful at fleecing the industry on multi-million dollar tours. Once big business gets its greedy paws on music, the bands and their sounds are branded and packaged out of existence, with Grunge seen as the latest style ruined by commercialism, 'an uninspired melee of sounds, created by eating its own words and noises', opines the author. At the crux of Arnold's analysis is the clichéd idea of pop's cyclical behaviour. It is 'sometimes exciting, sometimes very dull – and unfortunately, this is an extremely fallow period in its story. Moreover, it'll continue this way until kids stop forming bands in the hopes of getting popular and rich' (47). Arnold's vision of the pop world before the fall heralded in by big business co-option is one populated by joyous mavericks with not a thought of making a buck, when the reality, of course, is that commercialism and artistry have always gone hand in hand. However, despite the reactionary indie fetishism of some of the analysis, *Punk in the Present Tense* is a feisty read from an original punk who is still in love with music. If Arnold is bewildered and disaffected by 1990s' youth culture, then the befuddlement and sense of disappointment still makes for excellent reading.

Please Kill Me: The Uncensored Oral History of Punk, by Legs McNeil and Gillian McCain is a superbly engaging read and an important piece of investigative journalism. Based on hundreds of interviews, it lets the protagonists tell anecdote upon anecdote, sometimes bitchy and trivial, at other times bringing genuinely fresh insight into the punk moment. *Please Kill Me* is, in fact, not just a history of punk. Rather, the authors trace punk's origins back to the Iggy Pop and Warhol crowd, through Anglo-American glam rock and into the angularity of the US New Wave scene and beyond. British punk gets a mention, but the focus is overwhelmingly Stateside. Read as a counter to Jon Savage's canonical *England's Dreaming* (Faber 1991), *Please Kill Me* never fails to deliver, capturing the scene's energy-overload with breathless, articulate, sometimes sardonic stories from the likes of Wayne County, Patti Smith, Angela Bowie, Malcolm McLaren, William Burroughs and Richard Hell. This is a journalistic account that will repay the attention of popular music scholars.

If punk was seen both as a 'back to basics' reclamation of the spirit of early rock'n'roll and as a democratization of music in the wake of progressive rock, then the origins of the 'do-it-yourself' approach to pop are closely connected with the skiffle boom of the mid-to-late 1950s. Chas McDevitt was one of the leading skiffle musicians and in *Skiffle: The Definitive Story* offers an insider account of the scene. Skiffle was primarily a reaction against the perceived blandness of the dance-band tunes of the immediate post-war period. At its height, it was a genuinely democratic movement with a huge cultural impact. 'Every town could muster a dozen groups', recalls McDevitt: 'every barrack room, youth club and church hall now echoes to the pounding of the washboard'. In 1957, according to McDevitt, it was estimated that there were between 30 and 50,000 skiffle groups in the UK. McDevitt is a judicious historian who leads the reader through the origins of skiffle in the music of Chicago in the 1920s, before detailing all the major skiffle acts and describing how skiffle first caught on in the coffee bars of post-war England – exactly the sort of venue singled out in Richard Hoggart's *The Uses of Literacy* (Chatto and Windus, 1957; Penguin, 1992) as an example of the corruption of working-class culture. McDevitt then turns his attention to what he calls 'pseudo skiffle', the era when skiffle went mainstream and began parodying itself. A final chapter, 'They All Played Skiffle', shows how numerous pop musicians, including the Beatles and Van Morrison, started their musical careers as skiffle players. The book also boasts an extensive bibliography and is fully illustrated too, including ads from women's magazines on what casuals to buy for a skiffle party.

If the books on punk have shed new light on a well-trodden historical path, and the analyses on progressive rock have opened up pop history to new debates, then Chuck Eddy's *The Accidental Evolution of Rock 'n' Roll: A Misguided Tour Through Popular Music* takes the format of history and parodies it, replacing objectivity with a wildly subjective analysis of contemporary music. Many of the existing academic histories of popular music are predictable and dull, rehearsing the same litany of events, facts and faces, and describing and explaining the same canon of music. Not so with Eddy. His stance is personal (with a first-person narrative) and iconoclastic. His anti-intellectualism reveals itself in a flagrant disregard for the vast majority of canonical artistes or acts generally regarded as being influential (he hates Kraftwerk, Can and Faust, calling them 'Baader-Meinhof buddies'), Joy Division, and most of 1990s' UK pop, from the Chemical Brothers to Oasis. For Eddy, the weirdest music of the 1990s was made by Garth Brooks and the Gypsy Kings. He admires music that 'doesn't feel like too much second-guessing went into it' (11) and his central thesis is that 'unoriginality is indeed the essence of rock'n'roll' (51). Eddy's pop world, however, is not as maverick as it may seem, for all he ultimately achieves in his critical thrashing of the pop canon is the construction of a new story of heroes and heroines out of the shunned and the ignored. This is still a history of pop with winners and losers, but now it is Silver Convention's 'Get Up And Boogie' which is read as a 'classic text' rather than 'A Day In The Life'. Eddy's narrative is crammed full of lists of the arcane and the trivial, rendering it one long discography. Nevertheless, there are some wonderfully eccentric passages. This is one of the few popular music books that has actually made me laugh out loud. His sections on repetition and 'redundancy rock', 'The Power Ballad Revolution', 'Fucking Sound Effects Records', and 'Equestrian and Pedestrian Rock' are witty and unique, and his wildly eccentric categorizations actually seem quite normal and sensible by the end of the book, a tribute to his perspicacity and an indication that behind the craziness of the narrative is an intelligence matched by very few other popular music writers. As a counter to the accepted rock canon, *The Accidental Evolution of Rock'n'Roll* is essential reading.

Cultural studies often deals with the effects of popular music, but seldom with the actual music itself. John Shepherd and Peter Wicke's brief in their book, *Music and Cultural Theory*, is to 'feed musicology into cultural theory, to consider the implications for cultural theory of a viable theory for the social and cultural constitution of music as a particular and irreducible form of human knowledge and expression'. Shepherd and Wicke regard music as inherently social, as a medium with a particular trajectory and inherent qualities which have so far remained under-theorized or have been analysed using word-based theoretical models, models which they suggest are largely inappropriate for an understanding of music. However, the authors demand a command of theoretical protocols which perhaps only a couple dozen of fellow academics have, and the result, despite some helpful sections, is a book pitched so high that it will unfortunately doubtless remain of extreme minority interest only. However, it does make it very clear that there is a need for a book for undergraduates which bridges the gap between cultural theory and critical musicology.

Beneath the Diamond Sky: Haight-Ashbury 1965–1970, by veteran rock journalist Barney Hoskyns, ought to be consulted as much for its illustrations and photographic material (making up around half of the book) as for the text itself. As a visual history of the counter-culture, including moody shots of Ginsberg, images of tripped out fans at be-ins and love-ins, posters and cartoons, and action shots of the main musicians on stage, this is a valuable source. The narrative itself is useful, as Hoskyns paints a vivid picture of a time before LSD was criminalised, of the Acid Tests and the Pranksters, and of one of the most important sites of musical production in the 1960s. Hoskyns argues that, by early 1968, hippie culture had become diluted, and idolization rather than communality between audience and performance had broken the spell of the counterculture. Hoskyns quotes Joshua White, a light-show artist: 'we were now applauding the presence of the artist, rather than the performance' (169).

The emergence of 'Britpop' in the early 1990s deluged the British media with a wave of nostalgia, since much of the music sought to re-articulate a heritage-culture version of pop history in the immediate post-slacker, post-grunge period. While there have been any number of books aimed at disentangling mythic America, since George Melly's brilliant *Revolt into Style* (Allen Lane, 1970) there have been very few wholly devoted to the UK. *England is Mine: Pop Life in Albion from Wilde to Goldie*, by journalist and novelist Michael Bracewell, is far from being the last word on the relationship between 'Little Englandism' and popular music, being essentially a short monograph rather than an expansively detailed academic history, but it does make for sporadically brilliant reading. In Chapter 1, 'England as Arcady: Before Pop', Bracewell essentially updates Raymond William's paradigm, developed in his book *The Country and the City* (1973), concerning how culture mythologizes the past in order to critique the present. Bracewell shows himself to be a wonderfully eclectic analyst, placing discussions of Alexander Pope and Oscar Wilde next to succinct and telling readings of the likes of perennial favourites such as Bowie, Rotten and Morrissey. The author's canvas is broad: he touches not only on music, film, literature, philosophy and sexuality, but also throughout this searing polemic revels in and challenges England's myths. Bracewell's England is a land in which boundaries between high and low culture have totally collapsed. He sets up a feral dialogue between cultures, where traditions recognize no temporal boundaries, a dialogue of Englishness that includes both Geoffrey Chaucer and Paul Weller. Invigorating reading.

4. Short Notices

Space is the Place: The Life and Times of Sun Ra, by John F. Szwed, Professor of Anthropology, Afro-American Studies, Music, and American Studies at Yale University, is that rarest of birds: an academic popular music biography, painstakingly researched and accessibly written. Another biography, *The Ballad of the Thin Man: The Authorised Biography of Phil Lynott and Thin Lizzy*, by journalist Stuart Bailie, is a slight but sensitive portrait of a rocker more influential than the histories of popular music sometimes credit. David Buckley's *No Mercy: The Authorised and Uncensored Biography of the Stranglers* chronicles the still-continuing career of the original 'Men in Black', who in the year of punk, 1977, outsold all the other new wave acts put together in the UK. Paul Zollo's *Songwriters on Songwriting*, Expanded Edition, collects together fifty-two interviews with many of the American pop greats, from Paul Simon and Bob Dylan to REM and David Byrne. The focus is very much on mainstream singer-songwriters though, so anyone expecting interviews with the Butthole Surfers or Hole will be disappointed. Fred Goodman's *The Mansion on the Hill: Dylan, Young, Geffen, Springsteen and the Head-On Collision Of Rock and Commerce* is in the tradition of Frederic Dannen's 1990 critique of the music industry, *Hit Men* (Times Books). Journalist, manager and record-producer John Landau has his career laid bare in Goodman's polemic and Neil Young emerges as the rarest of birds: as a pop star with the integrity to have never 'sold-out'. Readers interested in the relationship between politics and pop would do well to consult John Street's eloquent *Politics and Popular Culture*, an attempt to feed political theory into a study of popular culture and music and a further indication of the diffusion of popular music studies throughout academia. Likewise, *Keeping Score, Music, Disciplinarity, Culture*, edited by David Schwarz, Anahid Kassabian and Lawrence Siegel, demonstrates that critical musicology is interfacing more enthusiastically with popular music too. It contains contributions by popular music scholars such as Sara Cohen, Susan McCalary and Robert Walser, as well as useful essays by Kassabian and McCreless on music theory, and by John Covach on rock music and music analysis. Finally, Alan Clayson's well-written, though slightly flippant, *Hamburg: The Cradle of British Rock*, assesses (and overstates) the importance of the city in helping a whole generation of Anglo-American rockers to hone their talents.

5. Articles

Useful articles published in 1997 include Dave Harker, 'The Wonderful World of IFPI: Music Industry Rhetoric, the Critics and the Classical Marxist Critique' (*Popular Music*, 16: ii. 45–80); Andrew Bennett, ' "Going Down The Pub!": The Pub Rock Scene as a Resource for the Consumption of Popular Music' (*Popular Music* 16: ii. 97–108); Tom McCourt and Eric Rothenbuhler, 'SoundScan and the Consolidation of Control in the Popular Music Industry' (*Media, Culture & Society* 19: 201–218); Martin Cloonan, 'State of the Nation: "Englishness", Pop, and Politics in the Mid-1990s' (*Popular Music & Society*

21: 2. 47–70); Mike Daily, 'Patti Smith's Gloria: Intertextual Play in a Vocal Performance' (*Popular Music* 16: iii. 235–254); and David Hesmondhalgh, 'Post-Punk's Attempt to Democratise the Music Industry: The Success and Failure of Rough Trade' (*Popular Music* 16: iii. 255–274).

Books Reviewed

Abbott, Kingsley. *Back to the Beach: A Brian Wilson and The Beach Boys Reader.* Helter Skelter Publishing. pp. 254. pb £12.99. ISBN 1 900924 02 1.

Arnold, Gina. *Kiss This: Punk in the Present Tense.* Pan. pp. 205. pb £39.99. ISBN 0 330 352588 X.

Bailie, Stuart. *The Ballad of the Thin Man: The Authorized Biography of Phil Lynott and Thin Lizzy.* Boxtree. pp. 193. hb £15.99. ISBN 0 7522 0384 3.

Buckley, David. *No Mercy: The Authorised and Uncensored Biography of the Stranglers.* Hodder & Stoughton. pp. 313. hb £17.99. ISBN 0 340 68062 8.

Chadwick, Vernon, ed. *In Search of Elvis: Music, Race, Art, Religion.* Westview Press. pp. 294. pb $22.00. ISBN 0 8133 2987 6.

Clayson, Alan. *Hamburg: The Cradle of British Rock.* Sanctuary. pp. 287. pb £12.99. ISBN 1 86074 221 1.

Collin, Matthew with contributions by John Godfrey. *Altered State: The Story of Ecstasy Culture and Acid House.* pp. 314. pb £10.99. ISBN 1 85242 377 3.

Du Gay, Paul, Stuart Hall, Linda James, Hugh MacKay and Keith Negus. *Doing Cultural Studies: The Story of the Sony Walkman.* Sage Publications in association with The Open University. pp. 150. pb £11.99. ISBN 0 76 19 5402 3.

Du Noyer. *We All Shine On: The Stories Behind Every John Lennon Song 1970–1980.* Carlton Books. pp. 128. pb £12.99. ISBN 1 858 682841 3.

Eddy, Chuck. *The Accidental Evolution of Rock 'n' Roll: A Misguided Tour through Popular Music.* Da Capo. pp. 436. pb £11.95. ISBN 0 306 80741 6.

Fabian, J. Byrne, D. and Green, S. Groupie. Omnibus Press. pp. 200. pb £39.95. ISBN 0 711 96318 5.

Gelder, Ken and Sarah Thornton. *The Subcultures Reader.* Routledge. pp. 599. hb £50.00. ISBN 0 415 12727 0.

Goodman, Fred. *The Mansion on the Hill: Dylan, Young, Geffen, Springsteen and the Head-on Collision of Rock and Commerce.* Jonathan Cape. pp. 431. pb £12.95. ISBN 0 224 05062 1.

Greenfield, Robert. *A Journey through America with the Rolling Stones.* Helter Skelter Publishing. pp. 191. pb £12.00. ISBN 1 900924 01 3.

Hewitt, Paolo. *Getting High: The Adventures of Oasis.* Boxtree. pp. 396. hb £15.99. ISBN 0 7522 0395 9.

Hoskyns, Barney. *Beneath the Diamond Sky: Haight-Ashbury 1965–1970.* Bloomsbury. pp. 221. hb £18.99. ISBN 0 74575 3327 X.

James, Martin. *State of Bass: Jungle: The Story So Far.* Foreword by A Guy Called Gerald. Boxtree. pp. 132. pb £9.99. ISBN 0 7522 2323 2.

Jones, Lesley-Ann. *Freddie Mercury: The Definitive Biography.* Hodder & Stoughton. pp. 466. hb £17.99. ISBN 0 340 67208 0.

Larkin, Colin. *Virgin Encyclopedia of Popular Music.* Virgin Publishing. pp. 1343. hb. £35.00. ISBN 1 85227 745 9.

Macan, Edward. *Rocking the Classics: English Progressive Rock and the Counterculture.* Oxford University Press. pp. 290. pb $17.95. ISBN 0 19 509888 9.

Miles, Barry. *Paul McCartney: Many Years From Now.* Secker & Warburg. pp. 654. hb £13.99. ISBN 0 436 28022 1.

McDevitt, Chas. *Skiffle: The Definitive Story.* Robson Books. pp. 294. hb £19.95. ISBN 1 86105 140 9.

McNeil, Legs and Gillian McCain. *Please Kill Me: The Uncensored Oral History of Punk.* Abacus. pp. 525. pb £8.99. ISBN 0 349 10880 3.

Neaverson, Bob. *The Beatles Movies.* Cassell. pp. 149. pb £13.99. ISBN 0 304 33797 8.

Numan, Gary with Steve Malins. *Praying to the Aliens* (an Autobiography). Andre Deutsche. pp. 276. hb £12.99. ISBN 0 233 99205 7.

Rogan, Johnny. *The Byrds: Timeless Flight Revisited: The Sequel.* Rogan House. pp. 720. hb £20.00. ISBN 0 95295 401 X.

Schwarz, David, Anahid Kassabian and Lawrence Siegel. *Keeping the Score: Music, Disciplinarity, Culture.* University Press of Virginia. pp. 307. pb £15.50. ISBN 0 8139 1700 X.

Shepherd, John and Peter Wicke. *Music and Cultural Theory.* Polity Press. pp. 230. pb £13.95. ISBN 0 7456 0864 7.

Shepherd, John, David Horn, Dave Laing, Paul Oliver, Philip Tagg, Peter Wicke and Jennifer Wilson. *Popular Music Studies: A Select International Bibliography.* Mansell. pp. 450. hb £85.00. ISBN 0 7201 2344 5.

Silverstone, Roger ed. *Visions of Suburbia.* Routledge. pp. 313. pb £14.99. ISBN 0 415 10717 2.

Strong, Martin C. *The Great Psychedelic Discography.* Canongate. pp. 386. pb £14.99. ISBN 0 86241 726 0.

Stump, Paul. *The Music's All That Matters: A History of Progressive Rock.* Quartet. pp. 384. pb £12.00. ISBN 0 7043 8036 6.

Szwed, John F. *Space Is The Place: The Life and Times of Sun Ra.* Payback Press. pp. 476. pb £12.99. ISBN 0 86241 722 8.

Whiteley, Sheila. *Sexing the Groove: Popular Music and Gender.* Routledge. pp. 353. pb £13.99. ISBN 0 415 14671 2.

Zollo, Paul. *Songwriters on Songwriting.* Expanded Edition. Da Capo Press. pp. 641. pb £14.95. ISBN 0 306 80777 7.

14

Virtual Cultures

IAN SAUNDERS

'Cyberspace is above all the trope for a new cybercultural imaginary which is reenergizing idealist social theory in its promise of a different (aesthetic) experience of culture in the form of technoculture.' Thus Amrohini Sahay writes, staking the claim for cyberspace in a typically sweeping, but revealing way ('Cybermaterialism and the Invention of the Cybercultural', *New Literary History*, 28:3, 542). The key is the invocation of the 'imaginary'. For Sahay and many of the other commentators whose work is reviewed here, the virtual is at least as interesting, and powerful, for the way it signifies, as it is for whatever its ontological status might 'in reality' be. For Sahay the nature of that signification is disabling: from his perspective, cyberspace works too readily in concert with a suppression of concepts such as production, labour, need, necessity, historical materiality, and collectivity which are essential to 'enable a politics of social transformation' (542); for many other scholars it is just such a politics that the virtual can promise.

Virtual Culture: Identity and Communication in Cybersociety (edited by Steven Jones) is an important collection of essays which are clustered around a key issue (and indeed the founding premise of this review chapter). If, as Benedict Anderson so persuasively argued, the invention of the printing press changed the very nature of what it was to be a community, what will follow in the wake of electronic communication? Can there be a 'virtual community'? Or indeed, does cyberspace present new possibilities for the restoration of a sense of community lost in contemporary society? Opening chapters by Steven Jones and Jan Fernback lay out the intellectual context which many such discussions draw upon, most notably Habermas's pursuit of the 'public sphere' as an epistemological and ethical guarantor and, within the context of American debate, the critique by Richard Sennett and others of contemporary social practice as suffering precisely the loss of public sphere. As both Jones and Fernback argue, there is little to support the claim that cyberspace is a public sphere of the sort Sennett mourns and Habermas celebrates; and yet, for all that, it remains a powerfully attractive idea. That power, Fernback suggests, can be seen in the energetic way users of the Net object to its control or censorship: what is at stake is less the content of what is being said but the idea of forum where anyone might speak, and in which anything might be said:

There is a 'virtual ideology' in cyberspace which is collective in orientation. There is a strong sense among users that, despite the tolerance needed for the space to be open-minded and despite the potential for oppressiveness, virtual interaction gives users back some of their humanity – a humanity which is authentically expressed among its constituents via a mass medium whose content is not wholly determined by corporate executives. It is an ideology that characterises collectivist rhetoric as something positive, not something anti-American or anti-democratic (46).

Fernback's conclusion – something of a long bow it has to be said – is that if we treat the environment of electronic communication as 'a virtual agora', or 'a place where the virtual collectivity is socially constructed,' rather than merely a communications technology, it has 'the potential to help us translate some of the ideology of virtual existence into our collective American psyche' (52–53). There are two parts to this claim: that praxis in cyberspace can engender a counter-hegemonic ideology, and that to do so we must think of the medium as a place, and not merely a form of communication, 'an underground newspaper of sorts'. It is not really clear why she needs to insist on the second part of the claim, or indeed who the 'we' is here. Moreover, the claim seems to forget Anderson's critical point: a new form of communications technology can have far-reaching ideological consequences, not because of how 'we' understand it, but because of the way it works. In Marxist parlance material practice underwrites social possibility, an insight to which Fernback's position points: 'for some, their experiential lives in cyberspace, their embrace of the collectivist virtual ideology, and their willingness to follow the norms and social expectations that comprise the virtual social contract constitute a rejection of the overly individualistic character of contemporary American social existence' (53).

Virtual Culture presents a number of different studies of candidate groups for 'virtual culture' status. In 'Virtual Commonality: Looking for India on the Internet' Ananda Mitra, notwithstanding her title, looks *not* for India on the Net, but at a particular site, soc.culture.indian, the online home of Indians in the United States who themselves are 'looking' for India. It is a curious case study in that the participants both find what they are looking for – identification with a diaspora based upon a common, albeit culturally and geographically distant origin – and yet fail to find either resolution as to the nature of that origin, or indeed contact with it. As Mitra observes, the first 'failure' is a consequence of the uncontrolled nature of the medium itself: whereas in a 'real' community the range of individual differences about the meaning of the community itself is always, more or less successfully, subsumed by the ideological understanding dominant at the time, in an online community there is no such regulating power. If this is so, though, then the usual perception that mass media and hegemonic power are intimately, and causally, connected seems implausible in the case of virtual media. Assuming hegemony is about consent, Mitra writes, 'it becomes clear that the question of gaining consent becomes unimportant in the electronic space because the traditional centres disappear on the Internet. [...] This is a space where power is manifest in discursive capital, and, given the varieties of ideological positions that find voice on the electronic space, there is no single dominant ideology that can be identified' (73–74). Rather than reaching resolution, or even having a sense of what the dominant view is, 'debate over the naming of Bombay, or the fate of the Muslims in India' never ends: 'no single argument appears to be convincing and persuasive enough to attract consent' (74).

One response to this, and one I suspect Mitra would endorse, is to say that this apparently non-ideological status of Net discourse is evidence of its liberatory potential. Equally, though, a conversation that 'never ends' seems itself a kind of trap, as indeed a community without ideology an illusion. Although not explored in the chapter, perhaps the difficulty here is the attenuated nature of this virtual, exemplified in the telling absence of the group's initiating referent, India itself. To take an uncharitable view, debate continues without end only when it doesn't matter.

More peculiar, even, is the case study described by McLaughlin, Osborne and Ellison ('Virtual Community in a Telepresence Environment') in which a virtual community is *invented* in order to enable its ethnographical analysis. The community's rationale – the maintenance of a 'garden' in cyberspace – is, one cannot help thinking, self-evidently without point; the fact that it generated committed membership (to earn the right to plant one's first 'seed' in the garden one has to accumulate 100 visits to the site) tells us less about how such communities work than about how impoverished a form of community we are willing to accept or, perhaps, how impoverished a need they answer.

It is just that kind of conclusion that Nessim Watson would vigorously reject. As the title of his 'Why We Argue About Virtual Community' suggests, Watson contends that arguing about whether or not 'virtual communities' like soc.culture.indian or Phish.Net are indeed communities misses the real political point, which is to consider why it is we *care* about what might, or might not, be justly a candidate for community status. It is a point well made, and not one I have seen before. As Watson cogently argues the issue is not about what a virtual community is, but how we wish to use the metaphor 'community' (and what is implied in the epithet 'virtual', regardless of what it describes). Watson neatly draws on Anderson's notion of an imaginary community to argue the case that there is no reason not to describe online collectivities as communities if they operate in every other way as such – and he effectively demonstrates that to be so in the case of Phish.net, the energetic fan-base of the popular band Phish. What then is the problem?

> Is there something so powerful about the word 'community' that some social groups would fight earnestly to keep the word from applying to other social groups? Does ownership of the term 'community' have something to do with the ability of a social group to be well represented in a democratic society? (121).

As his rhetoric makes plain, Watson answers in the affirmative to both. We do not get a clear identification of whom the gate-keeping group in this dynamic might be, but he does offer a suggestive account of why self-identification as community, on- as offline, is important. 'In Marxian terms, recognition of themselves as "community" is the first step to creating the common consciousness which enables attempts at improvement in the conditions of the participant's daily lives. When they understand their existence under a "community" metaphor, online participants become able to address their common situations of under-representation in the larger social democracy' (125).

One could make two points. First, not all community is to be desired, and against Watson's confidence in the democratic outcomes of going online one might well read Susan Zickmund's account of neoNazi, skinhead and other white supremacist Net groups in 'Approaching the Radical Other: The Discursive Culture of Cyberhate'. Disturbing as the material is, it is not entirely clear how Zickmund reads it. On the one hand, she argues that the Net has given such groups new prominence and organizational coherence; on the other hand she concludes that because of the uncensored nature of Net talk there is, even in the most inhospitable of sites, ample evidence of dissent. Anyone, regardless of political orientation can go online and, or so the argument goes, whereas in a neoNazi newspaper the moderate's letter would not see print, in the neoNazi newsgroup it is just as legible as any other. As Zickmund notes, however, the language game of these sites is reciprocated abuse. If that is so, what then is the bottom line: the moderate's anti-hate position, or the discursive logic of the exchange medium he or she helps maintain?

Second, as Harry Breslow reminds us (in 'Civil Society, Political Economy and the Internet'), it is not really the case that the phenomenon of the online community is an alternative to the offline one. Rather, the proliferation of online communications is one of the byproducts of the fundamental socio-economic shift from centralized to dispersed, or Fordist to post-Fordist, modes of organization. Critical to that shift has been the computer technology (and associated practices such as just-in-time delivery, horizontal monopolization, subcontracting and the like) that has enabled the transnational corporation to supercede the national, the dispersed and disorganized workforce to supplant the ethos of the shop-floor, and the atomized individual to replace the community. Of course, it is easy to fall into a nostalgia for a past that never existed, but Breslow's point is the important one that however much the online world might emulate, even create, community, it is the technological child of a process whose trajectory seems to be headed in the opposite direction.

An instrument of democratization or not, it remains the case that the most written about virtual communities are those dedicated to sex. There is some doubt about whether the scale of commentary – popular and professional – is in any way reflective of the quantity of sexual activity on the Net. As Wendy Grossman writes (in her *net.wars*), 'at a recent count there were 168 Usenet newsgroups with sex-related names – but there are 20,000 newsgroups overall' (116). Grossman offers an intelligently detached assessment of the issues concerning sex on the Net, although her conclusion is perhaps a little easy: 'the Net doesn't create real life, it only reflects it', and thus the fact that what it shows us is, at times, disturbing ought to prompt us to ask what it 'is teaching us about the society we built before we got wired' (126). More interesting, I think, is her discussion on evidence and the Net: the sheer size and semi-chaotic nature of the system means it is extraordinarily difficult to say with any accuracy just what is really happening in it. DEC research scientist Brian Reid observes that after nine years researching USENET readership and content he does 'not believe it is possible to get measurements whose accuracy is within a factor of 10 of the truth' (cited at 121), or, as Grossman remarks, 'the fact is that because the Internet is vast and the systems for measuring it poor, we may never be able to gauge accurately how much pornography is out there, any more than we know offhand how many of our neighbors have vibrators in their night-stands' (123).

One resident of the cyber-neighbourhood who makes it plain she does indeed have a vibrator on hand is Cleo Odzer, whose *Virtual Spaces: Sex and the Cyber Citizen* offers a first-person account of the possibilities of sex online. Odzer writes from an anthropological background, although it has to be said this book is less about analysing evidence than gathering it. The book offers an enthusiastically described cross-section of what's on in cybersex. In a way it is a refreshing change to have this material described without the usual (and usually unpersuasive) caveat that 'I'm only doing this for research and personally find it tiresome'. Odzer loves cybersex, and recounts numerous engagements in a number of different formats, but in the end the simplicity of the analytic thinking evidenced in the book means it can be little more than a record of participation. Her reflective, and thoroughly autobiographical, conclusion is worth pondering, though. As she tells it, her first sense of being 'at home', after years of dutifully following the hippie circuit of the 1960s, was finding Anjuna Beach in Goa. Time passed, and with it that haven; years later Odzer discovers life online:

> Cyberspace was so new, it was like a frontier territory with new laws, rules, and routines evolving day by day. And it was a community, a family. People jumped to offer support, praise, and help with a project. I gloried in being part of that world. When I created a virtual space called Anjuna Beach, Goa, on a MOO, I thought: 'Aha, I've come full circle. Home again' (182).

What is at first sight a bizarre analogy in fact reveals common ground, the logic of which is a fantasy built upon, but blind to, the economic and social structures that sustain it. It is easy to be censorious, though, and I should add that Odzer's book really does give a sense of the excitement of online (sexual) engagement and, as here, of the medium as it worked in its 'prehistory'. Returning to Grossman's *net.wars*, its pretty clear that the earlier, 'heroic' period of Net life is not long gone, but altogether gone for all that. A number of her essays attempt to give a sense of then versus now, and what the watersheds were: Delphi.com, the first national commercial online service (1993), the Canter and Siegel 'Green Card Lottery' mass posting (April 12, 1994), or the first paid-for advertising banner on Yahoo! (August 1995). Of course, there was not a clearly defined turning point, and nor was that prehistorical space the kind of folksy place some commentators enjoy reminiscing about; the change for all that is real enough, and Grossman's book is a useful record of its dimensions.

The kind of self-consciously addictive behaviour Odzer describes in *Virtual Spaces* receives an unexpected transformation in two papers in a special issue on addiction in *Diacritics* (27.3). In an extraordinarily dense essay, 'Welcome to the Pharmacy: Addiction, Transcendence, and Virtual Reality', Ann Weinstone explores the way the discourse of virtual reality often brings together a rhetoric of transcendence and a rhetoric of addiction. Weinstone suggests that the desire that fuels the virtual is the desire for the stuff that constitutes it: code. Code is read as that which transcends the normal, a late twentieth-century reinvention of the ideal world beyond Plato's cave: 'the rhetorics of world-as-code, fully saturated with the idea that organisms are nothing but information, are conjoined with rhetorics of Platonic hierarchies' (84). To achieve transcendence one 'ingests' code, but it is an act that must be endlessly repeated. The replacement of mortality for the immortality of code (or, in her rhetoric, DNA by code, real cells by 'junk cells') 'depends on repetition. The *pharmakon* is both drug and remedy. In order for it to "work," the user must become it; the user must become an addict' (86). Part of the reason for the necessity of addiction, she suggests, is that of the recurrent nature of anxiety: 'in VR discourses, the insistent rhetorics of addiction must work continually to reproduce hyper-real transcendence by repeatedly inoculating and intoxicating the anxious user with an idealized, vitalized, inFORMation Code' (86). But it is also because we expect it: we work in a tradition which links transcendence, writing and addiction (think of 'Kubla Khan'), and it is this tradition that the discourse of the virtual relies upon for its credibility. Without addiction, transcendence stops making sense. 'The thrill is gone. For those who have read *Neuromancer*, imagine that for Case, jacking in is just another day at the job' (86). Indeed.

In the same issue of *Diacritics* Margurite Waller develops a similar case, arguing that cyberspace is not about alternative positionality and potential, but rather it is about the construction of 'a clean, clear realm in which we can transcend positionality while remaining (or becoming more fully) "ourselves"' ('If "Reality is the Best Metaphor," It Must be Digital', 91). The myth of going online is best understood as a 'positivist dream of a common language in which noise, ambiguity, and misunderstanding are reduced to a minimum, and communication can aspire to transparency' (102). It is a myth, Waller argues, that sets aside the very condition of communication, the body itself; not 'body' as some kind of common essence we all share, but precisely bodies as sites of difference – be it in terms of biology, temporality, culture, gender – which enable meaning and communication. Meaning, she contends, is 'metaphorical, contextual, and relational,' not ontological, and this means (paradoxically) that it is 'by knowing that we do *not* understand, by encountering *aporias*, that we (incompletely) glimpse the contours and contingencies of our subjectivities and can begin to communicate otherwise than solipsistically or imperially' (102).

Digital Delirium, the latest offering of Arthur and Marilouise Kroker, is an edited selection of essays, interviews and 'events' from their online 'theory, technology and culture' journal CTHEORY. Accompanied by a CD in which the Krokers and others read/perform the essays with various degrees of electronic distortion, it is as eclectic as interesting, and not a little unlike a William Gibson novel without the plot. The editors themselves describe their project as 'theory from the academy without walls', and with breezy assurance grant it international, and cutting-edge, preeminence:

'everyday when the sun comes up over China Basin Landing in San Francisco, when cold digital winds blast the streets of Montréal, when guns and knives are silent for a moment in Sarajevo, and when pirate hackers band-talk from Amsterdam to Vienna and Bucharest, CTHEORY webs the globe, radiating back to its net readers a continuously updated media analysis' (xvi). The mainstay of *Digital Delirium* is a series of linked essays by the Krokers, '30 Cyber-Days in San Francisco', interviews from CTHEORY with 'leading cyber-thinkers' R. U. Sirius, Paul Virilio, Jean Baudrillard and Slavoj Žižek, and what the editors modestly call 'a major state of the digital union address by sci-fi writer, Bruce Stirling' (15). The collection as a whole, though, seems a little repetitive (much of the Krokers' material was better said in *Data Trash*, three years earlier, for example) and marked by a kind of pop-ephemerality. That should not be a surprise, I suppose: as a Bruce Stirling reminds us, this is a technology of accelerating obsolescence. Visiting the local landfill he finds a 'two stories high' computer graveyard: 'most [. . .] like they were in perfect working order. The really ominous part of the stack was the really quite large percentage of discarded junk that was still in the shrinkwrap. Never been used, and already extinct' (27).

Endearing trademark excesses aside, CTHEORY continues to make an important contribution to debate in the technology and culture arena, not the least in reminding us that the Net extends beyond California. Thus, for example, Lev Manovich examines Net activity in contemporary Russia ('Behind the Screen/Russian New Media', Vol 20, 3) and Janez Strehovec reports from Slovenia ('The Web as an Instrument of Power and a Realm of Freedom', Vol 20, 3). For both Manovich and Strehovec a key question is whether the 'non-Californian' web environment is indeed different from it, or whether, as Strehovec puts it, it has become 'a colonised and "Mc-Donald's-ised" field for enforcing the technototalitarianism, web fascism, machismo, and tribalism of new, distinctively yuppified elites'. In the projects Stehovec describes 'web-art' is both a form of social witness ('Programmer in Belgrade', for instance, documents the war in Bosnia and Herzegovina) and a form of art practice that works to undermine standard notions of art and the aesthetic: it is a 'radical questioning of the artistic' which proves that in the contemporary environment 'art has a raison d'être only if it explicitly questions and subverts its own procedures, if it escapes, like a satellite overhead, beyond the boundaries of the artistic system to the position of anti-art.'

For Manovich, the potential of web-art in Russia is – paradoxically – tied to its failure. 'Post-communist artists,' he contends, 'recognize that the nature of technology is that it does not work, that it will necessarily break down.' Rather than striving for a presentation of the prefect, then, the governing assumptions become those of Shannon's theory of communication: 'that every signal always contains some noise; that signal and noise are qualitatively the same; and that what is noise in one situation can be signal in another.' So, for example, he describes a project which, rather than the preciousness of artistic expression, collects 'found' web pages which 'were created not as art works but gave a definite "art" feeling,' and another which republished Pushkin via computer-generated translations from Russian to Finnish and then again from Finnish to English. For the perpetrator, conceptual artist and poet Dmitry Prigov, 'the final product was not a miserably misbegotten translation, twice removed from the source, but a new poem, its originality indebted – however ironically – to the operations of the lowest level of artificial intelligence.' It is certainly distinctly different from the San Francisco chic of the kind of project Holtzman describes in *Digital Mosaics* (see below).

In a special issue of *Modern Fiction Studies* (43.3), Stuart Moulthrop is also interested in the notion that what hypertext has to offer is electronic breakdown; it is, though, very much a Californian style of limitation where the inspiration is Heidegger's idea of an event or act that would break past our normal, confident 'being-in-the-world'. Computers break down, but Moulthrop argues that hypertext is, as it were, conceived in the logic of breakdown. 'If links and other interactive transactions are inherently confusing, traversing an invisible, nonspecific space, then these elements must also convey something of a phenomenological crisis or surprise even when they work as intended. Cybertextual work cannot deliver the infinite variation that its multivariate structure disingenuously promises' (664). And that, concludes Moulthrop, may well be its defining characteristic, although I suspect most readers would find Monavich's celebration of quotidian breakdown more plausible, and perhaps more reassuring.

While with that issue of *Modern Fiction Studies*, Jaishree Odin extends the flight from the American centre, contending that 'the intertextual and interactive hypertext or Net aesthetic is most suited for representing post-colonial cultural experience since it embodies our changed conception of language, space, and time' ('The Edge of Difference: Negotiations between the Hypertextual and the Postcolonial', 599). Because hypertext is perspectival we are unlikely to fall for a master narrative that insists on a singular truth and, in something of a twist, it is the very embodiedness of hypertext, the fact that it requires particular reading choices, that will enable our critical suspicion. 'Navigating in the "city of texts" can be liberating when the sites are approached not in the spirit of possession and control, but as the sites of active encounter that is marked by a self-awareness of one's positioning' (628). Odin's claim is a suggestive one, although it has to admitted that for the most part 'hypertext' is being used here as metaphor rather than actual practice: rather surprisingly given the paper's title, his favoured example turns out to be the film maker Trinh Minh-Ha. It is a useful connection nonetheless.

In *From Text to Hypertext: Decentering the Subject in Fiction, Film, the Visual Arts and Electronic Media*, Silvio Gaggi ranges over more than five centuries of creative work in a bid to get a handle on the postmodern claim (should that be cliché?) that we are now in the era of the decentred subject. Before turning to his discussion of hypertext, I should note the quite extraordinary range of Gaggi's work. His method is to concentrate on selected paradigmatic works, and he sets out with van Eyck's 'Wedding of the Arnolfini' before moving on to the photography of Cindy Sherman and Barbara Kruger, the fiction of Conrad, Faulkner and Calvino, and a variety of film texts including Coppola's *One from the Heart* and Altman's *The Player*. In all this Gaggi sees evidence of the evolution of the concept of subject along postmodern lines, and in the last section of the book – 'Hyperrealities and Hypertexts' – Gaggi investigates hypertext, and the communications logic enabled by the Net, as symptom and agent of yet a further stage in the process. Gaggi writes in an engaged and accessible way, but there is little in the chapter that surprises, or indeed that goes beyond the well-known texts he draws upon (chiefly, Landow, *Hypertext: The Convergence of Contemporary Critical Theory and Technology*, 1992 and Heim, *Electric Language: A Philosophical Study of Word Processing*, 1987). The result in the main is a rehearsal of their generalized claims for the medium. Thus for example, and drawing on Landow, Gaggi claims that 'the distinction between text and context will dissolve and intertextuality will cease to be regarded as such because there will be, in fact, only one text, one intertext, one hypertext' (103). Further, hypertext will undo notions of authorship and ownership, and that in its place it will establish a sense of communal good (106–107); that hypertext will unsettle the illusion nurtured in print texts of a single author speaking to a single reader (111); that it will in some ways return us to the forms and mechanisms of an oral, pre-print culture which may well have a new kind of collective intelligence that supercedes individual subjectivity (114–115):

> The *cogito* is both dispersed and enlarged, not by a challenge of philosophy or theory, but by the subject's experience in a decentered network that threatens to eclipse the 'individual' subject that understands itself as physically embodied and clearly localized in space and time. The groundless, shifting subject articulated by poststructural theory and represented in postmodern art and literature is actualized in the virtual space of hypertext.

The claim is now a familiar one, but without evidence or critique remains vaguely programmatic and, if anything, less persuasive for the retelling. To be fair to Gaggi, *From Text to Hypertext* does acknowledge that the hypertextual world could as easily be dystopic as not, but it is a recognition little developed beyond the obvious 'it is not difficult to imagine a future in which there is a polarization of society based on wealth and the ability of individuals to access information' (119). As Kroker and others would reply, it is not 'difficult' to imagine that particular future because it is, in fact, already here. Moreover if the subject in hypertext does indeed become detached from space and time this could as easily be read as retrograde than as an adavnce. As poet and self-conscious luddite Steven Heighton insists, 'the problem with electronic media in terms of writers and their evolving forms is that the media have pushed to the forefront and now lead the Western world's march into terminal abstraction, and the effect of this process is, predictably, to make writers more abstract, more detached from the sensual sources of imaginative power, more mediated – more remote and controlled' (*The Admen Move on Lhasa: Writing and Culture in a Virtual World*, 67).

Gaggi's book concludes with a discussion of two already much discussed hypertexts, Michael Joyce's 'Afternoon, a Story' and Stuart Moulthrop's *Victory Garden*. Again, this is a lucid presentation, although it is more than a little odd how the print medium seems to inevitably trap its practitioners into something like a retelling of the plot of hypertext, the very thing the latter is thought to eschew. As Gaggi makes clear, both thematize subjectivity and (more so *Victory Garden*) are interested in different ways of conceiving the subject. But that is not quite the same thing as demonstrating that 'the subject' has indeed changed, an altogether more difficult proposition.

As the subtitle of Steven Holtzman's *Digital Mosaics* signals, his aim is to work towards an 'aesthetics of cyberspace'. The book is divided into two parts: 'A Tour of Digital Worlds' and 'The Medium is the Message'. The 'Tour' gives a snapshot of experimental digital textuality in the year of publication. Holtzman notes that for the greater part commercial digitalization amounts to 'repurposing': the print text becomes available on CD, the telephone directory is published on the web, and so forth. His quarry, though, is text forms that are only possible within the medium of the digital, and the 'Tour' pays homage to phenomena such as the visualization of Mandelbrot's fractal geometry and other recursive processes that rely on computational power to deploy simple rule structures to build results of great complexity: the bifurcating triangles that seem to mutate into 'real' mountains, the program generated 'boids' that demonstrate independent flocking behaviour, the creation of digital species which evolve in unpredictable ways to better accomplish set tasks, and so forth. The last section of the 'Tour' describes Philip Glass and Robert Israel's collaborative *GhostDance* (Holtzman was himself project advisor), an aural-visual experience that takes as its inspiration the Ghost Dances performed by the Plains Indians in the latter part of the nineteenth century in order to drive the white men from their land. Holtzman does not seem overly concerned by the futility of the original project, preferring instead to give us something of a vicarious experience of its electronic descendent:

> I'm in a massive pipe, sliding downward, floating through a dark cavernous space with the expanse of a Himalayan valley. It appears to be miles from one side of this ethereal conduit to the other.
> The inner surface of this enormous tube is pockmarked with the texture of the moon. I'm still a little disoriented by the odd perspective. It's like being inside a hollow, tubular moon. [. . .]
> I'm stunned by the sight of a glistening cone and floating sphere profiled against a bright reflective mat. As I arrive at the base of the conical form, I look up in awe (110–112).

The second part of *Digital Mosaics* sets itself the task of trying to locate the essence of the digital, and thus the nature of the digital aesthetic. An initial response, of course, is precisely that it is digital: 'peeling the layers of structure from the surface of any digital world ultimately reveals the lowest level of abstraction in digital form: bits, 0s and 1s. A digital world's smallest element is a bit' (123). This, of course, is its great strength: in a code-world, reproduction is perfect. If the numbers are the same, the copy is the same. It is also its great weakness: to reproduce our experience of the natural requires just too many numbers for this, and perhaps any, generation of computer. This means, Holtzman writes, that 'the limits of the computer graphics engines of a given period in the evolution of the technology are evident in the accompanying aesthetic. [...] you know the image is computer-generated and you marvel at the rendering and how it dealt with certain complex issues of computation' (163). Moreover, he continues, there is a fundamental disparity between world and the digital that will always limit the latter because, unlike the virtual world, the real one is 'an analog place. It's a constant stream; our experience of time, our views of reality, our thoughts, and our consciousness are not broken into consecutive discrete segments' (164). Holtzman's chapter begins with a sketch of Derrida's contention that language is intrinsically limited, but the list here – experience, views, thoughts, consciousness – seems to forget language. It is a critical omission for, while we might wish to describe 'experience' as 'analog' (although I'm not sure what we are saying by this), it is difficult to see language, a series of discrete words, as anything but digital. Holtzman's rendering of a disjunction here, that is to say, in effect brings together a postmodern technology with a decidedly modernist, organicist account of the self, and one wonders if the disjunction is in fact not the result of that underlying dissonance.

In the final analysis, though, Holtzman wants us all to embrace the digital. The conclusion is titled 'Don't Look Back', and he means it. We may not know what the digital aesthetic will be, but we do know it is the way of the future. Holtzman decries the literati's defence of the book, the romanticist vision of reading 'while curled up in a chair' (Sarah Lyall, 'Are these books, or what?', *New York Times Book Review*, 14 August 1994), and counters with his own vision of readerly comfort:

> I imagine myself curled up in bed with laser images projected on my retinas, allowing me to view and travel through an imaginary three-dimensional virtual world. A story about the distant past flashes a quaint image of a young woman sitting and reading a book, which seems just as remote as the idea of a cluster of Navajo Indians sitting around a campfire and listening to a master of the long-lost tradition of storytelling.

'Don't look back', indeed: one has to ask, surely, why must an enthusiasm for a new expressive medium so often be disabled by the kind of political blindness that (for example) finds nothing offensive in using a stereotypical picture of lost indigenous culture to illustrate 'progress'?

In the special issue of *Modern Fiction Studies* (43:3) mentioned above, a number of scholars consider the 'style' of hypertext. Thus Michael Joyce recounts the experience of workshopping students of the medium, and exploring the different experiences of time hypertext enables. Sue-Ellen Case, in 'Eve's Apple, or Women's Narrative Bytes', offers readings of a number of iconoclastic works, including a collaborative hypertext fiction, a Grrl Website, and Adriene Jenik's CD *Mauve Desert*.

Reading Matters: Narratives in the New Media Ecology (edited by Tabbi and Wutz) is a collection that reexamines the fate of narrative in the context of electronic technology, for the most part arguing the case for the defence. Thus, for example, William Paulson argues for a conservation of the canon precisely because the texts that constitute may act as a kind of resistance to the 'hegemony of electronic information' (245): 'the mode of print, which now appears to us in its technological twilight as a particularism, offers for now at least an alternative to what Poster calls the mode of information' ('The Literary Canon in Technological Obsolescence', 246). In 'Virtual Textuality' Lynn Wells in like manner is less than enthusiastic about her topic, and draws back from the standard vision of an imminent 'democratization', noting that 'the view of technology's superiority over printed texts derives partially from an overestimation of the autonomy allowed the computer programs' users' (252). Indeed for Wells the chief virtue of the virtual is that it gives us a vocabulary that assists us to better appreciate postmodern fiction. Rereading *Midnight's Children* or *Terra Nostra* with that vocabulary allows us to describe them in terms of 'virtual meeting spaces,' or 'discrete artificial environments whose representational plasticity makes it feasible for historical actualities to be brought into improbable conjunctions with phenomena from several ontological origins' (260). Moreover, she suggests, the fact that this experience of the (psuedo?) hypertextual is nonetheless print based means that readers encounter the genuine resistance of an embodied medium, and must take into account its knowledge bases and discursive formations. The ensuing dialogue between one's own position and that of the text 'admits the possibility of texts having political effectiveness' (257). Wells is surely right in proposing that a text that merely reflected our own desires is unlikely to change much, and that political changes requires the resistance of the other; but then if this is the case her reservations about 'real' hypertext seem misplaced. If, as she observes, 'in spite of the exercise of choice that these technologies permit, the user must still interact with a previously established set of parameters' (252), this seems precisely a case of the medium offering a resistance to the reader, and thus on her own logic ought to be regarded as likely to engender a dialectic between the known and unknown in just the same way as the print texts she champions.

Stuart Moulthrop's 'No War Machine', also in *Reading Matters*, takes a line diametrically opposed to that of Wells, arguing that hypertext is a 'war machine' (the phrase is borrowed from Deleuze and Guatarri, and in their counter-intuitive usage, it means activity that *resists* the state apparatus – one would have thought the war machine does the reverse). Hypertexts are war machines because they 'require the reader to participate in the progressive unfolding of the narrative, hypertextual fictions necessarily undermine any singular fatalism, fostering instead an ethos of responsiveness and engagement' (275). And yet hypertext is more than its narrative and discursive elements:

> Outside this discourse lie scripts or routines created by the author; outside of these, the code that makes up the hypertext environment (Hypercard, Storyspace, HTML, etc); outside of that, the operating system of the machine on which this is running; and outside of *that*, the various layers of ROM and microcode that allows the machine's chips to function.

Following Martin Rosenberg ('Physics and Hypertext', *Hyper/Text/Theory* ed. George Landow, Johns Hopkins Press, 1994) Moulthrop goes on to observe all of these functional elements 'proceed from a state apparatus concerned with specificity, regularity, and constraint – something we might call the military-entertainment complex' (278). Given the nature of the machine that supports it, can hypertext be an iconoclastic 'war machine' after all? To the confusion of this reader, Moulthrop answers that question in both the negative and the affirmative. No, we were wrong to suppose it had any such potential: 'hypertext fiction cannot be a war machine [. . .] nor can its writers constitute a genuine avant-garde' (280). But then again, if we think about the nature of the virus, that which irrupts in a system, perhaps then a viral hypertext could dent the hegemony of the state. Moulthrop's example of such viral incursion, however, is Stephenson's *Snow Crash*, very much a print text. He remarks that 'we might consider viruses in the same way we do nuclear weapons: we are less concerned with their actual use, which remains "unthinkable," than with their rhetorical effect' (282), but this, or so it seems to me, leaves us even less certain about just what it is Moulthrop is arguing here and what, if anything, it tells us about hypertext. I should add, moreover, that for this reader the nuclear remains 'thinkable' and continues to signify something more than a rhetoric of ending.

Books Reviewed

Gaggi, Silvio. *From Text to Hypertext: Decentering the Subject in Fiction, Film, the Visual Arts, and Electronic Media.* Penn. pp. 169. hb $32.95. ISBN 0 8122 3400 6.
Grossman, Wendy. *net.wars.* New York University Press. pp. 237. hb US$22.00 (£17.75). ISBN 0 8147 3103 1.
Heighton, Steven. *The Admen Move on Lhasa: Writing and Culture in a Virtual World.* Anansi. pp. 157. pb US$18.95. ISBN 0 88784 588 6.
Holtzman, Steven. *Digital Mosaics: The Aesthetics of Cyberspace.* Simon and Schulster. pp. 206. hb US$25.00. ISBN 0 684 83207 0.
Jones, Steven, ed. *Virtual Culture: Identity and Communication in Cybersociety.* Sage. pp. 262. pb US$24.95 (£14.95). ISBN 0 7619 5526 7.
Kroker, Arthur and Marilouise, eds. *Digital Delirium.* St Martin's Press. pp. 318. pb US$15.96 (£11.99). ISBN 0 312 17237 0.
Odzer, Cleo. *Virtual Spaces: Sex and the Cyber Citizen.* Berkley Books. pp. 245. pb US$11.20 (£8.48). ISBN 0 425 15986 8.
Tabbi, Joseph and Michael Wutz, eds. *Reading Matters: Narratives in the New Media Ecology.* Cornell University Press. pp. 316. pb US$17.95 (£13.50). ISBN 0 8014 8403 0.

15

Film Theory

SUSAN PURDIE

I shall begin this chapter with discussions of a number of books that deal with specific aspects or genres of film, or with specific issues in, or approaches to, films' analysis. This will lead to a number of books whose specificity is defined in terms of films' historical period. This in turn will lead to books offering accounts of cinema defined in terms of nationality, before concluding with the 1997 republication of one of film theory's greatest monuments.

Audience Analysis by Denis McQuail is a useful book. It provides an overview of ways in which 'audiences' – as an empirical entity – have been thought of, for different and mostly pragmatic research purposes, in relation to all 'mass media'. Coverage is wide rather than deep, but the good lists of primary references for each topic make it easy to go further. McQuail is not concerned with theorizations of audience experiences. He is aware of some central debates, though his brief references might be misleading for a reader who has (as he seems to assume) no prior knowledge of these. For example, the two references to Bourdieu read, in their entirety, as follows.

First, summarizing factors to be considered in relation to audiences' choices of what they consume, as: '*social background and milieu*, especially as reflected in social class, education, religious, cultural, political, and family environment and region or locality of residence'. McQuail adds, 'we can also refer here to what Bourdieu (1984) calls "cultural capital" – learned cultural skills and tastes, often transmitted inter-generationally by way of family, education and the class system' (76).

Second, in a discussion of 'Lifestyle' within a chapter discussing 'Audience Practices: Social Uses of the Media':

> ... the pioneering work of the French sociologist Pierre Bour-
> dieu (1984) represents a long tradition of inquiry relating vari-
> ous expressions of cultural taste with social and family
> background. This has contributed to the debate about the
> hierarchical distribution of 'cultural capital' (Bourdieu's con-
> cept) and the nature of mass (or popular) culture (93).

However, any theorist engaged with empirical or 'ethnographic' research, or with debates about this, would be well advised to check their familiarity with the issues and research that McQuail surveys. His conclusion seems to apply to any kind of work that involves appealing to the actuality of an 'audience': 'we can no longer use the term without giving a clear indication of what we mean by it in a given instance, and any "measure" of audience will have to be understood in a specific way' (150).

The writing of Kenneth Mackinnon's *Uneasy Pleasures: The Male as Erotic Object* began, from his own account, with an audience reaction that he found puzzling. Presented with two videos of the chart band Take That, as examples of 'masculinity as spectacle', a usually responsive group of students reacted with embarrassed derision, denying that they themselves had any eroticized response to specularized males. The first thrust of Mackinnon's book is an empirical demonstration of 'the evidence for the male as object of the erotic gaze' in film, television, popular entertainment (male strippers) and, especially, the advertising and magazines of the 1990s. This is organized via a debate with Laura Mulvey's [in]famous assertion that, in Mackinnon's words, 'there cannot be a male object of the gaze'. His second intention, therefore, is 'to consider how the outing of the male object affects assumptions and convictions about the gendered identities of viewing subjects and viewed objects, particularly in relation to access to power' (14). The first objective is well achieved. This book would certainly be a good way to introduce students to a wide range of representations of males, of a kind that would allow 'masculinity', and thus all gendering, to be presented as problematic. Perhaps it is its foundation in undergraduate teaching that leads to the book's second intention being less fully realized. Mackinnon may be simplifying in order to address people coming to film theory for the first time; however, on the evidence of this writing, while citing subsequent debates and developments of Mulvey's position (including her own 'After-word'), he is not totally familiar with the foundations of the theoretical positions he discusses.

In summarizing the original article, for example, he suggests that 'the logic of Mulvey's position would appear to be that the female object of the gaze, in being invested with the trappings of greater power through fetishization, becomes more like the spectator (masculinized and thus, in fantasy at least, powerful). Given this logic, it is surely at least interesting to note in passing that the male object of the gaze is *already* like the masculine spectator' (15). Mackinnon seems to ignore the origin of Mulvey's argument in Freud's theory of fetishization as a defence against the female's genital castration threat; yet it is surely Freud, or else Mulvey's interpretation *of* Freud, that has to be debated here. (Mackinnon does not refer anywhere to Mulvey's work in the 1990s, collected in 1996 under the title *Fetishism and Curiosity* (BFI, reviewed in *YWCCT 96*). In this she extends her thinking, seeking a 'dialectical relationship' between fetishism and curiosity (Mulvey xi) and dealing, at least once, with a fetishized, abjected, male figure, in Sembene's *Xala*.) It is, of course, possible to debate any position that automatically equates 'the object of the gaze' with abjection and/or passivity.

Nevertheless, the sense in which Freud suggests that the fetishized object is 'masculinized' cannot simply be equated with the 'masculinity' involved in recognizing that an image is a representation of a male person.

Mackinnon is surely right to note the continued circulation of the 'Visual Pleasure' essay, as if it were a finalized position, especially in some teaching of film theory. However, in arguing for a more complex view of the power relations between the bearer of the gaze and its object than the original article offers, Mackinnon does not address its underlying assumptions.

Possibly an appeal to Foucault (e.g. the discussion of 'power' in Volume I of *The History of Sexuality*) would be useful to him. He makes no reference to Foucault, rather Freud and Lacan, and works that have developed from their thinking, are adduced. In fact, all references to Freud and Lacan turn out to come from other writers' discussions of them (there are no works by either of them in the bibliography either). When he writes that 'Lacan's Mirror Stage, through which the passage into subjectivity is effected, must have the presence of another (standing in, as it were, for the Other) corroborating, for example, that this mirror image is indeed the image of the self before it' (33). Mackinnon may again be making a necessary simplification to engage students. However, the references and explanatory quotations in this paragraph are all from an article by Kaja Silverman (in Modleski ed. 1986, *Studies in Entertainment*, Indiana University Press), as is this paragraph's concluding reference to the 'Great Masculine Renunciation'. When the next paragraph hurries on to begin 'Yet, it can be suggested that narcissism, being linked with psychic survival, plays a more important role in the unconscious than Oedipal crisis in its relation to psychic disorder' (this referenced to Joyce McDougal's 1990 *Plea for a Measure of Abnormality*, Free Association Books) it is difficult to feel that any argument, Lacan's, Silverman's or Mackinnon's, is being very fully investigated.

Further references to 'fetishistic thinking', e.g. in the conclusion (188–189), again suggest that Mackinnon's use of the term is rather different from Freud's. Whatever the reason for the absence of discussion about how, precisely, he intends such terms and how his use differs from more widely known ones, the result is confusing. His Conclusion begins 'After a review of the evidence, Laura Mulvey's suggestion that only females can be objectified (in narrative cinema) seems to be wrong' (187). It is not clear whether by 'evidence' Mackinnon refers to the instances of imagery he has cited, or to these and also the theories he has adduced. If we think that the effects or meanings of images are debatable, then no image in and of itself can be taken as 'evidence' of its own reading; we have to work out arguments. Mackinnon's collection of instances does raise a generative problem, but this book does not give evidence that he has really tackled the theoretical problematics it involves.

In *Looking for the Other: Feminism, Film and the Imperial Gaze*, E. Anne Kaplan investigates a question not unlike Mackinnon's. In Spivak's phrase, she asks 'can the subaltern look?' and also '*how* does the subaltern look?' (4). Her project is to redress problems which she now identifies in white feminist criticism of the 1970s and 1980s. She does not simply reject this or its psychoanalytic basis, but now brings that thinking to 'focus on the ways in which the "male" gaze and the "imperial" gaze cannot be separated within western patriarchal cultures' (xi). Thus issues of race, and also of gay/lesbian perspectives are given central attention, within a framework that references women's studies, postcolonial theory, history and 'literary-style textual analysis' as well as psychoanalytic film theory. Kaplan says that this coincides with the resources her own students bring, despite their lack of a 'film repertoire' and that it is 'such a reader and student that I am addressing in this book' (xiv). Such an address in no way restricts her searching and informed analysis of the deployments and effects of imaging human beings in cinema. From her initial distinction between 'gaze' and 'look' – the latter, unlike the former, relational – Kaplan lucidly and incisively asks us to reconsider and re-contextualize textual and critical practices as well as the politics within which both are produced.

Stella Bruzzi also takes psychoanalysis as a central axis in her investigation in *Undressing Cinema: Clothing and Identity in the Movies*. Her other main axis is 'fashion' – a subject that is, for once, taken absolutely seriously. Bruzzi starts from the fundamental premise that clothing exists as a discourse not wholly dependent on the structures of narrative and character for signification. Thus, she investigates, firstly, how far and in what ways 'clothes [seem] able to impose rather than absorb meaning' in film (xiv). Secondly, by considering the clothing of male, as well as female filmic characters, she is involved (again indexing a similar problem to Mackinnon's) with the problematics of masculinity's construction and of the eroticization of the imaged male. Thirdly, with persuasive logic, attention to filmic clothing as unsettling the 'basic' male/female binary leads towards a consideration of the instability of all absolute distinctions of gender or sexuality and thus to the 'fluidities of [all] identity' (xv).

In order to cover this subject, Bruzzi moves around a lot of (mainly American mainstream) films – her chapters are very usefully anchored in examinations of specific film texts – and a lot of topic definitions. Her first section includes a chapter about the overt use of 'couturier' clothes (i.e. related in publicity to the extra-textual kudos of the designer houses) to produce clothes as spectacle: films dealt with here include *Sabrina, Pretty Woman, Trop Belle Pour Toi!* and *Pret-à-Porter*. This section's second chapter considers the construction of 'woman' as the 'male's' fetish, with a discussion of the masculine 'Great Renunciation', accurately attributed as Flugel's hypothesis. Bruzzi's contention here is that film, with the instances of *The Piano* and *The Age of Innocence*, can 'make strange', or else appropriate such fetishization. Her second section brings together chapters on 'gangsters', black American cinema and modern versions of *femme fatales* to consider inter-relations of gender, sexuality and appearance. Specific examples are *Scarface, Pulp Fiction, Casino, Leon, Shaft, New Jack City, Boyz N the Hood, Waiting to Exhale, The Last Seduction, Disclosure*, and *Single White Female*. In the third section, Bruzzi distinguishes between 'The Comedy of Cross-Dressing' (*Glen or Glenda, Mrs. Doubtfire, The Adventures of Priscilla, Queen of the Desert*) and 'The Erotic Strategies of Androgyny' (*The Ballad of Little Jo, The Crying Game, Orlando*). The former category Bruzzi analyses as reaffirming gender divisions, by rendering their apparent confusion absurd. The second, however, operates to break down such divisions because, in them, uncertainty is rendered erotic.

(An interesting parallel to Mackinnon (above) emerges in one of her conclusions that 'despite the Great Masculine Renunciation, narcissism and the eroticization of the male body can exist as correlatives of heterosexual masculinity, even via the ostensibly unspectacular men's suit' (xviii).)

It is possible that Bruzzi slightly overstates the total originality of her conclusions (e.g. Introduction, xviii–xix); she does not, as one example, refer to Sybil DelGaudio's 1993 *Dressing the Part: Sternberg, Dietrich, and Cos-*

tume (Associated University Presses). This is, though, a readable and valuable book.

The Cinematic City brings together essays by a distinguished group of contributors drawn from disciplines relating to film theory and communications and to human geography. Geographer David B. Clarke edits and introduces the collection as well as co-authoring one of the essays. Clarke's initial perception that is 'so central is the city to film that, paradoxically, the widespread *implicit* acceptance of its importance has mitigated against explicit consideration of its actual significance' (1). Developing from this, the Introduction argues with incisive intelligence that we should now (following Benjamin and Deleuze, rather than the screen apparatus theorists) be treating cinema as possessing a hapticality such that 'cinematic space cannot be simply equated with a perspectival representation of (another) space, its dynamism contained by its narrative form (thereby offering the spectator a seemingly coherent position of phallocentric visual mastery)' (9). Thus the relationships between 'cinema and the city' are posited as those of two spatial entities that interpenetrate and inform each other, rather than ones in which the latter's reality appears as a reproduced content of the former's textuality. However, he adds that 'the aim of this volume is to provide for the *exploration* of the cinematic city without imposing, a priori, any single interpretation' (10).

Clarke's first contributor, Colin McArthur, demonstrates that within the binary 'city and country', the filmic city can be constructed to carry many different and contradictory significations. Guiliana Bruno studies the early Neapolitan film industry and its function for New York immigrant communities, as exported images of home. Contrastingly, John Gold and Stephen Ward jointly consider the construction of the modern[ist] city as a production of 'eternal and immutable' values, in British documentary film dealing with inter- and post-war city planning. Again contrastingly, the city's construction as a dystopia, in *film noir* and also in Capra's *It's a Wonderful Life*, is examined by Frank Krutnik. Will Straw investigates an even more extreme construction of the 'lurid city' in a genre of 'city expose' films (which claim a basis in actual investigations of municipal vice) that appeared in the USA in the 1950s. Antony Easthope examines the city in films of the 1960s (especially Godard and Antonioni), interrogating especially Foucault's 1967 announcement of 'the present epoch' as one of 'heterotopia'. Easthope suggests that, if in these texts we do indeed see the beginnings of 'the transition from modernism to postmodernism, [as] temporality gives way to spatiality, history to simultaneity, juxtaposition and heterotopia' (138), the loss of history's revolutionary potential cannot be simply welcomed.

Marcus A. Doel and David B. Clarke jointly question the 'oxymoronic status of a canonical postmodern cultural artefact' accorded to *Blade Runner*. Rather than viewing the film as a mirror, reflecting a dystopically imagined city, they argue (echoing Clarke's Introduction) that it is a dynamic construction of a dialectic between a modernist impulse towards order and a heterology which constantly troubles this, especially in the Replicants' disruption of the categories of 'life' and 'death'. Elisabeth Mahoney questions the politics of postmodernism, with specific reference to *Night on Earth*, *Falling Down* and *Just Another Girl on the I.R.T.* The two following chapters, by Rob Lapsley and James Hay, argue respectively for the continuing importance to film theory of Lacanian psychoanalysis and for a critique of this approach. Both writers are concerned that theorizations of the cinema should serve politically liberating intentions. For Lapsley, it remains an understanding of the subject's necessary, but manipulable, processes which allows 'the evaluation of the effects of particular ideals and illusions and, where possible, their displacement by less damaging configurations' (206). Hay argues against 'the tendency to see film practices [. . .] as discrete, albeit changing, unities and as a discrete set of relations producing a "cinematic subject" rather than understanding film as practised among different social sites, always in relation to other sites, and engaged by social subjects who move among sites and whose mobility, access to and investment in cinema conditions is conditioned by these relations among sites' (212). In the final chapter, Iain Chambers connects 'Maps, Movies, Musics and Memory', taking 'cinema and the city [. . .] not as a point of arrival, but as a point of departure for a further set of questions while employing aural, rather than visual, maps to orient my journey' (230).

Clarke's collection is, thus, far more than an examination of one particular cinematic topos. With its variety of energetically presented views, it challenges its readers to re-inspect their assumptions about cinema and its theorization, while reminding us that this is an exciting activity. An overall final index, which collections of essays do not always provide, is useful; an overall filmography would also have been useful.

The Road Movie Book, edited by Steven Cohan and Ina Rae Hark, also has contributors whose academic discipline is geography, brought together with others working (predominantly) in English departments. This is, more than Clarke's collection, an investigation of one particular cinematic genre, though the central interest of 'Road Movies' and the variety of their forms is well demonstrated.

In the first section, 'Mapping Boundaries', Bennet Shaber argues that 'the people' are constructed as the true destination of the journeys in mainstream Hollywood and European films of the 1940s and 1950s, while post-war films present that quest as an impossibility. Shari Roberts considers inscriptions of masculinity, especially in the films of Clint Eastwood, positing that road movies take over this ideological work from the Western. Ian Leong, Mike Sell and Kelly Thomas jointly consider the conjunction of sexuality, consumer capitalism and style in 'outlaw couple' movies, focusing on *Gun Crazy, Bonnie and Clyde* and *Natural Born Killers*.

The second section, 'American Roads', follows a history of the genre's Hollywood treatment. Steven Cohan examines films of the 1940s and 1950s as constructing a utopian association of 'the road' and 'the home', mediated by their introduction of 'Show Business Culture'. The television series *Route 66* is seen by Mark Alvery as the epitomal road narrative between the era of *On The Road* and that of *Easy Rider*. It is the impact of this last film's release which is analysed by Barbara Kilinger. Ina Rae Hark examines buddy movies' disappearance at the end of the 1970s and reappearance in the late 1980s, as a recuperative response to perceived, intervening, 'yuppie' excesses.

Finally, 'Alternative Roads' turns attention to non-US films and to productions by the independent US cinema. In this section Angelo Restivo finds in the Italian national highway system, and its cinematic representations, a source of a new national subjectivity in the late 1950s and early 1960s. Delia Falconer examines the construction of Australian national identity in relation to the *Mad Max* trilogy, in the 1980s. Pamela Robertson considers Australian nationalist, sexual and racial politics a decade later, in relation to *Priscilla, Queen of the Desert*. At what the editors term 'the sexual margins of the American road' (13) *To Wong Foo, Thanks for Everything! Julie Newmar* and *Boys on the Side*, are analysed by Sharon Willis. Where Willis identifies a final effacement of both racial and sexual difference in these films, both Katie Mills and Robert Lang find the films that they examine, *The Living End* and *My Own Private Idaho* respectively, offering genuine space for the representation of homosexual desire. Stuart C. Aitken and Christopher Lee Lukinbeal jointly consider troubled, 'disassociated' masculinities in *Priscilla, Queen of the Desert, My Own Private Idaho* and *Paris, Texas*. In the second two films, unlike the first, they find a mobility of gaze 'through which the subject of hegemonic masculinity can be contested' (37).

This book's contributors range from the professorial likes of Cohan and Hark themselves, to several graduate students, and not all of these writers wield their theory, which is mostly postmodern and prominently adduced, with the accomplished control of Clarke's experienced contributors. However, anyone with interests in or related to the genre should find *The Road Movie Book* stimulating reading. It has a general index and an index of films, which supplies director and date but is not quite reliable: *Priscilla, Queen of the Desert*, for example, is omitted.

The specific genre examined by Mikita Brotmann is deliberately extreme. That is to say that in *Offensive Films: Toward an Anthropology of Cinema Vomitif*, she examines a genre whose production is, intentionally, radically transgressive of normalized cinematic texts and which, because its transgressive intentions have commercial rather than ideological foundations, has generally been treated as beyond film theory's pale. Thus, her Acknowledgements announce that 'most of my support and guidance came from those editors and founders of horror societies and fanzines far beyond the walls of any academic institution'.

Brotmann offers an introductory defence of her chosen topic that is intelligent, theoretically informed and thought-provoking. She says that 'the main point of writing this book is to show that those films that have been shunned, mocked, and rejected are in fact – whether or not their directors and audiences are aware of it – of far more substance and interest than has previously been assumed [...] what separates *cinema vomitif* from most other forms of exploitation cinema is that it does not acknowledge any distinction between performers and performance. By displaying the nauseating, *cinema vomitif* induces nausea; it is both a spectacle to be witnessed and a part of our bodily lives. Everybody is a participant, because the very acts it involves embrace every body and every life' (3). Much of the following discussion is also useful, especially in its description of film material which is indeed largely excluded from critical notice and which does raise significant questions. The provision of a full filmography is especially welcome here. However, as her own discussion of work such as Carol J. Clover's 1992 *Men, Women and Chainsaws* (BFI Press) demonstrates, the territory of the extreme is not quite as neglected as Brotmann claims.

It is where a certain extremity creeps into Brotmann's own writing that some doubts may arise as to how thoroughly thought through this book's project is. She closes her first introductory section with the assertion that '*cinema vomitif* displays a bodily mirror world – the inverse of abstraction, philosophy, symbolism, tradition and analysis. But only in the mirror can we see humankind as it really is: a grotesque and freakish parade of bodily deformities and perversions' (4). As an academic assertion, the second sentence does not quite stand scrutiny (*all* humankind, *all* the time? – honestly?); but the necessity of offering introductory accounts of our work can drive anyone to rhetorical excess.

More troubling is the thinking – or lack of it – behind statements like 'the distinction between "us" and "not us" has always been a troublesome one to make, mainly because – while such distinctions tend to be based chiefly on the physical manifestation of racial characteristics – there is still no reliable way of distinguishing one race from another' (35). The point that is being pursued is the good one that the human displays in *Freaks* have parallels in the nineteenth-century display of 'primitive' individuals as if they were animals. However, Brotmann develops this statement by giving instances of scientific enquiry into the details of racial differences, suggesting that 'more to the point, perhaps, there are far more differences among races than skin color [sic] texture of hair, or facial features, ranging from the shapes of bones to the consistency of ear wax, to subtle variations in body chemistry' (35). Critical theorists of the kind Brotmann frequently adduces elsewhere, have suggested better reasons for the difficulty of distinguishing 'between "us" and "not us"', and for 'humankind's' perennial urge to construct such naturalized difference.

This is not an isolated instance, compare for example the discussion of the psychoanalytic concept of 'the primal act', pages 84–85. Is Brotmann's point that *all* the psychoanalysts briefly mentioned, Freud and Jung and 'both Klein (1952) and Lacan (1977) [who] also look back to the early experiences of childhood' (84) have identified a fundamental truth (which Hershel Gordon Lewis's *Blood Feast* also shares) despite the considerable differences in their theorizations; and does she take it for granted that all her readers know all about these differences? (The only other reference to Lacan, for example, is a similarly unspecific sentence about the trauma of the primal scene, 12.) Or is the point that all these analysts and the filmmaker share the same urge to *construct* a hidden, originary moment? Or what?

Thus it is more for the information about film texts, than for the analysis of them, that some readers will find this book of use.

Another way to acquire information about the kinds of film that not even Channel 5 shows is, of course, to follow Brotmann to the fountainhead of fan publications. The film theory chapters of *YWCCT 95* and *96* both note some relevant presses and their productions in those years. In 1997 Titan Books published Pete Tombs' *Mondo Macabro: Weird and Wonderful Cinema Around the World*.

Tombs' Introduction sums up the book's content, rationale and pitch:

> *Mondo Macabro* is a peek into the treasure trove of fifty years
> film from around the world. . . . The kind of films we're looking

at – action pics, horror films, sex exploiters and monster movies – are usually avoided by heavyweight histories. Which is odd, because in our encounters with Filipino action heroes, Hong Kong horror stars and Japanese bondage queens, we've learned far more about their respective countries than from any number of serious art films. Art cinema, from almost anywhere in the world, seems to follow the same gods of style; the French new wave and Italian neo-realist still reign supreme. Genre films, on the other hand, always grow out of their country's most deeply ingrained traditions [. . .].

But acquiring knowledge is only one of the joys of cinema. And probably the least important. There's another route to go. In reading about these films you can simply gawp the sheer awfulness of some of them while marvelling at the sheer weirdness of others. And that's a valid reaction too. After all, one of the purposes of 'fantastic' cinema is to be fantastic – to show you things you wouldn't otherwise see (7).

Thus the book continues with fourteen chapters covering film from Hong Kong, the Philippines, Indonesia, India, Turkey (co-authored by Giovanni Scognamillo) Brazil, Argentina (written by Diego Curubeto), Mexico (written by David Wilt) and Japan, with the same relaxed irreverence and firm intelligence and plentiful black and white illustrations. This is the sort of book that makes you glad to be a film theorist, because being engrossed in it can be explained to friends as 'work' – which in the context of many currently relevant projects, it really could be.

There is a very large index of film titles in very small print.

Creation Books' 'cinema culture' series is pitched towards a 'cognoscenti' rather than 'fan' readership. The mood of much of *Naked Lens: An Illustrated History of Beat Cinema*, written, edited and compiled by Jack Sargeant is rather solemn, although some at least of the film that it discusses might not unreasonably be described as 'sheerly weird' (some would say, also, as 'sheerly awful'). *Naked Lens* is a compilation of descriptive and analytic accounts and of interviews, covering a widely defined field of 'beat' cinema (Cassavete's *Shadows*, for example, is included). Other contributors are Stephanie Watson, Tessa Hughes-Freeland and Arthur and Corinne Cantrill. As well as an index of films and a bibliography which demonstrates the variety of source materials that have been located, there is a list of sources from which some of the film texts themselves can be obtained. There is clearly quite a lot to think about here, including the different critical idioms in which not wholly dissimilar cinemas get discussed.

In *Horror and Science Fiction Films IV*, Donald C. Willis provides a very, very large list that appears to aim to cover all – yes, all – films of the genre that remain extant. In the words of Willis's introduction 'top priority for *Horror and Science Fiction Films IV:* the most obscure films . . . titles which are mentioned virtually nowhere else in print, in English. The monster movies of Thailand, for example, are generally listed here under informal titles translated, on the spot, from Thai-language characters, by video and grocery clerks' (vi). Here we have almost 600 large-format pages of Halliwell-type listings, giving full filmographies and a paragraph summary of each

film, besides a number of introductory lists of Willis's personal selections
under different headings and apparatus for locating entries under alternative
titles. The only reason a theorist working in this field would not want this
book, is the daunting evidence provided of its extent and multiplicity.

Turning from the enthralling 'ridiculous' of extreme film, we might expect
to find a rather bland 'sublime' in *Shakespeare, the Movie: Popularising the
Plays on Film, TV, and Video* edited by Lynda E. Boose and Richard Burt.
However, this collection of sixteen essays is intellectually strong stuff.
Varying approaches bring deftly theorized analysis to issues raised by the
re-circulation within the realms of popular culture of the most securely
'canonized' of all literary texts. Importantly, coverage includes not only
direct transfers of the plays to screen formats, but also films that make
partial references; (such as *My Own Private Idaho*) or include parts of plays
or references to them within their diegeses (for example Valerie Wayne's
chapter on 'colonial specularity' and *Shakespeare Wallah*. Richard Burt's
chapter 'The Love that Dare not speak Shakespeare's Name: New Shakesqueer Cinema', which argues the positive power of 'degaying Shakespeare
[which] opens up the contrary possibility' (257) discusses a range of films
including *Porky's 2*, *The Goodbye Girl* and *Dead Poet's Society*); while
Katherine Eggert's chapter examines 'Warren Beatty's Bugsy as Hollywood
Cleopatra'.

This is not at all the sort of book designed to give academic respectability
to the book lists of courses that 'teach' Shakespeare by showing students the
BBC adaptation videos (though it will probably be used in that way). It will
be useful to readers whose interests lie in the current meanings of both the
plays and the cultural construction of Shakespeare and also to analysts of
film and other screen media who may never, normally, bother about the
Bard.

There is an overall index which includes film titles.

In *Understanding Animation*, Paul Wells argues against the 'scenario
[which] still consigns the animated film to its children's audience' (3).
Relating the development of animated images to that of live action film,
Wells argues that 'the very *craftsmanship* of the animated film became its
inhibiting factor at a time when the immediacy of the photographic image
was its novelty and its passport to industrial legitimacy and thus the name of
"cinema" itself' (2). His book offers a number of different approaches to a
study of animation that takes the subject seriously. In his first section he
considers the history of animation and then its different technical modes.
Identifying cel-animation (the standard 'cartoon') as 'orthodox animation'
he then categorizes 'experimental animation' which resists the cartoon's
maintained reference to some representation of the 'real' world (presenting
a 'hyper-reality') and 'developmental animation', which is representational
but 'resists[s] or redefine[s] the inherent vocabulary within orthodox animation' (51). He goes on to consider the narrative strategies that are uniquely
available to animation and then the strategies for producing humour that it
can command. The next section considers 'Issues in Representation'; specifically 'the complex ways in which animation problematizes the representation
of gender and race ... which are as much about the unique parameters of
expression available to the animator as they are about socio-political issues'

(187). Finally, the experience of spectatorship, in relation to animation, is examined.

This sectionalizing is slightly frustrating, and Wells seems a little defensively to acknowledge this in his Introduction. He says of his book, 'inevitably, it will be flawed, seeking not to be definitive but provocative ... in many ways it is a work in progress' (8); and also 'some areas of theoretical address, however, are only hinted at or partially addressed in the text. This is partly due to the limited space available to follow too many aspects of enquiry, and partly in the spirit of providing models which are only half-formed in the hope they will be developed' (9). Wells raises many and varied issues. He also tells his readers much about animation's different techniques and work that animators have created with them. There does seem to be a wholly unified book that could be written that would analyse at once the particular challenges (and pleasures) possible in animated film, the containment of these by the infantilization of the medium in dominant Anglephone cultures; the practices of animation outside these that challenge this containment and the issues for the understanding of live action film raised by all this. Furthermore, the advent of animatronic and digital technologies, which can both produce films that are indexed as 'animation' and also, silently, produce faked elements in what is announced as live action film, seems currently to blur the distinctions between the two methods of production without generally disrupting their reception as distinct. However, until someone writes the other book, *Understanding Animation* will remain not only the best work available on its subject but a good reason for those interested in other aspects of film to pay attention its topic.

It has a bibliography divided into 'References' and 'Further Reading', an index and a filmography that immediately demonstrates Wells' breadth of coverage.

In *Cinema and the Great War* Andrew Kelley examines 'those films which, generally, were recognised at the time of their release as anti-war by critics, commentators and – since then – by most historians' (1). He covers the period from just before the war's outbreak up to the 1964 *Paths of Glory*, looking at British, Danish, US, French and German film. Kelley is selective, concentrating on one or two films in each chapter, so that although there is an account of the more general cinematic activity in particular countries at particular points, which supplies a wider view of the topic than the Introduction might suggest, no attempt is made to offer its overall history. Published in Routledge's 'Cinema and society' series, it is social history that forms the book's approach and by and large we get factual description rather than analysis of any kind. Given the potential of this subject matter to generate enquiry into how and why dominant attitudes alter, towards something as central to Western experience and its constructions of national identity as the First World War, this is disappointing. Kelley's conclusion suggests how many questions are begged: 'while cinema is sometimes crass and banal – and most of the films made about the war can be characterised as such – in its reflection of the anti-war viewpoint there has been this crucial outcome: the belief that war is rarely just and peace must be maintained' (181–182). However, *Cinema and the Great War* does supply valuable information which may raise these questions. Especially given that some of the films discussed are not easily available for viewing, a full filmography, rather than an index of films giving only titles, would be welcome.

A number of books appeared in 1997 that deal with British film and cinema in specific periods or as a whole. These include Routledge's reprinting of the seven volumes of Rachel Low's *The History of British Film*, fifty years after the publication of the first volume (which was co-authored by Roger Manvill). This covers the years 1896–1906; Volume II covers 1906–14, and Volume III covers 1914–18, both the latter published in 1950. Low worked on the last four volumes following a fourteen-year break. Volume IV, covering 1918–29 appeared in 1971 and three more volumes, all covering the 1930s completed her work: Volume V deals with 'Documentary and Educational Films', VI with 'Films of Comment and Persuasion' and VII, subtitled 'Film Making in 1930s' Britain', covers the British cinema industry in that decade. This was published in 1985 (when volume V was also revised) and in that year the BFI decided to support four more volumes to bring the series up to the 1970s, decade by decade (only the first of these has so far appeared [1992]).

There is an enormous amount of information in these books not least because, especially in the first volumes, Low had access to people who had actually worked in early British cinema. She also had access to printed materials such as publicity material, reviews and letters, including items existing in private hands which could, just after the war, be discovered via appeals in the press as well as personal contacts. Making all this available again is a project greatly to be admired; though in an ideal world it would also be desirable to have some contemporary apparatus added to suggest, for example, where additional information is now available. Also, the direct photo-lithographic reproduction of the original volumes, while probably an economic necessity if the works were to reappear at all, makes the numerous and important illustrations very poor in quality.

What is newly provided is a twelve-page introduction by Jeffrey Richards. This usefully locates the *History*'s 1946 inception in a brief moment of confident optimism about the British cinema. However, he goes on to take a drearily predictable 'pop' at *Screen* and its pernicious effects on British film analysis. He approves Robin Woods quoted reaction to the appearance of such work as finding himself 'unrepentantly in favour of "art, democracy and . . . the value of individual life" ' (xiv). The lauded, and allegedly totally different, alternative offered is *The Historical Journal of Film, Radio and Television*'s reliance 'not on theoretical and scientific analyses based on semiology, structuralism or psychoanalysis like *Screen*, but on historical analysis, based on documentary evidence, on the circumstances of production and reception and the general social and political contexts of the age' [xv].

For Richards, Low's value lies in never succumbing to *Screen*'s diabolic practices. Their damnable nature is demonstrated (solely) by taking a particularly obscure paragraph of Christian Metz and announcing that 'this is mere verbal mystification, which neither enlightens nor informs or educates' (xiv). It is, admittedly, not very difficult to find a particularly obscure paragraph by Metz, especially if it is removed from any context. However, it is historically inaccurate to imply that ideological analysis and historical account have remained wholly separate and it is intellectually inadequate to claim that 'history' is better known when issues of meaning, desire and politics are treated as contaminating. It is also poor historical methodology to present a quotation referenced only from a secondary source: the Metz quotation is referenced via John Caughie's collection *Theories of Authorship* (1981), with no indication of the precise original date or even title. Rachel Low's achievement does need to be praised through such an impoverished and misleading comparison with other work.

Stephen C. Shafer's *British Popular Films 1929–1939: the Cinema of Reassurance* has, of course, some overlap with Andrew Kelley's book (above). This is also a book primarily located as social history, but its approach is rather different. Shafer distinguishes British film of the 'thirties that was aimed at a middle-class audience, from that destined for the working class'. Considering both the filmic texts and the whole experience of cinema-going, in the context of the Depression, he is fully aware that 'the prescription suggested for dealing with adversity was forbearance, not protest or action' (236). He also suggests that if 'the films [the working class] saw were reassuring and therefore not socially disruptive . . . it was precisely that kind of movie, that type of escape, which they apparently enjoyed' (237). Using a variety of paracinematic material, Shafer celebrates the under-discussed tradition of British film which stems from working class culture, especially music hall, while demonstrating the complexity of their social context and effects.

Shafer emphasizes the pleasure and excitement involved in visits to the 1930s' 'picture palaces'. Many of these are described and marvellously illustrated in Allan Eyles's *Gaumont British Cinemas*, which recounts the history of the rise, merger with rival Odeon and eventual fading away of this cinema circuit. It also lists all the Gaumont cinemas ever with indications of what, if anything, remains of them and there is a complete list of circuit releases between 1932–59. This is 'straight' information of the kind Jeffrey Richards extols, written with authority and committed enthusiasm. It offers a sense of the detailed workings of the British cinema industry, at the level of the managerial organization of the distributor and as it impinged on almost all the population's lives through its choice of films, publicity materials and promotional activities, as well as the extraordinary cinema buildings themselves. It is perhaps for the vivid sense of this 'cinematic experience' that it conveys, especially through the illustrations which occupy more than half its page space, that this book is valuable; as well as being an absolute delight. A full index, in addition to the already mentioned alphabetical list of cinemas, would be helpful. (The copy reviewed is the 1999 reprint, which is partly updated.)

Jeffrey Richards's own *Films and British National Identity: from Dickens to Dad's Army* is published in Manchester University Press's 'Studies in Popular Culture' series,' which he edits. It offers a set of lucidly written 'linked essays' that discuss different and roughly historically selected topics that have a connection to the idea of 'national identity'. Richards does acknowledge problems inherent in his topic – for example, some less pleasant aspects of what he takes as 'British national identity', such as 'the idea of English superiority to foreigners' (13) and he offers a brief argument as to why 'the character of [post eighteenth century] *Britain* was provided by *England*' (8). He includes a section on 'Region' (chapters on Scotland,

Wales and Ireland, and Lancashire) as well as sections on 'Empire', 'Nation', and 'Culture'. Within the section on 'Empire' there is a discussion of 'popular prejudice within the majority population' against 'the Irish, the Jews and black and Asian Commonwealth immigrants' (60). However, not surprisingly, some readers will find more to question in the area his title indicates than Richards does.

There is a general index that only gives proper names and an index of films that gives only titles.

Sarah Street's *British National Cinema* appears in Routledge's excellent National Cinema series. Street manages to give considerably detailed and sensitive descriptions of a great many film texts within a clearly organized and comprehensive account of the British cinema industry as a whole through its first century. She tackles the subject thematically, covering 'The Fiscal Politics of Film', 'Studios, Directors, and Genres' 'Genres from Austerity to Affluence', 'Genres in Transition, 1970s–1990s', 'Acting and Stars', 'Borderlines I: Modernism and British Cinema' and 'Borderlines II: Counter-cinema and Independence'. In a short, succinct 'Conclusion' Street considers some of the problems that the industry has faced and its current position, about which she is generally optimistic. Noting the economic and aesthetic impact on British cinema of Hollywood she suggests that 'the success of many British films which did not look as if they were American, or cost as much, indicates that Hollywood did not entirely call the shots' (198). In relation to the 'significant impact on British films' of class and gender, Street says 'that for much of the century there was a social distinction between audiences (primarily working class) and filmmakers (primarily middle class), lends credence to the possibility of readings against the grain which are not purely the province of film scholars'. The increasing number of women directors, and increased acknowledgement of past non-directorial contributions from women, leads her to speculate that 'the tendency in many recent films to collapse gender boundaries altogether is perhaps a development towards the depoliticisation of gender' (199). Finally, Street considers the critical bias against British film which prevailed through much of the century. However, she concludes, 'in the 1980s and 1990s this situation has been in good part rectified, with journals like *Screen* and *Sight and Sound* giving serious attention to questions of British cinema' (199–200). Here is at least one historian of film who does not find the influence of contemporary theory baneful.

There is a subject index, a name index and an index of films and television programmes, giving titles. The bibliography is extensive.

(A 1996 addition to the National cinema series, received too late to include in *YWCCT 96*, was Tom O'Regan's *Australian National Cinema*. The importance of Australian film texts and the particular problematics of 'nationality' that may be explored through them, have been increasingly recognized in the last decade. O'Regan takes his readers through his subject intelligently and probingly, dividing it into in three sections, 'Making a National Cinema', 'Making a Distinct Cinema' and 'Problematizing Australian Cinema', with introductions to Australian cinema and its theorization.

As well as offering, again, an extensive bibliography, the book provides a name and subject index and a list of films that gives directors and dates.

Also from 1996, Maria Ornella Marotti edits and introduces *Italian*

Women Writers from the Renaissance to the Present: Revising the Canon
which includes a short section on Italian women filmmakers.)

Stephen Teo provides a very thorough and most interesting survey of his
subject in *Hong Kong Cinema: The Extra Dimensions*. Beginning from the
observation that 'ironically, as Hong Kong cinema has become better known
internationally, its predominance in the domestic market has increasingly
been eroded by Hollywood' (vii) and writing at the moment when Hong
Kong was on the brink of handover to the mainland Chinese authorities,
Teo begins by considering Hong Kong cinema's relationships to aspects of
wider Chinese cinema, including the Shanghai cinema of the 1930s. His
second section looks at the martial arts stars and his third, working within
an 'auteur' theoretical framework, examines aspects of New Wave cinema
in Hong Kong. His final section considers various ways in which the
hybridities of his subject operate in the 1980s and 1990s. The contradictory
forces operating in Hong Kong's history and culture make its cinema an
important site for anyone interested in films' interactions with ideology and
experience and Teo's book provides a valuable study of its roots, relationships and variety of forms.

Besides its name and film title index, the book offers a full listing of bio-
filmographies.

If Stephen C. Shafer (above) represents a North American writing insightfully about British cinema of the 1930s, Giuliana Musico is an Italian writing,
also insightfully, about the cinema of North America in the 1930s. Specifically, in *Hollywood's New Deal*, she considers the relationship between
Roosevelt's response to the Depression and the US cinema industry. As she
sums it up, in this period 'politics transformed its "public" into "spectators"
at the same time cinema transformed its spectators into a public' (1). Her
treatment is by no means as mechanistic as this very neat phrasing might
suggest. Appealing to a contemporary interpretation of hegemony theory,
and insisting on the continually dynamic inter-relationship between popular
culture and society's formations, Musico charts the process by which Hollywood and Washington came to co-operate in the production of a unified
national conscious that allowed the US, with crucial ideological support
from its cinema, to enter the Second World War. She focuses on ways in
which the cinema industry was subjected to or resisted political control of its
content via the Hayes Code and of its economic organization via the
attempts at anti-monopoloy legislation. She concludes with a study of 'The
Paramount Case', demonstrating how the prolonged Antitrust case against
the company ended in 'a fairly ironic destiny' whereby it was the New Deal's
judicial and political establishment that successfully acted against an industry
where 'arguments by reformers and pressure groups' had failed; and
whereby 'while the majors held an almost total control of production and
distribution, they controlled a small (but crucial) section of exhibition; and
yet it was for this sin that they were punished' (195). This is a valuable book
not only as a study of one particular period in one particular place, but also
as a revealing case-study study of the interactions between mass communication industries, institutional powers and social forms. It has an index but,
unfortunately, no collected bibliography.

The evolution of the Hollywood cinema industry is one of the many topics
which are illuminated within the biography of Mary Pickford written by

Eileen Whitfield: *Pickford: the Woman who Made Hollywood.* This clearly written account intelligently considers its remarkable subject's life with an eye to the issues raised by her rise and fall, her fatal entrapment within the 'little girl' image, and the collapse of her private life when she could no longer supply what her public wanted. It also emphasizes the business acumen of 'America's Sweetheart', her canny negotiation of contracts and her co-founding (with W. D. Griffiths) of United Artists. Thus Whitfield's book is of interest beyond the particularities of one star's life. It is well illustrated and besides its index and bibliography it has a full filmography of Pickford's work.

Andrew Horton's *Buster Keaton's Sherlock Jr.* collects essays focused on one film by a great star of silent Hollywood. Again, wider contexts and issues are evoked, not only in terms of this film's position within his whole career, but of Keaton's filmic *persona*, its relationship with the vaudeville background out of which he emerged and also, interestingly, its arguably ambiguous construction of masculinity. As well as its index, and select bibliography, the book provides some opening reviews of *Sherlock Jr.* and also a full filmography of all Keaton's work.

In *Lovers of Cinema: the First American Film Avant-Garde, 1919–1945*, Jan-Christopher Horak edits a collection of essays which bring attention to a body of film that is often over-looked. As well as an Introduction, Horak supplies a first chapter offering a wide overview of the field and its inhabitants, including its relationship to amateur and to documentary film-making in the period. Kristen Thompson explores 'The Limits of Experimentation in Hollywood' while Brian Taves takes a more enthusiastic view of 'Robert Florey and the Hollywood Avant-Garde'. William Moritz looks across to 'Americans in Paris: Man Ray and Dudley Murphey'. Patricia R. Zimmerman concentrates on 'Amateur Film and the Early Avant-Garde' and Lisa Cartwright on 'US Modernism and the Emergence of "The Right Wing of Film Art": The Films of James Sibley Watson Jr., and Melville Webber'. Chuck Kleinhans examines 'Theodore Huff: Historian and Film-maker' while Scott Macdonald writes on 'Ralph Steiner'. Charles Wolfe's subject is 'Social Documentary and the Avant-Garde in the 1930s'. Concentrating on specific texts, Horak also provides a chapter on 'Paul Strand and Charles Sheeler's *Manhatta*' and William Uricchio on 'The Films of Leyda, Browning, and Weinberg'. Lauren Rabinovitz rescues the reputation of the once-recognized woman filmmaker 'Mary Ellen Bute' and Tom Gunning celebrates the work of 'Douglas Crockwell'. As well as its index and bibliography, this book provides a full list of 'Filmmakers of the First American Avant-Garde' which includes lists of all their films.

Hollywood films' representation of 'Russians' is the inciting topic of Michael J. Strada and Harold R. Toper's *Friend or Foe?: Russians in American Film and Foreign Policy, 1933–1991*. They note in their introduction that, following the blurring of terminology in American cinema, they are often using the term 'Russian' when it would be more accurate to refer to 'Soviets', or indeed to note the particular ethnicity of Soviet citizens. This is basically a descriptive book, following in seven chapters the development of official US policy towards the USSR and detailing films of the corresponding period which represent Russian people. Strada and Toper identify in each period two or three films that they propose as 'retrospective bellwethers', which are described at some length, and then go on to give more summary treatment to other contemporary releases. Beyond description, the authors give rather perfunctory judgements, labelling films CRI (critical), FAV (favourable) and MID (middle). From the point of view of critical theory, a lot of questions remain unraised and a lot of issues undiscussed. Strada and Toper do not develop any overall thesis about the film texts' operation in shaping dominant US constructions of 'the Russians', for example, or the relationship between these constructions and the wider pattern of US ideology. However, there is a huge amount of information here, including a four-page filmography, giving title, director and date of Hollywood films representing 'Russians' from 1933–1991. Anyone who wants to take their analysis further would be well advised to begin by reading this book.

In *Based on a True Story: Latin American History at the Movies*, historian Donald F. Stevens has gathered essays by other historians which both discuss specific aspects of Latin American history and their representation in film. Sonya Lipsett-Rivera and Sergio Rivera Ayal jointly consider the representation of Columbus in Ridley Scott's *1492: the Conquest of Paradise*. Thomas H. Holloway considers the more obscure sixteenth-century conquistador Lope de Aguirre, presented in Werner Herzog's *Aguirre, the Wrath of God*. The seventeenth-century poet Sor Juana Ines de la Cruz is discussed by Susan e. Ramirez in relation to Maria Luisa Bemberg's biographical film *Yo, la Peor de Todas*. James Schofield Saeger considers filmic and other misconceptions about the work of Jesuit missionaries in eighteenth-century Paraguay, analysing Roland Joffe's *The Mission*. Maria Louisa Bemberg's *Camila* is the site upon which Donald F. Stevens discusses 'the connections between patriarchal power in the family, the state and the church' (85) in nineteenth-century Argentina. John Mraz compares contrasting views of Cuban slavery in Sergio Giral's *The Other Francisco* and Tomas Gutierrez Alea's *The Last Supper*. Barbara Weinstein considers the changing course of Cuban women's history in, and after, Humber Solas's 1968 *Lucia*. The modernization of sexual relationships in Brazil is considered by James D. Henderson via Bruno Barreto's *Gabriela*. Confusions about Mexican culture are discussed by Barbara A. Tenenbaum, in relation to Laura Esquivel's *Like Water for Chocolate* and Alfons Arau's film of the novel. Mark D. Szuchman compares representations of family and politics in two films of the 1980s, Bemberg's *Miss Mary*, predominantly set in the Argentina of the 1930s and 1940s, and Luis Puenzo's *The Official Story*, set during the 1983 collapse of the military dictatorship. Finally, Robert M. Levine analyses the interplay of fact and fiction in Hector Babenco's *Pixote*, telling the story of a Brazilian street child. Stevens also provides an opening chapter 'Never Read History again? The Possibilities and Perils of Cinema as Historical Depiction', arguing that 'just as fact and imagination are not always clearly separable, the advantages and disadvantages of using film to study history are not necessarily distinguishable either' (10).

The list of contents demonstrates this book's range of coverage. The textual analyses are intelligently aware of their subject's filmic effects as well as their contents and the historical discussions are (as far as I am capable of judging) authoritative. Full details of the films are given at the beginning of each chapter, but there is no index.

Finally, it may be useful to note here the reprinting of three volumes collecting articles from *Cahiers du Cinema* from, respectively, the 1950s, the 1960s and 1969–72. The first two are edited by Jim Hillier and the third by Nick Browne. The selection strategy included the aims of making each volume 'representative of the period covered' and containing 'largely newly translated material rather than material already easily available in English' (viii). As Hillier notes in his Preface, fulfilling the latter has inevitably militated at times against the former, though the reprinting of some already available material has somewhat redressed the imbalance. Besides the *Cahiers* articles and the editors' general introductions, the first two volumes have introductions to their separate sections. These are, in *The 1950s*, 'French Cinema', 'American Cinema', 'Italian Cinema' and 'Polemics'; and in *The 1960s*, 'New Wave/French Cinema', 'American Cinema: Celebration' 'American Cinema: Revaluation', 'Towards a New Cinema/New Criticism'. The third volume, subtitled *The Politics of Representation*, is not divided into sections. Each volume has an appendix listing as far as possible all the material from the *Cahiers* of the covered period that is available in English and another briefly summarizing the major issues covered by the journal in the periods covered by the other volumes, and a name and film title index. The first two volumes each also provide listings of *Cahiers'* Best Films Listings from its decade.

Books Reviewed

Boose, Lynda E. and Richard Burt (eds.) *Shakespeare the Movie: Popularising the Plays on Film, TV, and Video.* Routledge. pp. 269. hb £50.00 pb £15.99. ISBN hb 0 415 16584 9 pb 0 415 16585 7.

Brotmann, Mikita. *Offensive films: Toward an Anthropology of Cinema Vomitif.* Greenwood Press. pp. 197. hb £43.95. ISBN 0 313 30033 X.

Bruzzi, Stella. *Undressing Cinema: Clothing and Identity in the Movies.* Routledge. pp. 199. hb £45.00 pb £12.99. ISBN hb 0 415 13956 2 pb 0 415 13957 0.

Clarke, David B. (ed.) *The Cinematic City.* pp. 240. Routledge. hb £50.00 pb £15.99. ISBN hb 0 415 12745 9 pb 0 415 12746 7.

Cohan, Steven and Ina Rae Hark (eds.) *The Road Movie Book.* Routledge. pp. 370. hb £45.00 pb £14.99. ISBN hb 0 415 14936 3 pb 0 415 14937 1.

Eyles, Allen. *Gaumont British Cinemas.* British Cinema Association (distributed by BFI Publishing). pp. 223. pb £14.99. ISBN 0 85170 519 7.

Hillier, Jim and Nick Browne (eds.) (1986) *Cahiers du Cinema.* (4 volumes; vol. IV 1973–78 available March 2000). Routledge. £200.00. ISBN 0 415 23016 X.

Horak, Jan-Christopher (ed.) *Lovers of Cinema: the First American Film Avant-Garde, 1919–1945.* University of Wisconsin Press. pp. 395. £39.95. ISBN 0 299 14680 4.

Horton, Andrew (ed.) *Buster Keaton's Sherlock Jr.* Cambridge Film Handbooks Series, Cambridge University Press. pp. 186. hb £30.00, pb £10.95. ISBN hb 0 521 48105 8, pb 0 521 48566 5.

Kaplan, E. Ann. *Looking for the Other: Feminism, Film and the Imperial Gaze.* Routledge. pp. 302. hb £40.00 pb £12.99. ISBN hb 0 415 91016 1 pb 0 415 91017 X.

Kelley, Andrew. *Cinema and the Great War*. 'Cinema and Society' series Routledge. pp. 208. hb £45.00. ISBN 0 415 05203 3.

Low, Rachel. *History of British Film*. (7 volumes). Routledge. £425.00. ISBN 0 415 15451 0.

Mackinnon, Kenneth. *Uneasy Pleasure: The Male as Erotic Object*. Cygnus Arts. pp. 240. £17.50. ISBN 1 900541 30 0.

McQuail, Denis. *Audience Analysis*. Sage Publications. pp. 150. hb £28.00 pb £11.99 (US$21.95). ISBN hb 0 7619 1001 8 pb 0 7619 1002 6.

Marotti, Maria Ornella. *Italian Women Writers from the Renaissance to the Present: Revising the Canon*. The Pennsylvania State University Press. pp. 272. hb £33.95, pb £15.95. ISBN hb 0 271 01505 5, pb 0 271 01506 3.

Musica, Giuliana. *Hollywood's New Deal*. Temple University Press. pp. 248. hb £47.95, pb £18.50. ISBN hb 1 56639 495 3, pb 1 56639 496 1.

O'Regan, Tom. *Australian National Cinema*. National Cinema Series, Routledge. pp. 391. hb £45.00 pb £14.99. ISBN hb 0 415 05730 2 pb 0 415 05731 0.

Richards, Jeffrey. *Films and British National Identity: From Dickens to Dad's Army*. Studies in Popular Culture Series, Manchester University Press. pp. 374. hb £45.00 pb £14.99. ISBN hb 0 7190 4742 0 pb 0 7190 4743 9.

Sargeant, Jack (ed.) *Naked Lens: An Illustrated History of Beat Cinema*. Cinema Culture Series, Creation Books. pp. 238. £12.95. ISBN 1 871592 67 4.

Shafer, Stephen C. *British Popular Films 1929–1939: The Cinema of Reassurance*. Studies in Film, Television and Media Series, Routledge. pp. 258. hb £50.00. ISBN 0 415 00282 6.

Stevens, Donald F. (ed.) *Based on a True Story: Latin American History at the Movies*. SR Books. pp. 243. hb US$50.00 pb $15.50. ISBN hb 0 8420 2582 0 pb 0 8420 2781 5.

Strada, Michael J. and Harold R. Troper. *Friend or Foe? Russians in American Film and Foreign Policy, 1933–1991*. Scarecrow Press. pp. 233. US$59.00. ISBN 0 8108 3245 3.

Street, Sarah *British National Cinema*. National Cinema Series, Routledge. pp. 217. hb £45.00 pb £12.99. ISBN hb 0 415 06735 9 pb 0 415 06736 7.

Teo, Stephen. *Hong Kong Cinema: The Extra Dimensions*. BFI Publishing. pp. 294. hb £36.34 pb £12.97. ISBN hb 0 85170 496 4 pb 0 85170 514 6.

Tombs, Pete. *Mondo Macabro: Weird and Wonderful Cinema Around the World*. Titan Books. pp. 189. pb £14.99. ISBN 1 85286 865 1.

Wells, Paul. *Understanding Animation*. Routledge. pp. 249. hb £40.00 pb £12.99. ISBN hb 0 415 11596 5 pb 0 415 11597 3.

Whitfield, Eileen. *Pickford: The Woman Who Made Hollywood*. University of Kentucky Press. pp. 492. $25.00. ISBN 0 8131 2045 4.

Willis, Donald C. *Horror and Science Fiction Films IV*. The Scarecrow Press. pp. 642. US$89.50 (£85.05). ISBN 0 8108 3055 8.

16

Art Histories and Visual Culture Studies

ANGELICA MICHELIS

In recent years 'visual culture' has become a more and more ubiquitous term and has developed into an umbrella heading under which we can find a wide range of fields of studies. But what exactly is meant by 'visual' in that context? And how does the compound affect and redefine the meaning and structure of 'culture'? These are just two of the many questions John A. Walker and Sarah Chaplin's book *Visual Culture: An Introduction* introduces and attempts to tackle and illuminate. As is indicated by the title, this is an introduction to the domain of visual culture and thus mainly aimed at undergraduates and graduates involved in the burgeoning area of visual culture studies. The volume is very thoroughly researched and refers to a wide range of recent publications in the field of visual culture, history and theory of art, critical theory and cultural studies to mention just some of the major disciplines. The authors' main interest consists of providing a well-researched overview of their subject by discussing it in relation to its inter- and multidisciplinary make-up. Walker and Chaplin define visual culture roughly as:

> ... those material artifacts, buildings and images, plus time-based media and performances, produced by human labour and imagination, which serve aesthetic, symbolic, ritualistic or ideological-political ends, and/or practical functions, and which address the sense of sight to a significant extent (1–2).

This might sound rather clinical, and there is a tendency to undercut the complexity of specific issues by compressing them into definitions which can be rather narrow at times. On the other hand, students will find this style very helpful, particularly if they are new to the field and need easing into the rather complicated areas of critical theory, poststructuralism/modernism, psychoanalysis etc. In this respect, *Visual Culture: An Introduction* is a very successful book which will help introduce readers to the subject in a clear yet critical way. Of further support will be the structural lay-out of the text which divides all of its thirteen chapters into small sections where issues such as the juxtaposition of culture and nature, culture and class, culture and barbarism etc. are discussed by referring to the main publications in the field and the arguments underlying them. Every chapter is closed by a short summary which recapitulates the main aspects the respective part of the book was concerned with. This, again, emphasizes the didactic and pedagogical character of the book and how it presents the discussion and analysis of its themes.

From a theoretical perspective, Walker and Smith's text manages to introduce a wide spectrum of approaches and theories which are explored in relation to visual culture. Barthes's work on semiotics and mythologies features as well as Bourdieu's sociological take on the meaning of culture; the various models of postmodern thinking are dealt with as well as a wide range of developments in the field of postcolonialism, feminism and gender studies, psychoanalysis and discourse theory. The authors offer informative and explanatory introductions to the different concepts, supported by thought-provoking and stimulating examples originating from a wide choice of genres: architecture, advertising, literature, history of art, contemporary, modern and early modern art is referred to in order to clarify ideas and theoretical models. By doing so the authors succeed not only in delivering a profound discussion of subjects such as 'concepts of culture', 'concepts of the visual', 'looks, the gaze and surveillance', 'visual literacy and visual poetics', 'the canon and concepts of value' to mention just a few, but also manage to introduce and explain the major terms students will encounter again and again when engaging with critical and cultural theory.

In addition to the more theoretically and art-theoretically informed parts of the text, *Visual Culture: An Introduction* also offers an illuminating and informative analysis of how art and visual culture is institutionally managed in contemporary society. It provides a thoroughly researched and well-documented overview of the various institutions which not only participate in the social organization of art and its cultural dissemination, but also contribute to the construction and understanding of what and how art means as a social discourse. As Walker and Chaplin argue:

> However, power is not evenly distributed within society: consequently the power to define what is art, and who is an artist, is concentrated in the art world, a subculture consisting of people with specialist knowledge of art – artists, critics, curators, dealers, collectors etc. – and a constellation of art institutions (81).

The final chapter of the book is devoted to recent developments in the area of new technologies and how they have redefined and culturally resituated the visual in contemporary society. In my opinion, this is the most interesting and innovative chapter of the text (together with the second chapter 'The Concept of the Visual' which consists of an exploration of the notion of visuality in relation to the physical and mental experience of the visual). The chapter discusses issues such as multimedia, cyberspace, virtual reality and computer technology by relating them dialectically to questions of gender, perceptions and constructions of subjectivity, economy, the production of art, the uniqueness of the art object, to mention just the main themes. Although some subjects might have deserved a more thorough and complex analysis (gender being one of them), on the whole, this chapter engages in a critical and stimulating way with complicated and wide-ranging theoretical questions.

Visual Culture: An Introduction is a model textbook (which would have been even better had it included a bibliography) and will be welcomed by students of the many disciplines that find a home under the umbrella of 'visual culture'. The book provides an excellent introduction to the field and its wide range of references will enable its readers to access more specialist subjects.

Photography: A Critical Introduction (edited by Liz Wells) is also aimed at students in further and higher education and offers an introductory account of photography, its historical development and its position in relation to political, social and cultural discourses. The book approaches the subject of photography consciously from a theoretical perspective, pointing out that it is not so much interested in providing a chronological history of the genre and technique, but more in locating photography in the critical and cultural framework of historical, socio-political and artistic issues. On the whole, the book's structure is to a great extent determined by its pedagogical and didactic objectives evident in the inclusion of specific case studies, summary diagrams and glossaries which are interspersed into the textual body. Additionally, photographic material is frequently used to illustrate individual points and thus employed in order to support a certain argument in the discussion. However, photography itself being the subject of the book as such, photographic images are in many cases presented less from an illustrative perspective but are used in order to critically locate the genre in relation to practical and theoretical questions. Thus the most notable feature of *Photography: A Critical Introduction* is its commitment to serve as an introduction which inevitably results in concentrating on issues predominantly of interest for a student reader.

However, the book accomplishes the task of demonstrating the diversity of photographic practices and to what extent they are linked with specific political and cultural questions by generally taking into account the interrelation between aesthetics and technologies. For instance, in 'Thinking about Photography: Debates, Historically and Now', Derrick Price and Liz Wells explore the subject by referring to the wide range of historical studies of photography and commenting critically on the respective summaries. Furthermore, the photographic genre is then considered in its contemporary context, from the viewpoint of the museum and archive as well as from technological, theoretical (here especially: postmodern theories as challenging 'photographic realism') and generic positions. As Wells and Price conclude:

> The photograph, therefore, might be conceptualised as a site of intersection of various orders of theoretical understanding relating to its production, publication and consumption or reading. Central to the project of theorising photography is the issue of the relation between that which particularly characterises the photographic (. . .), and theoretical discourses which pertain to the making and reading of the image but whose purchase is broader, for instance, aesthetic or sexual politics (51).

Thus the emphasis of approaching photography in the present volume is clearly a conceptual one which challenges the idea of meaning as intrinsic to the photographic image by understanding it as being generated and constituted in relation to photography's position in the various cultural and political processes and discourses. The following chapter 'Surveyors and Surveyed: Photography Out and About', takes a similar theoretically and critically informed stance in relation to the subject by considering photography as being essential to the mapping and categorizing as part of imperialism. By doing so, Price situates the discussion in the framework of psychoanalytical (the gaze, the Other) and postcolonial debates and thus succeeds in producing an informative and theoretically informed illumination of the genre. Other issues that figure in this chapter include the documentary function of photography, authenticity and visual representation, war photography and the genre in relation to its key role in social investigation in general.

Chapter 3 resumes the discussion by shifting the focus onto personal photography and its function in the private-public dichotomy as crucial to modernity, gender identity and the construction of subjectivity. Similar to the preceding chapter, photography is reviewed and addressed in a genealogical way by tracing it back to its beginnings in the nineteenth century and investigating its active contribution to the perception and appearance of capitalist, imperialist and bourgeois social reality.

At the centre of the following chapter are questions concerning the relationship between photography and commodity culture, focusing on fashion, advertising and tourism; the discussion of photography as art (particularly as part of modernism) and its position in the institutions of museums and galleries. In the final chapter 'Photography in the Age of Electronic Imaging' Martin Lister contemplates the complex relationship between photography and new technologies and the intrinsic fallacies of what is called 'post-photography' brought about by developments in digital image technology.

Photography: A Critical Introduction is a useful volume, mainly for students, but not exclusively. With its clear structure, wide range of theoretical material and excellently referenced contributions, the book will also be of great interest for readers interested in the history and development of visual culture in general.

Roland Barthes's critical and theoretical work was not only in many ways concerned with aspects of the visual and the image as specific signifying systems, it also impacted heavily on studies and research in the field of art and visual culture. Barthes's influence on the critical analysis and study of the visual can be found in the thriving 'business' of deconstructing advertisements which, one could say, was propelled into being by the publication and dissemination of *Mythologies* in 1973. His work on photography (such as 'The Photographic Message' and 'The Rhetoric of the Image', published in *Image, Music Text*, and *Camera Lucida: Reflections on Photography*) examined the visual field from a structuralist point of view, and by doing so explored the phenomenological concept of photography as a signifying system. It is in particular Barthes's writing on photography which informs the selection of essays in *Writing the Image After Roland Barthes* as its editor Jean-Michel Rabaté emphasizes in the introduction:

An investigation of the role of photography in Barthes's work is crucial, for it not only permits a fresh and unprejudiced re-examination of the medium itself but also provokes a reappraisal of what seems to have baffled most commentators: the shift between the first Barthes, who demystifies messages by exposing their hidden codes before embracing a more systematic structuralist methodology, and the later Barthes, who seems more concerned with personal 'ecstasies' (4).

To a certain extent this question of where to locate Barthes from the point of view of critical theory (where does Barthes the structuralist end and Barthes the poststructuralist begin?) can be identified as the unifying principle of the essays gathered in this volume. Rabaté's intention is above all to document the shift in Barthes's thinking which for him is manifested in his work on photography and the image when he explains: 'Photography, or perhaps more broadly, the technological or historicized image, can be situated at the hinge between structuralism and what has been called poststructuralism' (4).

Like Baudelaire and Benjamin before him, Barthes, in his theoretical as well as his essayistic writing, is fascinated by two major themes: theatricality and the spectacle. Being already implicitly informed by visuality as such, it is not surprising that these themes also impact on his interest and writing on the visual, in particular on photography. In his last book *Camera Lucida* (Barthes's major work on photography) photographs are explored as found objects which haunt their spectators, making it impossible for them to detach themselves from the image whose message always refers to an absolute loss which thus initiates the wish to talk or write about it. This aspect of the tragic and mourning is imbricated in Barthes's notion of the image as such, because the photographic image is constituted by an intrinsic 'emptiness' which, paradoxically, is precisely what turns photography into an effective technology. Nancy M. Shawcross's essay 'The Filter of Culture and the Culture of Death: How Barthes and Boltanski Play the Mythologies of the Photograph' focuses exactly on this underlying paradox of Barthes's concept of the photograph when, discussing Barthes's *Camera Lucida* (a critical analysis of the cultural role of photography and, simultaneously on a more personal level, a moving document of Barthes's pain about the loss of his mother) she remarks:

> In *Camera Lucida* Barthes is arguing from the spectator's perspective; he empowers the spectator to retrieve from the insulation of culture the madness – the pain and ecstasy – of the photograph ... No culture can 'speak' the grief and suffering that he experiences by his mother's death; ... Instead of offering a transformation of his grief – which to Barthes would be a diminution of his pain – the photograph affirms the existence or reality of his mother and affirms or keeps desire 'alive' [meta-phorically speaking] (63–64).

Not surprisingly, *Camera Lucida* features in a variety of essays gathered in *Writing the Image After Roland Barthes*. Marjorie Perloff, similarly to

Shawcross, investigates the themes of mourning, melancholia and remembrance when she pairs off a series of Christian Bolantski's photographs with Barthes's theses developed in *Camera Lucida* in order to discuss to what extent Barthes's views are still part of the tradition of modernism, particularly if compared to the self-referentiality which marks Boltanski's work. Derek Attridge takes issue with Barthes's last work in relation to its underlying 'structuralist predicament' (81) which for him is mainly the result of Barthes's non-systematic use of the *punctum* (in distinction to the *studium*, the scientific approach to photography). On the other hand it is exactly Barthes's awareness of the failure of his project in *Camera Lucida* which, according to Attridge, shows the links between Barthes's text and Derrida's concept of deconstruction.

Other contributions investigate Barthes's writing on film and its impact on film theory (as for example Victor Burgin's 'Barthes Discretion' and Colin McCabe's 'Barthes and Bazin: The Ontology of the Image'); explore the relationship and differences between Benjamin's and Barthes's concepts of photography from a genealogical perspective which draws on psychoanalytic theory and semiotics (Liliane Weissberg's excellent 'Circulating Images: Notes on the Photographic Exchange); or investigate the position of the mother and the maternal in Barthes's work on photography (for example Carol Schloss's 'Narrative Liaisons: Roland Barthes and the Dangers of the Photo-Essay' and Diane Knight's 'Roland Barthes, or the Woman without a Shadow').

The second part of the collection is entitled 'Seeing Language, Seeing Culture' and collects essays which explore Barthes's work in relation to language, history and culture and thus shift the focus from the first part ('Reflections on Photography') which is mainly dedicated to Barthes's direct writing on the medium of photography and the photographic image as sign. Similar to the first part of the book, these essays are very much informed by an interdisciplinary approach and investigate Barthes's writing and theories from a wide range of perspectives. Phillipe Roger, for example, concentrates on Barthes's early years by exploring Barthes's self proclaimed Marxism, triggered off by his interest in Brecht's writing and theories on theatre. Again, theatricality and the spectacle seem to take centre stage in Barthes's intellectual curiosity, an interest which led to the writing of *Writing Degree Zero*, simultaneously an acidic critique of proletarian literature and a celebration of Brecht's dialectical theatre. The final part of the collection consists of Bob Perleman's imagined postmortem confrontation between Barthes and Frank O'Hara. This is a quirky and highly enjoyable piece of writing which shows that critical theory and a sense of fun are not exclusive of each other.

On the whole, this is an excellent collection of essays, each original in its approach and innovative in its discussion of Barthes in relation to visual culture. In the fickle world of changing fashions in critical theory it is good to know that Roland Barthes will always be a force to reckon with.

Theatricality, performance and spectacle are also the key terms in Dorinne Kondo's exploration of the worlds of Japanese fashion design and Asian-American theatre. This is a rather unusual book in that it combines two subjects which – at least in academia – are very often regarded as inhabiting disparate worlds. Whereas theatre, even when reproached as being elitist in certain circles, is recognized as an intellectual space which has to be taken seriously from a theoretical point of view, fashion is looked at disparagingly as a rather unintellectual, shallow and superficial world which functions as the ideological gloss of capitalism, covering up the harsh realities of its exploitative practices.

Kondo's book *About Face. Performing Race in Fashion and Theater* is based on the very deconstruction of the above mentioned binary opposition and approaches its subject by drawing on what she regards as the most salient features shared by both discourses. The emphasis on performance and theatricality which, as she is suggesting in the introduction 'The Politics of Pleasure', illuminate 'the politics of pleasure, the performance of race, and the possibilities for intervention in a regime of commodity capitalism' (5). As she explains further fashion and theatre could at first glance be:

> dismissed as a problematic domain of elite culture, yet these essays contend that both can offer opportunities for aesthetic/ political contestation. Both are key arenas for the performance of identities, from the 'individual to the 'national'. Spectacle and staging are necessarily elements of each, whether on the theatrical stage, on a runway, or in the more mundane settings of everyday life, as we perform ourselves with the costumes, props, and theatrical conventions at our disposal. Accordingly, both fashion and theatre highlight the performativity of gender, race and nation (5).

Kondo is aware of the more ambivalent role of fashion in our current consumer society when she argues: 'It is fashion that is the more obviously problematic, a highly fraught arena for a discussion of cultural politics and pleasure' (14). However, it is precisely this critical awareness which shapes her scrutiny of the features shared by the discourses of theatre and fashion in relation to gender, race and national identity. Coming herself from an Asian-American background Kondo utilizes her own experiences and interests by focusing on the dramatic work of David Henry Hwang and the Japanese fashion designers Yohij Yamamoto, Rei Kawakubo and Issey Miyake, interrogating how the discourses of theatre and fashion are complicit with the dominant white, supremacist, Western and capitalist culture and simultaneously provide strategies which enable us to deconstruct hegemonic representations of Asian identity.

About Face is divided into three parts: 'Orientalisms'; 'Consuming Gender, Race and Nation'; and finally 'Strategies of Intervention'. Each chapter discusses Asian-American Theatre and fashion from a specific theoretical and critical point of view mainly informed by the discourses of gender, race and national identity. The last chapter is devoted to the question of subversion and the possibility of the development of alternative strategies in the domains of theatre and fashion and thus dedicated to the problematic issues of power, oppression and resistance in contemporary society. Kondo's theoretical approaches derive from analytic readings of the works of Roland Barthes (here especially the deployment of pleasure as a critical discourse), Michel Foucault, Judith Butler's concept of performance in relation to identity and subjectivity, the postcolonial writing of Edward Said, Homi

Bhabha, Minh-ha Trinh and Gayatri Spivak. Other influences include Walter Benjamin's thoughts on mass culture which Kondo draws on in her analysis of fashion as a potential discourse of resistance by arguing that, as part of mass culture, fashion 'could contain the seeds of historical awakenings that might spur socially transformative change' (106).

This argument is further supported by her deployment of Bhabha's concept of mimicry which enables her to illuminate the relationship between the Japanese designers and the world of fashion dominated by Western images by arguing that 'Japanese designers in their very entry into the domain of Western clothing destabilize the East-West binary even as, at another level, they reinscribe it through mimesis' (60).

The link between Kondo's interrogation of fashion as a discursive cultural practice and her analysis of Asian-American theatre is provided by the emphasis on performativity as a possibility of questioning the concept of a unitary and fixed identity. Her reading of Hwang's 'M.Butterfly' explores the play as an intervention in Orientalist and racist discourses that shape Asian and Asian-American subjectivities by 'providing an acute refiguration of the humanist subject upon which the Puccini opera is based, supplying us with critical tools we can use in order to appraise currents in feminist deconstructive literary criticism' (23).

In summary, *About Face* is a fascinating and innovative book which discusses its subject in a lively, interesting and truly interdisciplinary mode. It covers a wide range of themes and is an outstanding example of what cultural studies should stand for. The book is very readable, partly because of the way in which it supports its argument with the help of photographic material; but it is above all the vignettes interspersed between the chapters and the more personal stories they narrate which interrupt and enrich the process of reading and turn it into such an enjoyable experience. *About Face* will contribute new and inspiring ideas to the fields of anthropology, history of art, theatre studies and cultural and visual studies in general.

'About face' is also partly what the following book is concerned with. Although no longer at the cutting edge of contemporary art, naturalistic portraiture has not yet completely vanished as a particular form of visual representation. Monarchs, prime ministers and other persons in the public limelight are still portrayed by famous painters, and time and again the finished product is reproduced in the newspapers and scrutinized in relation to questions of likeness and whether it is appropriate to depict a person of high public standing in a specific way (for instance, the issue of Queen Elizabeth's realistically painted hands in a recent portrait). However, it is in the past and in the history of the portrait, its role in Western art, its changing iconography and its relationship to issues of class, gender and social power in general where the relevance of this particular art form is located. The essays gathered in *Portraiture: Facing the Subject*, edited by Joanna Woodall aim to introduce major issues of portraiture from the Renaissance onwards and by doing so provide a significant contribution to the development of the portrait in Western art and art theory. The book is divided into seven parts which structure the collected thirteen essays in a thematic and theoretical way. Recent critical and theoretical developments in the domain of subjectivity and representation function as the overall framework and accommodate a variety of approaches to the topic: matters of sexuality, social identity, questions of likeness and identity and the position of the portrait in the discursive practices of art and art theory are discussed and taken issue with. Historically, the different chapters proceed from the Renaissance onwards, covering the following centuries up to the last decades of the twentieth century. Though clearly centred on the portrait in Western, and specifically Western European, culture the volume also includes a discussion of photographic portraiture in central India in the 1980s and 1990s, and an afterword by the anthropologist Marilyn Strathern explores the meaning of portrayal in the visual tradition of Papua New Guinea which is different from the twentieth-century Euro-American view of attending to people's features in order to depict them as unique individuals. Conceptually, this last chapter complements and critically relates to the informative introduction by Joanna Woodall which provides a critical overview of the history and development of portraiture in Western culture and by doing so establishes a framework which situates the subsequent essays in relation to their specific relevance for the discourses of subjectivity and identity. In her introductory chapter the author demonstrates convincingly how the social and cultural role of the portrait was always inextricably linked to wider issues of social reality. Whereas in the sixteenth century portraiture played an important ideological role in consolidating the dominant position of the nobility and the patriarchal principle it was built on by coupling likeness with the relationship between (holy) father and son, the following century shifted the function of the portrait generically and iconographically as well as socially. Woodall proceeds with her visual genealogy to the eighteenth century which saw a vast proliferation of portraits because of, among other factors, technological progression in print culture which expedited the wide dissemination of honorific images. Changes in the nineteenth century brought about by the new technology of photography, the significance of the science of physiognomy and its specific influence on the form and meaning of the portrait challenged and problematized the genre in its claim to achieve truthful and realistic likeness as well as in its contingent relationship to questions of subjectivity and identity. This not only impacted on the artistic significance of the portrait as such but, additionally, led to a questioning of the principles of portrayal by repositioning the role and status of the artist and the relationship between painter and sitter and had thus wide-ranging effects on the meaning of visual art in general. As Woodall argues:

> Portraits depicting the friends and family of the artists had existed since at least the fifteenth century, but in the late nineteenth century 'avant-garde' portraiture was markedly confined to uncommissioned images of these categories of sitter. This enhanced the authority of the artist by making worthiness to be portrayed depend upon one's relationship to him or her. It implied a lived intimacy between painter and sitter, imaginatively reproduced in the viewer's relationship to the painting (7).

Woodall then moves on to investigate the altered role and position of the portrait in the twentieth century which is followed by an extensive exploration of the social, theoretical and cultural conditions which historically and critically have informed this specific genre. The author discuses the problems which underlay portraiture as naturalistic representation, explores concepts of identity – particularly in relation to femininity, masculinity and class – how different models of subjectivity, as for example constructed in psychoanalysis, semiotics, postcolonialism and deconstruction, question the idea of identity as ontologically and epistemologically distinct from representation, a question which will inevitably affect the interplay between viewer, artist and sitter and the meaning of portraiture as such.

This discussion establishes the theoretical and thematic framework for the following essays which approach their subject in the light of a variety of methodological perspectives. The different contributions focus on the sexualized and gendered character in portraits produced in the Renaissance period and on possibilities of deconstructing masculinized concepts of self and identity; others utilize the methodological tool of the masquerade in order to demonstrate the performative character of selfhood and representation. Other themes covered include the discussion of the formation and empowerment of social categories of identity and individuality as simultaneously aided and interrogated by the historical role and development of portraiture. Further contributions address the subject of portraiture in the light of psychoanalysis, particularly Lacan's work on the constitution of the self, and its implications on understanding portraiture in its dialectical relationship to self-fashioning and the concept of the self.

These are just some of the themes taken issue with in *Portraiture: Facing the Subject*. This is an indispensable book for readers who are interested in the complexities of subjectivity and identity and its relationship to the disciplines of art history and visual culture. Additionally the interdisciplinary approach underlying the majority of the essays gathered in this volume will establish its value for other disciplines and fields of study. This is a highly recommendable book.

Sarah Hyde's *Exhibiting Gender* developed out of the exhibition *Women and Men* held at Manchester's Whitworth Art Gallery between December 1991 and August 1992. Thus *Exhibiting Gender* is less an art theoretical exploration of the relationship between gender identity and art than an example of how the question of femininity and masculinity in relation to artistic production can be used constructively as informing the processes of curating and exhibiting objects of art. As Hyde explains:

> The main aim of the exhibition was to provide visitors with a means of engaging actively with the works on display. This was done by showing about fifty works from the Gallery's collection in unlabelled pairs, consisting of one work by a woman and one by a man. Each pair was accompanied by a label asking 'Which is the woman's work?'(5).

In the light of theoretical developments in the field of gender studies this does strike as a rather problematic approach to the relationship between gender and the production of art. However, Hyde is able to circumvent a too simplistic interpretation by drawing attention to the very problems underlying the aims of the exhibition. Furthermore, *Exhibiting Gender* is aimed at 'readers who do not consider themselves particularly knowledgable about "art" '(6), as Hyde explains, and at teachers who can use the volume as an introduction to the subject of gender and art. Thus, although the book does work with theoretical concepts developed in the context of how gender impacts on the production of art (the author refers in particular to work by Griselda Pollock, Roszika Parker, Lynda Nead and Linda Nochlin), its main interest consists of a critical investigation of the various aspects informing the process of exhibiting art. And it is precisely there that the critical strength of *Exhibiting Gender* lies. In this respect the book is more than just an accompanying catalogue to an exhibition. Hyde uses the text to include examples which could not be exhibited in the gallery, but more importantly she uses them to create a context which allows her to discuss the concept of the exhibition in a more critical and complex way. For example, Hyde explores in great detail to what extent the history of the art gallery in question and the cultural space of the gallery and the museum itself impact on the construction of 'art' and its meaning in society. As a cultural space the Whitworth Gallery – which was founded in the nineteenth century and funded by money left by the engineer Sir Joseph Whitworth – is inextricably linked to its geographical and historical location which is contingent on the initial focus of its collection on textiles 'which would stimulate and inspire the textile industry in and around Manchester' (6). By giving an account of the history of the Whitworth Gallery and its choice of collections as well as the ways they are displayed, Hyde is able to relate the specific, local history of the museum with more general questions concerning the social and cultural function of exhibiting art when she argues: 'The function of British art galleries, in particular in defining and policing the boundaries between certain categories, such as fine art and craft, or art and pornography, is of fundamental importance to the examination of the gender issues raised here'(7).

Although *Exhibiting Gender* focuses, obviously, on the connection between the production, collection and exhibition of art in relation to sexual and gender identity, it is also a very informative account of more general problems in relation to the work of curators and organizers of exhibitions. And it is exactly this choice of discussing the issue of gender in a wider cultural context which prevents a too narrow and simplistic representation of the subject as such. Hyde imbricates her gender specific argument in a more fundamental analysis of the nature of art itself and how it is affected by ideological concepts of the artist, the process of artistic creativity and how the museal space informs and shapes the process of the reception of art. Interspersed with a wide range of examples, the occasional anecdote and the illustrations themselves, *Exhibiting Gender* manages to engage the reader in an active and inspirational way in the representation of its argument. It also gives an interesting and informative account of the development of contemporary feminist art history and its interventions in the processes of exhibitions, collections and re-conceptualizations of the relationship between art and the social and cultural space. Thus, although not predominantly a new and innovative text on the discursive links between gender and art, the book nevertheless offers a useful and interesting discussion of its subject. As Hyde herself explains: 'The aim of the present writer is not to introduce further advances in theory; rather it is to present new research about, and interpretations of, individual objects and their producers in a format which is approachable for the non-specialist reader' (15). In that respect *Exhibiting Gender* is a stimulating and provocative text which will be useful for teachers, students, visitors of museums and galleries and museum and gallery curators.

In his book on Baudelaire, Walter Benjamin comments on the process of looking and recognizing art in the following way: '[T]he painting we look at reflects back to us that of which our eyes will never have their fill. What it contains that fulfils the original desire would be the very same stuff on which the desire continuously feeds' (Walter Benjamin, *Charles Baudelaire: A Lyric Poet in the Era of High Capitalism*, NLB, 146–147). A similar view of the artistic object and how it is rendered meaningful informs David Phillips's book *Exhibiting Authenticity* which, as is indicated by the title, debates the issue of authenticity as the basis for the practices of art historians, conservators and curators. Phillips's intention is to develop a critical scrutiny of the idea of the 'authentic' object of art, arguing that authenticity itself is nothing else but the effect of specific historical, social and cultural discourses which can be dismantled if questioned from a critical point of view.

Exhibiting Authenticity begins with the chapter 'The Cult of Saints and the Cult of Art' which takes a closer look at the institutions of the church and the museum, and their role in controlling supposedly authentic objects of art. This is an 'authenticity' which, as Phillips demonstrates convincingly, is effectively the discursive result of the very political and economical domains art is supposed to transcend: 'Transcendent aesthetic values cannot be kept distinct from cash values' (12). In his analysis of authenticity and its construction, Phillips refers extensively to the work of Pierre Bourdieu who argues that museums work by putting into practice a mechanism of social distinction and conclusion in order to police what is to be appreciated as authentic art. Drawing additionally on Walter Benjamin's theoretical work which demonstrates how uniqueness and authenticity in a work of art is always politically constructed, Phillips produces a critical grid which can accommodate his own approach. However, the book offers more than just an exploration of Bourdieu's and Benjamin's writing in relation to the question of authenticity. As Phillips argues:

> The problem for anyone who wants to retain a more transcendent and cross-cultural role for aesthetics and artworks is that it is very hard to stand outside the kind of socially conditioning processes that Benjamin or Bourdieu propose, to study art other than as a participant. The approach I shall follow in the chapters to come is ... to take a close look at what it is that is done in the name of authenticity, as art historians identify, conservators intervene and curators display (25).

Thus the following chapters are devoted to the various pitfalls in relation to the concept of authenticity and the general fallibility of the process of authenticating art. 'The Connoisseurs' Paradox' explores how evaluation of the experience of the observer is confused with the assessment of characteristics of the art object, by looking more closely at different strategies of authenticating paintings and revealing forgery. Phillips explicates very persuasively, and with the help of a variety of examples, that there is no objective ground on which the authenticity of an artefact can be proved without fail, since attribution of paintings to specific artists can never exclude the possibility that what is identified as the property of the object is in reality the result of the connoisseur's assessment itself.

Similar problems are taken issue with in the following three chapters which in a critical way survey how in the current century the process of authenticating is based on scientific characteristics of material and/or the ability to document the history of the ownership of an artefact in order to render it authentic and unique. However, as Phillips shows persuasively, these processes cannot exclude that even extensive scientific evidence is only rendered meaningful if interpreted and explicated. This is also the case if evidence is based on historical documentation, which according to Phillips's comprehensive discussion in the chapter entitled 'The Evidence', is never more than loosely suggestive and therefore unsuitable as a method to ascertain authenticity. As Phillips comments: '. . . attribution remains obviously a matter of probabilities, and the key issue becomes not just the evidence, but the weight that should be attached to it' (68).

The subject of authenticity and attribution can be regarded as a question of judgement which shifts the focus on the fact that art and its definition is inextricably linked to the process of delivering a verdict based on the evidence given to the judge. Consequently, the following chapters of *Exhibiting Authenticity* explore the problem of attribution by comparing the art historical method to the ones performed in courts, institutions which, at least eventually, have to deliver a verdict and thus differ fundamentally from the recalcitrant attitude displayed in the domain of art historical expertise. This is a particularly fascinating chapter which refers to mathematics as well as to the process of decision making as such, in order to show the inherent problems of the art-historical attributive debate. In the next chapter Phillips takes the juridical jargon a step further when, under the heading 'The Judges in the Dock' the tables are turned and Phillips deconstructs the process of art authentication and attribution as being discursively connected to the procedure of art history's academic self-fashioning. He comes to the conclusion:

> Art historians are guilty as charged, but can be dismissed with a caution. What they have done over the last century of scientific classification is to plot for us a map of the production of artefacts, and one of unrivalled precision, so long as we always remember that it is bound to be selective in what it shows, and to reveal as much about the society that produced the map as it does about the societies that produced the artefacts (3).

The final chapters of the book are devoted to the questions of 'Conservation', 'Intention' and 'Curators and Authenticity' and offer additional perspectives from which the subject of authenticity can be viewed and analysed. *Exhibiting Authenticity* is an extremely informative, witty and well-written book which engages with art-theoretical questions by demonstrating their relevance for the discursive practice of the production, exhibition and conservation of art. Many art historians will be enraged when reading the book, but that is not necessarily a bad thing to happen.

The time after the First World War and before the takeover of fascism – Weimar Germany – was one of the most innovative and prolific decades in respect of the visual arts. W. L. Guttsman's book *Art for the Workers: Ideology and the Visual Arts in Weimar Germany* is dedicated to this period of the history of art production in Germany. Specifically, the author is 'concerned with works of art from the point of view of how they were received by German workers and their families, and the potential impression which art may have made on them' (2). Although Guttsman focuses mainly on the period 1918 to 1933 he does contextualize his examination more broadly from a historical point of view by also considering paintings, drawings, prints and culture produced at an earlier point in the history of the German Labour Movement. This is a necessary move since the book intends to explore the relationship between art and the working class from a political perspective, and thus needs to look at the beginning of the Labour Movement in order to evaluate to what extent the two main left-wing parties, Social Democrats and Communists, utilized art as part of agitation and propaganda and as a tool towards mass education. Accordingly, *Art for the Workers* is mainly interested in investigating the relationship between art and politics which is based on an exploration of the institutional links between artistic production, dissemination and reception and working class politics in the Weimar Republic. In that respect Guttsman's perspective is rather different from the majority of art historical studies of this period which predominantly focus on avant-garde art and its development in 1920s Germany. This shift of focus not only impacts on the author's approach which is less informed by questions of theory in that it concentrates 'on documentary evidence on the history and institutions of the Labour Movement and the bodies and individuals connected with it' (1); it is also noticeable in his choice and selection of visual representations which consist of posters, home decorations, plates and reproductions in articles, prints in workers' journals, newspapers and magazines and specially commissioned art by the two main left-wing parties. Thus Guttsman's study does not only introduce a wide range of material which hitherto has been rather neglected in major works on the Weimar Republic, it also provides an interesting and informative historical account of the German socialist and communist parties and their attitude towards art on the one hand, and how, on the other hand, this specific stance has shaped their concept of politics in general and propaganda, agitation and education of the working class in particular.

Art for the Workers is a meticulously researched book and approaches its subject from a variety of perspectives. By taking a closer look at the political parties and their political ideas devoted to art and education, Guttsman not only re-narrates and re-evaluates the story of German left-wing politics in relation to art, he also manages to introduce a wide range of artistic material by artists who have been forgotten or were not well known in the first place outside of Germany. Naturally, the artists discussed in the book do also include such internationally renowned ones as Käthe Kollwitz, Max Pechtstein, Walter Gropius, George Grosz, E. L. Kirchner and others. But as already mentioned earlier, Guttsman's critical inquiry does not predominately centre on individual artists and the interpretation of their work; its main aim consists of analysing the gist of left-wing cultural politics and the encounter between the working classes and art. By giving a broad overview of the history of working-class education, the author shows how, on the one hand, this was traditionally always regulated, if not dictated, by the demands of the state and the economy, and, on the other hand, to what extent the objective of an educated working class had always been central to and inextricably linked with socialist (and later communist) political aims in Germany. Guttsman also demonstrates convincingly how this ideal of an educated working class was from the outset shaped by ideas based on philosophical concepts originating in the Enlightenment and its concept of *Bildung* (education). Thus, paradoxically, theories of the emancipation and liberation of the working class were greatly dominated by bourgeois notions of the acquirement of knowledge as the prerequisite for a moral and cultured life (a view which is particularly central to Lasalle's and Wilhelm Liebknecht's thoughts on education and culture). Guttsman concludes accordingly:

> The culture which workers and working-class organisations were thus expected to strive for was essentially the German high culture described earlier. Workers were to be encouraged to become acquainted with the works of the great thinkers and with the masterpieces of literature and the arts, and above all with those which reflected the workers' struggle (9–10).

This attitude is, naturally, also of great consequence for the relationship between the Labour Movement and the visual arts and is at the core the chapter 'Artistic Utopianism versus Committed Art'. Here Guttsman discusses the work of expressionist artists, painters, illustrators and architects, and their ambiguous relationship towards political change, artistic past and traditions and the sceptical reception of expressionist art theory and practice by the main left-wing parties. This is a very interesting chapter – very informative and thoroughly researched – but from a theoretical point of view, the debate between Brecht and Lukàcs concerning socialist politics and its evaluation of realist versus avant-garde art could have been included in order to situate the discussion in a more art-theoretical framework.

In general, *Art for the Workers* is a very knowledgeable book which introduces and takes issue with a wide range of material. The book's foremost scope is a historical one, thus theoretically informed aspects do not feature to a great extent. Although the text makes up for this by offering some highly interesting debates, certain subjects (in particular ideology, social and cultural reception of art) could have profited from a more critical approach at times. But, nonetheless, this is a recommendable book for readers who are specifically interested in the relationship between visual art and politics in Weimar Germany.

The Modernity of English Art: 1914–30 by David Peter Corbett covers roughly the same period as the previous book and 'is about a struggle in English painting to address the experience of a modern culture at a time when such an ambition had become in important ways unacceptable' (1). By exploring the development of English art between 1914 to 1930 Corbett offers a cultural history of the modernist movement in English visual art by referring to its specific national characteristics and discussing the facts and events which impeded its advancement. Corbett's argument evolves chronologically, commencing with the art before and around the outbreak of the First World War and the optimism surrounding the modernist art movement and its participants who enthused about the immense possibilities of avant-garde painting in the future. But, as the author convincingly demonstrates, not only did the outbreak of the war prove to be a fundamental sea change concerning the advancement of modernist art and the concept of a radical modernism; its practice and reception in pre-war England had always been a compromised one and could not be reconciled with the views and hopes expressed by the artists involved in the movement:

> Its promise of a radical public language with which to evaluate and comprehend modernity depended on a shaky anchorage in the shifting sands of English culture. Once the war had begun to enforce a reformulation of priorities, modernism could not withstand the consequent changes, and rapidly ceased to be allowable as an idiom or set of concerns (18).

Corbett supports his contention of modernism's potentiality as an accepted public discourse in pre-war England by closely and critically examining the underlying theoretical objectives and the artistic practice of Vorticism and the artists who subscribed to this movement. The first chapter of *The Modernity of English Art*, 'Radical Modernism, 1914–18', focuses on the aesthetic and social particularities of Vorticism and challenges its presentation as a powerful and radical artistic discourse by linking its success to its complicit relationship with modernism as fashion movement based on providing entertainment and novelty. Corbett's view is imbricated in a wider discussion of modernist art which concentrates its critical attention on the complex and contradictory relationship between modernism and capitalist social and cultural reality. Thus, on the one hand modernism can provide a powerful counter-discourse directed against a consumerist society by acting as a socially engaged critique of capitalism, but, on the other hand, by being preoccupied with its own autonomy and development it can also be involved in the legitimation of dominant culture and its elitist structure. Corbett's foremost intention, therefore, is to discuss modernism by discriminating within its different categories and relationships to modernity, the most important distinctions being between modernism as avant-garde, secondly a less radical modernism which is more concerned with its own formal aspects, and thirdly a pre-avant-garde modernism and its relationship to modernity as apparent in the Royal Academy and the paintings produced under its umbrella. By representing modernist art as different types of relationships with modernity, Corbett is able to establish a discursive link between English culture and its art practices by suggesting that:

> the understandings of modernity that English practice advances are linked to the particularly fraught relationship with its own modernity displayed by English culture. Like the culture as a whole, English art proved unable to derive an idiom of investigation and critique of the conditions of its own existence from the available languages (10).

By exploring the artistic practice of modernism not pre-eminently through modernist painting itself but by inextricably linking its development and formal characteristics with wider questions of modernity in relation to culture, *The Modernity of English Art* avoids the pitfalls of other investigations into modernism which view the movement predominantly from a stylistic perspective, or as being determined by a dialogic relationship between native traditions and foreign, mostly continental European, influences.

The main achievement of this approach consists of an innovative and productive method of how the relationship between visual art and culture can be investigated and evaluated without being reduced to either a too narrow formalism or theoretically diminished to just indicating mimetically the state of cultural reality.

Corbett manages to maintain his critical attitude in the subsequent chapters which are concerned with the periods after the war which saw the unfolding of a sense of modernity in England and English culture. By looking at the changes from the point of view of questions concerning aesthetics, public reception and adaptation of modernist principles, *The Modernity of English Art* explores the cultural and artistic dissemination of modernist painting and art. Other chapters are dedicated to individual artists (in particular Paul Nash and Wyndham Lewis), their work and their response to the changes in modernism as a critical and artistic practice in the 1920s. Attention is also paid to the increasing 'privatization' of modernity itself which augmented modernism's inability to act as a public idiom which could address modern life. As Corbett argues: 'In the years after 1918 modernity became an intimate, subjective, experience, pressing closely on the self, which could neither be admitted nor made sense of' (153). The study closes with a critical re-evaluation of Royal Academy painting and the presence of the modern within its established practices.

The Modernity of English Art offers an innovative and theoretically informed contribution to the debate of modernism and its relationship to national identity and the cultural formation of English society between 1914 and 1930. It takes issue with a wide variety of subjects and introduces ways of exploring and evaluating paintings and art theoretical statements produced, informed by the discourse of modernism often neglected by other art historical studies of this kind.

Many of the essays gathered in *Socialist Realism without Shores* edited by Thomas Lahusen and Evgeny Dobrenke engage with similar issues to those of Guttsman on art and the Labour Movement. However, in this volume the debate is clearly directed from a theoretical perspective. The collection of essays presents an enlarged version of a special issue of the *South Atlantic Quarterly* (volume 94, number 3, summer 1995) which was devoted to the subject of socialist realism, its development and its position in relation to current critical theoretical discourses. Socialist realism itself being a literary-centric discourse, it does not come as a surprise that the majority of essays gathered in this volume focus on literature and literary theoretical questions. However, some of the selected texts approach the subject from the point of view of art (mainly visual art, architecture and film) and art theory, and rather than giving a critical account of the complete volume, the following review will concentrate on those.

As the various essays collected in *Socialist Realism without Shores* show, although the discourse of socialist realism is of particular relevance for Russia and the states of the former Soviet Union, it is not exclusive to these countries. The volume brings together authors from among others China, East Germany, Hungary, France and Poland and it is indisputable that the respective national identities shaped by their specific cultural frameworks have impacted on how the subject is approached. Additionally the respective genre and art form discussed by the different authors is also not without effect on the critical evaluation of the meaning of socialist realism and its current status as a methodological tool. Leonid Heller's contribution 'A world of Prettiness: Socialist Realism and its Aesthetic Categories', for instance, situates its discussion of aesthetics and the position and function of the sublime in Socialist realism primarily in the domain of Russian literature and literary theory although art historical issues too are considered and relevant for his conclusions:

> The only unconstrained sublimity permissible in socialist realism was to be found in the image of unlimited power, an image that did not inspire horror at all (as it did in the old theorists, such as Burke or Kant). It neither deprived the subject of freedom nor opened up before itself the abyss of chaos (70).

Boris Groys, too, conducts his critical inquiry into socialist realism in relation to aesthetics. However, 'A Style and a Half: Socialist Realism between Modernism and Postmodernism' shifts the focus to an investigation of the affinities as well as the differences between the aesthetic concepts of Western modernism and socialist realism and asks to what extent they inform the divergent strategies employed respectively by Western postmodernism and Russian post-Sovietism. Central to Groys's argument is his discussion of *sots art*, also known as Moscow conceptualism which emerged within the Russian capital's 'unofficial art' circles in the 1970s and usually thought of as the Soviet version of postmodernism. However, as Groys argues persuasively, the differences between the two discourses eclipse their shared features and, on the whole, *sots art* and Western postmodernism should be ranked as disparate discursive practices:

> In the West, postmodernist appropriation occurred in the real context of real cultural institutions such as museums, universities and publishing houses. In Russia, on the other hand, the context for this appropriation had to be first created by the artist or the theorist himself. The creation of such contexts was complicated, above all, by the uniqueness of the Soviet/non-Soviet borderline, which, within this context, had to be at once drawn and transcended (83).

Groys's contribution is one of the most interesting in *Socialist Realism without Shores* providing a fascinating insight into post-Soviet developments in the visual arts and art theory. In a similar vein, Greg Castillo's article 'People at an Exhibition: Soviet Architecture and the National Question' which takes issue with exhibition architecture from pre-revolutionary Russia to the post-Stalinist era of the Soviet Union, is greatly relevant from a theoretical point of view in that it furthers the debate surrounding questions of national identity especially in relation to the problems intrinsic to the multinational state. Svetlana Boym's contribution 'Paradoxes of Unified Culture; From Stalin's Fairy Tale to Molotov's Lacquer Box' directs its enquiry from yet another perspective by considering the practical and theoretical effects of socialist realist mass culturization which aimed at a synthesization of 'the old opposition between culture and civilization, high and low art, public and private genres' (121). Antoine Baudin's essay ' "Why is Soviet Painting Hidden from us?" Zhdanov Art and its International Relations and Fallout, 1947–53' is dedicated in particular to the development of post-war Soviet visual art and in a more methodological sense to the cultural status of the visual arts and their secondary position in relation to the literary arts in the former Soviet Union. Baudin focuses on the years between 1947 and 1953 in order to 'illuminate the paradoxical strategies of the diffusion and presentation of Soviet art, as well as the issue of the very 'exportability' of socialist realism in this domain' (227) and by doing so explores the reasons for the absence and insignificance of Soviet art in the Western art world.

Socialist Realism without Shores unites a variety of engaging essays and offers some very conducive and innovative approaches to the field of socialist realism. Reading the different essays one cannot but notice how many of the contributions are still to a great extent preoccupied with the Stalinist era and its impact on art and art theory. And it is precisely there, in the critical engagement with the past and its contingent impact on future developments, that the real strength of the present volume is to be found. The possibility of socialist realism gaining a dominant position in the current field of critical theories seems to me, even after studying the various arguments presented in the selected essays, rather doubtful.

Books Reviewed

Corbett, David Peter. *The Modernity of English Art: 1914–30.* Manchester University Press. pp. 234. pb £17.99. ISBN 0 7190 3733 6.

Guttsman, W. L. *Art for the Workers: Ideology and the Visual Arts in Weimar Germany.* Manchester University Press. pp. 226. hb £47.50. ISBN 0 7190 3634 8.

Hyde, Sarah. *Exhibiting Gender.* Manchester University Press. pp. 120. hb £45.00. pb £17.99. ISBN 0 7190 4242 9, 0 7190 4243 7.

Kondo, Dorinne. *About Face. Performing Race in Fashion and Theater.* Routledge. pp. 277. pb £13.99. ISBN 0 415 91141 9.

Lahusen, Thomas, and Evgeny Dobrenko, eds. *Socialist Realism without Shores.* Duke University Press. pp. 369. hb £56.95. pb £17.95. ISBN 0 8223 1935 7, 0 8223 1941 1.

Phillips, David. *Exhibiting Authenticity.* Manchester University Press. pp. 234. hb £45.00. pb £16.99. ISBN 0 7190 4769 X, 0 7190 4797 8.

Rabaté, Jean-Michel, ed. *Writing the Image After Roland Barthes.* University of Pennsylvania Press. pp. 296. hb £35.00. pb £16.50. ISBN 0 8122 3369 7, 0 8122 1596 6.

Walker, John, and Sarah Chaplin, eds. *Visual Culture: An Introduction.* Manchester University Press. pp. 231. hb £45.00. pb £15.99. ISBN 0 7190 5019 7, 0 7190 5020 0.
Wells, Liz, ed. *Photography. A Critical Introduction.* Routledge. pp. 307. hb £50.00. pb £16.99. ISBN 0 415 12558 8, 0 415 12559 6.
Woodall, Joanna ed. *Portraiture: Facing the Subject.* Manchester University Press. pp. 282. hb £45.00. pb £16.99. ISBN 0 7190 4612 2, 0 7190 4614 9.

17

Cultural Policy

ROBIN TROTTER

This review covers a two-year period: 1996–97.

Introduction

A relative newcomer to both cultural and policy areas, cultural policy has been defined succinctly as policies that 'regulate' the 'market of ideas' (DiMaggio, 1983:242), or more exhaustively by Augustin Girard as:

> A policy is a system of ultimate aims, practical objectives and means, pursued by a group and applied by an authority. Cultural policies can be discerned in a trade union, a party, an educational movement, an institution, an enterprise, a town or a government. But regardless of the agent concerned, a policy implies the existence of ultimate purposes (long term), objectives (medium-term and measurable) and means (men [sic], money and legislation, combined in an explicitly coherent system (Girard,171–172).

Cultural policies may be 'direct' and explicitly defined as such, or 'indirect'. The latter refers to policies which, although not specifically cultural in jurisdiction do have an impact on cultural production (DiMaggio, 1983:242–244). It is, however, the former type of cultural policy with which this review is concerned. It is these cultural policies that are increasingly being initiated by national governments such as the various European states (at various dates), Australia (1994), and Britain (1992) – even though Britain's decision to establish a Department of National Heritage has been described more as a 'Clayton's' cultural policy (see Hewison, 1996 below). Cultural policy development is not restricted to national governments but may extend downward to subordinate levels of government – to state and local governments. At the city, municipal or regional level cultural statements and strategies are also becoming the norm rather than the exception. Cultural policy is increasingly being used as a tool of government for a number of reasons. The major themes this review will be exploring, and which have emerged from a reading of key texts on cultural policy published during 1996 and 1997, give an indication of some of the catalysts for this phenomenon.

It is apparent there is a renewed concern with *national cultural identity and national and/or regional autonomy.* Although nationalism has been associated closely with cultural policy, it is re-emerging again as an issue in the face of an intensification of globalizing forces and, ironically not only as a defensive measure *against* globalization, but also as a means of breaking down national barriers in order to facilitate broader and more inclusive cultural policies. This development is evident in the context of the European Community. At the same time, the notion of national identity is being renegotiated in numerous contexts, particularly where a politics of identity is converging with nationing strategies.

Globalization and convergence are, therefore, dominant issues – not only in respect to their impacts on the nation-state and to relationships within nation-states, but also in respect to the ways in which these developments are shaping and transforming cultural forms and institutions and engendering modification of regulatory structures.

Community cultural development (CCD) continues to be an ongoing theme in community arts and culture but it is increasingly being promoted as a more holistic form of community development, one that incorporates quality of life, creativity and social issues. However, CCD is also converging with a *cultural industries* model through culturally led economic development strategies (either urban or regional), cultural tourism and commodified forms of cultural consumption.

Another theme emerging in the period under discussion is that of *decentralization* – be this in terms of geographical space or in terms of delegation of responsibility to lower levels of government, to state or local authorities or to the private sector through various *deregulatory* processes. This shift brings with it an emphasis on consumption in line with a cultural industries approach.

There are, obviously, *theoretical* and *practical implications* associated with these developments and these have been variously and with varying degrees of success, dealt with in numerous texts published in the review period (1996–97). Key analysts for and of cultural policy tend to draw on either Antonio Gramsci and the theory of hegemony, or Michel Foucault and his writings and reconstruction of cultural studies around the notion of governmentality. However, in this review a number of alternative theorists and alternative constructions of cultural policy will be found. These, I believe, provide an analytical richness to debates which should be brought to bear on empirical studies and on the framing and implementing of polices in the cultural sphere. Hopefully, such research will also be directed at crossing policy boundaries to influence contingent policy and policy research areas – education, sciences, economic, social policy, etc.

The broad aim of this review is to reflect on studies relevant to broad cultural policy issues rather than to include writing on particular cultural sectors, areas which often comprise their own area of study such as arts management, or nationally specific areas. That being said, however, there are inevitably cultural policy issues that, although sectorally or nationally specific, do have either theoretical or practical implications for cultural policy studies in general or for comparative purposes. This, then, qualifies my preliminary statement of aim, but also provides a selection process.

1. National Culture and Identity

Although there are differing domains in which cultural policy is developed – governmental, institutional, civil society and commercial spheres (Bennett and Mercer, 1997) – it is the policies articulated by governments that are the dominant area of debate and this focus is represented in the texts discussed below.

Characteristic of cultural policies to date has been a concentration – either explicitly or covertly – on a platform centred on ensuring national identity and social cohesion. Cultural products, cultural production and cultural heritage are not only called upon to define a country (or community's) identity and uniqueness, but also to contribute to quality of life and, increasingly, to contribute to economic development. That forces for either colonization by more dominant cultures, or universalization of culture into a global culture, are seen as threats is evident in cultural policy debates and this has emerged with particular vehemence in two contexts – Canada and Europe.

Franklyn Griffiths, a professor of political science at the University of Toronto, puts the case for defending Canadian sovereignty through nourishing local culture in *Strong and Free. Canada and the New Sovereignty*.

Griffiths takes as his central theme, the statement from the Massey Report of 1951: 'If we as a nation are concerned with the problem of defence, what, we may ask ourselves, are we defending? We are defending civilization, our share of it, our contribution to it'.

He then puts this into the context of contemporary Canada and the 1995 referendum, to claim that Canadians are:

> Fragmented and increasingly dispossessed by the globalization of economic life, disabled by deficits and debit of our own making, and now beset by an onrush of separatism and regionalism, we are coming apart ... Defence of our sovereignty is now of the essence of securing our country ... [and] Defence of sovereignty is, *au fond*, a matter of culture – political culture very much included' (3,5,7).

There are two forms of sovereignty with which Griffiths deals: one spatial, territorial and legalistic in action, the other a broadly political condition – 'a condition of being supreme and free from external control in the governing of a given territory' (16) and it is the latter form which Griffiths considers to be most under threat. This is due, in large part, to disunity (in particular Quebec separatism and broader regionalism (17)), to an over-emphasis on Canada–USA relations (20), and to inaction and uncertainty in responding to globalization (21).

Griffiths is less concerned about high culture and more with popular culture and mass media because:

Canadian people need to experience themselves, their country, and the world around in newscasts and current affairs programs, in television and radio programs, in movies and books produced by Canadians, and not by others for foreign markets' (56).

A more sophisticated, less polemical account that takes a cultural policy perspective reveals, nevertheless, a similar concern and, interestingly, an interpretation that parallels Griffiths' argument in terms of 'defence' but relates this even more explicitly to cultural products. This is Michael Dorland's edited collection: *The Cultural Industries in Canada. Problems, Policies and Prospects.*

Dorland, like Griffiths, argues that, for Canada, cultural protection is a question of national security. What is of interest, in looking at these two texts, are the commonalties between a political scientist and culturalists. There are, inevitably, in the Dorland collection differing points of view in the fine detail, and more theoretically sophisticated approaches, nevertheless, like Griffiths, these writers also link cultural policy to national security.

A large section is devoted to sectoral analyses – the print industries (books, periodicals, newspapers), the sound industries (recording, radio), and the image/data industries (film and video, broadcasting and narrowcasting television) and policies relating to convergence, new technologies and to copyright regulations governing forms of media. The thrust of the cultural policy arguments is contained in several chapters briefly summarized below. However, these sectoral analyses indicate the increasing pressure on Canadian cultural forms from the convergences of new technologies and changing forms of market pressures that not only blur industry or sector boundaries but also create problems for regulatory bodies.

In the Introduction (ix–xiii) and concluding chapter, 'Cultural Industries and the Canadian Experience: Reflections on the Emergence of a Field' (347–365), Dorland discusses the field in respect to nation and nationalist ideals. First, he defines cultural industries as industries that produce cultural commodities and as a concept used in the policy arena (ix–viii). He goes on to point out that Canadian policy concerns are largely articulated around the need to 'demarcate Canadian activities from American ones and provide the space, ranging from the economic to the symbolic, in which such activities might be undertaken, continue and even flourish' and that culture has been fundamental to these ends (ix). Dorland explores this process through a discussion of filmmaking and broadcasting to trace a shift in the 'stream of Royal Commissions, white papers, public and parliamentary inquiries and legislative and regulatory modifications' from a discourse of culture to one of economy (xi).

One of the aims of this collection is to re-assess an earlier study of Canadian cultural industries undertaken by Paul Audley in the 1970s in which Audley defined these industries in terms of a 'nationalist model'. Audley's study acknowledged a degree of dependency on America but expressed confidence that Canadian distinctiveness would prevail. Subsequent events, Dorland suggests, reveal a gap between nationalist rhetoric (and expectations) and economic realities; a gap that calls for re-evaluation of the 'nationalist model' (349). Despite the facts that Canada was one of the first countries to acknowledge the role of the state in the production of film images to support both immigration and industrial development (347), and that Canada also set up its national broadcasting system based on the BBC model, Dorland maintains that:

> Canada remains a fragile communicative entity, plagued by recurring problems of national identity, both internal and external and more particularly by threats to cultural domination from its neighbour, especially in respect to media output (348).

And this is also despite wide-ranging measures introduced to 'police' and protect Canadian culture such as:

> Border controls, tariffs, censorship of the mails, censorship of the movies, regulation of the airwaves and an associated panoply of administrative and legal measures affecting everything from content to ownership (348).

In these chapters, Dorland charts the connective links established between Canadian cultural industries and the North American marketplace in which Canadian media as well as state media agencies have been complicit (355). However, he also notes the difficulties for the Canadian government and its intentions to establish and maintain 'Canadianness' in content when faced with political and economic imperatives to uphold international agreements on tariffs and free trade (356–357). Facilitating what he describes as a shift to 'post-nationalism', Dorland identifies a form of policy making oriented to 'operationalization' and a concomitant concern with increasing cultural production over the production of national product for Canadian audiences.

In Kevin Dowler's chapter on 'The Cultural Industries Policy Apparatus' (328–346), it is argued that a 'mandate for Canadian culture' lies not in an economic imperative but in 'the quest for national security' (329). This is largely an internal problem emerging post Second World War, when:

> An insecure internal frontier opened up, geographically located in the west, metaphysically located in the racial tension between Canadians of British origin and the new Central European immigrants.

This 'internal' threat was augmented with threats of colonization from American culture. Extending this argument, Dowler goes on to show how nationalizing for Canada has involved two stages – the first revolved around the construction of a national communications and transportation system. This failed to secure a national space and led to further dependency. A second front was opened up to counteract this failure and its consequences – 'this second front was culture' (329). So, in effect, failure to achieve economic and/or military dependency in a physical sense was addressed by attempts to construct a metaphysical national space (329–330). Consequently, Dowler argues that the 'cultural policy apparatus [is] a set of structures and procedures designed to bolster security, not to shape identity' (330). Basing his case on Foucauldian notions of tactics, he asserts that

Canadian cultural policy is a set of ' "tactics" to enhance security and ensure the continual reproduction of the Canadian state', while Canadian culture is 'a regime, or a regimen, that functions as a form of security' (330). The empty space of the nation is filled by foreign mass culture while in the empty metaphysical space – a space which is the 'locus of identity' – 'cultural policy emerges as the content' (334). According to Dowler, the Massey Report acknowledged that Canadian isolation created disunity and the report writers set out to overcome this by proposing the unification of the regions and bringing them into cohesive national life by implementation of national cultural programmes. But, because of concerns about the totalitarian state, culture needed to be seen as divorced and separate from government. At the same time, private capital did not wish, nor have the capacity, to fulfil this role, but expected the state to do so: 'If culture was to be Canadian, the government would have to build it' (335). Hence, the principle of 'arm's length' cultural regulation and administration and the establishment of a raft of agencies. Dowler claims this represents a 'simulated civil society' (336) where culture comes to function 'as a security mechanism that compensates for dependency and works to secure the continued existence of the Canadian state' (336).

Culture, instead of being free and quarantined from commercialism has become, for Canada, a core economic activity. At the same time industrialization of culture has become a means of strengthening the nation's industrial base, decreasing dependence and increasing security (340). Cultural and industrial policies have converged, and cultural industries have emerged with an economic agenda taking priority over cultural priorities.

The Presumption of Culture by Tom Henighan is a passionate plea for protecting and revitalizing Canadian culture, particularly the arts. His concern is that Canadian arts and culture are 'in crisis' due to funding cuts, a crisis of morale, instability and uncertainty in the cultural industries, internal tensions (between national and provincial governments, and between Quebec and Anglo-Canada), a vacuum in policy and the need for reform of administrative structures. Henighan claims 'I regard culture as one of the essentials of any good society' but his primary concern is that what he terms 'aesthetic culture' or 'serious culture', is under threat from 'entertainment culture' and that this also involves a national threat:

> My belief is that the Canadian national vision, made manifest, articulated, and shaped by its culture, is in danger, and that the danger is coming from the 'universal entertainment culture' that is largely a product of American industry ... I believe that Canadian aesthetic culture (and to some extent our more distinctively Canadian popular culture) represent the best national defence Canada has against assimilation into the American cultural hegemony (4).

In an overview of Canadian cultural history since the 1950s (i.e. from the time of the Massey Report of 1951), Henighan mounts an attack on ideologies of both left and right, academics (in particular those inclined to radicalism or revisionism), the politicization of arts as articulated around concerns where 'political correctness', 'appropriation of voice' and 'cultural diversity' threatened fundamental notions of excellence' (63). But the depth of his scorn is directed to television 'and other mind-numbing pleasures' such as the mass media. Television substitutes the personal experience for a subversive simulation (33), it fails the arts because it 'allows, almost demands, the manipulation of reality, but does little to enhance the power of art to communicate truth' (35) . . . [it is] also a sphere of idolatry . . . it is hopelessly superficial at conveying ideas and even information' (45). Exacerbating this threat from television, and other forms of mass media is the American origin of much of this product and Canada, because of its location and size, is especially vulnerable to colonization by American cultural (and ideological) hegemony disseminated through the American mass media (47).

Henighan claims 'only a comprehensive national plan to strengthen and develop its [Canada's] aesthetic culture will maintain our national integrity into the next century' (59). Such a plan should entail a shift from the British model and adoption of the European practice of a national cultural policy, a Ministry of Culture to administer that policy and a restructuring and re-evaluation of the role of the Canada Council. A new, but separate Ministry for Mass Communications should also be established. Concurrent with this restructuring should be a re-assessment of the relations between the federal government and its provinces.

Irrespective of the idealistic and, what some might consider, provocative views of the writer, *The Presumption of Culture* does provide an informative account of arts policy in Canada in the last decades, and again demonstrates the linkages between cultural policy and nationalism.

'Nationing' is, however, not only concerned with external threats as the Canadian texts indicate, but internal differences can also generate cultural tension, and, as indicated in the introduction, monocultural constructions of national identity are increasingly becoming the subject of review and modification in numerous nationalist contexts. As Henry A. Giroux comments in a Foreword to *Culture and Difference. Critical Perspectives on the Bicultural Experience in the United States:*

> Increasingly, the fractured realities that constitute diverse cultural traditions and experiences have called into question the meaning of national identity, what it means to be an American, and how as educators we address the formation of new publics of difference as a defining principle of democratic society (ix).

This volume of critical essays is edited by Antonia Darder, who, along with a number of contributors, is intent on presenting a range of perspectives of different 'communities of colour' and to 'extending our political understanding of culture and difference'. The themes and experiences are the material on which cultural policy is written and reshaped, however, several chapters deal explicitly with policy areas or with aspects of community culture. This illustrates not only the difficulty of imposing boundaries around cultural issues but also the penetration of cultural issues into other terrains. Alberto M. Ochoa, professor in the Department of Policy Studies in Language and Cross Cultural Education, writes on bilingual education and language policy and stresses the importance of policy reform in this area to ensure cultural and structural access ('Language Policy and Implications' (227–253)). David R. Diaz, with an interest in urban planning, discusses 'street culture' and its importance in bilingual communities. This is a culture of minorities, of ethnic people, and it is a culture that challenges 'the elite barons of culture and white suburbanites' (133) and contests urban spaces, particularly public spaces and middle-class usurpation of these locations.

2. Globalization and Convergence

Although the Canadian cases above focus on neighbouring USA as the predominant threat, the increased globalized environment for communications networks creates a climate of concern for cultural policy across a wider field. In the European context where there are pressures for unification and counter pressures of nationalist ideals, a complex and delicate balancing act has been played out through the GATT negotiations. An account of this process is provided in *Trading Culture. GATT, European Cultural Policies and the Transatlantic Market*, edited by Annemoon van Hemel, Hans Mommaas and Cas Smithuijsen.

The immediate context for this collection was the final round of GATT talks of 1993 between the USA and the European Union and the differences of opinion regarding international trade agreements in respect to the audiovisual industry. The European Parliament was voting for a system of quotas that would first, protect their respective countries from Americanization via media products and the concentration of media corporations and, second, stimulate European cultural products. The terms of the debate turned on those advocating global culture and those supporting a 'polycentric' culture.

As a follow-up to these negotiations the Boekman Foundation (an Amsterdam-based study centre for arts, culture and management), organized an international conference in 1994 on *GATT, the Arts and Cultural Exchange between the United States and Europe*. The publication, *Trading Culture*, comprises a number of papers from this conference and its purpose is to contribute to this debate, to put it into a 'scholarly context', to show the weaknesses and strengths of the European cultural system and to explore the opportunities and limitations on cultural co-operation within that system (Foreword). Following are brief summaries of those chapters most relevant to the themes of this review.

The contributors offer differing perspectives on 'the rhetoric and realities of European-American cultural exchange' (16) with the central issues being those of cultural protectionism, Europeanization of the audiovisual market, and the influence of an American media industry on the European media market (16). In the introductory chapter and 'The Politics of Culture and World Trade' (11–23), Hans Mommaas sets the context for the 1993 talks within a long history of cultural differences between Europe and the United States expressed as differences between traditional culture and modern, mass produced culture, and between protectionist as opposed to free trade ideologies and policies (12–14). He suggests that the 'old' vocabulary once used to position the 'European' fine arts domain *vis-à-vis* 'American' popular culture has become rather obsolete and misleading', and that what has emerged is a new 'created' culture based on the principle of a regulated 'public pluralism' and one which recognizes the role of the state in protecting cultural diversity and pluralism within a market economy (23).

The GATT conflict of 1993, as Michael Palmer points out, was a replay of earlier skirmishes. In 'GATT and Culture: A View from France' (27–38), Palmer explores the bases of these disputes and points out that these did not simply represent differing values between Europe and the United States but involved a number of divisive relationships not only between participating nations but also within the respective groupings. There were divisions among the European Union Commissioners. Within France there were further divisions between government, industry and public. At the height of the negotiations, while French delegates argued ways and means of protecting French audiovisual industry and pressed for continuation of an earlier agreement to exclude cultural products from trade agreements (the 'exception culturelle' clause), large numbers of the French public were thronging to American release movies (27–38).

In an environment of disunity and divided loyalties, aggressive lobbying by Hollywood undermined the French position. Against arguments for protection of European and French cultural interests, Jack Valenti (for the Motion Picture Association of America) argued for an international audiovisual industry based on a liberal free market approach, one that 'must be able to leap beyond its national borders' (Valenti's address to the American Chamber of Commerce in France, Paris, 28 Sept 1994, quoted 34).

Palmer concludes that argument and counter-argument have continued. Underlying this is the ongoing concern about Americanization, transnationalism, modernization and dilution of national identity – all of which are made more complex by a European infatuation with American culture. Consequently, a free trade agreement is seen by most French cultural policy makers as American cultural imperialism, while for American interests it promises economic flexibility, expanded markets, and protection of the industry's common interests (36).

Another grid of interests surrounding the GATT negotiations is identified by Arjo Klamer in 'Economic Aspects of Cultural Exchange' (39–48). There are the pragmatic liberal free traders whose ideologies inform the GATT agreement. Their objectives are to reduce tariffs, liberalize protected trade (especially in agricultural products), extend GATT to cover services, and protect intellectual property rights (of corporations but not of people). And on the other side are the 'romantic' protectionists who reject market forces for political intervention and call on various arguments in support of this strategy, such as 'infant industry status', the preservation of cultural identity and national autonomy, the ensuring of access and educational resources for citizens.

Klamer concludes that cultural value is fragile but also 'contestable' so that negotiation about the value of cultural products is healthy: 'It keeps us sharp and makes us realize what we have and what we would like to have – or perhaps rather, what we are and what we would like to be' (47).

Those cultural values are, in Richard Pells' opinion, the basis of European resistance to Americanization. His chapter, 'Resistance and Transformation: Europe's Response to American Mass Culture' (49–66) takes up the issue of Americanization and suggests this is the 'root of fear' among Europeans who are concerned about:

> The disappearance of national languages, customs, tastes and attitudes. They were also disturbed by what they (sic) seemed to them the decline of traditional family relationships, neighbourhoods, work habits, the manner in which people courted their spouses and raised their children, and the ways they had once entertained themselves at nights and on weekends. Presumably, everything familiar and cherished was being obliterated under the onslaught of American merchandise and American culture (49).

Pells goes on to detail the futile efforts of Europeans to resist Americanization from the 1920s through to the 1990s and the GATT negotiations but then queries the depth and impact of Americanization in the face of ethnic and national cultural revitalization in Europe. He proposes that the interaction between America and Europe is more complex than the Americanization thesis would have it (50–51). It is more a question of hybridization, of 'Creolization' or 'cultural reassembly'. Moreover:

> We are all highly selective in our acceptance of other cultures and value systems. We do not simply submit; rather, we use what we want, and discard those elements that are irrelevant to our public and private lives. In this sense, Europe was not thoroughly 'Americanized'. Instead, it adapted American culture to its own traditions and tastes, thereby 'Europeanizing' and domesticating what the United States sought to export (51).

Another explanation of the GATT controversy is offered by Annemoon van Hemel in 'The Complex Debate on Audiovisual Policy' (83–95). Van Hemel compares the development of the American film industry in the postwar period with the history of protectionism in Europe and notes divisions in the European camp with the European Union treating the film industry as an economic activity, the Council of Europe being concerned with culture in international conventions and agreements, while the European Broadcasting Union represents the public service broadcasters. Each of these bodies had its own response to GATT initiatives and objectives. Van Hemel also points out that these responses and positionings are not necessarily fixed but are open to compromise and negotiation. Moreover, the European Union is committed to balancing national and regional differences with emphasizing a common cultural heritage (Article 128 of the European Union agreement). In contrast American interests represent a universal culture. Further complicating the European position is the increasing commercialization of the audiovisual sector. This has seen a retreat of national governments with deregulation and introduction of market services into the public sphere, and an invasion of American interests and products. In this context:

National public service broadcasters have had to adapt their social and cultural objectives to accommodate the wishes of a mass audience (89).

Divisions among member states emerge with some states opposing the French position, the development of a north/south divide, and differences about the role of the state in cultural areas. Other divisive factors are industry based; size of the respective national industries, of audiences, and differences in languages. Mostly the audiovisual industries are advocates of free markets, but against this has to be set the field of cultural policy which is seen by many Europeans as a government responsibility. However, in the audiovisual area national barriers are increasingly being breached with production and distribution often in the hands of international corporations – many American. All these factors are the source of ongoing conflict that emerged during the GATT negotiations.

The theme of globalization shapes Philip Schlesinger's article. He asks, 'Should we Worry about America?' (96–110), and asserts that although the aim of the European Union is to pluralism, it is being 'undermined' by globalizing forces (97). The problem, he suggests, is in how the EU will negotiate its new role of 'sovereign cultural actor' without 'inflaming nationalistic reactions'. It is, he suggests, a conflict between cultural and economic imperatives but, at the same time, he agrees with Pells that European people are less concerned about Americanization than are their governments so we should consider the ways in which Europe 'takes' what is appropriate or acceptable of American culture and rejects the balance (98).

Denis McQuail in 'Transatlantic TV Flow: Another Look at Cultural Cost-Accounting' (111–125), argues that the cultural imperialism debate has obscured the real cause of crisis of European audiovisual industry – a misbalance between global communication flows, and the relations of dependence this establishes between first and third world countries. Moreover, he goes on to claim the debate is 'flawed' being based on fallacious notions about cultural change (111). Instead of seeing Americanization as a result of cultural policy, it should be recognized as a repercussion of industrial policies (112).

The traditional European notion of TV was as a national organization in the service of the community or public interest. 'There is', he goes on:

> No place in such a system for the eccentric, uneconomic and inefficient diversity of European national television. The American way of television is the essence and embodiment of commercialization in its pure market form . . . driven by money, with profit as its primary (and secondary) goal (114).

The American system has qualities and deficiencies. It can produce popular programmes but fails to produce 'challenging topics' – an area in which the European model excels. Consequently:

> American TV is subsidizing Europe culturally and possibly economically, giving Europe the best of both worlds, Old and New. In return, American viewers receive almost nothing of

what Europe has to offer. They also lose out in terms of the cultural specificity and diversity of their own television, partly because of the need to produce for global markets (116).

Turning attention back to America, Rob Kroes looks at the American strategy of cultural imperialism, in 'Advertising: The Commodification of American Icons' (137–147). It is, he suggests, a strategy based on messages of 'Freedom' and a 'New World' era which creates a 'craving for material that could visualize the image' (139). Pictures and images become tools of advertising and in the process 'the iconography of America has become international' (139). American images thus become a 'visual lingua franca'; 'they have been turned into free-floating signifiers, internationally understood, free for everyone to use' (140). But it is not simply a form of collective memory that these images construct, they also form a 'transmission belt' of American culture that carries with it an ideological message, a message 'blending the rationale of capitalism and democratic theory' (142), and where 'the right to choose' represents the 'commodification of political discourse' and these political discourses also confirm and reinforce a commercial culture. He goes on to suggest that the American icons and symbols transcend the nation to become international symbols.

More sectorally oriented views on GATT are presented by William Uricchio who discusses film and national culture, Portia Maultsby and Simon Frith on the music industry, and Vera Zolberg who looks at museums and the internationalization of art. Although concerned with specific cultural sectors, these commentators also contextualize their analysis within the broader frameworks of nation and globalization.

As Uricchio notes in 'Displacing Culture: Transnational Culture, Regional Elites, and the Challenge to National Cinema' (67–80), cultural arguments, historically and today, mask economic interests (67–68) as well as 'tension between the interests of elite and mass culture' (68). Accordingly, the contested nature of national culture is based on differing cultures. In Europe it is language, folklore, and the deep pasts of elites and institutions that give legitimacy to commercial and/or popular culture (68–69); in America it is the experiences of migration, the multiplicity of cultural traditions and power bases, more limited shared traditional and linguistic life, and a more democratic structure (68–69). These differences become translated as differences between authentic and deep culture and more superficial cultural expression – hence the fascination/repulsion that Americans have for European culture, and vice versa. In debates about film culture a parallel transformation occurs; nationalism is deployed in constructing an elite/mass dichotomy. Uricchio asserts that this trend must be transcended in order to address issues of collective national experience and memory (78).

Maultsby looks at 'Intra- and International Identities in American Popular Music' (148–156), and Simon Frith asks: 'Does Music Cross Boundaries?' (157–163). Music is an interesting case for studying intra- and international identities because 'music traditions are expressions of lifestyles shaped by social histories, political systems, class structures, cultural values, and aesthetic ideals' (Maultsby, 148). But music is also subject to external influences so when considering American popular music as a world trade it is necessary to consider the impact of socio cultural forces and technologies on adoption, adaptation and transformation of style, production and marketing of popular music as commodity for national and transnational consumption, and transnational identities (148). Maultsby concludes that: 'The free trade market and western capitalist economic systems provide avenues for cross-cultural and transatlantic musical borrowings in the global market'. The result is a 'transnational hybrid popular musical style, marked by multiple national identities' (155).

Frith, on the other hand suggests it is not technology that is responsible for this phenomenon; it is due to the 'qualities of music – a cultural form unconstrained by national boundaries, mobile in time and place, source of our most intense emotional experience of both social and individual identities' that has enabled the growth of the record industry across borders. He argues that music is defined in terms of ethnicity or sociability (162) rather than in terms of national identity. Because of this capacity to cross national borders fear of globalization is really about market forces (162). Although he concedes there is need for concern, he sees this not as a need to protect content so much as a need to protect national structures of broadcasting, intellectual property rights, and to redress negative impacts on local industrial components – artists, producers, consumers (163).

Museums are perceived as the custodians of national culture, therefore any threat to museums and their content is seen as an attack on a nation's patrimony. Vera Zolberg in 'Museum Culture and the Threat to National Identity in the Age of the GATT' (164–178), examines the fine art world in the context of the internationalization of trade in art works.

Fine art, Zolberg claims, is a commodity like any other, it is increasingly 'portable' and part of the market system and there is a symbiotic relationship between museums and the market – either directly or covertly. Moreover, 'the trend towards loosening national trade barriers to other nations has provided the impetus for rethinking how society considers art and whether art works should receive special protection' (166). It is apparent there are new notions about national identity brought about, largely, with the shift from monocultural to more pluralist ideas about nationalist identities. Museum are inevitably 'intertwined' with this new thinking about nation and national identity (169). She notes that while Europe and third world countries tend to legislate for protective measures for cultural and historical material, this is not the norm for the US where such measures would be seen as interfering in the market. The relationship between art or artefact and national identity, is therefore an area of distinction between Europe in particular and the United States.

The diversity of interpretive frameworks in *Trading Culture* reveals the complexity of cultural policy issues in contestations of nation versus economy, and nation versus nation.

3. Community Cultural Development and Cultural Industries

Although often perceived as contradictory, community and community culture are converging more and more into a cultural industries model. It is a trend that is problematic for many community cultural development workers but one that is welcomed by government agencies as well as many cultural workers – individuals, communal groups and organizations inclusive. Many of the concerns circulating around community cultural development and the cultural industries were explored in a collection of papers originating in a conference (Cultural Policy: The State of the Art) held in Brisbane in 1994 and hosted by the Institute for Cultural Policy Studies (the forerunner of the Australian Key Centre for Cultural and Media Policy). A selection of papers from the conference make up *Cultural Policy Case Studies* edited by Jennifer Craik.

The chosen papers represent the views of a range of commentators, academics, arts/cultural administrators and consultants involved in the cultural field. The editor has chosen papers which 'offered analyses of cultural policy-in-practice' but suggests the gap between theory and practice raises questions about the 'analytical void between cultural policy and public policy' (v). Craik concludes her preface by referring to shifts in the political scene since the Conference and to the politicization of policy making. History, she suggests, demonstrates that attempts to 'underpin cultural policy with conceptual, theoretical and practical girders' appear doomed to be subsumed by external political forces (vi). Among the high ideals that Craik refers to in the various chapters are access and equity, cultural diversity, sustainability, accountability and community.

Christopher Bowen, in 'Cultural Diversity in the Arts: Potentials and Problems' (1–12) examines ways in which a multicultural policy has been introduced into arts and cultural policy, mainly to comply with social justice principles and policy. Bowen perceives various potentials for advancing diversity in the arts but also acknowledges that public policy 'is framed in a value-laden domain' (see also Davis et al., 1993:2) and that adding 'culture' exacerbates subjectivity and the irrationality of policy making. Nevertheless, he concludes on a positive note that, despite contestation and scepticism, principles of diversity are slowly being recognized and incorporated into policy in the Australian context.

'Community' and its articulation in respect to regional cultural policy, and to development of community museums is explored by Helen Tyzack in 'Policy Inclusions and Exclusions: Whose Agenda?' (79–88) and Jane Lennon in 'Hidden Heritage: A Development Plan for Museums in Queensland 1995–2001' (55–78). Tyzak looks at contemporary developments in regional Queensland to assess 'the extent to which community policies are from and for the community' (79). Like Lennon, Tyzak's primary interest is the museum/art gallery and who makes policy, the subsequent content of that policy and the interests such policies might serve. Her study shows that:

> The initiative for policy has not been a grassroots, broad groundswell development; rather, it has come from a few, and mostly from motivations which are not firstly concerned with community benefits ... The reality is that policies which claim to be community policies are including most of the goals of councils, but only some of the community's goals. The degree of access by the community to the opportunity for contributions is a major issue. It has a direct bearing on whose agendas are reflected in the final policy document (88).

Lennon, on the other hand, provides a descriptive account of the development of a specific plan. This was an outcome of a broad policy reform
agenda in Queensland during the early 1990s and a subsequent assessment
of regional and community museums – their needs and the needs of their
respective communities – and an access and equity survey. The major issues
revealed by the assessment were: marginalization of museums *vis-à-vis* arts,
extensive collection management problems, a paucity of trained staff (both
paid and voluntary), lack of access to training (particularly for volunteers),
little recourse of marketing, and low levels of funding and local government
support. For the balance of the article, Lennon outlines the recommended
steps to address these deficiencies and shortfalls, and at the same time
proposes a statewide museums' policy. Of interest is a cultural industries
inflection to the recommendations with four of the eight recommendations
having an 'industry' agenda aimed at moving museums into cultural tourism.
There is an emphasis on industry training, development of a cultural tourism
strategy with community museums being nominated as important components of such a strategy, professionalization of the sector to enable museums
to contribute to the economic resources of their respective communities, and
industrialization of the sector to assist in the development of an integrated
cultural industry (69–77).

An extension of the community and access theme is picked up in Ruth
Rentschler's study of the role of local governments in the management of
local collections (29–54). Renthschler's research is concerned with how
'creatively' local government collections are currently being managed, how
this might compare with 'best practices', and what might be the impact of
change on such collection management practices (34).

Specific cultural policies are also examined. Tim Jacobs looks at a state
policy: '*Arts 21* – The Victorian Government's Strategy for the Arts' (15–28);
Helen Millicer describes a local government cultural programme put in place
by the City of Wyndham (a municipality of metropolitan Melbourne) that
implements a cultural policies approach (111–125); Richard Brecknock
evaluates South Australian cultural policy with an emphasis on regional and
local government cultural planning and the need for an integrated approach
with all tiers of government working together (89–96); and Francois Matarasso examines the process of implementing a cultural policy framework for
Belfast.

Arts 21 is Victoria's cultural policy directed at developing the state's arts
and cultural sectors along a cultural industries model and to bring cultural
policy into line with broader policy aims of restoring public and business
confidence, revitalizing economic social and cultural life, reforming and
rebuilding public infrastructures, and redefining the role of government and
its agencies so as to create the climate for prosperity (17). The Victorian
strategy is somewhat re-ordered in the Belfast approach described by
Matarasso. Here the strategy comprised both a cultural and an economic
agenda directed at integrating community cultural development with a 'new
model' for urban regeneration – one that puts 'people's creativity' and
'social regeneration' as a necessary precursor to regenerating the urban
infrastructure and its economy (103–104). It was the aim of the strategy,
therefore 'to promote social and urban regeneration in Belfast by enhancing

community confidence through access to and control of arts activity at neighbourhood level' (Matarasso, 1995, quoted 104).

These reports from the 'coal face' touch, sometimes fleetingly, on the themes of this review – community, cultural industries, cultural development – and the complex interaction between theory and practice. As noted in the introduction, there is evidence of a convergence of community cultural development (CCD) with the cultural industries. An article from *Cultural Policy* by Thomas Tresser illustrates this through an American case study. In 'How Do the Arts Build Communities?' (Vol. 3, No. 1, 145–162), Tresser writes of the interest in the United States in bringing together cultural planning and community development and undertakes an overview of this process through a study of Community Development Corporations (CDCs).

CDCs are non-profit organizations which are dedicated to developing their respective communities. In 1996 there were approximately 3000 CDCs in the United States, located in urban and regional areas, and targeting low income earners (145). These organizations developed over 300,000 units of housing, have been responsible for 90,000 jobs 1986–91 and have also lent money to support micro enterprises. They are lobbyists, community organizers, counsellors, provide health services, youth programmes and a range of community building work (145–146).

In charting the development of a typical CDC organization – Peoples Housing, Chicago – Tresser shows how initially concerns were centred on basic housing justice, acquisition of properties and property renovations. The organization then moved on to incorporate into its agenda community development and civic improvement projects (146–147). In the late 1980s the organisation's management started to investigate what might make a community strong and concluded that critical factors were: a stock of affordable and decent housing units, safe and neighbourly streetscapes, strong and effective public school system, and *a set of vibrant and accessible cultural resources*. This represented a shift from physical to human development for People's Housing – from buildings to 'human development, community coalition building, crime and safety projects, gang intervention, programs and economic development' (147).

Tresser stresses the importance of the local in the relationship between student/teacher so 'we should strive to employ artists who live in, or close by, our neighborhoods whenever possible'; and the empowerment power of arts projects which can give people 'a voice to speak out and express themselves'. Moreover, arts programmes for youth can, from this perspective, provide alternatives to anti-social activities or even rehabilitating juvenile offenders (150–151).

CPCs also offer opportunities for community input into the physical infrastructure of the community and in this respect Peoples Housing has generated over $23 million of work in fifteen years and Tresser notes the diversity of possibilities for involving creative art and craft work, in design, landscaping, interior and exterior finishing, apprenticeships, and for-profit enterprises such as a tile-making project at Peoples Housing which has grown to a small business designing hand-made tiles (152–153). CPCs not only provide public spaces but nurture them and promote community use of such spaces (154–155).

More directly referring to the cultural industries are two more articles from *Cultural Policy*: Robert Hewison's 'Cultural Policy and the Heritage Business' (Vol. 3, No. 1, 1–13); and Howard Hughes and Danielle Benn's article on 'Tourism and Cultural Policy: The Case of Seaside Entertainment in Britain' (Vol. 3, No. 2, 235–255).

Hewison's engagement with the 'heritage debate' which has raged since the mid-1970s turns here to incorporate this with the cultural policy debate. First, he observes that the term and the idea of 'cultural policy' is anathema to the British way of thinking informed, as it is, by an outmoded romantic ideal of culture as 'organic' and rooted in some vague and unattainable historically authentic past; and representing an over-reaction to the term 'cultural policy' because of its association with totalitarian regimes (1–2).

Hewison notes, ironically, 'Britain has had a policy of not having a cultural policy ever since January 1940 when the Board of Education decided that, in the face of German aggression, it was essential: "to show publicly and unmistakably that the government cares about the cultural life of the country"' (Levinthal, 1990, quoted 2). However, the cultural policy and supporting ideals, structures and funding, he characterizes, in Lord Keynes words, as 'informal, unostentatious and decidedly half-baked' (2) but one which he goes on to suggest has some virtues: 'It is gradualist, it is pragmatic, it is empirical, it is founded on tradition and precedent, above all it is pluralistic. It is indeed, organic, in that as a system, like Topsy, it just growed'. But, despite these 'virtues' – or because of them – he asserts that the system is in crisis (3).

The catalyst for the crisis, according to Hewison, was the Thatcherite revolution that brought about first, a breakdown in consensus regarding culture; and second, a slide into a market-driven notion of the arts with the subsequent commoditization that has 'so deformed our thinking that the only value judgment we are prepared to make is that of "value for money"' (4). With the new Department of National Heritage in place by 1996 Hewison claims there were no indications of a 'coherent policy' (5) and that the munificence of the National Lottery falling to culture has not only been mismanaged but has also been used to replace government funding programmes. Exacerbating this has been the use of Lottery money to fund capital development and while this, in itself, might have been a positive step, it is enabling buildings to be restored and refurbished while funding for operations is cut or non-existent. Hewison proposes, simply, that Lottery money be gradually redirected from capital development to revenue funding through an endowment strategy (7–13).

The Hughes and Benn article is important too because it flags a new direction in cultural policy, that of the cultural industries, and within that framework, the increasing interest in tourism as a cultural activity and in cultural activities as sources of revenue. The initial points that the writers make regarding the, until recently, exclusion of 'entertainment' from the concerns of cultural policy, represent a number of issues picked up by other writers considered in this review – particularly the themes of cultural industries, new social classes and their cultural needs and wants, and the expansion of the notion of culture.

Hughes and Benn consider an area not generally seen as germane to cultural policy – local government support for entertainment at seaside resorts – but point out that there has been a long history of local government involvement in culture at these locations (235). Moreover, seaside resorts have traditionally had a strong 'cultural' element evident in professional theatres and forms of popular entertainment. After a peak period for the seaside resorts, mass consumption and competition from other leisure forms, as well as attractions of overseas holidays and more 'novelty' activities, led to a decline in visitors, and shorter visits (especially a growth in day visitors). Urry (1990) has suggested another factor has been the decline in 'spectacles' and the 'extraordinary' that once characterized seaside resorts. Alongside the decline of the resort itself there has also been a decline in entertainment at these centres.

This article focuses on the issue of entertainment in tourism and the, to date, concentration on high arts and heritage as the important content areas of cultural tourism and the subsequent failure to engage with those forms of culture which are categorized as 'entertainment' because of the 'overtones of being light, pleasurable and undemanding'. Hughes and Benn, then, are concerned with redressing this gap: 'the concern of this paper, however, is the viewing of light performances of presentations such as variety shows, band concerts, cabaret, musicals, street performance, pop concerts, circus and similar activities' (238).

The writers conclude:

> Entertainment is conventionally considered to be the concern of the private sector: the seaside resort is a special case however and entertainment needs to be part of the local government's cultural policy ... the economic rationale has always been dominant: issues relating to preservation of cultural heritage, increasing access, community involvement and the encouragement of local cultures have not featured in seaside cultural policies in the same way that they have in national or inland city deliberations ... this economic perspective may need to be reconciled with other issues relating to culture policy ... linking the debate on the future of cities ... to that on the future of citizenship and local democracy – This grand vision applies as much to coastal holiday towns as it does to cities (251).

4. Decentralization

One aspect of decentralization is the shift from state to market in the provision, administration and regulation of cultural resources. The American model of philanthropy has been taken up as a model for governments intent on rolling back their responsibilities for funding art and culture. In an issue of *Cultural Policy*, (Vol. 3, No. 2, 207–232) Joan Jeffri provides valuable insight into the development and contemporary position of philanthropy in 'Philanthropy and the American Artist: A Historical Overview'.

In tracing the origins for American philanthropy, Jeffri points to a number of factors: the diversity of ethnic and racial groups involved in the traditional 'melting pot', the struggle and efforts of the lucky few to establish social status in a new society and one where the social infrastructures (libraries, museums, universities, voluntary associations, etc.) were put in place by the private sector 'with the government as a (sometimes late and sometimes reluctant) partner' (208); and English precedent with its classed notions of social responsibility. On the artists' side, they have largely had fluctuating fortunes and contradictory images, ranging from that of prosperous citizen, to pauperized struggler or even perceived as 'threats to a democratic society' (208). Their roles have been seen as critical to the nation or irrelevant and unworthy of government subsidy. For the most part, however, there was 'a lack of critical discourse about art in the United States' (209).

Jeffri's history covers the period of establishment of key endowments such as the Smithsonian, the growth of philanthropy in the nineteenth century and development of a close relationship between artists and the corporate world by the early twentieth century. When tax incentives were introduced in 1913 this move, Jeffri contends, was responsible in large part for the growth of private philanthropy. Roosevelt's New Deal did, however, bring the state into a supporting relationship with the arts and under this regime philanthropy became the subject of scrutiny and distrust, being seen as 'self serving and manifesting societal control rather than altruism'.

Jeffri asserts that by the time of the postwar period 'cultural competition and the Cold War propelled the United States towards federal arts support' (220) and by the 1950s a 'high-water decade for foundations' had been reached. By the 1960s, however, federal and local government had started to set up arts agencies and also had become more involved in public/private partnerships. This interventionary trend was confirmed in 1965 with the establishment of the National Foundation for the Arts and Humanities (with its dual public bodies, the National Endowment for the Arts (NEA) and the National Endowment for the Humanities). This represented a watershed in cultural policy development in America and confirmed the combination of private and public sector support for culture.

Arts crises in the 1980s were represented by lack of funds for non-profit organizations (including drastic cuts to NEA), AIDS which brought the need for more money to help afflicted artists, the fear of privatization and debates about public versus private funding, and finally censorship and the cultural wars. These events, especially the cultural wars have had their effects on philanthropy:

> Political conservatism, a gradual dilution of social programs starting with President Reagan, economic downsizing by corporations, and finally the very public discussion about the morality of taxpayer money supporting 'obscene and offensive art' – whether legally justified or not – had caused the issues of multiculturalism and changing demographics to make it seem as though there were at least two different Americas (231).

Jeffri concludes that it will have to be seen whether philanthropy (corporate and private) will re-emerge from this period of withdrawal. Of especial interest in this account is Jeffri's inclusion of women and black artists.

5. Theory and Practice

In *Culture and the Public Sphere*, Jim McGuigan moves the discussion of cultural policy into a more theoretically informed debate. His mission is to examine how cultural studies addresses cultural policy which he defines broadly as being about 'the politics of culture in the most general sense; it is about the clash of ideas, institutional struggles and power relations in the production and circulation of symbolic meanings'. He also sets out to critique what he describes as an 'agenda mapped out for "cultural policy studies" in Australia' (1), an agenda which takes as its informing theory, the work of Michel Foucault. In its stead, McGuigan proposes a 'more critical approach' (2) based on Jürgen Habermas's notion of culture. This, then, is a contrast of Foucauldian cultural policy with a cultural studies approach based on Habermass' notion of culture which, McGuigan claims, is not only more critical but is also 'corrective to a certain kind of instrumentalism which is implicit in the economic reductionisms and technological determinisms that frame much policy debate in the cultural field' (28). While *Culture and the Public Sphere* occasionally looks beyond Britain (America and the culture wars, Australian cultural policy studies, and French nationalizing strategies), it is, in essence, an overview of cultural policy in Britain; an overview that incorporates an historical perspective but concentrates more expressly on issues which are germane to contemporary cultural policy.

In the subsequent nine chapters, McGuigan examines: (1) cultural policy studies; (2) cultural values; (3) the shift from state to market; (4) the cultural industries; (5) urban regeneration; (6) national heritage; (7) identity, 'race' and citizenship; (8) censorship and moral regulation; and (9) the public sphere. While his study covers the key issues in cultural policy debates, what is more important for McGuigan is the interpretive and theoretical frameworks. Taking what have become traditional interpretations of the cultural policy field, McGuigan offers a set of evaluative analyses informed by a Habermassian understanding of culture.

In discussing cultural policy studies (5–29) McGuigan refers to certain 'constraints' on cultural policy. His concern is about too close an association with 'regulatory processes' (5). He puts this issue in the context of differences between Foucauldian and Habermassian theories, the former associated with postmodernism and poststructuralism, the latter with an ongoing modernism. Of concern to McGuigan is the Australian 'cultural policy school' (originating with Tony Bennett et al. at the Australian Key Centre for Cultural and Media Policy) which takes as its theoretical base, Foucault's notion of governmentality. The Key Centre's aims are to bring together theory and practice and, just as importantly, to bring into a fruitful relationship academia, government and industry. McGuigan contests the theoretical underpinning of the Key Centre's programme which he describes as an attempt to replace Raymond Williams' use of 'culture' and a neo-Gramscian critique of cultural practices with a form of cultural studies that is more 'useful' and one which perceives culture 'as a historically specific set of institutionally embedded relations of governments' (Bennett, 1992:26). The implications of positioning both culture and power in this way is first, to broaden the concept of government beyond the state apparatuses to include power/knowledge relations and 'the mechanisms of social management' (14), second, to perceive culture, and its regulation as diffused throughout society and its institutions – hence Foucault (and Bennett's) use of the term 'capillary' action in respect to both power and dispersion of cultural capacities (Foucault, 1981:92–93 and Bennett, 1995). A consequence of the Foucauldian framework is recourse to the notion of 'cultural technologies' – these include institutional structures and processes whereby power is constructed and employed. McGuigan joins other critics of the Australian cultural policy studies movement who have suggested that under this rubric too close an association is formed between agencies of the state and academia that leads to an uncritical, instrumental agenda where academic pursuit becomes the pawn of government.

McGuigan finally returns to his critique of a Foucauldian approach for its instrumentalist nature and because it promotes a 'deliberate lack of normative purpose' (176). His aim in this study is to apply:

> certain norms of social criticism and democratic egalitarianism to a number of concrete and substantive issues of cultural policy ... to identify and interrogate urgent issues of cultural policy from the point of view of an emancipatory knowledge interest ... [not] to come up with a handy set of immediately practical policy proposal (176–177).

He is not concerned with policy proposals *per se*, but with policy 'as an object of praxis, an object of theoretical interpretation and of public debate' (177).

In discussing the strengths and weaknesses of various approaches to cultural studies and cultural policy McGuigan argues for a Habermassian framework as more valuable for evaluating 'formation of cultural and governmental relations according to modern principles of democracy' (21) on the basis of Habermas's work and his belief in the power of liberal democracy, the citizenry and 'the public will'. He proposes a Habermassian approach to cultural policy 'as a corrective to a certain kind of instrumentalism which is implicit in the economic reductionisms and technological determinisms that frame much policy debate in the cultural field and from which a critical political economy of the media is not always immune' (28).

McGuigan then proceeds to review and unpack contemporary issues in cultural policy and, looking first at questions of value, he sets out to address Bourdieu's sociological argument regarding the production of cultural 'tastes' and 'dispositions' that have become the basis of bourgeois aesthetic cultural value. His intent here is to re-evaluate Bourdieu's notions in the light of contemporary culture and cultural developments – the collapse or blurring of boundaries between high art and popular culture, new methods and patterns of consumption, the hybridization of cultural forms and the blurring of class differences. After reviewing various explanations of class and 'classed culture' – ranging from Marxian and neo-Marxian to Galbraith's 'new class' argument, Wright's 'contradictory class locations', Ehrenrichs' and Pfeif's 'professional managerial class thesis' and Jameson's 'postmodernist' position – McGuigan reasserts the Habermassian argument that economic political structures are increasingly intruding into everyday life to impose a 'communicative rationality'. This involves practical and moral agencies, democratic and participatory processes, and the resources of cultural tradition' (Habermass, 1990:401 quoted 47).

In 'State to Market' (51–73) McGuigan looks at the reasons for the shift of regulation of social and cultural life from state to market and from dominance of national economies to global and international. More specifically, he is concerned with the increasing intrusion of market reasoning into the public sector. His exploration of this is undertaken by an analysis of the BBC in which he identifies a shift in discourse from public arts patronage to a new rhetoric of public service delivery that promises value for money, access and choice.

Under Reagan and Thatcher, not only was the state 'rolled back' but it was, according to McGuigan, also 'rolled forward with the insertion of 'the new managementialism and market reasoning into the state and state-related agencies of the public sector' (62). This ideology was quickly 'normalized' in the public sector of art and culture and this has enabled a new visioning that accepts market forces as determinants of cultural activity and forms. Nevertheless, McGuigan concludes that this shift from state to market has been resisted in some areas and not been completely successful, in fact: 'The effect of business sponsorship has been rather more ideological than material' (72).

This leads McGuigan to a consideration of the cultural industries (74–95). The notion of culture as an industry is not only inherent to the New Right economics and ideology but has also been taken up by factions of the Left who have drawn on the neo-Marxian line associated with Benjamin and Brechtian notions that the new technologies in communications are 'more democratic' than traditional forms of high culture. A 'socializing' of the market has grown out of attempts to broaden access to arts and to stimulate community arts. Various strategies have linked cultural industries with urban regeneration. Moreover, policy shifts around the issue of access have emphasized 'a materialist model of cultural exchange, signified by a terminology of "industry" and "markets"' (83). These processes have seen a 'coalescence of goals and objectives of Left and Right' and the emergence of a cultural industries model based on what Simon Frith (1991, 145) has described as a symbiotic relationship between 'small/creative/marginal' groups and 'big/exploitative/central' organizations (87).

The chapter on urban regeneration (95–115) develops the cultural industries issue further by examining in more detail the question of urban regeneration and how this might be linked to culture, cultural development, and cultural policy. Taking up Ken Worpole's contention that 'urban policy' is now 'inseparable from cultural policy' (1991:143) and David Harvey's view that contemporary emphasis on culture 'has directed attention away from the general problem' (1993a:14) of wealth creation, McGuigan's aim is to show that there is, in fact, no contradiction between these two positions. He does this by focusing on: (1) globalization and localization and relationship to urban culture and economy; (2) the connection between urban regeneration strategies and cultural policy; and (3) civic boosterism and the connection with social unrest and marginalization (96). In respect to these three themes, he also identifies two models of urban regeneration – the American and the European; the former inspiring 'conservative central government policies' that tend to promote 'private-property-led redevelopment strategies and out-of-town leisure and retailing complexes' and the latter 'an alternative approach for the more ambitious Labour-controlled local authorities' which have favoured 'attempts to recover the city centre for public culture' and to revitalize 'the public realm' (104). There are, obviously, differing implications for cultural policy under these two models – the former neutralizing or reducing the need for public policy, the latter linking with a broad social-democratic agenda and broader notions of culture to incorporate quality of life and with 'ideas of expanding one's mental horizons, of experiment, adventure, discovery, surprise' (Bianchini and Schwengel, 1991:229, quoted 104).

McGuigan goes on to examine urban cultural policies in Europe and Britain, the ways in which 'a new consensus regarding culture, economy and policy at regional and local levels' has been forged (106). However, as a study by Franco Bianchini and Michael Parkinson revealed, in spite of the rhetoric and aims there has been little direct economic benefit from policy-led developments. McGuigan appears to support Bianchini's advocacy for a holistic approach to urban cultural planning, one that is democratic and creates 'conditions for the emergence of a genuinely public, political discourse about their future [the city's], which should go beyond the conformist platitudes of the visions formulated by the new breed of civic boosters and municipal marketers' (1991 quoted 108).

In looking at heritage (116–134), McGuigan enters a long running debate, one which has raged in Britain since the mid-1970s. Along with those whose work he critiques, he sees heritage in less than glowing terms. Rather it is:

> An international phenomenon promoted by governments concerned with national identity and tourist revenue and, also, by the commercial exploitation of ubiquitous and popular fascination with the past in diverse forms of entertainment, including theme parks and the nostalgia mode in cinema, television, music, fashion, home decoration and furnishings (118).

He points out that the 'heritage' around which this particular discourse has largely been constructed was that of an aristocratic class but with elements of working class heritage 'appropriated' into the fabric of British heritage so as to become the leisure grounds of a general middle-class public or, where gentrification has occurred, the domestic residences of middle-class yuppies. Mythologizing of this constructed heritage works across classes to construct a national consensus (Hewison 1995, Wright, 1985 and 1992). Yet as a form of popular culture, McGuigan sees heritage as 'anti-elitist' and as with other forms of popular culture, 'in creative tension with, though not necessarily direct opposition to, mass-consumer culture' (126). He, nevertheless, sees as problematic the commercialization of heritage, especially as this is 'creeping' into the public sector. This is particularly evident in museums where museum products are promoted as 'cliched versions of the nation' incorporated to attract foreign tourists, while 'cliches of other nations are absorbed and re-articulated for internal consumption' (129).

Heritage, of course, includes the material (and ideas) of the past found in collecting institutions and this leads McGuigan into an engagement with various museum-oriented debates around the museum versus the theme park and with debates about the changing purpose and positioning of museums *vis-à-vis* popularization, traditional museum roles and functions, representation and postcolonialism, authenticity etc. He draws on Robert Lumley's agenda of issues (1988): postmodernism, representation, audience-related issues of interpretation and communications, commercialization, authenticity and media and its new and expanding technologies. He concludes with Kevin Walsh's argument, and we assume, agrees with this view, that there is need for a 'renewal of public responsibility towards the past and the principles of a critical "new museology" to be applied' (134) and that entertainment and education be balanced and openly accessible 'at the point of consumption' (134).

In regard to social policies, McGuigan rewrites the history of social policies in Britain in the second half of the century. He comments on how the categories of identity, race, and citizenship have become issues of concern as the Cartesian self has dissolved into a twentieth-century self that is 'for ever in flux' (135), while the solidity and certainty of the national state has been undermined so as to make the notion of citizenship more complex and more problematic. In such a climate, McGuigan points out that 'cultural policy may seek to address these matters in a desperate attempt to keep abreast of shifting conceptions of identity, "race" and "citizenship" but that inevitably "cultural politics vastly outpaces the lumbering discourses of cultural policy"' (136). He focuses on the shift from multiculturalism and anti-racism of the 1970s and 1980s as a response to earlier assimilationist policies, to 'the new cultural politics of difference'. He agrees with Stuart Hall's suggestion that what has happened has been a shift from 'nationalism' to 'ethnicity' (1987, 1988b) and a shift from 'a struggle over the relations of representation to a politics of representation' (1988b quoted 140).

In reviewing the literature and debates on race relations, and on the black diaspora, McGuigan identifies the emergence of an internationalized 'black cultural space' formed from the common experiences of oppression, exclusion and struggle. These experiences have enabled the transcendence of national public spheres (142).

In then engaging with the citizenship debate McGuigen moves on to explore the historical shifts in the meaning of 'citizen' and 'civilization' and the resultant contestation around these concepts (147–153). Drawing on Hazel Carby (1992) and Kobena Mercer (1994), he asserts that:

> The relationship between identity and citizenship, then, is at the heart of the matter whether we are talking about the cultural constructions of the self or the rights to cultural resources that contribute to the politics of changing material conditions. Cultural rights should also, however, and much less instrumentally, be about our sense of human dignity and meaning, the pleasures and knowledges that make life tolerable (147).

Again he resorts to Habermas and his notions of citizenship as involving 'social emancipation in order to rectify injustice' (150), the need for 'open and sensitive' decision making, and for 'interplay between institutionalized processes of opinion and will formation and [those] informal networks of public communication' if citizenship is to be 'more than an aggregation of pre-political individual interests and passive enjoyment of rights bestowed upon the individual by the paternalist authority of the state' (Habermas, 1994b quoted 151).

McGuigan's concern in respect to censorship is less to do with its immediate effects and more to do with censorship as a form of moral regulation and as a way of constructing normality (Rojek, 1995 quoted 155). More specifically, he looks at 'inovert forms of censorship' – the panopticon and the market (157), and the 'two faces of surveillance' – one concerned with governance of the welfare state and the other with social control and consumer exploitation (Rojek, 1995 quoted 158) and the associated decline of the public sphere. Recalling George Gerbner, and Habermas, McGuigan appears to support a call for 'the construction or reconstruction of a public sphere in the field of culture to articulate issues that routinely affect everyone's lives on a daily basis' and 'for more public participation in making decisions about cultural investment and cultural policy' (Gerbner, 1995 quoted 175).

Culture and the Public Sphere is a timely assessment of cultural policy and McGuigan undertakes a comprehensive review of the literature on contemporary issues, melding them into his objective – the re-evaluation of theory and the relationship between cultural studies and cultural policy studies.

It is also timely for a review of cultural policy practice and in 'Deconstructing the Difference-Engine: A Theory of Cultural Policy' in *Cultural Policy* (Vol. 2, No. 2, 189–212), Michael Volkerling undertakes a comparative study of the history of cultural policy in Britain, New Zealand, Canada and Australia. Defining cultural policy as 'purposive action by the state in the cultural', Volkerling brings together arts, culture and sport to identify an assemblage of what he calls the modern 'leisure economy'. Volkerling advances four principles: (1) the state maintains a cultural capital strategy aimed at maintaining a hegemonic coalition; (2) cultural policy represents the state's commitment to culture and to the social relations that culture constructs and maintains; (3) policy authority is a discursive construct where public agencies are responsible for defining what is culturally significant and allocating funding accordingly; and (4) that there has been a shift from subsidized art production to contemporary policy concern with consumption and also a shift of focus from 'high culture' to cultural diversity. The analysis is based on four periods – Foundational, Professional, Reaction and Incorporation, and a transformative period between Fordist and post-Fordist forms of economic and social organization (194).

During the 'Foundational' period Britain adopted an 'idealist' notion of culture. This shaped a cultural policy 'derived from the interaction between the cultural preferences and values of its leisured middle class and postwar state welfarism', and became a model for the former colonies (195). This 'idealism' was maintained through the Arts Council's system of peer assessment and post-war 'cultural welfarism' when public money promoted links between 'high culture and the National-Popular' (196). In the exportation of the model, however, Volkerling suggests, a more 'altruistic' motive came to the fore while also under the banner of welfarism state support for high culture 'emerged as a status culture of a class in formation' (DiMaggio, 1992 quoted 197) – in this case – the 'new Professional middle class' or 'Salaried middle class' (Enerenreich, 1979 and Gould, 1981, respectively).

During the 'Professional' period questions were raised around the questions of class, ethnicity and region and the Eurocentric nature of the arts tradition. There were calls for 'cultural democracy' that generated a raft of arts policies with a social democratic flavour. Volkerling notes that the discourse of this period was predominantly 'materialistic'; it proposed closer relations between culture and community and, in Britain, there was advocacy for increased government involvement in sport and recreation which was motivated by aspirations to use these areas not only for expression but also for social control (198). This period saw new institutional structures (or modifications of established structures), new professional categories, as well as conflict between the new materialist view and traditional idealistic notions of culture (198–199). Community cultural development was a child of the period as were cultural diversity policies and strategies, cultural planning and management programmes, and new governmental strategies. It was a period which also saw the professionalization of cultural policy but as the new professionals espousing new policies and practices moved into the cultural policy-making areas the welfare system, which was critical to their agenda, started to come apart (200).

A transformed political economy enabled the organization of new 'cultural power relations' and the emergence of a 'new constellation of interests' – finance, capital, the professional and bureaucratic middle classes – and ensured the reshaping of culture to include 'social' consumption of high culture and material consumption of leisure products and activities. Niche market products, internationalization of consumption and an expansion of cultural goods and services – all are designed for specialist rather than mass markets and to meet the needs and desires of those new middle classes. Accompanying the transformation is also a restructuring of the public cultural sector to minimize government involvement and funding of culture, promoting a mixed economy of culture, emphasizing accountability, splitting of policy and delivery functions, and contracting out of services (202).

In the period of consolidation of the market society and appropriate values (entrepreneurship, spectacularization, individualism and new forms of 'cultural capital') a new phase has been entered that evokes a new form of nationalism. Along with this, cultural policy is increasingly privatized and incorporated into the commercial world and culture itself is now being 'mediated through the marketplace and through commercial transnational telecommunications companies to which the state is an accessory' (207).

Volkerling concludes that in the last fifty years in Britain, as well as in its former dominion states, 'the educated middle classes have been the primary beneficiaries of the state's cultural policies' (207); that policy in the initial phase 'concealed a two nation strategy' wherein a subsidized middle class culture was distinguished from other social groupings. However, when cultural diversity became the policy objective, it has again been the middle classes (but mostly a new faction of the middle classes) who have benefited from opening up of new leisure products and services. He agrees, with Oliver Bennett (1995) that what is required is a 'new vision' of cultural policy but that this will only be possible in a transformed political economy capable of creating a 'hegemonic coalition' (208).

Conclusion

The above key texts and selected writings show that cultural policy is an extraordinarily dynamic field, partly because its theoretical frameworks are under constant review but, more critically, due to the interaction of cultural policy with broader public policy areas. Moreover, in a period of rapid technological change more pressures are imposed on the material conditions of cultural production. Management of cultural resources, in these changing contexts, is therefore a challenge for policy makers, and an area of critical analysis not only *of* cultural policy but also *for* cultural policy.

Books Reviewed

Craik, Jennifer (ed.) *Cultural Policy Case Studies.* Australian Key Centre for Cultural and Media Policy, Brisbane. pp. 125. A$15.00. ISBN 0 868 57766 9.

Darder, Antonia (ed.) (1996). *Culture and Difference. Cultural Perspectives on the Bicultural Experience in the United States.* Bergin & Garvey Inc. pp. 266. A$69.50. ISBN 0 89789 384 0.

Dorland, Michael (ed.) (1996). *The Cultural Industries in Canada. Problems, Policies and Prospects.* James Lorimer & Company. pp. 376. A$24.95. ISBN 1 55028 494 0.

Griffiths, Franklyn. *Strong and Free. Canada and the New Sovereignty.* Stoddart Publishing Co. Limited. pp. 106. A$19.95. ISBN 0 7737 5798 8.

Henighan, Tom (1996). *The Presumption of Culture.* Raincoast Book Distribution Ltd. pp. 143. ISBN 1 55192 013 1.

McGuigan, Jim (1996). *Culture and the Public Sphere.* Routledge. pp. 220. $75.00. ISBN 0 415 11262 1.

Van Hemel, Annemoon, Hans Mommaas and Cas Smithuijsen, (eds) (1996). *Trading Culture. GATT, European Cultural Policies and the Transatlantic Market.* Boekman Foundation. pp. 191. NLG30. ISBN 0 96650 046 8.

18

Aboriginal Identity, Culture and Art

DENISE CUTHBERT, SUSAN LOWISH,
STEPHEN PRITCHARD AND CERIDWEN SPARK

This essay has nine sections: 1. Introduction; 2. Making and Unmaking Histories; 3. Pauline Hanson and the 'Resurgence' of Racism; 4. Stolen Children; 5. Aboriginality and Emplacement: Home, Travel and Tourism; 6. Media, Representation and Identity; 7. Aboriginality, Law and Legislature; 8. Aboriginal Art; 9. Education.

1. Introduction

While there are clear lines of continuity between works published in 1997 and the work discussed in previous reviews (*YWCCT 4, 5, 6*), there is also a number of striking lines of departure which mark the profundity of the change in political climate in the year following the election in March 1996 of the Liberal/National coalition government led by John Howard. Many of the works published in the year under review, including major reports such as the final report of the Human Rights and Equal Opportunity Commission's inquiry into forced Aboriginal and Torres Strait Islander child removal (reviewed below), began in a climate radically different from that which prevailed as they were being concluded and published. Some writers struggle to account for the paradigm shift in what appear to be hastily rewritten conclusions or afterwords; others are defeated by lengthy publication lead times with words appearing in 1997 which quite simply no longer apply to the situation. Engaged criticism of contemporary cultural and political issues always runs this risk: nothing is fixed and precisely because change can be precipitated by critique, the imperative for criticism remains paramount and more urgent than ever before. While to a large degree reeling palpably from the impact of a return to regressive policies particularly in the conduct of Aboriginal and Torres Strait Islander affairs and a resurgence of racism, it must be said that the Australian intellectual community rallied quickly with trenchant criticism of the return to what Deborah Bird Rose has, in an exceptionally fine essay ('Dark Times and Excluded Bodies in the Colonisation of Australia' in Geoffrey Gray and Christine

Winter, eds. *The Resurgence of Racism: Howard, Hanson and the Race Debate*, pp. 97–116, reviewed below), characterized as 'dark times'.

The darkness in Australian culture and politics has and continues to intensify, prompting Tony Birch, an indigenous critic, commenting on the gaps between the promises of postcolonial theorizations and the lived experience of Aboriginal and Torres Strait Islander people, to observe that postcolonialism remains merely a job held down by a few academics in the Australian context and has little or nothing to do with (or say about) the situation in which indigenous people find themselves in this decidedly colonial society ('Black Armbands and White Veils': John Howard's Moral Amnesia', *Melbourne Historical Journal*, 25:8–16). In our view, it is important not to read Birch as advocating a binary between lived indigenous experience and academic theory (as if there are neither indigenous academics nor theorists). He is, we argue, calling for more engaged and committed theory to account for and to assist in the task of transforming Australian culture and politics and creating new and different possibilities for Aboriginal people and communities within contemporary Australia. Many of the works reviewed below amply signal this prospect; not least because of the speed with which their authors have changed tack to outrun ill winds.

In terms of threads of continuity, 1997 sees the continuation of a number of debates and important areas of research and inquiry. In the legal area, questions of land rights, protection of Aboriginal cultural and intellectual property rights and heritage sites as well the ongoing challenge of achieving compensation for the policies of former governments in areas such as the forced removal of Aboriginal and Torres Strait Islander children continue to receive attention. In the areas of art and media, questions of representation and authenticity are addressed by a range of writers, including practitioners and critics. Issues pertaining to the relationship between traditional Aboriginal forms of cultural production and forms which have been adapted are also considered in relationship to the visual arts and other forms of artistic expression. Beyond these areas, there is a body of literature reviewed below which takes up – from a variety of viewpoints – questions concerning the place and emplacement of Aboriginality in the Australian landscape and cities and the significance of 'hybrid' Aboriginality and urban Aboriginal culture, experience and identity. A small number of publications deal with Aboriginality and education: both the education of Aboriginal people and the place of Aboriginality in mainstream curricula in schools and universities.

2. Making and Unmaking Histories

A public debate on the status of history and the politics of Australian historiography occupied significant space in the first year of John Howard's prime ministership. The debate uneasily reflected the contribution made by revisionist histories (as discussed by Bain Attwood and others in his edited collection *In the Age of Mabo*, Allen & Unwin, 1996, reviewed *YWCCT 6*) to the prominent position of Aboriginal issues in Australian polity and culture from the mid-1980s and the particular role played by the work of Henry Reynolds in informing the High Court's crucial *Mabo* decisions and its overturning of the principle of *terra nullius*. In a number of well-publicized statements and most notably in his address for the Sir Thomas Playford Memorial Lecture at the Adelaide Town Hall in July 1996, the newly elected Australian Prime Minister John Howard – not otherwise known as a student of history – offered his critique of the current state of Australian historiography.

Howard's view of Australian history and the cultural meaning of the contest over 'which history?' and 'whose history?' which emerged into public prominence in 1996 are the subjects of Tony Birch's essay, ' "Black Armbands and White Veils": John Howard's Moral Amnesia' (*Melbourne Historical Journal*, 25:8–16). In his Playford lecture, Howard announced to his audience that this occasion provided him with the opportunity to 'set the historical record straight' by 'exposing one of the most insidious developments in Australian life over the past decade . . . that being the attempt to re-write Australian history in the service of a partisan political cause'. Ordinary Australians were 'being force-fed by those self-appointed cultural dieticians in our midst whose agenda has more to do with divisive political strategies than the facts of history' (quoted by Birch, p. 8). In the lecture which followed, Howard assumed for himself the position of historian as neutral arbiter of facts but, as Birch argues, Howard's accusations of the bias and revisionism of the so-called 'black-armband' brigade only thinly mask the political motivation of his own position.

While disagreeing with Howard on the nature of history, Birch is in agreement with him as to its importance to the resolution of issues such as native title and indigenous rights more generally. Howard fully realizes 'that a more open and honest account of white Australia's colonial past may . . . inhibit the ability of the Liberal-National government to roll back the (limited) recognition of indigenous land rights which resulted from the . . . 1992 Mabo decision' (9). Howard criticized recent attempts to 'hijack' Australian history which 'set Australian against Australian' and attempted to impose guilt for deeds long past and announced his vision for a truer history which Birch characterizes as an 'uplifting, relaxed and comfortable Australian history project' which in the words of the Prime Minister would be a unifying story 'of all our people . . . broadly constituting a scale of heroic and unique achievement against all odds' (quoted by Birch, p. 9).

As Birch argues, what the Prime Minister opposes is the concept of *histories*. A history 'for all of us' is *one* history for *one* Australia. Significantly, in the Playford lecture, Howard makes virtually no reference to Aboriginal people at all – their exclusion remains implicit in all of his 'inclusive' rhetoric of national harmony and unification. Tracing the source of many of Howard's ideas about history to the work and public statements of Geoffrey Blainey (*The Triumph of the Nomads: A History of Ancient Australia*, Macmillan, 1975), Birch shows the ways in which conservative views of what constitutes history and the historical narratives they enable a number of moves: the exclusion of Aboriginal people from history and the perpetuation of myths of their 'pastness'; the impression that Aboriginal culture is effectively a thing of the past and that those Aborigines who see a future for themselves need to take their place alongside Europeans as 'one nation'; the fantasy that the white conquest of Australia was an uncomplicated heroic undertaking; the belief that the colonial moment is past and that all Australians now stand subject to the much vaunted egalitarianism so beloved by the right; and that no responsibility need be assumed for the well-intended 'accidents' (such as forced child removal) of former administrations and that all of us should leave the unpleasantness of the past behind us and move on to our sunny, comfortable future.

Birch draws on and extends comments made by Raymond Gaita ('Genocide and Pedantry', *Quadrant*, 1997, July-August:41–45 and 'Genocide: The Holocaust and the Aborigine', *Quadrant*, 1997, November:17–22) that Howard's contention that 'on balance' white Australian history is a 'fine one' requires us to accept 'the sheer weightlessness of the evil done to Aborigines'. Birch argues that:

> This weightlessness, and the forgetfulness that often accompanies it, places an unfair burden on Aboriginal people, who are subsequently forced to remember white Australia's past for it. Aboriginal people must act as the conscience of a sector of white Australia unwilling to acknowledge its history ... The history of assimilation [with particular reference to white Australian 'forgetfulness' on the subject of stolen children] is one of bureaucratic deception; it is a history of the quack science of social Darwinism; it is a history of the dominant racial fear of white Australia in the first half of the twentieth century, the fear of miscegenation; it is a history of child abduction and abuse. Rather than repeatedly call upon Aboriginal people to relive the horrors of assimilation, we could have a version of South Africa's truth commission, with the bureaucrats, politicians, police and social workers explaining the so-called misguided motivation behind their actions. If this seems unfair, is it more reasonable to expect Aboriginal people to relive this trauma in the knowledge that if they do not speak white Australia is unlikely to do so? (15).

While such retrograde views as those of the Prime Minister hold sway and while Aboriginal people await justice on the myriad of claims they have against the state – on stolen children, on rights to land, on social justice – Birch holds little hope for change. Quoting Patrick Dodson's words that 'the past shapes the kind of society we now have' (16), Birch concludes that postcolonialism remains merely 'a job' in this country 'a luxury enjoyed only by the academy' (16). Australia was and is a colonial society; and John Howard's manifesto for Australian history will ensure that it remains one.

Geoffrey Blainey – never far from the fray when Eurocentric expressions of dismay at the demands of 'sectional' interests such as Aborigines and their 'politically correct' supporters are called for – added weight to the debate with the publication of an opinion piece titled 'Reverse Racism in Australia: The "Black Armband" View of History', *The Social Contract* Winter:106–108; also published as 'Black Future', *The Bulletin*, 8 April:22–23). As Verity Burgmann astutely comments in another context ('Refashioning Australian Racism', *Arena Magazine*, 30:15–16, reviewed below):

In responding to Wik, the standard rejoinder of those who have always favoured the equal treatment of the unequal has been to insist upon an absence of discrimination, the equal treatment of all before the law, regardless of history and circumstances. Given that satisfactory outcomes for indigenous peoples will never emerge from mere freedom from discrimination or a commitment to equality of opportunity, it is precisely such a futile freedom and spurious form of equality that the corporate sector and its Coalition allies favour. On their much vaunted level playing field, there is no room for the practical exercise of native title and the pre-modern form of group-based rights such title aims to protect (16).

The same neo-liberalism – or hyper-liberalism – can be seen at work in Blainey's arguments against the 'black armband' view of history. Blainey narrativizes the influence of revisionist histories of Australia's colonial past in terms of destruction and disaster reaching into the highest court in the state:

In the past two decades, a tidal wave of opinion has swept across a big section of educated Australia. It has challenged and changed the way people think about the nation's past, and especially about Aborigines. This new wave is a mixture of compassion and political cunning, high principle and lack of principle. Curiously, a citadel of the new attitude is the High Court (22).

Contrary to both the traditional view of the last ninety-seven years and 'common sense', revisionist histories of Australia now 'run wild', completely refuting the successes and achievements of white society in Australia and tipping the scales in favour of minority interests – the environment, women, minorities and above all Aborigines. While protesting the inequities of Australia's past and 'pretending to be anti-racist', the wearers of the black armband are themselves advocates of inequality by calling for the redress of past inequities and are themselves 'intent on permanently dividing Australia on the basis of race' (22). Blainey finds such 'divisiveness' abhorrent and through a series of emotive illustrations seeks to demonstrate the unsustain-ability of such demands in relation to Australia's future as a legitimate nation or, even, as 'one' nation.

The folly of imagining that actions such as the reparation of land rights might see Aboriginal people return to their pre-1788 way of life is dealt with by Blainey in the assertion that 'the Aborigines of today clearly have no serious wish to return to the way of life, often unattractive, which their ancestors lived in 1788' (22). This tired old chestnut is deftly dispatched by Ian Anderson in another context arguing against the bio-cultural stasis demanded of 'authentic' or 'real' Aboriginality: 'There is no society which is able to reproduce itself from generation to generation in perfect replica' ('I, the "Hybrid" Aborigine: Film and Representation', *Australian Aboriginal Studies*, 1:12, reviewed below). That contemporary Aboriginal people may seek to do different things on their land from their ancestors is not sufficient grounds to nullify their title to that land. The hyper-liberal principle of equality even in the face of inequality is also at work in Blainey's attempt to illustrate the racism at the heart of the *Mabo* decision: the absurdity of granting 'vast tracks' of land to people of 'one race' becomes clear when we consider the nonsense of granting the land around Circular Quay as a reserve in perpetuity for people of, say, Irish descent. For a nation in economic turmoil, such nonsense is more than we can afford. We need to forget about divisive and sectional interests and put the interests of the nation as a whole first. This, of course, is easy to say when your own interests as, say, a property-owning white male are deemed by both 'tradition' and 'common sense' to be at one with the interests of the nation; less easy to endure when your interests, your culture and your history are held to be marginal to those of the nation as a whole.

Further critique of Howard and Blainey is provided by Verity Burgmann in 'John Howard's Assault on the Black Armband View of History' (*Labor Review*, 27:2–13). In this piece, Burgmann considers the debt as a student of history owed by the Prime Minister to Geoffrey Blainey and singles out a statement by Blainey published in Melbourne's *Age* newspaper (26 October 1996) for comment. Blainey, calling for the re-instatement of balance argues that there is much of merit in both the Aboriginal era of history and the era of European colonization. In positing the existence of two eras of history in this way, Blainey implies that Aborigines belong to the period before European settlement; and not properly to the era initiated in 1788. This, Burgmann suggests, is of a piece with his own historical scholarship, most notably *The Triumph of the Nomads* (see above) which offers a celebration of a version of traditional Aboriginal life which may be read as a relegation of Aboriginality to the distant past, leaving the recent past and the present the preserve of non-Aboriginal culture.

This division between the admirable Aboriginality of the distant past and the marginalized Aboriginality of the European era suits John Howard's political aims. Three themes recur in Howard's attack on revisionist history within the ideological context of his neo-liberalism and commitment to economic rationalism. These are the rejection of the need for white guilt, the desire for balance and the need for celebration. In his articulation of arguments on these points, Howard remains committed to a neo-liberalist individualism, which remains resistant to the idea that any individual, black or white, be treated as part of a group seen as exhibiting the traits, sharing the travails or the responsibilities, and bearing the structural advantages and disadvantage that attach to such membership. While Howard's attempts to minimize the kinds of harm done by Europeans to the indigenous populations yet falls short of David Irving's brand of revisionism, significant distortions are worked in his version of the 'facts' of the past.

While Howard may concede in determinedly non-specific language that some Aboriginal people were treated 'badly' in the past, the focus of his dispute with the 'black-armband' view of history becomes the significance of this past to present day politics. As Burgmann comments:

Neo-liberalism necessarily affirms the primacy of the present over the past, for the present is construed as a more or less clean slate to be acted upon by discrete individuals devoid of meaningful linkages with the past (7).

Within such an asocial and utilitarian universe, the continuing consequences of historically produced and inherited disadvantage cannot be admitted. Nor are the shrillness of complaint or the hint of 'bias' tolerated. 'Balance, the notion of impartiality, is a classic trope in liberal thought' which is applied not only in the declared commitment to dispassionate inquiry but in liberalism's portrayal of the role of the state as disinterested arbiter between contending forces and its notion of the importance of checks and balances in the political system. Given Howard's dissatisfaction with all histories written since his own school days, Burgmann inquires into the kind of history read and admired by the Prime Minister. He was taught at Canterbury Boys High School by Frank Driscoll who authored the popular textbook, *The Story of Australia* in which the following passages appear:

> Scientists have rated the aboriginal low on the intelligence scale because he made little or no attempt to build himself a useful dwelling or to devise the furnishings and the pots and pans that go with such dwelling.

> Australia was a white man's land and they wished to remain white. It was not class distinction, but simply a big family of white British people saying in effect: 'This is our home and surely we are entitled to say what friends we shall ask under our roof' (quoted by Burgmann, 7).

This, we must presume, is the history Howard remembers as a model of balance, neutrality, and the epitome of dispassionate intellectual inquiry. This is the history which, in Howard's view, is not in need of rewriting and which can offer the Australian nation a palatable version of its past with which to proceed into the future.

One-time speech writer for Paul Keating and an important conduit through which revisionist Australian history was communicated to the Labor governments of Hawke and Keating, Don Watson makes a contribution to the Australian history debate in 'Back to the Past' (*Australian Review of Books*, 9 July:6–9). While the crises in Australian history which Watson singles out for comment go beyond John Howard's attack on the black armband brigade, he spends time on the 'philistine political assault' of Howard and his ilk alluding to the actions and comments of writer and critic Kerryn Goldsworthy who wore a black armband to a Melbourne seminar telling the audience that she wore the armband (as some wear a red poppy) so as to remember the dead: 'I care about the dead. I don't want to forget the dead'. For Watson, the sanitization of history being pushed by Howard and others holds great dangers for the future of history and for the nation:

> when we ignored the dark side of the frontier – in fact, ignored the concept of the frontier itself – we ignored much more than the implications for the dispossessed. We ignored the moments

of our creation. And creation, we surely know *always* has a dark side. (9).

A gendered approach to the public debate on history is taken by Marilyn Lake in 'New Privacies for Old in Historical Discourse?: Incorporating Gender into Historical Practice' (*Tasmanian Historical Studies* 5(2):7–16) in which she addresses challenges to politically engaged, specifically feminist, historiography from proponents of older forms of history suspect or hostile to emergent 'identity' driven modes of writing history. Lake intervenes in the Australian debate on the alleged hijacking of public history by 'private', sectional or partisan interests by way of reference to a parallel debate played out in Canada in 1991 prompted by Michael Bliss' address for the Creighton Centennial Lecture at the University of Toronto entitled 'Privatizing the Mind: The Sundering of Canadian History, the Sundering of Canada'. Bliss's rhetoric of 'sundering' and his fears of national division and disintegration strongly parallel conservative anxieties for the future of 'one nation' in the Australian context. Lake's essay is useful in providing a transnational context for the history debate in Australia and while her focus remains on feminist history – particularly the attacks to which *Creating a Nation*, the book which she co-authored with Patricia Grimshaw, Ann McGrath and Marian Quartly (Melbourne: Penguin, 1996), was subjected – her arguments also encompass Aboriginal history.

2.1 Historical Imagination

Chris Healy's *From the Ruins of Colonialism: History as Social Memory* considers the formulation and constituents of historical imagination in Australia, drawing on both Aboriginal and non-Aboriginal history making in the post-settlement period. Healy uses the markedly different status accorded to, and meanings made of, Captain Cook in the bicentenary celebrations of 1970 and 1988 as the starting point of his study of the ways in which social memory, both local and national, officially endorsed and counter-hegemonic, works with and against other modes of history-making, including museums, schools, civic celebrations, and commercial historical reconstructions in the settler (post)colonial context of Australia. In his consideration of non-Aboriginal and Aboriginal histories of Captain Cook, Healy poses questions about the status of history and the status of myth, directly challenging the divisions perpetuated even by practitioners of the new Australian history such as Bain Attwood for whom Aboriginal histories never amount to more than myth making, remaining the 'raw data' for historians (as if this category necessarily excludes the possibility of an academic Aboriginal history) to work with and not themselves 'critical understandings of the past' (quoted by Healy, p. 51). In comparing Aboriginal and non-Aboriginal narratives of Captain Cook, Healy compares the European iconography of Cook as heroic Enlightenment figure of progress, technological/scientific prowess, and progenitor of modern nationhood with Aboriginal narrativizations which use tropes of death, disease and dispossession to tell the story of Cook's impact.

By looking at these histories alongside each other, Healy is not concerned with assessing their relative worth or validity, nor with arriving at authoritative non-Aboriginal and Aboriginal versions of the past but rather with exploring how the perspective provided by one narrative or group of narratives highlights the limitations and the merits of the other stories in circulation at any one time and over periods of time. Healy's insistence on giving recognition to multiple narrativizations of Captain Cook also demonstrates the degree to which an historical icon like Cook is taken up and remembered in different ways by different groups at different times, revealing at the same time the ways in which the making of history is an ongoing social process involving constant revision as the past is reprised into the present, with present concerns being frequently written into histories of that past. Healy's comparative analysis of different versions of Captain Cook usefully ranges from Cook's self-fashioning in his journals, to the historical memorial of Cook's putative cottage which was transported brick by brick from Yorkshire to Melbourne's Fitzroy Gardens in 1933, to Aboriginal stories of Cook such as that told by Hobbles Danaiyairi to Deborah Bird Rose (*Hidden Histories: Black Stories from Victoria River Downs, Humbert River and Wave Hill Stations*, Aboriginal Studies Press, 1991), stories from the Kimberleys collected by Erich Kolig ('Captain Cook in the Western Kimberleys' in R. Berndt and C. H. Berndt, eds., *Aborigines of the West: Their Past and Their Present*, University of Western Australia Press, 1980) and the story 'Too Many Captain Cooks' of Paddy Fordam Wainburranga which circulates in text, painting and film. Also of interest is Healy's commentary on the debate between Marshall Sahlins (*How Natives Think: About Captain Cook, For Example*, University of Chicago Press, 1995) and Gananath Obeyesekere (*The Apotheosis of Captain Cook: European Myth-making in the Pacific*, Princeton University Press, 1992) particularly with respect to the question of the historicity of Hawaiian versions of Captain Cook.

Beyond Captain Cook, in the second part of the book, Healy takes up history making in the contexts of museums and schools. In his discussion of the history making in both sites, Healy addresses the strategies by which officials in education and museums overcame the perceived lack of history of the new nation by turning to Aboriginality as pastness, which, of course, has significant implications for the ways in which Aboriginality has been constructed in the non-Aboriginal historical imagination since settlement. That is, Aboriginality as ineffably of the past as if frozen in prehistory, whether this is viewed scientifically as an extant specimen of human life at the dawn of time, pejoratively as unredeemable barbarism, or romantically as transcendent and mythic primitivism.

In the final section of the book, Healy examines the impact on the Australian historical imagination of two quite different foundation stories. The first is the Eureka Stockade which marked a significant moment in settler labour history and in relations between settlers and colonial authorities, and by extension the metropolitan authority of London in relation to this southern reach of empire. The second is the history of Eliza Fraser, which has been the subject of considerable attention in recent years, including Kay Schaffer's book-length study *In the Wake of First Contact: The Eliza Fraser Stories* (Cambridge University Press, 1995) which was reviewed in an earlier chapter (*YWCCT* 5). For Healy, the enduring currency of stories of Eliza are revelatory of the operation of history in social memory in the Australian context: Eliza Fraser is important less as a historical figure and event and more as an event and figure constantly under description, whose very description and redescription take place in a historically charged field such that she can only be described in terms of her, albeit shifting, historicity. 'It is precisely historically embedded events such as "the rescue of Eliza Fraser" which can be used to trace the outlines of colonial historical imagination to ask about its circuits and rules, its forms and effects' (165). Healy concludes his study of history, history making and social memory in Australia by arguing that the various versions of many histories which circulate nationally and locally are yet colonial histories, either remembering or resisting crucial moments of colonial domination and dispossession. A truly postcolonial historical imagination is yet to be developed.

Intensely local, personal and community history is the subject of *Karijini Mirlimirli: Aboriginal Histories from the Pilbara*, edited by Noel Olive. The volume comprises thirty-nine life stories of Aboriginal people from the Pilbara region in Western Australia. The Aboriginal men and women whose stories are included are linked by region, by family, by experiences of mission and station life, by the enduring power of Aboriginal law amongst members of the older generation and the impact of alcohol on their children, and by the devastation caused by employment in one of the region's main industries, the asbestos mine at Wittenoom. Also presenting local Western Australian history is the work of Neville Green and Susan Moon, *Far From Home: Aboriginal Prisoners of Rottnest Island, 1838–1931*, which is Volume X in the *Dictionary of Western Australians*. Part One of the volume provides a history written by Neville Green (12–93) of the Rottnest Island Aboriginal Establishment. Rottnest Island, off the coast of Western Australia, became a prison for Aboriginal offenders in 1841 and was declared out of bounds to the general public. While the nature of the prison facility changed over time, from prison to penal out-station to reformatory, it continued to hold indigenous prisoners until 1931. The second part (99–332) of the volume comprises a biographical dictionary of Aboriginal inmates of the Rottnest Island facility, with entries varying in length and detail from mere names, classification of offences and terms of imprisonment, to far fuller entries which frequently include statements from prisoners such as that provided by Bob Thomas in 1884 to the *Commission to Inquire into the Treatment of Aboriginal Native Prisoners of the Crown in this Colony* (282). The volume will prove an invaluable resource for researchers in this field.

Another but quite different community-focused Aboriginal history published in 1997 is Jeanie Bell's *Talking About Celia . . .: Community and Family Memories of Celia Smith* which Bell produced in collaboration with Celia Smith's eldest son Charles. *Talking About Celia* presents the life of its subject, a prominent Murri activist and matriarch through the memories of friends, political associates and members of her large family in a montage of voices, texts and photographic images. Bell writes in her introduction that she 'has chosen to present this story in a minimalist way' (xiii), allowing gaps and silences in the story to remain and allowing the many voices and fragments to sit alongside each other with Bell's voice simply one of many in the text. This textualization of Celia Smith's life is presented by Bell as a memorial to Smith and as a gift to the community in which she lived and worked. The many stories which make up the text are spoken of by Bell as being 'given' to her, reminding readers of the networks of reciprocity, obligation and exchange which underpin Murri sociality and community in which Celia Smith played such a central role for many years.

In *Imagined Destinies: Aboriginal Australians and the Doomed Race Theory, 1880–1939*, Russell McGregor explores the intellectual and ideological origins, political and governmental implications, and gradual demise of the 'doomed race' theory which was a dominant force in European thinking about Aboriginal people from the late-nineteenth century through to the 1930s and which survived residually in the non-Aboriginal popular imagination until much later. McGregor's history, which is richly documented with passages from scientific and governmental texts, demonstrates how Enlightenment narratives of the progress of civilization converged with branches of Darwinism to produce the theory of Aboriginal people as unalterably primitive with a culture so markedly inferior to that of all other races from whom history and geography had long protected them that the contact brought about by white settlement would ultimately prove fatal. As McGregor also points out, there was a high degree of political wishful thinking in such theorizations of inevitable Aboriginal extinction, as the prospect of the 'passing of the Aborigines' left vast tracts of land unpeopled and available for easy European possession at the same time as it conveniently released Europeans from discomfiting sentiments of guilt at the destruction of Aboriginal populations and their culture. While European violence against Aboriginal people, the destruction of the environment and restrictions on Aboriginal access to hunting and fishing grounds, and the impact of European diseases were major causes of population decline in Aboriginal communities and threatened the survival of traditional life, the narrative of the doomed race allowed Europeans to distance themselves from their agency in these matters by suggesting that no matter what action was taken by Europeans, Aboriginal life had remained unchanged for too long for it to adapt to change and 'progress'. Aboriginality was held to be too primitive and fragile to survive, and the law of nature as interpreted by Darwinian precepts of the survival of the fittest dictated that it must inevitably give way to more advanced and robust civilizations.

The forecasts of the imminent disappearance of the race which was politically troublesome and inconvenient to settler aspirations for unfettered access to and control over land occasioned something approaching a sense of emergency in the Australian and international scientific communities with calls for redoubled efforts in the gathering of information about Aboriginal language, culture, and diet before these disappeared from the mainland as they were believed to have 'disappeared' from Tasmania. The value of Aboriginal culture to science was precisely in terms of its alleged status as the extant remnant of a primordial form of human life – virtually the link which had hitherto been missing in speculations about the descent of man from simian which underpinned the very evolutionary theories which were then used to classify Aboriginal culture as tragically doomed, and unfit for survival in the modern age. The policy response to this was the protection and preservation (for the purposes of scientific investigation) of Aboriginal populations where possible on reserves and missions, where they might eke out their remaining time in relative isolation from the onslaught of European culture.

While Aboriginal populations declined in most coastal areas and the hinterland which was transformed into farming and grazing land, predictions about the imminent demise of the native populations proved by the early decades of the twentieth century to have been greatly exaggerated. Aboriginal communities, while dramatically affected by the impact of European settlement, proved more robust and adaptable than the doomed race theorists postulated. As they survived and interacted with Europeans in a variety of social and economic relations, the half-caste problem emerged as a major challenge for governments, churches and humanitarian concern and prompted theorists and commentators to re-formulate but not entirely abandon earlier views. Aboriginality was held to have become irreparably debased through interbreeding, with half-castes being attributed with a whole suit of degenerate characteristics and few of the marks of virility and integrity that were now held to have characterized full-blood Aborigines. It was inconceivable to many that populations so compromised by interbreeding could survive, but again the continued survival and in some areas the growth of mixed Aboriginal communities forced a reconsideration of the status of Aboriginal people as inevitably doomed to extinction. It was as state and territory governments attempted to address the management of the half-caste problem that the seeds of the ultimate demise of the doomed race theory took hold, giving rise to the theorizations of the possibility of absorption of the Aboriginal population within the European population – or what McGregor calls 'civilization through blood' – which ultimately and unevenly was to supersede the earlier view and the policies of protectionism it promoted and was to give rise to the fully developed and articulated policy of assimilation in the post-war period.

The fragility of Aboriginality and its vulnerability to the incursions of Europeans, both culturally and genetically, would become the salvation of the descendants of the original inhabitants of the country while at the same time sounding the death knell for traditional Aboriginal culture. Half-caste, quadroon and octoroon children in Aboriginal communities, while subject to degeneracy within the Aboriginal context, were deemed to be more malleable than their full-blood ancestors and hence capable of being civilized where earlier generations of Aboriginal people were considered irredeemably primitive. But the supersession of the doomed race theory by the complex of theories which ultimately gave rise to assimilation was a halting and uneven process, marked by intense disagreement among anthropologists, moralists, church people and politicians. Disagreement was particularly intense over the question of managing marriage between Europeans and mixed descent Aboriginal people. Absorption relied on progressive intermarriage and the consequent dilution of Aboriginal blood by more robust European bloodlines, but proscriptions against interracial sexual relations and intermarriage ran very deeply in many communities and mooted shifts in attitudes and legal sanctions attracted public outrage and opposition from such organizations as the Women's Section of the United Country Party which greeted discussions of an open policy of absorption in 1933 with outrage: 'That, it is greatly to be deplored that the Federal Government is so lost to the knowledge of our deep rooted sentiments and pride of race, as to attempt to infuse a strain of aboriginal blood into our coming generations . . .' (quoted by McGregor, p. 174).

McGregor's history is a valuable discussion of the philosophical, scientific and ideological genesis of the doomed race theory and of the ways in which this conviction that Aborigines were doomed to extinction shaped subsequent policy and other activities, such as scientific research. It is also useful for charting the gradual demise of this theory and its replacement by the idea of the absorption or assimilation of the indigenous population into the non-Aboriginal population. As documented by McGregor both the rise and the fall of the doomed race paradigm were uneven and marked by contention and disagreement, with alternative views never entirely losing sway. McGregor skillfully maps a terrain in which vested interest – in the acquisition of land and in the careerist promotion of scientific reputation – jostled with other considerations in the shaping of policy. McGregor's history is also valuable in charting the adaptations and survival of Aboriginal people and their culture literally against all odds and for historicizing this survival in terms which, like the doomed race theory, have themselves been superseded by subsequent paradigms in the management of Aboriginality by the Australian state. It is, thus, salutary to be reminded that for many Aboriginal activists and their non-Aboriginal supporters in the inter-war and post-war years, assimilation was held to offer great hope for Aboriginal survival and equality. As McGregor argues, the political position of an Aboriginal activist such as William Cooper – while providing a direct line of descent to the trenchantly anti-assimilation activists of the 1970s and beyond – needs to be understood in terms of the history which preceded Cooper by over 150 years in which questions of whether Aboriginal people could survive into modernity and if so, on what terms, dominated debates.

Aboriginal people viewed as primitive but noble and tragically doomed emerge from *The Civilised Surveyor: Thomas Mitchell and the Australian Aborigines* in which D. W. A. Baker examines the relations between Mitchell and Aboriginal people in the course of his four major survey expeditions into New South Wales, Victoria and Queensland in the period between 1831 and 1846. The Mitchell revealed in Baker's study is a compassionate and humane man, largely horrified by the instances of violence, brutality and exploitation exacted against the native population by Europeans in and around the settlement of Sydney. In his surveying work, Mitchell's experiences with Aboriginal people are mixed and ambivalent, involving both co-operation and respect; and fear, betrayal and violence. But, consistently, as with his meeting with a tribal elder and his family group in a camp near Mittagong on his first expedition, Mitchell was moved by the degree to which contact with Europeans had wreaked disease and destruction on the people of the Sydney region compared with Aboriginal people in areas remote from European settlement – areas which were to be opened up for inevitable settlement through the very survey work in which he was engaged. For a man of Mitchell's temperament, this awareness produced no small degree of moral anguish. Believing initially that Aboriginal people might be humanely persuaded to join European civilization and partake of its benefits, he came ultimately to the view that European culture offered nothing but harm to the native population and that the most humane solution to the problems posed for their well being and way of life was for them to be segregated from Europeans on reserves. Towards the end of his life, Mitchell became convinced that Aboriginal culture would inevitably be supplanted by European civilization – with devastating consequences which he hoped could be averted by the exercise of philanthropy. As Baker argues, 'Mitchell did not use the phrase but it is clear that he had been reduced to the hope that government policy might, at best, merely smooth the pillow of the dying race' (195).

Tony Austin's *Never Trust a Government Man: Northern Territory Aboriginal Policy, 1911–1939* covers some of the same territory as McGregor (reviewed above) but is focused exclusively on the Northern Territory and on the development of what Austin writes 'might euphemistically be described as "government policy" during the period from the Commonwealth takeover of the Northern Territory in 1911, until the announcement in 1939 of a "new deal" for Aboriginal people' (1). Austin's politically engaged analysis examines the administration of native affairs in the territory over this thirty-year period during which predictions of the inevitable extinction of the native population and the attendant obligation this created for administrators to 'smooth the dying pillow' of this doomed race competed with distressing evidence of the sexual exploitation of Aboriginal women by white men and the subsequent growth in the half-caste population and problems in subordinating an indigenous labouring class to the demands of the growing pastoral industries of the territory as dominant and largely irreconcilable concerns.

Retelling the story of the European mission of 'civilizing' Aboriginal and Torres Strait Islander peoples is also undertaken by Rosalind Kidd in her significant history, *The Way We Civilise* which details the management of Aboriginal affairs in the state of Queensland during the twentieth century. The title of the work is taken from the title of an editorial in *The Queenslander* newspaper from 1880, the text of which Kidd reproduces in full, which is striking for its critique of the brutality with which the drive for land was being pursued and the inhumanity of European treatment of Aboriginal people, calling for 'a more rational and humane' way of dealing with blacks which may go some way in '[effacing] some portion at least of the stain which attaches to us' (quoted in Kidd, p. xvii). Kidd's study details all aspects of the Queensland government's management of the indigenous population. Of particular interest is her demonstration of the rise of an Aboriginal affairs bureaucracy in the 1920s and 1930s, whose activities, at times, appear almost independent of Parliament; and the way in which Aboriginal affairs provided career paths for a number of individuals whose expertise underpinned aspects of the administration. Of great interest in this regard is Kidd's work on the management of Aboriginal health under the direction of Raphael Cilento.

The task of making and remaking histories, with a special emphasis on issues of gender, racial/cultural difference and indigeneity is undertaken by a valuable cluster of essays published in Volume 9 of *The Bulletin of Olive Pink Society*. The journal, named in honour of the eminent female anthropologist Olive Muriel Pink, aims at a broad readership but nonetheless presents theoretically engaged criticism across the fields of anthropology, race and gender. It has been a source of valuable, if somewhat eccentric, work for many years and the 1997 issues prove no exception. This volume contains the text of a dialogue/performance piece 'Not Speaking, listening ... "and representation"' (4–14) by Efi Hatzimanolis, Gillian Fuller, Paula

Abood and Brigitta Olubus which, while not dealing explicitly with Aboriginal issues, offers a provocative intervention in contemporary cultural debates on identity and cultural difference and, in particular, challenges to current feminist theorizations of the 'other woman' who is, in Hatzimanolis's words:

> often compelled to become a channel for privileged women's theorising about the production of their own identity and like Trinh [Minh ha] may be despised for reminding them that the question of differences amongst women precludes the innocence that makes guilt so desirable for privileged groups (6).

Roslyn Poignant's essay 'Looking For Tambo' (27–37) provides a critical reflection on the research process of looking for Tambo, an Aboriginal man removed from Australia in the 1880s and taken to the Northern Hemipshere by R. A. Cunningham, agent for Barnum's circus, as part of a troupe of nine 'captured Aborigines' who were put on display and required to perform in circuses and fairs, dime museums and events such as Barnum's Ethnological Congress alongside Zulu tribes people and other exotic human exhibits. In the event, Poignant was in the United States in October 1993 when news of the discovery of Tambo's mummified remains in the basement of a recently closed funeral home in Cleveland, Ohio, was announced and her essay juxtaposes this event and the overlap between her own research and the researches of Tambo's collateral descendants from the Palm Island community, Walter and Reggie Palm Island and Kitchener Bligh who travelled to Cleveland to perform a ceremony to release Tambo's spirit from its American limbo and bring his remains home where they were finally laid to rest in his own country on 23 January 1994. Poignant's essay thoughtfully considers the continuities between the nineteenth-century commodified freak show version of Aboriginality to which Tambo and his compatriots were subjected and the manner in which the contemporary media handled the discovery of Tambo's remains and the significance of his mummification; just as it balances the implications of her own search for Tambo with the re-evaluation of identity within the Palm Island community which was set in motion by their travel to America to collect his remains and the various performances and rituals occasioned by these important events. As Poignant argues the chance event of the discovery of Tambo's remains at the very time that she was in the United States researching him served as a fulcrum in which past collided with present and tilted into the future, precipitating a range of meanings for Tambo and the various images of him which were the subject of her inquiry. Her essay reflects on the status, function and meaning of images, the image-making process and on the ways in which these interact with cultural performances (the release of spirit ceremony, Tambo's funeral, and the associated funeral feast) to enable particular re-evaluations of culture and identity. Poignant draws on the work of theorists such as Roland Barthes and Walter Benjamin on image making and the concept of montage; Arjun Appadurai on culture, identity and globalization; and a range of poststructuralist anthropological writings, including the work of George Marcus and Michael Taussig, to formulate her account of the 'search' for Tambo. Poignant's essay, which is presented as work-in-progress towards a larger project (see also her 'Captive Aboriginal Lives' in Kate Darian-Smith, ed. *Captured Lives, Working Papers in Australian Studies*, Sir Robert Menzies Centre for Australian Studies, 1993) is a highly provocative and useful consideration of the issues of representation and otherness.

Faith Walker in 'The Reinvention of the "Noble Savage": Archibald Meston and "Wild Australia"' (38–43) covers some of the same ground as Poignant's work in documenting the 'Wild Australia' shows convened by Archibald Meston, during his period as Southern Protector of Aborigines in Queensland. The 'Wild Australia' shows, which were performed in venues such as the Brisbane Exhibition Building, the Brisbane Opera House and the grounds of Government House, presented Aboriginal people in performances of song, dance and corroboree, and Aboriginal men in warlike displays of fighting with spears and nulla nulla – Meston himself, on occasion, participated in these martial exhibitions sparring with an Aboriginal opponent. Meston's work as Protector was encapsulated in the notorious 1897 Act (to make provision for the better protection and care of the Aboriginal and half-caste inhabitants of the Colony, and to make more effectual provision for restricting the sale and distribution of opium) which was profoundly to determine the conduct of Aborignal affairs in the state of Queensland for the next eighty years. What Walker's research into Meston's involvement in the 'Wild Australia' enterprise shows is how sadly naive and romantic Meston's views on Aboriginal people were and the direct links between his subscription to the romantic 'Noble Savage' view (and its concomitant distaste for the contaminated half-caste) and the policies which ultimately worked great destruction on the very people they aimed to 'protect'. For Meston, nothing was as 'proud and stately' as the 'Australian blacks in their wild state' and it was this wildness which he sought to represent for white settlers in his 'wild' performances. Partly pedagogic, the shows aimed to inform non-Aboriginal settlers about details of indigenous culture and life; monies raised through these performances were contributed to the Aboriginal Protection Fund, a coffer established to furnish comforts to these noble but doomed creatures who were unable to withstand any contact with 'civilization' and once 'contaminated' were to be removed to sequestered reserves for the 'period which spans the abyss between the present point and the unknown point of their final departure' (Meston, quoted by Walker p. 42). Meston is an articulate proponent of the doomed race theory, the subject of Russell McGregor's study (reviewed above) and offers poetic inscriptions of the demise of this noble race in his writings: 'the shadowy forms and naked feet of a doomed race marching swiftly and softly by us where the dark ocean of oblivion ruthlessly swallows them all' (Meston quoted by Walker, p. 38).

Also in this issue is Julie Marcus's '"... like an Aborigine' – Empathy, Elizabeth Durack and the Colonial Imagination' (44–52) which uses the contemporary controversy over the Western Australian artist's admission that she has painted under the assumed Aboriginal identity of Eddie Burrup as a starting point for a consideration both of Durack's work in its biographical and historical contexts, towards which she provides much valuable research on Durack; and a critical consideration of the vexed and politically charged issue of the appropriation by non-Aboriginal people of Aboriginal art and culture, which continues to be a major issue for Aboriginal cultural activists within Australia (see below). Marcus provides a largely sympathetic portrait of Durack, revealing the degree to which connections with and sympathy for Aboriginal people, with whom she associated closely in her childhood and youth in rural Western Australia, have influenced her art. Marcus uses the biography of Durack to problematize any easy equation between Durack's assumption of an Aboriginal persona and exploitative appropriation. While not in any way diminishing the claims of Aboriginal people that such appropriation is unacceptable to them, Marcus invites her readers to see in Durack's indigenous inspired art and her incarnation as Eddie Burrup a more complicated picture of profound empathy on the part of this privileged white woman for the plight of Aboriginal people in the wake of colonization and enormous respect or 'homage' for the integrity of their culture and its artistic expression. However, as Marcus concludes, Durack's response, while personally and artistically complicated, is in the end politically inadequate:

> Reconciliation and 'homage' to another culture are concepts which cannot miraculously fall outside the politics of human and land rights that characterise Australian society today. They also slide inevitably away from themselves and towards appropriation; they become the values of a 'tolerant' liberal humanism through which the relations of power governing everyday life are translated into apparently benign and individual sentiments . . . It comes as a shock to understand that noble sentiments and good intentions cannot be dislocated from the broader economic and political processes which they seek to ameliorate. That shock is part of Elizabeth Durack's pain, but the pain cannot be healed through Eddie Burrup. If only it could (50–51).

In 'Just Looking: Miss Pink and the Camera' (15–24), Catherine Rogers subjects the handful of photographs of the 'outspoken, feisty and difficult' female anthropologist whose working life was spent with Aboriginal people in the Northern Territory, Olive Muriel Pink, to a reading which draws on Pink's own views on the power of photography as a tool of documentation and biography, a power which she resisted strenuously throughout her life with respect to being photographed herself. In considering the few extant photographs of Pink – photographs of her as a girl in Sydney, with her camels in the desert, a romantic studio portrait, and a photograph of her as a very old woman – Rogers speculates on the resistances of Pink to the demands of the camera, both in terms of refusal to be photographed on many occasions and, when photographed, her refusal (with rare exceptions) to engage in the performances required by the photographic conventions of her times.

The early Australian anthropologist and contemporary of Olive Pink, A. P. Elkin is the subject of Geoffrey Gray's '"Mr Neville did all in [his] power to assist me": A. P. Elkin, A. O. Neville and Anthropological Research in Northwest Western Australia, 1927–1928' (*Oceania* 68(1):27–43) in which the relationship between Elkin and Neville, Chief Protector of Aborigines in Western Australia, is examined. Gray reveals that in the close relationship between Elkin and Neville, we can see the emergence of what Gillian

Cowlishaw ('Helping Anthropologists: Cultural Continuity in the Constructions of Aboriginality', *Canberra Anthropology* 13(2):1–28]) has called
anthropology's 'discourse of helping' through which anthropologists, particularly in the 1930s, sought to render themselves and their science of use to
the government of the day with respect to the management of Aboriginal
issues. The problem with such close and 'helping' relationships, as Gray's
essay shows, is that the work of Elkin in the northwest is largely silent on
issues pertaining to government policy and administration of native affairs
requiring critical intervention. The picture which emerges of Elkin is one of
self-interest: '[h]is was the voice of authoritative knowledge about Aborigines. The keystone to Elkin's influence and collaboration with government,
mission and pastoralists was his strategy not to publicly criticise these
agencies, particularly government and mission policies in which he had a
vested interest' (39). Another consideration of Elkin's work is provided by
Glen Ross in ' "Dreamtime", Who's Time?: A. P. Elkin and the Construction
of Aboriginal time in the 1930s and 1940s' (*Journal of Australian Studies*,
54:55–62). Ross uses Johannes Fabian's (*Time and the Other: How Anthropology Makes its Object*, Columbia University Press, 1983) critique of the
construction of temporality in Western evolutionary and anthropological
discourses on non-Western cultures as the basis for his examination of
Elkin's construction of the 'dreamtime'. As Ross argues, the obvious failure
of the doomed race theory in accounting for the Aboriginal race occasioned
something of crisis for those like Elkin attempting to theorize Aboriginal
temporality in modernity concluding that, like Freud (most notably in
Civilisation and its Discontents), Elkin 'was concerned with the threat posed
to civilization by signs of the presence of the primitive in Western society.
To combat this threat, Elkin sought national unity through the strengthening
of white Australia and the eventual assimilation of the Aboriginal people'
(55–56).

In 'Divergent Experiences of the Frontier: Jews and Aborigines in Early
Colonial   Australia'   (*Australian   Jewish   Historical   Society   Journal*,
14(2):23–37), Paul R. Bartrop considers the available evidence of Jewish life
in colonial Australia with particular reference to evidence of Jewish interactions with and attitudes to Aboriginal people and tentatively posits the
argument that the relatively easy situation faced by the majority of Jewish
settlers in colonial Australia was facilitated by the fact that the position of
feared and despised other, which had been the allotted place of Jewish
people in many European cultures, was on the colonial frontier occupied by
Aboriginal people. Bartrop finds no evidence that their own experience of
persecution made Jews in colonial Australia any more or less sensitive to
the plight of Aboriginal people with the onslaught of European settlement.

2.2 Museums

The making of particular understandings of the past through the exhibiting
of Aboriginal art and cultural artefacts in western museums and galleries is
the subject of the essay by Nicholas Thomas, 'Indigenous Presences and
National Narratives in Australian Museums' (*Humanities Research* Winter:
3–16). Thomas bases his argument about the curatorial processes for both
museums and galleries on their necessary process of decontextualization –
cultural artefacts are necessarily decontextualized from their cultural uses

and meanings when exhibited in a museum, just as works of art are displaced from their various spiritual, social and economic contexts and defined by the gallery space precisely in terms of their apparent 'function-lessness' (4). Thomas goes on to consider in some detail the curatorial practices which led to the mounting of the Aboriginal Art exhibit by the Australian Museum in 1941, the Voices exhibition of the Museum of New Zealand Te Papa Tongarewa in 1993, and the rehanging of the Australian Galleries collection, which includes important indigenous and colonial work, by the National Gallery of Australia unveiled in June 1994. In his consideration of the last of these exhibits, Thomas usefully takes up the criticisms of cultural historian Humphrey McQueen ('Capital Outlook for Homegrown Art' *The Weekend Australian*, 1994, 18 June:25) and argues that the implications of this exhibit go beyond any remedial project of offering 'two sides' to the story of the settlement of Australia, with the colonial narrative of achievement and accomplishment being balanced by the indigenous story of dispossession. What Thomas finds in the juxtaposition of colonial pieces and indigenous work is a powerful compulsion to acknowledge the discrepancies between the two: in short, to acknowledge that the indigenous presence cannot be readily assimilated to the available narratives of national identity which are commonly celebrated in exhibitions of this kind. The exhibition provides testimony to the disjunctions, disruptions, disorder and incommensurability that remain the characteristics of a cross-cultural settler colonial society such as contemporary Australia.

In 'Museums Inside-Out'(*Australian Leisure Management*, 1(1):34–36), Christopher Anderson turns his attention to the historical place of indigenous cultural objects not in galleries but in natural history museums, such as the Museum of South Australia of which he is Director. In considering the difficulties facing such museums in contemporary culture, Anderson points to the economic challenges of drawing a public and the political and ideological challenges of findings ways to exhibit cultural material in their collections which, in many cases, has been acquired in ways which are by contemporary standards unacceptable. The Museum of South Australia is a case in point with, as Anderson argues, Adelaide by virtue of its geographical location acting as a funnel ' "draining" the heart and top of the Australian continent and the western Pacific of natural and cultural material'. The co-location of indigenous cultural artefacts with the minerals, flora and fauna of a given region is problematic, but not entirely negative. While it can be argued that such co-location promotes unacceptable stereotypes of primitivism, it is possible that indigenous cultural objects in natural history collections may also promote an understanding of these cultures as intimately linked with their environments. Anderson also uses the essay to flag developments currently underway at the Museum, specifically the development of the Aboriginal Cultures Gallery which opened in 1999.

2.3 Taking Stock: Land Rights and Citizenship
Marking thirty years since the referendum of 1967 in which the Commonwealth government was granted the right to legislate on Aboriginal matters and twenty years of the formal struggle for indigenous land rights following the passing in 1976 of the Northern Territory's Aboriginal Land Rights Act, is *Our Land is Our Life: Land Rights – Past, Present and Future*, edited by

Galarrwuy Yunupingu. The volume presents essays by indigenous community leaders, activists and academics and usefully reproduces in a series of appendices key historical and legal documents in the Australian indigenous land rights struggle, including the statement from the 1963 Bark Petition, extracts from the 1971 *Milirrpum* case, extracts from the 1974 Aboriginal Land Rights Commission Report, the text of the Barunga statement and a summary of the Commonwealth's 1993 Native Tile Act. While the essays in the volume lean towards the insights to be gained from the twenty years' experience of Aboriginal communities in the Northern Territory with the operation land rights legislation in that jurisdiction, many contributors address the more recent developments following the High Court's *Mabo* decision and the passing of the Commonwealths native title legislation in 1993. The essays in the collection link the raft of contemporary Aboriginal cultural, social and political issues to the question of land underpinning the central contention that without access to their land there is no way forward for Aboriginal and Torres Strait Islander people on questions of health, welfare, education and social justice. The volume contains significant contributions by Marcia Langton ('Grandmother's Law, Company Business and Succession in Changing Aboriginal Land Tenure' 84–116); Barbara Cummings ('Talking History' 188–195); Aden Ridgeway ('Rights of the First Dispossessed: The New South Wales Situation' 63–79) and Mary Yarmirr ('Women and Land Rights' 80–83). Prominent Tasmanian Aboriginal leader Michael Mansell considers the subject of indigenous cultural and intellectual property rights in his essay 'Barricading Our Last Frontier – Aboriginal Cultural and Intellectual Property Rights' (195–209).

Citizens without Rights: Aborigines and Australian Citizenship jointly written by John Chesterman and Brian Galligan uses the thirtieth anniversary of the 1967 referendum as an occasion to consider the kind and quality of citizenship afforded to Aboriginal and Torres Strait Islander peoples in the intervening years and historical considerations leading to the referendum itself. The volume contains seven chapters which provide a partial history (partial due to its focus on colonial Victoria and Queensland) of the framing of Aboriginal legal subjecthood in the colonial period, the assumption of citizenship by indigenous people in 1967 which the authors argue was understood largely as a citizenship without rights; and the 'slow path' from this largely evacuated concept of citizenship to the concept of civil rights for indigenous people, and from this point to the development of the concept of indigenous rights as they are understood in contemporary political debates. The book is an extraordinarily detailed study, which encompasses constitutional and administrative law and historical theorizations of democracy, citizenship and representation. The story it tells is a remarkable and shameful one which shows the 'sheer amount of legislative ingenuity and administrative effort that went into devising and maintaining [the] discriminatory regimes' (9) which left indigenous people in Australia with virtually no rights under the law from the earliest colonial times until well into the twentieth century. This study, in common with many of the titles under review this year, was commenced under different political circumstances than the ones which prevailed when it was concluded. Chesterman and Galligan are not optimistic about the future, at least in the short term:

the continued evolution of the common law regarding indigenous rights, the viability of native title legislation, the possibility
of constitutional change, and the future of self-determination
(and in particular the Aboriginal and Torres Strait Islander
Commission) will all be decided in the short-term future ... It
remains to be seen whether Australia's shameful treatment of
Aborigines will enter its fourth century and second millennium
(222).

A further consideration of Aboriginality and citizenship is provided by
Geoffrey Stokes in his contribution to his edited collection *The Politics of
Identity in Australia.* In 'Citizenship and Aboriginality: Two Conceptions of
Identity in Aboriginal Political Thought' (158–171), Stokes rehearses and
applies to the issue of Aboriginal identity, and the evolving face of public
and political Aboriginality, arguments with which feminists are well familiar
pertaining the tensions between an agenda focused on equality and that
which recognizes difference and works to achieve social justice and other
rights without compromising cultural distinctiveness.

A further volume which revisits the referendum of 1967 is co-written by
Bain Attwood and Andrew Markus in collaboration with Dale Edwards and
Kath Schilling, *The 1967 Referendum, Or When Aborigines Didn't Get the
Vote.* This book, which is informed by a great deal of valuable research
through primary materials, including oral accounts from Aboriginal people
collected by Edwards and Schilling in early 1997, takes the assumption of
the referendum as a 'watershed' event in the history of Aboriginal affairs in
Australia and problematizes it; and in the manner of many of the histories
under review this year, looks at the ways in which this event is made and re-
made, being accorded different meanings and significance by different
groups, both in 1967 and in the thirty years since the passage of the
plebiscite, including previous anniversary commemorations, such as those
held in 1977, 1987 and 1992. Attwood and Markus are as much concerned
with what the referendum meant for Aboriginal and Torres Strait Islander
peoples as they are with what these people, and non-indigenous Australians,
think it meant (or means) to them:

> [T]he significance attributed to the referendum is a matter of
> interpretation and perspective, and these are subject to change
> over time. With the exception of the first decade after the
> referendum – when there was much disillusionment about its
> value among its proponents, particularly Aborigines whose
> expectations had been raised so high – the passing of time has
> seen the precise terms of the referendum disappear from histor-
> ical consciousness only to be replaced by myths which uncannily
> resemble the campaigners' representations of it at the time (65).

As Attwood and Markus argue, a great deal of mythologizing attends the
popular understanding of the significance of the referendum both then and
now. The referendum which asked Australian voters to decide on two
matters – whether the constitution should be altered to give the Common-

wealth power to legislate on Aboriginal affairs which were at that point the exclusive domain of the states and whether Aboriginal people should be reckoned as Australian citizens for the purposes of the census – readily slips into a range of other roles, frequently highly symbolic, for both Aboriginal and non-Aboriginal people. In 'Citizenship in Australia: An Indigenous Perspective' (*Alternative Law Journal*, 22(2):57–59), Michael Dodson uses the anniversary of the 1967 referendum to consider the kind and quality of 'citizenship' afforded to Aboriginal and Torres Strait Islander people under the Constitution and concludes that without a thorough overhaul of this document indigenous people will remain at best holders of a 'concession' citizenship and at worst will remain exiles in their own country. Also providing comment on the significance of the 1967 referendum is Lois O'Donaghue's 'The May 1967 Referendum: 30 Years Down the Track' (*Indigenous Law Bulletin*, 4(3):4–5).

While not dealing with the referendum of 1967, Terry Threadgold takes up many of the same issues of Aboriginality, citizenship and the constitution of nationhood in her *Feminist Poetics: Poiesis, Performance, Histories* – the title of which, while accurately flagging a number of the book's concerns, may not adequately alert readers to the valuable consideration of indigeneity and the discursive production and management of difference (both gendered and cultural) within the historical framework of Australian Federation which the book contains. With respect to these issues, *Feminist Poetics* offers in Chapters 7 and 8 a richly theorized, while at the same time historically and materially grounded, account of the discursive regimes deployed by nascent Australian nationalism to dispose of 'blackness' (and to a lesser extent femininity) outside the margins of nationhood. Threadgold builds her arguments around the formulation of the 'outlaw' figure in Australian popular culture, with reference to the exploits of the infamous (but revered) Ned Kelly and his gang which are then contrasted sharply with the treatment by colonial media of the Aboriginal outlaw Jimmy Governor. Threadgold argues that while Jimmy Governor fashioned himself in the romantic tradition of masculinized outlaw action which Kelly and others had operated within and helped to form, those interpreting his exploits saw him in a vastly different light. On the basis of his race, Jimmy Governor was excluded from this tradition of masculine action, regardless of the fact that this tradition was able to accommodate lawlessness, murder and brutality of the kind practised by Kelly and his gang: the category of the 'bushranger' as such, was open only to white men. Threadgold argues that understanding the historical context of the Governor episode is crucial to a reading of the complex dynamics of race and gender at work in the actions of Governor, their depiction in the colonial press (to which she alludes generously), his treatment by the law, and the ways in which the details of his story have been narratavized and re-narrativized by subsequent generations. For Threadgold, the critical factor in reading the Jimmy Governor 'texts' is the movement from a collection of colonies to a Federated nation which was taking place during the period of the commission of Governor's crimes, his flight from law and his ultimate capture. As Threadgold argues, the nation is formed by means of certain exclusions far more than it is formed through inclusions: Governor came to serve as exactly that which (white) Australian nationhood was not.

The details of Governor's situation are subjected to considerable scrutiny by Threadgold who draws heavily on press reports, transcripts of trials and other historical documents to demonstrate the ways in which these discourses worked to constitute Governor as an extreme alterity, wholly unassimilable and incapable of domesticization within the framework of Australian nationhood. There is further, as Threadgold argues, a strongly sexualized dimension to the Governor saga: he had a white wife, Ethel, and his crimes included the murders of white women. In her consideration of Governor's wife, Threadgold examines the colonial taboo of miscegenation and its gendered asymmetries: white men could consort with native women with relative impunity (as long as they did not attempt to bring these liaisons within white kinship structures as Bird argues, see below), while sexual relations between a white woman and a black man remained utterly unspeakable and incited as much (or greater) loathing of the white woman concerned as they did the black man. In this regard, femininity itself remains largely outside the masculinized structure of white nationhood, with women only participating in the nation via their relations with white men: as daughters, mothers and wives of citizens. Sexual liaisons between white women and black men provoke deep-seated fears in the white patriarchy with respect to both power and sexuality, fears which are highlighted in Thomas Keneally's novel based on the Governor story, *The Chant of Jimmie Blacksmith* (Fontana Collins, 1972):

> Gilda [Ethel Governor] always avoided him if she could, but he rolled up to her on his horse, vaulted out of his saddle and exposed his patriarchal blunt genitals, slug-white and sitting in his hand for her information.
> 'When yer find a bigger'n than that on a nigger, Mrs Blacksmith, let me know' (Keneally quoted in Threadgold, 145).

While demonstrably part of the discourses of nascent nationhood which accompanied the transformation of the Australian colonies into states which were federated at the turn of the century, the Jimmy Governor story has enjoyed a rich after-life throughout this century. Similar to the story of Eliza Fraser which Chris Healy (reviewed above) has characterized as being part of the social memory by which white Australia knows itself, the Jimmy Governor story has been subject to many re-tellings, including film versions. Threadgold examines in detail both Keneally's novel based on the novelist's own research and on the version of events provided by Frank Clune in his 1959 book *Jimmy Governor* (Horwitz); and Fred Schepsi's 1978 film *The Chant of Jimmie Blacksmith*, based on Keneally's novel with a screenplay by Schepsi. While the contemporary context in which Governor was first 'read' was that of Federation, for Keneally the circumstances surrounding Australia's participation in the Vietnam war and the parlous state of Aboriginal affairs in the 1960s provided an historical frame which paralleled that of the turn of the century in many relevant areas. As Healy also argues, history is rewritten as much for the present as for the past: it may be added that in the Australian context and with respect to constructions of Aboriginality, the distance between past and present is seldom very great. Threadgold's book, which may be easily overlooked by readers with an interest in the construction of Aboriginality in white Australian culture, makes a valuable contribution to the field. Threadgold's deft handling of a wide range of texts, her application of semiotics and discourse analysis, and her thorough research makes *Feminist Poetics* a fine example of locally nuanced and globally theorized feminist cultural studies.

3. Pauline Hanson and the 'Resurgence' of Racism

A number of publications in 1997 take up the alarming rise in public racist sentiment with the arrival on the federal political stage of Pauline Hanson in February 1996 during the campaign leading to the March election in which the conservative coalition led by John Howard swept into power. Hanson, a Liberal Party endorsed candidate for the Queensland seat of Oxley, a long-time Labor stronghold and former seat of Bill Hayden, was disendorsed after making public statements maligning Aboriginal people and criticizing Asian immigration in highly racist terms; she went on to run, winning the seat as an independent. While Howard made some effort to distance the Liberal/National coalition parties from such extreme statements, it was clear that the conservative parties saw considerable electoral mileage to be gained from this emerging race-based politics of resentment. As Geoffrey Gray and Christine Winter write in the Introduction (3–5) to their edited collection of essays exploring the Hanson phenomenon, *The Resurgence of Racism: Howard, Hanson and the Race Debate*:

> [t]he matter of race ... lay buried at the heart of the Liberal Party campaign. Its carefully chosen slogan, 'For all of us', was designed to appeal to the feelings of grievance and resentment which 'Howard's battlers', as they were called, were expressing towards what they saw as the Keating Labor government's 'pandering' to 'special' or 'sectional' interest groups such as Aborigines.

As prominent Aboriginal lawyer and activist Noel Pearson noted at the time, the apparent inclusiveness of the Liberal slogan masked a determined exclusion: 'For all of us' really meant 'For us, but not for them'. While, as Gray and Winter argue, the possibilities of who can be defined as part of the mainstream were and are almost limitless, as the election campaign progressed and in the first months of the Howard government's administration it became indisputably clear that the prime target for exclusion from the mainstream were Aboriginal people. John Howard wasted no time in signalling that his government was to usher in major changes in the administration of Aboriginal affairs in the country. He launched an assault on the Aboriginal and Torres Strait Islander Commission (ATSIC); cast doubt on the efficacy of the Human Rights and Equal Opportunity Commission (HR&EOC) inquiry into forced child removal; and flagged his government's intention to overhaul the 1993 Native Title Act. As Mick Dodson, an HR&EOC Commissioner observed, Howard was 'exploiting for political purposes a fear and loathing about Aboriginal people' (quoted by Gray and Winter, p. 2). Hanson's extremism worked in conjunction with Howard's politics of resentment, opening a space in which attacks on Aboriginal people and politics could be masked as a return to decent and traditional Australian values, with one standard of 'fair play' for all, and no concessions to special groups or sectional interests. Bound up with this was Howard's attack on the so-called 'black armband' view of history which, in his view, imposed irrelevant guilt on white Australians for the colonial dispossession of the past.

The Resurgence of Racism comprises eleven essays originally presented at the *Is Racism Un-Australian?* Symposium at the Humanities Research Centre, Australian National University in February 1997. The volume includes Judith Brett's 'John Howard, Pauline Hanson and the Politics of Resentment' (7–28), an analysis of Howard and Hanson's appeal to 'the battlers', lower-middle class Australians for whom the politics of resentment against the perceived concessions made to Aboriginal people and other special interest groups by the Labor government of Paul Keating struck a chord. More historically oriented are the essays by Henry Reynolds, 'Racism and other National Discourses' (29–38) and M. C. Ricklefs, 'The Asian Immigration Controversies of 1984–85, 1988–89 and 1996–97: A Historical Review' (39–62). In 'The "Robespierre" of the Air: Talkback Radio, Globalisation and Indigenous Issues' (63–78), Steve Mickler offers a further examination of race-based resentment among poor white Australians through his examination of Perth radio personality Howard Sattler. Andrew Markus in 'John Howard and the Re-Naturalisation of Bigotry' (79–86) challenges the view that Pauline Hanson represents a resurgence of racism, but merely a recentring of it on the main political stage. Peter Read in 'Pain, yes: Racism, no: the Response of Non-British Australians to Indigenous Land Rights' (87–96) examines the views of non-British Australians including Chinese and Southern Europeans on questions of indigenous land rights concluding that Aboriginal groups need to work harder to include non-British Australians in their address as these groups represent a large and potentially very supportive audience which is yet to be invited to join the debate.

More speculative contributions are made by Deborah Bird Rose and Ann Curthoys. In 'Dark Times and Excluded Bodies in the Colonisation of Australia' (97–116), Rose begins by relating the view of Aboriginal people with whom she worked in the Victoria Downs region of the Northern Territory that they believed whitefellas to be in a state of epistemological crisis precisely related to their inability to know 'what to remember and what to forget' (97). Rose speculates that this crisis does not so much affect white western views of time and of the relations between past, present and future as it is produced by the particular view of time, of history, and of the relations between times present and times past on which western European culture is organized. Rose then takes up Hannah Arendt's notion of 'dark times' – which may be times of disruption, pitilessness and horror and also times of epistemological crisis – and embarks on a wide-ranging survey of the ways in which time is organized and punctuated in the West alongside the ways in which highly hierarchical socio-biological schema have allowed Western societies to exclude certain groups and relegate them always to the outside of their organizations. Rose argues that '[t]emporal and moral issues in the contemporary world converge around the power to insulate one's self from the damage one causes, and thus around the power to allocate privilege' (103). The 'headlong' rush towards the future which, Rose argues, characterizes Western socio-temporal action, facilitates the divisions between those with power and those without. Crucially, it distances actors from their own agency by producing the present as a disjunctive moment between the desired future and the past which is always in the process of being transcended. Bird writes:

> Our lives are . . . thus suspended in a web of conceptions of time that tell us we are always about to be that which we would believe we truly are. The qualitative differentiation of past and future means that the present is discontinuous with both. In this disjunctive moment, it can appear that our responsibilities can be understood to be most properly directed towards the future rather than toward the people and places of this moment because the present is always already becoming the past which is in the process of being transcended. The present becomes a place in which we are estranged from the actual conditions of our lives, where agency is alienated, responsibility cast else-where, and morality subjected to a double deflection as it aims toward a future which will, in due course, become the past (101).

Rose extends her considerations of the ways in which conceptions of time produce this alienation to the specific circumstances of the colonization of Aboriginal people in Australia through an analysis of the federal minister for Aboriginal and Torres Strait Islander affairs, Senator John Herron's handling of issues pertaining to the HR&EOC's inquiry into stolen children. In a number of well-reported statements, Herron expressed views which attempted to minimise the ordeal of stolen children and the families from whom they had been removed, either by suggesting that these events had occurred, in many cases, a long time ago; or, that some children removed from their families had benefited enormously from increased educational opportunities. In addition, Herron alludes to his own ability to feel pain, thus '[deflecting] attention from the pain of others and . . . from any action toward alleviating that pain' (113). As Rose argues, drawing on a number of theorists of trauma and torture, the experience of pain is increased when it fails to meet with acknowledgement. By failing to acknowledge that the practice of forced child removal caused pain which is continuous and ongoing, not simply a past event but a traumatic thread which links the past with the present, Herron augments Aboriginal suffering.

Quite clearly an expression of the colonial power of European settlers over the indigenous population, Rose provides a further analysis of the power dynamics of child removal along gendered lines. The position allowed white men in these practices exemplifies her proposition that power is primarily the capacity to be distanced from the consequences of one's actions. It was irrelevant whether the sexual act which brought the children into being was an act of intimacy or an act of violence; what mattered was that it was between black and white, which was illicit, to be tolerated only as long as men did not seek to transform the liaison into familial relation-ships. Thus, Bird continues, 'liaisons were separated from kinship, and the offspring were removed from all systems of kinship' (111). The genitors of the children who were removed did not bear the consequences of their actions, like the men who made the policy and those who put it into practice. The pain was borne by others – quite precisely Aboriginal women and their children. And, then as now, this suffering is accompanied by a blanket of denial and the mobilization of distancing narratives: mixed-race children are not really valued by communities; Aboriginal mothers felt no real grief at their loss, or recovered very quickly from whatever pain they felt; or, as deployed by John Herron, the notion that whatever pain may have been occasioned paled in comparison with the long-term benefits to the child.

Rose concludes by positing the need for an ethics of care, a full and compassionate engagement with past injustices and present wrongs. Echoing the conclusion to her 1996 essay 'Rupture and the Ethics of Care in Colonised Space' (in T. Bonyhady and T. Griffith, eds., *Prehistory to Politics: John Mulvaney, the Humanities and the Public Intellectual*, Melbourne University Press, 1996, pp. 190–215, reviewed *YWCCT 6*), Rose contends that this turning towards each other in quiet gestures of care constitutes our best chance of asserting our presence (and *present*) and our 'most world shaping opportunities in these dark times' (113).

Taking up the question of white Australia's failure to deal adequately with our colonial past and the relationships between this failure and the present resurgence of racism is Ann Curthoys' essay 'Entangled Histories: Conflict and Ambivalence in Non-Aboriginal Australia' (117–127). In this essay, Curthoys poses a number of questions about what non-Aboriginal people know about Aboriginality, what Aboriginality means to non-Aboriginal Australians and what they do with this knowledge. For Curthoys, the history of non-Aboriginal knowledge and uses of Aboriginality are marked by deep ambivalences. Most significantly, they are characterized by the double-edged sword of racism, and uncritical and frequently exploitative admiration of Aboriginality which renders it the possession of all Australians. That is, transforming Aboriginality into a symbol, or resource or commodity, which is deployed in a variety of ways to shore up non-Aboriginal feelings of deficiency and guilt with respect to the only partially acknowledged spectre of our colonial past. Curthoys sees a critical engagement with history as one way forward.

The volume also includes essays by David Hollinsworth and Alan McKee which take up the particular problems associated with defining and resisting racism arising from the ways in which contemporary racist discourses are frequently presented as *not* being based on principles of biological causation or racial hierarchies, but rather obfuscate the bases of their differentiation. Hollinsworth's contribution 'The Work of Anti-Racism' (129–138) draws on the work of anti-racism theorists such as Paul Gilroy (*There Ain't No Black in the Union*, Hutchinson, 1987) and Phil Cohen ('"It's Racism What Dunnit": Hidden Narratives in Theories of Racism' in J. Donald and A. Rattansi, eds., *Race, Culture and Difference*, Sage, 1992; and 'The Perversions of Inheritance' in P. Cohen and H. Bains, eds., *Multi-Racist Britain*, Macmillan, 1988) and presents a schematic review of the range of sites and structures of contemporary racism, ranging from the overarching meta-structures of capitalism, imperialism and global economics, to more local sites such as local media idealogues such as John Laws and Howard Sattler, school curricula, and racist groups and organizations. In 'The "Lack" of Racism in Contemporary Australia' (139–147), Alan McKee examines the manifestation of particular forms of racist discourse which present as radical non-racism; that is discourses which proceed on the grounds of assuming or insisting on the absolute equality of all people but which nonetheless go on to make distinctions which are racially based but efface their racist bases. McKee cites John Howard's avowed commitment to equal treatment for 'all' Australians specifically regardless of race, which effectively denies the long history of systemic and structural inequality for indigenous Australians, as an example of this phenomenon. Anti-racists need to adapt their strategies to take into account the 'lack' of explicit racism in contemporary racist politics.

Notwithstanding a certain unevenness in the kind and quality of the papers in the collection – with some contributions reading very much like conference presentations and others, most notably Deborah Bird Rose's, showing the signs of reflective revision, *The Resurgence of Racism* makes an important contribution to scholarship in the fields of anti-racist and Aboriginal studies.

Another collection of essays on racism in contemporary Australia which began life as conference presentations is *Bringing Australia Together: The Structure and Experience of Racism in Australia*, edited by Bernadette Foley on behalf of the Brisbane-based Aboriginal organization FAIRA (Federation of Aboriginal and Islander Research Action). The conference on which the volume is based is an attempt to formulate the kind of dialogue advocated by Peter Read (see above) in which Aboriginal and Torres Strait Islander people confer with non-British Australians on strategies for combating racism and discrimination. The volume contains contributions from a wide range of people and communities – activists, bureaucrats, academics, politicians, community leaders from indigenous, Anglo-Australian, Greek-Australian, Chinese-Australian, and Jewish-Australian backgrounds. A number of contributions deal specifically with issues of race and racism pertaining to Aboriginal and Torres Strait Islander people. Hazel McKellar in 'Searching for My Country' (5–8) writes of the discrimination faced by Aboriginal people particularly in rural areas as they attempt to go about the work required by the native title process in gathering evidence for their claims; she is particularly critical of the obstacles created by landowners and pastoralists and the degree to which local authorities collude with these vested interests to the disadvantage of Aboriginal people. In 'Justice: Whose Interests?' (13–18), Robert Mills reflects on the great inequities faced by indigenous people under the law, particularly Aboriginal and Torres Strait youth in relation to the criminal justice system. Aileen Moreton-Robinson's essay 'White Race Privilege: Nullifying Native Title' (39–44) draws on theorists of whiteness such as Montag ('The Universalisation of Whiteness: Racism and the Enlightenment' in Mike Hill, ed., *Whiteness: A Critical Reader* New York: NewYork University Press, 1997) in her argument about the resistances to native title represented by vested property interests and critically unaware manifestations of white privilege: 'White values and the interests of the nation are centred and represented as being right and proper and the values and claims of Indigenous people are positioned as being improper, unjustifiable and ignominious' (42). Eve Fesl in 'Racism' (47–55), considers the progressive institutionalisation of racism against Aboriginal people over the course of Australia's colonial history, arguing that racist structures are now deeply embedded in the fabric of Australian society. In 'Queensland: Is the Clock Still Back 100 years?' (56–60), Jackie Huggins uses the occasion of the centenary of Queensland's 1897 Aboriginal Protection and the Restriction of the Sale of Opium Act to reflect on a century of Aboriginal affairs in that state. Mick Dodson addresses the challenge facing the nation in the aftermath of the High Court's Wik decision in 'Extinguishment or Co-Existence: A Crucial Choice for Australia' (89–96) arguing against the federal Liberal/National coalition's position on the relationship between native title and pastoral leases. Co-existence, argues Dodson, is crucial to the process of reconciliation and the necessary mechanism for all parties to share in the wealth of the nation.

'In Refashioning Australian Racism' (*Arena Magazine*, 30:15–16), Verity Burgmann offers a reading of the differentiated response of Australian corporate interests to Pauline Hanson's double-pronged racist attacks on indigenous people and on the 'Asianisation' of Australian culture and business. As early as 1988, in her guise as a fish and chip shop proprietor, Hanson expressed anti-Asian views in the form of fears that fish and chips were in danger of being swamped by stir-fry noodles and curry shops, 'By 1990 potato cakes and battered flake will be nothing but a food memory for Australians'. While both the virulence and provenance of her anti-Asian sentiments have increased, big business in Australia has coolly distanced itself from these sentiments but remains sanguine on her attacks on Aboriginal people. The explanation for this is clear: 'The response of business . . . to the Wik judgement indicates clearly that, while business links with Asia are becoming increasingly valuable and valued, capital continues to view indigenous rights at home as a hindrance and a hazard' (16).

Further considerations of the Hanson phenomenon are provided by Lili Tuwai in 'The Hanson Debate' (*Pacific Islands Monthly*, 67(8):27–29) and Richard Nile in his editorial essay, 'The Pauline Hanson One Person Party'(*Journal of Australian Studies*, 52:1–9) in which he deals, among other issues, with the media coverage of the race debate. The media coverage of Pauline Hanson and the debate she engendered on race and racism within Australia are also taken up by Kalinga Seneviratne in 'Race Debate Exposes Media Shortcomings' (*Pacific Islands Monthly*, 67(8):33–34); and by Bruce Shearer's report on a seminar conducted at Victoria University of Technology (with the involvement of the Communications Law Centre, the Faculty of Arts and the Koori Development Unit) on the representation of Aboriginal issues in the Australian media ('All there in Black and White?', *Communications Update*, 135:18–19]).

In *Football and Racism: The AFL's Racial and Religious Vilification Rule* (Koorie Research Centre, Monash University, Discussion Paper 6), Greg Gardiner considers the impact of the Australian Football League's introduction in 1995 of the Racial and Religious Vilification Rule over the first two years of its operation. Gardiner's paper provides an analysis of the inception of the AFL's rule and its relationship to the Racial Hatred Act (1995), a piece of Commonwealth legislation which substantially amended the Racial Discrimination Act of 1975. Gardiner also discusses the Aboriginal experience of racism in football and a number of key incidents leading to the

AFL's ruling, as well as the agitation of indigenous players for some action from the AFL on the matter of racism in football. Augmenting the work of such historians as Colin Tatz (*Obstacle Race: Aborigines in Sport*, University of New South Wales Press, 1995), Gardiner also provides a survey of the known players of Aboriginal descent in the AFL (formerly the Victorian Football League) since the league's inception. On the operation of the AFL's racial vilification rule, Gardiner concludes that while there remain some problems with the implementation of the rule, the League is to be commended for taking the issue of on-field racism seriously. The introduction of the racial vilification rule marks a major development in the sophistication and cultural relevance of rules governing player conduct which would be well emulated by other sporting authorities. Football, particularly AFL football, is an important element in Australian cultural life. Through signalling unequivocally its intolerance of racism, the AFL sends an important message to thousands of fans about the rights of indigenous people and people from other minority and ethnic groups.

A further contribution to analysis of the 'race debate' which occupied much space in the twelve months following the election of the coalition government is provided by Leigh Dale in her 'Mainstreaming Australia' (*Journal of Australian Studies*, 53:130–145). Dale uses the term 'mainstreaming' to refer to the tactics of conservative groups and individuals to present their views as normative and quintessentially 'Australian' and pejoratively to dismiss the views of others – particularly marginal groups including Aboriginals – as occupying positions which are 'unAustralian'. Dale bases her arguments on analyses of the representations made by Pauline Hanson, John Howard and popular social commentator Hugh Mackay (*Re-Inventing Australia: The Mind and Mood of Australia in the 1990s*, Angus and Robertson, 1993).

Also published in 1997 is the collection *Race Matters: Indigenous Australians and 'Our' Society*, edited by Gillian Cowlishaw and Barry Morris. The majority of the twelve essays in the collection are reprints of previously published works, some with alterations and some in their original form. The anthology usefully gathers together work by Tony Birch, ' "Nothing has Changed": The Making and Unmaking of Koori Culture' (11–28, first published in *Meanjin*, 1992, 51(2):229–46); Julie Marcus, 'The Journey Out to the Centre' (29–52, first published in A. Rutherford, ed. *Aboriginal Culture Today*, Dangaroo Press, 1988); Marcia Langton 'Rum, Seduction and Death' (77–96, first published in *Oceania*, 1993, 6393):195–206); Roberta James, 'Rousseau's Knot: The Entanglement of Liberal Democracy and Racism' (53–76, first published in *Oceania* [1993] 63.3: 207–210; Merridy Malin, 'Mrs Eyres is no Ogre' (139–160, first published in *The Aboriginal Child at School*, 1990, 18(1):9–29) Barry Morris, 'Racism, Egalitarianism and Aborigines' (161–176) and Gillian Cowlishaw 'Where is Racism?' (177–190, both published originally in *Journal for Justice Studies*, 1990, 3; Ian Anderson, 'The Ethics of the Allocation of Health Resources' (191–208, originally published in *Choice or Chance? The Ethics of Resource Allocation for Minority Groups. A Summary of Papers Presented to the Public Health Association Seminar*, Australian Health Ethics Committee, National Health and Medical Research Council, 1992); Andrew Lattas, 'Aborigines and Contemporary Australian Nationalism: Primordiality and the Cultural Politics of Otherness' (223–258, first published in *Social Analysis*, 1990, 27:50–69); and Noel Pearson, 'Mabo: Towards Respecting Equality and Difference' (209–219) which was delivered as part of the Boyer Lecture series on Aboriginality in 1993. New essays in the collection have been contributed by Marilyn Wood 'The Breelong Blacks' (97–120); Deborah Bird Rose 'Australia Felix Rules OK!' (121–138); and Mudrooroo 'Tell them You're Indian' (259–267) in which Mudrooroo responds to the revelations appearing in the press in 1995–96 concerning his non-Aboriginality. The volume is certainly useful in gathering together pieces which have proved to be significant in shaping the field of Aboriginal and race studies in Australia – such as the essays by Langton, Birch, Lattas, and Marcus – into easily accessible form. And while recognizing the difficulties entailed in doing otherwise, it is a shame that the balance of the volume tilts so decidedly towards previously published work and the work of non-indigenous writers.

4. Stolen Children

The Human Rights and Equal Opportunity Commission handed down its report into the forced removal of Aboriginal and Torres Strait Islander Children in May 1997, occasioning renewed coverage of this issue in all media. The Commission concluded its inquiries and the completion of the report in a political climate radically different from that in which it had commenced its work in 1995. Significantly, the federal government of John Howard pre-empted the Commission's findings by announcing precipitously that compensation for victims of the child removal policies and practices of former administrations was out of the question. The report, *Bringing Them Home: Report of the National Inquiry into the Separation of Aboriginal and Torres Strait Islander Children from Their Families* is a lengthy and harrowing document which has not yet achieved its twin political goals of securing a formal apology from the federal government for the harm done to indigenous communities and individuals by forced child removal and gaining compensation for those affected. The first battle continues to be fought in the political arena; the second is now being fought in courts in many jurisdictions in the Commonwealth. *Bringing Them Home* summarizes evidence and submissions presented to the inquiry organized on a state-by-state basis. Sections of the report deal, in turn, with the consequences of removal, the case for reparation for victims of child removal practices, the range and efficacy of services presently available for those affected, and the continuation of high levels of child removal from Aboriginal families by welfare and other agencies. Arguably, Aboriginal activism on the issue of stolen children, the inquiry of the HR&EOC and its report *Bringing Them Home* has had far more impact culturally than politically, not least of all because of the ways in which Aboriginal activists on this issue have been able to secure media attention. An important part of this media appeal is the dominant methodology of focusing on the stories of individual men, women and children who were victims of this policy: the life story/case study approach characterizes a range of Aboriginal utterances on this issue, from *Telling Our Story: A Report by the Aboriginal Legal Service of Western*

Australia (Inc.) on the Removal of Aboriginal Children from their Families in Western Australia (Perth: Aboriginal Legal Service of Western Australia, 1995, reviewed *YWCCT 5*) to the method of the HR&EOC inquiry and the form of its final report.

A number of publications in 1997 take up the stolen children issue. The majority of these are written by legal practitioners and deal exclusively with legal issues – primarily the question of whether the principle of fiduciary duty may provide legal remedy for victims of forced child removal – and hence are of limited interest to cultural critics. Some, which may be noted here, include: Rebecca La Forgia 'Truth – But Still Waiting for Justice' (*Alternative Law Journal*, 22(4):192–195); Trevor Nyman 'Another Generation of Stolen Children' (*Law Society Journal*, 35:9–10); Karen King 'A Search for Justice: Wik and the Stolen Generations', *Legaldate*, 9:5–7).

A more broadly cultural consideration of the issue of stolen children is provided by Melinda Hinkson in 'The Politics of Aboriginality' (*Arena Magazine*, 30:30–31). Other publications in this year take up the stolen children issue in more broadly cultural terms, these include Alan Luke's 'The Material Effects of the Word: Apologies, "Stolen Children", and Public Discourse' (*Discourse: Studies in the Cultural Politics of Education*, 18(3):343–368). Luke's essay provides a detailed linguistic analysis of John Howard's ill-received opening address to the Australian Reconciliation Convention in May 1997 in which he failed to apologize on behalf of the Commonwealth for the damage done to indigenous people through forced child removal, to which the indigenous people present responded one by one by standing and turning their backs to the Prime Minister. Drawing insights from speech-act theorists and Foucault's idea of discursive 'effects', Luke undertakes a critical discourse analysis of Howard's speech revealing its narrative structure and the power dynamics which shape it. As Luke demonstrates, the federal government is the only entity to be given agency in Howard's speech, all other parties – the Australian people, and indigenous people in particular are cast as the objects of government action. This is in stark contrast to Howard's treatment of past actions and past policies such as child removal which appear to have simply, and quite regrettably, occurred. Luke's analysis reveals the ways in which the Prime Minister's lexical choice effects a distancing from the past and a narrowing of interpretations of what that past means, as in 'we need to acknowledge as a nation ... what European settlement has meant for ... Aboriginal and Torres Strait Islander peoples' (quoted by Luke, p. 358) in which, Luke argues:

> the acknowledgment is due not of the action *per se* but, instead, of the meanings assigned to them by those whose lives, families and communities were fundamentally and irrevocably altered. First note the lexical choice of 'European settlement': not 'colonisation', much less 'invasion', with settlement constructed as a benign, completed process affiliated with a geographical location and culture (European) rather than any specific national or military entity. Second, note the shift of attention from the details, intents and material effects of the 'settlement' towards indigenous peoples' interpretation of that action – as if

the problem is, in part, the 'meaning' assigned to settlement and related actions by Aborigines and Torres Strait Islanders (358).

Echoing a point made by Deborah Bird Rose in relation to John Herron's deportment on the stolen children issue, Luke notes the way in which Howard repeatedly expressed his personal sorrow at the suffering of these people – 'Personally I feel deep sorrow for those of my fellow Australians who suffered injustices under the practices of past generations...' or 'Personally I am sorry for the hurt and trauma many people here today may continue to feel as a consequence' (quoted in Luke p. 358). Howard's personal statements of sorrow fall far short, as members of the audience registered, of the explicit performative required: 'I apologize'.

Thus the speech act the Prime Minister failed to perform and continued indigenous demands for an apology have become a nodal point in discourse for the assertion of identity and rights, and for coming to terms with colonial history. Luke concludes that Aboriginal demands for an apology are neither a grab for capital nor a retrospective laying on of guilt, they are demands for 'a reconsideration and discursive framing of history, and a demand that indigenous peoples ... will never again simply be positioned and defined as deficit subjects for government "treatment" of the day' (366). In Luke's view, this is something that John Howard fails to understand. Of course, another view is that this is something he understands only too well. In his eagerness to avoid blame and guilt (and apologies), John Howard reconstructs a past without agency and a future where there is a surplus of technical legal responsibility with nobody but the government around to accept it. Aboriginal people are positioned either as objects of advantage or disadvantage, but never as agents of power. Likewise, the citizenry, 'we Australians' (a formulation which excludes Aboriginal people when uttered by Howard) may be impelled or cajoled towards various sentiments but the only responsible actor in this universe is the government and it does not require any material intervention or social action from anyone.

In the Best Interests of the Child? Stolen Children: Aboriginal Pain/White Shame, by Link-Up (New South Wales) and Tikka Jan Wilson is based on the submission prepared by the New South Wales branch of Link-Up, the organization which has worked since 1980 to assist and provide support for Aboriginal people removed from their families, for the HR&EOC inquiry into forced child removal. Much material in the book was gathered at twenty-two community forums held throughout New South Wales and sponsored by Link-Up. The volume liberally incorporates testimonials primarily from people removed as children with fewer statements from the mothers whose children were taken as 'the level of grief and pain that mothers who lost children have felt is so deep, that most women were unwilling and unable to open up these old wounds ... One woman ... who had been taken away as a child subsequently lost her own children. Although she said she would readily talk about her own experiences as a separated child, she could not bear to speak about the loss of her children' (25–26). Like *Bringing them Home, In the Best Interest of the Child?* is harrowing reading. The testimonies of scores of Link-Up clients are contextualized in an historical narrative which traces the long history of Aboriginal child separation practices in New South Wales and the growth and systematic development of these practices into the dominant feature of the management of Aboriginal populations by the middle of the twentieth century. The book examines the near impenetrable blanket of silence and administrative obfuscation around the issue of indigenous child removal and chronicles the pioneering research of people like Peter Read and Coral Edwards (*The Lost Children*. Doubleday, 1989) in bringing the extent of the practice to light and facilitating Aboriginal access to vital archives, such as the Register of Wards of the State, in an effort to seek out information about birth families and the whereabouts of stolen children. The book also contains discussion of the ongoing impact of child removal, both in terms of the long-term psychological impact of these experiences on parents and children, but also in terms of the persistently high levels of state intervention into family life endured by Aboriginal people in New South Wales. While child removal as such is no longer officially part of the policy which governs Aboriginal affairs in New South Wales, Aboriginal children are still removed from their families in greater numbers than the children of any other racial/cultural group.

In response to the HR&EOC's inquiry, the Minajalku Aboriginal Corporation, an indigenous ecumenical centre based in Melbourne, conducted its own inquiry into indigenous child removal, the findings are published in *Home – Still Waiting: Report of the Minajalku Aboriginal Corporation into Aboriginal Children and the Churches in Victoria* (Thornbury, Vic: Minajalku Aboriginal Corporation). The report details the activities of a range of church-based organizations in Aboriginal child removal and placement. The agencies investigated include Copelen Child and Family Services, Orana Family Services, Mission of St James and St John, St John's Home for Boys and Girls, St Joseph's Babies and Family Services, and the Good Shepherd organization. In addition to providing a detailed picture of the extent of the involvement of church agencies in Aboriginal child removal and placement through to the present, this report will prove a valuable resource for those engaged in research on stolen children as it describes, in detail, the extent, condition and accessibility of archival material in these agencies.

5. Aboriginality and Emplacement: Home, Travel and Tourism

5.1 Tourism
Gordon Waitt's essay 'Selling Paradise and Adventure: Representations of Landscape in the Tourist Advertising of Australia' (*Australian Geographical Studies*, 35(1):47–60) provides an extremely detailed analysis of the Australian Tourist Commission's (ATC) 1992 international advertising campaigns, employed to promote Australia specifically as a 'paradise' and 'adventure' destination to international tourists. While Waitt's major concern is with the depiction of landscape in these print and television advertisements, he makes a number of interesting points regarding the representation of Aboriginality within this context. An ATC-sponsored survey of international tourists to Australia revealed that 49% were interested in experiencing traditional Aboriginal culture. In appealing to this market, the ATC's representations of indigenous people 'communicates,

amplifies and reinforces' a suite of highly primitivist tropes and images. Visual texts reproduce images of lean black male bodies with spears and boomerangs in settings suggestive of remote and traditional life, against colourful backdrops including red rock and sunsets. Other images depict activities, including rock art and body painting, which are suggestive of secret and ancient rituals. The conjunction of these features imply that Aboriginal people are living in harmony with nature as they have for untold centuries and that their culture provides an insight into the very dawn of human life. The representations are both ahistorical and deeply romanticized. Similarly, verbal texts promise visitors to Australia an escape to a 'primitive world'; 'to witness strange customs'; and the opportunity to 'experience directly a world of myth and legend extremely different from their own' in a 'land that time had forgotten, a place like nowhere on earth' (quoted by Waitts, p. 51).

Covering some of the same territory as Waitt is Paul Miller's essay 'Would I Lie to You?: Illustrating Indigenous Australians in the Travel Narrative' (*Coppertales*, 4:109–124). Miller draws his formulation of the genre of illustrated travel literature from the work of B. M. Stafford (*Voyage into Substance: Art, Science, Nature and the Illustrated Travel Account*, Massachusetts Institute of Technology, 1984) arguing that the popularity of popular travel genres is based on an 'ardent yearning for facts rather than fictions' (Stafford quoted by Miller, p. 109), not least of which is the yearning for visual facts. Photography has proved a boon for travel literature holding as it does the promise of truth prevailing over deceit. Miller goes on to consider the use of illustrations of Australian Aboriginal people in popular travel literature, including discussions of D. W. Carnegie's *Spinifex and Sand* (first published in 1899; reprinted Penguin 1973), Ernestine Hill's *The Great Australian Loneliness* (first published in 1937; reprinted Robertson and Mullens, 1943); and Robyn Davidson's *Tracks* (Jonathan Cape, 1980). In his consideration of these and other quite different texts, Miller argues that despite photography's claims to truth value, it is frequently the case that there exists a discrepancy between what is said in the text and what the photographs show. Miller contends that, in the face of this discrepancy, the reader of the text leans more towards the veracity of what is said than what is shown. While it is not made clear what Miller concludes from this, he goes on to argue that with the advent of visual technologies such as CD-ROMs, the power of photography stands to be increased; that is, its powers of representation and misrepresentation may become more persuasive as visual media hold even greater sway.

5.2 Aboriginality and the City

Brett Martin's 'The Battle for Redfern' (*The Bulletin*, 11 February, 16–19) exemplifies several of the problems associated with the media's portrayal of Aboriginality. Discussing Aboriginal children from 'the block', an Aboriginal-owned housing estate in Redfern, Sydney – the article purports to reveal Sydney's 'inner-city in the raw' (16). Because of its association with poverty, crime and drugs, the block provides a particularly easy target for journalists seeking the 'raw material' for sensationalist stories. In this instance, as in most cases where the block is publicly represented, Martin heightens prejudice, highlighting the negatively construed differences between (panicked) non-Aboriginal *Bulletin* readers and the Aboriginal inhabitants of the block. Furthermore, he adds his own special touch. On the basis of a belatedly acknowledged conversation with Ray Vincent – the one Aboriginal resident from the block with whom Martin actually talks – Martin foregrounds an association between Aboriginal children and Asian (specifically Vietnamese) 'heroin gang' (17) members. The Vietnamese 'gang members' are then constructed as bearing primary responsibility for the area's drug problems. Wholeheartedly accepting and indeed appropriating Vincent's claim that Vietnamese heroin dealers 'needed another outlet' and 'the block was the perfect place' (118), Martin manages to reproduce damning stereotypes about *two* of Sydney's ethnic minority groups. In addition, '[a]lleged paedophiles' (18), including one whom Martin names, are represented as having contributed to the social, mental and health problems of the block's teenagers. However, Martin makes no attempt to situate the daily struggles of Redfern's Aboriginal residents in the wider contexts of institutionalized racism and dispossession. An inserted piece by the Aboriginal writer Roberta Sykes (19) raises these issues, but Martin fails to address them at all, choosing instead to represent the views of the local police commissioner, one disgruntled resident and the Aboriginal Housing Company (AHC). The AHC (though not in this article) is accused of wanting to sell the highly valuable land for redevelopment purposes (see ABC TV *Four Corners* 'The Block' 1997). Mentioning a 'spate of media horror stories' which fuelled a 'full-scale [police] operation' (17), Martin seeks to distance his own article from other problematic media 'beat-ups'. The damaging claim that Redfern's Aboriginal people are 'cultureless' is headlined in a section entitled simply 'No Culture' (19). Manipulating the words of Mick Mundine, the head of the AHC, Martin reinforces the populist and highly problematic view that 'urban Aborigines', in contrast to their idealized outback counterparts, lack anything positive or worth while in terms of culture. Had Martin spoken with other Aboriginal locals, he might have produced a more complex account of Redfern as an Aboriginal place for, despite Mundine's claim that '75% of residents want to get out' (19), many Aboriginal inhabitants continue to resist relocation (ABC Radiotapes, *Women Out Loud*, Radio National, 2 December, 1998). In contrast, several other texts of the same year (see Museum of Sydney, *Guwanyi Exhibition Catalogue* and ABC TV *Four Corners* 'The Block') produce a strong sense that Redfern and the block – despite inadequate housing conditions – have and continue to provide a 'homeplace' for Aboriginal people in Sydney.

The issue of representation, especially as it relates to Aboriginal inhabitation of urban spaces, is taken up very differently in two other 1997 articles. The first, Ian Alexander and Oren Yiftachel's 'Sacred Site or Sacred Cow? The Frontier of Urban Racial Struggle in Australia' (*Progress in Planning*, 47(4):275–290) concerns the protracted struggle between various groups, including Aboriginal people, heritage conservationists, developers and the state government, over the future of the Swan Brewery site in Perth, Western Australia. Alexander and Yiftachel provide a brief account of the site's non-Aboriginal history before highlighting its significance to Aboriginal people who claim that the area is the home of the Waugal serpent (see also Jane M. Jacobs, *Edge of Empire*, Routledge, 1996, reviewed *YWCCT* 6). This essay can be critiqued for the tidy tale it wants to tell about a 'deprived indigenous minority's' (275) efforts to resist the 'inherently conflicting goals and aspirations of the capitalist-settler state' (289). The authors' pre-Foucauldian analysis – they conceive community groups as coming 'from below' (289) and the state as in effect being able 'to control the Aboriginal community' (289) – is too simplistic to be of much value for scholars seeking to theorize the contradictions and complexities which comprise battles over land in contemporary Australian cities. The authors' conclusion that 'in this head-on conflict the economic "sacred cow" proved more resilient than the indigenous "sacred site"' (289) betrays their oppositional structuring of the groups, issues and discourses involved in the struggle. Furthermore, it indicates their failure to appreciate how the perceived non-resilience of sacredness – its partial unavailability to non-Aboriginal Australians – has frequently resulted in it being denounced as insubstantial when pitted against the cold hard 'facts' of 'economic gain' or 'job prospects'.

Romanticism strongly informs Alexander and Yiftachel's understanding of Aboriginal people. Defining indigenous people as the 'occupiers of settler states prior to the arrival of European colonisers' (276), the authors unthinkingly exclude the very (contemporary Aboriginal) people whom they discuss in their paper. In addition, it is difficult to tell who might comprise the implied audience for their broad-ranging summation of pre-colonial Aboriginality. The few paragraphs on this subject reduce highly complex and little understood pre-colonial Aboriginality to something which was highly democratic, 'in tune' with nature and anti-capitalist (277). The authors' description of 'the Aboriginal mode of production' (277) depicts Aboriginality as something which was always already singular, thereby eliding the many differences between indigenous groups which continue to this day.

The essay has a tendency to reduce, simplify and generalize. While it contributes little to discussion about more abstract concepts such as space, place and sacredness, Alexander and Yiftachel reveal a strong commitment to justice for Australia's indigenous people. The essay's depiction of some of the 'power brokers, personalities, dates, bills and legislations' (285) provides a key to understanding the authors' framing of the struggle over the site. While a Labor Member of Parliament (MP), one of the authors witnessed the various 'waverings' and 'dilemmas' (285) of several other MPs and Ministers on the issue of the Brewery's future. This may help to explain the authors' way of framing the treatment of Aboriginal people and their interests. The essay serves as a reminder that while neat narratives of power and oppression may not always prove sufficiently intellectually rigorous, they can sometimes serve the function of highlighting the genuine power disparities that continue to exist between indigenous and non-indigenous Australians.

The second article which relates to the subject of Aboriginality in the city is Kay Anderson and Jane Jacob's 'From Urban Aborigines to Aboriginality and the City: One Path through the History of Australian Cultural Geography' (*Australian Geographical Studies*, 35(1):12–22). The title of the article makes reference to Fay Gale's important book *Urban Aborigines* (Australian National University Press, 1972) which was significant in bringing critical attention to bear on the category of urban Aboriginality and enabling subsequent work but whose conception of urban Aborigines has been substantially challenged by the terms in which identity is formulated in the work that followed. The essay productively highlights the inadequacies of 'narrow and constricting essentialisms' (14) of the kind which can be identified in Alexander and Yiftachel's article. Confirming the political value of challenging rigid categorizations of identity and power, Anderson and Jacobs attempt to answer the charge of apoliticism which has been directed at cultural geography as a 'sub-discipline'. Through reference to their own undergraduate experiences at the University of Adelaide, the authors depict their introduction to issues of cultural and racial difference and the associated power inequities. Challenging those shortsighted critics who oppose culture and politics, the cultural and the economic, the lived and the representational, Anderson and Jacobs argue that these oppositions result when critics forget that the history of cultural geography *is* political. They also suggest that critics from 'the Left' may be 'conditioned by an ambitious, universalising northern disciplinary perspective, which seems oblivious to the fact that there were other styles of cultural geography in other (southern) spaces' (13). Elegantly negotiating various issues to do with cultural geography, 'urban Aborigines' and representation, the essay successfully rebuts the claim that cultural geography 'lacks a sense of politics' (13). Indeed the reader is left with no doubt as to the significance of contemporary cultural geography's contribution to and engagement with feminist and postcolonial politics.

The essay takes as its chief example the shift in emphasis from the category 'Urban Aborigines' to 'Aboriginality and the City'. The authors represent the changes that have taken place since the 1970s, 'the questioning (though not necessarily abandonment) of positivist methods, the problematising of cross-cultural research, the shift in emphasis from description of a different sub-group to a politics of difference' as 'for the most part . . . for the good' (16). The most significant difference that Anderson and Jacobs identify between *Urban Aborigines* and contemporary cultural geographies relates to identity. Conceptualized in postmodern and postcolonial rubric as contingent rather than absolute, identity in contemporary cultural geographies is unlikely to be conceived as given. Rather, the processes by which it is made are recognized as centrally important to analysing power relations and cities. In contrast to earlier work in which a (white) academic researcher studied Aborigines as a 'category' and the city as 'context', Anderson and Jacobs argue that contemporary cultural geographers attempt to consider the ways in which Aboriginality is articulated *in* and *through* the spaces of the city. This includes considering how researchers' own involvement, experiences and frames of reference impact on and transform this 'fluid and intersubjective' process of structuring difference (18). The authors contextualize differences between approaches, relating them to broader changes in explanatory schemes in the fields of cultural studies and social inquiry. In addition, they note that while some strands of the geography discipline have embraced these changes, others have been less inclined to do so.

Acknowledging the value of their own hindsight and the political potency of their undergraduate teacher Fay Gale's *Urban Aborigines*, the authors resist the temptation to represent their own more recent and self-reflexive work as unequivocally progressive and Gale's – because of its assimilationist traces (15) – as purely problematic. Furthermore, their essay gives those who practise forms of cultural geography in Australia the opportunity to consider 'one local lineage'(20). Anderson describes two instances of her own work in Redfern, showing through this how the refusal to presume difference and disadvantage opens up possibilities for destabilizing neat categorizations of subject and object, power and resistance. In contrast to the depiction of Aboriginal groups in Alexander and Yiftachel's essay, Aboriginal occupants of the block are shown to be an internally differentiated group who no more embody resistance than do non-Aboriginal researchers embody objectivity. The particular, the complex and the contingent come into view in Anderson's cultural geography which show 'how divisions of ethnicity, language, social class, gender and so on unsettle the authority of the analytical grids we seek to impose on them' (17). However, Anderson's concern that resistance stories 'suffer from their own political essentialism' (17) derives from her assumption that political essentialism is essentially problematic. As the indigenous activist Michael Dodson has pointed out: 'charging black people with "essentialism" is little more than a modern extension of the politics of control over knowledge that has been going on since colonisation'(*Australian Aboriginal Studies*, 1994, 1:10). Citing Said, Bhabha, hooks and Trinh (18), Jacobs and Anderson document some of the many reasons to abandon essentialist notions. However, their failure to acknowledge that there are contexts in which 'political essentialisms' might be necessary for indigenous groups creates a gap in their otherwise balanced argument (see also the work of Ian Anderson, reviewed below). This is not without its ironies for in her own important contributions to Australian cultural geography both in this article and elsewhere (see Jacobs and Rita Huggins and Jackie Huggins 'Kooramindanjie: Place and the Postcolonial' *History Workshop Journal* [1995] 39: 165–181; and Jacobs, *Edge of Empire*, Routledge, 1996), Jacobs reminds readers that the Aboriginalization of urban space involves drawing on a variety of Aboriginalities, some of which reflect and reinforce essentialist notions, including primitivized Aboriginality and Aboriginality as resistance (19). Aware that there is an 'ambiguous cultural politics associated with these engagements with Aboriginality' (19), Jacobs reminds readers that the Aboriginalization of urban space can be interpreted either as a 'new phase of non-Aboriginal enthrallment' (19) representative of neo-colonialism or conversely, as evidence of postcolonialism which while 'a far cry from urban land rights' (19) unsettles colonial authority in the city. The fact that the revalorization of identities 'made' under the force of colonialism is part of counter-colonialism reminds us that it is not possible to dismiss identity, essential or otherwise as inherently problematic. While this criticism may be charged with making too much of one line in the essay, given Anderson and Jacobs' central argument that cultural geography has a sense of politics, it seems important to question how this moment might relate to the tendency to dismiss too easily the possibilities of identity politics. While the domination/resistance script (17) is necessarily challenged, for indigenous peoples and those fighting racial and ethnic oppression, 'political essentialism' may also be a necessity.

    In this article Jacobs and Anderson also identify a 'new racism' based not on the idea that 'Aborigines are "lesser", "other", "uncivilised", but rather around a view that Aborigines, despite their economic and political marginalisation now have *too much . . .*' (19). Linking this new or 'postcolonial racism' to the 'unsettlement of authority' (19) associated with the Aboriginalization of space, they point out the irony of the fact that this discourse arises out of various political attempts to compensate for the injustices of the past. The political climate of 1997, the rise of Pauline Hanson's One Nation party and the associated proliferation of the claim to marginality make their recognition of this new racism particularly pertinent. In *No Road (Bitumen all the way)* (reviewed below) Stephen Muecke also registers the significance of discourses of dispossession to modern subjects (152), however, unlike Jacobs and Anderson he does not draw connections between the claim to marginality and 'postcolonial racism'.

Anderson and Jacobs make important points about the value of non-Aboriginal scholars continuing to risk the charge of 'speaking out of place' (20). Reminding readers that 'speaking only about how Aboriginality is "made" by non-Aboriginals may well work to give further voice to those who for too long have had the last say' (20), Jacobs and Anderson also question the notion that there is a 'self' which can be independently located, discussed and theorized. Returning to a theme which runs through the essays, and which Muecke also takes up in *No Road*, Anderson and Jacobs remind readers that blurring the boundaries between centre and margin may open up, rather than preclude, the possibilities for reforming politics.

5.3 Aboriginality, Architecture and Planning

In contrast to the productively sophisticated way Jacobs and Anderson theorize Aboriginality and space, Tom Stannage's *Lakeside City, The Dreaming of Joondalup* unwittingly depicts some of the absences, gaps and refusals which persist in Australian town planning, history writing and politics. The book is worth mentioning in this context because these very refusals and disavowals reveal much about interracial relations in the Australian context. Essentially an attempt to render the extraordinarily dull process of planning and making the 'satellite' city of Joondalup interesting, *Lakeside City* is a somewhat sycophantic and touristic promotion of the apparent wonders of 'Australia's only environmental and post-modern city' (xv) – a claim not supported by any attempt to explicate terms such as 'post-modern' and 'environmental'. Obsessed with the end point of the creation of this town, Tom Stannage's linear and forward-thrusting history is littered with enlightenment metaphors and unexamined assumptions about the 'wonders' of ongoing European 'settlement' in the contemporary Australian context. For instance, though he relies throughout the text on images of light and shimmering implied by the name, it is not until well into the book that Stannage recalls one of the Anglo planners asking two *non-*Aboriginal anthropologists about the meaning of Joondalup, which is apparently 'the place of the glistening' (49). Stannage's approval of what he perceives to be the 'decisive' and 'progressive' actions of men such as Charles Court, the former Liberal premier of Western Australia and the Australian entrepreneur Robert Holmes à Court is all too evident. Describing Charles Court, for example, he states:

> Court looked on the world as a field of action. As Minister for
> Industrial Development . . . he had released and harnessed the
> State's north-west mineral resources and had dammed the Ord

River in order to make the Kimberley region a productive garden. He was not a man to sit around waiting on events. If a new city was needed for Western Australia, and the arithmetic said it should be at Joondalup (Court was an accountant by trade), then at Joondalup a new city would be built. And if the Commonwealth Government of Whitlam reneged on its own responsibilities, so what? This was what it usually did. . . . In any case it was very important for Western Australia not to be seen as a State claimant on the Commonwealth. Indeed, the future of the State depended on Western Australia showing Canberra, Melbourne and Sydney that it could stand on its own two feet and lead the nation (17).

Attempting to naturalize the process of damming and mining by depicting the Kimberley region as a 'garden', this passage constructs the Kimberleys as a place which is not only necessarily subordinate to 'culture', but also to the desires of productive (read non-indigenous, non-environmentalist) 'action' men such as Court. Furthermore, the 'progress' narrative encoded here – and even less subtly elsewhere in the text – reveals the not-so-submerged sense in which Joondalup is conceived by those involved as a vehicle for Western Australia to assert not only its apparent maturity (it *will* 'stand on its own two feet') but its right to lead the nation into the future. Joondalup *as* the future is never in doubt – the primary players are visionaries and the 'Edenic' town is something 'about to come down from the clouds' (8).

The most notable absence in the text relates to the denial that race is an 'issue' in the Australian context. Stannage suggests for instance that '[r]ace riots in American cities from the mid-1960s might seem a world away from protest-free Australian cities, but the flight of the middle classes from decaying central districts of cities was not' (9). At the risk of asserting the obvious, it is necessary to point out the profound irony of placing these issues in apposition for the very perception that the inner city was decaying is intimately connected to the increasing arrival of migrant and previously rural-dwelling Aboriginal people to inner city spaces. The image of Australia as 'protest-free' has its counterpart in the perception that Australia is 'happily multicultural'. In failing to theorize difference both these myths effectively reify whiteness as an all-accepting but still dominant Australian norm. Hence racial difference and the 'problems' it represents can be conveniently 'forgotten'. An early suggestion that the Joondalup project be allocated 'more land for lower cost housing, even housing for people of Aboriginal descent' (17) is described later in the text as an interest which has been 'lost' – 'Maunsell's interest in Aboriginal housing had been lost, but not the concern for a social mix' (49). Furthermore this has been ordained from the outset – 'designed as a beautiful place for beautiful lives' (p. xv), Joondalup is thus described in the preface: '[i]t began as the place of the shining for the first peoples; it became a shining city for those seeking freedom and some independence in the golden lands of Australia' (xv). The journey from past to present is one in which a largely unspoken Aboriginality is left behind in order to make a seemingly all-embracing (non-Aboriginal) modernity possible.

Two essays which focus on the theme of Aboriginality in architecture go some way to addressing the blindness exhibited by Stannage's rose-coloured view of Joondalup. These are Mathilde Lochert's 'Mediating Aboriginal Architecture' (*Transition*, 54–55:8–19) and Paul Hogben and Stanislaus Fung's 'Landscape and Culture, Geography and Race, Some Shifts in Australian Architectural Commentary' (*Voices*, 7:2, Winter:5–14). Expounding on issues to do with the 'place' of Aboriginality as raised for instance by Anderson and Jacobs, these articles focus particularly on its incorporation into the built environment.

If, as Mathilde Lochert claims, the effects of colonial discourse on Aboriginal culture and identity have not been 'critically addressed' in 'mainstream architecture' (8) then 'Mediating Aboriginal Architecture' can be seen as an achievement in itself. Despite her somewhat problematic use of terms such as 'mainstream architecture', 'critical' and 'public', Lochert provides an interesting discussion about two very different instances of collaboration between Aboriginal groups and non-Aboriginal architects. These are Brambuk Aboriginal Cultural Centre – which has a curvilinear design often seen to exist in harmony with the natural landscape – and the inner-urban located Victorian Aboriginal Health Service (VAHS), which has a 'high tech/industrial form and structure' (16). Lochert is not interested in the buildings themselves as much as in how these different collaborative efforts between Aboriginal groups and non-Aboriginal architects have been discussed in the architectural media.

The essay performs the important function of subjecting the often highly dubious pronouncements of some well-known architects to critique. The inherent nostalgism of Brambuk architect, Greg Burgess, is, if not completely deconstructed at the very least, exposed as fallacious (13). Lochert makes some salient (though not revelatory for those familiar with the field) points about issues of authenticity, primitivism and judgement. For instance she notes that the 'gossip' (13) that occurs among those in architectural circles has tended to focus on the Brambuk building as a representation of Aboriginality that promotes 'primitivism' (13), while an article on the VAHS, in contrast, implies that this building's 'industrial finish' (Hyatt quoted in Lochert, p. 16) and 'high-tech' minimalism is in some sense 'not Aboriginal'. Highlighting the unexamined nature of the assumptions involved in these architectural pronouncements, Lochert suggests that, '[a]s part of any evaluation, the fact that the building itself was a result of discussion and that Koori people were active agents in its design and construction, needs to be acknowledged and addressed' (14). In such moments, Lochert demonstrates her appreciation of the complexities involved in interpreting and analysing buildings which are, after all, constructed for and in consultation with Aboriginal people.

However – and this is perhaps the biggest irony of the essay – Lochert herself fails to depict the views of Aboriginal clients and users, despite the criticism she aims at the architectural media for not doing so (10). Though she suggests that VAHS clients consider the health centre building to fulfil their 'very specific requirements' (17), Lochert neither adequately supports this claim nor does she provide insights into the meanings Aboriginal clients and users of Brambuk have and continue to make of this building. Thus, the possibility that 'artful politics' (Stephen Muecke, 'Captain Cook's Shoes',

Island, 1994, 60(1):126–9], reviewed *YWCCT 4*) might comprise Aboriginal people's own involvement in perpetuating primitivist and romanticized notions of Aboriginality remains unexplored. As a result, the article suffers from an unnecessarily pessimistic interpretation of these collaborative efforts. For instance, though Lochert acknowledges that within mainstream architecture there is an increasing 'focus on the Aboriginal client "speaking" and the non-Aboriginal architect "listening"' (8), she highlights the dangers rather than the positive potential of this approach (9). Making the well-observed point that '[w]hen the non-Aboriginal architect is represented as "listening" in the design process ... he [sic] can be seen in effect as remaining silent' (9), Lochert does not acknowledge that listening – not necessarily equivalent to silence – is part of dialogue and therefore an integral aspect of challenging the dominance of the 'monologue' which she has identified as characterizing 'mainstream architectural discourse' (10). In some respects, the opposition between mainstream architecture and its invisible but implied 'fringe' is repeated in Lochert's overly simplistic structuring of the relation between the two forms of Aboriginal architecture under discussion. Significantly, given her claim that mainstream architecture has been less than self-reflexive about its own involvement in reifying images of the Aboriginal 'other' (9) Lochert contributes to the development of a dialogue between critical theory and architectural discourses.

Supporting some of Lochert's contentions about the racial politics of mainstream architecture, Hogben and Fung's 'Landscape and Culture, Geography and Race: Some Shifts in Australian Architectural Commentary' opens up a context in which to address the question of how Aboriginal groups participate in what might be deemed primitivist or romantic representations. Pointing out that architectural commentary has a tendency to rely on the easy rhetoric of '[t]he international marketplace and its forms of cultural tourism' (12), the authors foreground the idea that architecture does not exist independently of the state and the market (12). However, in doing so they risk reducing Aboriginal involvement in cultural tourism to a form of co-option. While Aboriginality matters to the global market, to Australian nationalism and to 'some of our most prominent architects and commentators' (12), cultural tourism as evinced in places such as Brambuk cannot be reductively interpreted always and only as exploitation. Without denying the validity of the authors' claim that 'Aboriginal otherness ... is considered a positive value for cultural growth in Australia and [that has] been appropriated by cultural industries in signifying Australianness to the world' (11), it is necessary to recognize the limits of this perspective which parallels Lochert's implied devaluation of places such as Brambuk. Although all three authors (rightly) seek to challenge the simplistic and romantic equations between primitive Aboriginalities and authenticity that apparently abound in architectural discourse, we encounter the limits of their argument when they fail adequately to attend to the possible and actual benefits for indigenous groups of such associations. Nevertheless, by highlighting the hypocrisy of architects who deem Aboriginality in buildings important, while failing 'to speak about the actual conditions of Australia's indigenous people' (12), Hogben and Fung make a valuable contribution to discussion about Aboriginality's relation to the architectural landscape.

5.4 Aboriginality, Home and Travel
Several publications take up the issue of 'home' which was raised earlier in relation to Redfern, Sydney. The increased interest in the construct 'home' relates to other efforts to explore concepts such as dispossession, displacement and belonging. In the introduction (1–31) to *Home/World: Space, Community and Marginality in Sydney's West*, a collaborative production by five authors connected with the University of Western Sydney, the contributors specify several aims – these include the desire to examine issues such as home, community and belonging, their hope of engendering a positive image for western Sydney and their goal of opening up the possibilities for 'representing' this area. This last one rather than being about the discovery of truth is conceived in terms of the shared desire 'to unseal' (16) the western suburbs, and thereby to undermine totalizing visions of this often stigmatized part of Sydney.

Having established some of the terms which will underlie the essays, *Home/World* presents four individually produced, self-contained and very different essays on western Sydney. Lesley Johnson's 'Feral suburbia? Western Sydney and the Problem of Urban Sprawl' (31–65) provides insights into the links between 'official' town planning perspectives – particularly the view from above, as challenged by de Certeau – and the marginalization of the desires and attachments of those who are constructed as the 'feral' and non-rational inhabitants of places such as Sydney's western suburbs. Johnson's analysis of the 1948 *Planning Scheme for the County of Cumberland* (35) demonstrates how the everyday lives of western Sydney's inhabitants, characterized in many instances by a desire for 'home', were consigned to virtual insignificance as planners sought to sell their 'solutions' to what they perceived to be the 'problems of urban sprawl' and 'inner-city decay' (54). Although Johnson does not explicitly discuss the ways in which race and migrancy impacted upon the planners' capacity to define western Sydney in these ways, her essay opens up the possibilities for thinking about the ongoing construction of much denigrated places, including western Sydney – and we might also think of the inner-city suburb of Redfern – which have strong associations with indigenous peoples. For instance, she states that: '[t]he complexity of the city and the needs and desires of the diverse urban populations – the lived experience of the urban – are reduced to this surface, to that which can be known and documented through population statistics and the mapping and monitoring techniques of social administration' (60). Ignoring daily meanings produced by community members, this process resembles contemporary efforts by state and housing authorities (such as are depicted in Brett Martin's article) to argue – despite evidence to the contrary – that Redfern's Aboriginal residents want to leave their home here and relocate to the suburbs. Johnson's analysis of the county planning scheme also shows how aspiring home-makers who protested the recommendations of the council were 'asked only to give their views on the solutions proposed by this agency, not to debate the way in which the problems themselves had been conceptualised' (61). Her essay is a challenge to critique the ways in which 'urban problems' are framed from the outset and by whom.

In his essay 'Outside the Spaces of Modernity' (66–98) in the same collaboration, Michael Symonds delves into the history of Western philosophy in order to historicize the western suburbs conceptualization as 'central Sydney's other, relating Sydney as a necessarily divided city to Hegel's effort to theorize the European-Western tradition. Symonds discusses aspects of Hegel's *The Phenomenology of Spirit* in order to demonstrate the ways in which Sophocles' *Antigone* represents 'how the city, as the site of the human law, was formed in relation to a specifically enhanced nature as the place of the divine law of Antigone'. In this Hegelian logic, nature appears as the enchantment which must be left behind if modern subjectivity is to succeed as such. Because, in the Australian context, nature has been constructed as foreign and antagonistic, it is, according to Symonds, only recently that subjectivity and home have been seen as able to be enacted in Australian spaces. For Symonds this explains the relation between the recent aestheticization of the Australian 'natural' landscape (which he argues has tended to include the Australian Dreamtime) and the birth of parts of Australia as 'modern cultural' spaces. Envisaged as neither central and cultural nor natural and beautiful, until the 1960s, the western suburbs had been represented as unhomely and as a space unable to produce the modern subjects that Sydney required in order to achieve the status of 'world-class' city. In an otherwise intricately constructed essay, Symonds' conclusion that 'the western Sydney of the future will almost certainly fit into the Hegelian dialectical pattern of city and home as surely as is now the case for the rest of Sydney' (92) stands out as being somewhat reductive.

In his contribution to this volume, 'At Home in the Entrails of the West' (99–153) Ghassan Hage argues that if multiculturalism is not to become/remain a fetishized and empty concept it is necessary to ground debates about multiculturalism in migrant home-building practices and intercultural interaction. Hage contrasts these practices with what he calls 'cosmomulticulturalism', suggesting that the former can be associated with Sydney's western suburbs and the latter with central Sydney. He describes cosmomulticulturalism as being 'part of a more general practical field of a "multiculturalism without migrants": a multicultural reality made of institutions that seems to exist without any migrants to sustain it' (118). Dividing his essay into three parts Hage analyses migrant (in this case Lebanese) home-making in the western suburbs suggesting that food production and sharing among ethnic groups are a crucial part of home-making for Lebanese-Australians. Pointing out that such practices are less about the desire for a past home than the desire for home in the present, Hage rereads nostalgia, suggesting that, rather than representing homesickness 'the fostering of nostalgic feelings is one of the main aspects of home-building' (105). Offering a new way of conceptualizing the relation between nostalgia, homeliness and homelessness, Hage's redeployment of nostalgia is a significant intervention into contemporary theorizations of home. In this first section, Hage begins to establish his argument that the 'feeling of being a subject' (117) is crucial to homeliness – a point which he addresses in his third section which examines the consumption of ethnic food in the western suburbs of Cabramatta. Hage makes the point that for cosmomulticulturalists the experience and encounter with authority is fuelled precisely by the perception that the ethnic food-producing 'other' of the western suburbs is in no sense actively and deliberately seeking to 'seduce' them. In this self-deceiving, non-egalitarian and (subtly) racist discourse, the western suburbs ethnic restaurateur becomes a kind of coy object to be 'discovered' by the cosmopolitan subject who is then rewarded for 'daring' to venture into Cabramatta. Hage's occasional acerbity is mitigated by his acknowledgement that illusions characterize all cultural practices and by his repeatedly reminding readers that his critique is not directed at cosmopolitan eating as such (118) but rather that it is meant to 'deconstruct the relation between cosmopolitanism and multiculturalism' (145). Challenging those who reductively interpret migrant food production and dancing and singing as simply performances for the other, Hage reminds readers that for migrants, such moments of cultural display are often matters of great pride as well as constitutive aspects of home-making (101). In a similar vein Hage condemns the 'vacuous journalist' who has declared multiculturalism to be a 'myth' (144). His countering and crucial point – that it is cosmomulticulturalism which has contributed to the attack on the genuine multiculturalism which exists in places such as western Sydney – is extremely pertinent and well made. The essay is a highly readable and perspicacious reminder to the often hegemonically positioned cynics of multiculturalism that the 'real lives' of Australian migrants are in danger of being displaced as a result of these particularly problematic definitions of this concept. Challenging multicultural theorists to debate but not discard multiculturalism, Hage suggests that the concept's potency may depend on the spatialities in which it is grounded.

The only obvious connection between the final essay 'Icon House' (154–195) by Helen Grace and the themes of the text as a whole is that the discussion purports to focus on Homeworld 11, which exists in the western Sydney suburb of Prospect. Moving between Moscow, Britain, the United States and Australia and only partly successfully through various theorists, the essay is a difficult-to-access pastiche. While Grace raises some interesting issues about the politics of archaeological design, her discussion of these is less fully realized than it could be, perhaps because the essay is overly ambitious.

The production of a text such as *Home/World* reflects the interest in home as a potentially enabling concept with a troubled and often politically conservative history. Theoretical engagements with 'home' in the Australian context arise both because of Australia's history as an 'immigrant nation' and also, perhaps to a lesser extent, because indigenous claims rest for their discursive power on the claim to be 'at home'. Described as having 'nowhere to go, according to white expectations, but more "at home" in this context (in this case the fringes of Australian towns) than any Australian can ever quite be' (Muecke, *No Road*, p. 14, reviewed below) indigenous people especially rural-dwelling individuals and groups have come to embody the 'homeliness' that non-Aboriginal (and perhaps particularly Anglo) Australians appear to desire. Bob Hodge's 'Aboriginal Iconographies of Home' (*Communal Plural*, 5:47–68) needs to be read in the broader context of discussion regarding the valuation, incorporation and/or appropriation of Aboriginality in the Australian context.

Hodge aims to demonstrate the relevance and explanatory power of Aboriginal iconographies of home. The recent proliferation of Aboriginality in urban spaces (see Anderson and Jacobs above) makes nonsense of Hodge's claim that 'non-Aborigines are still . . . stumbling around an unfamiliar new land, getting lost but too arrogant to ask for help from Aboriginal people' (66). Rather, it seems to be the case that non-Aboriginal Australians are doing exactly what Hodge recommends in his essay, that is, asking Aboriginal people to 'help' design spaces. Unfortunately, the fact that their participation in this process is by no means straightforwardly libratory is not discussed by Hodge.

In this essay Hodge expresses his hope that (Aboriginal) Western Desert art 'could become the basis of a *lingua franca* for all Australians'. Initially there seems to be a positive perspective from which to read Hodge's attempt to incorporate the spatialities of Western Desert art into Western knowledges. However, this becomes increasingly difficult to sustain. Reminding readers that Aboriginal rights to land have been disavowed by judges' separation of ' "art" from representation systems which have political and legal force' (54), Hodge endeavours to show how an appreciation of the similarities between Western systems of representation (for example maps) and Aboriginal ones might advance the legal and political causes of Aboriginal people. Indeed much of this essay is dedicated to demonstrating the similarities between ancient Greek conceptions of home and Aboriginal vocabularies of space. Although it is theoretically possible such acts of 'translation' might prove politically expedient for Aboriginal people seeking to represent their rights in a Western law court, Hodge's tendency to employ Greek words to describe Aboriginal concepts (see pp. 59, 62, 64) seems to arise out of a more general desire to render Aboriginality transparent to non-Aboriginal Australians. Attempts to articulate methods for cross-cultural communication ought not to be abandoned, however, it is necessary to question who ultimately benefits when terms are made 'equivalent' and meaning becomes something which is 'shared'.

The implied starting point for Hodge – which he aims to contest – is that by and large Australians do not value Aboriginal ways of understanding and representing space. The problem is, that while this particular Eurocentrism certainly underpinned assimilationist housing programmes for Aborigines (see pp. 55–59), Aboriginal ways of conceptualizing space are by no means straightforwardly devalued in the differently racist 1990s (see Anderson and Jacobs). Thus, the issue becomes not so much whether or not Aboriginality is valued, but how, when and to whose benefit. Hodge's attempt to counter what he calls 'Aboriginalist' (47) myths – for instance he reminds readers that the ' "timeless" wisdom of Aboriginal people isn't timeless' (47) – must be measured against his own less obvious romanticization of Aboriginality. Suggesting in the somewhat strange section entitled 'Aboriginal versions of home' (60) that Robert Bropho, an Aboriginal activist from Perth, is an 'effortlessly acute critic of modern suburban housing for whites' and that 'Aborigines have been experts in using space for a long time' (66), Hodge implies that Aboriginal people are the natural possessors of useful and (inherently different) spatial knowledge. He postulates that contemporary Western Desert art 'speaks a universal language simultaneously available to Aborigines and speakers of a diverse range of world languages' (54). Thus, he attributes its increasing popularity and recognition as an important art form to the notion that it is equally meaningful to Aborigines and non-Aborigines. As such, Hodge fails to consider the range of ways in which Aboriginal art – having come to signify authenticity – has been increasingly commodified in a global market which deems this characteristic both valuable and elusive. As with Hodge's claim that Western Desert art 'could become the basis of a *lingua franca* for all Australians' (54) and his concluding statement that reconciliation will help provide the 'shift or stratagem of language which could make Australia truly "home" for all its people' (67), this account does not acknowledge the possibility that there might be times and places in which Aboriginal people want to refuse non-Aboriginal people 'access' to their meanings, art, spatialities and constructions of home. Having acknowledged that Aboriginal people do not always want their paintings 'decoded' (64), Hodge, using Greek phrases, proceeds to 'explain' the spatial concepts which underlie a particular Western Desert painting. The attempt to theorize the possible incommensurability of Aboriginal knowledge with non-Aboriginal knowledge might have improved this essay's wide-ranging foray into Aboriginal and non-Aboriginal notions of home.

Hodge suggests that the popularity of Western Desert art reflects the 'still inadequate recognition of the power, scope and relevance of Aboriginal resources for making sense of complex spatiality in the postmodern world'(63–64) and that elements of tradition provide Western Desert Aboriginal people with the 'capacity for commenting on any narrative, any phenomena' (66). Hodge's suggestion that 'Aboriginal iconography seems simple, reductive and strongly constrained' (63) begs the question – to whom? In such instances, Hodge undermines his own efforts to validate Aboriginal art, concepts and frames of reference.

Home, especially as it relates to nationhood, is only one of many topics addressed in Stephen Muecke's *No Road* – an amusing, engaging and challenging text which reflects the cross-fertilization of 'theory' and 'fiction'. Combining wit with a theoretically informed perspective, Muecke explores the tensions that inhere in the relation between theory and practice:

> I'm vulnerable, I'm thinking half the time that being a plumber would be a whole lot more useful than doing Aboriginal studies. I mean, you can imagine turning up in some community in the North-West to fix the plumbing. *That* the people would see the point in doing. But the other? – 'Hi, I'm a cultural critic, I've come to fix up your representations' (91).

In addition to examining the complex issues of representation, *No Road* is committed to theorizing language, writing and words in relation to journeying, emplacement and belonging as well as power. The relation between location and narratives is creatively explored in the text and Muecke's tone oscillates between ironic distance and a more engaged and even occasionally enraptured perspective. Meaghan Morris' illuminating essay 'At Henry Parkes Motel' (*Cultural Studies*, 1988, 2(1):1–47) provides an obvious springboard for Muecke's own thinking about travelling and home in Australia. Having cited Morris, Muecke replicates something of her invigorating and often 'undisciplined' (43) style, as well as carving a new space for himself and others who may wish to explore complex theoretical questions in innovative ways. The wide-ranging nature of the text enables Muecke to make salient contributions to an immense variety of debates and topics, including tourism, travel, hybridity, essentialism, identity, Aboriginal drinking and postmodern architecture to name but a few. While the implied reader of *No Road* is a theoretically informed one, likely to be attuned to the complexities of these discussions, most readers with an interest in any of the above issues, for example, will find themselves newly challenged and refreshingly engaged.

Capitalism's relation to Aboriginality is interrogated throughout the book and Muecke – despite what we perceive to be his own differently constructed desire for relations with Aboriginal people – demonstrates his acute awareness of the ways in which Aboriginality, frequently constructed as 'Other' has been re-made in recent years. Exploring the somewhat disturbing overlaps that exist between tourist and research practices, Muecke discusses the difference between 'mixing with them' and 'parallelism' (34). Drawing on a wide variety of sources and traversing various places, he quotes an 'ancient' Yoruba proverb: 'No matter how long the log lies in the water it will never become a crocodile' (53) reminding readers that the desire to transcend oneself which frequently underlies the search for cross-cultural encounters can never be fully realized. Cognizant of the ways in which the discourse of 'discovery' is bound up with various progress narratives and with tourism – pioneering's contemporary counterpart – Muecke seeks to bring other travel stories to the fore, stories which convey roads on which ritual and repetition, rather than the quest for novelty prevails. Describing an Aboriginal story in which 'the two men, because they are Creation Beings, create, name, bring places into being, so that from that point on people will always travel this road and always find these things. This road is not a pioneering road, it is not part of progress, novelty or modernity' (60), Muecke reminds readers that travel is about the *recovery* of ancient space, layered with conflicting stories, which include colonial bloodshed, white mythologies, 'the promise of Asian investment' and 'future development' (58).

Muecke's exploration of the relations between people refigures sameness and otherness. While the paths of individuals are always 'parallel lines', there are moments in which meeting places arise and unity (however temporary) can be experienced. Drawing on sources as diverse as his friend 'Abdelkarim', St Augustine and Newtonian physics, Muecke's imaginative and often poignant exploration of difference, incommensurability, knowledge and convergence is as much about the relations between strangers from similar 'textual suburbs' (20) as it is about exploring broader questions such as the relation between Aboriginal and non-Aboriginal philosophies. Claiming that 'there is too much invested in liberal white demands for authenticity which preserve distance in relation to Aboriginal lives, making them apart in time and space', Muecke suggests that as a result 'passionate and public encounters are increasingly rare' (102). In contrast, his own refusal to shy away from depicting the more 'negative' aspects of Aboriginal culture alongside the 'positive' ones makes him something of a pioneer in a field in which a variety of representations of Aboriginal people might become possible. Exploring the various shapes and forms that 'Otherness' and relating to it takes, Muecke juxtaposes his letter, about the 're-making' of Coonardoo, to Trinh – 'the most sought after feminist film-maker in the world' (95) – with his friend's fascination with 'getting a bit of the other', in this case Joy, an Aboriginal woman. Here, the author's ambiguous 'J'ai envie' (108) makes it impossible to construct his own fascination with 'Otherness' as something which exists outside colonialism. However, this is a rare moment in *No Road* – the book's own desire for novel (frequently Aboriginal) stories and philosophies goes largely unchallenged. Despite Muecke's innovative weaving of theory – including Lingis and Trinh Minh-ha on otherness – humour and politics, *No Road* does not traverse the path of self-reflexivity to the point where Muecke's own quest to 'open up' new ways of becoming other is itself sufficiently problematized. The author's desire for a 'lightness of touch – 'we drift if we can' (191) – is bound up with wanting to imagine himself 'already gone' (135). This, surely, is a desire which approximates the quest for objectivity, the effort to absent oneself which characterizes imperialist ethnography. For all its cleverness, *No Road* stops short of divulging what might be at stake for the author in critiquing the (indeed, his own) desire for cross-cultural encounters.

Despite the author's apparent compulsion to occupy the position of 'knower' on occasions – a tendency which Muecke humorously alludes to several times – for instance, 'I got out my papers, the intellectual showing off even as we were almost lost' (132), and when he tries to 'teach Patience how to walk the Aboriginal way' (195), *No Road* provides 'something new' (184), in contrast to 'the old (which) is always the confident step, the almost cliched, the acceptable' (159). Against roads which have 'done all the thinking for us' (125), Muecke concatenates ideas, some of them previously expressed elsewhere, in an effort to disrupt the certainties of Imperial grids and to keep theory moving. Muecke is the 'affective academic subject whose complex intersubjective relations are part of his writing' (138) and *No Road*, partly because of its idiosyncratic style, makes an immensely valuable contribution to thought about a variety of complex subjects, including Aboriginality, subjectivity and nationhood. A further review of Muecke's book written by David Brooks may be found in *Meanjin* (56(3):486–494)

6. Media, Representation and Identity

In 'I, the "Hybrid" Aborigine: Film and Representation' (*Australian Aboriginal Studies*, 1:4–14), Ian Anderson locates himself as a 'hybrid' Tasmanian Aboriginal, less in conformity with the demand of many contemporary cultural critics for a 'transparent and reflexive strategy in cultural productions' and more in response to Aboriginal protocol which usually links the right to tell a story with a 'declaration of involvement or connection to that story' (4). The subject of Anderson's essay is the depiction of hybrid Aboriginal identity in a range of Australian films, including documentaries and feature films such as the 1955 feature film *Jedda*. Anderson's essay reviews the early history of colonial Tasmania with specific reference to the place of descendants of the Pallewah peoples and white sealers who formed the hybrid population so disparaged in anthropological accounts: 'In social terms, [these people] belong to neither race (and are shunned by both), and lacking a racial background they have no history' (N. J. B. Plomley, *The Tasmanian Aborigines*, published by the author in association with the Adult Education Division, Launceston, 1977). In the work of Plomley, a prolific commentator on Tasmanian Aboriginal society and others including Tindale and Elkin, the 'hybrid' Aboriginal becomes 'a code for destruction', the hybrid in the context of Australian colonial discourse being both (self)destructive and sterile. And, yet, imaginatively and discursively, the category is endlessly productive, such are the anxieties concerning racial purity in the dominant culture. Illustrating this point, Anderson lists some of the myriad phrases used to account for hybridity in popular Australian usage: half-castes, quadroons, octoroons, mixed blood, mixed breeds, half-breeds, quarterbreed, touched by the tar brush, of the descent, coloured, dis-coloured, and bit of a splash.

The primary site for the visualization of hybrid Aboriginality in Australian film is in what Anderson calls the assimilationist text, a genre produced during the forty-year period when the assimilation program dominated government administration of Aboriginal affairs. Charles Chauvel's *Jedda* (1955) is read by Anderson as an assimilation parable which points to the ultimate failure of attempts to acculturate 'full-blood' Aborigines, for whom 'the call of the wild' will always prove irresistible. The assimilationist impulse in the film is focused on the figure of the half-caste stockman Joe, who narrates the story, as pointing the way forward for Aboriginal culture. While Jedda and Marbuck meet a savage end, Joe, with his aspiration to become head stockman and his desire for a home and wife, marks out a future for hybridized Aboriginality which is ultimately indistinguishable from whiteness.

A somewhat harsher vision is provided in *The Fringe Dwellers* which charts the journey of an Aboriginal family, the suggestively named Comea-ways, from the 'implicitly "mixed blood" fringe camp' (8) into the realm of white small-town suburbia. As Anderson argues, the film presents 'only one escape route from the grinding degradation and poverty of Aboriginal camp life: into town where they could adopt the mores of white suburbia' (8). For these people, there is no recourse to 'authenticity'. While softened by comic and sentimental interludes, the film's message is a harsh one, particularly with respect to the character of Trilby whose aspirations for a white middle-class life eventually cost the life of her child and her relations with her family: 'such are the necessary costs of assimilation' (8).

Anderson's discussion of the 1978 documentary *The Last Tasmanian* is highly critical of the pervasiveness of its representation of holocaust and genocide, to the extent that it conveys the impression that there are no contemporary Tasmanian Aborigines. In this film, hybridity is equated with cultural extinction. *Manganinnie* (1980), set in the early Tasmanian frontier, demonstrates that the transgression of essentialized tropes of 'whiteness' and 'blackness' while frequently centring on the figure of the hybrid are not necessarily restricted to it. This film uses the figure of a white child adopted by an Aboriginal woman in the 'in-between' role of cultural intermediary – with Aboriginality used as a means of access to nature. Anderson argues that a highly troubling, colonialist model of hybridity is continually mobi-lized in Australian film. Even a film such as Rickettson's *Blackfellas* which deals explicitly with social issues outside an assimilationist framework, in this case the highly problematic position of Aboriginal youth in relation to the criminal justice system, resorts to earlier formulations of the hybrid to provide 'an explanatory framework' for the problems it narrativizes. The distinctions between the character of Dooligan, who has a white mother, and his darker and more wayward relation Pretty Boy appear to centre around Dooligan being 'less' Aboriginal than his cousin.

In the second half of the essay, Anderson turns his attention to a critique of the Tasmanian film *Black Man's Houses* and to a review of the film by Karl Quinn (*Cinema Papers*, 1993, 42–43). The film, a collaborative venture between filmmaker Steve Thomas and the Flinders Island Aboriginal Association, focuses on a series of events surrounding the reclaiming by the community of the Wyabelenna cemetery, their efforts to clean and restore it, and their engagement of an archaeologist to assist them in the process of identifying and recording grave sites. Community members then memorialize these significant events by a ceremonial re-enactment of the burial of Man Ner Le Lar Gen Ner and the installation of a plaque in memory of those who died in the times of frontier violence. These community events are framed by a historical narrative provided by the filmmaker and with extensive interviews with community members, including such elders as Auntie Ida West. The film also includes interviews with members of the local white community which highlight the persistence of racism and essentialized views of Aboriginality which marginalize 'hybrid' Aboriginal culture, as in the comment of one elderly white woman: '[Aboriginal people] were just part of the community, some of my best friends were Aboriginals [pause] or what they call Aboriginals' (quoted by Anderson, p. 10).

The disparaging 'or what they call Aboriginals' runs counter to the proud, unqualified declarations of their Aboriginality by members of the Flinders Island community and for reviewer Karl Quinn this raises problems with which Anderson engages. For Quinn, the film is problematic because through its:

> desire to maintain complete solidarity with the cause of these people, it baulks at the largest gate, preferring to leave racial identity in the hands of innate, interior blood links rather than moving to an understanding of race – particularly when genetic explanations are so blatantly problematised – as a social construct (quoted by Anderson, p. 10).

In response to Quinn, Anderson argues that while theorizing race may be the proper concern of cultural critics and postcolonial theorists, for the filmmaker, as for the Aboriginal community concerned, there are other priorities. Foremost among these is, quite simply, to assert a contemporary Aboriginal presence in Tasmania, where Aboriginal people live their lives in a context which denies their very existence, under the shadow of Trugannini – putatively the 'last' of her tribe. Where Quinn is uncomfortable with statements of Aboriginal identity which convey to him the sense that Aboriginality is held by these people to be somehow innate 'as a feeling within (which [Quinn] feels is suggestive of essentialism)' (11), Anderson points to the nuanced and historicized understanding of Aboriginality expressed by the Aboriginal people in the film. Discussing the segment in the film in which the community prepares for the re-enactment of the burial of Man Ner Le Lar Gen Ner in which certain players don period costume and 'blacken up' for the camera, Anderson makes the following points:

In darkening up for the event, participants repeatedly affirmed
... that this was not confronting to their sense of identity. What
this important segment reveals is that Aboriginal people have a
very sophisticated and nuanced sense of their own identity. This
understanding extends to the way in which people mobilise
aspects of racial discourse. At the same time they acknowledge
the profound changes in how they look or act relative to their
ancestors. But the engine for this transformation is explicitly
identified as colonialism (11).

Anderson concludes by arguing that *Black Man's Houses* represents a
significant improvement in the representational strategies employed in relation to Aboriginality – particularly hybrid Aboriginality – in Australian film.
While it is true that aspects of the film may be seen to essentialize Aboriginal
identity and culture, Anderson suggests that it is not essentialism but rather
the type of essentialism which should be the issue: 'In a colonial context that
emphasises invisibility and fragmentation, the task for Aboriginal people is
to re-present themselves as coherent people with a sustainable historicised
subjectivity' (12).

Also taking up the issue of representing Aboriginality is Alan McKee's
'Film vs *Real Life*: Communicating Aboriginality in Cinema and Television'
(*UTS Review*, 3(1):160–182). Drawing on a wide range of scholarship on
Aboriginality, McKee argues that despite arguments promoting the understanding of Aboriginality as cultural, Aboriginality remains in many domains
something which is *seen*: with acceptance of Aboriginality, in courts of law,
in anthropology, in the administration of government, and in visual media
such as cinema, frequently resting on the spectatorial element of skin colour.
McKee makes a particular case for film relying on and promoting a specific
and visually persuasive mode of Aboriginality pointing to the 'authentically'
Aboriginal features and dark skin colour of many prominent Aboriginal
screen actors such as Robert Tudawali (in Charles Chauvel's *Jedda* 1955),
David Gulpilil (in Nicholas Roeg's *Walkabout* 1970 or Peter Weir's The
Last Wave 1977) and David Ngoombujurra (in Rickettson's *Blackfellas*
1993). McKee alludes to the fact, covered clearly in a documentary on the
making of Fred Schepsi's *The Chant of Jimmie Blacksmith* (1978), that many
of the Aboriginal actors performing in the film were required to 'black up'
for the camera. McKee also finds in the film industry's excitement over the
success and 'authenticity' of Rickettson's *Blackfellas* contradictions which
point to the persistence of spectatorial Aboriginality based primarily on skin
colour. McKee argues that most praise was directed at the performance of
David Ngoombujurra (in the role of Pretty Boy), whose appearance clearly
met with white settler expectations of what an Aborigine should look like.
Far less attention was directed to the performance of John Moore – who
played the role of the film's central character – because he less readily fitted
audience expectations of Aboriginality due to his markedly lighter skin
colour. While McKee acknowledges that some filmic attempts to represent
Aboriginality, such as *Black Man's Houses* discussed by Ian Anderson
above, break with these conventions, there are remarkable continuities in
Australian film with respect to the representation of Aboriginality-as-
blackness.

Where McKee sees a break with convention is on the small screen. McKee argues, by way of reference to the prominence of Ernie Dingo and Stan Grant (presenter of the soft current affairs programme *Real Life* which screened on the 7 Network from 1991–1994) and other indigenous television personalities such as Rhoda Roberts and Aaron Pedersen, that television has shown itself prepared to take risks with the presentation of Aboriginal faces which depart from the kinds of indigenous faces required by the film industry. A point not made by McKee is that Dingo, Grant, Pedersen et al. are just plain good looking, Aboriginal or not: and television and the advertisers which fund it love good-looking folk. While Dingo, Grant and Pedersen are visually marked as different and to varying degrees 'appear' to be Aboriginal, their Aboriginality is registered primarily by means other than visual ones: either through identification with explicitly Aboriginal subject matter in the case of Roberts and Pedersen or through clear statements of Aboriginality. McKee attempts to argue that a range of other cues – including audio cues – may work to establish Aboriginality on television in contrast to the heavily spectatorial function of Aboriginality in cinema, but these arguments remain less convincing. The argument that television lacks the 'insistent visual communication' of cinema needs more work. Also less than convincing is McKee's confidence that the alternative or non-stereotypical Aboriginal faces seen on the small screen represent a breakthrough in representational practices. In the prime-time weekly travel show on which he worked as a member of a small team of roving reporters, did Ernie Dingo ever get to go to the Louvre? He remained, with few exceptions, in the great outdoors, complete with Akubra and moleskins. Not Robert Tudawali perhaps, but visually, at least, not too far from Jacky Jacky. While McKee explicitly rejects any simple equation of cinema as a bad medium with respect to its limited repertoire of Aboriginal representations and television as a good one, he concludes that television 'allows for more flexible, and more useful, representations of Aboriginality in contemporary Australia'. The presence of more and different kinds of Aboriginal and Torres Strait Islander faces on the Australian screen, both large and small, is something to hope for but it is a little too soon to congratulate the Australian television industry on its progressive attitude to Aboriginality. We think it advisable to wait and see how it responds to the changing tide in Aboriginal affairs: not that we are so cynical as to believe that it was only the perception of television executives that there was money to be made which prompted them to present 'acceptable' Aboriginal (that is, Aboriginal but not *too* Aboriginal) faces on the small screen.

Further examinations of Aboriginality and the media are provided by John Hartley in 'An Aboriginal Public Sphere in the Era of Media Citizenship' (*Culture and Policy*, 8(2):43–63) in which Hartley contends that an Aboriginal public sphere exists within the *mediasphere* in two different, sometimes antagonistic, manifestations. The first are the fora for discussing/representing Aboriginal issues in the mainstream media in which Aboriginal people participate at various levels and in diverse capacities but which remains outside Aboriginal control. The second manifestation comprises Aboriginal media organizations such as NIMA (National Indigenous Media Association of Australia) and NIRS (National Indigenous Radio Service). In considering the relationships between an Aboriginal public sphere, as outlined by Hartley, and 'ideological atrocities' such as the resurgence of open statements of racism in the Australian media, Hartley calls for media researchers to sensitize themselves to 'the positive potential of the media as a whole' and the view its treatment of Aboriginal issues 'in that context' (44). Helen Molnar takes up the second of Hartley's manifestations of the Aboriginal public sphere in her essay 'Radio: The "Heart and Soul of Indigenous Aspirations"' (*Australian-Canadian Studies*, 14(1)–2:71– 88). The essay provides a valuable and detailed overview of indigenous radio production and broadcasting in Australia, examining the activities of both metropolitan and regional stations, focusing on the extraordinary success and growth of CAAMA (Central Australian Aboriginal Media Association). As Molnar argues, radio is relatively cheaper for indigenous communities to access – in terms of production, transmission *and* reception – than television and offers a flexibility that makes it ideally suited to the needs and the aspirations of Aboriginal communities.

6.1 Literature and Representation
A small group of publications take up the question of Aboriginality and literature: both writings by Aboriginal people and the representation of Aboriginality in literature. These include Kerry Reed-Gilbert's edited anthology *Message Stick: Contemporary Aboriginal Writing* which contains the poetry and short prose pieces by twenty-seven indigenous writers and includes work by well-known writers such as Lisa Bellear and Cec Fisher as well as the work of lesser known writers. A collection of critical essays on indigenous literature is provided by Mudrooroo in *The Indigenous Literature of Australia: Milli Milli Wangka*. This volume contains thirteen essays including important considerations of the works of Oodgeroo (67–78), Kevin Gilbert (165–178) and Lionel Fogarty (79–88). Mudrooroo also gives consideration to the diverse musical and literary/cultural influences at work in popular Aboriginal music in the essay 'Reconciling Our Songs' (107–123). In the essay 'Tiddas Writing' (180–190), Mudrooroo discusses the work of several Aboriginal women writers (tidda is an Aboriginal term for woman) including Ruby Langford Ginibi, Rita and Jackie Huggins and Sally Morgan focusing on the ways in which the requirements of 'getting published' frequently work to curtail expressions of Aboriginality as evidenced most obviously by publishers' anxiety over non-standard or Aboriginal English. Prominent Aboriginal writer Ruby Langford Ginibi talks about her writing and her Aboriginality in an interview with Elizabeth Guy (*Westerly*, 42(2):9–17).

Mickey Dewar's *In Search of the 'Never-Never': Looking for Australia in Northern Territory Writing* examines representations of the Northern Territory in a wide range of Australian writing, both from the Territory and elsewhere. Understandably central to notions of the Territory are ideas about and representations of Aboriginality which, while covering a wide range, tend to cluster around the idealized image of the remote Aborigine as hyper-spiritualized being: 'the initiates of a spiritual paganism and a religiosity that they draw from their closeness to the forces of nature' (D. Myers, *Bleeding Battlers from Ironbark: Australian Myths in Fiction and Film, 1890s–1980s*. University of Central Queensland, 1992, quoted in Dewar, p. 169). In 'Representing Indigeneity: Aborigines and Australian

Children's Literature Then and Now' (*Ariel: A Review of International English Literature*, 28(1):89–99), Clare Bradford provides a brief historical survey of depictions of Aboriginal people and culture in literature for children, focusing on three texts which are illustrative of three major phases in the relationship between Aboriginal and non-Aboriginal people in the settler colonial context of Australia. The texts examined are: *A Mother's Offering to Her Children by A Lady Long Resident in New South Wales*, first published in 1841; *The Australia Book* by Eve Pownall published in 1951; and *Tjarany Roughtail* by Gracie Greene, Joe Tramacchi and Lucille Gill published in 1992 by the Aboriginal publishing house, Magabala Books. In the first two texts, Bradford finds, not surprisingly, versions of the Aboriginalism characterized by Bob Hodge and Vijay Mishra (*Dark Side of the Dream: Australian Literature and the Postcolonial Mind*. Allen and Unwin, 1990) as the Australian corollary of Said's Orientalism. In *Tjarany Roughtail*, however, Bradford finds a marked shift in the depiction of Aboriginality from the two earlier texts. Unlike the earlier texts which valorize colonialism and homogenize Aboriginality, the story about the roughtail lizard 'carries broader political meanings about history and . . . Aboriginal cultural production . . . we read [of] the survival of the indigenous, not merely by outlasting the colonisers but by strategies of resistance and subversion, and by those delicate negotiations through which indigenous cultural production appropriates Western forms and technologies, at the same time maintaining its Aboriginality' (98).

7. Aboriginality, Law and Legislature

7.1 Overview
Apart from publications and articles which dealt directly or specifically with the decisions from *Mabo* v. *Queensland* (No. 2) (1992), *Wik Peoples* v. *Queensland* (1996) or the Native Title Act (1993), 1997 saw a continued discussion of such legal and legislative issues in terms of their intersection with other legal decisions, legislature, Government Reports and Royal Commissions. In particular, publications and articles from a broad range of disciplinary areas extended and developed concerns relating to the *Mabo* decision and the legal and legislative recognition of Aboriginal customary law, society and rights to consider their relevance to the protection of indigenous intellectual property and heritage, Aboriginal imprisonment rates, legal process and criminal justice. What remained common in nearly all cases was an attempt to consider these issues in a manner that was sensitive to the links between the violent settlement of Australia, the destruction and displacement of Aboriginal society and culture, the effect this has had on the lives of contemporary Aboriginal peoples, and the role Anglo-Australian law and legislation has played in this. Unified by broad issues concerning social justice, representation, equality and the lasting effects of colonialism, the reviews in this section consider publications and articles which address and engage with a wide range of new and old legal cases, legislature and events: the Commonwealth Aboriginal and Torres Strait Islander Heritage Act (1984) in light of the Evatt Report (1996) and

the Royal Commission *Report on the Hindmarsh Island Bridge* (1995), the 'Heritage Act' and the Hindmarsh Island Bridge Bill (1996) which went before the Senate and was passed in 1997, the Copyright Act (1968), the Patents Act (1990) and the Trade Practices Act (1974) in light of a number of cases including *Harold Thomas* v. *David George Brown and Another* (1997), *George Milpurrurru* v. *Indofurn Pty Ltd* (1995), issues raised by the Human Genome Diversity Project, and issues concerning legal process, criminal justice and Aboriginal imprisonment in light of the *Royal Commission into Aboriginal Deaths in Custody* (1991) and subsequent reports such as *Keeping Aboriginal and Torres Strait Islander People Out of Custody* (1997).

7.2 Protecting Aboriginal Rights: Heritage, Intellectual Property and Hindmarsh Island

The effectiveness of the Commonwealth's Aboriginal and Torres Strait Islander Heritage Protection Act (1984) was brought into question following the outcome of the Royal Commission's *Report of the Hindmarsh Island Bridge* (1995) and the related legal cases. In 1996 Hon Elizabeth Evatt tabled the Review of the Aboriginal and Torres Strait Islander Heritage Protection Act 1984 (Canberra: Minister for Aboriginal and Torres Strait Islander Affairs, 1996), a review commissioned by then Minister for Aboriginal and Torres Strait Islander Affairs, Robert Tickner, to determine whether or not legislative change was necessary. The Act itself was brought into being by the first Hawke government in response to Aboriginal demands for some form of legislative recognition of significant sites and objects. The Act's track record, however, has not been good: of ninety-nine areas subject to applications for protection under the Act, only one, Niltye/Tnyere-Akere (Junction Waterhole) near Alice Springs, has received enduring protection from a declaration. If there were any doubts about its effectiveness, these were surely dissolved by events relating to the Hindmarsh Island Bridge 'affair' (see *YWCCT 6*) where two successive Reports commissioned under the Act were overturned and invalidated by legal challenges. Under the current system and following current precedent, for example, the dictates of 'procedural fairness' require that all relevant information be available to all interested parties, regardless of how sensitive or sacred such information might be. Thus, in instances like the Hindmarsh Island and Broome Crocodile Farm cases, where sacred/secret information has been the basis of a Heritage Act claim and legal decisions have demanded the disclosure of such information, the Act has proven to be ineffective. As Justice Jane Mathews noted in the *Commonwealth Hindmarsh Island Report* (Adelaide, S.A.: Government Printer, 1966):

> The events precipitated by the [Hindmarsh] bridge proposal have thus far revealed many deficiencies in Commonwealth laws designed to protect and preserve areas and objects of traditional Aboriginal significance ... This latest episode in the Hindmarsh Bridge saga has provided graphic illustration as to how little our apparently beneficial legislation has accommodated to the realities of Aboriginal culture (1).

Consequent on the change in government at the federal level in March 1996, both the Evatt Review and the Mathews Report were completed in a considerably different political climate from that which existed at the time they were commissioned. The newly elected Liberal/National Party Coalition government led by John Howard made it clear from the beginning where it stood with respect to the Hindmarsh Island 'affair' and the Minister for Aboriginal and Torres Strait Islander Affairs, John Herron, suggested that he would like to investigate ways of relieving the government of their obligations with regard to section 10 reporting on the area. And yet, the Mathews and Evatt documents are not only exceptional in that they are both marked by the peculiar positions they found themselves in politically, they also offer highly significant commentaries and critiques of the way in which the government handled the Hindmarsh Island 'affair' and similar cases.

A critical summary of the findings in Mathews Report can be found in Hilary Charlesworth's review ' "Little Boxes": A Review of the Common-wealth Hindmarsh Island Report' (*Aboriginal Law Bulletin*, 3(90):19–21), while Russell Goldflam's 'Noble Salvage: Aboriginal Heritage Protection and the Evatt Review' (*Aboriginal Law Bulletin*, 3(88):4–8) provides a good discussion of the issues and events which lead to the Heritage Review and a critical summary of its conclusions and recommendations. Charlesworth suggests that despite the fact that Justice Mathews did recommend that the Minister grant a declaration under the Aboriginal heritage legislation, the Review, perhaps unintentionally, demonstrates the inadequacy of the legis-lation in place to protect Aboriginal heritage. Similarly, Goldflam commends the Evatt Review, 'given the modest resources and time frame it was allowed, and the volatile climate in which it was conducted' (4) but also finds good reason to be sceptical about both its intentions and its ability to bring about significant changes. As he points out, 'the timing of the Review, shortly following the quashing in quick succession by the Federal Court of two Ministerial declarations made under section 10 of the Act [the Saunders Report and the Mathews Report, both concerning the Hindmarsh Island Case], strongly suggests the application of the if-it's-broke-fix-it principle, rather than the keep-your-promises principle' (5).

Without direct reference to the Evatt Review, but with similar con-clusions, Maureen Tehan's 'To be or Not to Be (Property): Anglo-Aus-tralian Law and the Search for Protection of Indigenous Cultural Heritage' (*University of Tasmania Law Review*, 15(2):267–305) discusses the inadequa-cies of the legal and legislative regimes in place for the protection of land-based indigenous cultural heritage. Tehan's central argument is that the manner in which Australian legal and legislative bodies have recognized indigenous rights only to the extent to which they conform to already existing principles, rules and categories demonstrates their failure to deliver just and fair legal and legislative protection. Indeed, considering the impli-cations of the *Mabo* decision upon heritage protection she notes that, arguably, it 'has had a negative impact on the limited heritage protection that does exist, since it demonstrated that the common law is unable to recognise interests in land which are different to, or not derived from, its own concepts of property and which do not meet the stringent test for the survival of native title' (268). Tehan finds further evidence of this failure with the Kumarangk or Hindmarsh Island Case where cultural heritage was taken to be based in a past and specific physical reality rather than a contemporary set of beliefs and practices. This relates to more general problems with legislation currently in place insofar as it implies, as Tehan observes, heritage claims under the current regime must be 'capable of, and must be subject to, transparent evaluation and assessment according to criteria imposed by the dominant legal system' (296).

As Tehan suggests, the Hindmarsh case not only illustrates some significant problems with the way in which Aboriginal claims are approached within the field of law, it also, through recognizing the problematic relationship between legal representation, recognition and reconciliation takes us some way to a far more radical approach to social justice. The demand currently made within law that claims be demonstrable, for example, highlights the way in which the law, in order to consolidate hegemonic interests, often operates as one or another version of the law of exchange, as a closed structure in which mutually recognizable opposites circulate. While the law requires that all things before it be reduced to terms recognizable to it and be able to be integrated into its economy, justice allows that we affirm and admit the difference, incalculability and untranslatability of that which is brought before it. Bearing in mind that the issue here is indigenous rights or beliefs, this 'before' or 'before the law' should be read both as temporal or historical as well as suggesting 'being in the presence of' or 'subject to'. Justice or just recognition, then, would necessarily exceed the bounds of law, being both within law and beyond its inauguration – 'before'. It would acknowledge, as much as possible, the injustice of the reduction of difference to the terms of law, to 'the spoken', the heard or recognized.

In 'Should Parliament enact the Hindmarsh Island Bill 1996?' (*Aboriginal Law Bulletin*, 3(88):15–18) Jennifer Clarke examines the constitutional validity of the then proposed Bill and in doing so signals its relevance to the future of native title rights. The Hindmarsh Island Bill 1996, which was before the Senate at the time Clarke wrote the article, effectively exempted Hindmarsh Island from claims under the Heritage Act, removing the need for any further inquiry and thus allowing development to proceed. The arguments that were put forward in favour of the Bill characterized both the opposition to the construction of the Hindmarsh Island bridge and the continued efforts to have the site protected under the Act as 'anti-development' and an 'indulgence' to minority interests at the expense of 'average Australians'. According to the Coalition government, the remedy which would provide security for 'development' and 'business' was the removal of the right to lodge a claim under the Act and the subsequent removal of the government's obligation to conduct another 'expensive' inquiry. The possibility that there were also other larger and more 'fruitful' objectives in view did not escape the critics of the proposed Bill. As Clarke notes, the Commonwealth government's power to enact the Bill seemed to fall within the Commonwealth Parliament's power to make laws with respect to the people of any race for whom it is deemed necessary to make special laws, Section 51 (xxvi) of the Constitution otherwise known as the 'race power'. It was this very power which would later be shown to provide the basis for the proposed, and now enacted, Native Title Amendment Act. Clarke's conclusion with regard to the Hindmarsh Island Bridge Bill 1996 is that it is 'probably constitutional. However, it adds nothing to the "security" of the bridge proposal [and leaves open the possibility that] . . . the Bill may place Australia in breach of its international obligations [with respect to the United Nations Committee on the Elimination of Racial Discrimination]' (18). In many ways this anticipates and mirrors debates that would later emerge regarding the constitutional validity of native title amendments proposed by the Coalition government in 1997.

Another article which addresses problems with the way in which the Royal Commission on the Hindmarsh Island Bridge and the media approached the Heritage claim is 'Women's Business: Sex, Secrets and the Hindmarsh Island Affair' (*UNSW Law Review*, 20(2):333–351) by Joanna Bourke. Bourke argues that the Hindmarsh case reveals the ways in which the intersection of gender and race places Aboriginal women before the law in a doubly disadvantaged position. With reference to Homi Bhabha, she goes on to note the difference between a recognition of difference, as a difference-in-itself, and the conceptualization of such difference within legal and legislative regimes as mere diversity, as a difference reduced to its relations to 'the norm', 'the Self' or Eurocentric law. As Bourke points out, '[t]he compulsion to embrace diversity, while simultaneously disadvantaging and normalizing difference, is very apparent in most considerations of Aboriginal heritage claims'(338). In this particular case, the institutional biases against feminist anthropology both mirrored and complemented a similar refusal within the law to recognize Aboriginal customary law or belief. The refusal to recognize the position of the Aboriginal women in terms except those of the law not only consolidated and secured legal authority, it established and reinforced a relation of difference in terms of the hegemonic patriarchal norm.

Thus, despite the claims which are often made concerning the law's universality, impartiality and objectivity, the terms of law are blind to difference and, as such, are unable to do justice to the specificities of each case or to weigh and consider the devastating effects of colonialism while recognizing the hand law has had in this. The reduction of difference is revealed to provide the law with the basis of its authority, what Derrida in another context has called its violent and 'mystical foundations'. The interpolation implicit within the 'we' and 'us' of law already assumes and passes over a considerable violence, an assumption of authority that proceeds with the denial of all others. 'Real' justice here finds its opening where such foundations are unable to contain such violent exclusion and effacement. Law and matters of legality foreclose such a possibility, as Bourke points out: '[i]n theory, it is acknowledged that Sandra Saunders, the Director of the Aboriginal Legal Rights Movement is right to claim that "technicalities are white fellas business"' (338).

'Promiscuous Sacred Sites: Reflections on Secrecy and Scepticism in the Hindmarsh Island Affair' (*Australian Humanities Review*, June) by Jane Jacobs and Ken Gelder also considers the entanglement of gender, Aboriginal rights and cultural politics. Like Bourke, Jacobs and Gelder discuss the ironic fact that in order to verify a claim, such as the one made in the Hindmarsh Island case concerning sacred/secret 'women's business', a claim must be talked about, a requirement, they note, that 'often seems entirely at odds with the structures of exclusivity which attend the Aboriginal sacred and which work to make it a special thing'. The only restriction the Royal Commission seemed to recognize, for example, were those concerning the Heritage and Racial Discrimination Act (1975). As we have seen in Tehan's article, this requirement that the secret be proved in some positive form, a symbolic demonstration of the power and authority of the law, demands that recognition be achieved in its terms only, that is, in a manner acceptable to the Commission. In this way, therefore, the pursuit of truth in this context is far more revealing of the problematic way in which Aboriginal claims are addressed in the legal or judicial context than it is of any truth about fabrication.

However, beyond this observation, the authors go on to consider the ways in which 'the sacred/secret' is, nevertheless, performed in a variety of contexts. The article, for example, describes the provisions that have been made to accommodate the protocols of secrecy associated with Aboriginal sites, noting that these provisions have also brought on concerns about the truth and validity of claims and the possibility of their use for purposes not entirely related to indigenous interests. In particular, as Jacobs and Gelder show, it is with such performances of 'the sacred/secret' that the authors consider both the alignment of the claim made in the Hindmarsh Island Case with anti-development movements and feminist anthropology and the manner in which the saga became emblematic of the nation's contemporary condition. Indeed, the government's claimed 'indulgences' in 'minority interests' and the decision by both the Royal Commission against the Heritage Protection claim can be seen as symptomatic of the change which led to the defeat of the Keating government. As Jacobs and Gelder note, '[t]he strangeness of this perspective lies in the way it takes the "majority" as restrained, even disabled, in relation to minority indulgences'.

A further and very ample consideration of the issues brought to prominence by the Hindmarsh Island affair is provided by Robert Tonkinson in 'Anthropology and Aboriginal Tradition: The Hindmarsh Island Bridge Affair and the Politics of Interpretation' (*Oceania*, 68(1):1–26). In characterizing the Hindmarsh Island Bridge affair as one of crucial importance to the conduct of Aboriginal affairs, the domain of heritage management and to the practice of anthropology in Australia, Tonkinson argues that it acted as the culmination and collision point between antagonistic views on Aboriginal self-determination and rights to land, between different views on 'tradition' and 'culture' within the Ngarrindjeri, and between methodological and other differences between anthropologists working primarily within classical research settings and those engaged in consultancy work with Aboriginal and other organizations.

In March 1997 a special edition of the *Australian Copyright Council Bulletin* No. 93 was published called *Protecting Indigenous Intellectual Property: A Copyright Perspective*. This publication is an extensive evaluation and commentary on the debates surrounding indigenous intellectual property protection and cultural appropriation. Addressing problems with the approach typically taken towards such issues in Australian law and legislation, the author Ian McDonald, critically examines preservationist and nationalist responses. According to McDonald, the preservationist approach seeks to preserve a tradition from outside influence, market forces, commercialization and exploitation. Similarly, the nationalist approach appropriates or 'preserves' aspects of indigenous culture for national culture or as part of a national identity. The first approach often bases the value it sees in 'purity' and 'authenticity' upon universalizing humanist notions of world heritage. Thus McDonald is led to ask 'why and for whom is the culture preserved?' (7). Indeed, as he observes, the universalizing tendency of the preservationists' approach means that the designation 'authentic' which bestows value upon an object, place or practice and makes it worthy of protection is often made in reference to non-indigenous definitions of 'the indigenous' and, thus, in a manner which places power and authority with non-indigenous institutions and individuals. 'Instead of local ownership and decision-making, archaeologists and anthropologists become the caretakers of the culture, and there is an implicit move against continuity or development' (7).

The positioning of the 'authentic' in opposition to the 'modern' or 'the European' has implications that extend beyond questions of legal or anthropological methodology and epistemology since the association of the purity or authenticity of other cultures' practices, beliefs or objects on the basis of their distinctness and autonomy from Western modernity has typically meant that authority and legitimacy are based upon these very cultural, temporal and conceptual divisions or differences. Consequently, the marks of colonization or contact upon the articulation of identities or the development of beliefs and practices which assimilate or appropriate 'Western' materials or methods are generally read in terms of degradation and the loss of authenticity and tradition. With respect to definitions of 'the indigenous', this inability of law and anthropology to integrate a sense of history within its central concerns is reflected in the fact that studies of the 'social change' genre always associate change with European contacts or some colonial presence. Moreover, the fact that such definitions now play a considerable part within the context of debates concerning the recognition and institutional legitimization of indigenous rights and beliefs means that such studies are generally disabling and limiting (although in ways necessary) insofar as they fail to provide provision for contemporary articulations of indigeneity. Here McDonald draws extensively upon the problems identified in the Government Issues Paper *Stopping the Rip-offs – Intellectual Property Protection for Aboriginal and Torres Strait Islanders* (Attorney General's Legal Practice, 1994) and in the work of Stephen Gray, particularly with respect to the difficulty of registering the difference between indigenous and non-indigenous appropriation of indigenous intellectual property or offering protection for both 'traditional' and 'non-traditional' Aboriginal artists under the Copyright Act.

McDonald goes on to consider problems concerning the use of copyright law for the protection of indigenous objects, practices or ideas, in particular, those relating to notions of 'originality', the material form of the thing protected, the duration of protection, ownership and the rights in derivative works. He notes that in each case these provisions significantly limit the extent to which copyright can protect indigenous intellectual property since indigenous discourse places little premium upon originality; Australian copyright requires that a work be in a 'material form' in order to be protected; copyright protection only lasts for the life of the artist plus fifty years; the systems by which indigenous society regulates the circulation of images or information does not translate well into any notion of ownership;

and what might be considered an 'original' work according to Australian law might still be regarded as offensive and damaging according to indigenous customary laws. After considering a number of other possible avenues for protection such as the Commonwealth Aboriginal and Torres Strait Islander Heritage Protection Act (1984) and international approaches, McDonald concludes that 'copyright is not an appropriate form of protection for indigenous intellectual property in its wider meaning' (68). Rather than attempting to find provision for such protection within existing law and legislature, he proposes an attempt to meet the challenge implied within the *Mabo* decision, a challenge to 'accommodate' indigenous needs and interests within existing legal frameworks or within purpose-built legislation: '[t]he challenge is urgent, in that successfully negotiating Aboriginal and Torres Strait Islander intellectual property protection may constitute a pre-condition of reconciliation between Indigenous and non-Indigenous communities' (70).

Cecilia O'Brien's 'Protecting Secret-Sacred Designs: Indigenous Culture and Intellectual Property Law' (*Media and Arts Law Review*, 2:57–76) considers a range of issues raised by the Government Issues Paper *Stopping the Rip-offs* and by a number of cases, such as *Bulun Bulun* v. *Nejlam Pty* (unreported, Federal Court, NT, 1989) and *George Milpurrurru* v. *Indofurn Pty Ltd* (AIPC 91–116, 1995), involving indigenous cultural or intellectual property. As O'Brien notes, the change of government since the report and the perceived difficulty of legislating to recognize and protect Aboriginal rights, as identified within the report, seem to have led to the side-lining of these issues. O'Brien re-addresses the issues raised within *Stopping the Rip-offs* and recommends that, in the absence of government action on the matter, 'those areas of our existing law which could potentially pertain to protection of Aboriginal sacred imagery warrant further investigation' (75). In particular, she identifies and considers the Trade Practices Act and the Copyright Act, recommending that the Copyright Act may be the most effective means of preventing 'rip-offs' and that '[i]t is most probable that economic torts regimes such as passing off and misrepresentation [associated with the Trade Practices Act] would provide protection in cases that fall outside the ambit of the Copyright Act' (75).

In addition to these studies, there is a number of articles that either reconsider or report back on recent and not so recent case decisions and events relevant to intellectual property law and copyright. In the editorial essay of *Media and Arts Law Review* (2:55–56), 'Copyright Ownership of the Aboriginal Flag' (*Art & Law*, 2: 8) and 'Copyright in the Aboriginal Flag' (*Australian Intellectual Property Law Bulletin*, 10(3):5–36) Colin Golvan reports on the case of *Harold Thomas* v. *David Brown and Another* (unreported, Federal Court of Australia, 9 April 1997). 'Custom, Currency and Copyright: Aboriginal Art and the $10 Note' (*Australian Intellectual Property Law Bulletin*, 9(10):150–152, 156) by Monroe E. Price and Aimee Brown Price reconsiders *Yumbulul* v. *Federal Reserve Bank* in a manner which draws upon legal theory and art history. Stephen Gray's 'Vampires round the campfire' (*Alternative Law Journal*, 22(2):60–63, 67) considers the relevance of issues raised by indigenous concerns about the Human Genome Diversity Project to the Patents Act (1990). Under this general theme, Gray's article covers a considerable range of topics, including the patenting of genetic material, traditional Aboriginal knowledge and patents registered by pharmaceutical companies and the bush 'tucker' industry. In addition to this, he goes on to examine the relationship between the protection of Aboriginal genetic resources, copyright law, international agreements and native title.

7.3 'Reconciling' Differences: Legal Process, Imprisonment and Social Justice

'Indigenous Imprisonment in Australia: An Unresolved Human Rights Issue' by Chris Cunneen and David McDonald (*Australian Journal of Human Rights*, 3(2):90–110) reconsiders the issue of the level of over-representation of indigenous people within the prison system six years after the recommendations included in the final *National Report of the Royal Commission into Aboriginal Deaths in Custody* were tabled in federal parliament in 1991. The authors observe that despite the measures that have been taken, '[t]he available data shows little sustained improvement in the overall situation of Indigenous people in the criminal justice system, if measured by imprisonment rates, police custodial rates, or the incidents of deaths in custody' (91). Framed by the issue of human rights and with constant references to current statistical evidence, this article explores a variety of alternatives for sentencing, policing and imprisonment.

'Language in Court: The Acceptance of Linguistic Evidence about Indigenous Australians in the Criminal Justice System' by Diana Eades (*Australian Aboriginal Studies*, 1:15–27) also considers the continuing high over-representation of indigenous peoples in the criminal justice system, with a focus on the relevance of linguistic evidence for issues of fair representation and judgement. As Eades notes, linguistic evidence has not been taken seriously by the legal profession until recently. Noting such a failure, she demonstrates its relevance through a study of two cases in which an Aboriginal man was convicted of murder on the basis of a signed 'confession', which the defendant alleged was fabricated by the police. According to Eades, in both cases, 'the accused man was a speaker of Aboriginal English, and expert linguistic evidence was presented in his defence to show that the language patterns of the answers attributed to him in the "confession" were not consistent with the way that he spoke English' (16). Eades then moves beyond these specific cases to show how the issues they raise are relevant for discussions about cross-cultural communication.

A further contribution to the body of research on Aboriginal people and the criminal justice system is made by Greg Gardiner and Michael Mackay in the discussion paper *Arresting Koories: A Review of Victoria Police Statistics 1995–96*, which is a continuation of the work of Gardiner and others on the unacceptably high rates of arrest, frequently for minor or 'good order' offences, of Aboriginal and Torres Strait Islander people, especially young men (see *YWCCT 6*). As Gardiner and Mackay argue, breaking the cycle of Aboriginal contact with the criminal justice system was a central thrust of the recommendations of the Royal Commission into Aboriginal Deaths in Custody. Their research examines first point of contact between Aboriginal people and the Victoria Police using police data to compare the number of Aboriginal alleged offenders arrested in the year 1995/96 with numbers in the year 1994/95. Gardiner and Mackay show that while there has been an overall decline in total numbers of Aboriginal alleged offenders arrested by Victoria police, numbers of arrests in certain categories – namely Aboriginal female alleged offenders and arrests for alleged drunkenness offences – show a marked increase in the period under review.

'Aboriginality and Lawyering: Problems of Justice for Aboriginal Defendants in Partner Homicide Cases' by Linda Hancock in S. Cook and J. Bessant eds, *Women's Encounters with Violence* (73–88) provides a close analysis of case involving Robyn Kina, an Aboriginal woman who was, as Hancock recounts, 'convicted of murder and sentenced to life imprisonment in September 1988 for killing her *de facto* partner, rapist, and tormenter, Tony Black, a White Australian' (73). In this context, the article considers both the complexities of Battered Wife Syndrome as a defence and the problems relating to cross-cultural communication which the case raised. Aligning this case with those identified by the Royal Commission into Aboriginal Deaths in Custody, she illustrates the doubly oppressed position of Aboriginal women before the law.

Two books which provide good introductions to a wide range of issues concerning the relationship between indigenous Australians and the legal system are *Indigenous Legal Issues: Commentary and Materials* edited and authored by Heather McRae, Gareth Nettheim and Laura Beacroft, and *Indigenous Australians and the Law* edited by Elliot Johnston, Martin Hinton and Daryle Rigney. The first appears to be aimed at students of law and related disciplines, while the second targets legal professionals. Despite the fact that both are directed at a reasonably specialized audience, both are generally accessible and lucid and offer a clear and relatively extensive introduction for those who merely wish to familiarize themselves with the field. This is particularly true of *Indigenous Legal Issues* which is a remarkable introductory text in its breath and the manner in which it interweaves textual material from experts in a variety of disciplinary areas with insightful and instructive commentary. Indeed, the diversity of its approach is reflected in the variety of textual sources used. For example, the text provides statistical information from studies of Aboriginal health, mortality, education, income, housing and geographic distribution in order to provide a background to discussions on criminality, rates of imprisonment and legal recognition, provides extracts from relevant historical, legal and legislative documents, Government Reports and Royal Commissions, complemented by newspaper exerts and cartoons, while also supplying commentary from scholars and activists as diverse as Michael Dodson, Deborah Bird Rose, Diane Bell, Frank Brennan, Gillian Cowlishaw, Marcia Langton, Stephen Gray, Tim Rowse and Stephen Muecke.

The sections within the book reflect this concern to move beyond the parameters of accepted law. The areas covered include: a general historical sketch of settlement, colonization, government policies and legal and legislative approaches to 'Aborigines' and 'Torres Strait Islanders' in the early years alongside a portrait of the position of Aborigines within Australian society today; a description of aspects of indigenous law and the (limited) extent of its recognition within Australian law, discussion of indigenous sovereignty, land rights, the recognition of native title and native title law and legal process; a consideration of equality issues such as racial discrimination, the (over) representation of Aborigines within the context of criminal justice and child welfare; and in the final section, a reflection on many of the issues discussed and possible avenues of change and reconciliation including self-determination, self-government, international law and constitutional change.

The prologue to the book, 'The Saga of Captain Cook' as recounted by Hobbles Danaiyairi to Deborah Bird Rose with Rose's commentary, sets up an interesting and engaging dialogue concerning the voices and narratives which have been excluded from conventional studies of law in Australia. As a narrative which supplements discussion of law and legislation in terms of mere legality, internal consistency and correct procedure, 'The Saga of Captain Cook' positions 'the law' culturally and historically, as imperial, colonizing and destructive. As Rose notes: 'Captain Cook's law . . . can be crudely summarised as the law that might makes right' (3). Such a narrative strikes at the heart of propositions that are frequently taken as fundamental to law: that the law is universal, generalizable and that all are equal before the law. Indeed, beginning with this narrative itself mirrors the temporal-historical priority indigenous customary law and narrative have over European-derived law and history, and in doing so suggests the irony of legal recognition of indigenous 'rights'. Even under *Mabo* prior rights are recognized, or rather *re*-cognized, only once provision is found within Eurocentric law and only in its terms. What is passed over in this temporal gap, between the before of the indigenous and the later 'recognition', is the 'violent' foundations upon which Australian law rests; a foundation which depends upon a repression and exclusion of the manner in which law was installed and the law(s), culture(s) and people(s) it displaced. This violent repression and exclusion, a silence within law and history for so many years, relates to what many have identified as the more radical aspects of the *Mabo* decision and to the motivation which issues a particular line of questioning frequently pursued within this book. An avenue opened, though not always directly addressed, is the question of whether the law is, in fact, *just*.

This critical dialogue established by the prologue is reinforced throughout the following sections of the book. Section one of Part One, 'Background and History', for example, juxtaposes statistical information relating to areas such as housing, income, health and mortality with textual fragments from a variety of sources including 'Contact History According to the Royal Commission into Aboriginal Deaths in Custody', 'Racial Thought in Early Colonial Australia' by Reynolds and 'Living in the Margins' by Pettman. The effect is clearly to demonstrate both that colonialism continues to have a devastating effect on the lives of Aboriginal people, and that what some take to be legal issues are thoroughly entangled within a complicated range of social, cultural and political issues.

Indigenous Australians and the Law similarly provides a basic guide to a broad range of legal issues concerning indigenous people in Australia. The first essay in the collection, 'Indigenous Australians and the legacy of European Conquest' (3–30) by Maria Lane, offers a number of historical sketches of early colonial policy and law, with a particular focus on South Australia, and in doing so registers both the effect of colonization on indigenous culture and society and law and legislature's complicity with colonizing power. In addition to this, Lane notes important similarities between 'protectionist' and 'segregationist' policies and practices, early 'assimilation' policies and some of the later 'self-determination' and 'self-management' policies, describing them as 'control' rather than 'enabling' policies. According to Lane, enabling policies have been rare and short lived and 'ironically, owe their existence to the broadened forms of assimilation, "equal rights", or "integration" policies from the mid-1960s onwards' (8–9). In this manner, Lane recognizes the ironic situation indigenous people find themselves in with respect to the restriction of *their* rights, indigenous rights granted on the basis of prior occupation, to those terms recognized by *European* law. Thus, emphasizing the similarities between early and recent approaches to Aboriginal rights, she observes much of what today appears 'liberal and individualist, rather than openly racist ... could fairly inherit the term "integration"' (29). In a similar way, Daryle Rigney, in 'Moving the Boundaries and Undoing the Restrictions' (31–38), begins an engagement with issues of social justice by asserting the need to 'move beyond merely making legal institutions safe and accessible places for Aboriginal and Islander people' (31). Rigney's argument follows two complementary paths. The first considers both the government's failure to act on the recommendations of the Law Reform Commission and its approach to the Hindmarsh Island 'affair', a demonstration of 'the chasm between recognition and realisation of rights for indigenous people' (31–32). The second is an attempt to 'shift the boundaries' through a description of some aspects of law according to the Ngarrindjeri, a tribe or language group from the Murray River region in South Australia.

Christopher Reynolds makes a similar attempt to consider the broader context of law through a study of the relationship between indigenous health and law in 'The Health of Indigenous Australians' (39–52). Reynolds justifies the relevance of a study about health in a book about law explaining that indigenous health can be taken as a social indicator that helps contextualize the specific questions posed within the legal field about 'the way we order our social structure and to speculate on what might be' (40). Thus, health problems, as a symptom of structural inadequacies and the continuation of the devastating effects of colonialism, not only reveal a connection between the way in which Australian law and policy have played a part in the dire situation Aboriginal people have found themselves in, they issue a challenge for present and future legal and policy decision making. Thus, as Reynolds notes, reconciliation would thereby be, at the very least, 'a recognition that land, health, housing, legal status and poverty are related to the process of reconciling past deeds with future hopes' (49).

Two essays discuss reconciliation, one, 'Reconciliation and the Constitution' (183–212) by Belinda Wells and John Doyle, examines references within the constitution of relevance to Aboriginal issues, and more specifically, the possibility of pursuing reconciliation through constitutional means. The second essay, 'Reconciliation' (213–224) by Irene Watson, asks, in light of the government's recent efforts towards reconciliation, 'who' and 'what' are to be reconciled in such a process? It seems clear to Watson that 'the "conflict" that is to be reconciled [in "real" reconciliation] has not subsided as a result of the Commonwealth Government's recent reconciliation initiatives' (213). Wells and Doyle also point to the shortfalls of attempts made by the Government to date in this regard. Arguing against the pursuit of reconciliation in terms of already existing law and policy, they suggest that the answer may lie with constitutional change. Indeed, they argue that while the Government has asserted its commitment to reconciliation and provided statutory protection of cultural heritage and some land rights, '[o]ur constitution, however, does not reflect any of these values' (184) Elliott Johnston's 'Aborigines and the Law', (101–110), Martin Hinton's 'Sentencing and Indigenous Australians' (111–132) and Bruce Debelle's 'Aboriginal Customary Law and the Common Law' (81–100) each consider both the differences between Aboriginal customary law and Australian law commonly ignored by traditional legal scholars and the failure of the legal system to acknowledge adequately and address the impact of colonization, displacement and dispossession within legal representations and sentencing. Michael Dodson's 'Human Rights and the Extinguishment of Native Title' (149–166), Anthony Moore's 'Aboriginal Land Rights in South Australia' (133–148) and Frank Brennan's '*Mabo* and its Ramification for the Future of Indigenous Australians' (167–182) discuss various issues relating to the *Mabo* and *Wik* decisions and their implications for native title, property rights and indigenous rights generally. Dodson's article is particularly interesting because it argues that the common law treatment of native title in *Mabo* (No 2) is 'in effect discriminatory' (155). While acknowledging the importance of *Mabo* for indigenous rights, his argument paints a picture of the decision as fundamentally discriminatory, revealing the terrible irony within what is 'given' to Aboriginal people in the decision: '[i]t is perhaps a legal nicety that the courts assume that the indigenous people of Australia became subjects of the Crown in 1788. But, if that is going to be the assumption, then a law which treats the property of one group of subjects in lesser regard than the property of all other subjects is patently unacceptable' (156).

8. Aboriginal Art

8.1 Rock Art and Traditional Forms

Josephine Flood's *Rock Art of the Dreamtime* is the first overview of new work in the field of Australian Aboriginal rock art written by an archaeologist in the past forty years. In what is intended to be an introductory survey, Flood plots the history of the development of rock art in Australia in a concise and interesting manner. Although there are many articles and essays on rock art, mostly to be found in the more scholarly journals, this data-based rather than theory-based work represents one of the relatively few books available on the subject. Her publication is noteworthy for reasons other than its rarity. In addition to the better-known sites, Flood provides useful information and reproductions of lesser-known bodies of prehistoric rock art and the results of significant new research – especially chapter five on new techniques for dating rock or desert varnish in South Australia. Arranged chronologically, each chapter is broken up by a number of sub-headings and condensed information and diagrams are presented in an informative and accessible fashion. She provides a wide-ranging discussion including engravings from the end of the last ice age and art of the deep limestone caves under the Nullarbor Plain through to the present, acknowledging the art of the first Australians as the oldest firmly dated body of rock art in the world.

Continuing the archaeological theme, Ian J. McNiven and Lynette Russell in ' "Strange Paintings" and "Mystery Races": Kimberley Rock-Art, Diffusionism and Colonialist Constructions of Australia's Aboriginal Past' (*Antiquity*, 71:801–809) summarize and present a range of arguments concerning the origins of some of the most striking ancient Aboriginal rock art: the Bradshaw paintings of the Kimberley region (also covered by Flood). Employing postcolonial critical methods, McNiven and Russell take issue with arguments that the Bradshaws (as these works are more commonly known) are not 'early Aboriginal' but rather 'pre-Aboriginal'. In a clearly written and well-structured report with over sixty references, McNiven and Russell critique much of this information for its underlying 'aspects of colonial intellectual ideology' (801). Concluding that the 'diffusionist debate' – their term for arguments that the Bradshaws were painted by non-Aboriginals – resurrects 'a colonialist standpoint that has played into the hands of political conservatives and again placed Aboriginal people in the position of having to demonstrate cultural authenticity and legitimacy' (807).

Dedicated to the memory of Lin Onus, *Kunwinjku Spirit: Creation Stories from Western Arnhem Land* is a unique collection of paintings, drawings and stories about the creator ancestors by Nawakadj Nganjmirra, a major artist of the Kunbarllanjnja (Oenpelli) region, and his extended family. Complemented by the superb photography of Neil McLeod, this beautiful book sets out both Kunwinjku and English language versions of the cultural history and mythology of the Kunwinjku peoples. There is a large glossary in the back of the book and this, coupled with Nganjmirra's biography, make *Kunwinjku Spirit* an invaluable record of a history and language not just for interested outsiders but for the Kunwinjku people themselves.

Moving from rock art to the less permanent medium of bark, the essay 'The Painters of the Wagilag Sisters Story' co-authored by Wally Caruana and Nigel Lendon (*Art and Australia*, 35(1):82–87) recounts the narrative of the Wagilag Sisters as told by the late Paddy Dhathangu, a Yolngu artist of senior ritual status. This essay explores the significance of bark painting as a means of recording information previously only stored as oral storytelling or visual memory. Bark paintings, as the essay explains, were originally used in ceremonies but later came to be produced as items of trade thus marking the beginning of a body of work that has been preserved. The exhibition charts the changes to the Wagilag Sisters story over six decades and four generations, dating back to the early days of contact between Europeans and the Yolngu peoples of Eastern and Central Arnhem Land. Also dealing with bark painting is Luke Taylor's *Seeing the Inside: Bark Painting in Western Arnhem Land*. Taylor's work is primarily a piece of social anthropology detailing the place of bark painting in Western Arnhem Land Aboriginal social and cultural life. While the detailed text is generously illustrated, it suffers from the inclusion of only black and white plates.

'The Land is My Foundation' (*Art and Australia*, 35(1):54–55) by Margaret Tuckson is a short review of the touring exhibition *Djalkiri Wänga: The Land is My Foundation: Fifty Years of Aboriginal Art from Yirrkala, Northeast Arnhem Land*. Based on the field work of anthropologists Ronald and Catherine Berndt, the exhibition consists of eighteen works on paper, eighteen bark pieces, much valuable information on moieties and language groups, stories and maps. Tuckson praises the show for its message as well as aesthetic. Other exhibitions of note include *Dreamings of the Desert: Aboriginal Dot Paintings* reviewed by Christopher Anderson (*Art and Australia*, 35(1):56–57) and commended for the lack of information about the works, forcing viewers to come to their own conclusions. In an interesting take on the politics of reviewing, Joyce Morgan in 'Sweet Dreams' (*Weekend Australian*, Sept 13–14:18–20) points out that there is no real critical rigour when it comes to reviewing Indigenous art. This article is basically a promotion for Sydney's *Festival of the Dreaming* – the first of four Olympic festivals and the largest celebration to date of indigenous culture in Australia – but curator Hetti Perkins, festival artistic director Rhonda Roberts and arts administrator Lydia Miller all agree about the tendency toward 'charity' in reviewing practice. That is, the situation in which critics tend to shy away from any harsh criticism of indigenous art in favour of reviews which are little more than descriptions of the works.

8.2 Authenticity

In 'Aboriginal Art Abroad: Responses to Touring Exhibitions in Europe, the United States and Asia' Djon Mundine (*Art and Australia*, 35(1):68–73) examines the growing popularity of Aboriginal art in relation to feedback from *Aratjara [The Messenger]: Art of the First Australians* 1993–1994 – on which Mundine was a touring curator. The show was distinguished by the diversity of works on display and also because it was controlled and directed by Aboriginal people. Mundine uses the critical reception of the show to point out the audience's preoccupation with romantic notions of purity, primitivism and authenticity giving a number of examples relating to problems of translation and misreading which occurred in this cross-cultural contact.

Recounting what must be one of the great scandals of the Australian art world, Jonathan Turner 'Aboriginal Sin' (*ARTnews*, 96:93) presents a brief but informative overview of the opinions of the art establishment, Aboriginal community and artists involved in the Eddie Burrup/Elizabeth Durack affair (see the review of Julie Marcus's essay above). In contrast, Marianna Annas 'Art, Originality and Authenticity' (*Periphery*, 33:6–8) discusses the constitution of a 'Label of Authenticity' for Indigenous art and cultural production and compares cases in Canada (Inuit), United States (Native American) and Aboriginal Australia. One of the major obstacles, as far as Annas is concerned, involves problems arising from understanding the differences in meanings of the term authenticity for Aboriginal and non-Aboriginal people.

Susan Congreve 'Painting Up Big: Large-Canvas Collaborative Paintings from Yuendumu' (*Art and Australia*, 35(1):88–93) tackles issues of authenticity and integrity of the Jukurrpa (Dreamings) as portrayed in art worked on by many Aboriginal artists. She writes of the practice of painting in large groups, sometimes utilizing designs owned by different landholders. For example there were forty-two Yuendumu artists working on the one canvas featured in the travelling exhibition *Aratjara: Art of the First Australians* (see above). Works painted by a number of artists present difficulties for categorization in gallery/dealer situations but, argues Congreve, this should not cast any aspersions on the authenticity or value of works.

8.3 Design and Textiles
The inseparability of art and life in indigenous society is the predominant theme in Doreen Mellor's 'Indigenous Australian Dyed and Printed Textiles' (*Artlink*, 17(1):46–49). By providing an informative overview of major developments and initiatives taken in Utopia, Ernabella in South Australia, and Tiwi Designs from Bathurst Island, Mellor hopes to bring about a greater recognition of textile-based art work by indigenous Australians. Maria Mann's short piece 'Magabala Books: The Politics of Design' (*Artlink*, 17(1):36–37) is an interview with Sam Cook, the designer from Magabala Books, Australia's first Indigenous publishing house. The interview covers the unique problems arising from use of Aboriginal designs in publishing. What makes Magabala unique is that it ensures the highest level of Aboriginal consultation over use and content of sensitive material. It also emphasizes the Aboriginal ownership of representation, something unusual in this context. Paul Counsel 'Desert Designs' (*Artlink*, 17(1):54–56) recounts the story of the birth and development of Desert Designs and the relationship between co-founders Stephen Culley and David Wroth and Aboriginal artist Jimmy Pike. Emphasis in this short piece is placed on the commitment to total lifestyle concept, establishing a vehicle for the promotion of images and designs of Aboriginal people.

8.4 Politics, Spirituality and the Land
In 'Divining the Spiritual' Joan Kerr reviews *Spirit + Place: Art in Australia 1861–1996*, an exhibition held at the Museum of Contemporary Art in Sydney, November 1996–March 1997. Kerr praises the exhibition's ability to show 'indigenous and non-indigenous art in partnership ... [and that] what the mixture purveyed was a sense of optimism for the future' (53). Similarly, Antonia Carver 'In Place (Out of Time): Contemporary Art in Australia' (*Flash Art*, 197:74) reviews the eponymous show (part of *New Images*, a year long project intended to 'heighten' Britons' awareness of Australian culture). The show, curated by Howard Morphy and David Elliott, is important as it mixes Aboriginal art, non-Aboriginal art, and traditional and contemporary styles. The interrelation of Aboriginal and non-Aboriginal art is explored in a different way by Cath Bowdler. In her article 'The Tyranny of Paradise or ... on being an emerging artist in Darwin' (*Artlink*, 17(4):70–71), Bowdler writes of her experience as a non-indigenous artist being inspired by close proximity to prolific Aboriginal art production and how this relates to her own practice which is inspired by the land which, for her, often defies definition.

This year, the quarterly journal *Art and Australia* has devoted one of its issues to Aboriginal and Torres Strait Islander art. *The Festival of the Dreaming* contains reviews of several important exhibitions, presents a number of essays on a wide range of topics affecting the visual arts and pays tribute to the recently deceased Aboriginal artist and arts activist Lin Onus. The magazine's editorial co-authored by Hannah Fink and Hetti Perkins, 'Writing For Land' (*Art and Australia*, 35(1):60–63), reflects upon 'a series of incongruities or paradoxes between the nature and perception of Aboriginal art' (60). The growing levels of appreciation (some might say appropriation) of Aboriginal imagery – the boomerang in the Sydney Olympics' logo is a particularly pertinent example in this instance – has caused symbol and meaning to be in an ever-increasing arbitrary relation, thus reducing Aboriginal iconography to a set of decorative functions. This function sits uneasily with the image of the boomerang as a traditional symbol of cultural resistance for Aboriginal peoples. Politics is also an important theme for Land Council Chairman Galarrwuy Yunupingu's 'Indigenous Art in the Olympic Age' 64–67). He points out important links between painting and politics for Aboriginal people in their struggles to maintain their culture and rights to their land, looking at *The Yirrkala Bark Petition* (1963) and the *Barunga Statement* (1988) as two prime examples of the way that painting in Aboriginal culture operates like writing. It makes a statement expressing a relation to the land of vital significance to the well being of Aboriginal cultural, social and political survival.

Judith Ryan, 'Abstraction, Meaning and Essence in Aboriginal Art' (74–81) examines the seemingly abstract patterns and designs in some Aboriginal art (Arnhem Land is used here as an example) revealing them to be a system of signs and symbols which represent a complex and intertextual visual language. Ryan describes the ways this visual form replicates its spoken counterpart: context, many-layers of meaning, a language that remains unwritten, secret-sacred and essentially abstract to those without the knowledge to de-code it. In one of the examples given, the diamond designs operate as symbols of origin and place 'like words in a sentence' (77). Ryan also compares Rover Thomas to Piet Mondrian with respect to Thomas's sparse symbolic composition and blocks of colour. She goes on to analyse the work of Long Tom Tjapanangka and Judy Watson in a similar fashion concluding that 'a great deal of Aboriginal art is abstract or non-figurative. It reveals through symbols and metaphors an unseen power or spirit essence abstracted from the land' (81).

'Blackness in the Art of Rover Thomas' (94–99) by Louis Nowra, is a fittingly eloquent essay which seems to take issue with Ryan's comparisons but not her conclusions, noting the superficiality of a comparison between Rover Thomas and Mark Rothko. Spirituality is pronounced in the work of both, but Rothko's is seen as intensely narcissistic whereas the spirituality in Thomas' work stems from the artist's deep connection to the land. While Rothko may not be a suitable comparison to Thomas, Australian landscape artist Fred Williams is deemed more appropriate for Nowra because Williams' work displays an attraction to the essence of the Australian landscape and an abstract sense of topography. In his description and review of several specific works, Nowra writes of the intense feelings that Thomas's works evoke in him, noting that even if one cannot understand the full spiritual significance, one can still appreciate the works for their beauty and the way that they subtly evoke the landscape of the East Kimberley Region.

8.5 Urban and Contemporary Aboriginal Art
Timothy Morrell's 'Art for a Banana Republic' (*Artlink*, 17(3):54–55) reviews the *Second Asia-Pacific Triennial of Contemporary Art* in Brisbane. He assesses curator Apinan Poshyananda's selection of artists – Fiona Hall, Luke Roberts, Destiny Deacon and Kathy Temin among those reviewed –

as one which promotes a version of Australian art 'which strenuously avoided anything slickly technological or expensive looking' (54). Indeed Morrell further describes those chosen by Poshyananda as artists who 'convey a sense of Australia as Third World country' (54) but ultimately praises the curator's choice of indigenous artists for displaying 'Urban Aboriginality' and promoting a different view of art than is usually portrayed.

Tom Byra Mixie Mosby in 'The Hell of Primitivism' (*Like, Art Magazine,* 5:18–22) compares the work of Ken Thaiday, Ellen Jose and Julie Gough in answer to the question of how to approach 'the "discovery" of new forms of indigenous art' (18). Mosby points out that in the majority of cases that indigenous art tends to be classified either as 'otherness' or under the rubric of art theory and that there tends to be no in-between. Similarly, 'Torres Strait Islander Art: An Outsider's View', an essay by Susan Cochrane (*Art and Australia,* 35(1):116–123), provides useful information and illustrations of a number of contemporary Torres Strait Islander artists but is confusing as it begins as an expression of resentment at the lack of attention paid to Islander art but ends by suggesting that the isolation is a virtue and gives the art its identity.

Janie Greville in 'Brenda L. Croft and Destiny Deacon' (*Creative Camera,* 345:42), a short review of Brenda Croft's *Strange Fruit* and Destiny Deacon's *Welcome to Never Never* praises the works of these artists for providing an alternative to dominant paradigms of Aboriginal art. In a similar way, Marcia Langton reviews several works by Melbourne-based artist Destiny Deacon in 'The Valley of the Dolls: Black Humour in the Art of Destiny Deacon' (*Art and Australia,* 35(1):100–107) and presents a reading of them as being 'a barometer of postcolonial anxiety, as a window of understanding for the new generations of Australians . . . seeking to establish a considered and meaningful grammar of images in an environment full of colonial memories' (107). For Langton, Deacon's work presents a 'deconstructionist reading of urban Australian Aboriginal survivors of the colonial wars now exiled in the Housing Commission "burbs"' (100). Deacon's humour is indeed 'Blak' – the spelling is deliberate and intended in respect of Deacon's own reclamation (for more information see Deacon's *Blakness: Blak City Culture,* Australian Centre for Contemporary Art, 1994). Nothing is sacred as Deacon satirises representations of Aboriginal women by Aboriginal men as well as Europeans. The humorous elements in Deacon's work are further emphasized by Langton as she likens it to the early comedy of Whoopi Goldberg for its acerbic wit and ability to 'cut the crap'.

In other reviews, noted Koori artist Brook Andrew looks briefly at the work of contemporaries Samantha Lau, Megan Jones and Josie Bri-Haines in an article entitled 'Between Heaven and Earth' (*Artlink,* 17(4):61–63) and Julie Gough in 'Time Ripples in Tasmania: Aboriginal Artists in Tasmania Today' (*Art and Australia,* 35(1):108–115) presents a round up of art practices by Palawa people. Palawa, as Gough tells us, is the name 'contemporary' Tasmanian Aboriginal people have chosen for themselves (much like 'Koori' for their nearest northern neighbours). For the Palawa it is impossible to separate political and cultural concerns from their artistic practice. This is true for visual artists as well as those maintaining traditional skills such as basketry, wood-working, shell necklace making, and tool making. These traditional forms or 'crafts' are imbued with a deep symbolic historical and cultural significance which is even more pronounced when they are exhibited as artworks. As Gough explains: 'Tasmanian Aboriginal people are creating and defending their own definitions of what is art today. Practices formerly externally labelled as "craft" . . . have undergone fundamental reworking. Palawa artists incorporate beliefs into practice, and insist that their work has meaning beyond form, and memory beyond materials' (112). Gough's essay also covers artists working in more 'contemporary' mediums including Ricky Maynard's photographs, Yvonne Kopper's prints, Julie Brown's textile designs and her own mixed media works. As a final point she reiterates the importance of interconnectedness and ties to the land despite all that the tide of history has thrown up at them.

In a short piece entitled 'Black Market' (*Art and Australia*, 35(1):126–127), Terry Ingram – (salesroom correspondent for the *Australian Financial Review*) reports on the fact that Aboriginal art has reached yet another new financial peak in terms of record prices and numbers of sales in the year 1996–97. This piece becomes interesting when read alongside Ian McLean's essay 'Aboriginal Art Since The Second World War' (*Australian Studies*, 11:78–88). The increasing market price of Aboriginal paintings, reflects a 'new public acceptance and prestige' for Ingram (126) and 'an accurate barometer of the Aborigine's enhanced legal position in land claims and other political struggles across the nation' for McLean (81). The most obvious difference between these two pieces is in terms of contextualisation. Ingram's two page market report is a dry round-up of the year's best sales whereas McLean traces the history and development of the Modern Aboriginal art movement – from its beginnings in 1963 with the *Yirrkala Bark Petition* (see Yunupingu's essay 'Indigenous Art in the Olympic Age', reviewed above) to the 'postcolonial' art of Gordon Bennett and Tracey Moffatt emphasizing the political nature of the art movement, its growth in self-determination and self-empowerment.

8.6 The Politics of Art Criticism

Providing something of the equivalent of a 'retrospective' of the art criticism and other work of Bernard Smith, with particular emphasis on his contribution to the re-visioning of Aboriginality and Aboriginal art in Australia, is Tim Bonyhady's intellectually generous but critical essay 'The Uncritical Culture' (*Eureka Street* October:24–32) which presents a challenge to art critics and historians to afford the work of Smith the rigorous criticism it deserves. Strategically locating the world of art and its criticism within the political domain of the impact of colonization on indigenous people, Bonyhady begins his essay with a consideration of Benjamin Law's imposing bust of Truganini, an image of which was chosen as the cover illustration for the published text of Smith's 1980 Boyer Lecture (*The Spectre of Truganini*, Australian Broadcasting Commission, 1981). In confronting this spectre, Smith argued that by 'trying to forget all the violence Europeans had done to Aborigines, white Australians not only skewed their understanding of the past, but also corrupted the present because there "is a close connection between culture, place and morality"' (24). However, Bonyhady contends, the spectre of Truganini continues to haunt Smith's own work, pointing to flaws and omissions in his writings which remain unaddressed as his groundbreaking books went into second and further editions. The essay goes on the consider the wide range of Smith's work in the fields of Australian art history and criticism, architectural criticism and activism on urban planning and redevelopment, as well as his contribution to Aboriginal issues. Drawing on the work of Peter Beilharz (*Imagining The Antipodes: Culture, Theory, and the Visual in the Work of Bernard Smith*, Cambridge University Press, 1997), Bonyhady writes that Smith is ' "best read ... as ... a theorist of peripheral vision" who has understood that the antipodes is not place but a relation' (25). In terms of his work specifically dealing with the impact of colonization (on both colonized and colonizers), Bonyhady assesses the primary significance of *European Vision and the South Pacific* (Oxford University Press, 1960) as lying in its critical disregard for the distinctions between art and ethnography. While Bonhady considers Smith's thesis concerning the progressive transformation of visual representations of natives from 'noble savages' to 'ignoble savages' flawed, precisely because it does not sufficiently take into account work as Law's sculptures of Truganini and Woureddy, the intellectual and political impact of the book should not be underestimated. Likewise, the flaws and omissions in Smith's scholarship should not be ignored. For example, returning to the trope of Truganani on which the essay turns, Bonhady argues that Smith failed to:

> weigh new curatorial evidence and art historical interest in Benjamin Law's bust of Truganini and Wourredy when Yale University Press republished *European Vision* in 1985. Perhaps Smith should have let his text stand and simply written a new preface of this lavish new edition, as he did when Oxford University Press republished *Place, Taste and Tradition* in 1979. Instead he claimed to have taken account 'of a good deal of original work' published since 1960, particularly where it bore 'upon major theses and topics considered'. But Smith did not live up to this promise. Even though art galleries across Australia had finally recognised Law's importance by including his sculptures in their displays and the Sydney art historian Mary Mackay had written the first substantial article on Law, Smith still ignored the implications of Law's busts for his thesis about the fall of the noble savage (32).

For Bonyhady, that the Australian art criticism community has for so long left these omissions unchallenged is one indication that its claims to being culturally mature are unfulfilled. Smith's work should not only be lauded for its theoretical sophistication, or for its remarkable depth and breadth of scholarship. A mature critical culture should show Smith's work the admiration it deserves through sustained critique.

9. Education

A number of publications in 1997 deal with the issue of Aboriginal education – both the primary, secondary and tertiary education of Aboriginal and Torres Strait Islander people and the inclusion of Aboriginal material into curricula, for both Aboriginal and non-Aboriginal students. *Aboriginal Studies in the 90s: Visions and Challenges II*, edited by Rhonda Craven and Nigel Parbury (Aboriginal Studies Association) is the collected papers of the sixth annual Aboriginal Studies Association Conference, held at the University of New South Wales in October 1996. The volume contains twenty-eight contributions from educators, policy makers and activists in the field of Aboriginal Studies in primary and secondary schools and offers a range of approaches to questions of policy, pedagogy, curriculum and student performance. While the majority of the essays are written by and for practitioners, a number of contributions offer wider perspectives on questions concerning the place of Aboriginal Studies in Australian culture and politics. A related volume, which also deals with tertiary education, is *Indigenous Education: Historical, Moral and Practical Tales* edited by Stephen Harris and Merridy Malin (Northern Territory University Press, 1997). This volume contains contributions from practitioners and commentators on educational theory and practice centring around the themes of history, access and equity, classroom practice, and in a final piece by Stephen Harris, 'Pay the Rent: Mabo and the Big Picture of Aboriginal Education' (138–143) on the role of the education of indigenous people (and the education of non-indigenous Australians in indigenous issues) in securing a political resolution to injustices which beset Aboriginal and Torres Strait Islander communities.

Also focusing on language and pedagogy in the field of Aboriginal Studies is *Ngoonjook* 13 published in the year under review. This issue of the journal contains contributions by indigenous and non-indigenous writers including Michael Christie's report on the Yolngu literature CD project (31–39); Robin Rogers and Carmel O'Shannessy discussing the status of Kriol in English teaching ('Using Kriol to Teach English – Help or Hindrance' 26–39); Rob McCormack's useful essay on the relations between academic discourse and Aboriginal discourse ('Academic Discourse', 55–67) which attempts to demystify the conventions of academic discourse for indigenous students by highlighting the degree to which all discourse is learned; and Veronica Arbon's 'Tracks of Knowledge: Sediments and Sentiments in Aboriginal Education Landscapes' (70–85) which focuses on the 'bothways' cross-cultural Aboriginal education experiences at Batchelor College in the Northern Territory via a consideration of the metaphors of land, land sediments, and tracks through the land.

Focusing on the popularity of indigenous popular music, Karl Neuenfeldt's essay 'Indigenous Popular Music: An Example of Cultural Vitality and a Curriculum Resource' (*Counterpoint*, February:42–46) considers the uses to which the music may be put in curricula, both for the education of Aboriginal and non-Aboriginal students. Nuenfeldt cites examples of the inclusion of indigenous musical material on school curricula, for example the New South Wales Higher School Certificate programme in Aboriginal Studies includes songs such as 'Blackfella, Whitefella' by the Warumpi Band and Yothu Yindi's 'Treaty' which are examined in terms of their musicality but also for the ideas conveyed in their lyrics.

Books Reviewed

Attwood, Bain and Andrew Markus with Dale Edwards and Kate Schilling. *The 1967 Referendum, Or When Aborigines Didn't Get the Vote.* Aboriginal Studies Press. pp. xi + 155. A$25.00. ISBN 0 85575 311 0.

Austin, Tony. *Never Trust a Government Man: Northern Territory Aboriginal Policy 1911–1939.* Northern Territory University Press. pp. x + 336. A$19.95. ISBN 1 876248 02 5.

Baker, D. W. A. *The Civilised Surveyor: Thomas Mitchell and the Australian Aborigines.* Melbourne University Press. pp. xvi + 213. A$29.95. ISBN 0 522 84763 3.

Bell, Jeanie. *Talking About Celia . . .: Community and Family Memories of Celia Smith.* University of Queensland Press. pp. xiv + 102. A$24.95. ISBN 0 7022 2833 8.

Chesterman, John and Brian Galligan. *Citizens without Rights: Aborigines and Australian Citizenship.* Cambridge University Press. pp. x + 277. A$29.95. ISBN 0 521 59751 X.

Cook, S. and J. Bessant, eds. *Women's Encounters with Violence* Sage. pp. xii + 268. A$39.95. ISBN 0 7619 0432 8.

Cowlishaw, Gillian and Barry Morris, eds. *Race Matters: Indigenous Australians and 'Our' Society.* Aboriginal Studies Press. pp. x + 295. A$29.95. ISBN 0 85575 294 7.

Craven, Rhonda and David Parbury, eds. *Journal of the Aboriginal Studies Association.* Aboriginal Studies Association. pp. 11 + 50. A$15.00. ISBN 0 64633 062 4.

Craven, Rhonda and David Parbury, eds. *Aboriginal Studies in the 90s: Visions and Challenges II (Collected Papers of the 6th Annual ASA Conference, The University of New South Wales, October 1996).* Aboriginal Studies Association. pp. vi + 217. A$25.00. ISBN 0 646 308866.

Dewar, Mickey. *In Search of the 'Never-Never': Looking for Australia in Northern Territory Writing.* Northern Territory University Press. pp. xvi + 234. A$30.00. ISBN 1 876248 06 8.

Flood, Josephine. *Rock Art of the Dreamtime.* Angus & Robertson. pp. xii + 372. £18.00. ISBN 0 207 18908 0.

Foley, Bernadette. ed. *Bringing Australia Together: The Structure and Experience of Racism in Australia.* Foundation for Aboriginal and Islander Research Action. pp. xii + 129. A$16.95. ISBN 0 646 35233 4.

Gardiner, Greg. *Football and Racism: The AFL's Racial and Religious Vilification Rule.* Monash University Koorie Research Centre. pp. iv + 29. A$5.50. ISBN 0 7326 12780.

Gardiner, Greg and Michael Mackay. *Arresting Koories: A Review of Victoria Police Statistics 1995/96.* Monash University Koorie Research Centre. pp. iv + 25. A$5.50. ISBN 0 7326 1298 5.

Grace, Helen, Ghassan Hage, Lesley Johnson, Julie Langsworth and Michael Symonds, eds. *Home/World: Space, Community and Marginality in Sydney's West.* Pluto Press. pp. x + 204. A$24.95. ISBN 1 86403 036 4.

Gray, Geoffrey, and Christine Winter, eds. *The Resurgence of Racism: Howard, Hanson and the Race Debate.* Monash Publications in History, Monash University, Department of History in Association with the Australian Institute of Aboriginal and Torres Strait Islander Studies, and the Humanities Research Centre, Australian National University. pp. viii + 170. A$17.00. ISBN 0 7326 1290.

Green, Neville and Susan Moon. *Far From Home: Aboriginal Prisoners of Rottnest Island 1838–1931.* University of Western Australia Press. pp. viii + 368. A$45.00. ISBN 1 875560 92 0.

Harris, Stephen and Merridy Malin eds. *Indigenous Education: Historical, Moral and Practical Tales.* Northern Territory University Press. pp. xiv + 143. A$19.95. ISBN 1 876248 05 X.

Healy, Chris. *From the Ruins of Colonialism: History as Social Memory.* Cambridge University Press. pp. viii + 249. A$29.95. ISBN 0 521 56576 6.

Johnston, Elliot, Martin Hinton and Daryle Rigney, eds. *Indigenous Australians and the Law.* Cavendish Publishing (Australia) pp. xi + 236. A$58.00. ISBN 1 876213 21 3.

Kidd, Rosalind. *The Way We Civilise: Aboriginal Affairs – the Untold Story.* University of Queensland Press. pp. xxvi + 390. A$19.95. ISBN 0 7022 2961 X.

Link-Up (NSW) and Tikka Jan Wilson. *In the Best Interest of the Child? Stolen Children: Aboriginal Pain/White Shame.* Link-Up (NSW) Aboriginal Corporation and Aboriginal History Inc. pp. xvi + 242. Price on application. ISBN 0 646 28789 3.

McRae, Heather, Garth Nettheim and Laura Beacroft, eds. *Indigenous Legal Issues: Commentary and Materials.* LBC Information Services. pp. xxviii + 540. A$85.00. ISBN 0 455 21468 9.

McGregor, Russell. *Imagined Destines: Aboriginal Australians and the Doomed Race Theory, 1880–1939.* Melbourne University Press. pp. xiv + 313. A$29.95. ISBN 0 522 84762 5.

Minajalku Aboriginal Corporation. *Home – Still Waiting: Report of the Minajalku Aboriginal Corporation into Aboriginal Children and the Churches in Victoria.* Thornbury, Vic: Minajalku Aboriginal Corporation. pp. 63. ISBN 0 646 34424 2.

Mudrooroo. *The Indigenous Literature of Australia: Milli Milli Wangka.* Hyland House. pp. vi + 233. A$24.95. ISBN 1 86447 014 3.

Muecke, Stephen. *No Road (Bitumen All the Way).* Fremantle Arts Centre Press. pp. 252. A$16.95. ISBN 1 86368 181 7.

National Inquiry into the Separation of Aboriginal and Torres Strait Islander Children from Their Families (Australia). *Bringing Them Home: Report of the National Inquiry into the Separation of Aboriginal and Torres Strait Islander Children from Their Families.* Human Rights and Equal Opportunity Commission. pp. x + 689. A$60.00. ISBN 0 642 26954 8.

Nganjmirra, Nawakadj. *Kunwinjku Spirit: Creation Stories from Western Arnhem Land.* Melbourne University Press. pp. xii + 276. A$49.95. ISBN 0 522 84773 0.

Olive, Noel, ed. *Karijini Mirlimirli: Aboriginal Histories from the Pilbara.* Fremantle Arts Centre Press. pp. 256. A$19.95. ISBN 1 86368 204 X.

Reed-Gilbert, Kerry (ed). *Message Stick: Contemporary Aboriginal Writing.* IAD Press. pp. xii + 96. A$14.95. ISBN 1 86465 001 X.

Stannage, Tom. *Lakeside City: The Dreaming of Joondalup.* University of Western Australia Press. pp. xviii + 270. A$45.00. ISBN 1 875560 88 2.

Stokes, Geoffrey. *The Politics of Identity in Australia.* Cambridge University Press. pp. xii + 222. A$29.95. ISBN 0 521 586 72 0.

Taylor, Luke. *Seeing the Inside: Bark Painting from Western Arnhem Land.* Clarendon Press. pp. ix + 283. A$49.95. ISBN 0 19 823354 X.

Threadgold, Terry. *Feminist Poetics: Poiesis, Performance, Histories.* Routledge. pp. x + 222. A$45.00. ISBN 0 415 02939 2.

Yunupingu, Galarrwuy (ed.) *Our Land is Our Life: Land Rights – Past, Present, Future.* University of Queensland Press/Penguin Books. pp. xviii + 242. A$29.95. ISBN 0 7022 2958 X.

19

Multiculturalism

VIJAY MISHRA

In recent years one of the more challenging areas of research in the field of cultural studies has been the study of multiculturalism. As the first survey of the field in *The Year's Work in Critical and Cultural Theory* I will be going over a number of texts and debates that do not necessarily belong to the year under review. This is essential for two reasons. First it gives us a good sense of where the debates come from and, second, it tells us where we are at. The latter is, obviously, the usual point of entry for all these surveys. I want to begin with my general comments on migration and the construction of the multicultural nation-state by looking at Canada. In more than one sense multiculturalism is a theory that began in Canada and continues to get much of its social payoff there. As Berdichewsky has noted '[multicultural-ism is itself largely] a Canadian term for cultural and ethnic pluralism' (1997: 53). So, in one sense, it is only proper that I begin the first survey with Canada. Statistics is always a good place to start and here there is a lot of it.

The Canadian government's five-year immigration plan for the period 1991–1995 allowed for a migrant intake of between 220,000 to 250,000 every year. In a decade this translates to around 2.5 million people. In 1992, 99,759 migrants (out of a total immigration of 252,842) came from the following countries:

Hong Kong	38,910	15.4% of total
Philippines	13,273	5.2%
India	12,675	5.0%
Sri Lanka	12,635	5.0%
China	10,429	4.1%
Vietnam	7,681	3.0%
Taiwan	7,456	2.9%

Given the increasingly high proportion of non-whites (largely Asian) who make up the annual intake, it is projected that the visible minority presence in Canada would rise to 9% (from the current 5%) by the year 2000. In 1991 the Canadian Asian population stood at 1,064,765. Of this number South Asians, for instance, made up 228,665. The number increases con-siderably if we add to the figure migrants from Fiji, Trinidad & Tobago,

Guyana, Surinam, Kenya, Mauritius, Tanzania, Uganda, Malaysia, Zimbabwe and South Africa (assuming that a large proportion of migrants from these countries are ethnic Indians). And of course, one has to add to the overall visible minority population Afrosporic and African peoples in Canada too. There are two conclusions that we can draw from this. The first is that the immigrant population in Canada has remained unchanged since 1951 (15%). The second is that unlike the composition of the 1951 immigrant population Canada now has a significant number of people who belong to the class called the visible minority.

The shift from a largely European derived population (which some would argue was in itself multicultural) to a more varied global one (where visible minorities became prominent) has meant that in the domain of culture there are many more signs of racial diversity: from the publication of small South Asian magazines such as *Ankur* (now discontinued), *Rungh, Watan* (a Punjabi quarterly), *Diva* (a quarterly journal of South Asian women), *Hum, Indian Currents, Trikone* (based in the USA), the scholarly *Toronto Review* (*TSAR*), *Mehfil, Sami Yoni, Samar, Serai*, and newspapers such as *Indian Voice*, the *Indo-Caribbean* to television programming in Chinese, Punjabi and Hindi. There is now an emergence of languages and voices hitherto relegated (in a negative fashion) to the Third World. In some instances, as in Sadhu Binning's recent collection of verse we find both the text and the poems given in both English and in Punjabi: *No More Watno Dur* (1994). In the title of this collection the negative is important because although the poems were originally composed in Punjabi, they speak of negotiation and accommodation, not of nostalgia and regret, which are the normal associations of the idea of *watno dur* ('away from home'). Binning, however, arrives at this 'multicultural' position not without some intense soul-searching. In the long polemical poem 'My thirteenth year in Canada' the theme is in fact the idea of loyalty to Canada. What constitutes loyalty? How can one ever outlive one's past, forget one's origins, adopt a new nation and forget the rest? Are visible minorities in a multicultural nation-state asked to sacrifice more than others? But even as the visible minority accepts and transforms, even as there is a will, a desire to produce a new sense of citizen (not one defined by an unproblematic belonging, and perhaps not even one that is locked into the (il)logic of the hyphen), the threat to the new self comes from both within and from a perceived questioning of one's loyalties by the dominant community. From within the diaspora there is another kind of danger, one that comes from the very fact of having redefined oneself; it comes from another amnesia, a forgetfulness about one's own working-class origins, the drudgery of work in the 'strawberry fields':

> we forget the crowded windowless trucks
> in which like chickens we were taken there

Canada recognized the demographic shifts mentioned above and is the only country in the world that has in place a Multicultural Act (1988). The key to the Act lies not so much in the section dealing with the definition of Multicultural Policy of Canada, but in the preamble to it in which the rights of individuals and communities are said to be self-evidently enshrined in the Canadian constitution itself. What the Act indeed lays down is not a new law nor, indeed, an addition to an existing law but the amplification of those fundamental human rights that a nation-state grants all its citizens. It could be argued that the Multicultural Act has a supplementary function to the Canadian constitution itself, its aim being to bring it in line with current social and political realities. First, it draws attention to the essential liberalism of the nation-state (something that may have been taken for granted or even lost to another generation of Canadians) and second, it foregrounds, out of the tradition of that liberalism, a series of definitions that reflect in a more particular fashion the new ethnic mix of Canada. Let me explain this by juxtaposing the first clause of the preamble, and item 3(1)(a) of the Act, which defines the aim of multiculturalism policy in Canada:

> WHEREAS the Constitution of Canada provides that every individual is equal before and under the law and has the right to the equal protection and benefit of the law without discrimination and that everyone has the freedom of conscience, religion, thought, belief, opinion, expression, peaceful assembly and association and guarantees those rights and freedoms equally to male and female persons.

> 3.(1) It is hereby declared to be the policy of the Government of Canada to (a) recognize and promote the understanding that multiculturalism reflects the cultural and racial diversity of Canadian society and acknowledges the freedom of all members of Canadian society to preserve, enhance and share their cultural heritage.

The nation-state as an abstraction (reflecting abstract enlightenment values) is then refashioned as a proactive agent in the Act. The abstract subject-addressee now becomes a political individual as the Act no longer spells out the obvious – that the nation defines itself in these enlightenment terms – but stipulates that the state has a multicultural policy with its enforcers, its agents to oversee that in the lives of people the constitution actually works itself out. In many ways this is a very real advance on abstract rights in the sense that the Act now spells out the ways in which the disadvantaged, whose rights are nevertheless a pre-given in the constitution (albeit only in an abstract fashion), would now have at their disposal apparatuses that would ensure the development of precisely those aspects of their lives that the nation-state has always valued as an inalienable human right. The advance that I speak of did not happen overnight in Canada. The Multicultural Act had a number of significant precursors: The Canadian Bill of Rights (1960), The Official Languages Act (1969), The Canadian Human Rights Act (1977) and The Canadian Charter of Rights and Freedoms (1982).

When the government of Canada decided to implement its policy of multiculturalism within the nation's pre-existent bilingual framework, this is how the then Prime Minister Pierre Trudeau addressed the policy on October 8, 1971:

> . . . there cannot be one cultural policy for Canadians of British and French origin, another for the original peoples and yet a

third for all others. For, although there are two official
languages, there is no official culture, nor does any ethnic group
take precedence over any other. No citizen or group of citizens
is other than Canadian, and all should be treated fairly ...
Canadian identity will not be undermined by multiculturalism.
Indeed, we believe that cultural pluralism is the very essence of
Canadian identity. Every ethnic group has the right to preserve
and develop its own culture and values within the Canadian
context.

It has been pointed out that Trudeau wanted to neutralize the endemic (and
growing) English-French antagonism in Canada by effectively placing the
two communities (and others who through assimilation identified themselves
with either) in a polyethnic Canadian nation-state. Since everyone else
except the indigenous peoples of the land are migrants, the policy of
multiculturalism simply confirmed this fact. The question of French or
English cultural hegemony (in reality very much a Canadian fact of life) is
theoretically set aside in favour of a loose, multiethnic national ethos. To be
a Canadian is quite something else yet again: it is to belong proactively to a
space that is defined by a number of enlightened liberal values. Canada
therefore ceases to be a land of absolute values and cultures that a race (or
two races) have built up; rather it is a field that has yet to congeal and
become intractable and to which people can bring their own values provided
these are not contrary to the nation-state's established framework of law
and order. As to the utility value of the policy this is what Gerry Weiner,
Minister of the new Federal Department of Multiculturalism and Citizenship, had to say about the function of his department:

At this time in our history, there is probably no more important
function any federal department can fulfill than that of helping
support and sustain our national unity ... Its (the department's)
programs and funding are focused mainly on removing barriers
to equality and full participation in our society.

In this markedly political speech the concept of national unity is made
paramount and multiculturalism is seen not as a policy of ghettoization or
of encouraging the maintaining of one's pre-Canadian way of life (although
it may do these) but of actually encouraging and making possible national
unity. Where once unity was linked to homogenization and assimilation into
either English or French culture, now it is linked to a heterogeneous
definition of the nation with the proviso that the key to the nation is not so
much its objective heterogeneity (true as this well may be) but a citizen's
attitudes towards such multiplicity. Writing from what Stanley Fish has
called the 'neutral principle' of enlightened liberalism, Will Kymlicka in a
particularly comprehensive study of multicultural citizenship notes: 'Canada,
with its policy of multiculturalism within a bilingual framework, and its
recognition of Aboriginal rights to self-government, is one of the very few
countries which has officially recognized and endorsed both polyethnicity
and multinationality' (1997:22). This is not the place to review the question
of multinationality and its relationship to polyethnicity. In Kymlicka's argu-

ment, however, the very idea of a multinational state is meaningful only with reference to first-nation peoples. For them, colonization should not have meant an end to their own nation (as indeed is implied in all preambles of settler nation constitutions), which, of course, means that first nations are already nations embedded within nations. They are a foundational constituent of a multinational state. For Kymlicka, the multicultural agenda is not about multinations (which is a separate debate); it is essentially about diasporas as constituents of a polyethnic social order within a multinational state. This distinction is important because as a multiethnic and a multinational state, Canada and other settler states have to address the claims of their diasporas and their first-nation inhabitants as two separate entities and agendas.

To bring this preamble to a close it must be said that however we look at it, at the core of a multicultural policy is an anti-racist agenda that arises out of the dramatic increase in the number of visible minorities within nation-states. Debates about multiculturalism, especially in the Canadian context, took a dramatic turn with the publication of Neil Bissoondath's *Selling Illusions* in 1994. This was an unusual book because it is the first major debunking of multiculturalism by a person of colour. If for no other reason, this fact alone demands that we pause to read this book in some detail before moving on to other works. 'Few silences', writes Bissoondath, 'are as loaded in this country as the one encasing the cult that has grown around our policy of multiculturalism' (4). And there are few other areas where opposition to them is equated, unconditionally, with racism. From the perspective of liberalism, Bissoondath has an important point here. Governmental policies must be debated, and there has to be accountability. There must also be some protocol (or at least a tacit understanding) by which the nation, as a 'Thing' or as an abstract but liberal and fair entity (in spite of the semantic contradictions here), must transcend individual self-interest. But Bissoondath seems to be asking a lot more. And it is here that he adopts the logic of the liberal assimilationist. 'Multiculturalism', he said in an interview *(Rungh* 1.4: 11) 'constantly throws your ethnicity or exoticism at you, thereby putting you at arm's length from society at large'. The discursive strategy adopted here is one in which a critic begins by denouncing racism, then speaks of decency, of the values of liberal Canadians who because they believe in equality and justice, will, finally, not accept the (il)logic of racism. The problem with Bissoondath is much simpler. Although Bissoondath declares his own difference, he does not understand that of others. Fundamentally he speaks from the position of the educated, enlightened, migrant from the colonial outposts of the West Indies where all British subjects were in one sense Anglophiles. These people lacked the force of an alternative, and total, culture with which to vigorously deconstruct imperial values. So Bissoondath comes to Canada already deracinated: no knowledge of an Indian language, no understanding of Hinduism, and unsurprisingly with a fierce desire to leave a racially divided Trinidad behind. Bissoondath, of course, can merge into Canada: he writes fluent English and French, and could aspire to the part of the unproblematic (linear) narrative of assimilation not available to other visible minorities. To be a Bissoondath is well beyond the latter: their children perhaps but not they themselves. Bissoondath was part of a third generation diaspora even before he migrated to

Canada. Bissoondath is thoroughly colonial; his early history (that of inden-
ture culture) is part of the classic modern movement of labour, when the
world was controlled by European metropolitan centres and the Mercator
projection was painted red all over. Many of the other migrants to Canada
do not share this experience. These migrants are part of a global, postmodern, post-imperial movement of labour; they are part of a world whose
centres have been constantly changing. And so Canadian values are neither
equally available to them nor read uniformly by them. In a very real sense
multiculturalism became an issue (or a way of defining racial difference)
once white nation-states allowed people of colour to immigrate. Visible
minorities cannot assimilate into the white mass, because into what would
they assimilate, and into whose values, and upon whose terms?

Some points made by Bissoondath are, of course, salutary. Silently
recalling Naipaul he says one shouldn't really think about race all the time
(210). It is also true that if a fair, non-racist society can be established
without the word multiculturalism that would be a great idea. That it hasn't
is not the fault of the word or of multicultural policies generally. Bissoondath
never really gets either of these arguments. Instead he invents, what Shiraz
Dossa said in a particularly good critique of *Selling Illusions*, a pernicious
and 'deadly image of multiculturalism as a dark, "counter-image" of Gothic
horror' (*Rungh*, 3(2):33).

The multiculturalism agenda also surfaces in a number of creative works
(both print and visual) that have been produced in the 1980s and 1990s.
Hanif Kureishi's novels and films, M. G. Vassanji's *No New Land* (1991)
and *The Book of Secrets* (1994) among a host of others are, in some sense,
critical texts about multiculturalism too. Here is a passage from Vassanji's
No New Land:

> Three years had passed since that blustery winter night when
> the Lalanis stood outside the Toronto airport, contemplating a
> mode of transportation. Much had happened in that period and
> there was, in a sense, no looking back. The children were well
> on their way, 'Canadians' now, or almost. There were many new
> faces in the buildings of Rosecliffe Park, and many others had
> disappeared, to Mississauga, Scarborough, and even as far away
> as Calgary. There were a few stories of success now.... For
> many others, Nurdin among them, life simply 'went along' (116).

The passage situates itself in the possibilities of a heterogeneous, complexly
hybrid social and racial condition where the subject seeks to find a new
ground, a new consensus, a new point of view that would build on the
successes of the Enlightenment ethos, but not be obstructed by its instrumentalist excesses. Vassanji's world is thoroughly multicultural as indeed he
declared in Deepika Bahri and Mary Vasudeva's edited volume (*Between
the Lines*). In this essay entitled 'Life at the Margins' Vassanji extends the
diasporic 'condition of multiplicity and contradiction', the condition he 'was
brought up with' (119), to the multicultural world. But Vassanji also draws
attention to the ways in which his own background – 'an Indian-African of
third generation' growing up in a very hybrid diasporic culture – leads him
to respond rather differently to the democratic nation-state (here Canada)

than someone, from the same ethnic background, but without his diasporic history. The point here is that some multicultural 'bodies' already carry prior multicultural histories. This fact needs to be taken into account in any examination of multicultural theory.

More recently the debates about multiculturalism have centred around boutique multiculturalism and critical or strong multiculturalism. Boutique multiculturalism (also referred to as the 'Benetton effect') is largely an expression of a liberal ethos where tolerance of other cultures is seen as one of liberalism's defining characteristics. In the boutique version of multiculturalism, however, tolerance does not lead to a redefinition of one's own 'core values' which remain the 'ground' through which the rest of humanity is read. At the heart of it is a liberal, non-interventionist ideology of the brotherhood of nations and of 'men'. Strong multiculturalism as explained in Stanley Fish's essay published in 1997, is something very different:

> The politics of difference is what I mean by strong multicultur-alism. It is strong because it values difference in and for itself rather than as a manifestation of something more basically constitutive. Whereas the boutique multiculturalist will accord a superficial respect to all cultures other than his own, a respect he will withdraw when he finds the practices of a culture irrational or inhumane, a strong multiculturalist would want to accord a *deep* respect to all cultures at their core, for he believes that each has the right to form its own identity and nourish its own sense of what is rational and humane. For the strong multiculturalist the first principle is not rationality or some other supracultural universal, but tolerance (382).

What Stanley Fish goes on to address is the demographic fact that other cultures do exist in white liberal nation-states and these cultures do call into question what Charles Taylor referred to as a country's 'philosophical boundaries'. To respond to the challenges that the questioning will give rise, Charles Taylor had suggested the future necessity of a degree of 'inspired adhoccery' (Fish: 386). It is a phrase that Fish takes very seriously and in a return to a kind of postmodern principle of the contingent, he believes that a serious look at the 'ad hoc' as a means of addressing issues as they arise may be the answer to racist and anti-multiculturalist rhetoric. The argument here is that liberals should 'stamp out' a racist agenda the moment it arises rather than give in to it because of their own commitment to a higher liberal principle of freedom of speech. The response of the Australian Prime Minister to the rise of the First Nation Party in Australia is one recent instance of the boutique multiculturalist's refusal to condemn a racist Party on the grounds that to do so would compromise fundamental democratic values such as freedom of speech. Fish would argue for a strong multicultural position that is linked to a vigilant and proactive liberal intelligentsia that believes in multiculturalism as a social movement that gets, as the Chicago Cultural Studies Group says, its critical purchase because it intrinsically challenges the established norms, and can link together identity struggles with a common rhetoric of difference and resistance (531). The Chicago Group makes the important point that for critical multiculturalism to succeed the public face of the state needs to be redefined: who reads news on television, who participates in films, who writes books, who are represented in the domain of culture, who represents the myths of the nation, and so on (553). Consequently, the group concludes:

> As critical multiculturalism redescribes the various public orders that are now undergoing change, it can help to realign what is now understood as simply insurgent or simply reactionary, simply dominant or simply marginal (553).

Appealing as Fish's and the Chicago Group's arguments are, there are, of course, a number of other problems that are never addressed head on. The first is the difference between the legislator and the interpreter (two terms that Donald Pease uses in his response to Stanley Fish's essay, see below). The second is an ontological issue relating to the very existence of multiculturalism and the role of the interpreter in it. And, finally, there is the question of power for the simple reason that because both boutique and strong multiculturalism are of interest only to the white person, how can one distinguish between a genuinely strong multiculturalist and a boutique multiculturalist masquerading as a strong one? Here, the logic of both Fish and the Chicago Cultural Group can only lead to Donald Pease's persuasive conclusion:

> Multiculturalism (whether the boutique form of appreciation or the strong form of tolerating) does not exist. It cannot exist because the laws regulating the norms internal to a specific culture necessarily result in incommensurable rationalities (398).

The reference to 'incommensurable rationalities' takes us back to Bissoondath's citation of the case of female circumcision among some Muslim communities. Bissoondath takes the position of the legislator to argue that when cultural positions are incommensurable, then the law of the state is paramount. In this view a liberal enlightened democratic state based on 'civilized' enlightened values has no choice but to outlaw female genital mutilation. Bissoondath makes the point that for many members of the Muslim groups in question not to participate in such practices may lead to communal ostracism because such practices are often social as much as religious or narrowly ethnic. However, Bissoondath overlooks the very simple fact (and which is understood by both Fish and Pease) that these cultural practices are 'grounded in rationalities' even though we may object to the absence of an historical critique in these 'rationalities' – that indeed the 'grounds' themselves were a function of a particular society at a particular moment in time, and are not (except in terms of religious absolutism) universal. It is here that (multi) cultural incommensurabilities must be understood and the need for a critical differend (after Lyotard), foregrounded without overlooking what Satya P. Mohanty understands as a cultural Others' capacity to evaluate 'their actions in light of their ideas and previous experiences, and of being "rational" in [a] minimal way' (198). The fact of multiculturalism may well mean, in terms of Mohanty's argument, that we do need various logics and ways of reading worlds so that we are rooted in some form of a realist version of multiculturalism. The need here is for agents who are both vigilant interpreters as well as committed legislators not unwilling to take some 'inspired adhoccery', which again may beg the question, 'Inspiration from whom?'.

Donald Pease's claim that multiculturalism cannot exist finds support in another quarter: the economic dimensions of multiculturalism. After all – and as the evidence of sweat shops as well as kitchen hands in 'ethnic' restaurants indicate – multiculturalism may well be in the economic interests of the nation-state, diasporic entrepreneurs and, on a much larger scale, multinational companies. In addressing this issue, one of the most interesting writers on questions of imaginary identifications of the subject from the Hegelian-Lacanian perspective, Slavoj Žižek, has called the process by which one's ethnic identity (as an Indian, Chinese, Japanese and so on), and one's universal identity as a member of a nation-state is 'surpassed', 'transubstantiation', a term that allows for a kind of passing of the subject as both 'ethnic' with ethnic roots and as a citizen. This doubling of the self is not necessarily schizophrenic (although it may be so) because the logic of multiculturalism allows for transubstantiation to be read as normal. From the position of the multinational company, however, the breaking of boundaries through transubstantiation and with it the recognition of difference as the norm translates itself into something altogether different. Multiculturalism becomes the 'ideology of global capitalism' because the logic of multiculturalism (and the logic that Žižek has in mind is Fish's boutique multiculturalism one suspects) sits comfortably with the neocolonialism of global capital. 'That is to say', writes Žižek:

> the relationship between traditional imperialist colonization and global capitalist self-colonizations is exactly the same as the relationship between Western cultural imperialism and multiculturalism: in the same way that global capitalism involves the paradox of colonization without the colonizing nation-state metropole, multiculturalism involves patronizing Eurocentrist distance and/or respect for local cultures without roots in one's own particular culture. In other words, multiculturalism is a disavowed, inverted, self-referential form of racism, a 'racism with a distance' – it 'respects' the Other's identity, conceiving the Other as a self-enclosed 'authentic' community towards which he, the multiculturalist, maintains a distance rendered possible by his privileged universal position. Multiculturalism is a racism which empties its own position of all positive content (the multiculturalist is not a direct racist, he doesn't oppose to the Other the *particular* values of his own culture), but nonetheless retains this position as the privileged empty point of universality from which one is able to appreciate (and depreciate) properly other particular cultures – the multiculturalist respect for the Other's specificity is the very form of asserting one's own superiority (1997:44).

Late modern capital does not need a gun to destroy (multi) culture; market forces provide the conditions for its demise just as efficiently (51). Thus goes

Žižek's argument in which it becomes clear that multicultural communities do not proclaim themselves as being multicultural; it is the nation-state and its dominant community that does. Ethnic communities continue to define themselves in terms of ethnic, national or linguistic difference. In terms of political solidarity there may be a unified multicultural position; among themselves the divisions are strong and incommensurable, as indeed the Canadian-Indian and Canadian-Pakistani response to the recent spate of nuclear tests on the subcontinent indicated so well.

The progressive diasporization of white nation-states, and especially the rise in them of diasporas of colour are clearly the reasons behind a state's own desire to invest in the ideology and apparatuses of multiculturalism which Žižek had earlier argued was a form of 'postmodern racism' (1993:226). As it should be clear by now, there are a number of texts reviewed here that were published before 1997. In this survey, I summarize the arguments of these texts because they are important in our understanding of where multiculturalism was at in 1997. Let me begin with three texts (two books and a newspaper article) by Appadurai, Radhakrishnan and Bharati Mukherjee, respectively. Although Appadurai does not address multiculturalism directly, or at least not extensively, the book is grounded in the twin concepts of media and migration both of which have had an enormous impact on modern nation-states which are becoming progressively multicultural. The multicultural space is, in one sense, a double space that also transforms (or 'transubstantiates' to use Žižek's religious metaphor) the relationship (hitherto one suspects unproblematic) that the subject has to the law of the nation-state, where nationalism is the 'ground' of a citizen's life. Multiculturalism, then, forces us to rethink older definitions of the nation-state. One approaches the latter not with high modernist or realist principles of unity and closure (the erstwhile semantics of the nation-state) but with postmodern (late modern) narratives of the 'transnational' or even the 'postnational'. To extrapolate from Appadurai's thesis about 'public spheres' one could claim that multicultural 'public spheres' too are no longer small, marginal or exceptional. In this sense multiculturalism is not something that needs to be 'managed' (because somehow the state feels obliged to create ways in which all the various ethnic components of the nation-state can represent themselves) as something that is simply intrinsic to the very definition of the late modern nation-state. However, in spite of this, when often thinly disguised state policies threaten to devalue the multicultural agenda, coalitional sodalities or mobilizations begin to take place. The other side of these mobilizations takes the form of ethnic, racial or religious 'self-imagining' (22) in transnational sites marked by a relocation of one's emotional energies towards homeland narratives of purity and ethnic absolutism.

Another text, and one again published in 1996, that is not directly about multiculturalism (the word does not occur in the book's Index) but where, nevertheless, multicultural issues are its central focus is R. Radhakrishnan's *Diasporic Mediations*. Although Radhakrishnan's central concerns are with the double subjectivity of diasporic peoples – their double consciousness, cross-constituency alliances, their location of bodies in hyphenated spaces, their struggles with the 'local' and the 'homeland' – his readings are really framed within a general discourse of critical multicultural theory. When he wishes to 'insist on a fundamental difference between hybridity as a comfortably genuine state of being and hybridity as an excruciating act of self-production by and through multiple traces' (159) we enter directly into questions about multicultural agency, the linear narrative of assimilation and the space occupied by heterogeneous bodies in the modern nation-state. This takes me to an important political agenda in Radhakrishnan's work. I have in mind his reference to the importance of a coalitional strategy among ethnic groups that would allow them to speak with one voice in a dialogue with the mainstream. The ethnic self is thus critically aware of the 'hyphen', of its rootedness in more than one history, its location in the present as well as in the past. This task of 'reciprocal invention' means that one is aware of the agonizing tension between two histories (176). But it also means a relationality that would encompass other ethnic communities and could lead to their collective, coalitional mobilization towards the goal of making the nation-state aware of its multiple ethnicities, those multiple historiographies that are the underside of its unstated grand narrative in which, in one sense, multiculturalism is finally located. Radhakrishnan is conscious of the move he makes here, a move that is clearly designed as a kind of consciousness-raising programme on the part of ethnic communities. The move is not only definitional in the sense that to rename the multicultural as ethnic inserts agency back into the subject. It is also, and fundamentally, strategic in the sense that it seeks to make difference a political fact of life. Let me quote extensively from Radhakrishnan here:

> but to me and many others in the diaspora, the politics of solidarity with other minorities and diasporic ethnicities is as important and primary as the politics of 'representations of origins'. It is in this sense, then, that I am in favor of the allegorization of the 'postcolonial condition': that the allegory be made available as that relational space to be spoken for heterogeneously but relationally by diverse subaltern/oppressed/minority subject positions in their attempts to seek justice and reparation for centuries of unevenness and inequality. Diasporic communities do not want to be rendered discrete or separate from other diasporic communities, for that way lies co-optation and depoliticization. To authenticate their awareness of themselves as a form of political knowledge, these communities need to share worldviews, theories, values, and strategies so that none of them will be 'divided and ruled' by the racism of the dominant historiography (177).

Radhakrishnan moves from a diagnostic position – the important location of the diasporic mentality in a double consciousness – to an interventionist and political one in that he now *wants* the diaspora to be redefined through an ethnic semantics so that it is no longer defined in terms of memory, trauma and loss (the usual semantics of the diaspora). It is this move on the part of Radhakrishnan that makes me read his diasporic mediations as an invaluable contribution to a critical multiculturalism. It is the kind of approach that one doesn't find in Bharati Mukherjee to whose *New York Times* essay, 'Two Ways to Belong in America', I now wish to turn. This is an interesting essay

because Bharati Mukherjee positions herself on the side of someone who
has been cured, for whom multicultural trauma is over and who no longer
sees her own ego as being empty. Against this position there is the life of
her sister Mira who in fact came to America a year earlier in 1960. Mira
arrived in the USA to study child psychology and pre-school education,
Bharati to study creative writing at the University of Iowa. After 36 years
Mira is still an Indian citizen, Bharati is American. They began with the
same ambitions – education, return to India, arranged marriage – and
harboured similar political beliefs, but now they have taken slightly different
paths. In 1962 Mira married an Indian student at Wayne State, in 1963
Bharati married a fellow student at Iowa, an American of Canadian parentage. In choosing a husband outside of her 'ethnic community' and not of her
'father's selection', Bharati Mukherjee writes:

> I was opting for fluidity, self-invention, blue jeans and T-shirts,
> and renouncing 3,000 years (at least) of caste-observant, 'pure
> culture' marriage in the Mukherjee family. My books have often
> been read as unapologetic (and in some quarters overenthusias-
> tic) texts for cultural and psychological 'mongrelization'. It's a
> word I celebrate.

Bharati Mukherjee speaks about discussions with her sister about the ethics
of obtaining American privileges and yet somehow belonging elsewhere.
Mira sees in Bharati 'the erasure of Indianness', the absence of an 'unvarying
daily core'. Bharati in turn reads Mira in terms of the 'narrowness of her
perspective', her failure to engage with surfaces, with popular American
cultural forms, its myths and so on. But Mira's life is threatened, in a manner
of speaking. There are pressures afoot in America with Al Gore's 'Citizenship USA' drive, with its sinister extension of the word 'alien' which could
now embrace even long-term legal migrants in the USA such as Mira. And
so Mira is incensed, berating America of ingratitude, for not acknowledging
her work, the taxes she has paid and so on. She lived in the country on the
understanding that her Indian citizenship was inviolate, like religion one
simply didn't change it because it was fashionable to do so. Shouldn't the
rule (that you take out US citizenship) apply only to those who have come
later, or after the new rules have been put in place?
   Writes Mukherjee: my sister is 'here to maintain an identity, not to
transform it'. Yet she can be manipulative, she will change her citizenship if
that is what Congress wants, but she will revert back to her Indian passport
when the time comes, when the moment of return arrives. What if that
doesn't happen? This question is important because it is not the reality of
the return but the magical nature of the passport itself, as a marker of an
unchanging identity, as a sign, a confirmation that even after thirty-six years
the self has not changed and one can return (in the mind so to speak) that
is important. It is that desire for continuity, so clearly present in religious-
identity politics, that surfaces in Mira's agonistic discourse here. Against
Mira's certainties there is Bharati's act of multicultural surrender:

> America spoke to me – I married it – I embraced the demotion
> from expatriate aristocrat to immigrant nobody, surrendering

those thousands of years of 'pure culture', the saris, the delight-
fully accented English. She retained them all. 'Which of us is
the freak?' Or to put it in another way, 'Who is still mourning?'

Mira's voice, Bharati concedes, is not proactive, let alone just politically
active. It is the voice of the millions of migrants, within the multicultural
nation-state, for whom migrancy means secure and permanent jobs so that
one can remain rooted in a city, in a place, and reconnect with the homeland
through a network of relationships among the migrants. Here the ancestral
culture is duplicated, the cuisine maintained, and the home simply transferred to the comfort zone of America. Mira interacts differently with
America from Bharati. Mira lives in America as an 'expatriate Indian' not
as an 'immigrant American'. Concludes Bharati Mukherjee:

> I need to feel like a part of the community I have adopted (as I
> tried to feel in Canada as well). I need to put roots down, to
> vote and make the difference that I can. The price that the
> immigrant willingly pays, and that the exile avoids, is the trauma
> of self-transformation.

In a sense multiculturalism for Bharati Mukherjee is linked to transformation, the kind of transformation signalled is her use of 'expatriate' and
'immigrant'. In this 'willed' act of transformation the multicultural 'body'
will lose many of its older certainties, the sense of belonging, but will, in
return, emerge as something new. In a very real sense, Bharati Mukherjee's
critical multicultural theory would be similar to that of Neil Bissoondath.
For both, multicultural debates (of the boutique or strong variety) are rather
pointless. If transformation – through the celebration of mongrelization – is
the condition of a postmodern ethnicity, then multiculturalism (as a theory
of culture) has little room to play in the debates. This may be true, but the
spate of books around the idea of multiculturalism tell a different story. In
the second half of this review essay, I want to address a range of texts that
deal with the subject. In many instances a multicultural world order is simply
assumed; in others multiculturalism is extensively debated in the context of
critical race, class and gender theory.

In *Mapping Multiculturalism* – a collection of twenty-six essays by as
many people, that went into its second printing within months of its
publication – the editors Avery F. Gordon and Christopher Newfield situate
multiculturalism in the larger context of race relations and 'new confronta-
tions with racism' in the USA. The point here is that multiculturalism cannot
be discussed without addressing questions of 'power and institutional authority'. Multiculturalism for whom? Who lays down the ground rules? Who are
its beneficiaries? In the end do hegemonic systems (like the nation) always
neutralize dissent by incorporating it within a relatively innocuous system.
In the opinion of the editors four major contradictions in multiculturalist
theory surface whenever we address the subject. These contradictions take
them to a broad scepticism about the ideology of multiculturalism. The
following questions are immediately posed: Is multiculturalism anti-racist or
oblivious to racism? Is multiculturalism cultural autonomy or common
culture revisited? Is multiculturalism grounded in grassroots alliances or

diversity management? Does multiculturalism link politics and culture or separate them? In one sense – and in a very real sense – the trouble with multiculturalism is that it never provides an adequate answer to any of these questions. So in the end – as the volume's contributors to a person show in their essays – is it a matter of racism? In the context of the USA, where multiculturalism as a theory is relatively new, systemic racial inequality has had such profound effects that any multicultural perspective will have to start from questions of race and justice.

Although there is much in this volume that adds significantly to our understanding of the field, especially in the American context, I want to begin with Angela Y. Davis' essay 'Gender, Class, and Multiculturalism' because this essay provides the theoretical lynchpin for most of the essays collected in the volume. Angela Davis sees current multicultural programmes – in the guise of the seemingly innocuous term 'diversity management' – as a means of 'preserving and fortifying power relations based on class, gender, and race' (41). For the fact is that multicultural programmes are not simply enlightened cultural credos, they are means of control that operate across the board from entrepreneurial organizations to the prison correctional system, where it is a means of reestablishing 'control over inmate populations' (42). In Angela Davis' argument one needs to be wary of the 'corporate compartmentalization of multiculturalism' and address how any cultural theory challenges those gender, class and race hierarchies that are at the heart of the American nation-state. In this task a critical multicultural theory should always gloss, even as it locates itself as a progressive idea, the historical mechanisms of 'control' that pre-date multiculturalism. Angela Davis mentions some of them: 'Assimilation', 'Cultural Pluralism', 'Desegregation', 'Integration', 'Black Nationalism', 'Black Power', 'Chicano Power', 'Affirmative Action', 'Reverse Discrimination', 'Difference', 'Diversity', 'Multiculturalism'. As we see in this sequence, 'multiculturalism', in one sense, is a signifier in a chain of signifiers. The difference is that it proposes to displace all of them, but without carrying the very precise (and often highly contentious and in some instances oppressive) histories of the other signifiers. In Angela Davis' reading, a multiculturalism that forgets its early avatars, and the uneven histories contained within them, will never be able to redress the crucial inequalities of race, class and gender. In this respect multiculturalism should never forget that racism persists even if 'race' is no longer a very useful idea to work with. For what one has to be wary of is the celebration of 'difference' and 'diversity' as if in doing so, racism itself is no longer an issue. 'Equal differences', is just as insidious as racial indifference, and both may lead to the marginalization of those very urgent voices (from beyond the rhetoric of multiculturalism) that scream for equality as a social fact. In the absence of these voices – voices that also speak of women's oppression across cultures – we may well find a resurgence of culture-specific ideologies of neglect that are defended in the name of multiculturalism. Angela Davis quotes Nira Yugal-Davis' insightful comment that fundamentalism defends multiculturalism because it sees the latter as preserving 'different mutually exclusive ways of life' (45). An appeal to culture of this kind does not help those groups who are doubly marginalized, such as women of colour in migrant communities. The divisions within ethnic groups, the silencing of the voices of women in particular, are what the new metaphor of the 'salad' (as opposed to the 'melting pot') fails to address. As Davis asks, 'Who consumes multiculturalism', the salad that it is? Is multiculturalism no more than a managerial strategy to get greater productivity from the work force? Unless one is rigorous in one's analysis, specifying the real, material conditions of racism and their relation to capital, in Davis' argument multiculturalism's claim to an 'unassimilated diversity' is no more than a control mechanism that keeps minorities where they are in the guise of (white) respect of cultural difference. What doesn't change is the 'unified self' of the 'managers' themselves.

There is, of course, a pedagogical dimension to a state's multicultural policy. This pedagogy takes the form of acquiring knowledge about cultural differences. So that a multicultural carnival in Toronto or the celebration of ethnic days in schools is a spectacle that helps erase racism because it 'informs' the dominant group about the lives of these other groups in society. Davis observes, 'If our difference is understood, consumed, and "digested," we simultaneously can be different and perform "as if" we really were middle-class, straight white males' (46). This, to Davis, is the insidious, ever-present agenda of a non-critical multiculturalism which assumes that projecting cultural difference destroys negative stereotypes of other cultures. As a means towards enlightenment, this is to be applauded but does it lead to a 'radical transformation of power structures?' (47). In a very real manner, the following observation of Davis sums up the agenda of a critical multiculturalism: 'A multiculturalism that does not acknowledge the political character of culture will not, I am sure, lead toward the dismantling of racist, sexist, homophobic, economically exploitative institutions' (47). In dismantling these institutions one should not reinvent the old essentialisms – essentialisms that created the negative binary of 'queers, coloreds and natives' that the discourse of liberalism, in Wendy Brown's words sought 'to bring to a formal close' (150).

The importance of examining the real, material conditions of marginalized groups – so that ethnic images can be fruitfully juxtaposed and critiqued and multicultural differences are not domesticated – is explored in Chapter Four of Lisa Lowe's *Immigrant Acts*. Exploring the dynamics (and the curriculum) of the September 1990 Los Angeles Festival of the Arts (Los Angeles – that most multicultural of all US cities) Lisa Lowe maps out the ways in which 'the terrain of multiculturalism is both a mode of pluralist containment and a vehicle for intervention in that containment' (85). The argument here is twofold. On the one hand the pluralist ethos of multiculturalism 'levels the important differences and contradictions within and among racial and minority groups' (86); on the other the performances that constituted the Los Angeles Festival of the Arts throw up the contradictions in the unstated principle of homogenization and aestheticization of cultural difference that underpins the multicultural agenda. In this respect, Lowe makes a number of valuable observations. Firstly, Lowe points out that the real owners of culture remain the white majority (not numerically as very soon the state of California may well have whites in a minority) since it is this majority that finally owns 'culture' – the 'culture' to which everyone else must aspire. Secondly, the connections made between Thai dance and the Thai diaspora in Los Angeles or that made between African music and the Black American community during the LA Festival of the Arts 'actually threw into relief the histories that disrupted and have rendered discontinuous the relationships between Thai immigrants and Thai artists and between Black Americans and Africans' (91). The disidentifications need to be noted, so that in the name of multiculturalism a city like Los Angeles does not begin to believe in what it said about itself in the festival programme: 'it turns out that most of that new world is alive and living right here'. The need for a constant critique of multiculturalism – so that its pluralism does not lead to the homogenization of all cultures under some large democratic cause – means that oppositional narratives, narratives that blast open the contradictions of pluralism, that signify complex subjectivities within the ethnic, are given adequate representations. Lowe examines the 1993 documentary video *Sa-I-Gu*, a video made after the 1992 Los Angeles riots in which a Korean/Black American divide was highlighted by the liberal press. What Lowe uncovers here are testimonies from Korean subjects that are contradictory and heterogeneous, work practices that are exploitative, and voices that contest the 'liberal myth of pluralist inclusion' (92). Reading *Sa-I-Gu* as an oppositional narrative, Lowe's analysis emphasizes the complex agenda of 'multicultural' subjects, of the need for a 'powerful particularism' (94) that would also show the tensions within multicultural communities. In some sense it is better for multicultural discourses to emphasize these particularities (within the domain of the 'ethnic') than to domesticate or universalize them. Lowe's conclusion is very important for our understanding of multiculturalism and where it has arrived: 'Narratives of multiculturalism which do not make the connections between historically differentiated forms of disempowerment or which do not make space for oppositional critiques risk denuding racial and ethnic groups of their specificity' (96).

In a symposium held in New York in 1991 a number of cultural theorists – Homi Bhabha, Cornel West, Chantal Mouffe, Ernesto Laclau, Etienne Balibar, Andreas Huyssen, Jacques Rancière, Joan W. Scott, Stanley Aronowitz, Wendy Brown, Judith Butler and Fredric Jameson – came together to discuss two pressing issues in America: 'multiculturalism' and 'political correctness'. The papers delivered at that symposium were subsequently edited by John Rajchman and published under the title *The Identity in Question*. Given the standing of so many of the participants, it comes as no surprise that the volume as a whole addresses the questions of minority identities from a number of perspectives. For the purposes of this survey, however, there is one essay that is especially relevant. The essay is by Joan W. Scott and is called 'Multiculturalism and the Politics of Identity'. Joan W. Scott takes up the two key themes of the symposium – 'political correctness' and 'multiculturalism' – and makes the connection between the two by pointing out that whereas political correctness is the 'label attached to critical attitudes and behavior', multiculturalism 'is the program it is attempting to enact'. In this respect the project of multiculturalism is itself part of a much larger discourse that effectively brings together under one umbrella a progressive discourse to counteract those of anti-feminists, anti-gays, anti-affirmative action, anti-minorities, indeed 'anti' virtually anybody who has problems with political correctness. For the latter group(s), multiculturalism is no more than a dangerously 'deviant' social ideology, so 'Europhobic' that it strikes at the very heart of the 'unity and the common culture of the American nation' (4–5). The threat becomes meaningful, even understandable, though not justifiable, if we read 'multiculturalism' very correctly it must be added, as an attempt to intervene into a unified, incontestable concept or national identity. In the American case it aims at providing qualitative histories of African-Americans, of Native Americans, and other oppressed groups so that American history itself could be read from other perspectives. The American Right takes this a step further, negatively of course. It argues that pluralism leads to the declaration of one's difference and hence to discrimination. In other words, if you didn't claim to be different we could all be the same. Taking her cue from Stuart Hall's observations about the historical constructedness of being Black ('Black is an identity which had to be learned and could only be learned in a certain moment'), Joan W. Scott points out that the American Right's argument forgets that non-declaration of difference does not lead to equality since minorities – and visible minorities in particular – would still be constructed in terms of a racist narrative of white superiority. And, at any rate, there is an insidious logic to the call for this tolerance of difference because the people who suffer most from the tolerance are minority women whose challenges to patriarchal pressures within multicultural communities are finally silenced because their voice, too, is contained within a pluralist notion of tolerance. What we get in American critiques of multiculturalism are re-statements of points made by Angela Davis about being conscious of the overall agenda of multiculturalism, a form in whatever guise – as managerial control, or even enlightened equality – that needs to be constantly deconstructed to uncover its underlying racism.

So much of what I have surveyed does not necessarily address the literary text and its role in the multicultural agenda. I have referred to the works of Vassanji and Bharati Mukherjee as being centrally located in the midst of multicultural debates. One book that does foreground the literary is *Cultural Difference and the Literary Text* edited by Winfried Siemerling and Katrin Schwenk. The book takes up the question of alternative voices in literature especially with reference to Chicano writing, North American tribal voices, the border writings of the Chicana-mestiza and so on. There is also in this volume an essay by Linda Hutcheon on the reception of a collection of Canadian multicultural writing *(Other Solitudes)* that she edited with Marion Richmond in 1990. The essay entitled 'Multicultural Furor: The Reception of *Other Solitudes*' is a survey of the reception of the Hutcheon and Richmond collection. In her opening remark in defence of her survey of the critical response to *Other Solitudes*, Linda Hutcheon writes, '[I want to] examine the problematics of *reading* multiculturalism, to look at the complex of reasons for this enormous diversity in the critical reception of a book about what is, admittedly, a touchy (if timely) topic these days' (10–11). The reception that Linda Hutcheon traces, however, says a lot about the way in which multiculturalism is read in Canada. But much of the criticism, in a sense, is quite expected, and should have been anticipated by the editors. Any collection that brings together representative writing of people of diverse ethnic backgrounds is asking for a range of critical responses. The principle governing the collection – an anthology of writers whose personal backgrounds are not English, French, or Native – was an implied principle of 'universalist' migrant experience that elides specific historical conditions.

Czechoslovakian, Russian, Greek, Italian, Ukrainian experiences are not the
same as Sri Lankan or Chinese, and nor are Sri Lankan and Chinese in any
way identical. The trouble is not simply a matter of avoiding 'particularism';
it has to do with an idealism that simply denies any exposure of questions of
ethnic, class and gender difference. Although in her defence Linda Hutcheon
draws our attention to the very different biographies of writers as they
emerge in the interviews and, indeed, as a contribution to Canadian literary
history, she makes the observation that 'from the first, [the canon in Canada
has been] a creation of women and "minorities"', it is clear that 'white'
Canada's entry into multicultural ethics has been one in which European
migrants have always had the option of an unproblematic entry into the
nation's linear narrative of assimilation. Although Linda Hutcheon herself
is conscious of the importance of 'historicizing analysis . . . in terms of time,
place, race, gender, class, and so on' (16), it is an argument that does not
surface in the ideological design of *Other Solitudes* where, in the end, one
simply gets a 'boutique multiculturalism' at work, a multiculturalism that
cannot address the different and uneven paths to inclusion within the
Canadian nation-state available to the Ukrainian and the South Asian.

   Whether universalism needs always to be particularized before we can
'acknowledge difference', is an issue taken up by Satya P. Mohanty and
Chantal Mouffe. Here I refer to Satya P. Mohanty's final chapter on
multiculturalism in *Literary Theory and the Claims of History* and Chantal
Mouffe's essay in *Radical Democracy: Identity, Citizenship, and the State*
edited by David Trend. Mohanty summarizes the project of his book as an
attempt to think through the place of a 'postpositivist realism' as an answer
to postmodern claims about the 'untenability of objective knowledge'. In the
context of multicultural theory, Mohanty examines cultures as fields of
'moral inquiry, with room for objective knowledge as well as for error or
mystification' (xii–xiii). In his view, multiculturalism is 'a form of epistemic
cooperation across cultures'. In what is arguably one of the finest discussions
of the phenomenology of racial identity and multiculturalism, Mohanty
makes a case for a realist version of multiculturalism against what are the
dominant 'relativist or liberal versions' (198). Mohanty returns to Kant as
his point of reference and begins by observing that the idea of 'individual
human worth' is a not-negotiable concept in any racialized society. It follows
that the primacy of 'human personhood' is a 'moral notion', something so
fundamental and basic to our very existence. Here of course, Mohanty is
aware of the criticism that such a move does not take into account particularities of social, ethnic or racial needs. Mohanty's argument at this point is
a transcendental one: value of human worth is such a 'radical principle' that
any move to particularize it effectively destroys the absolutism of the
principle itself. In one sense this is the kind of argument that grows out of
Kant's well-known essay 'What is Enlightenment?' and locates itself
squarely in the argument – notably that of Habermas – that modernity is
itself an incomplete project of the Enlightenment. The philosophical intervention that Mohanty makes is nothing new (philosophical anthropology, in
one sense, has underpinned many phenomenological readings of subjectivity) but it is nevertheless one that strikes us as unusual in the context of
current debates about multiculturalism. It must be said that Mohanty's
argument is not completely, or even centrally, about multiculturalism; he

wants to demonstrate the value of a realist theory of objective knowledge and to show that experience-based subjecthood requires testing and refinement. In this respect Mohanty makes short shrift of those claims that advance the unqualified primacy of experience: the 'I know because I've been there argument'. The problem with the latter is that it has not undergone a rigorous theory of what it means to make the claim and whether that kind of knowledge is true or false. In a sense reality testing would alone tell us whether the experience being recounted is capable of sustaining the epistemological claims being made about it. Of course, the postmodern solution is to read identity-politics of the kind presented in the above example as essentialist and therefore inadmissible since, in postmodern rhetoric, identities 'are fabricated and constructed rather than self-evidently deduced' (203). In case Mohanty's account is itself criticized for being in some sense essentialist or foundationalist, he defends it by saying that this 'naturalist-realist' account of identity politics is 'neither foundational nor skeptical' (205).

The crux of Mohanty's argument – insofar as the argument is valid for multicultural theory – is to make a case for 'personal experience' as being socially and 'theoretically' constructed. In the case of feminist 'consciousness-raising' groups, it is clear that the function of these groups is to test personal experience, to make it an effective critique of patriarchy and to transform personal experience into critical proactivism. This cannot happen if experience is essentially or contingently constructed. In this respect 'an objective explanation is necessarily continuous with oppositional and political struggles' (213). Mohanty goes on to summarize his proposal as follows:

> My proposal is that we reorient our theorizing of cultural identity in the following way: instead of conceiving identities as self-evidently based on authentic experiences of members of a cultural or social group (the conception that underlies identity politics) or as all equally unreal to the extent that they lay any claim to the real experiences of real people because experience is a radically mystifying term (this is the postmodernist alternative), we need to explore the possibility of a theoretical understanding of social and cultural identity in terms of objective social location (216).

Social and cultural identities are complex and historical as well and theoretical knowledge must be deployed to understand identitarian politics. It is important, in multicultural theory for instance, to be able to 'distinguish legitimate identities from spurious ones' (230), to be able to show how 'changes in our cultural identity reflect moral and political growth' (231) and to be able to explore that identities are both 'constructed' and 'real' at the same time. Drawing upon the racial politics of Toni Morrison's *Beloved*, Mohanty points out that the contrast between Paul D and Sethe is salutary: Paul D's experience needs to be tested and corrected against Sethe's fully articulated and theorized understanding of the identity and responsibility of a slave mother who is a part of the 'technology' of the production of slaves.

Where does this lead to in the more specific context of multicultural theory? Mohanty's implied argument is that multiculturalism is about justice, about the recognition of difference and about consciousness-raising on the part of dominant communities. Having said that one needs to address multicultural assumptions about oppression, about identitarian politics, about the role of experience within a realist theory that would enable objective judgements to be made. Mohanty writes:

> Since cultural identities are not mysterious inner essences of groups of people but are fundamentally about social relations, especially relations among groups, the realist view gives us a way to envision multiculturalism as an inevitable part of a theory of justice in societies defined by deep and pervasive cultural inequalities (239).

In democratic societies, identity-based political struggles will be 'inevitable components of general multicultural agendas' (240) which means that multicultural pluralism can take root only after some form of cultural equality has been achieved in the democratic nation-state. But multicultural communities (and subjects) must not be seen, ontologically, as 'othered' groups without a universalist moral underpinning. 'Multiculturalism' maintains Mohanty, 'should be defined as a form of epistemic cooperation' (240). A realist theory (of the kind suggested by Mohanty) makes all cultural experience available for critique and deconstruction, it maintains that the margin of error is available equally to all people. A realist theory of knowledge, in other words, celebrates cultural diversity because it is part of the general agenda of progress and 'moral inquiry'. In short, multiculturalism is 'morally' good for you just as, for the capitalist, it is good for business. Multiculturalism makes for a robustness about inquiries into the 'human good', and for nation-states such moral inquiries are good for their own well-being. To uphold multiculturalism implies holding on to the analytic of the Enlightenment itself since multicultural societies 'embody the advanced and complex cooperative structure of an ideal epistemic community'.

> Difference and individuality are not opposed to a deeper commonality, a community of purpose. Even in a world that is not fundamentally structured by (cultural) inequality, healthy pluralism is more likely than cultural homogeneity to lead to the fruitful coordination of our epistemic efforts. That is, I believe, the strongest argument that can be made for multiculturalism, and it is based not on moral or cultural relativism but rather on a realist account of the cognitive component of cultural practice and the objectivity of value (247).

Mohanty here opposes the 'relativist or liberal conceptions' of multiculturalism by a form of 'social cooperation, based on a [universalist] belief that humans, across cultures and societies, are creatures capable of rational agency and hence of cultural and political self-determination' (248). A critically self-aware moral and political universalist Enlightenment project does not imply the flattening out of difference or the celebration of cultural homogeneity. On the contrary, it respects all cultures (indeed *demands* that we do so) in much the same way in which Kant had declared *sapere aude*.

In this sense multiculturalism is a project that is intrinsic to democracy because it leads to a nation always willing to ask questions and adapt to change.
The question that Mohanty's thesis does not address is, of course, one of power and particularity. Although Chantal Mouffe does not, in the essay I examine now, look at the place of the 'particularist' analysis in any discussion of cultural difference, she also uses Kant but with a slightly higher degree of consciousness about the instrumental possibility of the Enlightenment project. For Chantal Mouffe (and Ernesto Laclau, in an earlier work) the socialist project itself may be reformulated in terms of a 'radical and plural democracy' (20) which would lead to a 'radicalization and deepening of the democratic revolution'. In these terms Chantal Mouffe's position is not particularly different from Satya Mohanty's because for both what is at stake 'is the nature of modern democracy as a pluralist democracy'. She continues:

Any modern democratic project must come to terms with such a pluralism. This means discarding the dangerous dream of a perfect consensus, of a harmonious collective will, and accepting the permanence of conflicts and antagonisms (20).

Although Mohanty had insisted on the historical and the social in discussing identity politics, one suspects that his project is not significantly different from those of liberals like John Rawls and Ronald Dworkin who also view politics in term of Kantian 'morally defined goals'. The criticism that Chantal Mouffe makes about the Rawls thesis of the 'priority of the right over the good' may be applied (though not to the letter) to Mohanty in whose thesis too 'conflicts, antagonisms, and relations disappear, and the field of politics is reduced to a rational process of negotiation among private interests under the constraints of morality' (23). To be fair to Mohanty, he is aware of the fact that the presence of diverse cultures guarantees that democracy (as morally envisaged) will have to accept division and conflict with no hope for a proper consensus ever. In this respect the common good is precisely a recognition of its impossibility. As Chantal Mouffe says, 'A radical pluralist approach, informed as it is by a nonessentialist view of politics, acknowledges the impossibility of a fully realized democracy and the total elimination of antagonisms' (24). In one sense this is remarkably close to Mohanty's realist theory of multiculturalism. The difference is that Mouffe does not speak about objective knowledge and its truth conditions. Instead she writes about the 'chain of equivalence' of the demands made by marginalized groups – women, blacks, workers, gays, lesbians, environmentalists – but without addressing, through a philosophical anthropology, whether the experiences are 'equivalent' or whether, indeed, their experiences have been adequately theorized. In this respect Chantal Mouffe is closer to the postmodern rather than to Mohanty's realist position. To her radical democracy can be understood or formulated only if the idea of the unitary subject is abandoned and replaced by a 'social agent constituted by a multiplicity of subject positions whose articulation is always precarious and temporary'. So Chantal Mouffe comes to the same position on multiculturalism as Mohanty but via a different (but overlapping) route. She concludes:

Only such a decentred view of the subject can enable us to theorize the multiplicity of relations of subordination in which a single individual can be inscribed and understand that one can be dominant in some groups while subordinated in others (25).

The argument – stated or implicit – thus far has been that multiculturalism makes us tolerant, mentally alert and creates a more robust democracy. A number of writers on art and aesthetics and on literature have made a similar point. One of the leading scholars of the literature of multiculturalism – Sneja Gunew – had made that point in *Framing Marginality* where she had noted that 'diasporic [multicultural] languages and cultures serve to deconstruct a nationalism based on those exclusive imaginaries which are structured around heritage in terms of kinship and genealogy, common descent and language' (21). In Wendy Steiner's brilliant book, *The Scandal of Pleasure* (1995) multiculturalism has a radical aesthetic function in that it brings a much-needed pluralism to acts of interpretation. Although Steiner's book, as the title implies, is about the scandal of pleasure with quite exceptional discussions of Robert Mapplethorpe and pornography and Salman Rushdie and the Iranian *fatwa*, it has a brief section on multiculturalism and canon reform that requires commentary. Although Wendy Steiner doesn't make the connection explicit, it is clear that debates about the canon in the academy are directly linked to the growth of multiculturalism. Steiner writes, 'Multiculturalism concerns not just who is admitted to universities and who teaches there, but what they teach and learn' (145). In this respect, it is directly concerned with bringing the realities of the outside world (the growth of ethnic diversity, the art of minorities, etc.) into the 'ivory tower'. The debates around the nature of the literary canon – and the direction in which it should go – often hinge around the question of a stable, homogeneous culture and shifting, heterogenous, even antagonistic, cultures which threaten to bring to an end the real achievements of the past in the name of political correctness. Wendy Steiner writes:

> We hear that multiculturalism is programmatically opposed to high culture, that its roots are in ethnic separatism and black nationalism, and that it is all part of a 'victims' revolution' in which women and minorities become a Moral Minority impatient for revenge against the dominance of Dead White European Males (DWEMs) who must be kicked out of the academy. Every time professors waver between Hemingway and [Zora Neale] Hurston, their deliberations take place amidst this din (149).

The significance of Wendy Steiner's account of multiculturalism and the canon is that it shows the ways in which the university curriculum has itself undergone changes in the wake of the kinds of cultural self-reflections that have come with multiculturalism. Just as democracy itself needs a politics of continuous contestations and disagreements, so the canon too needs to be interrogated and 'corrected' from the standpoint of those women and people of colour who had been denied self-representation in the domain of art. The kinds of demands being made by multiculturalists in the social sphere reverberate in the corridors of the academy as well: 'female and minority students [wish] to hear voices like their own in art, and thus both to learn about themselves and to be validated in the process' (150).

The issues surrounding multiculturalism and the canonical curriculum are taken up by Toni Morrison in her essay 'Unspeakable Things Unspoken' in *Criticism and the Color Line* edited by Henry B. Wonham. In her opening sentence, Toni Morrison makes her concern with the American literary canon clear: 'I planned to call this paper "Canon Fodder"' (18). According to conventional wisdom, she argues, the 'thing' called American literature is implicitly exclusive – it does not include Afro-American, Asian-American or Native American literatures. Part of the reason why this notion had not been seriously contested is linked to a liberal ethos whereby terms such as 'race' and 'white' could not enter into debates about the canon. The release of these terms from the confines of 'niceness', Toni Morrison argues, is one of the great cultural advances we have seen. It allows claims about white male domination to be aired and it has given rise to a healthy debate about the politics of judgement, hitherto conceived as being right and proper if made only by 'the dominant culture or gender' (17). A consciousness about alternative cultures – and the ways in which these inform the dominant culture and are informed by it – leads to a more thoroughgoing reappraisal of the canon. This reappraisal is epistemically different from an ongoing discovery or recovery of white authors because their 'discovery' – the reappraisal for instance of Mark Twain or Emily Dickinson, significant as it was – is 'serious but not destabilizing' (18). In her judgement it is not a matter of doing away with the canon (canonization is here to stay) nor is it a matter of dispensing with 'masterly' (17) texts (Aeschylus, Shakespeare, James, Melville) but rather it is a matter of examining the processes by which Afro-American writing was excluded from a transcendent understanding of the canon and what it means to bring minority literature into an American Eurocentric stronghold. There are two strategies that Toni Morrison advances in her interrogation of the canon. The first necessitates a deconstruction of what she calls the 'predictable sequence' of exclusion of non-white writing:

1) there is no Afro-American (or third world) art.
2) it exists but is inferior.
3) it exists and is superior when it measures up to the 'universal' criteria of Western art.
4) it is not so much 'art' as ore – rich ore that requires a Western or Eurocentric smith to refine it from its 'natural' state into an aesthetically complex form (20).

The second strategy, which she develops at some length with reference to Melville's *Moby Dick*, necessitates an examination of the ways in which race and slavery (and the master-slave ethos) become metaphorical tropes in the text. It is clear, for instance, that on the *Pequod* a mainly 'multiracial . . . proletariat is at work to produce a commodity'. This much is obvious enough. The critique of 'white notion of progress . . . of racial superiority' is less clear and one has to work at uncovering that critique. What Melville does, through the complex metaphor of whiteness and the whale, is to meditate 'on the fraudulent, self-destroying philosophy of that superiority' and this he could do only by building into the text both a metaphysics of racial exclusion that sustained the nation-state and a critique of it at the same time. This, Toni Morrison argues, is the 'unspeakable' truth of this 'complex, heaving, disorderly, profound text' which draws our attention to something that the canon has systematically denied, that is, the 'informing and determining Afro-American presence in traditional American literature' (29). *E Pluribus Unum* ('one from the many') taking its true form!

The issues raised by Wendy Steiner and Toni Morrison in the context of the canon are extended, with quite precise considerations of pedagogy and the curriculum, in a volume on research and scholarship in composition in America called *Writing in Multicultural Settings* (edited by Severino et al.). The essays collected in this volume – on linguistic diversity and English as a second language issues to the role of teachers and the politics of difference as it affects pedagogy – signal the extent to which a multicultural agenda is now a central tenet of education. In this context it is important to cite the editors' definition of multiculturalism as it is generally defined in the USA:

> [Multiculturalism encourages] citizens in the United States to embrace the racial, ethnic, class, gender, religious, age, and physical differences in our population; multiculturalism is an approach to living that respects, incorporates, and mediates the differences and similarities of our population. It suggests a reckoning with the erasure of cultural identities inherent in the melting-pot ideal . . .

In a very sensitive essay by Adrian Piper in *Passing and the Fictions of Identity* edited by Elaine K. Ginsberg, she explores some of the dangers of categories like race and ethnicity with reference to her own experience as a very white looking Afro-American woman. In this essay what we get is the narrative of an experience – marked by that ambiguous word 'passing', which some like Trinh Minh-ha have defined as self-empowering – that complicates some of the binaries surrounding multiculturalism. In a sense what is the 'epistemic' status of Adrian Piper's difference? Vilified by both white and black alike – and accused of getting it too easy by both – how does a person whose experience is not unproblematically marked, in this case, by racial oppression make a claim for her 'special difference' in a multicultural world order?

The point is made succinctly by Henry A. Giroux who writes in *Fugitive Cultures*, 'In the century to come, educators will not be able to ignore the hard questions that schools will have to face regarding issues of multiculturalism, race, identity, power, knowledge, ethics, and work' (17). A critical pedagogy is thus an essential component of the democratic process itself. It is here that critical educators need to know the multicultural components of national identity so that national identity is not defined 'through a primordial notion of ethnicity or a monolithic conception of culture, but as a part of a postmodern politics of cultural difference in which identities are constantly being negotiated and reinvented within complex and contradictory notions of national belonging' (200–201). Of course, Satya P. Mohanty would want to ground this claim to mobile identities in some understanding of realist, objective experience, and in that regard there may be a postmodern idealism (in a sense) in Giroux's definition of a postmodern ethnicity. But insofar as Giroux does draw attention to the dangers of the alternative position, we need to keep the critique firmly in mind. The dangers are in fact given urgent voice in Giroux's examination of the liberalism of, arguably, America's leading scholar of pragmatic philosophy, Richard Rorty, who declared in the *New York Times* that left-wing supporters of multiculturalism were in fact 'unpatriotic' as their position rocked the very foundations upon which national identity and national pride are based. The trouble with this position is not that it 'equates cultural differences with a threat to national unity' (197) but that it constructs multiculturalism as a monolithic conspiracy aimed at toppling the consensual basis of American democracy. In this regard it gets multiculturalism spectacularly wrong. What is surprising is that someone as astute, as careful, as Richard Rorty forgets that multiculturalism refers to a range of theoretical positions, some, like 'calls for separatism', may be dangerous, and others, like suggestions for 'new forms of democracy', are absolutely essential for the health and vigour of a democratic nation-state that understands, from the start, that 'national identity is always a shifting, unsettled complex of historical struggles and experiences' (198). Giroux concludes his book with the following very productive definition of multiculturalism:

> The discourse of multiculturalism represents, in part, the emergence of new voices that have generally been excluded from the histories that have defined our national identity. Far from being a threat to social order, multiculturalism in its various forms has challenged notions of national identity that equate cultural difference with deviance and disruption. Refusing a notion of national identity constructed on the suppression of cultural differences and social dissent, multiculturalism, especially its more critical and insurgent versions, explores how dominant views of national identity have been developed around cultural differences (198).

In America 'identity' and 'race' are the terms around which debates about the 'multicultural' are often constructed. In Canada where the term 'multicultural' invades the social as part of the overall agenda of the nation-state and where multicultural instrumentalities operate from the level of the local to that of the national, multicultural policy is often the target of essays on racial or gender difference. In a collection of essays edited by Himani Bannerji (*Returning the Gaze*) it is precisely the 'erasures' of visibility that get contested. Bannerji writes in her introduction:

> [The essays in this book] rest on a politicized notion of representation rather than the liberal notion of visibility which structures the discursive practices of multiculturalism and ethnic and race relations (xv).

Although the alternative project – an exploration of different subjectivities based on 'particularist' accounts of prior experiences – is in the end not unlike American discourses of power and oppression, we do tend to get theorizations that also take up ways in which colonial or neo-colonial assumptions underpin multicultural discourses in a much more systematic fashion. This is understandable because unlike America, Canada's vast visible minority has multiple histories of colonization behind it. As Bannerji's anthology demonstrates, the aim of the contributors is to spell out their colonial pasts, to seek fundamental changes in the ways in which the nation-state reads them and to rethink multiculturalism not as a management exercise but as an epistemology of margins reading the centre.

I will refer to a few texts that have gown out of a multicultural understanding of culture and the nation-state at the end of this survey. At this juncture, however, I want to refer to one of only a handful of single-authored books devoted to the subject of multiculturalism. Appropriately, this monograph is by the Canadian political philosopher Will Kymlicka to whose book *Multicultural Citizenship* reference has already been made in the context of the Fish and Pease debates on multiculturalism. The project of Kymlicka's book is to find 'morally defensible and politically viable answers' to an ongoing clash between minorities and majorities on a whole host of issues, including language rights, political representations, immigration, national symbols, and so on. The line of thinking that Kymlicka develops is not significantly different from those of Rawls, Dworkin or Taylor, since for Kymlicka too multiculturalism, finally, is a matter of managing individual/collective rights within a morally defensible, enlightened democratic framework. The move away from an 'idealized model of the polis in which fellow citizens share a common descent, language, and culture' to a polyglot nation-state means that traditional human rights need to be supplemented by a 'theory of minority rights'(5). For legislators – and in one sense Kymlicka's work focuses on the macro-dynamics of multiculturalism as a legislative fact – the increasingly multicultural nature of modern states means that minority rights have to be factored into universal human rights. An initial differentiation has to be made between the rights of first-nation peoples and that of all other minorities. This distinction – and a very valuable one – leads to two kinds of states: the 'multination' and the 'polyethnic'. For first-nation peoples Canada is a 'multination' state since it forcibly took over other self-governing cultures. For everyone else Canada is a 'polyethnic' state. In the latter conception of the nation-state, the question of self-government does not (and should not) arise; in the former conception any demand for it, although from the first-nation people's point of view very legitimate, would pose a 'serious threat to social unity' (9). In Kymlicka's argument, then, Canada – or the United States for that matter – is both multinational and polyethnic, terms that he feels indeed underlie the more popular conception of Canada as 'multicultural', but terms that, in his argument, keep the question of addressing minority rights – as ethnic rights – firmly in focus. Kymlicka observes:

> Some people use 'multicultural' in an even broader way, to encompass a wide range of non-ethnic social groups which have been excluded or marginalized for mainstream society. This usage is particularly common in the United States, where advocates of a 'multicultural' curriculum are often referring to efforts

to reverse the historical exclusion of groups such as the disabled, gays and lesbians, women, the working class, atheists and Communists (17–18).

Kymlicka overstates the generality of the term, but nevertheless draws our attention to the variety of ways in which the term 'multiculturalism' is used. In a valuable footnote, Kymlicka notes:

> In Canada, [multiculturalism] typically refers to the right of immigrants to express their ethnic identity without fear of prejudice or discrimination; in Europe, it often refers to the sharing of powers between national communities; in the USA, it is often used to include the demands of marginalized social groups (198).

A multiculturalism that arises quite specifically out of national and ethnic difference is where questions of rights and responsibilities become most marked. Of all the countries where multiculturalism is being seriously debated – in Canada, Britain, France, the USA, Germany, Australia, for instance – official recognition of polyethnicity or multinationality has taken place only in Canada. In Kymlicka's discussion of how to manage multiculturalism in the Canadian context, group-specific rights, which he classifies as self-government rights, polyethnic rights and special representation rights, need to be taken into consideration in any discussion of democratic rights. Of course, as Donald Pease remarked in his rejoinder to the Stanley Fish thesis, legislation however moral or enlightened does not translate into the social or the behavioural and may well be no more than attempts at containment and, in the end, paradoxically, even exclusion.

It is not uncommon to hear a phrase such as 'before the world became truly multinational'. Many of the texts we have reviewed, including those in which multiculturalism, as a word, figures only incidentally, are predicated upon a world that has 'truly become multicultural'. Thus books that I do not review here in any great detail but which are written in the 'shadow' of multiculturalism may be mentioned in these concluding paragraphs. I have in mind works such as Caren Kaplan's *Questions of Travel* in which many of the key terms and theories – travel, displacement, refugees, immigration, genocide, and so on – are connected to the truism that 'many of us have locations in the plural' (7). And postmodernism too – the theory that underpins Kaplan's work – has come about because of the emergence of destabilizing, contradictory, and contestatory 'unheard or unacknowledged narratives' (14). Roots, routes, mobility arise very much out of minority unease in an under-theorized (or even anti-theoretical) multiculturalism within nation-states. Theorizing about borders and cultural boundaries too are framed, implicitly, in a reading of the world as multicultural where alternative presences must be articulated. *Cross-Addressing*, a volume edited by John C. Hawley, is a good example of a work where postmodern culture is articulated through migrant experiences. And Patrick Brantlinger's very scholarly cultural history of Britain read in terms of British fiscal and monetary policies from the end of the seventeenth century onwards (*Fictions of State*) ends with a chapter in which literary evidence is adduced to show

how the emergence of 'ethnic and immigrant subcultures' exemplifies the contradictory, transgressive cultural and historical moments that are constitutive of British culture. The point is that any reading of late twentieth-century cultural politics or political economy must address the emergence of 'trans- or postnational identities' (250). This recognition, in a sense, underlies the thrust of most of the books surveyed here.

The ways in which 'multiculturalism, first nations, immigration policies' affect even the study of cultural studies in Canada is commented on, albeit very briefly indeed, by Ioan Davies in *Cultural Studies and Beyond*. Their appropriation by youth groups towards a fuller awareness that 'each moment is embedded within a range of cultural possibilities' is addressed in a collection of essay edited by Vered Amit-Talai and Helena Wulff (*Youth Cultures*). In this volume 'multi-culture' (hyphenated) is deployed in a manner for youth that carries many of the meanings of the term but has a more precise meaning for youths as they come to be 'socially effective' (231) and as they grapple with the historically very different cultural repertoires of their parents.

Multiculturalism surfaces even in the final paragraph of Rosemary Marangoly George's book on the representations of 'home' in the narratives of immigration and exile. Although 'home' is not theoretically located in the problematic context of diasporas (but one could, if one wishes to, read it as such) and in any active politics, it is nevertheless a principle to which Marangoly George returns in *The Politics of Home*:

> Perhaps the stance to take, while writing and reading fiction as much as in living, is to acknowledge the seductive pleasure of belonging in homes and in communities and in nations – while working toward changing the governing principles of exclusions and inclusions (200).

I want to end this survey with a book that deals with an area that is crucial to current debates about multiculturalism. The area is 'cultural appropriation' and the book in question is *Borrowed Power* edited by Bruce Ziff and Pratima V. Rao. Although the archives handled by the contributors to this volume are diverse, the message that comes across loud and clear is that 'cultural appropriation' is a central theme in multicultural discourses. Writes Jonathan Hart, 'the debate over what constitutes cultural appropriation by the dominant culture has become an important concern in multicultural societies' (137). But cultural appropriation is not to be read in an essentialist fashion. The Canadian poet and essayist M. Nourbese Philip writes, '[prohibiting] white writers writing from the point of view of persons from other cultures or races . . . is very flawed and entirely ill-advised [since] prohibiting such activity alters not one iota of that invisible and sticky web of systemic or structural racism' (101). M. Nourbese Philip's essay and those of many others in this volume draw our attention to the fundamental vulnerability of a project (of multiculturalism) that does not differentiate the 'ethnic'/ 'first nation' subject along the lines of class and gender and which, under the guise of a democratic utopianism, may even be complicit in a process that obliterates the corporeality of the Other. The 'liberal discourse of multiculturalism or cultural diversity', as Rosemary J. Coombe points out in her fine contribution to the volume, must 'emphasize, rather than obscure, the very real histories of colonialism which we must confront and the relations of power inherited from our multiple colonial pasts that continue to shape social relations of difference' (80). In the end, as the last two or three years' work on multiculturalism has shown, scholarly commentary has begun, finally, to address multiculturalism's multiple trajectories but also its incoherence.

Books Reviewed

Amit-Talai, Vered and Helena Wulff, eds. *Youth Cultures: A Cross-Cultural Perspective.* Routledge, 1995. pp. 239. pb £15.99. ISBN 0 415 10984 1.

Appadurai, Arjun. *Modernity at Large. Cultural Dimensions of Globalization.* Minnesota University Press, 1996. pp. 229. $30.95. ISBN 0 8166 2793 2.

Bahri, Deepika and Mary Vasudeva. eds. *Between the Lines.* 111–120. *South Asians and Postcoloniality.* Temple University Press, 1996. pp. 372. pb £15.75. ISBN 1 56639468 6.

Bannerji, Himani. *Returning The Gaze: Essays on Racism, Feminism and Politics.* Sister Vision Press, 1993. pp. 266.pb £12.95. ISBN 0 920813 55 0.

Berdichewsky, Bernardo. *Racism, Ethnicity and Multiculturalism.* Future Publications, 1996. pp. 105. ISBN 0 9698906 1 3.

Berdichewsky, Bernardo. *Cultural Pluralism in Canada: What It Means To The Jewish Community.* Canadian Jewish Congress.

Brantlinger, Patrick. *Fictions of State: Culture and Credit in Britain, 1694–1994.* Cornell University Press, 1996. pp. 291. pb £11.48. ISBN 0 8014 8287 9.

Binning, Sadhu. *No More Watno Dur.* TSAR Publications, 1994. pp. 118. pb $10.95. ISBN 0 920661 45 9.

Bissoondath, Neil. *Selling Illusions. The Cult of Multiculturalism in Canada.* Penguin Books, 1994. pp. 234. pb $12.99. ISBN 0 14 023878 6.

Chicago Cultural Studies Group. 'Critical Multiculturalism'. *Critical Inquiry,* 1992, 18(3), 530–555.

Davies, Ioan. *Cultural Studies and Beyond: Fragments of Empire.* Routledge, 1995. pp. 203. hb £47.50. ISBN 0 415 03837 5.

Fish, Stanley. 'Boutique Multiculturalism, or Why Liberals Are Incapable of Thinking about Hate Speech'. *Critical Inquiry,* 23(2), 378–395.

George, Rosemary Marangoly. *The Politics of Home. Postcolonial Relocations and Twentieth-Century Fiction.* Cambridge University Press, 1996. pp. 265. hb $80.00. ISBN 0 521 45334 8.

Ginsberg, Elaine K. ed. *Passing and the Fictions of Identity.* Duke University Press, 1996. pp. 298. pb £11.95. ISBN 0 8223 1764 8.

Giroux, Henry A. *Fugitive Cultures: Race, Violence, and Youth.* Routledge, 1996. pp. 247. pb £10.35. ISBN 0 415 91578 3.

Gordon, Avery F. and Christopher Newfield. eds. *Mapping Multiculturalism.* University of Minnesota Press. pp. 491. pb £13.60. ISBN 0 8166 2546 8.

Gunew, Sneja. *Framing Marginality* (1994). Melbourne University Press. pp. 158. pb £8.50. ISBN 0 522 84639 4.

Hawley, John C. ed. *Cross-Addressing: Resistance Literature and Cultural*

Borders. State University of New York Press, 1996. pp. 309. pb £13.29. ISBN 0 7914 2928 8.

Hutcheon, Linda and Marion Richmond. eds. *Other Solitudes.* Oxford University Press, 1990. pp. 374. pb $15.95. ISBN 0 19 540756 3.

Kaplan, Caren. *Questions of Travel: Postmodern Discourses of Displacement.* Duke University Press, 1996. pp. 238. pb £15.95. ISBN 0 8223 1821 0.

Kymlicka, Will. *Multicultural Citizenship.* Oxford University Press. pp. 280. pb £12.08. ISBN 0 19 829091 8.

Lowe, Lisa. *Immigrant Acts: On Asian American Cultural Politics.* Duke University Press, 1996. pp. 252. hb £34.00. ISBN 0 8223 1864 4.

Mohanty, Satya P. *Literary Theory and the Claims of History.* Cornell University Press. pp. 260. pb £12.50. ISBN 0 8014 8135 X.

Mukherjee, Bharati. 'Two Ways to Belong in America'. *New York Times.* 22 September 1996. E13.

Pease, Donald. 'Regulating Multi-Adhoccerists, Fish('s) Rules'. *Critical Inquiry*, 23(2), 396–418.

Radhakrishnan, R. *Diasporic Mediations. Between Home and Location.* University of Minnesota Press, 1996. pp. 217. hb $30.95. ISBN 0 8166 2641 3.

Rajchman, John. ed. *The Identity in Question.* Routledge, 1995. pp. 295. pb £10.90. ISBN 0 415 90618 0.

Severino, Carol, Juan C. Guerra and Johnnella E. Butler. eds. *Writing in Multicultural Settings.* The Modern Language Association of America. pp. 370. pb $19.75. ISBN 0 87352 584 1.

Siemerling, Winfried and Katrin Schwenk. eds. *Cultural Difference and the Literary Text.* University of Iowa Press, 1996. pp. 189. pb £11.95. ISBN 0 87745 566 X.

Steiner, Wendy. *The Scandal of Pleasure.* Chicago University Press, 1995. pp. 251. pb £10.25. ISBN 0 226 77223 3.

Trend, David, ed. *Radical Democracy: Identity, Citizenship, State.* Routledge, 1996. pp. 239. hb £42.39. ISBN 0 415 91247 4.

Vassanji, M. G. *No New Land.* McClelland & Stewart, 1991. pp. 208. pb £7.99. ISBN 0 77 10 8720 9.

Wonham, Henry B. ed. *Criticism and the Color Line: Desegregating American Literary Studies.* Rutgers University Press, 1996. pp. 299. pb £15.50. ISBN 0 8135 2263 3.

Ziff, Bruce and Pratima V. Rao. eds. *Borrowed Power: Essays on Cultural Appropriation.* Rutgers University Press. pp. 337. pb £12.11. ISBN 0 8135 2372 9.

Žižek, Slavoj. 'Multiculturalism, Or, the Cultural Logic of Multinational Capitalism'. *New Left Review*, 225, 28–51.

Žižek, Slavoj. *Tarrying with the Negative. Kant, Hegel, and The Critique of Ideology.* Duke University Press, 1993. pp. 289. pb £11.95. ISBN 0 8223 1362 6.

Index